The 124th New
Volunteers in the ... ..

The 124th New York State Volunteers in the Civil War

A History and Roster

CHARLES J. LAROCCA

McFarland & Company, Inc., Publishers

Jefferson, North Carolina, and London

Photographs are from author's collection unless otherwise noted.

Library of Congress Cataloguing-in-Publication Data

LaRocca, Charles J., 1946–
The 124th New York State Volunteers in the Civil War : a history
and roster / Charles J. LaRocca.
p.   cm.
Includes bibliographical references and index.

ISBN 978-0-7864-6697-9
softcover : acid free paper ∞

1. United States. Army. New York Infantry Regiment, 124th (1862–1865)
2. United States — History — Civil War, 1861–1865 — Regimental histories.
3. New York (State) — History — Civil War, 1861–1865.
4. United States — History — Civil War, 1861–1865 — Registers.
5. New York (State) — History — Civil War, 1861–1865 — Registers.
I. Title.
E523.5 124th.L37 2012   973.7′447 — dc23   2012031012

British Library cataloguing data are available

Front cover: The Kearny Badge (courtesy Betty Carey and Lillian Murray
from the William J. Murray Collection); background © 2012 Shutterstock

Manufactured in the United States of America

McFarland & Company, Inc., Publishers
Box 611, Jefferson, North Carolina 28640
www.mcfarlandpub.com

To my lovely wife, Katherine J. LaRocca.
All that is good in this life I owe to her.

Table of Contents

Acknowledgments

This book is the result of many years of research and plenty of help from a lot of people. In acknowledging those who have played a part, I hope that I did not leave anyone out and apologize in advance if I did.

Serious study of the 124th New York State Volunteers began for me in 1985, when I was awarded a grant through the Council for Basic Education. The grant, funded in part by the National Council for the Humanities, allowed me to spend the summer examining the newspapers published in Orange County during the Civil War. The study quickly centered on soldiers' letters home printed in the local press. A number of the letters quoted in this book were found during that CBE research.

At about the same time I met Ethel Gage and Betty Barry of Middletown, New York. Ms. Gage had, over many years, amassed an amazing collection of letters from two brothers, William and Henry Howell, who served in the 124th New York State Volunteers. Betty, as executor of Ethel's estate, entrusted me with preserving the letters and using them to tell the story of the soldiers who served in the regiment. Pam Hays, also of Middletown, found yet more letters from the Howell brothers and she urged me to use them in my research. I am grateful for the trust these ladies had in me and hope they are happy with the result.

In 1990, Pine Bush High School principal Ken Sherman suggested that I apply for a Christa McAuliffe Fellowship, which I received. The grant, funded in part by the Department of Education, paid the costs of publishing the letters, diaries, newspaper accounts, and photographs pertaining to the 124th New York that I'd found in my research. Titled *This Regiment of Heroes*, the book contained primary source materials that teachers could integrate into the curriculum at the grade levels where American history is taught. Five hundred copies were printed and distributed free of charge to every Orange County school library, public library, historical society, and local historian, and to those with an interest in the regiment. A copy was also sent to the National Park Service research center at each of the battlefields where the regiment fought.

It seemed logical to me that the next step was to use the letter collections to write a new regimental history of the 124th New York. It was a twenty-year project that grew as more and more letters, documents, and pictures came to light. Along the way I met a number people willing to help.

Larry Clance comes to mind immediately. He developed an interest in the 124th New York when he purchased letters written by Captain Henry Murray of Company B. He has been most generous in sharing his impressive collection of with me, sending along copies of letters and photographs he has purchased. We have walked a few Civil War battlefields together and look forward to walking many more.

Robert Cammaroto, a long time friend and fellow 124th New York reenactor, gave permission for the use of the letters and a diary written by Private James Irwin, as well as photographs from his collection. The 1864 diary is an invaluable day-by-day account of a time period about which little pertaining to the regiment is written.

Lynne Whealton has been very generous in allowing me to quote from the letters of Captain William E. Mapes, her ancestor. His candid observations add a great deal to the story and his earthy remarks and colorful vocabulary are humorous and insightful. In one letter, Mapes wondered if the people of his home town of Florida, New York, would remember his service in defense of the Union. Thanks to Lynne's efforts, he will be remembered.

The same is true for Sergeant Thomas Rodman, because Sandra and Robert Rodman gave me access to his letters as well as his photograph. His is an especially important collection because it covers the entire service of the regiment and provides an interesting look at the company level of the 124th New York.

Tom and Joan Frangos made their collection of Captain James Benedict's letters and their truly outstanding grouping of cartes de visite available. Captain Benedict ended the war serving as major and effectively commanded the regiment in the absence of Colonel Weygant. The pictures, in particular, add a great deal to this book.

Sue Gardner, Town of Warwick deputy historian and local history librarian at the Albert Wisner Public Library, brought Joan and Tom Frango's collection to my attention and was most helpful in securing permission to use that collection in this book. She also found and helped to transcribe the series of letters written by Corporal Frank Benedict published in the Warwick *Advertiser* thirty-five years after the Civil War ended. Her help in gathering materials related to Company D is greatly appreciated.

Stuart Kessler, author of *On Sacred Ground*, transcribed and sent copies to me of Private Henry Howell's second and third diaries, which took up where the diaries in my collection left off. Stuart's diaries included important new information on the battles of Brandy Station and Gettysburg. It was a pleasure working with him on this and we hope to publish all the diaries together at some not too distant time.

Tom Duclos of the New York State Military History Museum, Saratoga, New York, has been most helpful in making available to me the scrapbook clipping collection which contains Civil War letters written by members of the regiment. This collection may now be examined online. Many of these letters, especially those published in the Newburgh *Journal*, are available nowhere else.

Ted Sly, descendant of Private Norman Augustus Sly of Company D, and former Orange County Historian has always supported the research for this book. He brought the remembrances of his ancestor at The Wilderness and Spotsylvania to my attention. The handwritten document offers a unique look at the brigade level and is an important new source for those battles. Cornelia Bush, the current historian, has made it clear that she is interested in celebrating, during the war's sesquicentennial, the important role played by the 124th New York in the Civil War.

Mike McAfee, curator of history at the West Point Museum, is a well known historian who is always willing to share what he knows. He has been most helpful by opening his impressive CDV collection for inclusion in this book and was of great assistance with the two previous Civil War books I've done. A self-styled "curmudgeon," he is an incredible resource and a pleasure to work with.

I would not have been able to meet the publisher's deadline without the unstinting help and encouragement of Martin W. Husk. His *History of the 111th New York* is also published by McFarland. Martin proofread and edited the manuscript, offering helpful suggestions that improved the text. I especially want to thank him for providing the excellent maps which were far beyond my capability to produce.

There is little that Mel Johnson, curator at Washington's Headquarters in Newburgh, does not know about local history and the 124th New York. I have gone to him many times with questions and he has always proven to be a great friend and resource.

Marcus Millspaugh, of Walden, New York, has been very helpful in making items from *The Montgomery Standard* available to me from his "Orange Blossom" collection. Mr. Millspaugh also provided the stunning picture of Thomas Bradley, Walden's favorite son, wearing his sergeant's uniform. He first showed me the 1864 group photograph of Company H and has always been willing to share his knowledge.

Pat Eisley of the Walden and Wallkill Valley Historical Society brought a letter written by Andrew Bowman, Company H, to my attention and provided a transcription. I want to thank Barbara Imbasciani, president of the society, and Lisa Melville for their help in securing permission to use the Company H photograph and Private Bowman's letter.

I am grateful to Colonel Charles Umhey and his wife Tavy for making letters from Lieutenant John Houston, Co. D, available for this book. Both have my sincerest thanks.

No Orange Blossom correspondent tortured the King's English more than Private Henry Dill and I want to thank Cheri Cardone for bringing his colorful letters to my attention.

Lynn and Paul Ruback saved and preserved a number of enlistment documents and some very interesting letters written to Lieutenant Henry Ramsdell by his mother. I am grateful that she made me aware of the materials and offered them for use in this book. Paul, a New York City firefighter, met an untimely death on September 11, 2001, in the line of duty.

The Historical Society of Middletown and the Wallkill Precinct has a wonderful collection of local Civil War letters and related documents first brought to my attention by the late Charles Radzinsky. In recent years, Marv Cohen, who serves as president of the society, and the volunteer staff have always been helpful in research requests.

Pauline Kehoe, former director of the Goshen Public Library and Historical Society, has been most helpful in making available the impressive holdings in the library's local history collection. Ann Roche, history room clerk, and director Matt Gomm were helpful in locating specific items in the collection.

Pauline and her husband Bob Devino, good friends and fellow history buffs, have travelled with my wife and me on many trips to Civil War related historic places and made their summer house on Lake Champlain available as a quiet retreat where part of this book was written.

Chris Farlekis, *Times Herald Record* reporter, has, for nearly thirty years, been an enthusiastic fan of the 124th New York, Stephen Crane, and Orange County's role in the Civil War. He is the one most responsible for putting me on the path to discovering that Crane used the 124th New York as a model for *The Red Badge of Courage*.

Dennis Butticavoli made available from his collection letters written by William Howell, Henry Howell, and William H. Shaw. Shaw's letter in particular filled an important gap in the history of the regiment.

Shirley Mearns made available the diary of Private James Haggarty, Company I, who was wounded at Chancellorsville and spent the remainder of the war in the Veteran Reserve Corps.

Gregg Kelly, a member of the 124th New York reenactment group, has done extensive research on the role of the regiment and of Smith's Battery during the fight for Houck's Ridge on July 2nd at Gettysburg. My discussions with Gregg have helped me to understand the placement and actions of both.

A number of years ago, I purchased a copy of *The Civil War Letters of John Zephaniah Drake*, Company F, edited by Dr. Robert Drew Simpson and his wife, Megan Demarest Simpson. They graciously allowed me to quote from letters written by Private Drake to his sister Minerva.

The Huguenot Historical Society in New Paltz, New York, has a remarkable collection pertaining to the 124th New York. Private Joseph Johnston's letters home as well as those of his sister Hannah and of Lizzie Garretson, who was his nurse in Washington, add a great deal to the story of the regiment. Leslie LeFevre-Stratton, curator of collections, and Ashley Hurlburt, curatorial assistant, were enthusiastic in making this collection available for research.

Anita Goldsmith and Nancy Craig of the Mount Hope Historical Society contacted me last year about their purchase of fourteen letters from Henry and William Howell. Most were written in the late summer and fall of 1863 and fill an important gap in the story of the regiment.

When Larry Clance made me aware of letters written by Captain William Jackson in the Cornell University Library collection, I got in contact with the Ana Guimaraes, head of Reference Services. I must say that she and the staff were most cooperative in allowing me to copy and use the letters written by the captain to his friend Alsop Purdey. I very much appreciate their help.

My thanks also to Ted O'Reilly and the staff of the Manuscript Department at the New York Historical Society for their help in making available letters written by Captain Henry Spencer Murray, who led Company B into battle.

I want to thank Tom Holbrook and John Heiser of the Gettysburg NMP for critiquing the Gettysburg chapter and offering helpful suggestions. Tom recommended that I take a look at Troy Harman's *Lee's Real Plan at Gettysburg* for a new point of view on the battle.

Robert Krick, Jr., with the National Park Service at Richmond, answered questions on the North Anna crossing and critiqued Chapter 14. Jimmy Blankenship at NPS Petersburg did the same with regard to that battle and critiqued Chapter 15. Thanks to both for all their help.

I am grateful to my friend Dave Handzel for reading and critiquing several chapters and for answering questions about the types of rifle muskets carried by the 124th New York.

Mike Block of the Brandy Station Foundation read chapters on the battle but also on the Mine Run Campaign and the camp at Brandy Station during the winter of 1863–64. He and Bud Hall gave me an extensive tour of the battlefield that has helped me to understand the ebb and flow of the battle.

I would be remiss if I did not mention my good friend Gary Farbman. He was always ready to help with answers to questions about computer programs and has, on more than one occasion, saved this manuscript from obliteration by one virus or another. He is a computer guru with True Grit.

I'd like to thank Catherine and Chloe Williams, who helped transcribe the Captain William Jackson letter collection, and also mention Liam and Eleanor Fels. Their Grandpa hopes they will always share his interest in American history.

And, most of all, special thanks to my wife, Katherine J. LaRocca, to whom this book is dedicated. She read and edited many of the chapters, offering suggestions that improved the story. Her limitless patience and encouragement kept me going when the task seemed to have no end.

Preface

"Nothing does a soldier any more good than a letter."
— Private George Godfrey, Co. E, 124th NYSV

A reviewer of *The Red Badge of Courage* wrote of Stephen Crane, "The rank and file has its historian at last." Crane's novel was the story not of generals but of Henry Fleming, a private in the Union army. The author was able to accurately depict the chaos of battle so well that veterans were sure that he, too, must have fought in the Civil War. World War II hero Audie Murphy, who was chosen to play Fleming in the 1951 movie based on the novel, was amazed to find that Crane was born six years after the Civil War ended and that he had never been a soldier. "But he knew," commented America's most decorated soldier, "that in a battle you are all alone."[1]

Crane wanted to accurately depict how it *felt* to be in combat and he complained that accounts written by the generals offered nothing in that regard. He turned instead to the soldiers in the ranks. Local tradition has it that Crane learned what he wanted to know in a park in Port Jervis, a small city in western Orange County, New York. There he found men who, thirty years before, had volunteered to serve in the local regiment that marched away in the late summer of 1862 to save the Union. They had been members of the 124th New York State Volunteers, the famed Orange Blossoms, and they certainly could tell him what it felt like to be in a battle. Their war stories must have impressed the young author because he used the action of their regiment at the Battle of Chancellorsville as the setting for his war novel.

This book is the non-fiction version of their history told, as much as possible, in the words of the soldiers themselves.

The 124th New York was one of the great fighting regiments of the American Civil War and was made up of volunteers who served in the finest tradition of the citizen-soldier. Farmers, shopkeepers, mechanics, and tradesmen before enlisting, they returned to those pursuits when the war was done. In the intervening time period, from the summer of 1862 to the spring of 1865, they marched south in a sacred cause. They fought not for pay or bounty, but to save the Union. In the end, they accomplished their goal, but at great personal cost to themselves and to their families.

The last commander of the regiment, Colonel Charles Weygant, took it upon himself to write a history of the 124th New York which he published in 1877. Weygant was an eyewitness and an able historian. His book should be the starting point for any serious study of the regiment's experiences in the war. This book is in no way meant to supplant Weygant's effort, but instead to add to it. Since the publication of the *History of the 124th Regiment N.Y.S.V.*, masses of primary source material not available to Weygant can now be accessed. After-action reports, orders, maps, remembrances, and private letters which he never saw help to clarify the events he lived through.

1

Local newspaper accounts are also useful to the researcher because numerous daily and weekly newspapers were published in Orange County during the war years. These papers reprinted important stories from the metropolitan press in addition to letters sent home by local soldiers from the field. One example is Sergeant Charles Stewart of Company I, 124th New York, who used the penname "Felix," and was considered to be "Our Army Correspondent" by one of the local newspapers.

Private George Godfrey of Company E wrote, "Nothing does a soldier any more good than a letter." Of course he meant that nothing would better raise the spirits of a man far from home than a letter from a friend or family member. Such letters are rare because they often ended up in a knapsack or coat pocket and, vulnerable to wear and water, were read and re-read until they fell apart. But quite often the letters written by the soldiers themselves survived. Those at home were eager to hear that a son or father had not been killed in the latest battle or struck down by typhoid fever, cholera, or some other disease that took four men for every one killed by enemy fire. The soldiers' letters were treasured, often tied in a bundle and stored away for safekeeping. In so many cases, the letters would be all that remained of a loved one lost in the war to save the Union.

To the student of the Civil War, these letters can be treasures as well. They speak to us across a century and a half and show us the pattern of another time. The letters also give us clues to what the soldier was thinking as events were unfolding in front of him. Many were written close in time to the events they described. They bore headings like "In Our Old Camp," "Out in a Thick Woods, Virginia," or "On the battlefield." The privates in the ranks were not writing for posterity or for promotion, but simply to tell the folks back home what they were experiencing.

Private Norman Augustus Sly of Company D wrote that he preferred to read history written by a man who had actually seen or even participated in the events he wrote about. He was speaking of William Swinton, the *New York Times* reporter who had been arrested by General Ambrose Burnside and whom General Grant banned from the Union lines. Sly said he would like to read Swinton's *Campaigns of the Army of the Potomac* because "that is the kind of History to be written — by a man that was on the ground."

The soldiers who marched with the 124th New York were, most definitely, "on the ground" in the battles they fought as part of the Army of the Potomac. Theirs is a compelling story of great courage, endurance, and sacrifice. It has been my goal in this book to tell that story honestly and in such a way as to do them honor — to be, for this regiment, the historian of the rank and file.

CHAPTER 1

"But alas! our Country calls"
July 1–September 6, 1862

By the summer of 1862, the American Civil War had been raging for more than a year. Northerners had initially expected that the rebellion would be crushed in one swift, decisive battle. But a year before, on July 21, 1861, with the stunning Confederate victory at Bull Run, those expectations had been dramatically laid to rest, together with the bodies of 460 dead Union soldiers. An additional 2,400 of President Abraham Lincoln's men were wounded or missing. With this defeat, northerners came to the realization that the rebellion would be neither short in duration nor easily suppressed. To be successful, and to save the Union, they must mobilize all of their resources. The North quickly regained its balance, called for thousands more volunteers, changed army commanders, and brought considerable industrial and financial muscle to bear on the war effort.

In Washington, D.C., the Lincoln administration was so sure of success that in February 1862, some of the political prisoners who had been jailed for opposing the war were released. In April, Secretary of War Edwin Stanton began closing recruiting offices, certain that the Union troops already in the field were strong enough to put an end to the rebellion.[1] As summer approached, a huge army, brimming with confidence and led by Major General George B. McClellan, prepared to smash the rebel forces and capture their capital.

Then, in a string of spectacular Confederate victories in the Shenandoah Valley and on the Peninsula of Virginia, within sight of Richmond itself, the Union armies were again defeated. By mid-summer 1862, gloom and pessimism once more settled over what was left of the United States.

It was at last clear to the president and to realistic leaders in the North that the forces at hand — state militia regiments, United States Regulars, and volunteer regiments from the states — were not strong enough to reunite the nation. What was needed was a mighty army of longterm volunteers. The loyal governors of the North, led by New York's Governor Edwin D. Morgan, appealed to the president for "prompt and vigorous measures" urging him "that you at once call upon the several states for such numbers of men as may be required to fill up all military organizations now in the field ... and to speedily crush the rebellion that still exists in several of the Southern States."[2]

On July 1, 1862, President Lincoln replied to the governors by issuing a call for additional volunteers, "chiefly of infantry," and promised that the following day the War Department would fix a quota of men that each state was to provide.[3]

In New York, Governor Morgan issued a proclamation in response to Lincoln's message:

The President of the United States has duly called upon the country for an additional force of three hundred thousand volunteers to serve for three years, or the war.... This appeal is to the State of New York; it is to each citizen. Let it come to every fireside.... Present happiness and future greatness will be secured by responding to the present call. Let the answer go back to the President and to our brave soldiers in the field, that in New York the patriotic list of the country's defenders is augmented. It will strengthen the hands of the one, and give hope and encouragement to the other.[4]

The quota for New York was to be 59,705 men. The state was divided into military districts, each with a recruiting committee of prominent citizens appointed by the governor. Each committee had the power to expand its own membership and to select a colonel whose job it was to gather the men at a centrally located camp to begin their military training. That colonel would receive his commission when his regiment was at full strength. The 9th Recruiting District, covering two counties, was required to raise 1,800 men, 1,200 from Orange County and 600 from neighboring Sullivan County.[5]

Within military districts, towns were given quotas of men to be recruited. Newburgh, a thriving commercial center on the Hudson River, had the largest population so it was to provide 285 men to the new regiment even though numerous volunteers from the town had joined the 56th New York the year before. Rural Greenville was to contribute 23 men from among its farmers and herdsmen. The county seat of Goshen was to send 57 men while the prosperous farming community of Montgomery was to raise 76 men, and so on until the regiment was filled.[6]

It was easy to issue a call for volunteers, but getting men to actually sign up was another thing entirely. The recruiting committee members faced a daunting task and they knew it, but these were loyal Union men who pitched into the work with vigor. It was noted in the local press that most of the members lived in close proximity to one another at the eastern end of Orange County along the Hudson River. This permitted them to be called together quickly as the work at hand was pressing. The members' prosperous homesteads, some of the wealthiest in Orange County, were close to the population center of the county and also close to a neighbor they had in mind to lead the new regiment.[7] Meeting in Newburgh on July 11, the committee made an important decision: they would seek out Captain Augustus Van Horne Ellis of the 71st New York State Militia to offer him the command of the regiment they were charged to raise.[8] The 71st was stationed near Washington, D.C., but Captain Ellis, knowing full well that there was an opportunity to lead one of the new regiments, was home on leave. "Capt. Ellis, of the 71st is still here," reported the *Newburgh Daily Telegraph,* "having returned home in order to ascertain what steps are to be taken in regard to the new levy of troops." When the announcement was made that Ellis would lead the new regiment, the press was quick to lend its approval. "The Captain has what might be called a fighting reputation: i.e. he is a man who believes that the soldier's business is to do as much damage to the enemy as possible; and those who enlist under him may expect to be immediately taken into active service, and not left to vegetate in the useful but inglorious work of guarding posts remote from the scene of danger."[9] There can be little doubt that members of the committee contacted Ellis ahead of time, urging him to make himself available as it was likely he would be offered the command. When it came, Ellis accepted without hesitation, resigned his commission in the 71st, and immediately made his way to Albany for instructions.

That same day, the adjutant general issued the following order:

State of New-York
General Head-Quarters,
Albany, July 11th, 1862
Special Orders, No. 330:

Capt. A. Van Horn Ellis, is hereby appointed Colonel of a Regiment of Volunteers to be organized in the 9th Regimental District, composed of the Counties of Orange and Sullivan. Col. Ellis will without delay, establish his Head-Quarters at Goshen, in Orange County, and proceed in the organization of the Regiment in conformity with the provisions of General Order, No. 52, from this Department.

By order of the Commander-in-Chief
Thos. Hillhouse, Adj. General[10]

The order was official business and was published in all the local newspapers. Ellis took out the following advertisement and saw to it that it appeared directly below Special Order No. 330:

In accordance with above Special Order, I am ready to receive proposals from persons desirous of organizing Companies, or parts thereof. Applications may be made to me at Goshen on Mondays and Fridays until further notice.

Van Horn Ellis
Col. 9th Regt'l Dist. Goshen.[11]

The next day, Ellis was back in Newburgh to begin the work of recruiting. The new regiment would be made up of ten companies, each with a captain, two lieutenants, and over eighty enlisted volunteers, a fact noted with pride in the local press. "Orange and Sullivan Ahead!" was the bold title of the article detailing Ellis' new job.

Col. Ellis has received his appointment — the first issued under the new levee. The Governor was not a little astonished at the promptness of the action. The men who follow Col. Ellis will find something to do. The selection made for a colonel of the new regiment is an excellent one, and one that will command the confidence of our entire people. Col. Ellis is an energetic man of business, as brave as he is patriotic, a thorough disciplinarian, and by nature and education immanently fitted for the position. Men of Orange and Sullivan! you have already done nobly, more than your share, as men reckon a fair division of burdens, but now do better! Fill up the ranks promptly and well, show to the Union that the Old Tenth is never appealed to in vain when the country is called for duty.[12]

The creation of the 124th New York and the appointment of Ellis as its colonel drew very positive press coverage, but just as the work of recruiting the new regiment was getting underway, a cloud darkened the prospects for a good start. The *Newburgh Journal* published a report that during the Battle of Bull Run, when then–Captain Ellis led a two-gun battery as part of the 71st New York Militia, he had been knocked down by a piece of exploding shell and left for dead by the men of his command.[13] The story seemed to impugn both the behavior of the captain and that of his men. The accusation drew an immediate, heated reply:

Augustus Van Horn Ellis led an interesting life before becoming the colonel of the 124th New York. He'd journeyed to California during the Gold Rush where he was a tax collector, member of the Committee of Vigilance and a fireman in San Francisco, a tug boat captain, land speculator, and an advisor to the king of Hawaii. He came east to captain a steamer for Cornelius Vanderbilt, then married into a prominent family in New Windsor, Orange County, New York. On the eve of the Civil War, he was a captain in the state militia (Michael J. McAfee collection).

Mr. Editor:—As you are always willing to do justice to all, I would like to say something in reply to an article in The Journal of Saturday, in regard to Capt. A.V.H. Ellis.... Such is not true, for there was not a man in the Company who would leave a man under such circumstances; and the statement is not doing justice to the brave boys who always obeyed his orders. When Johnston's reinforcements were close upon us, at Bull Run, Capt. Ellis was as cool as on a parade, and the boys rallied around him, and came off in excellent order.

Ward Beecher.[14]

Mr. Beecher's letter was supported a week later by another member of Ellis's company in the 71st who signed with his initials, "SJR."

> We all concur in saying the committee appointed by the Governor could not have chosen a better man, a braver or more efficient officer, as commandant of the new regiment from Orange and Sullivan than Col. A.V.H. Ellis. One thing we feel assured of, that he will never disgrace himself or those under his command by a mean or cowardly act, if we may judge his future conduct by his past.
>
> July 24th 1862
> Company I, 71st Regiment, NYSM.[15]

This seemed to put to rest any inference that Ellis was lacking in leadership, military skill, or bravery. In fact, the newspapers redoubled their praise of the man named to lead the new regiment.

The colonel wanted as many volunteers as possible for his new regiment but he put a premium on those with experience. He sought out men from the 71st New York State Militia who were "well drilled and of great respectability" to offer them "non-commissioned appointments."[16] He was also looking for experienced men to fill company grade officer slots. He had been in contact with Colonel Thomas B. Arden, New York State's adjutant general, who recommended two officers. But here Colonel Ellis ran up against public opinion and the will of the local recruiting committee. He wrote back to Colonel Arden that "it is the wish of the citizens here to officer the Reg't from the District if possible."[17] Colonel Arden wrote again at the end of the month recommending Lieutenant Colonel Charles Bartlett, presumably for second in command of the regiment. Ellis replied, "I have to say that the local Committee have some time strongly recommended a Mr. Cummings, native of this place and Lieut. Col. of an Iowa Reg't. He served through the Mexican War and is highly spoken of. If he does not succeed in his transfer, I shall attend your advice."[18]

In the end the committee prevailed and forty-year-old Francis Marko Cummins of Goshen got the job. He was a Mexican War veteran who, since the start of the Civil War, had fought in the recent western battles of Wilson's Creek, Dug Springs, and Shiloh. Here was a soldier who had not only seen battle, he had led men in battle. It had been alleged that Cummins was drunk at the Battle of Shiloh, but the recruiting committee, at least, was confident that his leadership abilities did not come from the bottle. For the position of adjutant, Ellis chose William Silliman of Cornwall whose abrupt manner did nothing to endear him to the men. They soon took to referring to him as "Old Silly Man." For the time being, the major's slot remained vacant.

To spur enlistments across the state, Governor Morgan issued a proclamation offering a bounty of $50 for every new volunteer. At the same time, towns in Orange and Sullivan counties began raising additional funds to help in the recruitment effort. The Town of Montgomery voted a $60 bounty for each of fifty recruits. The Village of Chester held a rally that raised $900 in nine minutes for the same purpose. Chester quickly filled its quota of 36 men, 25 of whom went with Charles B. Wood to join Charles Weygant's company then forming in Newburgh. The rest allied themselves with Frederick F. Wood, who, together with the men raised by James Denniston of Blooming Grove, joined Captain Isaac Nicoll's company.[19]

Some of those trying to attract volunteers did so by assuming ranks of lieutenant and even captain before they were mustered into the regiment. The aforementioned Charles Wood, for instance, was referred to as a captain while recruiting but started his military career with the 124th New York as Company A's first lieutenant. Frederick Wood, gathering men together as a lieutenant, later signed on as a sergeant in Company G.[20] Charles Wood later did rise to the rank of captain before a Confederate bullet ended his military career at Spotsylvania Court House in 1864. Sergeant Frederick Wood's military career — and his life — ended the same way at Chancellorsville less than a year after his enlistment. As the ten companies were filling up, serious negotiations took place to determine who would assume which rank in the new regiment.

"All the towns in the county are waking up," a reporter noted in an article written about the recruiting efforts. As in most things, Newburgh took the lead, raising, through pledges, well over $10,000. The names of the major donors and the amounts promised were prominently listed in the newspaper.[21] This bounty money was an important inducement to enlist. A private in the Union army was paid $13 per month but, as the men soon found out, the paymaster did not appear at regular intervals.

The prospect of leaving one's family destitute caused many potential recruits to think twice about enlisting. The bounty money paid to a volunteer might exceed $100, which would certainly get his family through the first winter of his absence. William Howell, of Howell's Depot, New York, began to keep what he called a "record of military service" in which he detailed the money he received for enlisting: "September 2nd, $50 state bounty, September 4th, $10 from the town, September 5th, $25 from the U states."[22]

Howell volunteered for three years' service on August 7 and was immediately detailed to recruit others. He was in Goshen on August 18 with his brother Henry, where they were assigned to a barracks and began their training with drill. William did so well that on August 30 he proudly entered into his record, "Was appointed Corporal of Company E 124th NY Vols."[23]

During the first week of August, the *Goshen Democrat* reported that men were arriving in the village every day, much more rapidly than had been the case the previous year when the 56th New York was being recruited from the same two counties. This optimistic appraisal was tempered with an admonition in the same edition that there were plenty of able-bodied men in the area not willing to step forward to defend the Union.

Lieutenant Colonel Francis M. Cummins served in Iowa regiments at the battles of Wilson's Creek and Shiloh, where he was put under arrest for drunkenness. As the second in command, he led the 124th New York at Brandy Station and was promoted after the death of Colonel Ellis. He was highly thought of by the men because of his genuine concern for their welfare, although Captain William Mapes called him "a perfect old Cuss a drunken Old SOB." Cummins was wounded at the Battle of the Wilderness on May 6, 1864, and discharged the following September (Michael J. McAfee collection).

> In some sections of the County, however, we hear from the people who do not appear to be sufficiently awake to the vast importance of having our Regiment filled up at once. It appears to us that supineness at such a time as this, when our country is menaced by bitter and barbarous enemies, and when her noble defenders now in the field, are calling to us for reinforcements, is wicked and criminal in the highest degree.... The simple declaration that our liberties,—the Union itself is in imminent peril, should be potent enough to rouse the veriest sluggard, and fire the heart that has never before throbbed with a single patriotic impulse.[24]

Talk of rousing the sluggards missed the point: thousands of Union soldiers were already under arms and yet the war went on. Union generals seemed unable to win a single battle. At the same time, casualty lists of men who had gone off to fight early in the war were published in the newspapers for all to see.

The experience of the 56th New York on the peninsula of Virginia earlier that summer did nothing to lift the spirits in the mid–Hudson region. Mustered into service for three years on October 28, 1861, the regiment was the brainchild of local Congressman Charles H. Van Wyck. He pressed for and received authorization to form the regiment which went by the nickname "Tenth Legion" in honor of his Tenth Congressional District. The 56th recruited five companies from Orange County and five from Sullivan County so these were all local men. Van Wyck was a prolific writer and many of his letters home were printed in the local press.

At the Battle of Fair Oaks, Virginia, at the end of May, the men of the Tenth Legion had a chance to show their mettle when General Joseph E. Johnston smashed into isolated units of the Union Army, which included the 56th New York. In the battle that followed, the regiment, which was part of Casey's Division of the 4th Corps, fought well. In the end, Union forces held their positions but the cost in killed, wounded, or missing on both sides was high even by Civil War standards. Among the wounded was Col. Van Wyck himself, who had been hit in the thigh by a piece of artillery shell. The force of the blow bent his sword and metal scabbard at a right angle instead of taking off his leg. In the days following the battle, the names of more than seventy soldiers of the Tenth Legion were listed in the newspapers as casualties. Each man had family and friends to worry about his recovery or mourn his death.[25] Then, in a classic example of adding insult to injury, General McClellan accused the 4th Corps in general and Casey's Division in particular of behaving badly in the face of the enemy at Fair Oaks. These charges resulted in a storm of protest, forcing McClellan to withdrew the accusations. Withdrawn or not, the charge had a sting to it when viewed next to the loss suffered by the regiment.

Clearly, local men were aware of what was at stake and were hardly supine or unconcerned. What was also clear to them was that inept generals were leading brave men to their deaths. Further, some agreed that the South had every right to leave the Union, for where in the Constitution did it prevent a sovereign state from doing just that? The Constitutional issues aside, there were those in the North who felt the South, with its backward institution of slavery, was an embarrassment. They saw the hypocrisy of insisting on the freedoms guaranteed in the Declaration of Independence and the Constitution on one hand and enslavement based upon race on the other. And then there were the local Peace Democrats, known as "Copperheads," who opposed the war for a host of reasons ranging from fear that the freed slaves would swarm North to take jobs and to mix in white society, to virulent hatred of the Lincoln administration and all things Republican.

Even as the 124th was forming, law enforcement authorities were moving against those in Orange County who opposed the war. Citing an order issued by President Lincoln, Constable William A. Cooley of Cornwall arrested Dr. W.F.C. Beattie and John E. Ryder, who "opposed enlistments and otherwise manifested their treasonable sentiments." It was reported that the two men held in Cornwall would soon be delivered to the United States marshal in New York City.[26]

Opposition to the war was hardly confined to Cornwall. Middletown was home to two decidedly anti-war, anti–Republican newspapers. The first was the *Banner of Liberty* whose masthead proclaimed, "An Independent National Newspaper,

Officers of the 124th New York. Lieutenant Henry Ramsdell is at the right, the seated officer is probably Captain William Silliman, the officer at left is unknown.

Private Henry Howell, Company E. He enlisted with his brother William and served until he was wounded at Spotsylvania Court House, May 12, 1864.

Advocating Civil and Religious Freedom, the Constitution and the Union, and Exposing Priestcraft and all its Cognate Isms." The last part reflected an anti–Catholic nativist sentiment sometimes associated with the early Republicans, a party regularly reviled in the pages of editor G.J. Beebe's popular newspaper. It was widely believed that Beebe closed his paper in September 1861 to avoid arrest and to prevent having *The Banner of Liberty* suppressed by the administration he hated.

A second anti-war paper soon took up the cause of the Copperheads in Orange County. The *Mercury* was just as virulent in its attacks on the administration and its despicable policy of emancipation. Both papers played to a nascent racism all too prevalent in Orange County. Readers were urged to oppose the war, the Lincoln administration, the draft, volunteering, and anything else that might support the war. It was said that soldiers home on leave were attacked in the streets of Middletown for daring to wear their uniforms in public. John Hasbrouck, editor of the pro-war Middletown *Whig Press* was himself caned by D.C. Dusenberry for his editorial attacks on the Copperhead movement. The indefatigable editor would not be silenced and retaliated in the way he knew best: in the editorial columns of his newspaper.[27]

Into this hotbed of Copperhead activity came Colonel Ellis and members of the recruiting committee seeking volunteers. On Saturday evening, August 7, Gothic Hall in Middletown was packed to capacity with an overflow crowd that spilled into the streets. Local Union men and Ellis made patriotic appeals to the assembled crowd inside and outside Gothic Hall. Their efforts were met with approval but they were upstaged when the aged War of 1812 veteran Moses H. Corwin dramatically rose and said that if Colonel Ellis needed but one more volunteer to complete his regiment, he could be counted upon to be that man. The crowd went wild, enthusiastically cheering the old soldier and the cause he espoused. It was not recorded how many recruits volunteered that night but a very large subscription was pledged to encourage volunteering.[28]

As early as July 14, Colonel Ellis was lobbying to have the rendezvous site for the new regiment located near Newburgh or New Windsor, two towns in the eastern end of Orange County. Ellis lived in New Windsor and a number of men he had in mind to officer his regiment had homes nearby. As a militia captain, he had trained the 56th New York one year earlier on ground just south of Newburgh, so he was familiar with the advantages to be found in the area. He argued that the eastern sites had more convenient rail service from the interior, making it easier to reach than Goshen, even from the western end of the county. Mail service in Goshen was "uncertain" and the water was "poor, hard, and limy." In the end, Goshen was chosen for the rendezvous although the citizens of the town did not appear too eager to have it so.[29]

Now, Colonel Ellis needed to find an area of open ground in Goshen large enough to house, feed, and train his men, and he went right to the top of Orange County society to find one. He contacted Bridget McDonell Wickham, widow of General George D. Wickham, a militia officer of War of 1812 vintage. Ellis asked for permission to use her estate within the village as the campsite for the new regiment. She readily agreed, acquiescing to his further request that the camp be named in honor of her late husband. "Accept my thanks for the compliment and best wishes for a speedy success of the Regiment you command, in putting down this unholy rebellion," she wrote the colonel.[30]

The pace of recruitment quickened in the first two weeks of August. "Companies are organizing in all directions," reported the *Newburgh Telegraph*. "We met Col. Ellis this morning and found him in fine spirits. His regiment is progressing finely. By tomorrow night he will have 200 men in camp at Goshen, where they are under drill by Lieut. Cressy."[31]

The men recruiting in Newburgh were having such success that a company under Charles Weygant was at full strength and ready to report to Goshen with five sergeants, eight corporals, two buglers, two musicians, and 83 privates. A second company was forming in the county seat itself and a third in Cornwall would be full in a matter of days. Now it became a race to get the men to Goshen as soon as possible. The first company to be enrolled would be designated Company A, the second Company B, and so on. This established a seniority for promotion when vacancies occurred among the field grade officers (major, lieutenant colonel, and colonel) and also established the positions of the companies in the line of battle. Company A was given the position of honor on the right flank, Company B on the left flank, and Company C in the center. The rest of the companies, D through K, would be positioned based on the seniority of their captains, no two junior captains next to each other. Company positions could be changed later at the discretion of the regimental commander.[32]

Ellis set up his headquarters at Camp Wickham in Goshen, giving the village a decidedly martial appearance. He started to refer to his burgeoning military unit as the "American Guard," a tribute paid to his old outfit, the 71st Militia, which bore that nickname. It is likely that he did so as a remembrance of his brother, Captain Julius Ellis, who was mortally wounded while leading Company F of the 71st at Bull Run.[33]

"The recruits are a fine body of men, both physically and mentally," wrote a reporter. "They have a well fitting fine blue cloth frock coat, and a flannel blouse for undress uniform; good under-clothing in abundance is also on hand." The new colonel, who already had quite a reputation as a stern drill master, and a number of company commanders began to teach the recruits the rudiments of drill and military discipline.[34] Since no weapons were available from the state or federal government, the men were drilled using sticks or borrowed civilian weapons.[35]

By mid–August, Charles Weygant's men had been mustered as Company A, but before they could even get settled at Camp Wickham, at least five of Weygant's privates deserted.[36] Henry Spencer Murray's company from Goshen was next, being enrolled as Company B. These two groups were soon followed by a third recruited by James Cromwell and William Silliman, which became Company C from Cornwall. James Cromwell was to be the captain and his was designated the "color company," with the color guard included on the left when the regiment formed in line of battle.

Also ready were the Warwick boys, as they liked to be called. James W. Benedict, Daniel Sayer, and John W. Houston recruited this company from the prosperous farming community on the New Jersey border. Twenty-year-old 2nd Lieutenant Houston wrote, "Company D was filled and reported to Col. A.W.H. Ellis at Goshen and then the fun began."[37] Within a very short time, Colonel Ellis reported to the adjutant general of New York that he had nine hundred twenty eight men enrolled in his new regiment awaiting orders.[38] Provisions had to be made to clothe, feed, and house the recruits massing at the heretofore sleepy county seat at Goshen. By mid–August, five huge barracks had been erected, each one a hundred feet by forty feet in size, with additional smaller outbuildings for cooking meals and for feeding the men.[39] A restaurateur, Benjamin B. Odell from Newburgh, was given the contract to provide meals. "We had barrocks to sleep in and straw for beds with bread and milk, boiled rice, and white beans for grub," wrote Lieutenant Houston.[40]

While the papers reported that "the soldiers are well satisfied with the provisions furnished them," letters written after they departed the camp contain comments that the army rations they received later were superior to what was fed to them in Goshen.[41] In fact, the food, barracks, and the site itself left much to be desired. When the barracks were torn down, the townsfolk were relieved that the eyesores were destroyed. The site of Camp Wickham was chosen without input from local citizens, who could have told Ellis that the drainage and water supply on the property would be sorely taxed by so large a body of men.[42]

These problems notwithstanding, the local press continued to laud the new regiment. "A finer body of men, or more orderly and well behaved, could not be got together ... Col. Ellis and his officers are untiring in their efforts to have the Regiment ready to leave for the seat of War, at the earliest moment."[43] If indeed the men were orderly and well behaved, it was because Ellis sought to instill in his civilians-in-uniform an understanding that a well disciplined regiment was an effective fighting regiment and that drill had a purpose. The ability to move quickly and efficiently on the battlefield, to load and fire in unison, and to obey without question the orders of the officers meant that they would be able to inflict upon the enemy more punishment than the enemy could inflict upon them. Ellis had learned the importance of discipline in the gold fields of California, as a captain on one of Vanderbilt's steamers, and on the battlefield at Bull Run. Poorly led and poorly trained units had marched off to war with great promise only to dissolve into chaos when pressed by the enemy. Ellis knew that he must forcefully put the men under his command right away, before they had a chance to develop ideas contrary to his own. He set about doing it as soon as the men began to gather at Goshen.

Ellis may have tempered his famously profane vocabulary when civilians were around but an incident that took place a month after the regiment was mustered serves to illustrate his ability to instill fear in his own men. Sergeant William Wirt Bailey of Company K wrote home to his father that "The Col. sometimes does swear big, that is when he gets mad." The incident involved Bailey's friend, Sergeant Daniel Webb, who was serving as the 2nd sergeant of the same company during a drill. The manuals of the day placed great responsibility on the 2nd sergeant for positioning the left of the company during drill. When moving from a column of four men abreast into the a line of battle, the 2nd sergeant was to move up quickly to take the leftmost position in the line while the 1st sergeant did the same on the right. Between the two, they aligned the company in a straight front two ranks deep before moving on to another evolution. This movement had to be done correctly by each of the ten companies. Sergeant Bailey readily agreed that the job of the 2nd sergeant was critical. "If the second Sergeant does not guess the right distance, it will throw the whole Regt. out of mash. I think they have almost as much to do on parade as the Captains."[44]

Colonel Ellis had ordered a maneuver which required the unfortunate Sergeant Webb to move onto the left flank of his company, but for some reason Webb did not end up in the correct position. "The Col. came around and drew his sword as if to strike him and said, 'I will cut your

Colonel Augustus Van Horne Ellis, one of five Ellis brothers who served in the war. His brother Julius was killed leading a company of the 71st New York State Militia at the First Battle of Bull Run. Augustus commanded a two-gun battery of the 71st in the same battle. He raised the 124th New York and was its first commander. He led the regiment at Fredericksburg, Brandy Station, and Chancellorsville. Ellis was killed in action at Gettysburg July 2, 1863 (archive of the Historical Society of the Town of Warwick, gift of Joan and Tom Frangos).

God dam little head off and then skedadle.'" Bailey remarked that he and Dan's friends found the incident hilarious and teased him about it later, having a "good laugh" every time one of them related the story of how Dan's eyes bulged out like "peeled onions." Bailey also remarked that, at the time of the incident, he dared not laugh, for to do so would further inflame the colonel and have Ellis' anger directed at him instead of the hapless Sergeant Webb.[45]

Private Henry Dill of Company G, sometimes called the "praying company" because of the strong religious tone of some of its members, related another example of the Ellis temper. As Dill told the story: "Wee Ware marching Along the other Day and a man said that is A Damed purty Looking Regiment." The man making the derogatory comment was a teamster, a civilian wagon driver in the pay of the government, and his mocking tone brought a swift response from Ellis. The colonel rode right up to him, pointedly asking if he thought he could do better than the men marching past. "Yes," answered the man, "and a Beter son of Bitch of A Cornel to." This was too much for Ellis, who dismounted and ordered the man off his wagon. The driver, realizing too late that this particular colonel was in no mood for jokes at his own expense, refused to come down. Ellis pulled him to the ground then soundly beat him in front of the regiment. The man was put under guard, and marched four miles before being released. Private Dill was duly impressed. "I tell you Cornel Eles is A man and Wont Let His Boys Be imposed on."[46]

Ellis' assault on the teamster demonstrated a number of things: his quick temper, physical strength, and ability to brawl with the best of them—teamsters had to be tough to handle the stubborn, skittish army mules hitched to the heavy wagons. The fight also showed the colonel's unwillingness to see his men demeaned or to have his own competence called into question by anyone, including those same men in the ranks who watched the teamster take his beating. Ellis seized a dramatic moment to demonstrate that they, too, would obey him or suffer the consequences. He was also trying to instill pride and a fighting spirit in his men, an élan that would serve them well on the battlefield.

Colonel Charles H. Weygant, last commander of the 124th New York and author of the regimental history. At the time of his enlistment, Weygant was 23 years old and captain of Company A. He was wounded at Chancellorsville, at Spotsylvania Court House, and at Boydton Road, Virginia; he mustered out with regiment June 3, 1865, near Washington, D.C. (archive of the Historical Society of the Town of Warwick, gift of Joan and Tom Frangos).

But all this was yet to come. The men gathering in Goshen were still basically civilians and would continue to act as such until Ellis and his officers could get them away from familiar surroundings to begin their training. "It was very hard for the men to be compelled to remain in camp and many a one stole between the sentinels who were armed with sticks as there were no guns in camp at that time," wrote young Lieutenant John Houston.[47]

One evening in late August, as the regiment was formed up for dress parade, the cry of "Fire!" was heard from the direction of the village. Smoke and flames could be seen in the distance, rising from a private residence. Without being dismissed, the entire regiment broke ranks and went "helter-skelter across fields for Goshen." Ellis himself had belonged to a fire company during his California days and he was no doubt in the lead. Fighting the fire was hot work and the boys shared a "social glass" with the appreciative townspeople whose homes and property the new recruits had rushed to protect. After dark, they all came back to camp "of their own accord," none having to be rounded up. Lieutenant Houston commented that they were in "fair condition," having not imbibed too much while battling the flames. "So you see the discipline of the soldier had its good effect in that early day."[48]

The men were settling into the routine of camp life. Private John Z. Drake of Captain Ira Bush's Company F from Port Jervis wrote that he had not been feeling well, perhaps a victim of the poor drinking water. He had been so sick that "I didn't eat nothing but I can eat as much as any of them now. We have Plenty of fun here in Camp. We have got all of our uniforms all but our guns. We are to have miney rifles." Private Drake was referring the modern rifle muskets, American and foreign, that fired the Minié ball.[49] The most popular were the American-made Springfield and the British made Enfield. Technological advances in the weapon itself and in the design of the bullet made these weapons more reliable and accurate at greater distance. Just as important, the bullet packed a far more powerful punch than arms issued previously to American troops.

Colonel Ellis wanted modern arms for his regiment and wrote to Colonel Arden on August 4 to secure them. "My dear Colonel, can you put me in the way of getting Springfield rifled muskets for the Regt? I have a great respect for that arm and would do much to get them. I have a horror of these Enfield and Belgian concerns. I believe Comy. Genl Welsh has that distribution and I have the misfortune to be unacquainted with him."[50] The demand for arms was so great that large numbers of weapons, both good and bad, were imported from Europe to meet the need. Private Drake was to be dis-

Major James Cromwell, a Quaker, and the first major of the regiment at the age of 22. Much beloved by the troops, he was killed in action, July 2, 1863, at Gettysburg. Captain Benedict said of him, "He was to my mind the Noblest, Bravest, Best Young Man I ever Knew and one I am proud to be able to call friend" (archive of the Historical Society of the Town of Warwick, gift of Joan and Tom Frangos).

appointed, and the colonel outraged, when they learned that they would not be issued rifle muskets for many months but instead would have "2nd Class Arms" from Belgium, the very "horror" that Colonel Ellis so feared.

By late August, it was clear that there would be more than enough recruits to fill the regiment with just the men signed up so far: nine hundred and three of all ranks, including officers, staff, musicians, and wagoneers.[51] Colonel Ellis issued an order on August 12 that "all officers recruiting for this Regiment are hereby ordered to make a full report of their progress, and if possible, have their men mustered in at these Headquarters, by Friday evening, 15th inst., as the Regiment is ready to muster in." Rumors were flying that the recruiting district might be divided and Ellis, no doubt fearing that some recruits might change their minds, pushed hard to get his men mustered in as quickly as possible. On August 20 he issued an order for the recruiting officers to bring in their men "forthwith," as the 124th New York had marching orders for Thursday, August 27, and that "clothing, Arms, &c. are ready."[52]

Once Ellis reported that his regiment was at full strength, it was just a matter of time before the men would be mustered into federal service and entrained for points south. Orange County buzzed with the prospect of the emotion and pomp of such an historic ceremony. Then, just as over nine hundred of its sons, husbands, fathers, and brothers prepared to depart for the great war of the rebellion, distant, ominous rumblings of the Confederate victories at Cedar Mountain and the Second Battle of Bull Run reverberated through the land. These Union defeats enhanced concern for the fate of the Union and for the safety of the men and boys who would march with the 124th New York.

Some were concerned with more than just the physical safety of the men. On August 19, Hannah C. Johnston sat down to write a letter to her younger brother Joseph, whom she called Josey. He had only recently enlisted in Company E under Captain William McBirney. Their brother Frank Johnston had, the year before, volunteered to serve in a Missouri cavalry regiment.

My dear brother

It is with a sad heart that I now undertake the task of writing a farewell letter for you to read when you are many miles away from me ... but alas! our Country calls also for your services in regaining her honor and freedom and we must make the sacrifice, hard though it be to do so. I give you up to the care and protection of that Almighty Preserver who has so mercifully and wonderfully preserved our brother through many and fearful dangers. O do put your trust in him and try to do your duty as he would have you do it.... Then you will be kept from taking part in the many vices and bad habits which always attend in a greater or less degree, a Camp life. You will probably see many and frequent examples of drunkeness, lying, stealing perhaps and what is probably most frequent is swearing. O what my beloved brother sounds more sinful and degrading than taking the name of God in vain.... Never play cards with persons who would play for money or drink. If you want something to pass away the time pleasantly, either read some good book or read of the letters which you receive from home.... Spend much of your time in writing letters home. Write good long ones and give us all the particulars which you know.... You will not find a man in Camp worth quarreling with, and I hope you will treat them as if you thought so. Have no words with them when angry, this has been a great cause of anxiety with me in having you leave home so young ... but I know that if you are determined to do right whatever cross you have to bear you will by the grace of God most surely succeed. And now closing this with a sweet farewell I earnestly pray God to have you in his keeping, to help you bravely to do your duty, and return you safely to the ever fond embrace of your most loving devoted sister

Hannah C. Johnston.[53]

The war that split the nation likewise split the Johnston family. The Quaker Meeting to which they all belonged could not abide the fact that the brothers had joined to fight. Both Frank and Josey were expelled.

Throughout the north that late summer of 1862, nearly three hundred new regiments prepared for departure. Families again flooded the camps to make sure that their soldiers had with them all manner of Bibles, images of family members, extra clothing, preserves, handguns, knives, portable writing desks, toiletries, and other items. Some were useful or such powerful reminders of home that they found a place in the soldier's knapsack. But most would be discarded along the roadside on the first march.

A visitor to the camp gave Private Patrick Leach of Company B a pistol and, while he was examining it, the weapon discharged. The ball passed through a one inch wallboard and struck the wife of Private John Eckert while she was talking to her husband outside.[54] The wound was so serious and Mrs. Eckert in such critical condition that Private Eckert was furloughed to remain in Goshen to nurse his wife back to health. She had recovered sufficiently for him to return to the regiment in time for the Battle of Chancellorsville the following May.

Even the advertisements in the local press looked to the needs of the men. "Soldiers!" an ad read. "See to your own health, do not trust to the Army supplies; Cholera, Fever, and Bowel complaint will follow your slightest indiscretion. Holloway's Pills and Ointment should be in every man's knapsack — The British and French troops use no other medicines. Only 25 cents per Box or Pot."[55]

Soldiers made preparations for going off to war in other ways as well. In one issue of a local paper under the heading "Marriages" were listed the following:

Moses Ross, Chief Bugler of the 124th Regt., to Miss E. Vail
Curtis Ackerman, of Co. E, 124th Regt., to Miss Ann Hall
Ezra Hyatt, of Co. D, 124th Regt., to Miss Barbara Fitzgerald.[56]

Officers were expected to provide their own uniforms and weapons. Here was an opportunity for friends and family to present useful items of value and significance. The moulders of the Washington Iron Works of Newburgh gave 2nd Lieutenant Henry P. Ramsdell of Company C an engraved sword, a sash, and belt. He came from a wealthy family with varied business interests which included the ironworks and Hudson River steamships. In a letter to the young volunteer, iron workers wrote that they had the highest respect for his willingness to exchange his life of "refinement and luxury" for the rigors of the march and the danger of the battlefield. This feeling was due in no small measure to his "gentlemanly conduct towards us and to the fact that you seemed to take considerable interest in our business." They had hoped to make the presentation in Newburgh where Ramsdell resided but because of the demands placed upon him in Goshen they sent the sword and letter to him in camp.[57]

On August 24, orders were received setting August 27 as the departure date for the regiment. With so much left to do and so little time left before their loved ones departed, a feeling of urgency took hold of the county. It was soon learned, however, that the federal government was not ready to arm them or to provide travel and accommodations as so many other regiments were on the move at the same time. On top of that, the men had not received their advance pay. It was speculated that it would be at least a week before the regiment would finally depart.[58] The general public, however, still thought that the regiment would move out August 27. That and a flag presentation on August 26 meant that a sizeable portion of Orange County determined to make its way to Goshen to be a part of the historic event.

The Village of Goshen awoke that Tuesday to a flood of visitors. "Somehow the impression had got abroad that a 'big time' was to be had in connection with a flag presentation, and at an early hour the people began to pour in to the astonished town.... One can imagine what a time the residents had with such a crowd, and no provision made for their reception."[59] By noon, every hotel and inn with rooms to let was full and there was no more room for the horses and carriages. The sleepy village swelled to several times its permanent population, some estimates running as high as 15,000 people. The presentation of a stand of colors to the regiment would be a solemn occasion indeed and a great opportunity for Colonel Ellis to demonstrate how well his new recruits had been trained.

At 3:30 P.M., the regiment was ordered out for dress parade, a formal exercise which members would be required to perform throughout their military service. Each of ten companies marched out and took its place in line of battle, each captain at the right of his company until, at the command, he stepped out awaiting orders. At Ellis' command, the companies wheeled to the right forming a column of companies so that the regiment could pass in review for the huge crowd. The colonel, already well known for his martial bearing, looked every inch the soldier. Superbly mounted as always, he proudly

Lieutenant Henry Ramsdell, adjutant, came from a wealthy and prominent Newburgh family (Michael J. McAfee collection).

Flag of the 124th Reg't N. Y. Vols.,
PRESENTED BY
THE LADIES OF ORANGE, SEPTEMBER, 1862.
ITS BATTLES:
Manassas Gap, Fredericksburgh, Chancellorsville, Beverly Ford, Gettysburg, Woppings Heights, Auburn, Kelly's Ford, Jone's Cross Roads, Mine Run.

FOR SALE AT REMILLARD'S,
82 Water St., and at the Newburgh Bookstores.

Sergeant Thomas Rodman, Company C. He enlisted as a private and steadily rose in rank. A prolific letter writer, he told his parents, "I am going to end the War before I get back Or the War is going to end me" (Robert and Sandra Rodman collection).

watched his men pass in review. "The troops deported themselves creditably, and their short stay at camp had transformed them into a fine looking body of soldiers, who will certainly do honor to the county from which they hail...."[60] With the regiment again drawn up in line of battle, the highlight of the afternoon took place.

On a speaker's platform sat dignitaries awaiting the colonel's signal that he was prepared to receive the colors. But first came the obligatory political bombast presented in the form of a patriotic speech by the Honorable Charles H. Winfield, who just happened to be running for Congress. When he was done, Winfield handed the national flag to Colonel Ellis on behalf of the "Daughters of Orange," the patriotic ladies' group that had raised money for its purchase. The silk national flag was, at Ellis' request, made for "service and not for show." It would be carried at the center of the regiment by a color bearer chosen for his bravery and soldierly demeanor. A color guard of handpicked men would protect the colors at all costs. Also presented to the regiment was a pair of guidons. These small American flags were carried at each flank of the regiment, left and right, by sergeants chosen for the same qualities as the color bearer. With the colors at the center and the guidons on the flanks, the men could always align themselves even under the most trying circumstances.[61]

Ellis received the flag and dramatically held it aloft saying, "Should the Flag this day presented by the people of loyal Orange, never be permitted to return, the brave boys marching under its broad folds will share its fate; for we have sworn to die rather than that it should be yielded to the enemies of our country!"[62] The prophetic words told the fate of Colonel Ellis himself and of nearly two hundred fifty officers and men who heard them.

David F. Gedney, Esq., a local dignitary, was next to speak, accepting the flag in the name of the regiment. "His remarks were received with many demonstrations of gratification, and upon its conclusion the assemblage manifested its approbation by cheers and clapping of hands."[63] The *Whig Press* described his speech as "eloquent" but of "some length."[64]

Next, Miss Charlotte Coulter stepped forward, determined not to be overshadowed by any politician. She made a "grand little speech" and presented the guidons on behalf of the "Daughters of Wawayanda."

With all eyes upon him, Colonel Ellis carried the national flag to the center of the regiment, and held it aloft while the men gave their new banner its first salute, "which was done in true Military order with the right hand raised." He then handed it over for safekeeping to Color Bearer Jonas G. Davis, "which was the signal for a simultaneous outburst of enthusiasm upon

Opposite: First Battle Flag of the 124th New York. The Daughters of Orange ordered the first battle flag and two guidons from Tiffany and Co. of New York City. This flag was carried by the regiment until the winter of 1864, when it was replaced and sent home to be displayed at Washington's Headquarters in Newburgh (archive of the Historical Society of the Town of Warwick, gift of Joan and Tom Frangos).

the part of the whole Regiment and all joined in six cheers and a 'tiger'—three for the colors, and three for the 'Daughters of Orange' and Wawayanda for the highly valued gift." Just at that moment, the Middletown Band struck up "The Star Spangled Banner." "The effect was electrical, and the dense mass of people present, seemed carried away by the enthusiasm of the moment."[65] The official ceremonies complete, the regiment marched and countermarched to show off the new banner, which "looked very beautiful as it gracefully floated to the breeze."

The total cost of the national colors and guidons was $130. The flag was made of the very best oil boiled silk to regulation size. "The staff is surmounted with a silver spear, and decorated with a crimson cord and tassel. Upon the colors is the inscription, '124th Regiment, N.Y.S.V., American Guard.' On an engraved plate upon the Staff, is written—'Presented to the American Guard, by the Daughters of Orange.'"

The company commanders were then ordered to take charge of their companies. Captain Ira Bush marched Company F back to its barracks where soldiers were drawn up in front of the building. A ladies group from Port Jervis, the hometown of Company F, had raised $45 to pay for a truly magnificent sword made by Tiffany and Company of New York. In a stirring ceremony, Eliza Knight and Maggie Heller, representing all who had contributed, presented the sword to Captain Bush in front of his company.[66]

The festivities concluded, the officers and men were dismissed to visit with their families. Ellis seized the opportunity to make a quick trip home to New Windsor. There he found awaiting him a group of townspeople led by George Denniston, the town supervisor. In a brief and quiet ceremony, Ellis was presented with a sword.[67]

Thomas Rodman of Company C sat down to write his parents what he was sure would be his last letter from Camp Wickham.

> I am well and in good spirits at present and I hope I may always be the same.... This afternoon we have our Flag presented to us. Tell Father I am now acting as orderly Sergeant of my company as to what position I am permanently to hold I cannot say at present but am sure of an office. There is some talk of changing out our Captain. None of our Sergeants or Corporals are yet appointed.[68]

As it turned out, this piece of camp gossip was true: Captain James Cromwell, at that time serving as the commander of Rodman's company, had been promoted to major six days before and would be mustered at that rank the day before their departure from Goshen on September 5.[69] William Silliman, serving as adjutant, was promoted to captain of Company C and would be mustered on the same date.[70]

The daily routine of camp continued as the regiment awaited orders. Drummers woke the men at 5 A.M., when they were expected to wash and clean their quarters in time for roll call at 6 A.M. Close attention was paid to determine if anyone had deserted during the night. The regiment drilled until 7 A.M., when the men were excused for breakfast until 8 A.M., after which the men formed up for more drill. Dinner was served by Mr. Odell's workers at noon followed by yet more drill. The men were called to dress parade at 5 P.M., where orders were read, inspections conducted, and other general military

Captain William Silliman had been a lieutenant in the 7th New York Cavalry. He became the captain of Company C but left the regiment to become the colonel of the 26th U.S. Colored Troops. He was killed in action (archive of the Historical Society of the Town of Warwick, gift of Joan and Tom Frangos).

business concluded. Upon dismissal at 7 P.M., they were expected to return to their quarters until 9 P.M., when they were to retire.[71] And so the routine continued while the men and their families waited for the inevitable order to move.

Finally, on September 5, Captain William G. Edgerton of the 11th United States Infantry arrived at Camp Wickham to muster the regiment into the service of the United States. That same day a telegram was received setting Saturday, September 6 for departure as their weapons were awaiting them in New York City. It was, at last, time to leave behind their civilian pursuits and take up arms in the defense of the Union.

Just after noon on the appointed day, the regiment was formed up "and, without arms, but with banners flying and drums beating a lively tune; with knapsacks and haversacks swelled to their utmost capacity, with not only wearing apparel that would never be worn and food that would never be eaten, but with books to read, and keepsakes ... we moved through throngs of weeping ones to the depot, where the last hand-shakings and final adieus were given; and at two P.M. the heavily laden train, with wild shrieks to warn away the clinging multitudes, moved off, and we were on our way to the seat of war."[72]

CHAPTER 2

"To learn us our duty"
September 6–October 16, 1862

Two long trains were required to transport the regiment to New York City. The first pulled out of Goshen at noon, the second followed an hour later.[1] Before departure, Colonel Ellis handed Lieutenant Houston a tough assignment. The young officer and ten men from his company were detailed to act as a rear guard to watch for stragglers, deserters, and drunks until they reached their destination. "And it was a hard task he gave me, as some of the men would get tipsey after all my watching and some were trying to get home for a visit."[2]

The trip was not without incident. When the train stopped at Turner's Depot, just ten miles from Goshen, Private Hugh Foley of Company K jumped out of the window. Lieutenant James Roosa and several others of that company grabbed him, wrestling him back to the car, but the man continued to struggle. Captain Leander Clark, officer of the day, came up to investigate the disturbance and wasted no time on the man, striking him in the face and handcuffing him. "I tell you the blood flew," wrote Sergeant William Wirt Bailey. When the regiment arrived in New York City, Foley was made to "hug a tree all night," handcuffed with his arms around the trunk. The fight must have been something to see because Wirt, as he liked to be called, noted, "He has got an awful face."[3] About a month later, Bailey wrote to reassure friends back home that Private Foley was still with them. "Hugh Foley was not shot, nor anything done to him except he had to wear hand cuffs until he got to Phil[adelphia]."[4]

The train ran east and then south, through Rockland County, to the Jersey City Depot. The men made themselves as comfortable as possible, expecting that another train would come along to carry them on to Philadelphia. But so many regiments were converging on the same depot that there were not enough cars to accommodate them all. With no food, shelter, or transportation available, they were ferried across the Hudson River to New York City.[5] Once back in the Empire State, the 124th New York took up the march to City Hall Park Barracks. It was midnight before the men had supper, which they thought "an improvement on Goshen fare." Quarters were available inside the barracks for some, outside in tents for others, and "under the light of the moon" for the rest.[6] Sergeant Bailey shared a tent with three other men. "We had no straw, I laid my rubber blanket down on the boards and slept like a pig. I know if I was home, I would have the leg ache, but I do not mind it now. I feel first rate." Sergeant John D. Drake of Company F slept soundly "on the soft side of a board."[7]

Colonel Ellis kept the men confined to quarters with sentries posted that night and the next day. But at least one man, nineteen-year-old Private John Shepard, a sailor by profession, managed to slip past the guards into the dark streets beyond the barracks, never to be seen in the ranks of the 124th again.[8]

Corporal William W. Decker of Company F knew his father planned to take a different train into the city. Decker tried his best to get away a few minutes for a last goodbye, but he was one of the men assigned to guard duty. Although he managed to get out of the barracks twice, he did not have the chance to see his father.[9]

Colonel Ellis did his best to secure decent weapons for his regiment but equipment of all kinds was in short supply. Much to the colonel's disgust, his men were issued .69 caliber Vincennes rifles. The ordnance report showed that the regiment was issued these inferior European weapons along with cartridge boxes, waist belts, cap pouches, slings, bayonets, scabbards, and 15,000 rounds of .69 caliber "expanding ball cartridges."[10] There were not enough working rifles to go around and some of the men had to wait to be armed.[11]

By 5 P.M. on Sunday, the men had been fed dinner and were on their way back to the Jersey Depot to board the train that would take them to Philadelphia.[12] At every town along the route, they were cheered by crowds of well-wishers waving American flags to speed them on their way. Pleased by their reception, the men returned shout for shout and cheer for cheer.

The trained chuffed south to Camden, New Jersey, where, at about midnight, the regiment was ferried across the Delaware River to Philadelphia to be greeted by the ladies of the Cooper Shop Volunteer Refreshment Saloon. Corporal Decker wrote that he sat down to the best meal he'd had since he left home a month before. "And God bless the ladies or authorities of Philadelphia," wrote Chaplain T. Scott Bradner. The

Private John E. Kidd, Company H. He served throughout the war and brought home his rifle and accoutrements. This included his cartridge box which contained six rounds he did not fire in the last engagement of the 124th New York near Appomattox Court House.

men "found an immense building, with tables loaded with provisions in abundance. On the sidewalk a row of 100 wash basins. There the ladies stand all day and all night, feeding a Regiment at once.—The booming of a cannon when the boat is in the middle of the river, announcing to them to get the tea and coffee ready. Here, too, they have a hospital, and all men who are compelled to fall out of the ranks, are nursed with the kindest attention, and sent on after their Regiment." The same day that the 124th New York passed through, the Cooper Shop fed the 123rd New York, 11th Ver-

Chaplain T. Scott Bradner tried to cure Colonel Ellis of swearing. He served throughout the war, and was mustered out with the regiment (archive of the Historical Society of the Town of Warwick, gift of Joan and Tom Frangos).

mont, 37th Massachusetts, 40th Massachusetts, and a small group from the 3rd and 12th New Jersey regiments.[13]

After what one man called a "splendid supper," they lay down on the sidewalk and slept until dawn. The next day the regiment took up the march for the Baltimore Depot where the men were loaded aboard freight cars, since no passenger cars were available. As the train moved through the countryside south of Philadelphia, the New Yorkers noticed a subtle change in how they were greeted. The villagers along the railroad no longer turned out en mass to cheer them; instead the people "seemed to look on us with a sort of sneer and disdain. especialy in the city of Wilmington."[14]

At the Susquehanna River, the whole train was run aboard a ferry bound for Havre de Grace, Maryland. Some of the men went to fill their canteens on the Maryland side but were left behind when the train got underway for Baltimore without them. Although that city was well known for its secessionist sympathies, the men were treated to a fine dinner courtesy of the Baltimore Union Relief Association. Private Henry Losey was impressed by the citizens of Baltimore. "On arriving at Baltimore we met with a first rate reception, and were treated to a good meal of victuals, furnished by the Union Women of that Place. To see the flags waving from numerous housetops in the city, you would not think it was peopled by men three-fourths of who are secessionists."[15]

Thirty-two-year-old Captain James Benedict of Company D wrote,

Major James W. Benedict, captain of Company D, wounded at Spotsylvania (archive of the Historical Society of the Town of Warwick, gift of Joan and Tom Frangos).

At Baltimore we had to stay on the sidewalk for about 3 hours before we could get our meals at the Relief Rooms. When I ordered Halt an old Lady opened her front door and asked the officers in to wash and rest which came very acceptable as we had had no opportunity to wash since leaving N.J. In coming through it was amusing to see the different countenances and expressions and actions some would greet us with extravagant expressions of joy, others with sour looks and motions but nothing disrespectful when the cars were stopped, and it would not have been well for them to have done so, almost all the way the ladies would bring out a flag and shake it as long as we could see them and cheer them.[16]

The tracks did not run through Baltimore, so the 124th New York, like all regiments before them, marched to Camden Station on the other side of town. It was a hot day, and some of the men fell out due to heat exhaustion and were sent to the hospital. "We were obliged to remain in Baltimore until night, most of which time was spent by the boys in looking around and buying things that they thought would be needful in camp. Although there was a riot the day before, between the Union men and the secessionists, and some members of the 123rd Regiment [which passed through in the morning] were poisoned, we were unmolested."[17]

These Unionists notwithstanding, Corporal Decker did not like what he saw. "We arrived in Baltimore yesterday about 2 o'clock P.M. and if the truth was known the place is rotten with rebels and through fear were forced to raise the American flag. We had anticipated a row on passing through but fortunate for them they held there peace for we were armed to the teeth with French rifels with sabor banuts. Of all places of corruption and whoredom Baltimore is No 1. I never heard so much profanity and vulgarity in so short a time among pretty ~~ladies~~ women as I did there."[18]

Long Bridge, Washington, D.C. On September 10, 1862, Private Thomas Rodman wrote, "Passed the Presidents house and the Capitol building, down to the long bridge and over on the sacred soil of Virginia" (Library of Congress, Prints & Photographs Division).

The regiment departed Baltimore that evening, arriving in Washington after midnight where members "spread our blankets in the Street and turned in for a nap."[19] When they awoke, it was Tuesday morning, September 9. Until then, few among them had traveled outside Orange County, let alone New York State. Now, in just three days, they had moved by train through three of the nation's largest and wealthiest cities, crossed three great rivers and traveled through two slave states, and were now camped on the grounds of the Capitol building where the senators and congressmen met to write the nation's laws. This was all very exciting, but they had a lot to learn about soldiering and the first lesson had to do with room and board at government expense. The barracks offered to the regiment were so dirty that Colonel Ellis chose instead to have his men sleep in the open air amid the stone blocks that would be used to build the north wing of the Capitol. Breakfast was equally repulsive: "the filth and stench of that government soup-house was too much for the sons of Orange, and hardly a score of them entered."[20] Private John Drake's review of the meal was just as terse: "Then we got our breakfast. One slice of bread and meat and a cup of coffee. But I couldn't eat the Beef."[21]

Then, the new regiment found out what it was like to march in Virginia. About midmorning, Wednesday, September 10, soldiers were ordered to strap on their knapsacks, shoulder their weapons, form up, and move out for Secessia. The distances were short but they were not yet conditioned to carrying weapons, ammunition, food, water, and other gear on the march.

Starting down Pennsylvania Avenue, they "passed the Presidents house and the Capitol building, down to the long bridge and over on the sacred soil of Virginia," as eighteen-year-old Private Thomas Rodman sarcastically referred to it.[22] After marching about six miles they reached Camp Chase, "on the farm of the Rebal Genral Lee."[23] So many stragglers were scattered along the road behind that a detachment of fifty men was sent back to gather them up. Private Henry Losey was among those who walked almost to the bridge, where they were able to find some baggage wagons to carry their comrades into camp.[24]

Chaplain Bradner had a difficult time too. "It was intensely hot on the march, and we were enveloped in a cloud of dust, equal to a dry Goshen Horse Fair, with hundreds of wagons, horses and men passing both ways. No words can give you any conception of the realities of war. Since we have been on the ground, we have slept, eaten, and lived in the dirt. You cannot know the value of water, till you go a mile for it, and then not particular as to the quality. In addition from the great scarcity of teams and provender, we have hardly had enough to eat."

Mixed among the new regiments at Camp Chase were a number of older units, including some veterans of the recent defeat of the Second Battle of Bull Run or the equally disappointing battles on the peninsula of Virginia. "All these troops have been very much cut up, they number only from 150 to 300 in a Regiment, and still they are cheerful and as ready to move for action, as the first day they entered service."[25]

"The enemy are reported to be only ten miles from us," Corporal William Howell wrote. "We are on the tented field on Arlington Heights. Our tents are about three and a half ft. high seven wide and ten long."[26] There was excitement right away. "Our guards caught a rebel spy last night. He had a map of all our fortifications and encampments on his person."[27] The man was walking around the camp of the 124th New York dressed in civilian clothes asking how the men were armed. His rather obvious questions alerted the guards who seized him. The spy was found to have accurate written estimates on him as to the number of Union troops in and around Camp Chase. A closer search yielded a letter he planned to send to his friends farther south saying that the Yankees had new, clean uniforms and tents, so they must be raw recruits. Although they were about 50,000 strong, the spy had written, he was sure that if General Jackson moved quickly against them with a small force, he could capture the whole lot and take their new gear. "But," noted Private Thomas Rodman with obvious pride, "we are not so green as all that."[28] The boys had some fun with the spy, roughing him up before he was put under arrest and taken away.[29]

After the regiment arrived at Camp Chase, "Gov. Seward," as New Yorkers called the secretary of state, paid them a visit. Seward's hometown was Florida, New York, only a couple of miles from Goshen, so he was well known to the men who received him with "great cheers." With all the excitement of Seward's visit and the spy in camp, it must have been difficult for the men to settle into soldier life, but Colonel Ellis was a stickler for discipline, drill, and military decorum. He soon had the men clearing up the debris left by the last regiment, policing the grounds, and making sure that their tents were set up according to regulation.

Sergeant Bailey wrote home to complain about Camp Chase: "I don't like our place, for we can not see very far off, but as far as we can see, we see nothing but tents and soldiers." As he wrote, he could hear the men "pounding coffee" for breakfast. Coffee beans were issued whole to prevent unscrupulous contractors from mixing ground coffee with sawdust. The soldiers had to pulverize the beans, usually in a small bag, before adding the grounds to a tin cup of boiling water. It took some practice but the result was a potent, refreshing brew. "We have just had our breakfast," Bailey wrote, "our coffee, pork, and bread was very good, but the cheese was spoiled. The coffee was as good as could be."[30]

Officers were expected to provide their own meals. Captain Weygant had a servant, his "colored man, Jim Sailor," to cook for him as well as put up and take down his tent and keep his uniform and side arms clean and in good repair. Officers could buy food from the sutlers, usually an expensive proposition, or seek out locals to provide meals. Lieutenant Houston heard of a house nearby where one might purchase a good supper and he went in search of it. As about any good eatery, the word had spread. He was greatly disappointed when he found that "the house and yard was full of officers all bent on the same errand."[31] Captain William Jackson wrote that "our rations are first rate good salt meat, nice tea, coffee, beans, etc. We have two good company cooks who have done this thing before. We eat the same as the men. I don't want better as long as I keep well."[32]

Captain Benedict wrote,

As to our fodder, we are all right as near as it is possible to be. Our company and company I commanded by Capt. Leander Clark from the second Division of our Battalion and the officers have clubbed together and bought a mess chest and we have a cook and first rate meals. Ham and every day or two fresh meat good tea and coffee & c. so you see I am all right.... I am in better health than I have been in a long time, you may think this is blowing, but I feel much better than I did at home for I weigh but 159 pounds so you see there is no surplus bloat about me ... there comes the Drums again so good night and write.... Our Bully Colonel and Lieut. Colonel also have an especial eye upon the

Left: 1st Lieutenant John W. Houston, Company D. He was wounded in action June 9, 1863, at Beverly Ford, Virginia, and again May 12, 1864, at Spotsylvania Court House, then discharged for disability August 10, 1864. "Company D was filled and reported to Col. A.W.H. Ellis at Goshen and then the fun began." *Right:* Captain William A. Jackson, Company K. Last of the original company commanders, he was killed at Petersburg while rallying his men (both photographs, archive of the Historical Society of the Town of Warwick, gift of Joan and Tom Frangos).

Whortleberry Rangers [a nickname Benedict and his company officers had adopted] and as long as I have them to back me I do not fear the Devil or any other man. I am getting along first rate in my new business.[33]

On their second day at Camp Chase, a peculiar bugle call was heard from headquarters. The few veterans in the 124th knew it to be "strike tents," the signal to take down the canvas, pack things up, and be ready to move. Captain Charles Weygant hadn't a clue what the bugle call meant until a "small, dirty-looking drummer-boy from some New York city regiment" seized the opportunity to educate the officer and his fellow "fresh fish" from upstate. The lad told Weygant that "old sogers" like himself referred to the call as "git up and git." Having satisfied himself that he had done his part in helping the new troops, the youth tried to hustle Weygant's men out of some tobacco.[34]

A short time later when "To the Colors" was sounded, the men knew it was the signal to move out of their company streets into a battalion front, two ranks deep with the colors at the center. At Colonel Ellis' command, the men faced to the right, doubling up to form a column four men abreast, and set out for Georgetown Heights, four miles away, where on September 12, they established Camp Ellis. In a letter to his sister Emily, Corporal William Howell wrote that the regiment "marched in the heat of the day to this place, which is opposite Georgetown on the Virginian side of the Potomac. We are in plain sight of the Capitol and have a fine birds eye view of the city. We go down to the river frequently to Swim. I Swam across the river the other day when we were down."[35]

While at Camp Ellis, Private Joseph Johnston of Company E wrote to his mother,

I begin to think of wat thee told me about home. I have traveled over a great deal of land and can say there is no place like home. I am not home sick for I think it will not be long before Frank and Joe comes home ... if I could be there and have a drink of milk for my dinner and see Torney and Phebe annok I think it would do me some good tell phebe annok that I will get her a present from the rebels wen I go in a battle.... I must stop now for I am very tired after being up all night we have prawer meeting evry night and preaching evry Sunday and I never felt better in my life than wen I here them begin to sing for it seems so much like home.[36]

At Camp Ellis, the 124th became part of a brigade, the basic fighting unit of the Union army. The commander was Brigadier General Abram Sanders Piatt, described by Captain Weygant as "a tall, gloomy-looking Western man, and a strict disciplinarian." Piatt's Brigade was made up of three infantry regiments and one battery of artillery, about 2,200 men total. The 124th, of course, was green as green could be. The 122nd Pennsylvania Infantry, nine-month volunteers from Lancaster County, were just as green, having been organized August 12, 1862, only a couple of weeks before the 124th New York. The 86th New York, however, had all the characteristics of a veteran regiment. Greatly reduced in numbers, their line of battle was about half the size of the 124th. The 86th was a three-year regiment recruited in the fall of 1861 in and around Elmira, New York. It had been engaged at the Second Battle of Bull Run where it lost 118 men killed, wounded, or missing. Captain Weygant may not have known much about army life as yet, but when he saw this regiment, he recognized what he was looking at. When the 86th formed up beside the 124th, its "little companies of tanned veterans, in their faded, dingy-looking blue, formed on their tattered, weather-stained colors — dressed to a perfect line, with the slightest perceptible turn of their heads, and brought their guns to an order with a single thud — we were ready to doff our caps, as in the presence of our superiors."[37]

The artillery unit was Battery H, 1st Ohio Light, Lieutenant George W. Norton commanding. It had seen action in the Shenandoah Valley against Stonewall Jackson before being assigned to duty in the forts around Washington. Captain Jackson wrote, "This last and perhaps some of the others have seen service. The battery is just in front of us. The fellows are rough but look ready and are full of fight."[38]

The division commander was Brigadier General Amiel Weeks Whipple, who graduated fifth in the class of 1841 at West Point, a class that produced 22 Civil War generals. Before the war, Whipple served as an officer of topographical engineers, surveying the boundaries with Mexico and Canada and surveying a railroad route through the Arizona Territory to California. When the Civil War began, Whipple was given command of a brigade and then a division in the forts guarding Washington.[39] Weygant described him as "a small, slight, feminine-looking man," a "kind-hearted thorough gentleman," and "an able, true, and brave soldier."[40]

The commander of the 3rd Corps was Major General Samuel Peter Heintzelman, another West Point graduate, class of 1826, who had been brevetted for gallantry during the Mexican War. He served in the east from the First Battle of Bull Run with mixed success, being sent into the Washington defenses after the second Bull Run.[41]

Though Piatt, Whipple, and Heintzelman would soon be gone, the inclusion of the 124th in the 3rd Corps had far reaching implications for the regiment. It meant that the Civil War experiences for the volunteers from Orange County would not include guarding railroads, or being stationed in fortresses for long periods of time. There would be no obscure campaigns of little importance nor would they pass the ammunition forward while others did the shooting. In the 3rd Corps, Ellis would have ample opportunity to "render [the] efficient services at the front" he so desired.

At Camp Ellis, the regiment's preparation and training moved to a higher level, made urgent by rumors flying through the camps that Lee's army was moving north. The men were put to work digging rifle pits and felling trees, blocking any approach road with sharpened branches pointing in the direction of the enemy. Pickets were thrown out to warn of the approach of Confederate cavalrymen raiding to take prisoners and to gather information. All the while, Lee's main force moved north into Maryland and Pennsylvania. On September 16, the regiment was ordered to prepare to march at a moment's notice to the relief of Harpers Ferry. That very afternoon, Henry Howell wrote in his diary of that post's capture, along with 8,000 Union soldiers.[42]

Now drill became a daily exercise with a purpose. Colonel Ellis had taught them the manual of arms and a good deal of company drill back in Goshen even before they had weapons. With Casey's *Tactics* as their guide, the men learned to maneuver as a group, form a line of battle, wheel their company left or right, and move from a column of fours into a line of battle.[43] By mid–September, the men were quite proficient at company drill and were learning how to maneuver as a regiment, all ten companies moving at the direction of the colonel. Next came brigade drill, where the 124th New York, 122nd Pennsylvania and 86th New York learned to move at the direction of General Piatt. They were also taught to load and fire their weapons, a nine step process. Private Howell wrote, "We drilled in fighting dry loading and firing by motions and the falling on our faces so that the next regiment behind could fire too, then we went up behind the breastworks and went through the motions of loading and firing by ranks, the front rank first and then load while the rear went up and fired."[44]

"We have to go through with a pretty hard course of drill now days, but we are abel to stand it; our equipment are quite heavy and the neighboring regiments give us the Soubriquet of 'light Artillery.'" Private Joseph Brooks of Company D reported that Colonel Ellis himself was not happy with the weapons his regiment had been issued. "The cournel sayes that he will not take us in battel until we get better guns the guns that we have got now shoot very well but they are too heavy they wiegh sixteen pounds the others that he wants to get only wiegh ten pounds which make a considerable difference on a two days march with our knapsacks."[45]

Wirt Bailey agreed. "Our guns are heavier than any in Va., I guess and I have had hold of a good many others. The old soldiers all swear and say they would not have them."[46] Two weeks later he repeated a camp rumor, "We are to have new guns to night, they are called the rifle musket. The guns we have, they don't like and I am glad of it. For they are awful heavy. The ones we have are called the French rifle musket. We fired at a target today. I done well."[47] Private Drake heard the rumor about getting new guns too, and, as if to strengthen the argument in favor, he exaggerated the defects of their Vincennes rifles. He wrote as if the exchange of weapons had already been made. "We are going to have new guns. The others were so heavy they would take a Bullet as Big as my head. When we would shoot them off they would kick me back about a foot."[48]

Captain William Jackson was twenty-three years old, a graduate of Union College, and a teacher in Middletown before he headed up Company K. He may have been a soldier for but a short time but he knew a piece of junk when he saw one. He pronounced the Vincennes rifles "worthless," noting that they would "snap at half cock" which was supposed to be the safety position of the hammer. They were "very clumsy provided with a sword bayonet which I don't like as well as the old kind."[49]

For two days in a row, September 19 and 20, the regiment was marched over to Fort Corcoran, heavy rifles and all, for drill involving more units than just Piatt's Brigade. "Yesterday we drilled nine hours, and today I am on guard and they will not let us go away from the guard house, but a short time when off of duty."[50] There were complaints that Colonel Ellis had a habit of marching them too fast, he on horseback while they had to tote their knapsacks and heavy weapons. For one exercise, the 124th formed up in the center of the front line with the 86th and 122nd on either side. Behind them were three more regiments, veteran troops as seen by their small numbers and battle scarred colors. "One of them had been in ten different fights, and had to pull their flag off of the stick for the Rebels had a hold of it in the Bull Run fight." As part of the exercise, a bayonet charge was ordered. Forward they went, the veterans in the rear cheering so loudly that it frightened some of the new men who, glancing nervously behind, fell down and lost their caps.

Impressed, Sergeant Bailey wrote, "I bet it looked savage."[51] Corporal Howell thought they handled it all quite well. "Cavalry make a charge on us Several men dismounted We came out first rate."[52]

After two weeks in the army, Captain William Jackson wrote to his friend from Orange County.

> For the last two days in the afternoon we have had brigade reviews and parades.... The first time officers and men from Col. down were somewhat excited and did not do as well as this afternoon or as they will when more used to Generals. Some 4 or 5 thousand were reviewed. The old regiments of course took the shine off of us in going through the movements but look very small some of the companies having only about 20 men with a captain for colonel and sergeants for line officers.... By the way Sergeant Major Grier is a first rate fellow and understands himself. I get a great deal of useful information from him. Lieut. Roosa improves every day and is liked well by the men. Finnegan made himself unpopular by being rather rough to some of the men who complained to Col. and me. The Col. gave him some advice which he will remember. It won't do for an officer to be harsh with men unnecessarily. There are some who must be put down by hard measures but for the kind of men in this regiment kind usage is the most effectual, and most of the officers see it in this light.[53]

The Battle of Antietam had been fought three days before Jackson wrote his letter. The 124th New York was camped just a few miles down the Potomac and had even heard cannon fire echo down from the fight along South Mountain, but as yet they did not know the outcome. "Some of the boys are supposing that there is nothing left for us to do," wrote the captain, "but I think they are mistaken for if General McClellan is victorious we will push on to Richmond, if not we will have to support him, so some will get more fight than they want unless I am mistaken. Besides this we are under a fighting general, Heintzelman, who knows how to set his men to work and keep them at it."[54]

Daily camp life changed to reinforce military regimen. "Our rotine of duty is different now from what it used to be. In the morning at 5 O'Clock the Drum beats for us to tumble out for roll call. At 6 we go to Breakfast which consists of Coffee, Corned Beef, Bread and Crackers. Each man is allowed a pint of Coffee 2 slices of Bakers Bread a chunk of meat as big as your hand and 2 Crackers."[55] After breakfast the guards posted around camp and at the colonel's tent were relieved at regular intervals. Those who did not feel well or who wanted to shirk their duties reported to the regimental surgeon for sick call. It did not take the medical staff long to identify the chronic malingerers.

Between 8 A.M. and 9 A.M. officers and NCOs were required to attend a drill session. Colonel Ellis chose what was to be taught and the company commanders went over what orders they were to pass on to the men, where they would stand,

Left: Captain James A. Grier had prior service in the 71st New York Militia with Colonel Ellis. He enlisted in the 124th New York as a private but was quickly promoted to sergeant-major, ending his military career as a captain. *Right:* Captain James Finnigan. He served as 2nd lieutenant, Company K, and captain, Company C. He was wounded at Gettysburg and at Boydton Plank Road, and died of his wounds (both photographs, archive of the Historical Society of the Town of Warwick, gift of Joan and Tom Frangos).

what the sergeants and corporals would do, and so on. Both Captain Weygant and Private Nathan Hallock of Company K described these sessions as if the officers and NCOs were required to actually walk through each maneuver themselves to demonstrate proficiency. Under Ellis' sharp eye, those who wore rank were held responsible for knowing their own jobs and for teaching the privates in the ranks. And as poor Dan Webb knew from his own experience, woe to the man who was out of place.

From 9 A.M. until noon the men worked from small groups to progressively larger groups, squad drill to platoon drill to company drill. Each session reinforced the previous exercises as the men moved to larger units of drill. At noon came dinner, described by Thomas Rodman as "nothing different from breakfast except water in place of Coffee." After dinner, the men were expected to police the camp again, both inside their tents and all around the company streets. Rodman noted that the afternoon's lesson began with the men drilling by division, two companies adjacent to each other forming a division. "After Dd. [division drill] D[ress] Parade after that Supper which consists of boiled Rice and Molasses Bread Meat & Coffee." He told his father that he had gained seven pounds on this diet and never felt better in his life.[56]

After supper, the men returned to camp to look to their gear, write or read letters, read newspapers, or just sit around the fire and smoke. "Tattoo was sounded at a quarter of nine, and Taps at nine, when lights were extinguished, noise ceased, and all in camp, except the guards and the officer who commanded them, were permitted to sleep."[57]

Soldiers were always looking for the little extras to make their lives in camp more comfortable. "It is a great help to buy a pie once in a while," wrote Wirt Bailey. The soldiers did have some options when it came to purchasing canned milk, canned peaches, cheese, tobacco, candy, eggs, butter, baked goods, stationary, ink, and other things not issued by the federal government. "Our camp is full of women all the time, with fruit, milk, and butter and we have sweet potatoes. Lewis Wisner, Winfield Parssons, Dan and I bunk together and we have pickles and potatoes and live good enough."[58]

Army regulations allowed each regiment to have one sutler, a businessman who followed the regiment with a wagon filled with goods for sale. The sutler was appointed by the regimental commander, subject to approval from higher command. When the regiment was in fixed camp, the sutler might construct a small storefront from which to do business. His prices were to be set by the military and posted in a conspicuous place in his store or wagon. He was not allowed to sell on credit beyond one third of the soldier's monthly pay and could not charge more for purchases on credit than for cash purchases. At the end of the month, the sutler was to furnish the regimental commander with a list of those men who owed money and he was entitled to sit at the paymaster's table with his ledger books. The sutler got the money owed to him even before the soldier was "paid off."[59] Nathaniel J. Kelsey was appointed sutler to the 124th New York. He signed a contract with the firm of C. W. Reevs & Son of Goshen in which he agreed to travel with the regiment, conducting business in an honest manner. Reevs's end of the bargain was to provide the "money and means to carry on the business." His investment was to be repaid from the profits which were split evenly between Reevs and Kelsey.[60]

"Our Sutler has very high prices for everything he has Butter 25 cents sugar 20 cents eggs 3 cents apiece Lemons 5 cents and other thing to match there is peddlers brings in pies, cakes, apples, peaches, milk, and such other things as are wanted by the boys sweet potatoes with the rest."[61] Sergeant Bailey and 1st Sergeant Jacob Denton cultivated a good relationship with the company cooks by providing them with postage stamps, which were often used as currency. In turn, the cooks gave them corn and fresh meat for roasting when everyone else got stew. One Sunday morning in late September, the two sergeants wanted something different for breakfast. Bailey paid the sutler thirty five cents for a pound of butter and Denton got some tomatoes from the cooks. With these meager rations, they managed to put together "a first rate breakfast."[62]

Sutler's tent at Bealton, Virginia. Each regiment had its own sutler who, by army regulations, had to post his prices. Within limits, the soldier was allowed to buy on credit, but many wrote home complaining of high prices and asked that items be sent from home (Library of Congress, Prints & Photographs Division).

On occasion, they overdid it. Wirt Bailey once ate a small pork roast with potatoes and bread, then polished it off with some milk. At ten cents a quart he figured he had better finish it before it spoiled. He tried to relax while writing home but complained he was so full he could not comfortably sit with his legs straight out.[63] On another occasion he "ate so much stuf of different kinds and in the night I did throw up from way back. We have all had our turns but now I feel as well as I ever did, in good spirits and at home. This morning I drew the rations for the company and got on the scales and my weight was 129 lb. One day I ate six peaches, two apples, and all the watermelon I wanted. It did not hurt me a bit—but I won't do that every day."[64]

As it turned out, Wirt Bailey was quite an entrepreneur. The original equipment issue for the regiment shows that 1,015 woolen blankets were issued to the regiment but mentions no issue of waterproof blankets. Often referred to as "gum blankets," they were usually made of rectangular pieces of canvas coated on one side with "India rubber" or painted with a waterproofing substance. The gum blanket made a very handy, efficient raincoat with considerable insulating qualities when worn as rain gear or at night when the soldier might wrap himself in both his gum blanket and woolen blanket. The "Consolidated Return of Clothing, Camp and Garrison Equipage" for Company D, covering its entire period of service, shows that at some time during the war 34 waterproof blankets were issued to the Warwick boys, but that issue might have been as late as the summer of 1864.[65]

Early in their military careers, the Orange County soldiers may have had to supply their own rubber blankets or oil cloths, making these desirable items to have. While on the march, Bailey purchased an India rubber blanket from another soldier for seventy-five cents. When he got back to camp, he sold it for the tidy sum of three dollars. "So much for having a little change," he wrote. "It is very summer here. I have sixteen dollars in bills and two in silver."[66]

Soldiers might also have things shipped to them from home. By the 1860s, Orange County had an extensive rail system connecting the major towns with each other and with New York City. The Adams Express company could ship a box by rail from Newburgh that would reach Washington in just a couple of days. In the first few months of service, as the men found out what they needed, letters home began to list specific items that they wanted shipped. Wirt Bailey suggested to his parents that whatever they shipped should be put in glass bottles because all the boxes were opened for inspection prior to delivery as the authorities checked for whiskey or other items not proper for soldiers to have in their possession.

Most of all, the men wanted letters from home. "I received your letter of the 18th," wrote Sergeant Bailey, "and I guess every one of the company got one. So we had a good jovial time."[67] After three weeks in the army, Private Rodman was worried that he had not received any word from home. "I take this opportunity to write you a few lines to let you know that I am still alive and well and that I have not been sick an hour since I came to the sacred soil of Virginia. I have not received a single letter from you since I came here in answer to the 2 I wrote to you. I wrote one to you from Washington and one to Mother from Camp Chase and now I write again to you to see if I cannot get an answer."[68]

Finally, on October 3, he received a letter from home. "I received your kind letter of the 1st on last evening and was glad to hear that you and Mother was well. The reason I had, for not giving you the directions in my letter I wrote from Washington was, we did not know where we were going."[69] Private Drake was also quite upset at having received no mail from his family. "What is the reason that Dave and Ella Don't write to me. I have written David two letters and Ella two letters. I hain't got any letters from them yet. You must write often for I want to hear from you and the rest. And I will write as often as I can."[70]

The five sergeants from Company K bunked together in the same tent and often invited Captain William Jackson to join them. Military etiquette discouraged such familiarity but in Company K at least things were a little more relaxed when it came to this particular officer. They enjoyed eating oyster dinners together and sharing the local newspapers from Orange County as well as those from Baltimore and Washington which could be purchased in camp. The group especially enjoyed sharing letters from home. Wirt Bailey was receiving mail from a number of young ladies including one named "Bell B" and a friend of the family named Ida. His 24-year-old sister Ellen and his 17-year-old sister Augusta wrote often. "And what sport we do have. Jake [1st Sergeant Jacob Denton] tried to get the letters from me, because I would not tell him who they were from. Captain Jackson said Oh! How he wished he had some girls to get some letters from ... we had a good laugh."[71]

Captain Jackson notwithstanding, there was plenty of grousing about the officers. Private Henry Howell and his brother William were members of Captain William A. McBirney's Company E. "Some of the boys do not like the captain as well as they did and Beecher [2nd Lieutenant A. Whittenbeecher] is getting more popular, Verplank [1st Lieutenant William A. Verplank] does not come around very often and report says that he is intemperate, but I have not noticed anything of the kind."[72] Lieutenant James Finnegan, the fireman from Newburgh, had angered some of the men in Company K. "Finnegan has a great deal of trouble. He was reported twice to the Col." Those who saw Ellis talking to the lieutenant assumed the colonel was chewing him out but no one overheard exactly what was said. Later, Finnegan asserted that the colonel told him to shoot anyone who insulted him, but the men saw this to be just so much bluster.[73]

Sergeant Bailey was having his own problems with Finnegan. "Lieut Finigan has a spite against me for something. I don't know what for, nor do I care." The lieutenant ordered the sergeant to go get him some firewood and then shoved him to emphasize who was in charge. "I told him I did not have to carry wood, but he thought he would scare me. He had the right to order me to take a guard of men to get wood. But he can not make me carry a stick. All of the non officers hate him and if he ever gets in a battle he had better look for a place to lay down as well as some others in the Regt." The 18-year-old sergeant assured his father that he would not harm the lieutenant but told him there were plenty who would.[74]

Taking a dislike to his brigade commander, General Sanders Piatt, Private John Drake set his sights higher, literally as well as figuratively. "We have a bad General. He drills us from 3 o'clock until seven o'clock at night. If we ever go into Battle some of the men will Pick him with a chunk of lead." He did not think much of Captain Ira Bush, his company commander, either. "Our Captain has turned out to be very ugly. Some of them says if we ever go into Battle he will never come out alive." Drake sent no assurances to his mother that he would not be a party to shooting either man but, dutiful son that he was, he did say that he wanted to hear from her more often.[75]

Thomas Rodman spoke highly of all the officers, calling them "fine gentlemen" except for General Piatt, whom he disliked. "He marches us too much for our own good, every afternoon we have to go about 2¼ miles to division drill which last about 2 hours. Thence come home and go on dress parade which lasts about 1 hour then go to supper at 7."[76] Despite his grievances with the general, Rodman did not have any plans to shoot him.

"Col. Cummings has just recovered enough for duty," wrote Captain William Jackson.

> He is a jolly good fellow and tells some tough yarns and as a man and officer is liked but give me Col. Ellis for an officer. He is as quick as lightening hardly ever makes a mistake and when he does soon gets out of it. He makes some thick headed officers step around lively enough when they don't do just right and he tells them in a way they don't soon forget. The Major does very well but his office does not give him much to do except when Ellis is absent which is seldom. I like most of the other officers very well and the few that I don't like I need not associate with though we don't have much time to associate with any one for we have enough to tend to in our own companies, and to find good company I need not go out of it, for I think company K has got a first rate lot of boys in it and we all get on without jarring. One thing I wish we had about 15 more men we would then make more of a show and 100 men are as easily managed as 80.[77]

Thursday, September 25, the regiment was again on the march. "It is cold considering the time of year and climate. At noon we reecived orders to strike tents and be ready for further orders which we got about two oclock we started on the march with slow time on the road toward Centreville, we went about six miles I think, passing falls church, and camping on Minors hill." The men built bonfires to keep warm and waited for the quartermaster to arrive with their rations. When he caught up with the regiment, he had no cooking pots. The men happily cooked their meal on the hot coals that chilly night. The next day they moved back about half a mile to the east side of Minor's Hill where they again set up a regular camp, christening it Camp Cromwell in honor of the major.[78]

Second Lieutenant William E. Mapes was twenty-one years old when he signed on with Captain Henry Murray's Company B. "I like a soldiers life bully," he wrote to his brother Jesse in Florida, New York. "Marched 8 miles to Minors Hill ... we biavouked out under the canopy of heaven, in a woods we built fires all around & slept quite comfortable.... Old bill stands it well last night after my march my pins felt kindy weary but I laid down before the fire & toasted my shins well & this morning I was jay bird."[79]

Lieutenant Mapes had strong opinions and was candid with his brother. He didn't think much of Surgeon John Thompson — "Our seurgen is a damn ass he has no heart at all." He was particularly critical of 1st Lieutenant Wines Weygant of his company who did not appear up to the job. "Lieut. Weygant is not well. Camp life is too much for his slightly throwed together frame." Two days later he wrote to Jesse, "Lieut. Weygant is sick. He has applied for a leave of absence to go home 2 or 3 weeks until he gets better. He has got the 'Aisterics' he is discontented." With the company down to just one lieutenant instead of two, Mapes had to do both jobs. There was a rumor at home that Mapes himself was "discontented" but he said it was a "*damned lie* & a *damned mean cuss*" that raised that report." He hoped the author of the rumor would get drafted.

Captain William E. Mapes, Company B. He was wounded in action May 12, 1864, at Spotsylvania Court House, Virginia, and again August 14, 1864, at Deep Bottom, Virginia. He was discharged for wounds December 15, 1864. He said that with his sword he would "hew out my way to distinction" (archive of the Historical Society of the Town of Warwick, gift of Joan and Tom Frangos).

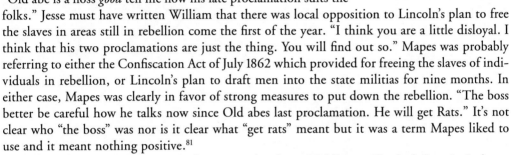

He concluded his letter, written on a Sunday, "I am writing to night while you are singing in the choir. So it goes. I am the boy that can stand it."[80]

Mapes approved Lincoln's Emancipation Proclamation — "Old abe is a hoss *good* tell me how his late proclamation suits the folks." Jesse must have written William that there was local opposition to Lincoln's plan to free the slaves in areas still in rebellion come the first of the year. "I think you are a little disloyal. I think that his two proclamations are just the thing. You will find out so." Mapes was probably referring to either the Confiscation Act of July 1862 which provided for freeing the slaves of individuals in rebellion, or Lincoln's plan to draft men into the state militias for nine months. In either case, Mapes was clearly in favor of strong measures to put down the rebellion. "The boss better be careful how he talks now since Old abes last proclamation. He will get Rats." It's not clear who "the boss" was nor is it clear what "get rats" meant but it was a term Mapes liked to use and it meant nothing positive.[81]

"How does the Presidents Proclamation take about Middletown?" asked Captain Jackson. "There is very little said about it here but all who mention it approve of it and every thing that will have a tendency to crush the rebellion. To my mind a strong argument in its favor is that it exasperates the south so much. It must hurt them or they would not be so much enraged at it. No one here favors compromise and nothing but unconditional by the south will suit."[82]

"How is it you talk about my filling an honored grave, as though I am going to be shot?" Mapes asked his brother Jesse in his next letter. "The lead has yet to be molten that kills me 'put that in your pipe' ... Capt Murray has been under the weather I have been in command for about 2 weeks at Briggade & Division Drills, Lieut Weygant I must say is a '*dead Beat*' he has a feminine voice & besides he has no *Military Genius*, a Disagreable cuss!! (Keep Dark) The Baby had his discharge made out & signed by Capt Murray (who did it with no reluctance) & was awaiting the signature of Maj Gen Heintsteman."

Then he turned to the issue of discipline in his own company. "I corrected a soldier who disrespectfully spoke to me ... but by golly they must obey orders, yesterday I put 3 in the guard house, they thought that because they were acquainted with me they could do as they pleased but I gave them some cheap jewelry to wear in the shape of hand cuffs. I am not afraid of Sam Schultz. If the men do not have Enemy enough to shoot at then let them fire at me. A fellow from the 8th N.J. Cavalry is going to bring me a six inch Navy revolver. I can get it for 5 or X Dols as we may go in battle. I will keep it until I get a chance to get another which I will send to you."[83] Private Schultz, thinking better of threatening an officer about to purchase a Colt .36 caliber handgun, deserted about a week later.[84]

The regiment's three week stay at Minor's Hill was remembered by Captain Weygant as a time when the regiment was drilled more than any other period during its service.[85] The men complained mightily about all the drill. "I had to laugh to hear [Corporal A.S.] Harlburt talk. He said he would not have come if he knew they would have to drill so much." The weather had been quite dry for weeks, the days warm and the nights surprisingly cool. The parade grounds, trod upon by thousands of men each day, became exceedingly dusty. "When we go on parade we are very thirsty and warm. Some places we go through the dust is so thick you can not see ten paces in front of you, and when we come out we look as though we had been rolling in the dust."[86]

While at Minor's Hill, Captain James Benedict wrote his wife with an unusual request. The officers had been ordered to ship home all their extra gear including dress uniforms in preparation for taking the field. He was sure he'd mistakenly sent the payroll document that each man had signed at Goshen and they could not be paid without it. He asked his wife to search his jackets for the document. He needn't have worried, for the paymaster would not visit the regiment any-time soon. "I am feeling first reate tonight for we (that is the commissioned officers) received a nice piece of parchment with the signature of Edwin D. Morgan and Thomas Hillhouse upon it and if we were at Lews or Boneys or any-where else where we could we would have Bully times." The parchments Captain Benedict spoke of were, of course, their commissions.[87]

Picket duty, together with guard duty around the camp, became a regular part of everyday military life. Colonel Ellis told the men that they had better pay attention while on duty, warning them that Confederate cavalry might attack at any time. "I guess he said so to keep the boys awake," Sergeant Bailey wrote. He noted however that only recently his friend Sergeant Winfield Parsons saw Union cavalry bring a captured Confederate trooper through their picket line. While at Miner's Hill, Private Joseph Brooks described picket duty to a friend.

> I was on guard for the last twenty four hours theare is three reliefs of us and we take turns two hours on and four off.... Theare is quite some diference between picket and guard the pickets have to go four or five miles from camp and if it rains they have no shelter but thoes that are guard a round camp have a good shelter wen they are off duty but theare is no danger to stand picket weare we stand for theare is two lines of Union picket farther out one of infantry and one of cavalry the cavalry go the farthest towards the rebel lines ... our pickets are only sent out to get them ust to picket and to learn us our duty I am sorry to say that one of our boys got in a dose las night while he was on his post the officer came a long and took his gun out of his hand before he knowed it, I stood on the post joining him but was not cloas enough to wake him up before the officer got to him they have got him in the guard house to day. I do not know what they will do with him the penalty is death but I do not think they will punish him for his offence for he complained of being sick I hope they will let him slip this time. It was John K. Clark from Belvale pleas do not say anything about it for if his folks should hear it they will feel bad about it.[88]

Beyond picket duty and drill, camp life remained much as before. As might be expected, church services were as important in camp as they had been at home. Most of the soldiers had been raised Protestant but with a surprising number of Irish born Catholics among them. The 124th, of course, brought a chaplain from home, Episcopal minister T. Scott Bradner of Goshen. Some of the men were critical of his lack of religious fervor, but there were many who thought highly of him. No matter his shortcomings, he stayed with the regiment right through the war. When photographed with the other officers, he could be seen looking heavenward as if searching for divine inspiration.

Most of the men would never even consider swearing at home but some were now becoming quite proficient at it. They had only to follow the example of a few of their officers. "Some of the boys that did not swear when at Goshen are getting so they can do it with out much trouble now. I think they do it because the Col. and other officers do sometimes. I know it is the nature of some, but I am happy to say, it is not mine. You never hear our little Capt. or first Lieut. swear, not a word."[89] Chaplain Bradner went right to work on the swearing issue, starting at the top. When he sermonized about the evils of profanity, he made it a point to stand close to Colonel Ellis, who apparently got the message. Soldiers noted that Ellis' intemperate language seemed to be improving. On Sunday, October 5, Bradner was in especially good form, reading from the 34th Psalm and from Proverbs. Hitting his stride, he "gave it to them big for swearing."[90]

Wirt Bailey's parents expressed concern that he would take up the evils of army life: swearing, drinking, card playing, or worse. They worried he might even throw away the Bible they had given him. They requested that he carry it in his pocket as a reminder of home and of their teachings as well as those of the church. Bailey reassured them that he would not take up the vices they feared, but the Bible was too big to carry in his pocket. He would not throw it away he told them, but instead carry it within easy reach inside his knapsack.[91]

"The boys here carry on as though they did not know when Sunday came," complained one soldier. "They will not let them play cards in camp, but they go out in the woods and play all the afternoon." Most soldiers, however, observed the Sabbath in camp as they had done at home. Prayer meetings and informal religious gatherings were very common among the men of the regiment. "We have some very good men to carry on a prayer meeting," Sergeant Bailey wrote to his parents. "I went last Sunday night and was very much pleased it was a good meeting and I believe there was quite a number of converts. Every Sunday morn we have inspection of arms and then close up in mass and have a short sermon. They are very good."[92] Bailey got a lot from these meetings although he did not like one thing about them: there were too many Methodists. In his opinion, they tended to be noisy and made foolish remarks. During the meeting one of them said, "The rebels are after us my brethern, you don't know when they will catch you, come make up your mind." Bailey whispered to his friend Lieutenant James Roosa, who sat beside him, "I thought we were after them!" They both had a laugh. "There are some very good men that attend the meetings," Bailey admitted.[93]

As the military regimen got tougher, more men fell by the wayside, some sick, others injured. A correspondent to the *Newburgh Daily Telegraph* made a point that explained a good deal of the medical problems: "The men are generally healthy, but I am sorry to say that a few men are in our regiment who were not healthy when they enlisted, and of course they are unhealthy still; of such, four were sent to the hospital at Washington on the 6th inst. The general good health in camp is attributable to the care the men take of themselves."[94] The perfunctory "physical" at enlistment weeded out only those most obviously unfit for duty and let pass many who would later prove unable to stand army life. Among them were privates in their late thirties and some even in their forties, most of whom did not last long in the ranks.

Those genuinely ill, as well as the shirkers, were taken to the hospital to see the regimental surgeon each day after sick call. Civil War field hospitals were notoriously dirty places, to be avoided if at all possible. "Orderly takes the sick down to the hospital every morning, he says some companys have 8 or 12 to be examined for the day while we don't have over three or four. It is very bad for those that are sick, it is so hot, and the flys light on you and you have to take a stick and pry them off, all most."[95]

"Some one falls out of the ranks every day, one did yesterday and he could not walk, they all have the same pain. It is a grasping pain in the stomach. It must be awful by the way they scream. I have not had it nor I don't want it. I think the watter we drink will make us sick if we drink to much."[96] On those occasions when the regiment moved to a new camp, tents were often set up on ground recently vacated by another regiment. All manner of debris had to be cleaned up before the place was made livable. With so many men in such close quarters, often with little attention paid to rudimentary hygiene, it is small wonder that the water supply might be contaminated. The results had serious implications for the efficiency of the army and could be traced directly to unsanitary conditions in camp.

The weather added to the sick list. It had been generally dry and warm into the second week of October when the rain brought cooler temperatures. "This day has been the coldest one that we have had since I have been in camp, as it is about the only day that we have had but what has been warm, a good deal like a summer day in Old Orange, but it has suddenly changed, and I fear a great many will take colds."[97]

There were a few who went to extreme measures in their efforts to get sent to the hospital or, better yet, sent home. "Our regiment overall enjoying good health except six that are very bad. One of them D. Odell was out cutting trees and his axe slipped and took off 2 of his toes, the great toe and the one next. He has got his discharge and is on his way home."[98] Some instances like this may well have been accidents but when Wirt Bailey wrote home asking that a pair of boots be made up for him, his sarcasm was clear. "I will send you my foot, for you to get me a pair of boots, that is if I can get it cut off. I think I can do it for some body is cutting themselves quite often. One man cut his own toes off and another cut his finger most off."[99]

Lieutenant James Roosa of Company K was among the sick, incapacitated for three weeks with chronic diarrhea. Assistant Surgeon Edward Marshall advised that he take a furlough and return home to recuperate, but Roosa fretted lest the folks back home think him unfit for duty. He knew that unless his condition improved soon he would end up in the hospital with the other sick men from the company. These included six foot five inch John Varmylia, who also had diarrhea, Stephen Frost, who had a rupture and would be discharged, and two others with high fevers, Henry Baker, who would survive the winter, and John Stalbird, who would not.

Roosa complained that Surgeon Thompson was not sending sick men to be treated. "If I was not an officer, would give the opinion of the Regiment from the Col. on down as to how well Dr. Thompson discharges his duties." Sick as he was, Roosa took comfort in the knowledge that he was popular with the men. "The boys all are anxious for me to get with them again and I hope to be with them before many days. The thing I know they all like me. Capt. Jackson stands high in the regiment."[100]

"The general appearance of the country is very similar to Orange County," wrote Captain Jackson, "but one acre there is worth a dozen here."

> Of course we can't get about to see the country for McClellan has issued very strict orders concerning leaving camp but make the most of chance when sent out on duty. I have been kept closer than usual the past two weeks as Lieut Roosa has been unfit for duty but to day he, with 3 or 4 others of the "diarrhea guard" as the Col. calls them have been detailed to act as a court martial with some other officers from 122nd Penn and 83rd N.Y. Quite a number of the officers have been a little unwell some three captains and 4 or 5 Lieut's and that gives the rest more to do. For myself I have never been beter have gained 10 lbs. scince we left Goshen and begin to feel quite a veteran taking things just as they come without grumbling.

Captain Jackson did complain about tents issued to the regiment, which were low and uncomfortable. As a company commander, he had a great deal of paperwork to do and he wanted more comfortable quarters in which to do it.[101]

And there were more desertions. "I am very sorry to tell you," wrote Bailey, "J.N. has been put down in the ranks, for leaving without permission his company. I am afraid John will do something yet that will hurt him ... I would not say anything about John Newton, for I don't want them to know that I wrote home about it." Bailey was correct in his assessment of his friend. By the end of the month, Newton deserted near Berlin, Maryland.[102]

On October 10, General Piatt was putting the brigade through drill when he was handed a dispatch. He quickly rode off, leaving "the whole brigade marching around." Colonel Ellis took charge and got the men back to camp. It was raining when, at about 9 P.M., "the bugle sounded for us to strike tents for to take to march, as we had been supplied with two days rations beforehand (as we were expecting to march at any moment) and in a very few minutes, each man had his knapsack on his back, and were formed in line, and then we commenced to march."[103] Before bidding farewell to Minor's Hill, the men made bonfires of tent poles, shipping crates, hardtack boxes, and unwanted gear. Chaplain Bradner wrote,

> I was sitting on a box by a fire just by the foundation of what had been my house, now rolled up by the side, I could still hear the Colonel's voice ringing on the night air, from a neighboring hill, and as I was meditating on the transitiveness of all things pertaining to soldier's life, who should drive in again but Dr. Thompson ... saying it was all a hoax ... the order had been countermanded, and the whole Brigade were coming back. It seemed at first to be a very sorry joke. But we have learned by this time to take everything in that light.[104]

Sure enough, half a mile from camp, General Piatt had received a second dispatch that brought the column to a halt. There had obviously been a mixup and the men were ordered back to camp, which "looked rather desolate, with the fires burning what remained, but the boys saluted the Colonel with three cheers as he dismissed them with the remark that they should make themselves comfortable for the night, and perhaps next week we would march for Orange County."[105] The chaplain, adjutant, and sergeant major unrolled their large tent, beginning the task of setting it up again, when they were "set upon" by Major Cromwell and Lieutenant Colonel Cummins, who goodnaturedly contested possession. By then it was raining hard and all that was gained by this "sorry joke" was to soak and chill several hundred federal soldiers. Henry Howell considered himself fortunate. He "escaped with only one shoe half full of water."[106]

During the next few days, the sick in the brigade hospital were sent to the hospitals around Washington. Included among them was Corporal William Howell, whose short note to his mother caused her great distress: "I am so unfortunate as to get in the Hospital ... and am unable to help myself most of the time. I have managed to write a little now. Hope for the best."[107] When her younger son Henry wrote a few days later, it did nothing to lift her spirits: "I have not heard from William since he left us a week ago last Friday."[108]

Wirt Bailey's parents received a similar letter. On the night before the regiment moved out, he'd spent an unusually cold and damp tour of duty on the picket line. He developed what the doctor thought might be a "touch of typhoid fever." When the regiment marched, Bailey was in such bad shape that he traveled by ambulance to Georgetown and from there to St. Eloise Hospital in Washington.[109]

Sickness, desertions, accidents, pompous officers, military rations, uncertainty, loneliness and more — all were facts of life for the men in the ranks that fall in Virginia. Again the rumors flew that the regiment would soon be called to action and the men tried to prepare themselves as best they could. "We are under marching orders," wrote Private Drake. "We expect to march Every day. But we are here yet. Night before last our Regiment was Declared in the field. But I don't think it will be long before we will be in the Battles.... But there will be a great deal of fighting to do and I suppose we will have to do some of it."[110]

Before he got sick, Wirt Bailey told his parents that he felt "Bully" and was prepared to meet the enemy in battle anytime. "I suppose if we go in a battle you will worry about me, but I don't want you to. I shall put my trust in God, and am willing for his will to be done, if I fall, it will be his pleasure and if not — the same."[111]

"Father I am going to end the War before I get back," wrote Private Rodman. He then added, "Or the War is going to end me," but thinking better of it, crossed the last part out.[112]

CHAPTER 3

"The Romance of the thing
is all gone and the sad Realities
of Ware Begin to Aper"

October 16–December 17, 1862

Following his victory at Antietam on September 17, Major General George McClellan did not immediately pursue the Army of Northern Virginia. President Lincoln repeatedly urged him to cross the Potomac and engage the enemy, but McClellan saw this as just an attempt "to push me into a premature advance into Virginia." On October 6 an exasperated Lincoln ordered him to "cross the Potomac and give battle to the enemy or drive him south" but it was not until October 16 that the "Virginia Creeper" got underway.

On the morning of October 17, the 124th New York marched out to join the Army of the Potomac.[1] The regiment crossed the Aqueduct Bridge at Georgetown and moved through Washington, past "old Abes house" and the Capitol Building. Privates Henry Howell and Sam Clark were part of the rear guard. "We got a sight at Washington and Jackson's statues last night," Howell wrote to his mother. "Washington looks natural with his fine horse rearing in air and his sword drawn ready to strike treason down. If we had a leader now who thought as much of his country's honor as he this unholy war would soon come to an end. As it is I hope and trust for the best. It looks now as though a powerful blow was about to be struck for the Union. God grant that it may prove successful."[2]

The regiment arrived at the Baltimore and Ohio railroad depot at about 8 P.M. and boarded a westbound train at midnight. The racket of the moving cars kept the soldiers awake for most of the eleven-hour ride to Knoxville, Maryland. Howell described Knoxville to his sister as "a small place of about a dozen houses with the Delaware and Chesapeake Canal running between it and the Potomac river.... Harpers Ferry is three miles further up the River which is our destination for the present."[3] Twenty-eight-year-old Sergeant William B. Van Houten of Company D did manage to sleep on the long ride; when he awoke, the train was well into Maryland and he marveled at what he saw. "We were also in a country presenting more the appearance of thrift and industry than any I've seen in the land of Secessia."[4]

When they finally left the train, the regiment went into camp with orders to hold itself in readiness. "We are situated in as pretty a farming section and as good a one as I have ever seen," wrote Captain Benedict. "We are camped on a large plantation the owner of which professes to be true Union and has a guard to protect his property while two of his sons joined Jackson with five Horses and the slaves say against their will." The owner of the farm visited Colonel Ellis before the men had even put up their tents. He threatened to shoot any soldier who disturbed his property. "Well we put up our tent and as the ground was wet we thought a little straw or hay would make it nice so over the boys or some of them went and while they were chatting with him about his hay they looked around and there went two of the 86th with a sheep on their back a bleeding. This morning he was in camp complaining that he was short 6 sheep 1 calf one or more hogs and thought he was very much persecuted."[5]

The next day the regiment marched to South Mountain, the site of one of the opening battles of the Antietam campaign. Private James Irwin wrote that they camped where the rebel army had been drawn up in line of battle just three weeks earlier. The positions held by their skirmish lines were clearly visible. Some of the men were curious to see what the battlefield looked like so they did some exploring. They found a mass grave where they estimated fifty Confederate soldiers were buried, and graves of sixteen Union men clearly marked with boards.[6]

The brigade remained near South Mountain until Friday evening, October 24, then headed back toward the Potomac River, halting after midnight near Berlin. Thomas Rodman wrote that the regiment was ordered to set up camp "for we are going to stay here till tomorrow morning. We are waiting for them to build a bridge of boards across the Potomac. We are going back into Virginia again where they say we may expect some lively times." He asked his parents for some money, "as many of them 25 & 50 ct bills as you can" because his recent purchases of a pair of boots and a pistol "cleared me out."[7]

Sergeant Van Houten took a special interest in the bridge under construction on the Potomac. "Here a pontoon bridge had been placed over the river, on which troops were continually crossing. It consisted of boats twenty-three feet long, six feet wide, and three deep, placed ten feet apart on the stream.—There were 76 of these in the bridge."[8] From Saturday morning until Sunday evening the entire army, one hundred thousand strong, crossed the Potomac. Corporal Isaac Decker of Company K wrote, "We crossed the Potomac at Berlin the 26th of Oct. I think that that day will long be remembered by the boys as it was an uncommon heavy rain and the wind blew very hard in the afternoon. We started about 12 oclock and marched six miles in mud often over our shoes."[9]

Once on the southern shore, Decker and some of his comrades took shelter in an old carpenter shop, where they tried to dry out and keep warm. They occupied themselves dressing and cooking some chickens, which Sergeant Van Houten maintained had followed them across the river. The men also found an eel snare and helped themselves, despite orders read to all the regiments forbidding trespassing and foraging of any kind.[10]

James Irwin intimated that even Captain James Benedict, his company commander, was involved, referring to his "scouting around" during the day. "I tell you the boys will not starve as long as there is anything alive around such as poultry and pigs."[11]

For the next four days, Piatt's Brigade marched south

Left: Private James G. Irwin, Company D. He wore a 3rd Corps badge on his forage cap along with the regimental numbers "124" and "D" to designate his company (Robert Cammaroto collection). *Right:* Adjutant William B. Van Houten, who was discharged January 23, 1865 (archive of the Historical Society of the Town of Warwick, gift of Joan and Tom Frangos).

with the Blue Ridge Mountains to the west. Their presence in Virginia was not warmly received. "All is secesh here. If you ask any persons you meet a question, the chances are he will not answer you or if he does it will be wrong."[12]

Captain Henry S. Murray, who commanded Company B, wrote from Snickersville on November 3 that roads were in terrible condition. Heavy firing had been heard ahead of them for the past two days as Union cavalry tried to force its way through a gap in the mountains to see what the Confederates were up to on the other side.

> We were just drawn up in line of battle on acct. of a body of troop being seen coming through the gap, but it proved to be our men, so we stacked arms & are lying around promiscuously. The people here are desperately Secesh & guards are put over all houses and officers are to be held responsible for the conduct of their men. Notwithstanding which, hog skins & chicken feathers are very numerous around camp & I never ask where fresh meat comes from when the boys offer me a piece. The only people we saw that appeared to be glad to see us, were four wenches & a big nigger, who waved their handkerchiefs & shouted to bring *Jeff Davis* back with us.[13]

Corporal Isaac Decker's company was left behind to guard the wagon trains at Piedmont, where he witnessed a memorable sight. "Gens McClellan and Burnside passed us on our march, and caught up with the brigade. Genl. McClellan said he wanted a brigade to go and clear the rebels out of Manassas Gap, and ours volunteered to go and do the job."[14]

Captain Murray wrote that the brigade marched from Upperville to Piedmont, a station on the Manassas Gap Rail Road, where it "turned in a field and while cooking our dinner of hard bread and bacon, Gen'l McClellan & Burnside rode by." At 2:30 P.M. the men were ordered to fall in. "Piling knapsacks & blankets together in a heap with a man to guard them, we started & are now just a half mile from the Rebels. There has been artillery skirmishing here all day.... We will probably have a fight tomorrow. Lord knows, & I say it with all reverence, with what result. I will finish this as soon as I have time. I am now holding a candle in one hand and writing on my knee."[15] Henry Howell noted in his diary that no fires were permitted as the enemy was presumed to be nearby. It had rained during the afternoon and now there was no way to dry the wet uniforms. The night turned frigid and damp, so cold that the order was countermanded and fires were built in the rear at the foot of a hill. The men settled in, hoping to get some much needed rest after their long march. "At precisely twelve oclock an orderly rode through the lines

stating that the enemy were advancing on our pickets. In less than two minutes the whole regiment was in line of battle but we got sight of no rebels that night." They remained on the alert and under arms until dawn.[16]

The next morning, the Union cavalry screen was ordered to rejoin the main force. To cover his own movements and to determine the intentions of the enemy, General Piatt deployed his skirmishers on either side of the road, then ordered them forward. "In the morning we started in pursuit. After a march of three miles we came up with them," wrote Sergeant Van Houten. As they moved through Manassas Gap, the skirmishers were fired upon by Confederate artillery. "They were prepared to send us their card in the form of a cannon ball," he added. Piatt moved quickly to establish strong positions that would give

Major Henry S. Murray, captain Company B. He was wounded in action and captured May 3, 1863, at Chancellorsville, then paroled, wounded again and captured October 27, 1864, at Boydton Road. Again he was paroled, then promoted to major and later to lieutenant colonel (archive of the Historical Society of the Town of Warwick, gift of Joan and Tom Frangos).

him the advantage. "The 122 Pennsylvania took the left the 86th N.Y. took the center and the 124th the right with two pieces of the 2d Ohio battery going each way."[17] Piatt sent the guns left to command the enemy's artillery position while the guns sent right were aimed at their main position. Each two gun section was supported by infantry but the general ordered that they stay out of sight; the 86th remained in the center, ready to support either gun position should it be pressed by the enemy. "Our battery was soon in position and throwing shell among them at a rapid rate. They fired two shots and then took to their heels; they did some tall skedadling I think."[18]

Piatt was still unsure of the enemy force on the left so he sent skirmishers forward to drive back the enemy pickets. He then moved the left section of artillery to the right to concentrate on the main Confederate position.[19]

The ground over which the 124th advanced was steep and wooded. A soldier described "climbing up the mountain, which in some places, was almost perpendicular, and with bushes so thick that only one could walk through at a time. One peak was ascended only to encounter another still higher, and so for a mile. When we reached the summit we could look over into the Shenandoah Valley, and it was the handsomest picture that I ever saw."[20] The purpose of this difficult climb was to get through the woods and brush, outflank the enemy, and trap any Confederates in the gap. But the enemy soldiers were familiar with the ground and did not wait around long enough to fall into federal hands. "At this juncture our Regiment was ordered to the right to cut them off, but again their heels proved true to them."[21]

Captain Murray wrote,

As soon as our artillery saw we were right, they opened against them. We thought we had them, when turning short to the left, they started up the Front Royal road. The 122d Col. lost himself in the woods & consequently they got off with only the loss of four horses. There was 250 Cavalry and battery & 500 infantry. The plan was good, but Col. Franklin, by losing himself, spoilt it all. We started back at about 3½ & having had no sleep the night before & nothing to eat all day but a cup of coffee & piece of hard bread in the morning, it was something of an undertaking, but we got home 14 miles at 9 P.M., tired, cold & hungry. In the morning we were sent out on picket, that is Co. B, & I am now in my tent with my feet sticking out to the fire."[22]

General Piatt was more gentle in his account of Colonel Franklin's performance: "The One hundred and twenty-second, owing to the inequality of the ground, and not fully understanding the order, failed to come up in time.... The One hundred and twenty-fourth having reached its point of destination, drove them completely out of the gap, passing to the valley beyond."[23]

This was heady stuff indeed: a long march through rebel territory, picket duty in the freezing darkness in the presence of the enemy, skirmishers moving forward under fire, an artillery duel against the backdrop of the Shenandoah Valley, and, best of all, seeing the enemy flee before them.

Piatt had done what he came to do. He'd determined that there were enemy soldiers in the gap but they were there to detect any thrust into the valley by Union forces, not to launch offensive operations east of the Blue Ridge. By now his men had eaten all their rations and had no tents or blankets to protect them from the elements. When a squadron of cavalry arrived to take up picket duty in the gap, Piatt marched his men back to Piedmont.

Compared to what they would witness in just a few weeks and what they themselves would experience in just a few months, Manassas Gap was not much of a battle. They lost not a single man killed, wounded, or missing but they had at last acquitted themselves under fire. Private John Z. Drake's pride was evident — he was the one who previously intimated that he might like to shoot General Piatt:

Last Thursday we had a skirmish with the darned Rebels at Mannases Gap. They held the Gap till we came up. We shelled them out of it and we tried to flank them but they ran too fast. When we came out of the woods we came out behind them. We drove them to the Shenandoah Valley. There we left them and returned back to camp that day. We marched thirty miles. I was tired enough when I got back to camp. When we started we left our knapsacks. That is what we call light marching orders. Col. Ellis told us we were going to have a Plug mess. Three cheers for that. We were all in good spirits for the fray.[24]

"I have smelt powder for once," wrote Thomas Rodman. "You must not think hard of my not writing oftener for we have no way of sending them to you, for we are marching all the time. I have not had any preaching for 4 Sabaths in sucession." He repeated his request that they send him some money and asked for a pair of lined buckskin gloves.[25]

The regiment did not reach Piedmont until midnight, a distance that Sergeant Van Houten figured to be about twenty-five miles. Knapsacks were retrieved and the men turned in for the night, rolling up in their blankets without bothering to set up the tents. By the time the New Yorkers awoke the next morning, a storm that would continue for days had covered them with snow. By mid-afternoon on November 7, the men were on the march again, moving southeast about five miles toward Salem, where they halted, pitched tents, and spent a "sleepless and most dreary night." The next day they moved on to Orleans, eleven miles away, where they made camp for three days.[26]

"It has been so long since I wrote a letter that I have forgot where we were when I sent my last one home," Henry Howell wrote to his sister Emily. They'd been on the move every day that week and had covered at least eighty miles. When the regiment neared Salem they found that Colonel Ellis had sent his orderly ahead to start fires so that the men could warm themselves. "We camped in the woods so we scrape the snow away with the leaves. We found a lot of hay to lay down on and we slept like pigs all night."

"We are getting so that we forage as we go along on any thing like a chicken, turkey or even a pig or sheep," wrote Henry Howell. "Our Orange County boys do not believe with McClellan about Rebel property and all that. I have stood this long march first rate and felt hearty and in good spirits.... It is reported that the Rebel have burnt the bridge across the Rappahannock river, if that is the case our advance will be delayed a short time, and I am afraid the Rebels will get in to Richmond before we can catch them, unless some of the other troops gets ahead of them and cuts them off in some way."[27]

While the 124th rested at Orleans, the men received the news of a change in army command. "I am glad Gen. Burnside is in Gen. McClelans place. I saw that in the Paper that some of the boys got today."[28] McClellan's lethargic pursuit after the Battle of Antietam was just one reason for his dismissal. McClellan did not hide his disdain for some of Lincoln's policies including the Emancipation Proclamation, and his negative opinions were made known to the public and press by his supporters. Lincoln knew that no civilian government could hope to survive in the face of such open political intriguing by one of its chief military commanders. McClellan simply had to go.

As might be expected, there was no cry of outrage from the 124th at "Little Mac's" departure. An unsigned letter published in the *Goshen Democrat*, written by an officer in the 124th, succinctly stated the men's opinion. "The removal of McClellan and the appointment of Burnside as Commander-in-Chief of the Army has given universal satisfaction. The majority think it is the fore-runner of a prompt energetic campaign, which will soon terminate in the discomfiture and overthrow of the rebels.... The manner in which affairs have been conducted is perfectly scandalous, and unless Burnside effects a change very soon, it is my opinion we might as well hang up our fiddles and go home."[29] Private James Irwin mentioned McClellan's removal in a letter to his sister, repeating what a friend said about it. "He is very much pleased to think that McClellan is removed. He thinks as much as to say that he wish they would hang him."[30]

Lincoln, ever the astute politician, was not prepared to hang up his fiddle or hang McClellan.

Instead, he waited until the fall elections were decided before replacing the general. He knew that the Democrats would likely gain seats in Congress, as the opposition party generally does in off-year elections, and did not want to give them an issue around which to rally even more support. The president waited for the New York results to see how bad things were before he acted — and they were bad. For the office of governor, New York elected Horatio Seymour, a Democrat who defeated the Republican candidate, James Wadsworth, then serving in the Army of the Potomac. When the tallying was done in Orange County, the Democrats had made substantial gains. Seymour carried the county by about six hundred votes of over eleven thousand cast. Voters chose Democrat Charles H. Winfield to represent them in Congress. From canal commissioner to state prison inspector, the Democrats won Orange County, giving the Copperheads in the towns of Wallkill and Crawford renewed hope that their activities were reaping political gain.

Little can be found in letters home to Orange County commenting on the election results. Lieutenant Mapes wrote, "I like the Wadsworth ticket bully" and he also liked Charles Winfield for Congress, but not on the Democratic ticket.[31] Most of the men were more concerned with brutal weather, long marches, and the likelihood of battle. Henry Howell asked his parents again about a rubber blanket, saying the best kind was one with a "place to put your head through so as to use it for a coat too."[32]

Several days later Howell wrote again, this time from Waterloo, a village southeast of Orleans. He'd injured his toe and now his right foot had swollen so much that he had to cut his boot to put it on. He did not like the prospect of the regiment moving on for fear he would be left behind. Otherwise, he reassured his mother, he felt fine and could get around quite well with a cane. "I am as fleshy here on hard crackers, and salt pork, as I used to be with all the luxuries of home.... Sometimes when we are on the march and our hard bread gets scarce and no prospect for any more for a few hours to come I often think of the plenty of good things I always had when I was home, but with all a soldiers hardships I would not exchange it for a citizens life with our country in the middle of this desolating war."[33]

Howell went on to describe Waterloo and its surroundings to his mother. "The country around here has been pretty well scoured.... If the war could end to day Virginia could not regain her old prosperity in a great many years. The inhabitants are nearly all gone, and what few are left are miserably clad and almost in a starving condition." He promised to write again as soon as he could, although his paper supply was "getting scarce." He asked that she send him news of the draft in Orange County. He heard that the full quota had been raised but doubted that a single person would actually serve.[34]

General Burnside abandoned McClellan's push south for a rapid move to the east. If he could get his men to Fredericksburg and across the Rappahannock before the Confederates could concentrate there, his army would be in a position to advance on Richmond with little opposition. But the bridges across the river at Fredericksburg had been destroyed. Success depended on getting pontoon bridges built before the enemy arrived to block his advance. Lincoln understood what was at stake. He told Burnside in plain terms that his operation would succeed if he moved quickly, otherwise it would fail.

Burnside acted with un–McClellan-like speed. Captain Benedict wrote,

> To-day the weak and complaining were ordered to take the cars for Alexandria and it reduced the Regiment at least one company it played the Devil with us for I had to report Alf Gray, Geo Decker, Tom Hyatt, Herrick, Ike Garrison, Jack Degraw, Wm Abram, John Ackerman, Henry Quackenbush, James McElroy, Coleman Morris, and Lieut. Houston none of them dangerous but unable to carry their packs and march.... This is the third time we have been sorted over and hope it is the last, I still hold my own, at least compared with the other companies. I said none of the squad were able to carry their packs but do not believe it for in my private opinion at the very least four of them were able to go as far as I if they thought so.[35]

The new commander reorganized the Army of the Potomac into three Grand Divisions of two army corps each. Piatt's Brigade, along with the rest of Whipple's Division remained in the 3rd Army Corps, now commanded by Brigadier General George Stoneman. The 3rd Corps and the 5th Corps comprised the Center Grand Division commanded by Major General Joseph Hooker.

The weather continued foul. Before dawn on November 17, the 124th was on the move through a heavy storm toward Libertyville, where the regiment camped for the night. Captain Clark was put in charge of guarding a large pile of straw to be used as bedding for the sick at the division hospital. An able-bodied group of soldiers from the 1st New York decided they would like dry bedding too, and tried to help themselves. They were "driven off" by the volatile captain. A much larger group from the 1st returned intent on overpowering the guard but Clark would have none of it. He drew his revolver and fired, seriously wounding one of their number. The captain had to "flee for his life" and hid out at division headquarters. Charges were brought against him, but Clark was tried and acquitted.[36]

On November 18 the regiment slogged through mud and rain to Hartwood Church. "This was in many respects the severest march we had made — all were exhausted and as wet as the rain could make us. At nearly every halt those who wore boots pulled them off and poured the water out of them, and the moment the order 'break ranks' was given, the men threw themselves on the wet ground, and had they been permitted most of them would have laid there until morning without putting up tents, building fires, or cook-

Captain Leander Clark beat a man and handcuffed him for trying to go home. He later shot a Yankee cavalryman in an argument over a hay stack (Michael McAfee collection).

ing any food, and not a few of them did lay in that condition until daylight."[37]

On November 19, it was more of the same: a march of six miles through ankle deep slush. While the storm continued for the next two days, the men were kept busy corduroying the roads so that artillery and wagons could move ahead. On that day, Private John Z. Drake wrote to his sister Minerva. "We haint had much to Eat. Our wagons went to Fredericksburg the 19th of this month and haint got back yet. All we had to live on was Beans and Beef. But now we haint got nothing to Eat but Beef. I suppose the wagons are stuck in the mud. The artillery started out but they got stuck in the mud. There is a string of them along the roads."

Drake stopped writing at this point, picking up the letter to finish it three days later. "I haint got patience to write much now because I am hungry. We are living on half rations. For about a week we have six hard crackers a day. But never mind there are better times coming when you and I and the rest will Be sitting around the table with two or three fat chickens on it if God spares my life which I hope he will." He heard that there had been a foot and a half of snow in Orange County. "You must slayride for me too." He told Minerva that the army was massing on the north side of the river and that "we expect to fight at Fredericksburg."[38]

On the 23rd they finally halted within two miles of Falmouth on the north side of the Rappahannock River across from Fredericksburg. The next day the regiment moved a short distance, cleared a piece of ground, and once again set up a regulation camp. Although the men were exhausted by the march, Colonel Ellis quickly re-established the usual camp routine of drill and picket duty.

Despite the weather, Burnside got his men to Fredericksburg relatively quickly, but the pontoon trains were not there. By the time they arrived — at least two weeks late — elements of the Army of Northern Virginia were on the opposite shore. Now the river would have to be bridged and crossed under fire. Burnside had a decision to make: should he try to cross in the face of an enemy dug in on the high ground beyond Fredericksburg, or should he call it quits for now and go into winter quarters? The latter choice would mean effectively putting off campaigning until spring when Virginia's muddy roads dried out. The pressure from Washington and from the northern press was already weighing on Burnside. Everyone looked to this self-deprecating general to reverse the fortunes of the Union with a stunning victory and he bowed to the pressure and chose to attack.

Captain Benedict wrote on November 27 that "Sayer and the Orderly obtained a pass this morning and have just returned from Falmouth they report that there are plenty of Rebs in sight from Falmouth they brought in some fresh meat soft bread and some other things for a Thanksgiving dinner not as great a variety as you have but with as good a relish and with as much contentment as any dinner eaten in the Old Dominion or in Yankee Land either, the only things necessary being to have our friends around us or we with them."[39]

Private Henry Dill's letters were short on spelling and grammar but certainly colorful. At the end of November he wrote, "I am Well and Hope this Will Find you same. Well We ar Here in old Virgine and The Romance of the thing is all gone and the sad Realities of Ware Begin to Aper I Have marched All Day on three Crackers and Barefoot at that." Ever willing to brag of his prowess with the ladies, Dill described an encounter with the natives. "Wee encamped on Rebel Farm the other night and I Went over to get something to Eat and the Women Wanted me to prochect them I told them I Would but I must Have my super First so I got my super and plenty of Whisky and Had a very plesent time about 12 oclock the Boys got in the Hen Roost I Went out But Was carful not to get out untill the chickens Ware All gone." Dill was assigned as an ambulance guard for a good bit of the march south. If he is to be believed, he spent most of his time drinking, foraging, or trying to get to know the local womenfolk.

"It is Fun to go out on picket and go in the Rebel Houses the Ambulance guard and Driver is A Hard Cuss put thar to get Red of Him He Liks Whiskey Will Not pass A chicken or a pig and is Aholyas on Hand For A Fight or Frolick if any of the Boys Want to inlist tell them the 124 is the place." As if to add to this appeal to join the 124th, he further described the benefits,

Wee Live good some times Have Fresh Beef Beens Rice Flour tea Cofey shugar it is one Doler A pound Cofey the same salt 2 Doler A pound thar is some perty girles Heare I Was talking With one the other Day Wee told Her Wee Was A goang to Whip the Rebels out Right off she said that Was A old story generl pope come ther and Was A going to do the same But Did Not she said Wee come Down Heare With our Bagege Wagons tents and Looking glases and thay Had none But Fight Fore thar Cuntry you may Bet High if the 124 is in Fight thay Wont Disgrace old oarnge Wee Had a grand Reveue the other Day generl Hooker Burnside Waren sickel sigal sykes sumener Whipel the Rebels Call Hooker old Fiting Joe thay youse to call Kerny the Fiting Devel I Have got so I Like it First Rate and Would Not Come Home If I could.[40]

While at Fredericksburg, Private James Irwin wrote to his sister asking her to get together a couple of shirts and a pair of socks, but told her not to send them until he wrote again because he was not sure where the regiment was going next. "As soon we stop long enough to get some boxes I want some of those apples and some nuts if they are very plenty." He also asked for lined buckskin gloves. "Get good ones and send by mail as soon as possible." For some reason he asked that they send a copy of the infamous Copperhead newspaper, the Middletown *Mercury*. Private Irwin had no delusions about what lay ahead. "We are expecting a fight in Fredericksburg."[41]

That same Tuesday, Sergeant John D. Drake wrote a letter that was printed in his hometown newspaper, the Port Jervis *Union*. "Our General says the 124th can stand more marching than any lot of men he ever saw, and the 86th N.Y.S.V., who compose the left wing of our Brigade, say they do not know what Orange County boys are made of as they (the 86th) have been in the field over a year, and now *we* are marching them to death. The health of our Company is good, considering what we have been through.... We have managed to live, yet sometimes pretty poorly. But I will leave my war stories untill I reach home."[42]

Early in December, Colonel Ellis issued "Special Order No. 3," which had to do with common hygiene in the camp. "Hereafter no nuisances shall be committed, except in the 'sinks' dug for the purpose. Company Commanders will be held responsible for the enforcement of this order applied to their respective streets, and any one is privileged to arrest another for the violation of the above order."[43]

The long march and exposure to the elements had taken a toll on the men, many of whom were sick. On December 1, Captain Leander Clark had a run-in with the medical staff over the care of one of his men. Lieutenant Isaac M. Martin was not getting proper care in the hospital and Clark said so, adding "I considered this Hospital arrangement a humbug. Dr. Marshall took offence and then I gave him a plain talk about the way the sick of the Regt. were neglected. About all he said was I and my sick men might go to the Devil. I told him I did not want to go just yet, and was not quite willing to let my men go there for fear they would get the same treatment they got at the Hospital. I immediately reported the Surgeon to Col. Ellis for neglect."[44]

Captain Clark's opinion of the surgeons was shared by others, including Captain James Benedict. "Our Hospital Department is not as well conducted as it should be, the D — lish Doctors are too lazy and selfish to attend to the sick as they should be, I prefer to take care of them myself in the company than to have them go to the Hospital." He had to go to Colonel Ellis to get the doctors to admit one the men too sick for duty. "Very low," was his comment. "James H. Bertholf is quite sick the Doctor said this morning that he had the Typhoid Fever but I hope, against hope, that he is mistaken, he is looking very bad so much so that I fear the worst but I should advise you not to tell his folks, for they would be the more uneasy about him, and they cannot do him any good nor can they get here to see him, and more, he will be cared for as well as it can possibly be done, he is sitting in front of My tent now by the fire, eating some soup we made for him."[45]

On December 2, Captain Clark wrote he "spent the hardest night's sleeping I ever saw. The dampness and cold struck through me as that I can hardly move, and I was very sick to-day." After the regiment stood for inspection, the camp was moved a short distance. The captain got his tent set up and was able to find a few boards to sleep on. He took some satisfaction in the fact that "after I had my talk with the Doctors, they issued rations to their sick and made some farina or corn starch for them for the first time."[46]

December 7 dawned a beautiful Sunday morning but very cold. "The ice froze in a running brook near our camp so thick that horses crossed it without breaking through." The next day, Private Bertholf was found dead in his tent. He had a fever but slept in his flimsy shelter tent, exposed to the freezing cold. As far as Captain Clark was concerned, this was simply inexcusable. "Some one is responsible for such cruelty and must answer for it at the bar of God if not to an earthly tribunal.... He leaves a wife and small family in Warwick." That afternoon, Clark and most of his company attended the funeral. Private Irwin wrote that the unfortunate soldier died of typhoid fever during the night but his tent mate, who slept beside him, did not realize his comrade was dead until the next morning.[47]

To lift his spirits, Clark did some shopping at the sutlers. With $2.50 he purchased two pounds of butter, five pounds of crackers, a pound of tea, and some candles. He invited Quartermaster Travis, Sergeant Stewart, and the recently promoted Sergeant Spencer Brooks to his tent to share in this simple feast. Clark heated the crackers and spread each with butter, then served them to the sergeants with hot coffee and apple sauce. "I thought the above named articles too good a treat to eat without my friends knowing it."[48]

On December 9, Private Drake wrote to his sister that

the Army of the Potomac is laying still. It is all quiet along the lines.... Our cooks have orders to cook five days rations. We expect to march one of these days. We are going to Richmond if we don't get stopped. I expect to hear the roar of cannons before a great many days. I can tell you how the roar of canons and musket sound in battle. It sounds like fifty wagons a running over a stony road ... only a good deal louder.... I hope there wont be a great many more Battles. You must not be surprised if you should get up one morning and see me in the Garden with my tent up cooking my grub over a little fire."[49]

On December 10, Private Irwin asked his sister to send him a box from home even though "we will be some where else when you [get this] ... as we have marching orders. There is various rumors as to where we are going." He asked for "2 pr w sock 1 camp knife of the Walden make 1 paper pepper make a bag to carry it in 2 cans concentrated milk some tea 1 lb. Also a bag to carry it in. Some dried apple or peaches or dried fruit of any kind. You tell Clara Dolson if she want to get rid of any of there apples to eat that she put them in this box."[50]

The regiment was issued four-day rations with orders to stow the food in haversacks and knapsacks. At about 4:30 in the afternoon, the men were called out for dress parade in heavy marching order. Captain Clark wrote that "every man in my company reported himself ready to march and was the only company that did not report quite a number of men unable to move. Yesterday I issued a pair of socks to each man in my company, and several drew new shoes. Sundown everything packed and ready to march." Two hours later, orders came for the regiment to turn in so as to be ready to march at 6 the next morning. Clark, in final preparation for the battle, had his Colt's rifle repaired by Private Samuel A. White.[51] Captain Weygant, who had been serving as brigade provost-marshal at headquarters, asked to be relieved of that duty so that he could take his place at the head of his company, a request that was approved.

The Battle of Fredericksburg began on Thursday, December 11, 1862. General Burnside planned to send his Grand Divisions across the river on pontoon bridges, then launch a two-pronged attack to drive the Confederates from the heavily defended ridgeline above the town.

The men were awake by 3 in the morning and ready to go soon after. Knapsacks, packed the night before, were dropped off at the quartermaster's tent. "We left camp on Thursday," Captain Murray wrote, "leaving everything behind us, except our blankets, canteens, haversacks, and arms, and marched about three miles, passing all the army moving toward where the cannonading had been going on at a prodigious rate, ever since 5½ o'clock that morning, which was kept up without intermission all day. We were here drawn up in line of battle and rested, waiting a chance to cross the river."[52] General Whipple noted that his division "deployed in the ravine to the left and rear of the Phillips house."[53]

Piatt's Brigade was positioned on Stafford Heights, a bluff overlooking the Rappahannock and the town of Fredericksburg. "Here they stacked arms and lay down to await the completion of a pontoon bridge which our engineers had, during the night, pushed two-thirds of the way across the river." Confederate riflemen in the town opened a deadly fire which periodically drove the bridge builders back up and over the bluff. Captain Weygant marveled at how these soldiers dragged their wounded with them, reformed, and dashed back down to renew their work. He described how the "floating blood-stained bridge was pushed out toward the hostile shore, bringing its resolute builders nearer and yet nearer their hidden foes."[54]

Yankee artillery opened fire on the town to silence the sharpshooters then stopped to allow the engineers to continue the work, but again the enemy opened fire on them and again the artillery replied. The drama played out before a vast audience which included the men of the 124th New York. Captain Weygant, ever the keen observer, wrote:

All of a sudden the earth trembled and the air was rent with a noise that cannot be described.... The bluffs disappeared; and in their stead was a long line of puffing curling smoke, filled with weird-looking forms of moving men, and lit up continually by ever changing flashes of shooting flame. The river, to, faded from our sight, and the crumbling city gradually disappeared under thick black clouds of powder smoke.... At length the cannonade ceased, the smoke raised a little, and lo! Two bridges spanned the river, filled with columns of Union troops, who were hurrying across into the battered city, which was not yet entirely cleared of the enemy, though our infantry crossing in boats under the smoke, had successfully, driven them from the river front.[55]

As evening approached, orders were received for Piatt's Brigade to remain in place for the night. Captain Weygant noted that all he had witnessed, the destruction of Fredericksburg, the loss of several hundred Union soldiers in laying the two bridges and in driving enemy from the town, "was but a side show. The main battle had not yet commenced."[56]

At about 10 A.M. on Friday, December 12, the 124th prepared to cross the pontoons in column, Company A in the lead, Company B in the rear. An unsigned letter published in the *Goshen Democrat* written by Captain Henry Murray described the initial attempt to cross.

The next morning we started, and marched toward the lower bridge where Gen. Franklin had crossed — laid in the mud there some time started back, and went up the river to the bridge opposite the city. As you go to the river you have to descend a bank at an angle of 45 degrees probably 150 feet. Just as the right of our Regiment had got on the bridge, (the 122d Pennsylvania having nearly crossed) and the left company just on the brow of the hill, wing! thug! went something over my head, and a shell struck right behind us under the horse of the Adjutant of the 86th N.Y. The Col. kept on, and the shells kept coming at the rate of one every five seconds, right in amongst us. I called to the boys to keep together and not be alarmed and succeeded in preventing much confusion. Just as I got them together in good order, I saw one man dodge a shell that came over us. "Don't dodge boys," said I, "you'll be just as likely to get hit as if you stood up." No sooner had the words left my mouth than buzz! wing!! thug!!! came another shell — down went my head, and I turned to the boys laughing at the absurdity of my not following my own advice; but remembering the anecdote of Gen. Taylor in Mexico, I said "boys, dodge the big ones."[57]

Company K was well toward the back of the column so Captain Jackson had a good view.

Our reg. was one half over, a band on the city side was playing "Bully for that" and we thought it a "big thing" to get over when all at once "Bang" "whiz" and chuck in the mud just on the side hill about us on the left came a shell followed by shot and shell falling and bursting among us in quick succession. It made us dodge very lively and to tell the truth it was enough to frighten any one not used to such things for the enemy had full view of us coming down the bank and had perfect range beside this we were the first who had crossed the bridge in plain sight and broad daylight.[58]

"I then looked down the bank toward the river," wrote Captain Murray,

and saw the right wing "about faced" and marching back, and the left wing filing to the right under the bank. So, running to the head of the Company, I led them at common time after the rest. Fortunately no one in our Regiment was hurt, although several in the 12th N.H. Vols., which was behind us were wounded, one fatally. The rebels had the range of the bridge exactly, and the shells flew in the water around the bridge and in the bank, at a fearful rate for a few minutes. One passed probably two feet over my head ... striking in the bank 30 feet above us exploded, throwing its pieces in all directions; one passed so close to the Major and Adjutant, who were together on horseback, that it knocked off the hat of the latter, and exploded covering them both with mud. They were mostly percussion shells, and the ground being soft they did not explode with a few exceptions. Had they been fuse, they would have knocked us higher than a kite.... They make a peculiar sound as they go over, and one cannot help involuntarily dodging them. Some think they say "Cousin," accenting and prolonging the last syllable Be that as it may, it is not at all pleasant to be "cousined" by them.[59]

"The Col. wanted to take us on over," wrote Captain Jackson, "but Gen. Whipple ordered us to draw back out of range, which we did in some little confusion for a moment or two for the Major at our end did not hear the Col's order at the head of the column and told us to stand fast."[60]

The regiment was under accurate and intense shelling for the first time and the men could easily have panicked, but for the efforts of the company-level officers. Captain Benedict wrote,

I had to lead the column *through*. It was in this way, after we had faced about, I saw the column breaking, and ran to the left of my company, and turned them, as we were ordered, and took them along the River, till I came to a small run, and as there was no officers there to command us, I ordered Halt, and down, and the last order was executed very sudden I can tell you, but we were hardly down when a part of companys I.F.C.A. and I guess almost every other company in the Reg, a part of the 86th N.Y., and a part of the N. Hampshire 12th, were huddled in with us, all in a heap, well in a few minutes along came the Col. Looking up his Reg (he had to jump off his Horse once, and just in time too, for a piece of shell hit his Blanket in front of his saddle) and ordered us to form again when I called the company up, they all *came to time* but one, who I found in another company some distance off the officers of the other Reg say I was the coolest one they saw among the whole.[61]

The regiment moved off along the river to the left where the soldiers lay until sundown. "To keep us awake and our spirits up," Captain Jackson wrote,

1st Lieutenant James H. Roosa, Company K, who was discharged March 7, 1863, for disability (Archive of the Historical Society of the Town of Warwick, Gift of Joan and Tom Frangos).

the rebs would bang away every few minutes. It was rather dangerous for a while at first. Some fell and bust uncomfortably near. One came within an inch of my head and burst right by my side in the soft ground. Another about as near Lieut. Roosa and two others fell in our company besides many which struck just over the reg. It was a great wonder that none in the reg. were struck. Five of the 12th N.H. just behind us were wounded severely. We all kept our places though somewhat alarmed for they had a perfect range on us from a battery up the road to the bridge. It is not very pleasant to be shelled with no chance to get a shot at any thing in return. Some of our old soldiers said they would rather any day be in close action.[62]

Captain Benedict summed up the day, "Well we could not cross and were ordered to march back about a mile where we spent the night in the mud."[63]

"The next day the shelling was very brisk, from 9½ until 11, with considerable musketry. We took a different route to get to the bridge from that of the day before so that the rebels did not see us. We crossed the bridge at a quarter to 12. The firing commenced again at that time and there was a continual roar.... After we crossed the river we were marched along the bank out of reach of the shell, which would occasionally come over our heads."[64]

Thomas Rodman was disgusted at not being able to cross on Friday. "Saturday morning got up took arms and loaded them made up our minds to cross that river or die in the attempt. So forward we went marched down to the bridge without any trouble but then came the shells but we did not stop to see where they struck, got safely across the River into the City.... Sat down on the river bank and ate our dinner under a very heavy fire from their guns."[65]

"When we were safely across," Captain Murray wrote, "we sat down under the bank where there were some other Regiments, the 19th and 20th Mass., being among them. One of the officers of the former was eating dinner, and gave me a cup of coffee. (Poor fellow he was killed that afternoon) While I sat drinking it, a shell burst in the street beyond, and a piece striking the ground half way down the bank, passing under the chin of one of our company struck one of their Lieutenants on the shoulder without hurting him."[66]

General Whipple placed his division to guard the right flank of army with "the One hundred and twenty-second Pennsylvania Volunteers deployed as skirmishers upon the Fall Hill road, between the two canals, above the city and upon the crest of the ridge upon which stands Mrs.

Washington's monument, and two companies of the One hundred and twenty-fourth New York Volunteers were advanced in front of Kenmore mansion."

The two companies mentioned by the division commander were E and F, commanded by Captain McBirney of F. From their vantage point, the men witnessed part of the assault by Federal troops on the Confederate position atop Marye's Heights. Once the battle got underway, the batteries they were to support came under rifle fire from Confederate marksmen who managed to pick off a couple of the gunners working the cannon. A volunteer from Company F crept forward and saw that the rifle fire was coming from an octagonal summer house. A section of the battery opened fire on the house, destroying it and killing or driving away the sniper.[67]

The remaining eight companies of the 124th were still under cover of the river bank where they had stacked their arms in a straight line that corresponded to the regimental front. When the order was given to form up and take arms, it could be done quickly and efficiently, every man retrieving his own weapon. That order came, but before the men got in line, a "prematurely bursting shell" sent chunks of metal flying among them, destroying several of the stacked weapons and wounding three of the men.[68]

Captain Murray wrote that the men "soon fell in as some musketry sounded on the hill, and went up to take a part. We laid there perhaps two hours, then fell in and moved about 40 rods up the river. When the Rebels saw some troops (our other brigade) coming down the opposite hill, they threw shells at them, which, passing close over our heads, we were ordered to go under the bank which we did, and let them pass over us. They sent all kinds of missiles. We could see long pieces of railroad iron come over, end over end. Their range was not as good as the day before and did no damage. As the firing slackened, Piatt's Brigade advanced through the town, "we fell in, and moved into the yards of houses, which form the suburbs of the city, and forming in line of battle, we laid flat on our faces, the shells from both our own and the enemy's batteries passing over us."[69]

About mid-afternoon, orders came for the brigade to prepare for a charge on a Confederate battery positioned on the high ground about a half mile to their front. The men hurried forward, the 86th and the 122nd moving to the flanks, the 124th in the center. Once in position, the men were ordered to lie down to escape the shells flying overhead from both sides. Here they had time to contemplate the likelihood of surviving a charge over open ground against dug-in artillery and infantry.[70] Most had no idea that only a short distance to their left, thousands of Union men were being needlessly sacrificed doing the same thing. Colonel Ellis came along the line, telling his "Old Goshen Blossoms" to make themselves ready.[71] According to Captain Weygant, it was at this critical juncture that General Piatt, "attempting to force his horse over a ditch, fell in, and was so badly injured that he had to be carried to the rear." Colonel Franklin of the 122nd Pennsylvania, who was senior, took charge of the brigade.

It is not clear who decided against the charge but Weygant noted, "fortunately for the Orange Blossoms, it never came."[72] Captain Jackson wrote, "At this the upper end of town we gained no ground and indeed it was not attempted for it would have been folly to storm their batteries one above the other with a deep canal to cross and go for a mile in face of rifle buts and intrenchments.... Of course if ordered we would have tried and might have taken the first line but with heavy loss as was done by Sumner in the center."[73]

"The roar of the canon on Saturday sounded like Thunder in the Heavens," a soldier wrote. "It was a continual roar all day. We had to support a Battery and at night we had to do Picket Duty next to the Rebels. We had to lay down flat on the ground. That was nice you better believe. Right in the mud."[74] Private James Haggerty of Company I noted that they pulled down a fence and used it to sleep on that night.[75]

Nineteen-year-old Private Daniel Dugan of Company D wrote that "we was not in the fite in the Day time but we was in a very bad place in the nite time we was on picket close by the reables I hear SharpShooters were firing on us during the night wile we layed on our Face and hands for 7 hours and could not move for if we did not do so they would fire on us. Some of our men they fixed on them During the night but killed none of them in the Day time they shelled us but killed none of them that is our redg."[76]

At dawn on Sunday, December 14, the regiment was pulled back a little, taking cover behind the drying yard of a large woolen factory. A high board fence provided additional cover from the ever-vigilant Confederate artillerymen. Thomas Rodman referred to this as a large cloth factory and noted that it provided ample cover until "the boys got running in and out of an old house and they got sight of us and began shelling us."[77] Meanwhile, Companies E and F were still on duty guarding the batteries near the Kenmore Mansion. Early in the morning, they moved into an open field to the right of the mansion "in full view of the enemy; and there we lay on our faces till night, the enemy throwing their shells all around us, but doing us no damage although several exploded near us. At night we were relieved and sent back to our Regiment which we found under the river bank near where we left it."[78]

As dusk approached, the regiment moved back toward the riverbank, where the men found a flour mill. Never shy about appropriating Rebel property, the men helped themselves and made such good griddle cakes that several mentioned the incident in letters home. While they were at the mill, another shell from their own artillery fell among them but did no harm.[79]

Captain Weygant wrote that the regiment spent Sunday night at the river and that the men took advantage of what the deserted homes had to offer in the way of bedding. "Not a few of our number slept that night on feather beds, and had spread over them soft white woolen, instead of course gray blankets."[80] Although Captain Murray maintained he did not visit the houses himself, he assured his father that the men of his company did not hesitate. "I did not go into the village, but they say it is sacked awfully, indeed from the feather beds etc. I saw the boys sleeping on I should say the inhabitants will sleep *hard* when they come back."[81]

While the boys pillaged the houses, Lieutenant Mapes wrote a quick note to his brother Jesse. "We have crossed the River, we had a little trouble in crossing. The Rebs saw us & shelled us, but hurt none of us. We have laid on our bellies since Friday under the South side of the river. Providence has spared us all.... Saturday there was a very heavy battle fought here. I have not heard the result. I suppose I will go on picket to night the papers will tell you."[82]

"It was hard to see nice furniture thrown out, when to take it could be of no possible use," wrote Captain Jackson. "As Col. Cummings said it seems as if a soldier would rather steal a bureau than a watch. Many of the houses were splendidly furnished. Some of the boys were in a house drumming on a piano when 'bang' came a shell into it when they soon left."[83]

It became clear to General Burnside that the enemy positions could not be breached by direct assault and the time had come to pull the army back across the river. Strong picket lines were sent forward to keep the enemy at a distance while the army quit the south bank of the Rappahannock.

"Monday until night we lay under the river bank as a picket reserve," Captain Jackson wrote, "falling in line every once in a while when picket firing in front was heard. Here at dusk two of my men turned up missing Henry J. Wright and Alfred G. Randall both painters of Middletown. They may have strolled off and got taken but I don't know any thing about them." Both men had indeed "strolled off"—they'd deserted that very day. "All day our wounded were taken out of the city in ambulances to the other side. There were a great number of them from Saturdays fight."[84]

During the day Monday, December 15, the regiment remained sheltered along the river. That night, the men were ordered out to picket duty along the Bowling Green Road.[85] "In the evening we went out about 300 yards as outer pickets changing our position in the night falling back of the canal and taking up the bridge. Then I got an idea of what was going on. Our troops were evacuating the town. Here we were and in danger of being left and taken by rebels. Col. Cummings some how found out what was up and got us together. We ran down to the river and formed on the edge." The enemy was so quiet that Captain Murray suspected that "some deviltry was on hand." The thought kept him pacing up and down his end of the line all night. At about 2:30 A.M. a staff officer from brigade headquarters came with news that the bridge over the canal had been destroyed and, should they have to fall back in a hurry, they should find another route to the pontoons."[86]

At about 4:30 A.M. Tuesday morning, orders came for the 124th to prepare to move back to the river. A short while later Lieutenant Colonel Cummins moved along the line from company to company telling each company commander it was time to leave. "Hurry in our vedettes without making any noise," he told Captain Weygant.[87] When Cummins got to Company B, he "ordered attention, left face, and marched us down to the river, when we countermarched and re-crossed the river. We were the last regiment to cross; the bridge being taken up immediately after us."[88] Two companies, I and K, held their positions to cover the retreat of the regiment and then "About day light left the road and fell back over the canal where we laid down in the mud about 10 min. then fell back to the river meet the rest of the regt. At the bridge crossed the river and came back to camp rain all the time & very muddy."[89]

"We crossed over the last regiment only a few skirmishers after us," wrote Captain Jackson.

I was afraid the rebs would take a notion to shell us when we crossed but it was just at daylight and in the rain with the wind in our favor. We breathed freer when over for if the rebs only knew it they could have driven us far on the right we were not very strong for our troops moved more to the left and all the time we were there we were in a very confined position, for we could not stir without drawing fire the rebel left extending far beyond our right of which our brigade was the extreme. Our regiment did nothing very brilliant but all that was required or ordered.[90]

The retreat, though smooth, was not flawless. Two members of Company I were captured. Private Robert Rose was soon paroled and served with the regiment until the end of the war. As Private Harvey H. Snider waited to be exchanged at Camp Parole near Annapolis, Maryland, he deserted; there is no record of his ever returning to serve with the regiment.

Private Benjamin Lancaster of Company A made a harrowing escape from the advancing Confederates. Just after dawn on Tuesday, he and three other men from his company were far to the front of the main picket line when they saw heavy lines of infantry coming toward them. They raced to the rear only to find that, not only had the regiment fallen back without notifying them, the entire Union army had crossed to the northern bank of the river and taken up the pontoon bridge behind them. Lancaster evaded the Confederates, swimming the icy waters of the Rappahannock to safety only to be arrested by Union pickets on the other side. Fortunately for him, he was taken before a general who sent him on his way before he froze to death. Fires were built in the old camp of the 124th to warm Lancaster and others who suffered from the cold. Captain Weygant, an unswerving temperance man, looked the other way as copious amounts of liquid stimulants were given to the men to help fend off the cold. By his own account, he paid for a good deal of the whiskey himself.[91]

"The morning after our return, nearly half the regiment answered the surgeon's call, and the names of nearly a hundred were placed on the sick list. Ten of this number died within six weeks, and many others never returned to duty with the regiment."[92] A member of the medical staff of the 124th confirmed the large number of casualties for the army, but his assessment of the health of the regiment was good news for the families at home. "We have had a number of cases of Typhoid Fever, since the return of the Regiment from Fredericksburgh, and seven deaths; but the disease has now assumed a milder form and the men are in good condition, ready (but not anxious) to go where they are ordered." He referred to the Fredericksburg battlefield as a "slaughter pen" and wrote that anyone seeing the place "would be astonished that our army was ever caught in such a trap, or that when caught they succeeded in making their escape. Our loss was not, I think, overrated, and you can add to the number about a thousand more who have since died from disease arising from exposure at that time. I was not present on the battle ground, having been previously detailed to take charge of the sick and disabled of our Division. I found myself in charge of three hundred and fifty-four men, one hundred and fifty-two of whom were unable to do anything for themselves, with but one able-bodied assistant."[93]

"We reached our old camp ground about 9 o'clock, wet, hungry, and tired, for it rained hard during part of the night," wrote "Scriptor" to a friend back in Middletown. "So you see that although not in battle, we were pretty close to the enemy."[94] Some of the men began to reflect upon the hardship they had endured, knowing full well that they had suffered none of the loss that shattered many Union regiments. "We do not look on it as a defeat and certainly not as a great Victory," wrote Captain Jackson, "but as a part of a game not yet played out.... We are curious to learn how this move is regarded in New York."[95]

Even though Fredericksburg was clearly a defeat, the regiment and its commander were noticed by General Whipple, who mentioned them in his official report of the action. "In the withdrawal of the pickets I would call attention to the coolness and presence of mind of the officers and men of the One hundred and twenty-fourth New York Volunteers, on duty at the Fall Hill road, beyond the canal. Colonel Ellis, who was in command, was perfectly prepared to contend, foot by foot, with any force the enemy might throw against him."[96]

Private Thomas Rodman summed up the 124th's part in the Battle of Fredericksburg when he wrote: "So we did not make anything by crossing."[97]

CHAPTER 4

"Who would be a soldier?"
December 18, 1862–April 25, 1863

Christmas 1862 was different for the soldiers from Orange County from any that had gone before. Most of the men had never been away from their families for any appreciable length of time, and they had always been home for the holidays.

Private Thomas Rodman wrote to his mother on Christmas morning, "Now I wish you a merry Christmas. I suppose you are going to have a Turkey or Chicken for dinner today. I hope that you may enjoy it and I want you to eat a leg and breast for me, for I am not there to do it myself. I suppose there will be a great time sleigh riding there today." He had hoped that the religious nature of the holiday would be observed in camp and was delighted when the regiment was called out and formed into a hollow square for the purpose of having a "divine service." Much to Rodman's annoyance, Chaplain Bradner did not show up. "I am quite provoked for we have not had any preaching since we left Minors Hill, it is a shame for a chaplain to act so."[1] The celebration at New Years started out on a high note when the regiment had apple dumplings for dinner. Then the festive mood was spoiled when "some half dozen of the boys got Whiskey and got Drunk and was put in Irons all night."[2]

Private Joseph Brooks of Company D wrote to "Friend Sarah" in much the same vein, "We had a green crissmast and New Years I spent my New Year on picket I suppose Old santy brought you a great manny nice things. Old santy did not bring me any thing I think he is a hard Old Felow." Sarah had written chastising him for not putting enough postage on the last letter he sent her and for asking that she send him stamps in her letters. "I am sorry that you could not Find an extry stamp to put on your letter," he answered, obviously annoyed. "You was so hard on me because I did not put stamps on the one that I sent you I have an excuse for not putting an other extry stamp for it is hard to get them hear I think it is no more than wright if the girles want the boys to write to them for to keep them in postage stamps and paper wel I shall not say any thing more a bout that now."[3]

It is not known how Sarah replied or if she sent him any more stamps. If their relationship blossomed through the mail that winter, it would have been that much harder for her to receive the news the following spring that the twenty-two-year-old private had been shot down near the crossroads at Chancellorsville.

A note of bitterness crept into Private John Drake's letter to his sister, "I suppose you had Christmas like you do every time. But I did not. It didn't seem no more like Christmas to me than any other day."[4]

Private Gouverner M. Legg, Company H, wrote to his wife, "Dear you ask me what I had at crisamass I had nothing and I did not want anything there is only one thing in this world that I want and that is peace sow that I can go to my home with my family." As regards to his children he wrote, "I Gess it makes me feal Glad to hear that Santa Closs did come the poor little ones thought that he would not com because I was not home but thank God that he did come to them." Previously his wife wrote of getting a box together to send to him; he emphatically told her to do no such thing. He said that he was getting along fine and did not want her depriving herself or the children of anything by sending him a box. There was another much more urgent problem: although the regiment had been in service four months, the men had yet to be paid. Legg was unable to send any money home for his family, a situation that bothered him a great deal. It must have weighed heavily on many soldiers that their families would be dependent on the generosity of relatives and friends to make it through the winter.

In desperation, Crissey had secured a loan to be repaid with her husband's army salary. She wrote to ask him if she had done the right thing. "Of corse you did what Else Could you do and God knows I am Glad that you can do that I hope that I will Sune be paid of Sow that you can have sum money of your own." He reminded her that when the regiment was raised the previous summer, promises had been made to the recruits that wives and families would be cared for in their absence with money donated for that very purpose. "Do thay let you have a nuff to live on" he wanted to know. "You must not be a fraid to ask them for all you want for thay promist me that my family should not want that they would see to them if thay do not ceap thear word I want to know it and you must tell me."[5]

On January 4, Colonel Ellis issued "General Orders No. 7," a good indication that the men were getting lax in winter camp. "Hereafter all men absent from roll calls without permission, or who have dirty guns will be fined one month's pay to the United States Government." To that point, the men were owed four months' pay. A fine that would amount to 25 percent of their pay was probably motivation enough to make roll call and keep their weapons clean.[6]

With no paymaster in sight, the soldiers themselves needed money. Private Andrew Bowman wrote to a friend back home, "I received your letter ... & in it found $5.00. $3.00 in small change & two in one dollar bills & received it with much pleasure & I am mutch oblige to your for your trobble ... theare is no sutch thing in the Book as me deserting," he assured his friend. "I will stick to company H as long as captain Crist has got read hair in his head."[7]

In Newburgh, the ladies of the Soldiers Aid Society were working to help the soldiers' families in need at Christmas time. They held a fair which "netted the *snug little* sum of $650 an amount much exceeding their expectations.... More than one poor Soldier's family was treated to something like a Christmas dinner from the surplus of the bountifully supplied supper tables."[8] In the next issue of the same newspaper, it was reported that Private David Titsworth of Capt. Bush's Company F died of typhoid fever, leaving a wife and three children, underscoring the need to provide not just for soldiers' families but also for the newly created widows and orphans.[9]

As Private Legg fretted about the welfare of his family, his hometown of Walden was taking action to help the soldiers and their families. Sergeant Charles Stewart of Company I, who sometimes signed his letters to the press "Felix" and whom the editor of the *Daily Telegraph* referred to as "our correspondent in the army," wrote to the Newburgh paper. He said that the people of his city should take their cue from Walden, which had packed and sent two huge boxes to the men of Company H. "Every town but Newburgh that has a company in this regiment has sent them boxes and barrels full of good things, to remind them that they were not forgotten by the towns that sent them out.... We are often asked what we have done to make Newburgh forget us so." The citizens of Walden had, only the week before, sent a box of new boots to Company H, each boot filled with useful items. Walden had also sent each soldier a "nice sum of money" at New Year's and, "better yet, has employed two men to cut wood for the families of those who have gone to fight for their country." All this had been done by a community smaller than Newburgh, less prosperous, with no Soldiers' Aid Society, and without "a puff in the newspaper."

Then Stewart really twisted the knife: "We can say as did the boy of his mother when she would not give him butter on his bread. He did not care a darn for the butter; it was the mean disposition of the old women that bothered him."[10]

During the holidays John Cowdrey decided to visit his son Sergeant John Cowdrey, then serving in Company D, 124th New York. He and a traveling companion boarded a train in Warwick on Wednesday bound for the Union camps along the Rappahannock. They decided to drop in on President Lincoln but "owing to the pressure of business, were unable to see him, which we regretted exceedingly."

While in the capital, Mr. Cowdrey procured military passes for himself and his friend to depart for the "seat of war." On Friday morning, they set sail on a government steamer which took them to Aquia Creek, where they boarded a train for Falmouth Station. Another train took them to within a couple of miles of the camps. Then, "with carpet-bag in hand, we were obliged to take on foot, but the kindly greeting and happiness manifested by our dear friends, (among them my son), amply repaid for all our trouble and difficulties in reaching them."

They visited with the officers of the regiment and many of their friends from Orange County, then "we accepted the pressing invitation of our old chums — Capt. Benedict and Lieut. Sayer — to partake a soldier's fare while we remained." With new military passes in hand and accompanied by Lieutenant Colonel Cummins, Captain Benedict, and Sergeant Cowdrey, they went on a sightseeing tour of the Fredericksburg battlefield from the safety of the northern shore of the Rappahannock River. They saw the place where the regiment crossed the river and where they lay for several days exposed to enemy fire. "When, with the aid of glasses you see the enemy's works rising tier above tier, the guns in each succeeding line of entrenchments bearing directly upon the others, I must agree with many with whom I conversed, that the works cannot be taken.... They are not so discouraged as one would suppose, and find no fault with anything but the entire neglect of the Government to pay them their well earned dues, knowing as many do, that their dear ones at home are suffering for the necessaries of life." With that, John Cowdrey took leave of his friends in the regiment and his son "feeling fully impressed that we had seen what God knows we hope never to be compelled to see again, *the horrors of war.*"[11]

The soldiers had been reluctant, at first, to write about the battle, but time had made them better able to assess what had happened. Thomas Rodman wanted to know what his parents thought of the progress of the war to date, but wrote,

> For my part I think it is no more nearer to a close than it was when I came down here.... The reason I did not say more about the Battle of Fredericksburgh was because I was ashamed to say that I came all the way down here to fight and then got whipped (that's so). All I have to say about it is that it is not very pleasant to see whole ranks of men mown down like grass and they not able to make any resistance of any account. I saw about 500 men killed that time right in front of me not over ¼ off and I could not help their comrades avenge their death. But I am thankful that I came out alive.[12]

Private Joseph Brooks wrote to a friend,

> The rebels hold a very strong posision theare so strong that they can hold it against five to one it is a mistake for you or anyone else to think that the rebels canot fight I used to think so but I have found out the difference they are as good if not better than the union army I have come to the conclusion that the head men concerned in this War such as the government contractors and Major Generals and in fact the President and his cabinet is in no hury to bring this to a close they don't care how much hardships the soldiers have to endure so long as they feather theare nest. If the Oficers did not get any more Wages than privates this War would end in thirty days as it is theare is no knowing When it will end. The government is now at the Expence of two million a day and they have not accomplished any thing for the last five months if they don't do any more for the next five to come the army Will be in a Worse condition.

He laid the blame at the doorstep of the president and the party that elected him for all that had gone wrong. "I have voted the last republican ticket if I live to get back theare is a great manny more that have changed theare politics in the last three months."[13]

Corporal Francis Benedict, killed at the Battle of Chancellorsville. "I'd rather be laid up well riddled with honest bullets ... than be sick in camp" (Michael J. McAfee collection).

Corporal Francis Benedict of Company D was growing weary of the inactivity of winter camp. He called it "dreary and monotonous" and thought it had an adverse effect on the health of the men. "I'd rather be laid up well riddled with honest bullets, after an engagement, than to be sick in camp. It takes all the starch out of a fellow." Benedict must have read the same newspaper as Joseph Brooks. "The papers say half a million men have gone and five hundred millions of money have been spent; and yet these 'Secesh' have not had one good knock-down crack. But we'll help do it. Ellis is a fighter. We're got a colonel who means business. We're got a captain who is ready. Ellis can do two things; swear and fight. He does the former till the air is blue, when things don't go right—Let men do right then. If an officer isn't an out and out disciplinarian, he doesn't belong there.... We want to get to work and wipe this rebellion out."[14]

January 10, 1863, was a big day for the 124th New York. The men were marched to regimental headquarters to turn in their heavy Vincennes rifles in exchange for "1st Class Arms"—Enfield rifle muskets of British manufacture. The effect on the regiment was immediate. "All are rejoicing," wrote Captain Weygant, "from Colonel Ellis down to the contrabands." The men were all of the opinion that their inferior weapons had kept them on the fringes of the last battle but that now, with these rifles, they would surely be in the thick of the next one.[15]

Captain Murray wrote that he, Colonel Cummins, Adjutant Bronson, and Dr. Marshall had personally gone to Aquia Creek "to see about getting new guns in which I am happy to say we succeeded...." The regiment was issued Enfields, "and although not as good as the Springfield are infinitely preferable to our old Cannons with Cheeseknife accompaniment."[16]

"We have got guns cince we come out," wrote Joseph Brooks, "the first wheare very heavy and they had heavy saber bayonet wich we caried in a belt by our side the belt We had to have it buckled so tight that it hurt a man the doctor sayed that they was the caus of unfiting so many from duty. We have a verry light gun now."[17]

The Enfields were muzzle loaders just as the old Vincennes had been, so the drill they had learned in the fall was perfectly fine for the new weapons. More accurate than the Vincennes, the Enfields were a big improvement. The sights could be adjusted to 900 yards and while it was unlikely that an infantryman could pick out and hit a specific target at such an extreme range, the bullet could carry that far with a deadly punch. In addition, the Enfield had an appealing look to it, and was well designed and well balanced. The British import fired a cone-shaped minié ball propelled by a powder charge. Both powder and ball were packaged in a paper tube, folded and tied shut.[18]

The men also exchanged their old sword bayonets for slimmer, triangular bayonets designed to puncture a man rather than cut him. Such a wound was difficult to close so, in theory at least, the enemy soldier would bleed to death unless he got immediate medical care. After spending the day cleaning the new weapons, the men turned out for dress parade presenting "as happy and proud a line of faces as one could wish to see."[19]

The week before, Thomas Rodman wrote home that the weather was warm and dry. He assured his parents that his health was excellent. "Our grub continues to keep good and plenty. We have Pork, Crackers, Beef, Beans, Rice, dried Apples and Coffee." Quite a few soldiers wrote about gaining weight since their enlistment despite the rigors of the march and sleeping out of doors. The regiment had been out on picket duty but since Rodman was a member of Company C, the Color Company he was exempt.[20]

Except for picket duty, there had not been much action since the day after Christmas, when the army was to cook three days' rations in preparation for a march. Nothing came of it and things remained quiet until mid–January. The men settled into what they thought would be winter camp. Without orders to do so, they began to build small log structures, buttoning several of their shelter halves together to serve as a roof for each cabin.[21]

The second week in January, long wagon trains loaded with pontoons were seen moving in the direction of the Rappahannock. Yet another ominous sign of an impending battle was the order that no more boxes could be shipped to the soldiers from home.[22] This was followed by orders to move the sick from regimental hospitals to division hospitals. Extra rations were issued on January 17 with orders to prepare to march the following day. The order to move was twice delayed and the routine of camp life was again reestablished. On January 20, Colonel Ellis received orders to prepare to move at 1 P.M. At about noon the men pulled down their tents, built log fires to keep warm, and waited for the order to march, which, of course, did not come.[23]

Late in the afternoon it began to rain and, having been down this road before, the men pitched their meager cloth tents, crawled in, and went to sleep. They awoke to a steady, chilling rain, assuring each other that no sane general would order a march until the storm passed. But, just as the rain turned to sleet, the bugle call to "strike tents" was heard. They packed their gear, formed up, and headed out into the storm. The sleet turned to hail, adding to their misery. "When night overtook us, we halted, or rather, were stuck fast in the mud, scarce three miles from camp. The rain was still falling, and freezing as it fell. We were soaking wet, and chilled to the very marrow of our bones; and there in an open piece of woods, we added yet another to our already long list of nights of terrible suffering."[24]

"We left our camp on the 21," Private Bowman wrote, "marched about 2½ miles & every step for two miles the mud was over the tops of our shoes & rainen all the time. Our artillery could not get threw I seen twelve & sixteen horses hitched to one Batery & eight mules before an empty waggon & got stuck at that. You haint got no idea of viergina mud tonge cant tell."[25]

The rain continued for another twenty four hours sinking the army deeper and deeper into the mud. It was clear that the advance had to be called off and many soldiers were put to work corduroying the roads. The Confederates on the south side of the Rappahannock quickly assessed the situation and began shouting all manner of insults and raucous advice to the Yankees, who, for the most part, good-naturedly endured it as just one more torment. Private William Shaw, Company E, wrote his friends at home, "The boys say burnside got stuck in the mud up to his ear." He added that the Confederates painted a huge sign clearly visible from the north side of the Rappahannock with the words, "Burnside grand army stuck in the mud."[26]

Thomas Rodman described the latest fiasco to his father: "I take my pencil in hand again to write you a few lines to let you know that I am not discouraged yet, although we have tried Fredericksburgh again and got stuck in the mud." He went on to describe the march in much the same terms as the others had, adding that on "Thursday morning orders came that we must get back to Camp the best way we could. The mud was so deep that our provision train and the artillery could not move one foot, so I suppose this movement is about the same as the other only no destruction to our troops as there was no fighting. I think we will not move again until Spring."[27]

Weygant, Irwin, Bowman, Rodman, and thousands of other Union soldiers, east and west, marched countless miles down nameless muddy roads throughout the war. But this latest shared experience become known ever after as *the* "Mud March," the last gasp of Ambrose Burnside's lackluster tenure as commander of the Army of the Potomac. Through it all, Private Bowman remained optimistic, "I think if the weather had bin favorable we would give the rebbles very hard brush I think it will be some time now before the army of the Potomac can make another move ... the Peopple say out here that it rains or snows about every other day the snow is about twelve or forteen inches deep on the levil."[28] Private James Irwin wrote in parentheses as if whispering: "(The boys has for a big word who is stuck in the mud — Burnside)."[29]

When the 124th returned to the old camp, members found the place a shambles. Most of the winter quarters that had been built had been dismantled to use the logs for corduroying the roads. The men built bonfires to clear the debris, dry their soaked clothing, and warm themselves. Shelter tents were pitched in regular company streets and work began on reconstructing their log quarters but, as usually happened, they were no sooner started when orders came that the camp would be moved. They marched to within a mile and half of Stoneman's Switch, set up their canvas tents again and set about making a permanent winter camp. Trees were cut and the logs loaded on to wagons for the trip back to the camps. The whole region was virtually denuded of forest, replaced instead by "fifty thousand muslin and canvas-covered log cabins grouped in from three to four hundred miniature cities, each a petty kingdom."[30]

Much to the relief of the men, the ban on shipping boxes to the army was lifted. Having had some experience with Virginia mud, Andrew Bowman wrote home: "I want my boots very bad theare is no troble now about getting boxes some of the company got boxes yesterday & we expect some more in a few days for they are down at acqua creak." Mr. James Gram from Orange County had been to the army for a visit and brought the welcome gift of sixteen papers of smoking tobacco, one for each tent in Bowman's company.[31]

James Irwin said that the box he received from home

> arrived in fine condition. It was about a week in coming. Their was not a thing spoilt in it.... If you will send another small one I would like it very much as I think we are going to stay here some time now for it is so muddy that Burnside has got stuck into it.... You need not send me that Bible as I have got one given me by the Orange County Bible society. You will please send me the following articles: Pepper another box mustard, tea as I do not drink coffee any more it does not agree with me, Can or, two of milk, Licorice, the pepper send a box with it, I would like to have five dollars sent by mail as soon as possible. I will send it back when we get paid off. Send all as soon as you can send me some postage stamps.[32]

In the middle of January, Colonel Cummins heard that boxes from home addressed to members of Company D were at Stoneman's Switch. He said, "Boys, if those boxes are there, they shall be here," and he ordered an ambulance to retrieve them. "And what do you think the boys dipped into first — the apples. We all knew just the trees they grew on.... But we've had something better than all, our new Springfield rifles. We got our Co. letters with them, 124. We all will be more satisfied with them when we are exchanging pops at those rebels and winding this thing up."[33]

Rodman also requested a box from home, assuring his parents that it was safe to send it now "as we are not likely to move very soon." He asked for writing paper and envelopes as well as "Cakes, Pies, Candies, Sigars or anything you think best — a Chicken if you have a mind to, some pepper and mustard the kind that comes in tin boxes. And send me a box of Figs and a little mony $2.00 in a letter as soon as you get this. We are going to be paid off in a few days then I will pay you for your kindness. I wish you would send me a little bottle of ink one of those that are intended to carry in the Pocket and a pen holder and pens.... Don't forget the BOX."[34]

On January 29, the long awaited paymaster came for the first time to the regiment. Although they had been in the service for almost five months, they were paid for only a month and a half. Most men sent money home either in the form of an allotment check or in cash. Andrew Bowman gave specific instructions:

We got Paid off yesterday for one Month & seventeen days I received $20 80 cents that Paid us up to the first of November leavin the Government indet to us three months tomorrow the Army of the Potomac is very mutch dissatisfied about the way they are paid off some redgments they onley Paid them three monts out of seven the camp reports is that they will Pay us all off in Forteen or fifteen days enclosed you Will find my enlotment for the amount is fifteen dollars & you Will find five dollar bil witch makes the amount $20.00. Pleas put this with the other & ablidge me & let me know in your next letter wether you received it or not.[35]

This was big news for families back home in Orange County whose resources were stretched to the limit. The Goshen *Democrat*, under the heading "Military Items" ran the following in the February 5 edition: "The 124th Regiment, N.Y.S. Volunteers having been paid off, the alotment money of the men is beginning to arrive hereabouts. The payment was not in full up to this time."

At about the same time that the paymaster arrived, there was a change in command for the Army of the Potomac. Few soldiers mentioned that General Burnside was to be replaced with Major General Joseph Hooker, but one who did was Captain Murray. "I don't blame Burnside," he wrote to his mother, "he knew he was not capable of managing so large an army but the Command was thrust upon him in defiance of his wishes." While the change meant little to them at the time, it would have far reaching consequences for the 124th New York and for the army as a whole.[36]

The newspapers called him "Fighting Joe," a nickname he disliked because he thought it made him appear to be rash and aggressive. Tall, handsome, and with a reputation as a drinker, Hooker set out to reshape the army and rebuild sagging morale. He reorganized his men into seven infantry corps which would be the way the Army of the Potomac would go to battle for the next year.

Other changes were more important to the men in the ranks. Ovens were built so that the soldiers could have soft bread on a regular basis. This was a welcome change from a diet of hard-tack. Fresh vegetables were put on the menu to improve their health and ward off disease. Camps were ordered to be cleaned and officers were put on notice that their men were to drill and observe military decorum. This was much more than just the whim of another martinet. Hooker knew the army had been dealt a serious blow at Fredericksburg that might affect its ability to fight. Many had lost confidence in their military leaders and Hooker meant to replace that with pride in the army and in themselves.

There would be regular inspections of weapons, uniforms, accoutrements, and quarters. Those units found to be up to par would be allowed to begin sending men home on furlough, two at a time per company, for up to two weeks. If a man did not return, his company would have the privilege reduced accordingly. In the 124th, the companies had been recruited largely by town and just about everyone in the company had known everyone else before the war. This resulted in significant peer pressure not to mess things up for the next men in line for furlough. That is exactly what happened when Lt. Finnegan and Private James McCoy of Company K went home for six days. Finnegan returned but McCoy did not. Corporal Nathan Hallock noted in a letter home that no one else from Company K could get a furlough until McCoy returned.[37]

Once things were settled in the camp, Colonel Ellis applied to Brigade Commander Piatt for a fourteen-day leave of absence. He'd gotten wind of a group of men attempting to form a nine-month regiment back home. They had been able to raise only about four hundred men of the nine hundred needed and Ellis was sure he could persuade at least half of them to sign up with the 124th. In addition, Ellis was a man of property and his business affairs had been neglected for almost six months. He included "personal business" as a reason for his request.[38]

Hooker hit on another idea to raise morale. Union soldiers tended to take great pride in their regiment but usually did not identify with their division or army corps. He borrowed the idea of insignia for each corps from General Phil Kearny, a famous one-armed division commander killed in the late summer of 1862. Kearny wanted to be able to readily identify the officers under his command. It is said that he cut up a red blanket and issued small square pieces to the officers with instructions to wear the badge prominently on hats or jackets. The idea caught on and soon some of the enlisted men were doing the same, showing their pride in being part of a fighting division. It is also said that they began to wear them rotated ninety degrees to take the shape of a diamond, a very distinctive insignia indeed.

Hooker ordered General Daniel Butterfield, his chief of staff, to regularize the insignia for the seven infantry corps of the Army of the Potomac. Kearny's old outfit was still part of the 3rd Corps, so that corps badge would be the diamond or lozenge shape. As most army corps had three divisions, their badges would be red, white, and blue accordingly. The 124th was part of Whipple's Division, 3rd Corps, they were to wear a blue diamond but it was difficult to determine if the men actually did so. Better food, furloughs home, drills, inspections, reviews — Hooker's efforts had the desired effect. Over the course of the winter months of 1863, the Army of the Potomac regained some of its old confidence.

Private Nathan Hallock of Company K landed in the hospital prior to the Battle of Fredericksburg. He remained there most of the winter suffering from the same camp ailments that afflicted thousands of fellow soldiers. He carried on a correspondence with his father and with his friends in the regiment, who returned the favor. In early February, Corporal George Van Sciver, also of Company K, wrote Hallock describing their winter quarters. "We moved about a mile and are now encamped in a heavy piece of woods where the wood is plenty. As soon as we reached our new place, we had to go cutting down the woods, in order to get ourselves in shape, and then we went to work and built a log hut up high enough to stand *up* in and then we stretched our tent over it, and then we have built a fire-place in it, and we live as comfortable as you may imagine."

Then the letter took a decidedly risqué turn. Hallock was in the hospital near Washington, D.C., a city known to have a seamy side. He must have bragged about his adventures in a previous letter. "Allow me to congratulate you on the receipt of such a splendid '*valentine*,'" Shiver wrote. "I have not had the '*luck*' to receive '*such*' a '*valentine*' or any other this year. Allow me as a virtuous young man, to warn you, to beware of these '*sporting*' young women, that you do not get caught in the '*hymenial*' noose, — that she does not make '*game*' of you. And as for me, taking a '*walk*' with a young lady, why you know that I would '*not*' do such a thing!! If I received such a splendid '*valentine*' — I'd '*proffit*' by it! I'll bet." He concluded his letter with the admonition, "Remember me to all of my male friends and some of the 'fe-male.'"[39]

Camp news and opinions were not always so lighthearted. A soldier who signed himself "D.J.G." wrote a letter that was printed in the Goshen *Independent Republican*. The author may well have been Corporal Jonas G. Davis, the color bearer who was discharged for disability about a month after the letter was published.

> Well I have seen what I came here to see, and a devilish site more than I bargained for; but I came here to be a soldier and there is no use of grumbling; but it goes against the grain the devilishest to fight for the nigger. You know the old proverb, that "experience is a dear school, but it makes fools wise," and so it has been with me. I came down here with a good will to fight, to re-establish the old Union; but little dreamed of being forced to fight to emancipate a lot of black heathen, which will not do the country as much good as planting Butter Hill with potatoes, for half the crop in which I think you will agree with me. But let old Abraham and his apostles work, and if they don't destroy this country then I am no judge of a horses foot that has got the gravel in.

He took a dim view of Abolitionists, especially those who visited the military camps. "The thought then struck me very forcibly, how I would like to deal out Uncle Sam's new clothes with brass buttons on, and say to them, now d-n you, if you want the niggers freed go and fight for them! When you write, tell me if you don't think such a suit would look well on Mr. L., of Cornwall."[40]

Private Dan Dugan of the Warwick company similarly complained about the abolitionists and draft dodgers at home and about Horace Greeley, quixotic editor of the *New York Tribune*. He had no use for any of them. News of the impending draft in the North terrified those who had no wish to serve but delighted those already in uniform. "I am glad that they have to come to war that is to say some of the hot headed republicans and I hope they will Bring ould Greeley and his troupes if ould Greeley will have to come I will be very much plesed at it wich I hope he will come and take charge of the nigar rigments. Send Down your conscripts and we will sho them how to march and fight," he wrote. He resented the young men who espoused the abolition cause but were not in uniform. "I tould them that they had sompthing to fite for what I had not."[41]

His disgust with Abolitionists was shared by many in the North and by many who served in the Northern army. The war was for the preservation of the Union they said, not for abolition. Lincoln's Emancipation Proclamation, which took effect on January 1, 1863, sent a ripple of resentment through the army. The *Newburgh Daily Telegraph* ran a story under the heading "The Bone Doesn't Fight," which ridiculed the efforts to get blacks, or "the bone," to enlist in the 54th Massachusetts, an all-black infantry regiment then recruiting throughout the North. "They can't fill up the famous 54th regiment in Massachusetts — as fast as they catch a 'bone,' it somehow slips through their fingers — and so they have sent a recruiting officer all the way to Newburgh." The article also ridiculed *The Journal* for its "pathetic appeal to the 'Bone'" to "face the music, both for its own sake and for that of its friends, who have done and suffered so much for them, but it is *very* doubtful whether the appeal will be effectual. So far as we can judge of the Newburgh portion of the 'Bone,' it prefers to lounge on street corners, for the chance of odd jobs, to any regular employment. We don't believe the dark-complexioned officer will be able to get a platoon fairly over the river."[42]

In mid–February, soldiers returning from furloughs to Orange County brought news that resistance to the expected draft was strong in the North and especially so in New York City. Authorities there had searched the city for weapons in anticipation of armed resistance to conscription. Lieutenant William Mapes was irate and hoped the city would "sink in hell" if the Copperheads tried any such thing. "I wish they had to go through what the poor private and soldiers do. They would damn soon become Union & for war. The more I go through the more I love my country & so would they."[43]

Sergeant Charles Stewart, also known as "Felix," wrote to the *Newburgh Journal*,

> Most of us are beginning to discover that it is indeed no joke to be a soldier. — One of our greatest difficulties is to keep our skin and garments clean. Here we are always dirty — not dirty by chance or accident say twice or three times a day, but dirty at all times and in all places. We can never get rid of dirt, it sticks to us like a brother — there is dirt in the skin, dirt in the blood, dirt in the flesh, and dirt in the bone. Take the hand of a common soldier, even after it has been washed and dried, and you would think it was the hand of a newly imported Egyptian mummy. I have seen as much pure dirt washed off the feet of some of our non-commissioned officers at a single sitting as would have served to raise half a bushel of potatoes in Orange County. Everything here struggles under this calamity. The streams and puddles are dirty, the bread we eat and the water we drink, as a necessary consequence, are dirty. The sweet soft rains, as soon as they touch the soil, are turned into filth.

The letter was reprinted in at least two other local newspapers, which soon found their way into the camp of the 124th New York. Another member of Company I, who signed his letter "Felix, Jr.," responded, assuring the readers that while Felix and his friends might be filthy, the rest of the company kept clean habits. In fact, Jr. asserted, "There is not a cleaner regiment in the whole army of the Potomac than the 124th, and there is not a cleaner company in the 124th than Company I. Felix and one or two others excepted."[44]

February turned bitter and snowy but picket duty continued as usual; a three day shift on the outer lines was cold, wet, and boring. On February 25, however, there was excitement enough to write home about. That day the brigade was marched to Hartwood Church, a crossroads village northwest of Falmouth. Colonel Bailey of the 86th New York was in command of the brigade with Lieutenant Colonel Cummins commanding the 124th New York in Colonel Ellis' absence. The brigade took up position behind the Federal cavalry screen on the Warrenton Road. Captain Weygant reported that the 124th first relieved the grand reserve, then sent four companies forward to relieve the pickets closest to the front. Private Edward Carpenter of Company B wrote, "We had just got to our post when the Rebles made a dash on our cavalry pickets Driving them in."[45]

The Confederate troopers were part of Brigadier General Fitzhugh Lee's brigade out on a reconnaissance north of the Rappahannock River. Lee had crossed at Kelly's Ford the day before with four hundred men in his command in an attempt to find out what Federal units were opposite them.[46]

At about 2 P.M., the Confederates suddenly fell upon the Union cavalry, driving them back. Weygant reported that as the 124th approached its picket post, they saw cavalry fleeing to the rear in great confusion, with riderless horses adding to the chaotic scene. Their officers were waving their swords in a fruitless effort to rally the Union horsemen, many of whom lost their hats in the headlong flight. The young captain knew that the Confederates could not be far behind so he ordered the reserve forward.[47] The Confederates came on the gallop, not expecting to find infantry so far out on the picket line. Lieutenant Colonel Cummins steadied his men with the words, "Now boys remember who you are and where you come from." Adding to the drama of the moment Captain William Jackson called for three cheers for the colonel "which were given with a will."[48]

Fitz Lee's troopers came on "untill thay came to us infantry the Rebs saw the 124 was coming out of the woods Double quick and not knowing what forse we had there thay turned Back."[49] Colonel Bailey wrote in his official report that then enemy was "within 20 yards, firing with pistols at the time. Lieutenant-Colonel Cummins opened fire upon them with our infantry picket and repulsed them. They skededdled back in double quick time. Lieutenant-Colonel Cummins says, if I will allow it, he will take his command and put the rebels across the river before night. This I cannot do without orders; neither would it be safe, as there has been considerable firing off to our right."[50] Captain Weygant wrote that when the enemy realized that there was a considerable force of infantry in front of them they "went fours about, and dashed off as wildly as our cavalry had come in."[51]

When Fitzhugh Lee wrote his account of the skirmish at Hartwood Church, he described the encounter and withdrawal somewhat differently. "On the 25th, I drove in the enemy's pickets near Hardwood Church, and attacked his reserve and main body. Routed them, and pursued them within 5 miles of Falmouth, to their infantry lines. Killed and wounded many of them. Captured 150 prisoners, including 5 commissioned officers, with all their horses, arms, and equipments. I then withdrew my command slowly, retiring by detachments."[52] Gen. Dan Sickles, 3rd Corps commander, was pleased with the action.

Major General Daniel E. Sickles commanded the 3rd Corps. The 124th New York served under him at Chancellorsville and Gettysburg. Sickles lost a leg at Gettysburg and received a Medal of Honor instead of the court martial many thought he deserved (archive of the Historical Society of the Town of Warwick, gift of Joan and Tom Frangos).

"Lieutenant-Colonel Cummins, One hundred and twenty-fourth New York, opened fire on the assailants, and drove them back with loss. The attack was not renewed. Considerable firing was heard on the right of Colonel Bailey.... General Whipple informs me that Colonel Bailey has taken a prisoner who states that he belongs to Fitzhugh Lee's cavalry, five regiments of which crossed the river this morning and made this attack. This man will be sent immediately to head-quarters as soon as he arrives."[53]

That winter both William and Henry Howell spent a good deal of time in the hospital at Washington, suffering from leg injuries, sore throats, and dysentery. As February drew to a close, Henry was making ready to leave Carver Hospital to rejoin the regiment and he was eager to do so. "I have seen enough of hospital life to satisfy me. We have better food to eat and nothing to do, but they are all strangers here, or at least they was when I came here." On February 13 he sat in on a session of Congress "and heard the great men of the nation." In preparation for his return he got a pass to go into the city to make some purchases. In particular, he wanted a frying pan as he did not like his "salt junk boiled & the only thing I had to fry on before was my little tin plate."[54]

Shortly thereafter, he was writing home from the winter camp near Falmouth. He assured his mother that he was up to the rigors of camp life. "I live fine on salt junk and hard tack and although I have not been in camp but a little over a week I have come up to 160 pounds and if I keep on gaining like I have for the past two weeks I will soon be a young giant."[55]

He and his brother William built new quarters in much the same manner as the others in the regiment had done. Henry described how they built a bed in the cabin: "We drove a couple of crotches in the ground and laid straight poles on them and upon these we spread a few pine brush and a rubber blanket. This makes a hard bed but it is a great deal better than the cold and wet ground. All we lack is a bundle of straw and then we would have a regular pig pen and glad we are to have a chance to live in such a place this cold weather." As his health improved, he started to draw duty, the first being guard duty at brigade headquarters. "It takes twelve men and a corporal up there to take care of a few trees and salute the officers as they pass these are all the orders we have, but it is military I suppose." He asked that a box be sent with "some butter, cakes, sausage if you have it to spare, biscuit well baked so it will keep, some flour, apples, etc."[56] Neither he nor William had yet been sent out on picket duty, probably because exposure to the elements might land them back in the hospital.

Charles Stewart, 2nd sergeant, Company I, had written a letter in January to the *Daily Tele-graph*, taking the townspeople to task for ignoring the men of Newburgh by not sending them boxes as other towns had done. It did not take long for Newburgh to respond and Sergeant Stewart wrote back to the paper to thank the town, and in doing so left a detailed account of how important these shipments were to the soldiers. Two huge boxes came by rail and sailing vessel to Stoneman's Switch, where the provost marshall opened each and closely examined the contents. The boxes were then sent on to Company I and dumped in the company street right in front of Stewart's quarters. The company turned out en masse to admire them. Also present were "dead beats" and "sinks" from other companies who hoped to partake in the feast. Stewart assured his readers that there were no such characters in Company I as "we got rid of them long ago at Berlin."

When the boxes were opened,

we found a bountiful supply of everything the heart of man could wish — apples, cheese, butter, ham, smoked beef, tea, sugar, pickles, condensed milk, mustard, pepper, tobacco, soap, cider vinegar, &c. *ad infinitum*. As the day was fine we turned everything out on the street, and left them for exhibition, till we got ready to commence the task of distribution. This was rather a hard and delicate job — but seeing it must be tackled, and the boys had looked at the good things long enough — we called in the help of two or three willing hands and commenced with the apples — these although long on the way arrived in good condition — then we cut up the hams, smoked beef, butter and cheese, and gave to every man his part, and the daylight beginning to fail, we closed the labors of the first day by giving to each a ration of cider vinegar — this last was so good that the boys smacked their lips after taking it — you would have almost supposed it had been apple jack, if you didn't know that the Provost Marshal didn't allow such things to come into camp *when he knows of it*. We crowded what remains of our undivided stuff into our shanty, and satisfied that we had done a fair days work, prepared to rest. That night our tent presented the appearance of a well filled store, we could neither sit nor stand — but feeling tired we cleared enough space to let us lie down, and went to sleep. We slept sound that night, and had some pleasant dreams — next morning about daylight a few of the boys felt as if they would like another ration of the vinegar. So we had to get up and finish the work of distribution. Company I was a happy and envied company about these times. I noticed tears of gratitude rolling down the cheeks of my tent mates while eating our first dinner after the boxes came. We had boiled ham, with mustard, horse radish and pepper sauce for dinner that day. Such living we had been strangers to for a long time. From that time we felt proud of Newburgh. When she gives a favor she does it without stint... Your boxes commenced a streak of luck for us, and we have lived high, and fared sumptuously every day since. About the same time a great many of us got boxes on our own hook. Joe Hooker took up the hint, and built up bakeries all over for us, and we have had our good loaf every day since fresh from the oven; he gave us also plenty of potatoes, onions and other good things to which we had long been strangers. Some benevolent person or persons sent us a supply of gloves, tippets, and other things of that sort to keep us warm. I have never been able to find out who did sent us them. Some think they were sent by the Goshen folks, and some again say the Newburgh Aid Society sent them. I hope when they send us anything again, they will let us know who our benefactors are.

As usual, Stewart signed his letter "Felix."[57]

As spring approached, the men began to speculate on the next campaign. "I think that we will march or go across the Raphanick once more if we go across the Raphanck we will conker or be conkered with the loss of 50,000 men," Private Dugan wrote. His captain, James Benedict, had been down to the river to inspect one of the other companies whose officers were all home on leave. While there, the rebel pickets across the river kept up a lively banter with the Union troops on the north shore asking if they were the regiment that had been kind enough to leave their blankets for them in their hasty departure from Fredericksburg in December.[58]

After a long absence, William Wirt Bailey of Company K returned to his regiment. He had taken sick on the march toward Fredericksburg and been sent to the hospitals around the capital, where he stayed for some time. As he began to recuperate, he was given a leave to go home, a trip that cost him his sergeant's stripes. The regiment needed to replace those NCOs who were absent so he was reduced to the ranks as a private for no other reason than he was sick. He tried to take it in good stride but privately considered it "as mean as can be" and resented not so much those who took his place as those who made the decision.

By March 19 Bailey, Dan Webb, and Nathan Hallock were back at Camp Stoneman with the regiment. Although former sergeants Bailey and Webb were now privates, they got to take their meals with the other sergeants, at least for the present. Their friend Jacob Denton expected to be promoted to 2nd lieutenant, opening a slot for someone to be promoted to sergeant, a position to which both Bailey and Well aspired but neither attained. As always, Captain William Jackson made sure his men wanted for nothing, seeing to it that they had plenty of building materials for a cabin and a choice spot. That night, as Bailey sat down to pen his letter home, a flute could be heard in Denton's tent. Bailey wrote, "I can hardly write it sounds so nice.... That flute is playing 'Home, Sweet Home.' I wish you could hear it, it is enough to make tears come in anybody's eyes." As he wrote he noticed that General Sickles and his staff were slowly riding through the camp. Bailey quickly took the measure of the man who would lead the 3rd Corps in the coming battle. Of the general he wrote, "He looks like a warrior."[59] He shared his opinion of the regimental commanders too. "The Col. is very stif, but the Major plays ball with the Captain and men."[60]

The regiment's turn at picket duty began again in early March in a new section of the line on the north bank of the Rappahannock. The Confederates could be clearly seen drilling on the plain beyond the town, doing the evolutions in much the same manner as was done by Union soldiers.[61] Even though spring was approaching, the weather could quickly turn cold. In early April storms hit the picket line with unusual ferocity. "On the 4th of this month it stormed all night. The wind blew very hard too. I had to stand on Post for hours during the night. It was the hardest night I ever put in since I have been in the Army or out of it. I thought I would freeze."[62]

The regiment was often out for days at a time, exposed to the elements. The men sometimes returned soaking wet, their rifles showing signs of rust, and their leather gear in need of cleaning. After one such stint in late March, Private Henry Howell arrived back in camp with little time to get his gear in order before a review scheduled that very afternoon. Exhausted from several days on the picket line, he would have much preferred a nap but he and his friends quickly set to work. "We got all of our guns and equipments in good order. We drawed leggings for to make a show, and that is all they are good for those who have boots, but for those who wear shoes they are very good. The General said we must take them so that we would all look alike."

They were to be inspected by Major General Sickles. "We marched around in front of him and then he rode around and his sharp eye took every thing in at once glancing at us after he had made a circle around he dismounted and went along the lines and examining it more closely. This ended the performances and we went back to camp." But Sickles was not done with the 124th N.Y. He and his staff visited Colonel Ellis at his headquarters tent, the general telling him that he was "highly pleased" with the troops' appearance. Sickles further commented that he never saw a regiment come off the picket line and get itself ready for inspection so quickly.

Henry Howell's sister Emily asked how they saluted officers when on guard duty. There had been an argument at home about this and Henry was being asked to settle it. "I would like to know who of you was arguing about this saluting business and who was right. I guess neither one of you." He went on to describe the correct procedure in detail. Since Henry did not have his letter ready in time for the mail pickup, his brother William decided to add to the page which was addressed to their mother. He thanked the family for the box from home and commented that it contained just about everything they wanted, including some flour which they used to make flapjacks, dumplings, and crullers. "Our Company numbers 54 men but we have several dead beets who do no duty."[63]

 April 1 was William's 22nd birthday, and his first in the army. "Who would have thought that I would be a soldier in Virginia on this day three years ago. But it is so." He had been on guard at General Headquarters the day before where he had a run in with Lieutenant Henry Ramsdell, whom he regarded with disdain as a person who owed his rank to his father's wealth and social position in Newburgh. "Young Ramsdell is on the Generals Staff & we think he is one of the most self conceited all important persons that ever disgraced a pair of Shoulder Straps. His Company is well pleased when he left them for they thought their Captain was bad enough." Howell was referring to Captain William Silliman still known to his men as "Old Silly Man."[64]

Instead of leaving the corporal to run the guard, Ramsdell intruded on what Howell regarded as his job. He ordered Howell to report to him and demanded to know why there were only two men on the relief. Howell replied that such were his orders and had been the same the week before. Ramsdell overrode the corporal and put four men on as relief, then ordered the squad to stand for inspection of their arms and accoutrements. "This he had no business to do as we had an inspection of arms at guard mounting. Neither had he any business with the guard at all." To lighten the mood of this letter to his mother, William wrote, "My sheet just caught fire by the candle as it sets on the board I'm writing on." The scorched corner of the blue paper he was using no doubt amused his mother.[65]

The March weather continued severe. Thomas Rodman wrote that it had rained or snowed on each of the past three days.

It is also quite cold. One afternoon last week it rained hailed thundered and Lightened all at the same time. There has been no new moves in the army of the Potomac lately except a skirmish last Monday across the Rapahanock between 1400 of Stonemans Cavalry and some Infantry and artillery and the Reb Cavalry. We captured about 40 of their men I saw them come in myself they were a pretty rough looking set of fellows. No two of them dressed alike. Some looked as iff they had just come out of a grist mill, and other a coal pit. They seem to be well supplied with provisions one of them had on 3 haversacks full of Grub others 2 and some 1. The snow is about 2 inches high down here at present a pretty hard day for Virginia at this time of the year. When you write again let me know what you think about the War by this time. I do not see as it is going to end this spring but I think that next fall will tear the thing all to peaces. You see the 124th has not had a chance to try their hand at it yet but look out when they do. The health of our Regt is quite good for such bad weather. Another man in our Company by the name of Odell brother to the one that cut off his toes at Minors Hill shot off his thumb the other day by accident.[66]

As April began, the many farmers in the regiment thought back to the spring rituals on the farm. "Where are you to have corn this year?" Henry Howell asked his brother at home. "I won't be there to break the plows plowing sod. Did you get any of the meadow by the hog pen plowed last fall? I suppose James will be chief plowman now. Did you have snow enough this winter to keep the manure drawed away on sleights?"

Spring also meant that the muddy roads of Virginia would dry enough to support marching men, horses, wagons, and artillery, and that would mean a campaign. All the signs were there. "We expect to march before a great while. An order is posted to the effect that men must dispense with extra clothing &c. Only carry what is actually necessary. Officers will have from 20 to 35 pounds carried for according to rank. Ammunition trains are to be carried by pack mules."[67] About two weeks later their readiness was improved once more: "We have marching orders with eight days rations, five in our Napsacks and three in the Harvey sacks and sixty rounds of cartridges."[68]

The first week of April, the soldiers were ordered to clean up their camps, get their weapons and gear in order, and prepare themselves for inspection and a big review. On April 6, Henry Howell wrote in his diary, "Abraham Lincoln had a grand cavalry review near Stoneman's Switch which was a grander sight to those that saw it than any Orange County horse shows. I did not know that the President was to be there or I should have went there as I had nothing in particular to do and it was not far away. Some of the boys went up and they said the cavalry and artillery flew around through the mud was a caushen."[69]

The next day the regiment was ordered to pack up knapsacks and be ready for a review at 8:30 in the morning.[70] Company officers closely examined the quarters, uniforms, rifles, cartridge boxes, and personal appearance of each man. This was followed by an equally close inspection by Colonel Ellis, Lieutenant Colonel Cummins, and Major Cromwell. Weapons were stacked in each company street and the men were dismissed but ordered to remain close at hand, taking cover in the tent or cabin nearest their stacked arms. The colonel, as usual, wanted to make an impression on the approaching generals and dignitaries. To Captain Weygant, he pointed out a nearby regiment which stood at attention with arms at the shoulder. "A picket fence like that is well enough, but I want to show these fellows that there is at least one *live* regiment in the army." At about 3 o'clock, a sentry alerted the colonel that the reviewing party was approaching. An aide from division headquarters raced into camp with orders to form up lest General Whipple be embarrassed that one of his regiments was not ready to salute the commander of the Army of the Potomac and the commander-in-chief. But Ellis was ready. He ordered "to the colors" be sounded, at which every man sprang to his post. The regiment was formed in an instant, every man in his place and colors flying at the center.[71]

Ellis did indeed make an impression. General Whipple was relieved to see the 124th in line. The president rode along the front of the regiment, head uncovered and "a smile on his careworn features." He seemed interested in the men's cabins and looked into their faces, all the while chatting with General Hooker.[72] "As they passed we gave 2 times 3 cheers for Abe and 3 more for the Commander in Chief of the Army."[73]

The Orange County soldiers had not served long enough under McClellan to adore him as others did, and never grew fond of Burnside, but among them there was a growing respect toward General Hooker. As for the president, the jury was still out. Henry Howell wrote, "Old Abe is a very plain looking man but he has got a long head when he has his old 'beaver' on top of it." Thomas Rodman thought "Uncil Abe looks as if he had pretty hard times. He looks more like sitting in a rocking chair by a good fire than Reviewing Troops. He was dressed in plain black clothes."[74]

The next day the official grand review took place about five miles from camp. General Sickles' 3rd Corps, some forty regiments strong in three divisions, was deployed in double columns with nine batteries to the left. Behind them stood the ammunition, baggage, and supply train of the corps, some four hundred wagons in all. As Lincoln, Sickles, and Hooker approached on horseback, many of the teamsters left their wagons to get a better view of the spectacle. Just then the batteries opened with a salute that caused the skittish mules to stampede, creating pandemonium and a great deal of damage in the rear.[75]

Private Howell took a somewhat jaundiced view of the whole affair. "We had our knapsacks on six hours in the middle of the day. We were paraded around for some time for them to examine our efficiency in drill and discipline." Then he got to what really interested him: "There were several Ladies present on horseback and in coaches." Howell described the grand review as "a big thing," but noted "we do not want to see many more such days. We were all pretty tired when we got in camp."[76]

All their efforts were recognized in an order read at dress parade to every regiment in Whipple's Division "His Excellency the President, and the Commander-in-Chief of the Army of the Potomac, were pleased to express themselves gratified with the reception given them by the various regiments." The order went on to recognize for "especial praise" the 124th New York, the 12th New Hampshire, and Berdan's Sharpshooters.[77] Private Howell noted in his diary, "It is pretty generally understood that this regiment ranks with the best in the army."[78]

The next week was filled with division drill, brigade drill, more inspections, a sham battle, and picket duty. On April 15 William Howell wrote in his diary, "A soaking rain return to camp. Ford the streams on the way sign the pay rolls and get paid up to the 1st of March." Now this was, indeed, a "big thing." Privates were paid $13 a month so unless the private had some outstanding sutler bill or fine to pay, he received $52 in greenbacks or in the form of an allotment check.[79] Thomas Rodman gave specific instructions to his parents: "I send the Check to you and after you get it cashed you must send me $5.00 for I do not like to be without it if we go on the march for I do not think it will be long before we move as the army is now beginning to move away from Falmoth. All the Cavilry has moved towards Kelleys Ford and quite a large force of Infantry."[80]

The next day Henry Howell made a chance decision to sent $31 home with Lieutenant Mapes, who had a furlough. This turned out to be a fortunate choice because later that same night someone stole the mailbag. It usually hung outside Chaplain Bradner's tent, and was then entrusted to postal authorities for delivery to Orange County. The chaplain must have left it out a bit too long, giving the thief his golden opportunity. As soon as the bag was missed, guards were placed around the camp to stop anyone from entering or leaving, and officers searched the tents but to no avail. The men were confined to their company streets and fires doused so that if the culprit was in the regiment, he could not burn the allotments and keep the greenbacks.[81] The next day the chaplain got the serial numbers of the checks and quickly went to Washington, D.C., hoping to catch the thief in the act of cashing them. "Nothing has been discovered yet and

I am afraid the thief will get away with his booty unpunished. There was a great many letters in the bag that did not have any money in. I had two such which I shall have to write over."[82] Nathan Hallock also sent his money home with Lieutenant Mapes in the form of an allotment check to be mailed from Goshen to the Hallock family.

There followed several days of picket duty in the rain during which a man from Company B shot off his forefinger on his right hand. On April 16, Sergeant Charles Stewart, Company I, "Our regular Army Correspondent," wrote that the army expected to be marching soon.

> We have done a good deal of picket duty during the winter, and while in camp have played a good many excellent games of base ball. I expect ere this reaches you that Joe Hooker will change the base of operations, and give us for a change a good deal of fighting. We have got eight days rations all ready to lug when the roads dry up, and he says, "come boys." The army is in excellent condition and spirits, and I expect we will give a good account of ourselves before many weeks roll past. As soon as anything turns up worth writing about you will hear again from FELIX.[83]

Captain Jackson wrote home on April 25 that the army had been under marching orders and was on the point of starting. "The weather had disappointed us so often that I begin to think that we will wait for settled weather before we move, but I can form no idea when we will start."[84]

On April 27 Felix wrote again to the *Daily Telegraph*. He admitted he was wrong in his prediction that the army was to move but did not hesitate to make another.

> Well, I will again stake my reputation for veracity by telling you that we will move tomorrow morning. I mean the army of the Potomac, Co. I, of the 124th included, also its second sergeant.... Should anything happen to me, B. will let you know, if he is left. I don't feel that I would be anxious to have my body buried in Newburgh. It will rot as easily here as there. I care not where it is buried.... May God hear the prayers that have been and may be offered up for us here, and if we meet not again here, I hope we will meet above. I have the presentiment that I am to come through the fiery ordeal unscathed. I don't know why, but I have it, I have often feared death more, when it did not stare me so in the face. Felix.

He ended his letter with a postscript: "P.S. Tuesday morning — everything looks propitious for our move — orders have not been countermanded, so in a few hours we will have left camp for parts unknown."[85]

CHAPTER 5

"Our men fought like tigers!"
April 26–May 4, 1863

On the eve of battle, a young soldier mailed his brother a letter that was sent over to the Middletown *Whig Press* for publication. He had been raised in "democratic, conservative sentiments, having been reared in the pro-slavery school." His eight months of service with the 124th New York had changed his attitude about the war.

> We have a good man at the head of this army; and he has the power to dismiss from it any officer under him who does not work with him. Had Burnside had this power, Fredericksburgh today would have been ours, and I think the 124th would have had a sight of Richmond. But he did not have it, and the consequence was that we were defeated, driven back across the river, and many a soldier breathed his last on the Rappahannock shore, not to say anything of the suffering of those who were made cripples for life.

There were rumors back home that the men were demoralized but the author attributed that to the "worthless devils" who joined for the bounty, had seen the "elephant's tail," and wanted to give up. He considered those men "worse than traitors" and thought the regiment was better off without them. "Out of 550 men in this regiment that are fit for duty, I doubt if you could get a dozen but what are for fighting and not for a compromise with the rebels…. We do not want a compromise, but want to fight the rebels till they get enough of it and come back in the Union, and the old flag again floats over every city North and South."[1]

Now the Army of the Potomac made ready to cross the Rappahannock once more. No one, from the privates in the ranks to the generals commanding each of the seven army corps, had any idea what that plan would be. "Fighting Joe" Hooker kept his own council, knowing full well that the more officers, politicians, and newspapermen in on his plan, the more likely General Lee would be in on it too.

The troops would have been reassured to know that General Hooker was not about to repeat the mistakes made at the Battle of Fredericksburg. He planned no frontal assaults against the strong position on the hills behind the town. Hooker would indeed make a show of crossing at the same place Burnside had tried, just as "Felix" predicted, but this would be only a diversion to mask the movement of three full army corps sent on a swift march west to cross far upriver at a place lightly defended by the enemy. Once over the Rappahannock River, this force would cross the Rapidan River, a tributary that joined the Rappahannock above Fredericksburg. Then, the three Federal corps would sweep down the southern bank, driving the Confederate defenders away from the lower fords so that more troops could cross by a shorter route. If successful, Hooker would have a large force on the left flank of Lee's outnumbered army. The Union troops remaining at Fredericksburg could threaten Lee's front while Hooker's flanking corps could threaten Lee's left, his lines of supply and communication, and his line of retreat.

Hooker would use speed, surprise, and superior numbers in a way no other commander of this army had done. His plan bore little resemblance to those of the pondering, over-cautious McClellan or the fumbling Burnside. It was, quite simply, a work of genius.

Those not convinced of Hooker's brilliance need only read the opinion of one of the rising stars in Lee's army, General Edward Porter Alexander. "On the whole I think this plan was decidedly the best strategy conceived in any of the campaigns ever set against us. And the execution of it was, also, excellently managed, up to the morning of May 1st. At that time Hooker had reached Chancellorsville on our side of the river and only about twelve miles from Fredericksburg, & had with him five corps of infantry, while two were threatening our front at Fredericksburg."[2] Alexander wrote this critique after the war was over. He thought Hooker's battle plan superior, not just to those that had gone before, but to Grant's Overland Campaign of 1864 as well.

On April 27, while the 3rd Corps was being reviewed by General Hooker and Secretary of State William Seward, "heavy columns" were seen marching west, out of sight of the Confederates. The next day orders were issued to Sickles's Corps that would take them in the opposite direction, past thousands of roofless, abandoned log cabins. This told the men that the entire army was in motion and that they were among the last to move.[3] Every man in the 124th knew something big was underway.

Henry Howell penciled into his diary that the march took seven hours, passing near White Oak Church on the way to the north side of the Rappahannock. Before leaving camp, most of the men rolled up their overcoats and stored them in the orderly's tent until the quartermaster could gather them up, but "if he could not they were to be lost for we could not carry them, no way."[4]

"Felix" got rid of his overcoat before the march began along with his "extra pants, shirts, boots, shoes, &c., &c." He regretted leaving the old camp, a place he thought a comfortable, safe spot. "The pile of dry goods and furniture that we had to leave was enormous," he wrote.

Stacked rifles. When the soldiers halted on the march, they stacked arms and, at the order of their officers, broke ranks. When ordered to fall in, each man was near his rifle and could "take arms" when ordered to do so (Library of Congress, Prints & Photographs Division).

The men could only bring along "one suit and one change of undergarments." With eight days' supply of hardtack, bacon, coffee, and sugar packed into their haversacks and knapsacks, there was little room for much else. Felix did manage to tuck away a small Bible, a writing portfolio, two books on tactics, and his sewing kit. He observed that if they did not live to return, the farmer on whose land they had been camped that winter could have gathered up all the items left behind and made a fortune in the secondhand clothing business.[5] One soldier, probably Captain William Jackson of Company K, said it best: "Rendered wise by past experience, we took with us as little as possible."[6]

"We struck tents and commenced our march about ½ past four o'clock," wrote Corporal William Howell. "Marched 8 or 10 miles Striking the rapahanock by a circuitous route a few miles below Fredericksburg. The 6th army corps crossed on pontoons during the night & took the rebel pickets. I went up to Prof. Lowes balloon and saw him go up to watch the enemies movements."[7]

The march, though relatively short in distance, was severe. When they finally halted and stacked arms, "Felix" was relieved. He ached where the knapsack straps cut into his shoulders and he was soaked through with sweat. He cut some pine boughs to lie upon, spread his blanket, and was quickly asleep.[8] At daybreak the men awoke to the sounds of gunfire coming from the direction of the river. Instead of moving immediately, they were given time to kindle fires and boil coffee, sending up clouds of smoke visible for miles. Hooker wanted to make sure that the Confederates in Fredericksburg saw lots of Yankees. After they had eaten, the whole corps was moved forward, halted, and drawn up in sight of the enemy pickets across the river. Rumors flew that a pontoon bridge had been thrown across the Rappahannock and that the 3rd Corps would support two other Federal corps in an attack south of the town.[9]

Artillery fire could be heard above and below Fredericksburg, "our troops only crossing and forming in long lines of battle a short distance from the river, and the rebs, slowly falling back apparently taken by surprise, for the great move was expected on the right above. The balloon was up most of the time very near us reconnoitering the movements of the enemy. In the afternoon quite a shower came on and the boys put up their tents. Our corps encamped on a beautiful piece of land. This night we got a good rest."[10]

Sergeant Peter P. Hazen of Company C, writing as the events were taking place, described this movement forward as a march of about a mile before they halted and dropped their knapsacks. He took advantage of the clear sky and level, open ground to have a "very good nap." When he awoke, the sky had turned cloudy. He and his friends, Corporal Charles Knapp and Corporal Charles Chatfield, "soon pitched our tent on the side hill, and got some pine boughs and laid in on the ground, and then with our case-knives we dug a trench around our tent to lead the water off. I had mentioned only Knapp, Charley and I as pitching our tents, but of course we were not the only ones, for thousands of tents were soon pitched, and it was not long before it commenced raining, and it continued all night and until near noon next day. We slept dry and soundly, and no water ran under us."[11]

It was while the regiment rested on the north side of the Rappahannock, that Colonel Ellis saw to it that each man was given an orange ribbon to wear in a button hole of his jacket "by which the men of his regiment might be known, in case of death or wounds." But the colonel had another purpose—he wanted to instill pride by means of a unique insignia. Lewis Wisner, a Medal of Honor recipient, writing thirty years later about the incident noted that the Orange County men got their ribbons before they ever wore any "distinctive mark of brigade, division and corps badge."[12] By Wisner's account, the men of the 124th had not adopted the blue diamond insignia of the 3rd Division, 3rd Corps, as they headed for Chancellorsville.

Captain Leander Clark, Company I, had a somewhat different recollection. He stated years after the war that Colonel Ellis issued the orange ribbons in 1862, "to distinguish the officers in case of being slain, in order that the Regt. might claim its own." Clark said that the ribbons were issued "just previous to entering a battle" but he alone placed the date in 1862, meaning, by his account, the ribbons were issued prior to the Battle of Fredericksburg. As there is no other source placing it so early, it is likely that Clark remembered the date incorrectly. It is possible that Ellis issued ribbons to the officers before the enlisted men received theirs. In any case, there is no doubt that the men in the ranks were wearing orange ribbons at Chancellorsville.[13]

By mid-day, April 30, Hooker had three corps of infantry across two rivers and massed near Chancellorsville. Hooker's feint on the north side of the river coupled with the rapid march upriver did the trick: Lee was caught flat-footed, but he quickly regained his balance to do what he did best. Leaving a small force on the south bank of the Rappahannock near Fredericksburg, Lee divided his army in the face of an opponent superior in numbers and marched west to take the measure of this latest Yankee commander.

Great armies were now in motion with nothing less than the fate of the Union in the balance. If Hooker would only follow up on his initial success, strike fast, and strike hard, real damage could be done to Lee's army and to the cause of secession. The Army of the Potomac, confident and strong, substantially outnumbered Lee's forces. The plan itself was excellent, but the big unknown was the man himself. Could Hooker set aside the mystique that surrounded the names of Lee and Jackson and, using his strength in numbers, pitch into them? On the eve of battle, President Lincoln, his military intuition equal to that of the best professional soldiers, told "Fighting Joe" and Major General Darius Couch, his second in command, what they needed to do to be victorious. "I want to impress upon you two gentlemen," the self-taught Illinois lawyer told the West Point graduates, "in your next fight put in all your men."[14]

Once Hooker's flanking columns were in position near Chancellorsville, the 3rd Corps was ordered to cease the charade and march west. At about nine o'clock on the morning of April 30, "we were called in line to hear an order from Hooker to the effect that the operations of the 5th, 11th, and 12th corps on the right had been very successful. We all cheered and began to think that the rebs would be whipped without any help from us, and a good many began to growl that we were on the reserve and would have no chance to fight. After events showed that the reserve is not a very enviable position; that its business is wherever there is fighting, there to be and take part."[15]

The 3rd Corps marched up the north bank of the Rappahannock, crossed over, and massed near Chancellorsville. Sergeant Coe Reevs of Company B, in a letter to his father wrote, "We started about 3 o'clock, on what they call a forced march — marched all night Thursday."[16] A soldier from Middletown noted the starting time as 2 P.M. He wrote that the order to march "came suddenly in, for the rebs were pressing on our right and we were needed there. So off we started, moving back not far from our camp."[17] Some of the men optimistically speculated that they might stop at their old camp for the night but they were ordered to keep going. "About 11 at night we halted and were ordered to make a cup of coffee. (On the march when tired there is nothing like this to freshen us up.) After a half hour's stop we left our blazing fires and pushed on up the Warrenton road, leaving it at Berea church, and taking a miserable road for the United States Ford. At 2 am we halted about two miles from the Ford and lay down for a short nap."[18]

"It was our Company's turn to be on guard," wrote Sergeant Hazen.

> Knapp was Corporal of one relief, and Charlie of another. We had marched all the way just as fast as we could march, and with our heavy load to carry, I can assure you we were very tired; and then to sleep only two hours was rather tough. At four o'clock in the morning [Friday] the General ordered the drums to beat reveille, or at least gave the orders to the Colonel, so we had to get up, and roll up blankets, &c. I then went about half a mile after some water to make us some coffee, and then had to get it out of a muddy brook; but anything, you know, must answer for a soldier.[19]

After a breakfast of hardtack and salt pork, the men moved out again, crossing the Rappahannock at the United States Ford a little after noon. Sergeant Reevs wrote that they reached the ford in the morning, "—crossed without any opposition. Our forces were in the rear then, as you will learn by the papers. We had about 5 miles to go after crossing, before we came to the front. We had then marched about 20 miles, I was pretty well tired out, I threw away my blanket and everything I thought I could possibly get along without."[20]

Once across the river, the regiment marched up a hill where the men halted, stacked arms, and rested. Sergeant Hazen got a look at the enemy earthworks and rifle pits. "I can assure you that they had them in a very advantageous position" on the hill with clear fields of fire right down to the river, but the works had been abandoned.

> The sun was shining very hot, and I can assure you we were nearly exhausted. We thought sure that we were going to have a long rest here so most of the boys in our brigade soon threw off their things, and laid down to rest; and some to sleep, and some boiled a cup of coffee. Some with sticks and bayonets fixed up a shelter with a piece of tent to shield them from the burning sun. But there is but little rest for the wearied and tired soldier when on a forced march. We had rested about twenty minutes when the order came to "fall in," which order of course had to be obeyed.[21]

Sergeant Hazen admitted that he could not keep up. He dropped by the side of the road where he lay for a few minutes to recover. Fortunately, the regiment had stopped just ahead and Hazen had no trouble catching up. Again the men moved forward but after a short march, they halted and were ordered to load their weapons. This got everyone's attention and weariness was replaced by excitement as it was assumed the enemy must be nearby. But it was just a false alarm and the men moved into some thick woods where they stopped to rest.[22]

Corporal William Howell, who wrote that they crossed the Rappahannock on pontoon bridges, also noted the halt in the deep woods. They were in "the Wilderness" of Virginia, a singularly unpleasant location for marching or fighting. The woods stretched for miles but this was no ordinary forest of the type the boys had roamed back in Orange County. In colonial days this had been an active iron mining region where the trees had been almost clearcut to provide charcoal for refining iron ore. The second growth of pine and scrub oak took root so close together that in areas the forest was quite impenetrable. The Wilderness was cut by a plank road and a turnpike from Fredericksburg but most byways were roads in name only. Dirt paths twisted through a foreboding forest that seemed to close in and swallow the troops. Maps of the area were inadequate and the natives were uncooperative or on the other side. This was no place for an army to linger, especially one that did not know the way.

The regiment was on what many would later consider to be its most important battlefield of the war and one it would return to the following year. Although the men had seen no real combat since their enlistment began, the regiment bore distinct signs of the hardships it had so far endured. When the 124th boarded the trains in Goshen the previous September, it numbered over nine hundred men of all ranks. On May 1, 1863, the regiment was down to about five hundred fifty men, assuming all the stragglers caught up. Included were George W. Camfield and John N. Cole, two drummers just sixteen years old.[23]

Company K, composed of men from Middletown and Newburgh, was a good example of the reduced strength of the regiment. At Goshen the previous year, the company mustered with its full complement of officers and NCOs: one captain, one 1st lieutenant, one 2nd lieutenant, five sergeants, eight corporals, and sixty five privates. When Company K crossed the pontoons at United States Ford, on the way to Chancellorsville, William Jackson was still its captain but 1st Lieutenant James Roosa was out of the service, disabled, and replaced by the fireman from Newburgh, 2nd Lieutenant James Finnegan. 1st Sergeant Jacob Denton moved up to 2nd Lieutenant whereupon 2nd Sergeant Lewis Wisner became 1st sergeant. Former sergeants Bailey and Webb, as previously noted, had been returned to the ranks due to their long stay in the hospital. Their spots among the file closers, the rear rank composed of sergeants and lieutenants, were taken by former corporals Woodward Ogden and Watson Rich. There were now just four corporals, three having been promoted to sergeant, one demoted to private, and two who deserted — one while home on furlough. Two privates, Daniel Carpenter and Jason Conning, had, during the winter, been promoted to fill the vacancies among the corporals. Standing in the ranks that Friday night were just forty-two privates making Company K one of the smallest companies in the regiment.[24]

Colonel Ellis, in his after-action report to his brigade commander, stated that upon crossing on the pontoons his regiment "proceeded about three miles westerly and formed columns of division in an open space with a large building to the left. Here was collected a large body of troops and an engagement took place in front of us with some severe cannonading in which the enemy appeared to have the worst."[25] The engagement Ellis mentioned was brought on by Hooker's men pushing out of the Wilderness onto clear ground in the direction of Fredericksburg — and Lee's rear.

At this point, Hooker made what many would argue was a fatal mistake — he chose to abandon the offensive. He ordered those brigades marching east to fall back closer to Chancellorsville. Instead of pressing his advantage in men and position, he dug in, fully expecting Lee to send wave after wave of Confederates against his entrenched army. Hooker was, after all, right where he planned to be from the start: threatening Lee's flank and front at the same time. In Hooker's mind Lee had only two options. He could smash his army to pieces against the strong Union line at Chancellorsville or retreat. Lee, of course, had in mind some different options.

But there are other interpretations of Hooker's decision to halt. Historian Stephen Sears noted that "it was the intelligence concerning the enemy that as much as anything else decided Hooker on his course."[26] One of the reforms instituted by the new commander of the Army of the Potomac was a complete overhaul of the intelligence gathering system. He replaced McClellan's operatives with the much more efficient and accurate agency that came to be known as the Bureau of Military Information. To head it, Hooker chose Colonel G. H. Sharpe, formerly of the 120th New York, a regiment raised primarily in Ulster County, just north of Orange County in the Hudson Valley.

Colonel Sharpe's reports told Hooker that a combination of Stonewall Jackson's Corps, McLaw's Division, and Anderson's Division were in front of him, deployed perpendicular to the Orange Plank Road and the Orange Turnpike. Sharpe estimated these forces at about 48,000 men. Later returns showed their actual strength to be but three hundred men more, an incredibly accurate estimate by any measure.[27] This meant that Hooker was outnumbered, not in fantasy as McClellan had so often been, but in reality. The prudent thing to do in the face of these numbers was to pull back and bring up reinforcements.

While the two forces probed each other's lines, the 3rd Corps moved forward. The three divisions of Sickles's Corps were positioned a mile or so west of the crossroads at Chancellorsville, occupying what would become the center of Hooker's line of battle.[28] Here Sergeant Hazen continued his letter: "After resting awhile in the woods, about four o'clock our division was ordered to fall in without knapsacks, and we were then marched forward toward the enemy where heavy firing was going on. We marched nearly a mile and halted in the woods again, and then in a few moments crossed the woods again and were placed in an open field in a mud hole; we stood here awhile and then moved forward where it was drier."[29]

Henry Howell penciled into his diary, "We marched 8 miles and laid down in the woods in hearing of the engagement that is progressing between the two armys. Out of 24 hours we were on the march 20. Then we rested about four hours and started towards the scene of action we were drawn up in line where the mud was half a knee deep. While we were here the most terrific firing was going on."[30]

"We marched on until about 3 o'clock P.M.," wrote Corporal Alexander Valet of Company I, when we halted in the woods an hour or two when we were again ordered up without our knapsacks to go and support a battery which was about 1 mile out in front of us engaged with the enemy; then was the first time that a feeling of fear took possession of me for I expected then that we would soon be engaged in all the horrors of battle, as we could distinctly hear the booming of cannon and rattle of musketry right in front of us, but we did not get engaged that night as our men succeeded in silencing them without our help; we had to lay in line of battle until nine o'clock that night, in a mud-hole with nothing to sit on as we had left everything behind us in the woods.[31]

Sergeant Hazen and his company commander, Captain William Silliman, thought they would be in this place for the night so each put down his rubber blanket and lay upon the damp ground with a tent half Hazen brought along to cover them. What little rest they were able to get was disturbed when, at about ten o'clock, the regiment was ordered to form up and was marched back to where they had piled their knapsacks. Here they got comfortable again and, as Sergeant Hazen wrote, "laid down and slept till daylight."[32] Corporal Valet made himself a cup of coffee, then settled in for the night.[33]

Captain Charles Weygant curled up under his blanket with the regimental mascot, a dog named Jack, and with Lieutenant Colonel Cummins, who had somehow become separated from his blankets. Weygant welcomed Jack and "Old Shiloh" since both would provide warmth against the damp night air.[34] They woke early Saturday morning, May 2, to the sound of heavy firing to the east. Lee's men were probing Hooker's line, looking for a weak spot.

Sergeant Hazen finished up his letter that morning as he brewed a strong cup of coffee to ward off the intense fatigue that had overcome him.

It was not long before we moved forward and halted again in the woods. There was scarcely anything else here but woods, though we occasionally came to a very fine clearing. There is some heavy firing in front of us, and I don't know how soon we may be ordered forward. I am too tired to write any more at present. I have a piece of tent spread in the bushes to keep the hot rays of the sun from me and am lying down writing on my haversack. I will close for the moment. You can scarcely imagine how tired I am and I can assure you I am not the only one. The order has just come to fall in, there is no use to murmer or complain, I must go. So for the moment, Good-bye. I do not know when I shall be able to write any more.

Yours truly, P.P.H.[35]

As Sergeant Hazen boiled his coffee, General Lee put in motion his plans for this soon-to-be historic Saturday. He was so confident that Hooker was stalled in the Wilderness that he divided his army yet again. His scouts, military and civilian, told him that the Union line, extending west from Chancellorsville along the Plank Road, tapered off into the woods just beyond the junction of the Plank Road and the Orange Turnpike. Hooker's right flank was "in the air," to use the military parlance of the day. No hill or easily defended topographical feature served as an anchor for the Union position. The men of the 11th Corps, who held that part of the line, had done very little in the way of building earthworks to improve their exposed position. Here was an opportunity that Lee could not resist, but it was more than just an opportunity. Lee was in a tight spot. He had an unknown number of Yankees in his front, more behind him at Fredericksburg, and no real idea of what Hooker might do. Lee's army was smaller and, while long on confidence, they were short on resources. In this respect Hooker was correct. Lee must attack, for to do otherwise was to invite defeat. Lee's plan to swing around the flank of Hooker's army, while audacious, was born of desperation.

Lee weighed his choices and made his decision. Ordering some of his forces to demonstrate in front of the Federal line to keep Hooker's attention focused there, he sent Lieutenant General Thomas J. "Stonewall" Jackson and his men marching to attack that unprotected Union right flank. If Jackson could get his corps in position perpendicular to the enemy line and launch his attack before he was discovered, the right wing of Hooker's army might be destroyed.

Lee knew he was taking a huge gamble. For a good bit of the way, Jackson would be moving roughly parallel to the Union lines. A column of regiments marching four men abreast would be a very tempting target for the Union forces arrayed just a short distance away. Jackson's men would be bunched together, making them easy targets for Union artillery. If the Union forces chose to attack in heavy lines of battle, they might hit the column and smash it to pieces before Jackson could deploy his men to return fire. Finally, the Yankees might figure out what Lee was up to, rush men and artillery to the point of attack, and dig in. Protected by earthworks, the Yankees might put overwhelming fire on Jackson's men as they emerged from the Wilderness to attack. But none of that happened. The general in gray postured to the east, riveting Hooker's attention in the wrong direction. Meanwhile, Jackson's men, hidden from view most of the way by the dense forest, stepped off on one of the most famous marches of the Civil War.

The soldier leading the attack against Hooker's flank would have been right at home among the ancient warriors of the Old Testament. He credited the Almighty for all his successes, prayed often, and had come to the conclusion that it was not enough to simply defeat the Yankees, they must be swept from the face of the earth. Repeated Confederate victories had not ended the war, so in Jackson's mind only the annihilation of Hooker's army would suffice. It was not enough to drive the Yankees back across the river, they must be driven *into* the river.

By mid-morning Jackson's column was spotted by Union skirmishers. Since Hooker had already considered the possibility that Lee might retreat, he assumed that the infantry, artillery, and wagons seen in the distance were just part of the Confederate flight.

In fairness to Hooker, it must be said that he sent warnings to Major General Oliver O. Howard, commanding the 11th Corps holding the right flank, to watch for Confederates who might turn and attack. Howard was told to make the proper dispositions of his regiments to receive just such an attack. Tragically for the cause of the Union in general and the fate of the 11th Corps in particular, Hooker's warnings and the warnings of Howard's own pickets out in front of the exposed position went unheeded.

Meanwhile, at the center of the Union line, Major General Sickles' instincts told him something was up. The commander of the 3rd Corps was not a West Point graduate but instead was the product of New York City's infamous Tammany Hall political machine. A Democratic congressman before the war, Sickles had a somewhat unsavory personal history, which included at least one charge of murder, but there was no denying that this fiery politician-turned-soldier had what it took to lead men in battle. As did many others that day, his pickets spotted Jackson's men moving across his front. Always ready for a fight, Sickles saw the opportunity; he asked for and received Hooker's permission to move forward to strike the column. Hooker, well aware of Sickles' aggressive nature, reined him in by ordering him to advance with one division, support it with a second, but leave his third division in place as a reserve.

Sickles ordered Brigadier General David Birney's Division forward; Major General Amiel Whipple's Division went as support, just in case the Rebels turned to fight. As Hooker ordered, Major General Berry's Division remained in reserve near Chancellorsville. Whipple's Division, which included Colonel Franklin's Brigade — the 86th New York, 122nd Pennsylvania, and 124th New York — moved toward the front via the Plank Road, turning left to march through the area known as Hazel Grove where Whipple's men began massing to support Birney's advance.

Captain Weygant noted that the regiment marched about half a mile down what he identified as the Furnace Road before being ordered to the right to relieve some of Birney's pickets.[36] Colonel Ellis' report corroborated this move. He described how his regiment deployed in the woods until "about noon when we marched along a plank road & taking a cut in the woods to the right formed a picket line relieving some of Birneys division there posted."[37]

The view from the ranks was more detailed. Corporal Valet wrote, "At an early hour we were again aroused to prepare for what ever the day might bring forth; after making a hasty meal we were marched out to the front and laid there for some time expecting every moment to be pushed in, but it was quiet all that forenoon with the exception of an occasional volley of musketry brought on by our pickets."[38] Captain Jackson described this movement in two phases, the first at 6 A.M. when the regiment moved "up near where we were the night before, remaining until 10." This was followed by a second march: "We then started out on the plank road and filed to the left to picket along some woods."[39]

Here the regiment remained until mid-afternoon, when they were relieved by troops of Howard's 11th Corps. Whipple's Division formed up and began the march south and east toward what Henry Howell described as the center of the line, where it was thought the enemy was making an aggressive move. Corporal William Howell, writing just two days later while still on the battlefield, noted that as they moved forward, the 124th and the 84th Pennsylvania of Colonel Bowman's Brigade were detached to support the 1st and 2nd U.S. Sharpshooters of Colonel Hiram Berdan's Brigade.[40] This would have drawn the two regiments away from the rest of Franklin's Brigade as the Sharpshooters sought out the Confederates near Catherine Furnace. After this little adventure in which the regiment was not actively engaged other than to witness the Sharpshooters bring in 300 prisoners, the "124th moved to the left" to rejoin Franklin's Brigade.[41]

The word quickly passed through the ranks that Birney's Division was driving the enemy and now Whipple moved forward in support. A 3rd Corps staff officer wrote, "Leaving the batteries at the farm about midway between the Plank road and our line of battle, when it formed in line, the Second Brigade and the One hundred and twenty-fourth New York on the right, connecting with General Ward's brigade, and the two remaining regiments of the First Brigade on the left, connecting with General Williams' command, of the Twelfth Corps. We advanced in fine style, the First Brigade firing a few volleys, and all feeling almost sure of success."[42]

The 124th reached its designated position and went into line of battle behind Scott's Run, about a quarter mile from the old iron furnace. As noted by Captain Dalton of Whipple's staff, the regiment formed the right of Franklin's Brigade, connecting with Colonel Samuel Bowman's Second Brigade. The left of Franklin's Brigade connected with General Alpheus Williams's Division of Major General Henry Slocum's 12th Corps. General Sickles placed Whipple's men there to close the "considerable interval" between Birney and Williams. Colonel Ellis wrote that they "formed line of battle under the directions of Major General Sickles in Company with our whole division and many other troops."[43]

Colonel Franklin wrote that after advancing about two miles "we met the enemy in force immediately after debouching from a dense and tangled thicket, and formed line of battle."[44] Lieutenant Colonel Edward McGovern of the 122nd Pennsylvania noted that he had moved his men

> in the direction of a battery, and forwarded obliquely to the right, passing a dense woods on my front in close column by Company, when I deployed column on emerging from the woods, and again advanced in line of battle across a swamp to within 250 yards of the line of the enemy. At this point the fire of the enemy opened, but as I was preceded by a line of skirmishers, I was prevented from delivering an effective reply. Our lines halted at this point, and I ordered my men to avoid that part of the enemy's fire which was delivered at our skirmishers. Our lines were not advanced from this point. I found it impossible wholly to restrain the fire of my men, as the fire opened on our left and rear, through our skirmishers had not yet retired.[45]

The Confederates in front of Franklin were probably men of General Ambrose Wright's Brigade of General Anderson's Division. These were some of the men whose job it was to fix Hooker's attention east until Stonewall Jackson completed his flank march. They did their job almost too well as they had attracted the attention of two big Yankee divisions looking for a fight.

Franklin's men moved forward, marching toward the sound of the fighting. Sergeant Sprenger, 122nd Pennsylvania, wrote that just as the brigade moved from woods into an open space, some rebels who had been hiding in tall grass rose up and fired a volley into his regiment, which was leading the brigade. The Pennsylvanians were halted by the surprise volley but attempted to advance again, only to be halted a second time. He commented that the enemy's aim was high and their fire inflicted few casualties; the 122nd retired "in good order."[46]

William Howell wrote a somewhat different account, "The 124th then moved to the left the 86th NY and 122 Penn ahead. They come unexpectedly on the enemy and are driven back in disorder. We take a double quick to their support and the rebs fall back in the woods."[47]

Sergeant Coe Reevs, 124th, wrote a similar account. "We were hurried on at double quick, and the balls began to whistle over our heads. We had orders to throw away our knapsacks. The rebs had planted themselves in the edge of the woods, and we had to cross an open field to get to them, besides a big ditch, (the 122d Pa. were ahead of us, they are nine months men.) The rebs fired a voley into them and they broke and ran and put us all in confusion." The sergeant took pains to note that the leading regiment was composed of short term volunteers but did not mention that their enlistments were nearly up. His meaning is clear: they broke and ran because short term men near the end of their service were thought to be unreliable. Reevs's letter was published in the *Goshen Democrat* on May 21 and the paper was soon in the hands of the Orange County men back in camp.[48]

Almost immediately, Henry Howell took exception to the sergeant's portrayal of the 124th as being put "all in confusion" by the route of the Pennsylvania men and he said so in a letter home to his mother.

> That letter in the democrat from Coe Reeves had a misstatement in it that does not suit this regiment very well. He says "when the 122nd broke and run back it threw us all in confusion." Now he might have been confused but I did not see anything of the kind near where I was. We were double quicking through the woods, and no regiment that ever fought could keep perfect on account of the trees and bushes. But as soon as we came out in a little opening every man was in his place like a flash. If that is confusion I do not understand the meaning of the word.

He further mentioned "We did not have any officers like they say McBurney was at the first Fredericksburg, dodging behind every little thing."[49] Howell's disparaging remark was directed at his former company commander, Captain William A. McBurney, who was absent at Chancellorsville. In fact, all three of the officers of Company E were absent for one reason or another. Lieutenant Henry Gowdy of Company H, the next company to the right, assumed command of Howell's company just prior on the battle.

Whatever the particulars of the skirmish on the edge of the woods, the 124th did not remain there for long. General Whipple detached Franklin's men again, sending them toward a wooded hill on their right front to support Colonel Bowman's Brigade, but upon arriving at the designated hill, neither Colonel Bowman nor his men were anywhere to be found. As they halted, awaiting further orders, artillery fire and musketry could be heard ahead.

Ellis ordered his men into a line of battle, and, placing himself at the head of the color guard, ordered the charge. A mighty "HURRAH!" that "made the woods ring" announced the presence of the 124th New York. The men, "cheering lustily," charged into the woods.[50] A soldier in the ranks noted that it was about 5 P.M. "when we formed battle line, unslung our knapsacks ready for a charge down a steep hill through brush and briars, but when we got down in the hollow, the enemy was not to be found — they had fled in the woods."[51] At that moment General Whipple rode up, personally ordered the halt, and directed Ellis to fall back toward Hooker's main line.

Both General Sickles and Private Howell had been optimistic about the advance of the 3rd Corp divisions that afternoon. "I found every indication that looked to a complete success as soon as my advance could be supported" the general wrote in his official report. The private agreed that they "were driving them pretty lively." Driving them, that is, until "Mighty Stonewall" ordered his men forward.

Jackson had indeed accomplished what Lee expected: his men had reached the vulnerable right flank of the Union army undetected. He then carefully deployed his divisions in the woods and when he was sure that everything was just right, he turned to the commander of the lead division and asked if he was ready. General Rodes answered that he was. "You can go forward, then," he replied.[52] It was 5:15 in the afternoon and the sun was already low in the sky.

The Confederate onslaught that overran the 11th Corps put the entire Union army in jeopardy. This was especially true of Sickles's Corps, which found itself in the position of being cut off from the rest of the army unless its members reversed their steps in a hurry. Ellis wrote, "Heavy cannonading was going in our rear now our front, and we found that the enemy had turned our position and taken several caisons and prisoners Stampeding our Mules & Nigroes."[53] Word quickly spread that the 11th Corps had broken under the force of Jackson's attack. Surgeon Thompson had not followed the 124th as it marched out with Sickles in the morning but instead he was ordered to report to the "White House," where the 3rd Corps hospital was established. From there he could clearly hear the battle developing as Jackson's men rolled up the Union flank.

> Late in the afternoon the engagement commenced on the left, and soon extended along the line until it became general. As it grew in fierceness and intensity the Surgeon-in-Chief of the Third Corps, suspecting that it must be engaged ordered me, in Company with the Assistant Surgeon and my Hospital attendants to report at my Division's Headquarters on the field, but first to stop at the Chancellor House on the way for information as to the whereabouts of Whipple's Headquarters. It was while attempting to execute this order that the most exciting scenes that I experienced and witnessed occurred.[54]

From this position, Thompson was able to see firsthand the effects of Jackson's attack.

> On reaching the Chancellor House I was brought under a very lively artillery fire of the enemy.... The enemy had thrown a heavy column on our right wing, and with an impetuous charge was driving our troops.... I was afforded a sight of our forces repulsed and fleeing before the pursuing enemy, and of the latter's checked advance by the reinforcements ... it was at this juncture that Jackson came so nearly successful in turning our right by the giving way of the 11th Army Corps.... At the moment it seemed to me that our retreating troops emerged from the woods at the right, down charged a rebel column upon our lines at the left. The fusillade of musketry, joined with the tremendous roar of artillery just at this moment was terrible beyond all description.[55]

At first General Sickles could not believe the reports about the 11th Corps but when aides rode up from Hooker's staff confirming the worst, he acted quickly. The 3rd Corps commander dispatched the 8th Pennsylvania Cavalry to check the rebel advance, then sent couriers to recall Birney and Whipple. Sickles rode toward the sound of the firing, cobbling together as much infantry and artillery as he could to hold the enemy at bay until his divisions could arrive. All around him were the "panic-struck hordes" of the 11th Corps "rushing between and over our guns," with Jackson's screaming infantry right behind them. When the pursuing Confederates broke into the open, they were hit by twenty-two cannons firing double canister at close range. The effect was devastating. "The

Surgeon John H. Thompson. He was discharged January 23, 1865, on flimsy evidence (archive of the Historical Society of the Town of Warwick, gift of Joan and Tom Frangos).

heads of the columns were swept away to the woods, from which they opened a furious but ineffectual fire of musketry. Twice they attempted a flank movement, but the first was checked by our guns, and the second and most formidable was baffled by the advance of Whipple and Birney, who were coming up rapidly, but in perfect order, and forming in lines of brigades in rear of the artillery, and on the flanks." Sickles was everywhere, directing artillery, inspiring the men, and pushing regiments into line. "My position was now secure in the adequate infantry support which had arrived; the loud cheers of our men as twilight closed the combat vainly challenged the enemy to renew the encounter."[56]

"The 11th Corps played a bad trick on the 3d Corps by letting the enemy get in to our rear on Saturday afternoon" wrote Henry Howell.

> General Hooker says they knocked all of his plans in the head by it ... we heard an awful roaring of our artillery commenced in our rear, and we were double quicked back to see what was up. We found that the enemy had advanced on the 11th Corps and they fell back, scarcely giving the slightest resistance to the Rebs until they reached our battery's which were stationed on a rise of ground by a house. Those batterys were what called us back and they poured grape and canister in to them so that they were forced to retire. We were close at hand but the shades of night were gathering around and they were in the woods we did not know how strong so we were taken on picket to the end of the woods.[57]

As Colonel McGovern of the 122nd Pennsylvania neared Hazel Grove, General Sickles rode up to him and said that everything depended on his getting his men into line. "In a moment the regiment was in line, ready to meet the enemy," the colonel wrote. Sickles directed him to move his regiment up to the edge of the woods, about two hundred yards in front of one of the batteries. Shells exploding around them, Sickles told McGovern that he was "in no case to yield the place to the enemy."[58]

All along the line, Sickles rallied his forces, put them where they could do the most good, and acted with resolve when others around him didn't seem to know what to do. In the gathering darkness, he massed his men in the area between Hazel Grove and the Plank Road, reinforcing General Hiram Berry's Division, the troops he'd left behind to cover the afternoon advance. In a series of bold counterattacks, Sickles used elements of the 3rd, 11th, and 12th Corps to drive back Jackson's exhausted men, stabilizing the situation and saving the day for Hooker.

Sickles has been excoriated by historians as just another "political general." But on Saturday, May 2, 1863, he demonstrated that the skills he'd learned in Tammany Hall politics — the ability to see the weakness of the opponent and marshal resources against that weakness, the ability to inspire followers and get them to the right place at the right time to secure victory in the campaign — translate well to the battlefield.

As the 3rd Corps units reached Hazel Grove, a cleared piece of high ground that would figure prominently in the fighting to come, they took up defensive positions. The 124th filed to the left of a road that ran north through a place known locally as Vista. "Saturday night we got on the field just in time to be too late for the mess," Private Ben Dutcher of Company H wrote. "The rebs skedadeled in the woods, but we slept on, or rather layed on, our arms all night — we did not sleep much as the firing kept up till a late hour in the night."[59]

Captain Dalton of Whipple's staff gave the official rendition of where Franklin's Brigade was placed. "The First Brigade was then out in position in two lines, to the left and front of the batteries, close to the woods on the edge of the open field, the Second Brigade supporting the batteries in the rear. Our troops remained in this position under arms all night, and repulsed several times the attempts of the enemy to force our lines."[60]

The 122nd Pennsylvania made up the first line with the 124th about "8 or ten rods" behind them, a distance of about fifty yards. Estimates vary, but sometime after dark the 124th New York moved up and relieved the 122nd along a fence line. "They drove our skirmishers but could not move the first line from under the fence. We were lying down flat so we could not be seen but

Chancellorsville, May 2, 1863

The 124th New York and the rest of Franklin's Brigade were positioned at Hazel Grove in front of Sickles' Corps. After dark, the 124th formed along a fence and sent patrols into the woods. It was while in this position that members of the regiment fired on a mysterious horseman whom some later assumed to be General Thomas J. "Stonewall" Jackson.

"The First Brigade was then out in position in two lines, to the left and front of the batteries, close to the woods on the edge of the open field...Our troops remained in this position under arms all night, and repulsed several times the attempts of the enemy to force our lines"—Captain Dalton of General Whipple's staff

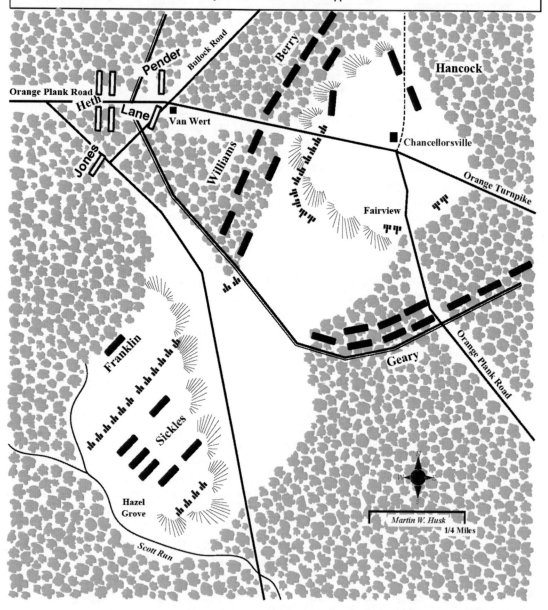

the way the bullets did whistle over and all around us we did not stir until the firing ceased for we could not do anything on account of our troops ahead."[61] Henry Howell penciled into his diary that they were in position just a short time when the enemy advanced on them. They were at the edge of a thick cedar grove behind a rail fence which they made into a breastwork and from there kept the enemy at bay.[62]

Whipple's Division was in support with the 3rd Corps artillery massed on the high ground in the rear. Sergeant Reevs described the scene: "We advanced in front of our cannon about fifty rods, near the edge of the woods where there was an old rail fence. We lay behind that all night (Saturday) firing most of the time. The balls from the rebs would whistle over our heads like bees. We had to lay on our backs and load for fear if we got up they would see us. We had no one hurt that night." Howell wrote that at about 11 o'clock they changed places with the front line. "About midnight they tried us again but we returned their shots with a heavy interest. Well we laid there until morning with out any sleep."[63]

Corporal Howell also put their location "behind a fence at the edge of a wood" and said that large numbers of the enemy were opposite them. He speculated that this was "said to be Stonewall Jackson just come down from Culpepper."[64] "They fired a volley at us but done no damage.... We lay flat and the bullets whistled all around us. We returned fire with interest. Our batery then shelled the woods. We sent out 40 men a few rods in the woods. If they saw a reb they fired and fell back. They fell back but once the reb picket fired and our regt discharge two or three volleys and they drew in their lines I think as they did not disturb us again."[65]

Corporal Valet put the time at 9 o'clock when they moved up to the fence line. He said the men were ordered to lie down with four men from each Company sent forward as scouts. "We all lay there for about one hour quietly, when all at once we heard the report of ten or fifteen muskets and our videts came in on the jump, then our Colonel gave us the order to fire; the next instant the woods in front of us was alive with balls, we all gave nine rounds then ceased as the rebs did not return our fire."[66]

Before any further attacks could be launched, and to ascertain the strength of the enemy, Ellis was ordered to send out patrols into the woods to their front. He noted that "a rude road ran from each flank of the regiment into the woods." Captain Weygant led "Sergeant Campbell and ten of my best men" to the right while Captain Henry S. Murray, Company B, took eight men to the left. Murray picked his way through the gloom before seeing a large force of the enemy in column, ready to attack. He retraced his steps and reported to Colonel Ellis.[67]

Meanwhile, Weygant, after proceeding only about thirty yards, found two caissons and two rifled guns abandoned by the 11th Corps. His men paused to help a wounded soldier who spoke only German; Weygent detailed two men to take him to the rear. He then split his patrol, leaving two men with the guns and sending Sergeant William H. Campbell and two men across the road. Again they moved forward, stepping over bodies; all around them the "piteus moanings and dying groans of wounded men" filled the night.

Weygant was startled by the discharge of a rifle from the opposite side of the road. Private James G. Ciles had moved ahead of the others who, mistaking their comrade for the enemy, shot him. He was carried to the field hospital where Assistant Surgeon Montfort found that Ciles's leg had been broken, a very serious wound. The only choice was to amputate, but the operation itself or the infection that set in afterwards proved fatal; the twenty-one-year-old private died three days later.

Weygant returned from his patrol and reported to Colonel Ellis just as firing broke out along the line of the 124th. As the two officers spoke, a horseman approached out of the darkness from the direction of the enemy. He spoke with authority, demanding to know what regiment was doing the shooting and further warned the colonel that he was firing into his own men. Ellis was not intimidated and replied in a loud voice, "This is the One Hundred and Twenty-fourth New

York, and by—we will give them shot for shot, friend or foe." The horseman, who had been joined by several others, quickly wheeled and rode off, followed by a volley from Company A and a ball from the Colonel's revolver.[68]

More than ten years later Charles Weygant wrote of this incident in his regimental history. While he let the reader draw his own conclusion, he had no doubt that the man on horseback was Stonewall Jackson.[69] A corporal in Weygant's Company witnessed the event and was of the same opinion. John W. Taylor stood in the front rank at the right center of Company A. More than twenty-five years later he sent a letter to the *National Tribune*, the Union veterans' newspaper.

> The night was very dark and we were told to be very watchful, as we were in the front and the rebels were very close to us. We were ordered to fire into the woods if we heard the least noise. At first it was very still, but after a while we heard something moving around out in our front and we began to fire according to our orders. We had fired several shots when we heard a horse galloping up the road and a man shouted at the top of his voice, "Stop that firing! You are shooting your own men." We stopped and he rode up to us saying "You are shooting your own men." We said, "There are none of our men in those woods; this is our front." He had then partly turned his horse, when he said: "What regiment is this?" We answered: "The 124th NY." As soon as he had heard this, he stuck his horse with the spurs, and away he went back down the road as if the very devil was after him and I guess he thought this was the case, for Colonel Ellis, who was standing a few feet away, shouted: "That's a reb, boys; give it to him," and all the guns that could be raised quickly enough were fired at him. He might not have been hit, but how he could get away with a whole skin I do not see as we all did our best. But we were excited and it was very dark. The rest of the night was spent in guessing who the man was and how he came to be there at that time of night, it being about 10 o'clock. Now I, for one, think this was Stonewall Jackson who called on us that night, if not, who was it?[70]

The problem with both accounts is that Jackson was wounded on the north side of the Plank Road about three quarters of a mile from the position held by the 124th New York. Weygant mistook the road through Hazel Grove for the Plank Road. The time frame was off as well; Jackson was wounded at least one hour and possibly as much as three hours before the mysterious horseman appeared out of the darkness. There is no question that Ellis and his men fired at someone on horseback, someone who spoke as if he was used to giving orders, but it was not Jackson. Although time and location make it impossible, it became an article of faith back home that the Orange County boys did indeed fire upon and possibly wound none other than Stonewall Jackson himself.

After this incident, which probably occurred between 10 P.M. and midnight, quiet settled in. All that was heard was an occasional rustling in the trees and the cries of the wounded. The soldiers were exhausted by the day's events and did their best to stay alert on the fence line. Ellis wrote that they were bothered only once by the enemy, who opened fire, "which we returned lustily." The enemy, just as exhausted, annoyed them no more.

During the night, General Hooker made another fateful decision. Just as he had done the day before, he decided to again pull in his lines. With dawn approaching, he ordered Sickles to abandon Hazel Grove and move his men closer to Chancellorsville. It can be argued that Hooker was again sticking to the battle plan. He was concentrating his forces inviting Lee to throw his men against a strong defensive position. But in doing so, Hooker gave up possession of one of the commanding positions on the battlefield and one that would soon be studded with enemy artillery. At the same time, Hooker fully expected the 6th Corps, ten miles away at Fredericksburg, to storm the heights above the town, march west for Chancellorsville, and attack the Confederate rear.

When Sunday, May 3, 1863, dawned, the battle was by no means lost. Hooker was about to surrender a key position on the field, it is true, but his men were concentrated behind three stout lines of earthworks supported by plenty of artillery. His flanks were secure and the enemy had to drive him from the field to secure victory. The nature of weapons, rifled muskets and rifled cannon, gave the defender, when skillfully positioned and supplied with lots of ammunition, the advantage. Finally, Hooker had a big ace up his sleeve: two fresh Union corps, the 1st and the 5th, were in a position that would bring the left flank of the advancing enemy brigades right across their front. Lincoln's words to Hooker about putting in all his men applied at no better time or place.

As dawn approached, Sickles got right to the task at hand. He had a regiment make a road over the swamp that blocked the shortest way to Fairview, putting his men and artillery on the march as soon as the road was ready. His troops got underway just as the Confederates began their advance.

With the wounded Jackson carried far to the rear, Lee called upon Major General J.E.B. Stuart to take up his command. Stuart was determined to follow up the successful Saturday attack as soon as it was light enough to see. His men were formed in three lines, each bisected by the Plank Road. The first, about 600 yards in front of the Union lines, was commanded by General Henry Heth. At about 6 A.M., Stuart sent his skirmishers forward followed by Heth's line of battle. With the cry "Charge and remember Jackson!" they surged toward two targets: Hazel Grove, for which they expected to fight, and the Union artillery position at Fairview.[71]

The Confederates were surprised to see Hooker's men retreating from Hazel Grove. Stuart recognized the importance of the position and pushed battery after battery forward to begin the process of shelling Fairview in preparation for seizing that position by direct assault. This early success, however, was deceptive. Stuart would find that attacking Fairview head on would turn out to be a difficult matter indeed. Lines of Confederates would smash themselves to pieces against the determined Union troops, dug in and ready to fight. In the end, Stuart would have to bring up his last reserves to carry the line of Union earthworks. The attacks would take all day and cost thousands of men.

The 124th was one of the last regiments of Whipple's Division to quit Hazel Grove. In obedience to his orders, Colonel Ellis directed Captain Weygant to take the two rightmost companies, A and F, fall back a short distance, and act as a rear guard. Weygant pulled the two companies from the retreating column and deployed them "at long intervals" as skirmishers, keeping half of Company A as a reserve. The thin line now faced thousands of advancing Confederates. Weygant must have been contemplating his slim chances of survival when out of nowhere a voice asked "Captain Weygant, what orders have you?" It was General Whipple, alone except for an aide. When the captain repeated his orders, Whipple replied "Oh! No! No! Check them a little if possible, and then make your escape — if you can. Don't you hear them; they are already advancing." Whipple quickly mounted and rode off in the direction of the retreating column. In the gathering light, Weygant looked back down the road and saw that it was full of enemy artillery moving into position. In the woods on either side of the road he could just make out masses of gray infantry coming toward him.[72]

The skirmish line held its ground, firing as rapidly as possible. Weygant ordered the skirmishers to fall back on the reserve and form a line of battle. The enemy "without deigning to return a shot, hastened forward," but soon bullets began to zip past Weygant's head. He calculated the odds against his puny line at about one hundred to one, sure that a single volley would have "swept us out of existence." He looked toward Fairview and saw what he hoped would be their means of escape, a ravine that curled around a knoll. He gave the order "Every man for his life" and headed for the rear at a "tremendous gait." Weygant, who was a young man, thought he could outrun anyone in either company, but he was soon left behind. The officers and men raced toward Fairview, where Union artillery pieces thundered at the enemy guns wheeling into position at the recently vacated Hazel Grove. Several times Weygant's little band threw themselves on the ground to avoid the screeching shells. Solid shot passed so close to their heads that some of them were pushed to the ground by the rush of air. "Turn right or left, grim death stared at us." They finally dragged themselves between the Union guns, rejoining their regiment.[73]

Corporal Valet also set the march at about daylight when

our videttes called in and we were marched by a round about way to an open plain that we had laid on the day previous, — we were drawn up in line of battle right behind one of our batteries; we had no more than got in line when the firing commences. We were ordered to lay down, which we quickly obeyed; we lay there with our faces in the mud, the shot and shell flying over us as thick as hail for about half an hour. While laying there I saw men carried back to the rear, some with arms and some with legs off, others wounded in the head and body; horses running around with one leg completely severed from the body. It was the most horrible sight I ever beheld.[74]

Henry Howell wrote that they started the march from Hazel Grove as the first hint of daylight was visible on the horizon and reached Fairview at sunrise "at which time the ball opened." Whipple's Division supported the artillery for about an hour "and during that hour some of the most terrific roaring mortal ears ever heard was going on. The prisoners say that they never saw artillery do so much execution as ours did then. The grape and cannister did tear the woods to pieces like everything."[75]

Captain William Jackson pinpointed the location of the regiment.

Very early the next morning, preparations were made for the coming battle. Our corps lay principally south of the plank road. The right of our regiment rested on the south side of the road, and we lay on our faces with our batteries in front of us. We were in the first long line of our corps, and there were two lines behind us, each distant from the other about fifty yards. About one-fourth mile in front of us were two other lines to receive the first attack of the rebs. We had laid in position but a few moments before the ball opened in front, and soon the roar of our artillery in the woods became deafening. The Enemy's artillery soon replied, and the shells flew over and around us very fast. Had we stood up many of us must have been killed. It is very unpleasant, to say the least, to be lying down and have the shells roaring and bursting near one with no chance to do anything. None of the regiment was hurt here, but a number of artillery men and horses just in front of us were struck. The rebs must have lost heavily from our grape and cannister.[76]

"Early in the morning before breakfast," wrote Sergeant Thomas Bradley, Company H, "we took our position supporting a battery that was shelling the rebels with a goodwill. We were here sometime, — the fight raging furiously in front of us, the wounded being brought up leaning on the arm of some comrade, and all the horrors of war we saw for the first time." At enlistment, Bradley gave his age as eighteen, but local tradition has it that he was much younger, so young in fact that he could not yet grow a beard or mustache. His comrades teased him, calling him "the beardless boy," but his rapid promotion to sergeant bore witness to their high regard for him and to his innate ability to lead. At Chancellorsville, he would demonstrate that he deserved the three stripes he wore.[77]

Veterans of many battles would say that the fighting at Chancellorsville on Sunday surpassed anything they had ever seen. A Confederate soldier who witnessed it from the other side of the field thought "this is hell sure enough."[78]

The right flank of Franklin's Brigade rested on the Plank Road just behind, as Colonel Ellis noted, a "brass battery," part of a line of nearly 40 guns under the command of Captain Clermont Best. The rebels repeatedly tried to overrun

Captain Thomas Bradley, Company H. He was wounded in action July 2, 1863, at Gettysburg, and again May 6, 1864, at the Wilderness and October 27 at Boydton Road, Virginia. He was the "beardless boy" who retrieved ammunition boxes under enemy fire at Chancellorsville and was awarded the Medal of Honor (archive of the Historical Society of the Town of Warwick, gift of Joan and Tom Frangos).

the position by direct assault, only to be thrown back by the Federal troops in the log works in front of the artillery. The Union guns, on slightly higher ground to the rear, could not do much damage to the enemy directly in front because they would be firing over the heads of their own infantrymen, a dangerous undertaking that could unnerve the steadiest of troops. Instead they concentrated their fire against enemy artillery and the infantry to the rear. For their part, it did not take the Confederate artillery long to get the range; their shells dismounted a Federal gun by knocking off a wheel and at least one caisson laden with ammunition exploded. Stuart's artillery had an advantage in that their guns were firing from the Plank Road and from Hazel Grove, a converging fire that was both accurate and demoralizing.

John Bigelow in his monumental work *The Campaign of Chancellorsville* noted that the line of Union guns at Fairview was really not a line at all. "I have been unable to determine the exact location of all the batteries. They were not in one line, nor were they all on the height of Fairview."[79] Some of the cannons were behind earth and log works while others stood in the open. It was the fire of the Union guns coupled with those in reply that gave this phase of the battle its terrifying, unforgettable nature.

Stuart's men succeeded in taking the first two lines of Union earthworks but at great cost. His troops would advance, carry a position and then be thrown back by a Union counterattack. Then the Confederates would attack again, regiments and brigades intermingling in the chaos of battle so that it became difficult for the commanders to control their troops. Brigade and division commanders and even General Stuart himself ventured far too close to the action. In this deadly back and forth battle, the Confederates gradually gained ground on the Union artillery at Fairview. But the price they were forced to pay for this nondescript wooded marshland was very high. Brigade and regimental commanders, leading by example, repeatedly exposed themselves to danger. They did so to stiffen the resolve of their men, but fell in alarming numbers. Some Confederate units with long and glorious histories, advancing into the hail of lead ran to the rear, took cover, and refused to advance again. But many more did advance, blasting a path over and around the earthworks north of the Plank Road. This put them within rifle range of Fairview to their right. They got behind the road's embankment and began to pick off the gun crews and the artillery horses. Without the horses to pull the cannons to the rear, and lacking an adequate re-supply of ammunition, Best's line might well be overrun.

The Union troops north of the Plank Road began to give way under the pressure of Brigadier General Dorsey Pender's North Carolina brigade and Brigadier General E.L. Thomas's Georgia brigade. These Confederates were "about to sweep away the last infantry protection on the right of the Federal artillery, and break in a surging mass on the flank and rear of the guns at Fairview when their victorious progress was arrested by opposition from two directions." The first came from Colonel Franklin's three regiments — 86th and 124th New York and 122nd Pennsylvania — advancing to halt the enemy attempt to flank and capture Fairview. Franklin's orders were simple: "Repulse any attack and cover the artillery at all hazards." At about 7:30 A.M., he prepared to lead his brigade across the Plank Road to engage the enemy.[80]

Captain Jackson's Company K was at the center of the left wing of the 124th New York. He hoped that they would not be called into action at all but after enduring the shelling for about thirty minutes "our Colonel called out, 'up my tulips,' and we crossed the road into the woods on our right. Just as we rose up to go into the woods, one of my men, McCanney, of Newburgh, was shot in the wrist by a rifle ball."[81]

Captain Weygant hugged the ground with the rest of the men, trying to keep as low a profile as possible. Then a caisson filled with ammunition exploded, horribly burning some of the gun crew, shell fragments randomly killing or wounding others within range. Just as his head cleared from the concussion, he "heard amid the tumult, in the familiar words and voice of Ellis, the order, 'Forward, my tulips,' and saw moving away through the smoke, our regimental colors."[82]

Chancellorsville, May 3, 1863

When the 3rd Corps was pulled back to Fairview, Franklin's Brigade took up a position south of the Orange Turnpike, just behind the Union artillery position. As Confederate units advanced north of the turnpike, they threatened to outflank the line of guns. Franklin's Brigade was called upon to cross to the north side of the road and drive off the enemy. It was here that Colonel Ellis called upon his Orange Blossoms to charge.

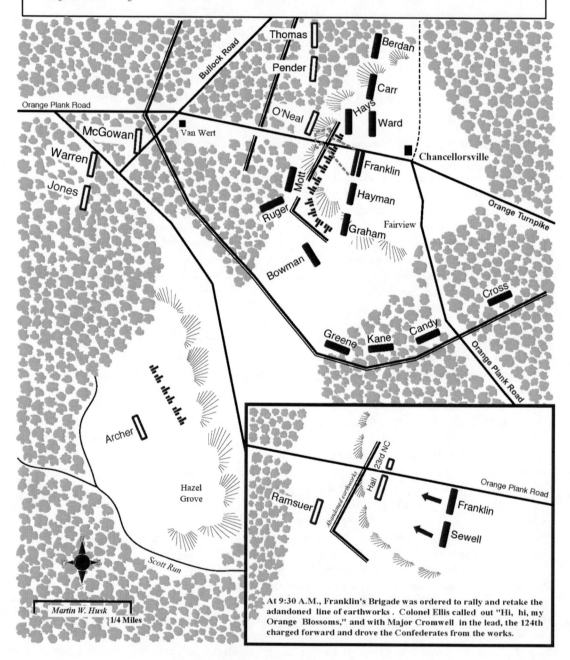

At 9:30 A.M., Franklin's Brigade was ordered to rally and retake the adandoned line of earthworks. Colonel Ellis called out "Hi, hi, my Orange Blossoms," and with Major Cromwell in the lead, the 124th charged forward and drove the Confederates from the works.

As soon as Ellis gave his unusual battle cry, the regiment moved by the right flank — from a line of battle to a column of fours facing right — and headed off into the woods. Once in position, Ellis halted his men and had them form a battalion front, a line of battle facing the enemy. Weygant and his two rightmost companies were still out of position, probably because they hit the ground as soon as they arrived at Fairview, not choosing to expose themselves while seeking out their proper place in the line. Now, as the regiment formed up, he hurried the men of A and F along behind the other companies until they reached their positions at the right of the regiment. Colonel Ellis saw them coming and greeted them with "Good! Good! Weygant; I was sure you had all gone to kingdom come," then added, "let the little girls of old Orange hear a good report of this day's work." Just then, George Weygant of Company I and John Judson of Company A were shot dead right in front of the two officers.[83]

From this position, the 124th linked up with some sharpshooters and pressed forward through thick underbrush and more woods, crossing Lewis Creek. "We went in the woods to our right as the rebs were trying to flank our baterys. The field was a half mile square surrounded by woods. We went in and were immediately hotly engaged with their Sharpshooters.... We held them in check an hour."[84]

Sergeant Bradley wrote,

It was time for us to "go in" as we term it. Our brigade went from the little hill where the battery was in a thick woods, to the right. We were soon aware of the enemy's approach — the whiz of a bullet past one's ear as a quick forerunner of what is coming. But we're in line ready to receive them and were soon forgetting of everything but taking human life. First to fall was Van Keuren Crist. Poor fellow! He died nobly — shot in the mouth — he never spoke. About the same time William L. Fairchild, in the Color Guard, was struck in the head. He fell on his back and never moved. Next came Foster; and then they were wounded so fast we knew not all that were wounded.[85]

"We lay in the woods about one-half hour when the crack of the rifles in front announced that the rebs were coming," Captain Jackson wrote.

Every man was ready. Our right was engaged first, but as they came on the firing extended along our whole line. How our boys did fire, each one for himself, as fast as he could load, but all taking deliberate aim. Adjutant Brownson was the first one I noticed shot. He was hit in the ankle, and went limping off the field. Soon the bullets came whistling by us thick and fast. David Quick was the first one of our boys hit. He was just in front of me and was struck in the left arm. The sight of blood affected us only to make us more angry, and when I saw poor Denton shot I called out to the boys, "they have killed Denton; give it to the rascals." I picked up his gun and was just going to fire when Wisner came up and said his would not go off, so I gave it to him and picked up another and had some good shots at the scoundrels.[86]

Corporal Valet also implied that there was a delay before the battle really got underway.

1st Lieutenant William Brownson, Company C, adjutant. At Chancellorsville, Captain Jackson wrote, "Adjutant Brownson was the first one I noticed shot. He was hit in the ankle, and went limping off the field." He was discharged for wounds September 17, 1863 (archive of the Historical Society of the Town of Warwick, gift of Joan and Tom Frangos).

After getting a respectable distance from the line of rebel infantry we were halted, our Colonel took one of the men's gun and went out in front of the line to see if he could get a pop at one of the Johnny's. In the meantime the rebels came up on our right flank, double quick, the men hollered at the Colonel but their voices were drowned with reports of the enemy's guns, and without further orders commenced firing, and in a few moments we were all engaged in the horrors of battle. The first volley that they fired at us caused many of our brave boys to bite the dust. A feeling of almost madness took possession of me at that time, as I witnessed one after another of my comrades fall; some dead on the spot, others badly wounded. I have often heard say that when a man once got engaged in battle he became so excited that he did not realize the danger he was in, and I did not credit it, but I know it to be the case now by experience.[87]

Colonel Ellis threw back his right wing to meet the attack and with obvious pride he wrote that the maneuver was done perfectly while under a heavy fire. He made no mention in his official report of his attempt to play sharpshooter while his men were being flanked.[88]

"We had not taken our position long, when the firing commenced in earnest. It was hard work I assure you," wrote Sergeant Charles Stewart.

The barrell of my gun was so hot I could scarcely touch it. I fired twenty-two rounds when a ball struck me on the head above the right eye. I felt the sting but thought nothing of it till I saw the blood pouring, then I made up my mind that the ball must have entered the skull, and that the wound was mortal. I dropped my gun and B took me to the rear, where I had my wound dressed. It was not so bad as I supposed. The skin was torn, and the skull a wee bit cracked. I was, and still am, weak from loss of blood.[89]

The commander of a nearby gun crew, quite possibly 1st Lieutenant Dimick, Battery H, 1st U.S. Artillery, whose six twelve-pound Napoleons were especially effective firing canister at close range, quickly sized up the 124th New York. He warned his men "to look out as he was supported by a 'green regiment' as he was pleased to call us," an Orange County soldier wrote, obviously annoyed by the characterization. "We had not fired many rounds when things took a turn, as the pig said on the spit and he told his men to blaze away, for there was no danger of them as long as the 'Orange Blossoms' lasted."[90]

For nearly an hour the battle raged while, to the left and rear, the Union artillery at Fairview began pulling back. Colonel Franklin rode up and down the line urging his men to hold on. One

of his aides, Lieutenant Henry P. Ramsdell of the 124th, received a scalp wound when his hat was shot off his head. Corporal Howell, who had previously been critical of the officer, wrote home that young Ramsdell had "done well" under fire. It was a fortunate observation for Ramsdell because several local newspapers printed the comment.[91]

Most of the casualties sustained by the 124th occurred during the fight in the woods. "Our color bearers were some of them shot," Corporal Howell wrote to his mother. Sergeant Thomas Foley was shot through the neck and fell backwards, still holding the flag staff. Corporal Hiram Ketcham of Howell's Company E seized the colors and was in turn shot down, but before the beloved flag could fall, Corporal William B. Hazen grabbed the staff and holster, waving the colors aloft. He bore the flag for the rest of the battle with such conspicuous gallantry that Ellis promoted him to 5th Sergeant of Company B. Not only

Captain Henry P. Ramsdell, Company C, discharged for disability December 13, 1863. Corp. William Howell reported that Lieutenant Ramsdell "done good" under fire at Chancellorsville (archive of the Historical Society of the Town of Warwick, gift of Joan and Tom Frangos).

did the nine man Color Guard draw heavy enemy fire, the companies on either side, C to the right and H to the left, were hit hard.[92]

Henry Howell was knocked off his feet by a ball that passed through his haversack, tin plate, coat, and vest, coming to rest just above his navel. He got quite a bruise and kept the bullet as a souvenir. His brother William had bullets pass through his canteen, pail, coattails, and the seat of his pants. He was staggered by the shot that hit his canteen, and when he felt the water running down his leg, he limped to the rear, assuming he was bleeding. To his great relief, he discovered the truth and "sprang back and pegged away again. I didn't care for the canteen, but I missed the water" was his flippant observation after the shooting died down.[93]

Sergeant Coe Reevs did not fire many rounds before he was knocked to the ground with a buckshot wound to the hip. Fortunately, Captain Murray saw him and told his brother, Sergeant Robert Murray, and Lieutenant Gabriel Tuthill to help him to the rear. As they were carrying him, a ball tore through Tuthill's haversack and hit Reevs in the back. The haversack was filled with hardtack which, in this case, lived up to its cement-like reputation — the force of the ball was absorbed and Reevs was only slightly wounded.[94] As Robert was tending to Sergeant Reevs's wounds he got word that his brother, the captain, "was shot through the head and killed instantly." Robert quickly rejoined his company but could not find his brother's body and, as the regiment fell back from Fairview, he too was wounded.[95]

Members of Company H, standing to the left of the colors, drew heavy enemy fire. Private James E. Homan was so eager to fight the rebels that he stood several paces in front of the line, firing as fast as he could load. He escaped without a scratch but both boots were "riddled with bullets." Private William McVey's cap was spun on his head by a passing ball. "Look out McVey," he yelled to no one in particular, "this is getting to be a hot place!" Sergeant Thomas Bradley managed to empty his cartridge box of all its forty rounds before they fell back. "John McCann had fired six rounds before he was wounded. Orderly Sergeant John Rowland had his nose slightly skinned by a passing bullet or piece of shell. Alfred Bowman fired twenty-two rounds, and he coolly expressed his opinion that they were not 'for nothing,' meaning that there were some rebels the fewer for them. Wm. Dawson had all the front of his clothing over his breast torn away by a passing shot or shell. Thomas O'Connell's clothes were riddled with bullets."[96] Of the 57 members of Company H who went into the battle, 29 were hit by enemy fire, a casualty rate of 51 percent.

In the stand up fight in the woods, Franklin's brigade halted the Confederate advance. In their eagerness to attack, the enemy soldiers moved far in front of any support, especially on their dangerously exposed left flank. Now a second blow hit them. It was delivered by elements of General French's Division of the 2nd Corps that had marched all the way from the other side of the battlefield. The leading regiments in this attack, commanded by Brigadier General Samuel Carroll, caught the Confederates in the flank and drove them back to the earthworks. The charge cleared the ground in front of Franklin, giving his men a respite and a chance to catch their breath.

As happened all morning, Carroll's attack spent itself and was in turn thrown back by Confederate artillery fire. Jeb Stuart's third line, his last reserves, now moved to the attack. The brigades of this division, led by Brigadier General Robert Rodes, passed through the second line of troops, many of whom had seen enough fighting for one day. Rodes's First Brigade was led by Colonel Edward O'Neal, another of those senior officers wounded while leading from the front; his command passed to Colonel Josephus Hall. As the brigade approached the Yankees, it split in two — one part, commanded by Colonel Hall, drifted right, picking up soldiers from the earlier attacks who still wanted to fight.[97]

The Confederates paused to gather their strength and steel themselves for yet another try at the Yankee batteries. But first they would need to deal with the infantry guarding the approaches to the artillery's flank. Most of the federal troops in front of the guns had by now been shot down or driven away allowing the twenty or so cannons still in action to freely use canister on any Confederates approaching them head on.

> Hall's men, accompanied on their left by five companies of Iverson's brigade under Colonel Christie, surge around the Federal right, and compel Dimick's guns north of the Plank Road to retire. Skirmishers and sharpshooters get within 100 yards of Winslow's battery on the new flank. They plant their colors by the side of the road, and commence picking off his horses. He loads with canister and blows them back. Again and again they return, to be as often repulsed.[98]

"The battle was now at its height, and the 124th was in the thickest of the fray," Weygant wrote. According to his recounting of events, the 23rd North Carolina and another North Carolina regiment, both commanded by Colonel Christie, swept toward them. At a range of less than fifty yards, the 124th poured a volley into their ranks that brought them to an instant halt and caused them to fall to the ground to escape the withering fire. The regiment behind the 23rd now began shooting but in a few minutes this one too was taking cover. "They had the advantage of us," Sergeant Bradley wrote. "They could load lying, raise, and fire, and drop again. Our men fell thick and fast."[99] As the men in the front rank fell, men from the second rank stepped up to fill the gaps.

Colonel Ellis described the fight in the woods as severe, lasting about an hour, "the enemy in force trying to drive us and capture the battery." He wrote that "our men fought like tigers cheering loudly but falling fast.... Three Color bearers were shot here but the colors never touched the ground." Sometime around 9:15 A.M., Ellis received word that the batteries had pulled back and that the federal troops on the left went with them. "To remain would be certain capture and previously passing word of the movement up and down the line to prevent confusion we fell back step by step to the road in the rear."[100]

"Our fire was so rapid and well aimed," wrote Captain Jackson, "that the rebs fell back for a few moments, but they came on again with reinforcements and we were ordered to fall back. We lost some men when falling back across the road. Here Dan Webb was wounded; one of the boys was helping him off but was soon hit himself and had to leave him, for the rebs were not far off. I knew nothing of it until afterward, for I was at the right of the Company."[101]

The brigade fell back under heavy fire across the road and to the rear of the Fairview position. "We stood up to the rack for about three quarters of an hour, when we were ordered to retreat as the battery had left us and we had no support. We fell back across a large open plain, through shot and shell, men falling on every side of us."[102]

"We held them in check an hour then fell back in good order. They scattered us as we passed the bank out of the woods. The artillery had retreated to the upper end of the field and the infantry too. The rebs began to pour out of the woods below in pursuit." Corporal William Howell, having recovered from his canteen wound and rejoined the regiment, wrote,

> Our wounded were thus far carried back but as we came up on the bank Josiah Harris fell seriously wounded just in front of me. He screamed and rolled about in agony, poor fellow. We could not stop for the bullets were whistling by us like hale and we sought to gain the top in safety before we began to retreat. John Staples, Corporal James W. Daly and Charles Newall were all shot dead. Adam W. Beakes had his left arm shot off or will have to have it cut off. Dora Robinson was seriously wounded. Bill Price had his left forefinger shot off and a shot in his arm. Abe Rogers in the leg others who you have never heard of were wounded there also.

He described again the many bullet holes in his clothing but as for himself, "nary a scratch."[103]

Before the battle, Lieutenant Henry Gowdy of Company H was placed in command of Company E. Even thought he was in charge of another company, his comrades from Walden still looked after him. During the retreat, the young officer was shot in the thigh. William Buchanan and several others rushed to his side, picked him up, and carried him to the hospital in the rear.

Civil War history book

whether it gets published or
ot."

Before the book was re-
ased, the author had two au-
orities check the section on
ettysburg. He said that's the
ie battle, where readers are
kely to pounce on mistakes
any part of the narrative
inaccurate. The reviewers
ad positive comments on
ie Gettysburg section, and
lr. LaRocca offered a brief
verview of what happened
1 the battlefield. He said
iat Gen. Lee's objective was
o take Cemetery Hill and cut
ff the road to Baltimore. But
ie Confederate troops were
istracted by a Northern unit
iat strayed out of position.

Although the student re-
earch project is no longer
1 existence, a couple of
oung students helped with
ie compilation of the cur-
ent paperbound volume. Mr.
.aRocca's granddaughters,
:hloe and Cassie Williams,
vere responsible for input-
ing several letters that were
vritten during the Civil War.
)ne sister read out loud while
he other one typed.

The book refers to several
eriod documents and offers
complete roster of the regi-

Photo by Ken Cashman

**Civil War author Charles F. LaRocca signs a copy of his
book for Anna and George Tilley at the Cornwall Public Library on Nov. 25.**

ment. The refreshments at
the library included cookies
that resembled the Orange
Blossom insignia. Before answering questions and sign-

ing books, Mr. LaRocca provided one final comment on
the project. "I'm very happy
to see it completed," he said.
And the audience laughed.

Obituaries

Send obits to reporter.local@verizon.net or fax (845) 534-3855
Read past obits online at www.thecornwalllocal.com

Jason M. Corbin Sr.

August 18, 1969-Nov. 21, 2012

Jason M. Corbin of Newburgh died in Newburgh on Nov. 21. He was 43 years old.

The son of Sharon and Bill Corbin Jr., he was born in Suffern on Aug. 18, 1969.

He is survived by his parents, his sons Jason M. Corbin and Kyle Corbin, his daughters Brieanna Corbin, Riley Corbin and AmyethEst Frye; his sisters Jaime Riegel of Scotia (formerly of Cornwall) and Melissa Sayers of Fuquay Varina, NC.; his grandmother Elizabeth Corbin and several nieces and a nephew.

The family received visitors and hosted a funeral service on Nov. 28 at Quigley Brothers Funeral Home Inc. in Cornwall-on-Hudson. The funeral was followed by cremation at Cedar Hill in Newburgh.

Aina L. Sullivan

July 3, 1922 - November 21, 2012

Aina L. Sullivan, a longtime resident of Cornwall-on-Hudson, entered into rest on Wednesday, Nov. 21 at Wingate at Dutchess. She was 90.

Aina was born on July 3, 1922 in Riga, Latvia. She came to the United States in 1951.

She worked for Lightron and was in the electrical union for almost 40 years. Aina loved watching the family race sailboats at Chelsea Yacht Club. Her favorite things included dining out with her family and going on vacations to Florida.

Survivors include her daughter Diana Kolfrat and husband Brett, and her grandson Tyler of Cornwall. She was predeceased by her husband, James Joseph Sullivan.

A memorial service and inurnment will be held on May 26 at the Latvian Memorial Park Cemetery in Tannersville, N.Y.

Arrangements are under the direction of James F. Lulves Fu-

Police

Town of Cornwall Police Department

There were seven arrest between Nov. 19 and Nov 25.

Nov. 19: A 16-year-old mal was charged with unlawfu possession of marijuana fo having a blunt and a lighte at the high school.

Nov. 24: Christian Kno chen, age 20 of Cornwall was charged with unlawfu possession of marijuana.

Nov. 24: A 17-year-old Newburgh female wa charged with criminal possession of a stolen car, unlawful fleeing from police and reckless endangerment She was turned over to the New Windsor police since the car was allegedly taken in Vails Gate.

There were three arrests for people driving with a suspended license or registration.

Incidents:

Nov. 19: Police moderated a dispute that involved threatening text messages.

Nov. 21: A car parked in a

Cyclist vee

"In going back we had to go up the rise of ground where the battery had been. While going up here the rebels in the woods poured into us very heavy.... Captain was also wounded slightly in the chin."[104]

When Private William H. Whiteside, another of Company H, saw a wounded comrade he quickly went to attend him. Absorbed in his mission and unaware that the regiment was falling back, he soon found himself under fire. Whiteside "played possum on them by throwing himself down and pretending that he was dead. The Rebs soon passed on, when he up and 'broke' in a double quick 'gait' in the direction of our men."[105]

By about 9:30 A.M., it looked as if this latest Confederate attack would overrun the center of the Union position. Only after tremendous, costly effort did Stuart's men finally take the artillery works at Fairview, but their moment of triumph was short lived. General French again attacked north of the Plank Road, the 5th Maine battery adding its weight in canister to the charge. The Confederates were again thrown back in confusion, exposing the flank of their comrades at Fairview.

Exhausted, with nearly half of their men down, the 124th New York was falling back, but the day was not yet over for them. Sergeant Bradley remembered that they had reached the high ground and a safer position when they looked back and "fired at seeing their traitorous flag floating in the place where our own spangled banner had floated, we rallied." Corporal Howell also saw the Confederate battle flag. "Well we retreated up on the level and ... the rebs came pouring out with their hated colors waving."[106]

The sight of that flag moving triumphantly forward halted their retreat and filled them with anger. At that very moment a young officer, whom Ellis identified as Lieutenant Blake of Sickles's staff, rode among them calling out in the name of their 3rd Corps commander to rally and to retake the artillery position. Ellis, sensing the drama of the moment, cried "Hi, hi, my Orange Blossoms," using an expression learned in his days as a fireman in California to rally his men. Major James Cromwell, "springing to the front, took position ten paces ahead of the colors to lead the charge. Hastily fixing bayonets the regiment once more, with a wild hurrah! rushed forward at their foes; driving them pell-mell over the works, capturing some, and opening a deadly fire on those who fled."[107]

The 86th New York was nearby, having come out of the woods with the 124th New York. "We were then ordered to fall back, as the enemy were outflanking us. We formed again in the open field, and in rear of the earthworks and in front of the enemy, under a heavy fire, and charged as far as the small house on the left, driving the enemy, and there forming line."[108] Captain Dalton of Sickles's staff wrote, "The One hundred and twenty-fourth and Eighty-sixth New York Volunteers reformed on the left of the Plank road, and charged vigorously upon the enemy, who were then coming down the road and over the works erected as a covering to the battery."[109]

Out of the confusion of retreat, the 124th New York and the 86th New York, with a portion of Sewell's New Jersey Brigade, had rallied, formed up, and roared back one more time. Their charge "recovers a number of cannon that the enemy had seized, and hurls him out of the works, taking the flags of Hall's 5th Alabama and 26th Alabama, and many prisoners."[110]

They held the position until all the Union troops, left and right, had pulled back and until

the flag presented to them at Goshen, by the Ladies of Orange County, and which Ellis promised the donors should never be disgraced, was the only emblem of liberty in sight; while the stars and bars of the Confederates waved in front and on either side of them. Then was Ellis again forced to repeat the order "Fall back," and the regiment retired toward the new Union line which was being rapidly reformed a quarter of a mile further to the rear, leaving their route over the plain marked by the blood and bodies of yet another score of Orange County's bravest sons.[111]

"We held them in check some time," wrote William Howell. "Our colors were the last to leave and then we had ⅕ of a mile to double quick before we came to our next rifle pit. They peppered us all the way back. Lieutenant Colonel Cummings said he never saw a regt fight braver new or old in his life."[112] Corporal Valet's letter home contained a short but memorable account as well. "Our Colonel rallied us again and we made a charge across the field and drove the rebels out of our earthworks, taking some prisoners, but again we had to retreat as their numbers were too large for us. This time we fell back to the reserve about 2 miles. Such a looking set of boys you never saw, faces and hands all blacked up with powder."[113]

Corporal Francis Lee, Company B, was not so lucky. He and a group of comrades helped retake the breastworks, firing on the retreating Confederates with such concentration that they did not hear the orders to fall back. By the time they realized their dilemma, "the Rebels were so close on us that we would certainly have got a ball in the back, had we run." Frank did not care to be shot down in such a manner so, using a mocking reference to General McClellan, he decided, "as a 'military necessity' we changed our base and compromised the matter." The group was told to go to the rear but for some reason the rebels did not take Lee's rifle from him. "I held on to my 'Shooting Iron,' which was loaded, primed, and ready to use should I see my cousin the General, I might 'draw a bead' on him." It didn't take his captors long to relieve him of his weapon, "three of whom 'lit upon me like a hawk on a June bug' and knocked the gun out of my hand. I thought they were going to swallow me, and as the nigger said, I was 'toted' to the rear."[114]

The regiment fell back in good order in the direction of the main Union line about five hundred yards to the rear. Once in position, Colonel Ellis was ordered to make ready to "support Meaghers Irish Brigade who it was said were about Charging with the bayonet we lay down behind them in line of battle with a battery on our right & were here shelled by the enemy in the liveliest manner a caisson blown up in front of us filled the air with fragments and the roar and bursting of shells was one continuous thunder."[115]

The 124th New York was now near to the crossroads at Chancellorsville. Confederate batteries were "raking the plain and turnpike with grape and canister, making the spot a very warm one, and causing the men of our regiment to hug the ground closely."[116]

Captain Jackson described how it felt to be under such intense bombardment.

We then moved to the right, a little to the right of a large brick house, and supported a battery. While lying here we were subject to a most terrible fire of canister, shell, and shrapnel. It was ten times worse than at Fredericksburg. Old troops say that they never heard anything like it. It was the last desperate effort of the rebs, to break still more our lines, but they failed. Only one man of our regiment was killed by the fire. I must say that I don't yet like shells. I did not feel the least fear when the bullets were flying after the first round or two, for I could stir around and cheer on the men, but to lie still and take it with no chance to do anything I don't like.... Several of our boys can show some marks of rebel balls through caps and clothes. I did not get a scratch, but they whistled very close.[117]

Lieutenant John R. Hays of Company H, a native of Walden, described a most remarkable event that took place while the regiment waited for whatever it might be called upon to do next. Since the charge at Fairview, the regiment had not been resupplied with ammunition and most of the men were out of cartridges. Colonel Ellis expected to be moved forward in support of the Irish Brigade and he was concerned that no ammunition had been brought up from the rear. Then he noticed between the lines a group of dead mules with ammunition boxes strapped to them. Here were thousands of cartridges that would go to the first side to reach them. Hayes estimated that the Confederates were about five hundred yards distant with the dead mules at about the halfway point.[118]

Ellis considered sending a detail, perhaps a whole company, to gather the boxes "but hesitated about doing so because of the hazardous undertaking." As Ellis weighed his options, Sergeant Thomas Bradley, "the beardless boy" of Company H, volunteered to go alone. He handed his rifle to a file mate, dropped his cartridge box, belt, canteen, and haversack and ran out between

Lieutenant Thomas Hart, Company A. Mustered in as a corporal, he was commissioned 1st lieutenant February 15, 1865 (archive of the Historical Society of the Town of Warwick, gift of Joan and Tom Frangos).

the lines "amid a heavy fire of shell, canister, and scattering rifle-shots, across the plain, to where the ammunition boxes lay."[119]

Lieutenant Thomas Hart watched as Bradley returned toward the Union lines dragging a couple of heavy boxes behind him. When the fire increased, "Bradley was seen to turn, and, facing the enemy's line, rapidly walk backwards." As Bradley faced toward the enemy, they recognized his bravery, the firing slowed, and they cheered him. Once Bradley was back within his own lines, the boxes were broken open and the cartridge packages, ten shots each, were distributed so that the battle could resume. When asked why he turned toward the enemy, Bradley replied, "I felt sure of getting hit, and wanted the stroke in front instead of in my back."[120]

General Sickles, in a letter to Secretary of War Daniel Lamont years later, wrote that he knew of Bradley's action at the time of the battle. "The incident of the supply of ammunition obtained by Bradley in the face of a terrible fire from the enemy — the only man who volunteered to get it, was reported to me at the time. It seems to me that this is distinctly one of the signal acts of devotion, courage and heroism, contemplated in the Act of Congress, authorizing these medals of honor, and that Bradley is worthy, both as a soldier and a citizen, to wear it." It would take thirty years, but eventually his brave act was recognized with a Medal of Honor.[121]

The 124th remained on the open plain under artillery fire for about an hour. Sergeant Bradley wrote, "We then went to the rear; here we laid down in line of battle, weak and tired out, the shells flying around us. One of our men named Fuller, was struck in the head and instantly killed by a shell."[122]

Corporal Howell wrote that "we got back past the rifle pits and lay under a terrible cannonading of shot and shell behind our baterys as they had made a determined stand. At the time our Company had eight left of 42." He listed the men present as "Myself, Corp George Godfrey, Privates Adam Miller, Sim Wheat, Freeman, John H. Little, Harris, and Codington." Just then, "Hooker came passed us and the colonel proposed three cheers, and then told him we had lost 400. He stopped short and asked what regt. It was a sad day for Old Orange but she had won glory."[123] At 4 P.M., Meagher's brigade was pulled back and the 124th was ordered out on picket in front of its own batteries where it remained all night. William Howell penciled into his diary, "About 125 men remaining with the colors out of over 500."[124] His brother's account was about the same. "Out of 540 men that went in 160 came out with the colors but there are quite a number taking the wounded back so we will increase the number after a while. We drove them at the start but we were not properly supported so we had to yield the ground to them in the end. But with a dear cost to them as well as ourselves at night we were out on picket again but did not have any trouble with them."[125]

At daylight on Monday, May 4, the regiment was relieved, moved to the rear, and were put to work digging rifle pits and putting up breastworks.[126] The men speculated that they would remain behind the protective barricades and await the enemy's attack "on our own ground" as Henry Howell put it.[127] Even this duty proved to be dangerous, as the Confederate snipers were in the trees and kept up a constant fire. At 10 A.M., Private Andrew Boyd of Company C was wounded and within a couple of hours three more men were hit.

At about 2 P.M., General Whipple stopped to talk to Captain Weygant, asking how his wound was doing and remarking on his fortunate escape from the skirmish line the previous day.

The general walked up the line to the 86th New York and Weygant went back to his work. Moments later he heard a thud and knew someone had been hit. He thought it was one of his own men but the sniper had set his sights higher. General Whipple had been mortally wounded; he fell into the arms of the man he was conversing with. That was simply too much to bear. Colonel Hiram Berdan of the Sharpshooters took a squad of handpicked men and set off to clear the woods. Returning sometime later, they told of snipers perched high in the trees and brought with them three rifles with telescopic sights as trophies.[128]

General Whipple was much beloved by the men in the ranks for his compassion and sincere concern for their welfare. Private Matthew Wood of Company E wrote "He was a good man and a good General and liked by us all."[129] It was said that Berdan himself shot the sniper who had killed the general.[130]

William Howell wrote,

> We are entrenched now with rifle pits and breastworks all around us, woods on every side of our position. This afternoon we sent our skirmishers and stirred up the rebs and took a stand of colors. Our batteries played on them a while and they returned the compliment. All quiet this evening. I got Emily's letter a few days before we marched. No mail since ... I have carried my knapsack all the way through. Henry's is lost. This is the first day that we got time to eat and sleep. We have endured more than we had any idea we could. We are well now and trust and hope God will bring us out safe.[131]

All day, stragglers who had become separated from the regiment during the fighting wandered in, sometimes in groups of two or three.

On Tuesday, May 5, William noted in his diary "lively skirmishing," but his brother gave a more detailed account of their activities. "We staid in our rifle pits all day, every once and awhile the rebs would commence and shell us a few minutes but did not do any damage. We live good on our beefsteak and hardtack."[132] By mid-afternoon the weather turned cooler and it began to rain. The men were ordered to pack up their gear and prepare to move. At first it looked as if they were going forward for another attack, but they reversed direction and headed toward the river, reaching the pontoons about daylight. "The mud was half a knee deep all over but the army was not at all demoralized. They kept up a constant talking, laughing, and cheering."[133] Private Judson B. Lupton of Walden was the butt of some good natured ribbing once the men were back in camp. He had always been fond of referring to "friends" he had south of the Rappahannock and often said he would like to visit them. Once back over the river a wag wrote home to the local newspaper, "Well, I guess he has seen them (his 'friends') to his heart's content at last. He thinks they did not use him very good, and he says he will not go and see them again."[134]

They reached their old camp after thirteen hours on the road. "We were tired out," Henry wrote. "5 of our skeddadlers were there with their tents up and fires built ... Leon is here but does not feel quite as well as common. I guess rest will fetch him around again all right. We got our letters and some papers last night that were mailed on the 27th. I lost my knapsack with my Bible portfolio and all in. I picked up another one and a blanket. Will is all right. I have no more room so good bye for this time."[135]

The defeat at Chancellorsville did not depress the men, in fact many like Corporal John H. Little of Company E, expressed "perfect confidence in 'fighting Joe Hooker'" and only awaited his command to renew the battle.[136] Captain Jackson said of his men, "One thing remarkable is, that they are all in the best of spirits.... This afternoon Gen. Sickles reviewed our Corps. Our numbers are less by far than when reviewed on the 27th, but we all marched with a proud step, conscious of having done our duty—Talk of being discouraged! Not a bit of it; we are just as ready to try it again, for we have confidence in the justice of our cause, and in the ability of our leaders. I am afraid that some of the papers will assail Gen. Hooker and call for McClellan. Hooker is our man yet."[137]

Upon arrival at their old winter quarters at Falmouth, the many empty huts drove home the enormity of their loss. But there was consolation in the knowledge that they had done their duty, successfully standing the test of battle. The doubts and uncertainties were assuaged by their courageous performance under fire. They knew, as Private Henry Fleming of *The Red Badge of Courage* knew, that they "had been to touch the great death and found that, after all, it was but the great death." Felix noted that the men "never flinched in battle. I believe they would have stood till the last man had been cut down had they not been ordered off.... The privates were as heroic as the officers and the officers as the privates."[138]

A rebel prisoner, making his way to the rear, paid them the ultimate compliment. He recognized their orange ribbons and said it made no difference whether he and his comrades lay down or stood up, the fire of the "red stringed devils" "fetched them." He was, of course, wrote a soldier in a letter home, "alluding to the pieces of orange tape worn by us as a badge."[139] Captain Jackson described a similar incident: "From prisoners taken it appears that the regiments against us were the 6th Alabama and 2d Louisiana. They asked what regiment that was with red strings in their button holes (meaning 'our orange blossoms') for said they 'they gave us h—l!'"[140]

They were proud of the appellation "red stringed devils," an indication of respect won in their first battle against a tenacious enemy. The ribbons — "our orange blossoms" — were powerful symbols of their prowess and skill in battle. They took pride also in the sobriquet Orange Blossoms, bestowed on them by Colonel Ellis himself in the desperate charge at Fairview. The colonel, who gave them their orange ribbons on the banks of the Rappahannock and then led them to battle, had made them into soldiers. From that day until the last of them died eighty years later, the orange ribbon was always a part of their formal attire whenever the veterans of Chancellorsville gathered.

CHAPTER 6

"We done our duty"
May 5–June 14, 1863

The *Goshen Independent Republican* for June 18, 1863, carried the following obituary: "Died May 3 — At the battle before Chancellorsville, George G., eldest son of the late Burns and Mary Wygant, aged 20 years. His remains were buried on the battle field."

"You will have heard before this reaches you how our regiment suffered," Private Matthew Wood of Company E wrote to John Hasbrouck, editor of the *Whig Press*. "It don't look in numbers at all like the once proud 124th it used to be, having lost in killed, wounded, and missing some 235 persons." Wood noted that many regiments were going home, having served their two year enlistments "and we can but wish that the rebellion was crushed and the war over that we might do likewise. This fine army of the Potomac is not as large as it once was by a great deal, and the worst of it is the rebs will know it; but we hope to make up in spirit and energy what we lack in numbers."[1]

"I have been the witness of many a hard sight," Thomas Rodman wrote to his mother.

> It seems as if the hand of God was with me and protected me from the Balls and Shells of the enemy. Whilst hundreds of my fellow creatures were shot down by my side I did not get hurt except a slight scratch on one of my ribs from a buck shot, but it did not keep me from doing my duty on the Battle-field.... Our company went into the fight on Sabbath morning with 47 men and came out with 13 but since we came into camp it has increased to 25 non commissioned officers and all. It was a hard sight to see my old comrades shot down like sheep on all sides of me.... I never wish to see such another sight, but if I do I shall do as I did then, put my trust in the Lord and he will be my everlasting strength and protection.[2]

Private Adam W. Beakes of Company K wrote to his mother that he had been wounded and his left arm was amputated, "but I am not discouraged at all, and I do not want you to worry about me, for I am getting along well. I have done all I ever can for my country, though I would do more if I could. I would do it all over again if necessary to save my bleeding country." He said his arm did not bother him much and he considered himself fortunate "when I look back and think how many poor fellows fell to rise no more. One fell on each side of me, and we lost 4 killed and 10 wounded in the Company."[3]

Felix, "correspondent of the *Newburgh Telegraph*," gave his opinion of their commanding general:

> If Hooker did not accomplish all we expected of him we know he is no coward, and we have lost no confidence in him. All the articles that could be written against him in the State of New York, from now till the fourth of July, could not make us alter our opinion. We do not believe he is a God, or even a man without blemish; but we do believe that he can handle an army well, and that for strategy his equal is not

to be found. The army of the Potomac is ready to a man I believe to follow fighting Joe Hooker, whenever and wherever he says "comeon."[4]

Captain Jackson agreed. In a letter to the *Whig Press* he wrote,

I don't know why we fell back for we seemed to have a strong position, and I think could have held it against all the rebel forces; but I suppose Hooker knows what he is about. Hooker is said to have told the 11th corps that their break on Saturday the 2d was a disgrace to themselves, to him, their country, and caused the failure of his plans. Our own division did some very hard fighting also our corps. Hooker speaks very highly of the 3d corps. That our regiment stood well the list of killed and wounded will show.... I am beginning to feel like myself. Our old camp does look deserted — 200 less than when we started. I can't seem to realize that they are gone from us. I feel very bad about my boys, such brave fellows they were.... Several of the boys can show some marks of rebel balls through caps and clothes. I did not get a scratch but they whistled very close."[5]

Jackson finished his letter a couple of days later after he and Captain Benedict visited the men in the division hospital.

Most of them are doing well. One thing remarkable is, that they are all in the best of spirits and indeed have been from the first. This afternoon, Gen. Sickles reviewed our corps. Our numbers are less by far than when reviewed on the 27th inst., but we all marched with a proud step, conscious of having done our duty.— Talk of being discouraged! Not a bit of it; we are just as ready to try it again, for we have confidence in the justice of our cause, and in the ability of our leaders. I am afraid that some of the papers will assail Gen. Hooker and call for McClellan. Hooker is our man yet. I am quite sure that if the 11th had held its ground all would have gone well. I hope the North will not be downcast at this reverse of ours, but will be still more resolved to put down this rebellion. The rebs can stand but few more such victories.[6]

Although outnumbered more than two to one, the Confederates lost just about the same number of men killed and wounded as had the Yankees. But the lives of thousands killed and wounded were overshadowed in their importance to the cause of secession by the death of one man. Stonewall Jackson's mortal wounding doomed the Confederacy. General Lee would reorganize his army in the coming months in an attempt to make up for the loss of his best subordinate but he would find no one as able to lead men in battle as Jackson.

Captain Jackson ended his letter to the editor with some advice and a prediction. "A draft to fill up our ranks is inevitable, and should be borne in the right spirit. It is far better to fight here than at home, and it is quite certain that if we don't fight on southern soil, we will have to fight on Northern."[7]

As early as Friday, May 8, the *Newburgh Daily Telegraph* had a letter written on Monday, May 4, by 2nd Lieutenant Charles T. Cressy of Company A. His "rough guess" listed six killed and twenty wounded from his company. Later, more accurate estimates put the number at three killed and eleven wounded. He mistakenly reported that Captain Murray of Company B had been killed and Lieutenant Henry Gowdy only slightly wounded. His estimates for Company I, also from Newburgh, were inaccurate as well. While this is certainly excusable considering the confusion of battle, Cressy's comment that "we have about two hundred men left in the Regiment" sent a shiver through anyone who read it. Two hundred left out of over five hundred engaged would mean that 60 percent of the regiment was killed, wounded, or missing in action.[8]

Captain Leander Clark of Company I sent a list of the wounded for the same issue of the *Daily Telegraph*. Among them were Sergeant Charles Stewart, who was shot in the head; James Bovill, shot in the arm; William Wallace, in the leg; Patrick Ryan, in the foot; and so on. A group of seven names was added to the list without specifying if the men were wounded or missing. Four names of men "supposed to be dead" completed the list.

The *Montgomery Standard* waited a week to publish the casualties from among the local boys. The *Standard*'s coverage started with the "Roll of Company H" listing all the men present at the battle. Then came the particulars:

Lieutenant Henry Gowdy, of Walden; shot through calf of leg, May 3d, and died May 11th.

Corporal William L. Fairchild, of Walden; shot through head and died instantly. Corporal David Mould, of Ulsterville; shot through head and died instantly.

Private Van Keuren Crist, of Walden; shot through body.

Private George O. Fuller, of Montgomery; struck in head by piece of shell, and died instantly.

Private Joseph W. Delamater, of Shawangunk; shot through both eyes.[9]

Listed under "Wounded" came the names of nineteen local men followed by a description of their wounds and to which Washington, D.C., hospital they had been sent, if that information was known.

The lengthy coverage continued under the heading "Incidents of the Battle." "Company H went into battle 53 strong. There were killed and wounded as to be disabled, 27." Then, as if to further horrify and dismay the families at home, the paper added, "The regiment mustered 162 men for Picket duty on Sunday evening. Nearly every man in the company received some token of the enemy presence by at least a bullet hole through some portion of their clothing."[10]

"Lt. Gowdy killed" was the heading Private Gouvernor Legg wrote at the top of the letter he sent home.

> I suppose that you have hurd of the death of my first lieutenant Henry Gowdy of walden it is a sad day for this company the day it lost him he was one of the best little fellows that ever lived every man that knowde him loved him i never saw him out of temper allways the same way never spoke a crows word to aney of us Go to him and ask him for any thing and if it was in his power to Grant he would never say no i lost my best frend in the army when I lost him.... God only knows how many poor famelys this day are mornin for the dear ones lost in battle but sow it is and seems as tho it was Gont to remane so till every man is Gon.[11]

When accounts of Captain Henry Murray's death reached home, his family mourned him as lost; the local newspaper even published his obituary. Meanwhile on the picket line, Captain Weygant had just finished reading the obituary when word came of an ambulance train approaching under a flag of truce. In the third wagon, Weygant found Murray "Why, Captain ... I was sure you were killed, and was told George Hawley had buried you on the field; besides I have just been reading your obituary in a Goshen paper." Murray's mumbled reply could not be understood. A bullet had "passed in between his lips, carried away his two upper and two lower teeth, gone through the back of his neck, and lodged just under the skin of his shoulder. His lacerated tongue and mouth were so swollen he could scarcely speak." But Murray tried again: "Worth a dozen dead men" he said with effort.[12]

A telegram was sent home with the news and he was soon joined in the hospital by his father, the Honorable William Murray, president of the Goshen National Bank, and by his uncle, the Honorable Spencer Murray, president of the National Bank of Orange County. Both had been members of Congress and were good friends with Secretary of State William Seward. When these well connected men reached the capital, a special engine was placed at their disposal to take them to the division hospital near Falmouth. Captain Weygant visited Murray there with another officer who, in a "doleful voice," read aloud Murray's obituary to him. As it turned out, he was not the first to tease the young captain but was surely the last. Murray had borrowed a revolver from the officer in the next bed and threatened to "put a hole through the very next person who unfolded a newspaper in front of him." Captain Murray was soon on his way home to recuperate.[13]

Murray certainly deserved the special care he got, but many others just as deserving were wasting away from the wounds they had suffered in the service of their country. Weygant wrote that every morning "could be seen in front of the hospital tents at Aquia Creek a line of stretchers, most of which held the dead form of somebody's husband, father, son, brother or loved one, in most cases waiting a soldier's unceremonious coffinless burial" in an unmarked grave.[14]

The care that the wounded received, or rather the lack of it, became a hot issue with the folks back home in Orange County when a letter from a soldier who signed himself "C.G." was printed in the *Newburgh Telegraph*. The author was Private Charles Goodsell of Company C, and he sent it directly to Mr. E.W. Grey, editor of the newspaper, describing the abysmal medical care he received following a wound to his foot at Chancellorsville.

Editor Grey took it upon himself to write a short introduction to Goodsell's letter, catching the public's eye and alerting them to a very serious problem.

It is with considerable reluctance, that we publish the following letter from a member of the 124th. We venture to say that nothing has been printed since the war began which will awaken such universal indignation. We were led to suppose that unprecedented efforts had been made to promote the comfort of our friends. The letter referred to must convince every one who reads it, that the truth has been concealed.

Within the last few days messengers have been arriving from the camps of our favorite regiment. They have knocked at the door of two hundred houses, telling children that they were orphans, wives that they were widows, sisters that their brothers had been butchered, and parents that the pride of their hearts had been made to bite the dust. But no one supposed that the shocking inhumanity which could leave the dead and dying on the field was present in the hospital.

Private Goodsell's letter originated from the hospital of the 3rd Division, 3rd Corps located near Potomac Creek, Virginia. He wrote it on May 11, 1863:

Sir: I believe that your paper is always ready to chronicle the grievances of the oppressed and as I, with many others, belong to this class at the present moment, I cannot help from telling you how we have been used since we received our marks of honor at the battle of Chancellorsville. After having our wounds dressed near the field we were told to make our way to the hospital of the 3d Division, where we would be well cared for. I was fortunate enough to get a ride in an ambulance. I could not have walked for I had a bullet in my foot. On reaching the hospital, my foot was looked at and bandaged up, and I was told to keep it wet till the inflammation was reduced, when the ball would be extracted. I got nothing to eat and had no place to go to—first come first served, was the rule and the hospital tents were crowded. When near night another tent was put up and into it eighteen of us 124th boys stowed ourselves—we had nothing to lie on, and very few of us had anything to cover us with, and to add further to our misery we could get nothing to eat and it had commenced to rain. Soon the rain came through our tent, and those who were able had to dig a canal through the center to carry off the water. We put in a miserable night but hoped for better things in the morning. We were, however, doomed to disappointment. We could get no doctor with time enough to look at our wounds. We could get nothing to eat and had to steal—Dr. Marshall was no cook, and referred us to Ward Master, who referred us to a cook that had drawn rations for us already. Mr. Cook referred us to the d—l as he had nothing for us. In the afternoon of that day we got some bread and coffee. We got along in this style til Friday, dressing our own wounds and feeding when we could get anything to eat. On Thursday night Drs. Marshall and a little New Hampshire doctor—came into the place where we lay in order to get the names of those worst wounded in order to send them to Washington. They looked as if they had just come from a good supper with plenty of fixings, and though they had two lanterns they did not see the worst cases. The result was that some were sent off who were wounded, but not badly—one even got off who had only a slight bruise on his foot the skin was not cut. I lay helpless with a bullet in my foot, another next to me had one in his arm, still another had one in his cheek, but they happened to be asleep and the good pious doctors would not disturb them.

On Friday afternoon I insisted to having my foot dressed and the

Dr. Edward Marshall, assistant surgeon, 124th New York. Private Charles Goodsell's letter home about the neglect he received may have led to Dr. Marshall's dismissal (Michael J. McAfee collection).

Wounded at Fredericksburg. Most of these men appear to have leg wounds but they are fortunate enough to have a building as shelter (Library of Congress, Prints & Photographs Division).

ball extracted — it was done — I was removed on a stretcher to another tent where my foot was taken off, had it been done at first I would not have cared so much, but I do feel badly when I think that the bullet might have been taken out and my foot saved, had there been a man worthy the name of a doctor here. I am now in a better ward where I have a good bed and plenty to eat, but some of my comrades are still badly off, two of them I fear will have to undergo my unhappy experience and in a few days lose each a hand. The doctors here are miserable specimens of humanity. The truth of what I have said I will prove to you by the experience of dozens. If we get over our wounds we will not have to thank the doctors. By publishing you will oblige.
C. G. 124th Reg't. NYSV[15]

Goodsell's accusations and Gray's willingness to print them for the public to read raised serious questions not just about medical care, but about leadership as well. Colonel Ellis had, after all, personally chosen most of the commissioned officers of the 124th New York. It did not take long for a reply to arrive at the newspaper from the pen of the short tempered colonel.

Sirs:- Yours of May 21st is just received. In reply I have to state, that the three Medical officers of my regiment have well and ably performed their duties, as their present standing in the Division testifies.... I can speak personally of the 3d Division, 3d Corps Hospital, as I was there to-day and inspected it thoroughly; and you can use my name to the effect that the wounded and sick of this Regiment are receiving every possible attention and doing well, many severe cases rapidly recovering. Any inattention to my brave wounded I would personally resent.[16]

Ellis' letter was printed in the *Telegraph* on June 4, the same day that Dr. Mary E. Walker wrote from Windmill Point, Virginia, to Dr. Lydia Sayer Hasbrouck in Middletown, New York. Dr. Hasbrouck, an early advocate of dress reform for women and the first woman to be elected to office in the state of New York, edited *The Sybil*, a woman's newspaper. Her husband was John Hasbrouck, the editor of the Middletown *Whig Press*, a supporter of the war and of Lincoln and the bane of Orange County peace Democrats and Copperheads. Dr. Walker was writing to calm the folks back home with regard to the care their relatives were receiving in the army hospitals. The short article was titled "Our Wounded in Hospital."

> There are a large number of sick and wounded at the various hospitals on the Potomac, and a number of ladies are staying in them. The men are, as a matter of course, better cared for than they would be if they were absent. At the 3d corps hospital where the "Orange Blossoms" are, I must say for the consolation of your county people that Mrs. Husband, from Philadelphia, Penn., is there. She has a son in the corps, and feels a mother's sympathy for all the men who are away from home.... Many of the sick told me that they would not know how to live without her.... The Orange county people would do well to send their hospital stores to her.... There are Pennsylvania men at her hospital, but she says she "knows no State," but treats all alike as soldiers.... I am in great haste this morning, as it is rumored that there is a move Towards the front, and I hope to be of service if there is professional work to be done. Yours as ever.
>
> Dr. Mary E. Walker.[17]

When Editor Grey published Colonel Ellis' letter, he prefaced it with the comment that it did not "invalidate" the accusations made about the neglect the wounded had experienced. He added, "The impression that the Surgeons of the Regiment have been parties to this neglect, we are happy to have the opportunity to correct."[18] Dr. Walker's letter and Editor Grey's supportive comments about the doctors attached to the regiment probably did calm the worried parents and spouses.

But the finer points of the argument were lost on Private Goodsell, the twenty-year-old soldier who originally raised the issue. He died of his wounds at the Potomac Creek Hospital nine days after writing his letter to Editor Grey. As for Dr. Marshall, the man accused by Goodsell of not having time to tend to his wounds, he was quietly dismissed from the service for unspecified reasons two months later.[19]

Not all the stories of the captured or wounded were so grim. Corporal Frank Lee, Company B, was among the men who did not hear the order to retire after the second charge at Fairview on Sunday, May 3. When the Confederates overran the position, those not killed were captured and "'toted' to the rear." Now a prisoner in the middle of a battle, Lee found himself under Union artillery fire. "Our shells burst in the woods where the rebels were, and I tell you there was some tall dodging." The Confederate soldiers lay all around him "as thick as hasty pudding, some yelling with pain, others taking it easy, others crawling and walking along as best they could. One fellow was wounded with a canister shot as large as a hen's egg and as I passed him he said, 'Yank, give me a drink.'" After Lee did so, the man wanted to know how badly he had been wounded. Lee could clearly see that the wound was mortal but did his best to reassure his enemy by telling him he really could not tell how badly he had been hit.

> The Confederates marched the prisoners to Spotsylvania Court House. "There we were put in the yard and locked up. It reminded me of the Park Barracks in New York City. They had us caged up like so many wild beasts. Next day they marched us to Guiness Station. We all thought we could get transportation from there, but we didn't. We were put in an open lot and managed to shelter us from the sun with our rubber blankets. As soon as we got our names registered, we drew rations which was some Flour and "Salt mule," which when cooked was so tender it was like eating pine chips. We made bread from flour, which after being baked was heavy enough for ballast on a "seventy-four," or would do for a grindstone. We dare not eat much of it for fear we could not get up when we lay down — it was ponderous. Our rations were about a pound of flour for each man.

The place Lee was writing about was Guinea Station, a stop on the Richmond, Fredericksburg & Potomac Railroad. Here they remained for two days and must have been marched to Richmond along a railroad track as Lee wrote, "We rode all the way by railroad, on foot." It was good that he kept his sense of humor because it was a forty-nine mile hike.

> We drew eight "Hard Tacks," that lasted us until we reached our destination, where we saw two niggers to one white man. They stowed us in their old Tobacco Houses, three hundred on a floor. We had to lay heads and points, spoon fashion and in every other way to make room. The room gave forth all sorts of villainous smells, besides being densely inhabited with "crawlin ferlie." At night they deployed as skir-mishers over us, and when we would turn over we could feel them "rallying by fours." Our rations were then half a loaf of bread per day.[20]

On May 11, the Richmond *Examiner* printed an account of the arrival of the prisoners taken at Chancellorsville. Under the heading, "A Streaming In of Yankee Prisoners," the rebel newspaper did not paint a very favorable picture.

> The city was inundated on Saturday afternoon by the arrival from different quarters of between two and three thousand Yankee prisoners of war, the main body marching from Guinea station, and pouring into the city through Brooke Avenue and Main street in a dark blue stream of Yankee uniforms, dusky with dirt and begrimed with blood and the battle smoke. The line reached three or four squares, and moved, flanked by a fringe of Confederate greys as guard. This body numbered two thousand and more rank and file of the "finest army on the planet." The mass of them gave unmistakable evidence, in their low, repulsive countenances, of their Teutonic and Celtic extraction, particularly the former, and "Yaw, yaw," sounded along the line, as they moved, like the grunt of so many pigs.... They will all be paroled and sent off as soon as possible to City Point, as it is not desireable to hold such an increased population when it can be reduced, especially as the Government has to pay for it.[21]

Frank Lee continued with the tale of his journey.

> We lay there two days and then were taken to Bell Island. At the latter place we were two days and all we got to eat was one hard tack; we then started for City Point a distance of twenty-one miles one way and thirty-two the other. They took us the longest way of course. At Manchester, near Richmond, two and a half hard tacks were issued to each man. We started again for City Point at one o'clock in the after-noon. They intended to have marched us all night, but there was a heavy shower came up and we got stuck in the mud, so we took lodgings for the night, having marched twenty miles that afternoon, and it was eleven o'clock when we halted. Next morning we started again, passed through Petersburgh at noon, and reached City Point, where our good old uncle Samuel's transports waited us. We were two weeks with the Rebels, and our rations were about one pound of flour, eleven hard tack and two loaves of bread apiece. I tell you I got as fat as a June shad, and my legs swelled to the fabulous size of bean poles. We were conveyed to Annapolis and from thence to Alexandria, where I now am. Write me as soon as you get this and tell me how Captain Murray came out. The last I saw of him was when the firing com-menced when I heard him say "Sock it to them boys!" Give my regards to our officers and men.[22]

William Wirt Bailey, the sergeant who was demoted to private just prior to Chancellorsville, had also been a wounded prisoner of the Confederates. As with most of the others, he wanted to communicate to his relatives as soon as possible that he was alive. He wrote to his father on the first day he crossed back into Union lines. "I suppose you gave me up for dead, but know the Lord saw fit to spare my life a while longer. It grieves me so to think how we were cut up that I can hardly write. I was shot by a ball under the left ear, and came out my right cheek on the bone. The men wonder that it did not kill me. I don't suffer any pain at all hardly, and it is doing well."

He told his family that Dan Webb was wounded in the thigh, and that Lieutenant Jacob Denton was dead. "The Rebs treated me very kindly indeed.... I long to get home.... I have got a bad wound, but not dangerous. We done our duty, as you know by the way we were cut up."[23]

For those men still with the regiment in camp at Falmouth, Virginia, the routine of military life returned to normal. "We are well as usual," Henry Howell wrote to his mother at the end of May. "We are drilling quite a good deal now days. Company drill in the morning and battalion drill in the afternoon. I was down to the hospital and staid a day and night with the wounded boys. They are getting along as well as could be expected considering the warm weather." Adam Beakes, who was related to Henry, and 1st Sgt. Theodore Robeson had their beds next to each other, "laughing with the rest of the boys all the while." Egbert Puff, who lost his right arm, got a horse and rode the short distance to the camp to visit his old comrades whenever he felt like it. His goal was to be home for the 4th of July, "have a nice horse and pretty girl," and take her to the holiday ball. "Such fellows that keeps up their spirits will get well a great deal quicker than others."[24]

The soldiers in the hospitals tried to stay together as much as possible. They had to rely on one another and on their friends in camp to tend to their needs. But now these men, who had shared the experience of battle, were more than just friends and relatives who knew each other back home in Orange County. Now they were comrades, veterans who stood side by side in the face of the enemy, their orange ribbons symbols of a hard-won reputation. One day, an aide to the slain General Whipple was touring the ward. He walked near to where one of the Orange County boys lay, stopping short when he saw the piece of "red tape" in his button hole. "Here is an orange blossom," he said, reaching into his pocket. He took out a dollar and gave it to the man so that he might buy some extra food. "Quite a compliment to old Orange and her soldiers," Henry Howell noted. "General Hooker went all through the hospital encouraging the men. He tells them to get well is all he asks them to do for he has got enough to whip the Rebbles without them. I don't know whether he has or not but hope he has."[25]

Lieutenant Colonel Francis Cummins, "Old Shiloh," was a constant fixture at the hospital, badgering division headquarters about furloughs for the wounded and tending to the needs of the men. "He is one of the best men to us wounded boys," Howell wrote. "He gives them money & anything else that is in his power. It is said that he gave out a hundred dollars in one day. I heard him say that he would give out all he had and then if any one wants any more he would borrow more. He wants to resign but says he wont as long as the Rebs are getting the better of us. I hope he wont for we would never get another man to fill his place as well."

The man who would take Cummins's place should he resign would be Major James Cromwell, whose reputation was quite positive among the troops before they departed for the war. Everyone knew that the colonel had his eye on a brigadier's star but Howell perceived that Cromwell had also changed. "Colonel Ellis thinks more of promotion. So does the Major."[26]

If that was the case, Ellis soon got his chance when, after the Battle of Chancellorsville, the 122nd Pennsylvania, a nine-months regiment, was mustered out and departed for home. With them went Colonel Franklin, who had commanded the brigade. Since the colonel of the 86th New York had been killed at Chancellorsville, that regiment was now commanded by an officer junior to Ellis. If indeed he was interested in promotion, here was the opportunity, for he was now in command of a two-regiment brigade with another battle likely soon. If things went well and if a couple of other regiments were added to form a brigade, Ellis might yet get his star. As for Lieutenant Colonel Cummins, he was senior after Ellis and would then command the 124th which, no doubt, was just fine with Private Howell.

The 124th had returned to its old camp after Chancellorsville, which relieved the men of constructing new quarters. The downside had to do with health conditions. "We did not remove our camp for Sanitary reasons but we had ought to. Other regiments did. It is impossible that a regiment can spend the summer in their winter quarters without getting a sight of vermin." To spruce things up, they cut evergreen boughs and planted small trees both for shade and for decoration. "We have made a regular little grove out of our camp.... We had built a new cookhouse and got a new cook. Wheat and Parson had been a little to free with the sugar, Potatoes and such things to be tolerated any longer." Henry did not say who replaced privates Simeon Wheat and James Parsons but he noted that the "boys have been finding fault with it for some time past."

As Howell was writing his letter home he could hear a brass band playing a short distance away. The band practiced a great deal "so we have plenty of music." He could not say the same for what he called "our common drum Corps" who "are not worth listening to especially if we happen to be close to them." But camp life did have its pleasant diversions. It was late spring and the weather turned decidedly warmer. The company streets were easier to keep tidy when the mud dried up, quarters could be cleaned and aired out, and bedding changed. The men took steps to rid themselves of lice that infested their bodies, uniforms, and bedding. Soldiers tried to keep themselves and their uniforms as clean as possible but in the winter bathing was simply not possible. Now they seized the opportunity. "We went down to the Potomac creek to bathe one night last week. I never seen so many men in the water at one time before."[27]

On June 2, a letter from Democratic Congressman Charles Winfield was read to the 124th at dress parade. He congratulated the regiment for its performance in the recent battle, telling the men "we hardly dared to hope the regiment would stand the first severe and terrible battle shock with the cool and unfaltering courage displayed on the occasion referred to." The people of Orange County were proud of them, he said. "May Heaven spare you all."[28]

Ellis was quick to reply with a letter that was, like Winfield's, published in the newspapers throughout the county. "We have striven to do our duty.... When asked for a list of officers and men who conducted themselves bravely in the fight, I could but say 'Here is the muster-roll of the regiment.'" Ever mindful of crediting the regiment for its exploits, Ellis wrote that with the death of General Whipple in battle, no after-action report had been written from the Third Division, which "made us fear our efforts might never be appreciated by the ones we cared most for, but these fears are now removed."[29]

With summer approaching, the peaceful interlude north of the Rappahannock was about to come to a dramatic end. Fighting Joe Hooker still had plenty of fight left in him and he planned to use his mounted arm to bring the fight to the enemy. In the coming battle, fought just south of the Rappahannock at Brandy Station, the war for the Union would take an historic turn. Not only was it to be the biggest cavalry battle ever fought in the Western Hemisphere, it foreshadowed mounted engagements for the rest of the war. At Brandy Station, the Federal cavalry ceased to be a joke, but instead demonstrated that it had become a lethal force. In this momentous battle, two divisions of infantry would act as support for the cavalry. The regiments chosen to go must be the most dependable foot soldiers in the Army of the Potomac and the 124th New York would be among them.

On May 27, the ever-diligent head of the Bureau of Military Information, Colonel George Sharpe, sent headquarters a detailed analysis of the Confederate positions south of the Rappahannock. He pinpointed the locations of the major infantry formations and then included a nugget of intelligence that caught Hooker's eye: "There are three brigades of cavalry 3 miles from Culpeper Court-House, toward Kelly's Ford. They can at present turn out only 4,700 men for duty, but have many dismounted men, and the horses are being constantly and rapidly recruited by the spring growth of grass. These are Fitz. Lee's, William H. Fitzhugh Lee's, and Wade Hampton's brigades." He followed this up with something that would move Hooker to action: "The Confederate army is under marching orders, and an order from General Lee was very lately read to the troops, announcing a campaign of long marches and hard fighting, in a part of the country where they would have no railroad transportation.... All the deserters say that the idea is very prevalent in the ranks that they are about to move forward upon or above our right flank."[30]

Enemy cavalry at Culpeper in such large numbers might mean a cavalry raid, a favored pastime of Major General James E.B. Stuart. Based upon Sharpe's assessment, Hooker ordered his new cavalry commander, Major General Alfred Pleasanton, to attack Stuart and scatter his formations around Culpeper before the raid could get started, and he said so in a dispatch to General Halleck, the overall commander of Union Cavalry. "As the accumulation of the heavy rebel force of cavalry about Culpepper may mean mischief, I am determined to break it up in its incipiency. I shall send all my cavalry against them stiffened by about three thousand infantry."[31]

What Hooker did not know was that the Confederates intended much more than just another joy ride around the Yankees. Lee was planning something really big: he wanted to strike north a second time, invade Maryland and Pennsylvania, and defeat the Yankees on their own ground. The benefits, if successful, would be monumental indeed. The British might yet insist on bringing the two warring sides to the negotiating table. A successful campaign might relieve pressure on Vicksburg and Virginia farmers might have a chance to complete the growing season and gather their crops without battles being fought on their land. Finally, a big Union defeat might cause Lincoln, already hounded by the Copperheads and those among his own party who had lost confidence in him, to sue for peace. Add to that the fact that in the two most recent encounters with the Army of the Potomac at Fredericksburg and Chancellorsville, the Yankee leadership had failed the men in the ranks. No such failure of leadership crippled the Army of Northern Virginia.

The Rebel cavalry reported to be in the vicinity of Culpeper were there to screen the movements of the Rebel infantry, two corps of which were already present. Once Lee had his men concentrated in the Culpeper area, he planned to march them over the Blue Ridge Mountains into the Shenandoah Valley, then north to Maryland and Pennsylvania. Confederate cavalry would block the passes through the Blue Ridge to keep the Yankees from detecting the move. The cavalry would then ride east and north to spread mayhem in the Yankee rear.

Another thing that Hooker did not know was that Stuart's cavalry was no longer at Culpeper. Stuart had moved his troopers forward to Brandy Station, a stop on the Orange and Alexandria Railroad five miles north of Culpeper. The flamboyant general had no inking that the usually lethargic Yankee horsemen were up to anything so audacious as seeking a battle with his legendary mounted brigades. In fact, he used the time to plan a series of reviews for the entertainment of General Lee and the local civilians — especially the ladies. To top things off, there would be parties and a gala ball.

To the men in the Federal ranks on the north side of the Rappahannock, nothing seemed amiss. Corporal William Howell's diary entries for the last half of May were full of the mundane: "draw new clothing"; "A couple of reb deserters come in. They said they were fighting against us on the 3rd. They said we red stringed fellows gave them a warm reception"; "Return to camp having had a pleasant time on picket for a wonder"; "go down to the creek for a swim"; "Reported capture of Vicksburg"; and constant drill. At the end of the month William was on picket duty along the Rappahannock. "The rebs are quite familiar on the opposite shore. They go in to swim & fish. First strawberries of the season." On the first day in June, "two deserters crossed the river and gave themselves up.... I have the diaheria very bad."[32]

On June 3, Major Cromwell of the 124th New York inspected the regiment. At three o'clock the morning of June 4, Lieutenant Colonel Cummins made the rounds of the company commanders telling each of them that he had just received orders to have the regiment ready to move at daylight. An hour later assembly was sounded and the regiment turned out in heavy marching order, each man carrying all his gear including knapsack, if he had not lost it at Chancellorsville, rubber blanket, wool blanket, extra rations, and extra ammunition. The men remained in line for an hour but were then dismissed and told to remain in the immediate area, ready to move out at a moment's notice. Needless to say, "the day passed quietly away without bringing us any further orders."[33] Private Howell noted in his diary, "At ½ past 3 this morning we were called up for some move or other but after waiting until after sunrise we were taken back to our quarters with instructions to be ready to fall in at any moment. No order came however."[34] William Howell wrote in his diary that day, "Called out & form in line rebs reported making a raid have a severe headache."[35]

Mid-afternoon on June 5, Captain Weygant was sitting on a cracker box outside his log hut pondering the events of the past few weeks and his prospects for the future when he heard artillery fire coming from the direction of Fredericksburg. The sound grew from a few distant thuds to a steady roar, leading him to the conclusion that some kind of river crossing was underway.[36] Private Howell was on guard duty at camp. "They all appear to be preparing for a move. At five o'clock this evening were roaring in the vicinity of Fredericksburg about an hour. It was reported that we have two Corps across before the City." Then he added, "I had a toothache for about an hour this afternoon."[37] His brother's headache had developed into a "severe cold in the head" but he added "a mustard plaster affords relief."[38]

Captain Weygant went inside his quarters, buckled on his sword belt and gave directions to his servant to fill his canteens and haversacks. He put boxes of sardines in his jacket pocket then he stepped out to alert his men. The company commander's quarters were at the head of the company street and the man saw him getting ready. Many of them had already slung their cartridge boxes over their shoulders, buckled on their belts, and strapped on their knapsacks "walking thoughtfully up and down by their gun stacks." Meanwhile a couple of "dead-beats" could be seen making their way toward the surgeon's tent, doing an unconvincing hobble to avoid marching to battle. But, as before, this was another false alarm and the men returned to their quarters.[39]

Lieutenant William Mapes took the opportunity to write a few lines to his brother Jesse.

> We did not march this morning but are under orders at 6 P.M. tonight. Colonel Ellis goes on a reconi-
> sance with 500 men we are ordered to report to Hartwood Church about 5 or 6 miles near Warrentons
> we may have a tough time. Cant say but I am ready. We go with 3 days rations &c Sheriff Cowdrey came
> here today his son is quite sick & not expected to live. Do not be uneasy about me. The paymaster
> wanted to pay us this afternoon but the Col would not permit him to we will get paid when we come
> back.
>
> I am well & hearty. I saw a letter from Mitt to Lewis Adams in it he wished he had the Eloquence of
> Webster the patriotism of Seymour & fearless-ness of Valandigham. I wished he possesed the Patriotism
> of a *Nigger*; *who* is willing to fight for a country in which he has no interest at stake. One in which he
> cant say his soul is his own. I think that the Rebs have stepped out of the Back door & we cant find them
> cant tell. I am the only officer with the Company.[40]

That morning a soldier from the 86th New York who served as a clerk at 3rd Corps head-quarters told of how he had just copied an order calling for picked regiments to form the infantry support that would accompany a large body of Union horsemen on a "secret expedition." Within an hour the rumor spread that Colonel Ellis' brigade had been chosen to go from the 3rd Corps. A while later Colonel Cummins, now in command of the regiment, received orders that all unnec-essary baggage including knapsacks, tents, and blankets were to be left behind as this was to be a "long and rapid march." At five o'clock in the afternoon the drummers beat the long roll, the signal to form up.

Shortly, Ellis and his staff rode up. They took their places at the head of the column of troops and the colonel ordered his bugler to sound "forward." Henry Howell wrote, "At five o'clock this afternoon we started with a blanket piece of tent and three days rations, expecting to be gone six days on a reconnaissance in the vicinity of Hartwood Church. We marched until one o'clock in the morning stopping at Cropps Tavern that being about 12 miles. 500 from our division were here being from the 86th and 124th."[41] His brother William had been on guard duty at headquarters that day and may well have been the source of the rumor. When he was relieved, he reported to camp in time to prepare himself.[42] With all the bugle calls, drum rolls, rumors, and clerks broadcasting what was going on at headquarters, it is a wonder that the expedition remained a secret from the enemy.

As soon as the column cleared the camp the rain came down, drenching the men and turning the surface of the Virginia road to gooey Virginia mud. "On Saturday evening we started from our old camp near Falmouth, to go as we were told, only to Hartwood Church, distant from the old camp only about six miles. We passed Hartwood Church, however, without halting; and on, and on we went, not stopping for the night for rest and sleep til about 2 o'clock, A.M." After a difficult march over rough terrain, the regiment halted near a place Captain Weygant called Cropp's Tavern or Spottsville. He figured they had covered nearly sixteen miles and all were thoroughly worn out by the effort.[43]

By Sunday morning the weather was much improved. A number of men exhausted by the march were sent back to Falmouth. The column moved forward under a bright, clear sky through a part of Virginia almost untouched by the ravages of war. But this was still Secessia and to prevent anyone riding to warn Stuart's pickets that a lot of Yankee horse and foot were headed their way, men and boys encountered along the route were placed under arrest. Despite Colonel Ellis' assurances that no harm would come to them, at least one woman fainted on her doorstep when her husband was led away by the despised Yankees. "After that we left at nearly every house a group of weeping women and children."[44] Henry Howell wrote, "We got our breakfast and started on. We made a forced march of 15 miles in 8 hours. We are on the Warrenton and Falmouth road. We were nearly all 'played' when we halted for the night. We pick up all citizens and make them take the oath of Allegiance. Co. I is patrol for the day. The country is quite fine along here."[45]

William Howell wrote on June 7, "The Harris light cavalry pass by us. We go through the crossroads hunting guerillas. Get on the Warrenton road & go to Bealton some 18 miles."[46] The column reached Bealton Station on the Orange and Alexandria railroad at about five o'clock. By Captain Weygant's reckoning they had covered about thirty-five miles in twenty-four hours. They spent the rest of Sunday and most of Monday in place. Just after dark they moved along the railroad toward the river, halting about a mile back from Beverley's Ford on the Rappahannock River. Private Howell wrote, "Struck the Warrenton Railroad at Bealeton, and followed that a couple of miles and then turned to the right and went up the river a piece and halted for the night. We drew six days rations. We passed by a couple of splendid plantations but they begin to show the effects of war."[47]

Pleasanton had been ordered to divide his command, sending one force across the Rappahannock at Beverly's Ford, the other at Kelly's Ford about seven miles downstream. The two wings would converge on Culpeper, there to "disperse and destroy" the enemy force, wagon trains, and supplies.[48] Pleasanton made his preparations accordingly and, on June 9, sent General John Buford with the First Division and the Reserve Brigade of cavalry and a division of infantry commanded by General Adelbert Ames toward Beverley's Ford.[49] The infantry would serve as "a moving *point d'appui* to rally on at all times, which no cavalry force can be able to shake."[50] In other words, the infantry would serve as an anchor; should the cavalry be forced to retreat, they would have a place to fall back upon and rally. In the *New York Times* account of the battle, the reporter wrote, "The infantry force selected challenged particular admiration. The regiments were small, but they were *reliable*— such for instance as the Second, Third, and Seventh Wisconsin, Second and Thirty-third Massachusetts, Sixth Maine, Eighty-sixth and One Hundred and Twenty-fourth New York, and one or two others of like character."[51]

Surgeon Thompson understood right away what it meant to be chosen. "Our main force in the expedition is constituted of Cavalry. The infantry part of the force is composed of only five hundred men from each of the corps, the 3d, 11th, and 12th. I may mention, by-the-by, that only those Regiments were chosen whose military record was unexceptionable, or that had gained a distinguished reputation in the army. This means of course a compliment for the 124th."[52]

Before daylight on the morning of Tuesday, June 9, "everything was stirring" as the 124th moved in the direction of the ford.[53] They had marched but a short distance when firing could be heard ahead. Hastening to the river, someone had the idea that a bridge could be put across but Colonel Ellis would have none of that. He waded his horse into the Rappahannock to check the depth then ordered his men to follow him across.[54] "The water was about three feet deep, but the bottom was good, and we got over with out any trouble, except, *wet pants*," wrote one soldier, who proudly added, "Some cavalry crossed before us, but the *124th was the first regiment of infantry* that went over."[55] The infantry headed up a road toward a heavy belt of woods.

"I think we rather surprised the enemy in crossing the river, as there was only a few pickets guarding the Ford where we crossed." wrote Surgeon Thompson.[56] The usually vigilant Confederates were totally unaware of the large body of cavalry and infantry with artillery support that had been just across the river for almost a day.

"We have again had a chance to 'smell powder,'" Isaac Decker of Company K penciled into his journal.

> We waded the Rappahannock at Beverly Ford. The water was about two and half feet deep. There were some cavalry crossed before us. The "rebs" did not try to hinder us from crossing, and there was no firing until they got about a third of a mile from the river, when they charged on the rebel cavalry and took some prisoners and drove the remainder of them. Our Regt. was the first infantry that crossed the river. We were sent to find out where the "rebs" were and did not expect to stay where we went.[57]

Private Henry Dill, writing from "Gum Springs, Virginy" a week later, noted, "Wee Had quite A Fight At Beryelys Ford Wee Ataked the Rebs In the morning they Was geting Brekfist thay Had Cakes miketed to Bake And thay Fight Like Devels But it Was No go the shells Come thru the Woods and made the Limbes Crack."[58] William Howell wrote in his diary for June 9, "We follow the cavalry over the river take the enemys pickets by surprise go in to a woods where we are exposed to a heavy shelling."[59]

The first mounted unit crossing at Beverly Ford was the 8th New York Cavalry led by Colonel Benjamin F. Davis, commander of the 1st Brigade. They encountered pickets from the 6th Virginia Cavalry, which, although taken by surprise, put up a spirited fighting retreat. The rest of the 6th Virginia was about two miles to the rear near St. James Church. Between them and the Yankee cavalry was a "mile wide belt of woods" that would figure prominently in the infantry part of the action.[60]

In the open stood the sixteen guns of Stuart's Horse Artillery, which might have been overrun had the Union cavalry pressed the attack right away. As it was, the guns, commanded by Major Robert Beckham, were pulled back 1,000 yards to a ridgeline. From this position near St. James Church, the artillery covered two approach roads and a wide expanse of fields which led up to the wood line where the Federal infantry would soon be posted. The Confederate cavalry brigade in Buford's front was led by his West Point classmate, General William E. "Grumble" Jones. During most of the morning, Union and Confederate horsemen waged a back-and-forth battle, each trying to gain an advantage over the other.

Private Howell wrote, "We forded the Rappahannock. Pleasantons Cavalry being in the advance and flying artillery and then our Regiment, the 86th, 33rd Mass and others. The whole force were picked men 500 being from each Corps. We were soon engaged with Stewarts cavalry."[61]

"The slope from the river, back, from about half a mile was clear, and then you came to a large piece of woods, and there the cavalry was at work with the enemy. As soon as we were acrossed we were ordered to the front, and as we marched up the slope we met cavalry men coming back, some of them with prisoners; others wounded or helping those that were. We soon got into the woods, on the Gordonsville road I think, and every little way we would see dead and dieing rebs."[62]

Weygant described these as scenes only seen "in rear of contending battle-lines." Wounded men on horseback, pale and bloody, made their way to the rear while others staggered by on foot. Some were carried to the rear by "apparently tender-hearted, but really cowardly comrades," who were, in Weygant's opinion, more eager to get out of harm's way than to save a fellow soldier.

"Colonel Ellis' regiments were the first infantry on the field. But ere long batteries on both sides opened fire, and we heard through the woods beyond, shouts of officers, shrill bugle blasts, and the southern squeal and northern yell of charge and countercharge."[63] As they got closer to the fight, bullets began to "hiss and whistle about us." Ellis ordered Weygant, his company in the lead, to halt and remain behind to cover the right flank of the column with companies A and F. "We were now moving along a rough road through a slight ravine, in woods so dense that we could not see twenty yards away." A general officer rode up and ordered the captain to halt his two companies while the rest of the brigade moved on.

About a quarter of an hour later, a staff officer came up with orders from General Ames to rejoin the regiment. He could not tell Weygant where he might find the 124th but helpfully offered that he had just seen two regiments moving through the woods and suggested he try to find them. The young captain had gone only a short distance when Colonel Ellis himself rode up and led them away in the opposite direction. The two companies made their way through the dense woods until they could see a large open field ahead. Ellis ordered Weygant to deploy his men at the edge of the woods but to keep them under cover. As he rode away Ellis called back, "If the devils charge you, make a determined stand — hold them at all hazards until reinforcements can be brought to you."[64]

Weygant formed his men into a loose skirmish line, four feet between each man, using the trees for cover; the captain chose what looked to be the biggest pine tree in the forest and got behind it. Across the clearing, about six hundred yards away stood a full brigade of Confederate cavalry drawn up in line of battle. As Weygant was examining the terrain from the cover of the huge pine, he noticed a Federal officer some distance to his left walk forward into the field to look at something on the ground. Weygant recognized him as Lieutenant Houston of Company D. After the departure of Weygant's two companies, Captain Benedict's Company D would have formed the right flank of the regiment. Weygant was most assuredly pleased to see that he was closer than expected to rejoining the regimental line of battle. Just then Houston "whirled about like a top, and I knew he had been hit by a rebel bullet." The lieutenant did not fall but quickly made his way back into the woods; Weygant assumed he had returned to his company.[65]

The 124th New York was positioned to the right of the Beverly Ford Road, the 86th New York to the left, the 3rd Wisconsin to the rear of the 86th. There was still a gap between Weygant's two companies and the rest of the regiment. What Weygant saw in front of him was an expanse of open ground rising to the ridgeline where Beckham had placed his guns. The Confederates, unsure who was in the woods and how many, opened a sustained rain of shells on them.

The battle now raged all around them, the two little companies under artillery fire for about an hour from a four gun battery. Their aim was high so they did no damage but the enemy was eager to see if any more Yankees were in the woods. Down the slope in front of them, several squads of mounted Confederates slowly rode forward, challenging the Yankees to open fire and reveal themselves.

Lieutenant John W. Houston. At the Battle of Brandy Station, Captain Weygant saw him "whirled about like a top, I knew he was hit by a rebel bullet" (Michael J. McAfee collection).

A man in Weygant's company could not resist the temptation and he shot a Confederate from the saddle. Now that it was clear there were Yankees in the woods, an entire regiment moved forward, dismounted in a heavy line of skirmishers with twice their number mounted and clearly visible in the rear ready to ride to support the skirmishers. Weygant estimated his little band was outnumbered about fifteen to one if the cavalry came on. He remembered Colonel Ellis' orders, which left no option for falling back.[66]

As the enemy drew closer, the men began to raise their weapons, taking careful aim to make each shot count. Weygant cautioned them to hold their fire but at the same time picked out a shrub in the field figuring it to be about one hundred yards away. Once the Rebel skirmishers got to the shrub, he would give the command to open fire. Just as they approached that point, the skirmishers seemed to disappear into the earth. Weygant was sure that they had dropped into a ravine so he ordered his men to wait, expecting the enemy to reappear as they came up the other side. The minutes dragged on but the Confederates remained out of sight. Just then the enemy artillery stopped firing and it came to Weygant in a flash: they were using the shelter of the ravine to turn his flank. At that moment, the captain heard a "peculiar half yell and half squeal" to his rear followed by a volley as the enemy charged from that direction. But the rebels cheered before they fired, attempting to frighten the Union troops, who had time to change their positions, still using the trees for cover. Weygant's men poured a volley into the gray ranks and they too sought the shelter of the trees. What followed was a "hand to hand Indian fight" as the enemy sought to drive them into the open field which would put them in the unenviable position of having enemy artillery at their back and the enemy dismounted cavalry at their front. The Orange Blossoms kept the Confederate troopers at bay with well-aimed fire, but Weygant grew concerned that the Rebels might overlap one or both of his flanks.[67]

At this critical moment, just as all seemed lost, Weygant heard from the woods, "Forward, men, forward." It was Major Cromwell leading a company of the 86th New York as they smashed into the exposed flank of the Confederates. At the same moment was heard the pounding of horses coming through the woods and the unmistakable shout of Colonel Ellis: "Give them the steel my honeys, give them the steel, the brigade will support you." Weygant's two companies, thinking hundreds of their comrades were coming to them, gave the "Yankee charging shout" and rushed the Confederates, who, "in utter dismay broke from their cover and fled before us, followed by a galling fire which left the ground, in their line of retreat out of the woods and over the plain, strewn with dead and wounded." Captain Weygant turned to greet the reinforcements only to discover they consisted of Colonel Ellis, Captain Ben Piatt, Lieut. Ramsdell, three mounted orderlies and the brigade colors.[68]

Weygant's relief was short lived; as soon as the enemy cleared the woods, its artillery opened again. The first shell smashed into Frank Rhinefield of Company A, tearing him to pieces and killing him instantly. Weygant was none too charitable in his description of the lad, calling him an "illiterate, untidy, careless boy, who would go to sleep on picket as quick as in camp." But the lad did have his good points: "Once on the line of battle, a braver or better soldier seldom handled a musket." His comrades buried the nineteen year old where he fell, in a shallow soldier's grave far from home.[69]

The whole action lasted about ten minutes, with the loss of two killed and twenty wounded, including quite a number from the men of the 86th New York, who came to the aid of the two companies of the 124th New York. Among the enemy dead were the major who commanded them and a lieutenant whom Weygant thought was quite young, with "fine features." He examined the body, drawing from the dead man's breast pocket a letter which he started to read. When he realized it was from the young man's mother, he quickly replaced it, and had the body removed to the roadside where it might be found and covered with a blanket. This man most likely found the same resting place as did Frank Rhinefield — a shallow soldier's grave far from home.

General Ames, commander of the infantry division that crossed at Beverly's Ford, wrote that, earlier in the day, just as Weygant's two companies were detached, the main body of infantry "moved up the road and through the woods to the front and center of our line." This was the position held by the eight remaining companies of the 124th New York commanded by Lieutenant Colonel Cummins. "After we crossed the river," Corporal Decker wrote in his journal, "we marched about a mile and a half and stopped in line of battle in the edge of the woods. In front of us was a cleared field and about fifty rods from us and on a hill the 'rebs' had earthworks thrown up and artillery planted. We had not been in this position but a short time when they began to shell us, but the shells all went over us so that no one was hurt. We were in sight of the 'rebs' but they could not see us."[70]

This was corroborated by Sergeant Peter P. Hazen of Company C who wrote home, "We halted just in the edge of the woods while the rebel cavalry were in the edge of the woods opposite us.... While lying here we were badly shelled from light batteries.... A piece of shell about two inches square struck my woolen blanket just over my shoulder, but fortunately did not hurt me." A soldier of Company K wrote, "When we had got into the woods about half a mile, we were deployed ... and then moved forward in line of battle till we arrived within about ten yards of the outer edge of the woods, there we were ordered to lay down and await the coming of the enemy. No sooner than we had got this position when they commenced to shell us, but they shot too high and no one was hurt."[71]

Private Henry Howell, whose Company E remained with the main body, wrote, "Our regt were stationed in the woods and the Rebs charged on to us we repulsed them finely. Then we were moved farther to the right and deployed as skirmishers. They advanced on different parts of our line several times but could not move us. The cavalry drove the Rebs two or three miles and then fell back in good order...."[72]

Isaac Decker wrote: "We noticed that they were preparing to make a charge upon us and we got ready to receive them. They were all Cavalry. They soon started and when they got within about fifteen rods of us some of the boys on the right of the Regt. fired into them and they wheeled around and left in a hurry. There was no order to fire, and if they had waited half a minute longer until the 'rebs' had got nearer, we would have emptied a good many saddles."[73]

Weygant says, "Soon the word was passed along the line that the rebel cavalry was preparing to charge on us, and that we must 'stand like a rock and shoot at the horsses.' In about five minutes we could see them as they came sweeping acrossed the open space in our front, and in another instance they were in close pistol shot of us, when we jumped on our feet and poured in a volley which throughed them into confusion and dismounted a great many while the next volley sent them rolling back a disorganized mob."[74] Sergeant Hazen wrote, "We fired a volley into them, at which they wheeled quickly, put spurs to their horses, and got out of range. We delivered our volley too soon.... If we had retained it about one minute longer, and allowed them to come close to us, undoubtedly we would have done greater execution."[75]

What all these eyewitnesses were describing was most likely the charge of three regiments of General William Jones's Brigade of cavalry across their front as they attacked the 6th Pennsylvania Cavalry and 6th U.S. Cavalry on the Beverly Ford Road.[76] The New Yorkers hit the left flank of the leftmost regiment, the 11th Virginia Cavalry. When the prisoners were gathered up, some of them said they did not know there was Union infantry in the wood or they would not have made the charge in the first place.[77]

The regiment remained in place for about an hour when it was discovered that the enemy was attempting to turn its right flank, possibly to bring rifles to bear on the ford, cutting the Union line of retreat. The 124th New York and a regiment from the 12th Corps were moved to the right to stop them. "When we arrived there, our cavalry had just made a charge on a reb battery and been driven back, and the enemy's skirmishers was following them up. (they were dismounted cavalry men.) Prospects did not look very bright at that time...." Two companies, Co. B and K, under Captain Jackson, were ordered to deploy as skirmishers, at the extreme right of the regiment, "within shooting distance" of the enemy skirmishers and a brisk exchange began before the two forces.[78]

The Confederates recognized the importance of a stone wall that ran down toward the river at about the same time as the Yankees did. The enemy soldiers got there first with more men coming up to reinforce them. "About a dozen of our company (myself among the number)," wrote Isaac Decker, "charge on them and took seven prisoners and killed and wounded ten or twelve more."[79] Another soldier on the skirmish line wrote "as we ran down along the wall, the balls flew around our head in very disagreeable manner." Once deployed, the soldiers opened on the enemy who fell back at the double quick. "We turned our attention to their grey backs and in about fifteen minutes we had driven them back out of range of our rifles, excepting a few that were not able to take themselves off on account of them getting in the way of our bullets. About a hundred yards *behind* our first line, was the house of *Capt. Dick Cunningham*, a rebel *gorilla*...."[80]

"After this the 'rebs' began to fall back, and our Cavalry came up and charged on them and drove them about half a mile and then the battle commenced in earnest. There was very hard fighting from about noon until five o'clock. It was all between the Cavalry."[81]

Private Howell wrote, "Their sharpshooters advanced upon us at one time and hit the tree that I was behind but we soon started them on the retreat. There were three wounded Rebs behind my post that belonged to the 9th Virginia cavalry. There were quite a number of charges made & I think it was the sharpest cavalry fight of the war."[82]

Sergeant Hazen wrote, "We were now ordered up, and moved to the right as skirmishers in the woods." The men struggled through the heavy underbrush, their visibility limited to but a few yards ahead. "We laid down behind trees and remained there in deep suspense, keeping a sharp watch for the approach of the enemy." Hazen could hear a constant fire to his right and a distant roaring to his left which may have been the "hard fighting" between the Union and Confederate horsemen, which now became a general back and forth cavalry battle.[83] William Howell succinctly described the action: "We then deploy out on the skirmish line. We held the line all day while our cavalry were engaged."[84]

"At 11 A.M. our entire line advanced in the afternoon," Gen. Ames wrote. "All of my available force moved toward a ridge of hills on our right. By this movement a very superior force of the enemy's infantry and cavalry was discovered. A section of the artillery crossed the river with the infantry, and was engaged first on the left, and afterward on the right. The remaining two sections crossed later in the day, as did the infantry left on this side, moved to the extreme front, and engaged the enemy. My command was withdrawn unmolested."[85]

According to Captain Weygant, the infantry support had served its expected purpose. Early in the battle, Buford's cavalry pushed the Confederates back about two miles but was then checked when reinforcements came up. Buford was pushed back on the defensive, placing his mounted regiments on the flanks of the woods held by Ames's infantry. The 124th New York, 86th New York, 2nd Massachusetts, 33rd Massachusetts, and 3rd Wisconsin did indeed serve as a *point d'appui*, a rallying point to stiffen the cavalry. The battle continued into the afternoon without, as the captain wrote, "any material advantage to either side."[86] Late in the afternoon, as reports reached Pleasanton that heavy columns of enemy infantry were approaching, the Union forces retired across the Rappahannock River. On the evening of June 9, the 124th New York and 86th New York were again encamped at Bealton Station.[87]

"Our Company did not have any one hurt. There were two killed and twelve wounded in our Regt.," wrote Isaac Decker. Among the wounded was Lieutenant John Houston, the officer Captain Weygant had seen wander in the field and get shot early in the fight. He was taken to Seminary Hospital in Georgetown where a stranger took the time to write home to his father.

"Dear Sir: Your son John W. Houston 2d Lieut. 124th Regt. N.S.V. was wounded yesterday morning near Banks Ford by a minie ball passing through the fleshy part of his thigh — The bone is not broken — He arrived here this morning in an ambulance and is very comfortable — having just taken his breakfast. He wished me to drop you this line that you may know how & where he is." The good deed was done by Russel Martin, who added a postscript to the letter. "The writer of this lives in Olean Cattasawgas County N.Y. I happened in his ward when he was brought in, and wrote this line for him."[88]

Surgeon Thompson, using his penname, "Esculapius," wrote home:

> The rebels in the early part of the day had decidedly the advantage in the score of artillery. Their guns were larger than ours, and were fired with great precision. Our Regiment showed great bravery, and heroically resisted several Cavalry charges. I am very happy to state, the casualties in the action of yesterday have not resulted so serious to our Regiment as that of the Chancellorsville fight. We had but two killed, and about ten, so far as I could learn, wounded; and none captured. I think I saw and treated most of our wounded. I was across the river and at the scene of the first encounter, in less than an hour after the first crossing and fighting. I staid near the front during the forenoon, at a place where I could intercept the wounded, as they came or were brought from the field. In the afternoon I was detailed on this side by Dr. Pancost, Medical Director on General Stoneman's staff, to assist as operating Surgeon at a Hospital established near the Ford. For the long period the fighting continued, and the large number engaged, the number wounded was certainly small. I think two hundred would include all I saw. I am fully satisfied that Infantry is the most destructive arm of the service, and cavalry the least so."[89]

In addition to Frank Rhinefield, Private Miles Vance of Company E was killed during the battle. Like Rhinefield, he was hit by artillery fire and his death was especially gruesome. Vance was just a short distance from Sergeant Hazen, taking cover behind a big oak tree, when a shell struck the ground about ten feet from him. It "plowed a furrow through the ground about six feet, then bounded and struck him in the side, tearing him in a dreadful manner." Vance let out several piercing shrieks, then begged his friends to take him to the rear where he asked them to put a bullet in his head to end his suffering. When they refused, he pleaded with them to bring his company commander, Lieutenant Charles B. Wood, "for we were schoolmates, and when he sees me, torn in this way and dying by inches, I know he will grant my request." Wood, who had seen Vance get hit, was sent for but before he arrived the eighteen-year-old farm boy from Otisville was dead.[90] Private Howell of the same company witnessed the event. "Miles Vance was struck with a shell and his left leg taken off close to the hip. He was carried back to the hospital but I doubt whether he lives or not. That was the only casualty in our Company but others had narrow escapes."[91]

Captain William Jackson wrote to his friend Alsop Purdy from the field immediately following the battle.

> Colonel Ellis took 500 of our brigade. This infantry was under Gen Ames. There were 500 from the 12th and 500 from 11th corps. The fight commenced early Tuesday morning principally cavalry. We acted as pickets and skirmishers and lost in the reg. But 2 killed 12 wounded and 1 missing. None of our company were hurt. Our regiment did well. The rebel cavalry charged us once but we soon scattered them. At 4 P.M. our cavalry withdrew having found the rebels in strong force. I am pretty well tired out for it is no light march to follow up cavalry. I will write more fully as soon as I get time.

In a postscript he added, "Don't let this get in the papers."[92]

In the days that followed, the opening moves in the Gettysburg Campaign began to take shape. Lee was on his way north followed by Hooker, who was careful to shield the capital while at the same time trying to find and engage the enemy. Brandy Station would soon be overshadowed by Gettysburg, but it remains an historic turning point in the war. The Yankee cavalry had gone looking for a fight. They not only found one, they did quite well. Stuart, initially caught off guard, rallied his men and held the field at the end of the battle but when the Union horsemen fell back across the Rappahannock, they did so at their own pace. A subtle change had come over the troopers in blue and therein lay the importance of the Battle of Brandy Station. The cavalry battles at Gettysburg and during the rest of 1863 would serve to demonstrate that the Northern horsemen had at last gotten the hang of it. They would still need to find that charismatic leader who could mold them into a truly dangerous force but that too would come in due time.

To the 124th New York, Brandy Station was a reaffirmation of its members' new-found status as top notch combat veterans. Private Howell concluded his diary entry for June 9, "The enemy cavalry were on the point of starting on a raid up in Maryland but I think this will delay it. We crossed at Beverly ford and there was another force crossed at Kellys Ford. General Stewarts staff was routed and part of them captured. One Major, one Captain and Lieutenant were among the prisoners."[93] Although Sergeant Isaac Decker was incorrect in what the enemy had in mind, he was not shy in assessing his regiment's part in the battle. "Some of the prisoners that we took said that the morning we crossed Genl Stuart with 15,000 Cavalry and thirty pieces of artillery were going to make a raid into Maryland. But," he added with obvious pride, " we stopped it."[94]

CHAPTER 7

"Wee Will Whip the Rebels yet"

June 10–July 1, 1863

The 124th New York was once again on the north side of the Rappahannock resting, but lying on their arms. "The Sharpshooters and some other regiments from the 3rd Division came down that night and joined us," Private Henry Howell wrote to his sister. "The next morning we moved back into the woods half a mile from the river, laid there a short time and then went to digging Rifle pits along the bank of the river. We worked all day. At night a small shower came up. We were moved back in the woods and staid there till morning."[1] Then he took up his diary, "I was detailed to go to the station to help load Forage, and one thing and another. There were about Four hundred prisoners sent to Washington. At night I was on guard around the camp."[2]

General Hooker concluded that Lee was indeed moving north and ordered the Army of the Potomac to do the same. Three days after the battle, the lead units of the 3rd Corps reached Bealton Station and the 124th was among its old comrades once more. But there had been some changes. The death of General Whipple at Chancellorsville, the heavy casualties sustained by the 3rd Corps, and the loss of a number of regiments whose enlistments were up led Hooker to reorganize the corps. Henry Howell gave his sister, who took a keen interest in military matters, a rundown of the command structure at that moment. "The 3rd Division has been broken up and the Sharpshooters, 86th and 124th are in the first Division 2nd Brigade. Col Berdan commands at present. General Sickles is away. Birney has charge of the 3rd Corps and Ward commands the 1st Div."[3]

The transfer meant that the Orange County boys would march with units already famous for their fighting abilities. Ward commanded the brigade once led by the colorful General Phil Kearny. Before his death in September 1862, Kearny also commanded the division now led by Birney. To be a part of Kearny's old unit meant that they would have to prove themselves all over again. The insignia of the First Division, 3rd Corps, was the Kearny Badge, a red diamond that was the very symbol of courage in the Army of the Potomac.

John Henry Hobart Ward, the new brigade commander, was not a West Point graduate but he was a veteran of the Mexican War and a career soldier. Born in New York City, Ward was just shy of his fortieth birthday in June 1863. He'd been educated at Trinity Collegiate School but at the age of eighteen enlisted in the army. Ward served in the Mexican War at Monterey and Vera Cruz, then held various military posts in the 1850s. When the Civil War began, he was commissioned colonel of the 38th New York, which he led at First Bull Run and in the battles on the Peninsula. In October 1862, he was promoted to brigadier general of volunteers and given command of the brigade he led at Fredericksburg and Chancellorsville.[4]

General David Bell Birney, division commander, was born in Alabama. He was the son of the antislavery leader and 1840 presidential candidate James G. Birney. The family relocated to Ohio, where Birney was educated, entered business, and studied law. He moved to Philadelphia to pursue business and the law but developed a third interest: the study of military procedures and tactics "which equipped him better professionally than most volunteer officers mustered into

service." Birney began his military career as the lieutenant colonel of the 23rd Pennsylvania. He went on to lead a brigade in Phil Kearny's division of the 3rd Corps, which he commanded in the battles on the Peninsula. When Kearny was killed just prior to the Battle of Antietam, Birney was given command of the division.[5]

Captain Weygant did not comment on the departure of Colonel Emlen Franklin who led the brigade at Chancellorsville but he did compare his late, beloved, division commander, General Whipple, with the new one. General Birney had, he said, "served with distinction," and was second to none when it came to his fighting qualities. What was lacking was a "fatherly kindness and solicitude for the welfare of those under him," the very qualities that endeared Whipple to his men.[6]

With the arrival of Colonel Berdan, who was senior, Colonel Ellis returned to his duties as commander of the 124th New York. During the next few days, the Howell brothers took advantage of the respite to make brief entries in their diaries. On June 11 William wrote, "Make ourselves comfortable as we can. Sleep on our arms." Henry found a Richmond newspaper and was annoyed to read an article about how the Yankees abused Confederate prisoners of war. "They print such stuff and pretend that they take it from the northern papers." Then he added optimistically, "It is reported that Vicksburg is ours." The next day William wrote, "Hard up for better food. At night we went down to Rappahannock bridge on guard." His brother added, "We staid in the woods until near night & then marched down to the river near Rappahannock Station. This station was burned down some time ago. The rest of our Corps has come up the river so we will not get back to our old camp again. We are close to the river but there is not many Johnny's to be seen." On June 13, William noted that the enemy scouts were plainly visible across the river.

Major General David B. Birney commanded the 1st Division, 3rd Corps. The 124th New York served under him from Gettysburg through Petersburg. "I don't think there is a man in the whole Division that likes him, for he wants to have this Division in the front lines all the while" (archive of the Historical Society of the Town of Warwick, gift of Joan and Tom Frangos).

"We dig rifle pits," he added and finished with the news, "We are put in the 1st Division which comes up & forms." Henry wrote, "We moved a short distance from the river into the woods. Then the whole Regt were taken close to the rivers edge and went to digging Rifle pits. At night Post got up with our provisions, and the Mail for all except Company E. There was quite a little shower in the evening."[7]

That day, Saturday, June 13, Commissary Sergeant Ellis Post's wagons arrived with three days rations and the mail from home. Private Henry Howell was annoyed that the mail came for every company in the regiment but his. He blamed a soldier who reported himself too sick to march as probably taking the mail with him when he went to the convalescent camp. Lieutenant Charles Wood, who now led Henry's company, was not happy either. He had been a lieutenant in Company A, but was moved to command Company E following the Battle of Chancellorsville. It was rumored that Wood planned to request to be "reduced" as soon as things got settled. The lieutenant's reason was not stated, but Wood obviously preferred to be second in command under Captain Weygant to leading Company E.[8]

The next day, at about 3 P.M., buglers throughout the camps blew the "attention," signaling another march. It was not "on to Richmond" this time, but back toward Washington as Hooker attempted to find Lee's army while at the same time he safeguarded the capital from attack. For the next two weeks it would be a foot race as each army tried to gain an advantage in position against the other. In the years to come, historians would fill libraries with analyses of what went wrong, missed opportunities, bungled orders, and misunderstandings up and down the chains of command, North and South. But to the men in the ranks, it was a swift, hot, taxing march they knew would end on yet another bloody battlefield.

The 124th followed the railroad through Warrenton Junction fourteen miles to Cattlett's Station, a seven-hour march that ended near midnight, when they finally halted to break ranks and get some rest.[9]

Early the next morning, the regiment was on the march again, this time for Manassas Plains. In a letter to his sister, Henry Howell wrote that they started after breakfast. "It was very hot and dusty. The water was very poor and scarce at that. I did not suffer for it but some of the others did. We were forced along so fast that it was hard to tell which was the regiments and which were the stragglers. There were quite a number sunstruck and fell down in the ranks." He added to his diary for June 15, "We march 15 miles and when the regiment halted there were not more than a quarter of the men with the Colors but they soon came up. We suffered quite a good deal for water."[10]

"This was a very severe march," Captain Weygant wrote. They stopped to rest at noon near Bristow Station and were fortunate in that the men of the 15th Vermont saw their condition. The "Green Mountain boys distributed to them their entire ration of soft bread and the hot coffee they had just prepared for their own dinner. And when our ambulances with the victims of sun-stroke came up, they voluntarily turned their camp into a temporary hospital, and themselves into nurses." When the 124th moved out a short time later, they gave three cheers to the "big-hearted sons of Vermont."[11] During this half-hour rest, some of the men took the opportunity to wash themselves in Deep Run, a nearby creek. Henry Howell washed his shirt but had no clean one to put on. He simply wrung it out by hand and wore it wet.[12]

After the short break they were off again. "About three o'clock in the afternoon Will got tired," Henry wrote, "and sick at his stomach so we fell out in the shade of a tree." The Howell brothers rested a while and, after William had something to eat, he felt better. "So I carried his gun and we went along slowly, resting often. In this way we caught up to the regiment in a couple of hours, but they had halted for the night. There were not more than a quarter of the men there to stack there arms and all the other regiments were in the same condition, but they soon came along. Most of them were only tired so after resting awhile they were better. Lew Wisner fell down in the ranks and was brought up in the ambulance. Captain Jackson and Lieut. Hays rode also."[13]

On June 16 the regiment marched three miles. "Start in the morning & go on the bull run ground," William Howell penciled into his diary. "Wash up & rest at Blackburns ford. Union and Secesh names engraved on the trees. I noticed one Miss Abbey Westmans, Abbeyville Dist. S.C."[14] Colonel Ellis and a number of others who had been present at the Battle of Bull Run with the 71st New York Militia reminisced, sharing stories about what all agreed had been a "series of military blunders that terminated in a general stampede."[15] The regiment drew up in line of battle near some old Confederate rifle pits and, when dismissed, took the opportunity to bathe in the famous creek that gave the battle its name. "We have all rested up now and feel pretty well. We are wishing very much to have another mail come in. Since I commenced this we had to go and whip a fire out that had got started in the woods back of us. We call it the third Bull Run Battle."[16]

During this much-appreciated rest, Henry Howell set his opinions on the military situation to paper. "I do not understand this backward movement. There are a great many different reports as to its meaning but I do not put faith in any of them. Some of the men have commenced grumbling about Joe Hooker, and talking McClellan. I have not given up on old Hooker yet. My feet have been pretty sore but are better. The boys are all here from Company E that came back from the fight with us."[17]

On June 17, they moved five miles to Centreville, where they rested for two days. Henry's diary entry read, "We staid around catching fresh clams and passing away the time in various ways until three oclock in the afternoon when we started crossing bull run creek at Blackburn Ford where the famous black horse cavalry made their last charge. We went nearly three miles and halted near Cub Run about a mile and a half from Centerville."[18]

Mid-afternoon on June 18 it looked like rain so the men put up their shelter halves. Experience taught them to dig shallow trenches around their tents so that the rainwater might flow to either side instead of right through their canvas-covered quarters. Fresh meat was issued to the men and William Howell took the opportunity to walk to a nearby village to buy some bread. The rain was so heavy that he sought refuge in an old church.[19] "We did not do any marching. It was so hot that we could hardly keep from melting." Henry wrote in his diary. "There was a drenching shower fell in the evening. This is the best place to get good water that we have been in since we left the old camp."[20]

The storm continued into the next day but the regiment set off again anyway, marching through a drizzle in almost total darkness. Captain Weygant noted that the mud sloshed over the tops of their low army brogans. "Occasionally one of our number would tumble into a hole filled with water which came up to his knee, and then another would trip or stumble over something, and fall head foremost in the mud."[21] William Howell wrote, "We strike tents in the afternoon & move slowly. Night dark & raining. We go into Gum Springs and halt." His brother wrote, "We marched up to Centerville and then took the road leading to Gum Crossing. It had been showering all day but just after dark it came down in torrents and it got so dark that we could not see the man ahead of us. We had a desperate time but halted at last in the vicinity of the Springs about 8 miles from Centerville."[22]

The men were ordered to file into a boggy field to camp for the night. This ridiculous order must have been given by someone at headquarters who had no idea the field was little better than a swamp. Horses foundered in the muck, throwing their riders and injuring nearby soldiers. "Colonel Ellis tumbled with his horse into a ditch, but fortunately escaped with no greater injury than an extra coating of Virginia mud." The colonel got his men into some semblance of a line and gave an order not heard before or since in the Army of Potomac. For the benefit of the officer who ordered his men into the morass, Ellis bellowed, "Squat, my bullfrogs!" The regiment passed a miserable night without blankets or a dry place to sit or sleep.[23]

The next morning the men were sore and covered with mud. Captain Weygant wondered what the "fair daughters of Old Orange" would think of their "dashing soldier boys" if they could see them in such condition. The foul weather served to point up the shortcomings of a piece of shoddy outerwear Weygant had purchased from the regimental sutler: a seamless felt overcoat meant to double as a blanket. A slight man, he'd ordered an extra large size to keep out the elements. During the rainy night while he slept in the new overcoat, the soaked garment began to shrink. He was awakened by the distinct feeling that someone was trying to tie his arms behind him. When he jumped up, all the buttons popped off and the hem, which when dry was almost to his feet, was now just below his waist.[24] While the captain was prone to exaggeration for comedic effect, many soldiers suffered from poorly constructed jackets, caps, shoes, and trousers purchased by the government from profiteering contractors.

At dawn, the soaked regiment moved to dry ground, stripped the nearest farm field of fence rails, and soon had fires roaring. They boiled coffee, then cooked breakfast and set to work cleaning themselves and their equipment. William Howell wrote that all the marching in the rain and sleeping on damp ground left him "quite stiff & wet." He was happy he had the opportunity to warm himself and dry his damp, filthy clothes. The trousers and jackets gave off a distinctly pungent aroma, a combination of wet wool, dirt, sweat, smoke — wood, gun powder, and tobacco — bacon grease, and a variety of other smells, none pleasant to the nostrils.

The exposure to the weather was causing their Enfield rifle muskets to show signs of rust. They knew full well that Colonel Ellis would fine a man a month's pay or worse if his weapon was not in good order, foul weather or not. Each man went to work with a will to "clean up our guns."[25] Henry wrote, "We put up our tents on the ground we stopped on last night. There is an old planters house a few rods from camp. He has got lots of Contrabands around. It was cloudy all day. The sun hardly showing himself. Gum Springs is composed of a Church & what was once a blacksmith shop & six or eight old houses."[26]

Despite the weather and trying marches, Private Henry Dill of Co. G seemed to be in his usual good spirits. He wrote to "Friend William" back home, "I Amm Well And Hope this Will find you the same We Have marched one Hundered miles thru A very Perty Cuntry thar Had Bin No troops Ahead of us." Capt. Weygant's assertions notwithstanding, Dill gave a different account of foraging, "And you can bet the pigs And sheep sufered some." Dill also took the opportunity to comment on the condition of the troops. "The Boys Are All Well thay are A Fighting in 8 miles of us And Wee Are Redy to go on As soon As Wee Are Wanted." He was a persistent recruiter for the 124th New York, giving advice to his friends at home and telling how much they would enjoy being soldiers if they enlisted. He asked William to tell a friend named Ed to write him more often but to send some postage stamps so that he might reply. He also urged William not to go to "Webs sow often but tou kepe Cool" perhaps giving him some advice with regard to the ladies. "I Wish you Was Down Hear," he wrote, "Fore I know you Would like it Wee got plenty of Cherys Heare And Like it First Rate Wee marched All Night Night Before last it Rained As Hard As I Every saw it I supose Hary And mark Will Come Now tell Hary thar is Lots of Black gals Down Hear it is very Warm Hear in the Daytime and Cool Nights I think Wee Will Whip the Rebels yet. give my Love to All inquing Freinds so No more At Present."[27]

On the morning of June 21, General Ward moved his brigade about half a mile, forming "column at full distance" so that the men would have enough room to pitch their tents in an orderly fashion. Henry Howell was detailed to brigade guard, nine men being assigned to guard duty from each of the eight regiments in the brigade. That evening he heard firing off to west, and thought it was probably a cavalry fight between Stuart and Pleasanton near Middleburgh. "There is considerable cannonading in front. It sounds as though it was in the vicinity of Snickers Gap.... About 2 oclock the bugle sounded marching orders and we were soon in motion. But we did not move more than a mile."[28]

Captain William Jackson started a letter from Gum Springs on Sunday, June 21, "Late on Friday night our corps reached this place which is about no place at all except the name like a good many other spots in Virginia. It takes its name from a large spring under a gum tree." He stopped when the order mentioned above came to fall in as firing was heard to the southwest. He continued his letter the next day. "We expect a big fight soon. I do very much hope we will give the rebs a good one. They will find a hard set to deal with in our corps."[29]

That morning, following drill and inspection, the regiment was assigned three days' picket duty, half the companies on the line, the rest "stationed in the woods in the rear of Gum Springs as a support to the picket line." Henry Howell wrote that the Yankee cavalry brought in six "guerrillas" caught in the act of burning supply wagons. "They had three on fire and were just starting the fourth one."[30]

Their position lay five miles beyond the main body of Union troops, giving the boys considerable opportunity for foraging. "Fresh beef, veal and poultry abounded," noted Captain Weygant. He maintained that he paid for everything he got from the local Virginians, as did, he assured his readers, the rest of the soldiers from Orange County. He went on to relate that his new cook managed to get hold of "a fine quarter of fresh veal" and a good sized beef steak from parties unknown. The captain hinted broadly that the food might well have come from the estate of a local secessionist—a "notorious traitor" as Weygant preferred to call him—who was then serving in the Army of Northern Virginia.[31]

For the next few days the regiment remained in place. On June 23 the men were issued five days' rations, but the New Yorkers were busy augmenting their fare. "We captured nearly all the Four Footed animals that came in camp in the shape of Fresh meat. There is a splendid spring down in the village."[32]

Along with the livestock, the pickets also captured more enemy soldiers, or guerrillas, as they like to call them, but neither of the Howell brothers said what was done to the prisoners. On June 24 William wrote in a bored tone, "In the same posish."[33] Henry noted that no mail had come in the past few days but the newspapers were available from "the newsboys" so they could not have been too far from civilization. He also noted that Colonel Cummins had been recently kicked by a mule and was so badly hurt that he could not ride his horse. The regimental bugler "captured" a cow and tied it outside Cummins's tent. Henry did not make it clear if the cow was to provide milk, beef, or transportation for the injured colonel.[34]

On June 25 the companies out on picket were ordered back to camp. As they approached, they saw that the army was on the march, so they sat by the side of the road to wait for their regiment to join them. When the men saw Colonel Ellis, they fell in with the column for another blistering march. "This was one of the severest marches, as to length and rapidity, we had ever made," Weygant wrote.[35]

Henry Howell wrote of the same day's march,

> We are called up before day light to get our breakfast and be ready to march. The pickets were called in and at six oclock we started. We marched on quick time and as the day was cool we got over the ground pretty lively. We passed a cherry orchard and the boys felt as though they would like to get a nip at them but we were marching to fast for that. We passed one home where the people were very kind to the soldiers. There were two men with a pail a piece drawing water for them. The Flowers around the house were blooming fine by showing the taste of the ladies who were standing in the gate as we passed. We stopped an hour for dinner. Then we started on again reaching the Potomac about three oclock. We crossed the River and canal at Edwards Ferry on a pontoon bridge. The Goose Creek emptys in the Potomac at this place. It commenced to rain about this time. Co. E was detailed for rear guard after we got on the Maryland shore. We did not camp for the night until nine oclock after marching twenty five miles.[36]

At the start of the march that day, the regiment was joined by a brand-new second lieutenant named Milnor Brown, recently appointed by New York's Governor Seymour. In May 1862, months before the 124th was mustered into service, Brown enlisted in the 7th New York State Militia, a unit that drew upon the sons of New York City's elite to fill its ranks. Private Brown served with the 7th as part of 8th Army Corps, stationed in Baltimore.[37] Most of their time was spent at Fort Federal Hill, a temporary installation built right after the secessionist riots of 1861. The cannons in the fort were not sighted to protect the harbor, but instead pointed ominously downtown, should the rebel sympathizers still active in Baltimore rise again.

Upon the return of the 7th to New York, Brown sought and received a commission in the 124th New York with the rank of 2nd Lieutenant dating from December 30, 1862.[38] When he reached the regiment, Lieutenant Brown was given command of Company I, whose officers had departed the service for one reason or another. Lieutenant Thomas Quick of Company F led

Captain Thomas J. Quick, Company F and G. He was mustered in as 1st lieutenant of Company F, and later promoted to captain of Company G. He was wounded at the Battle of Chancellorsville, May 3, 1863 (Michael J. McAfee collection).

them at Chancellorsville, where he had been wounded. When Quick returned to the regiment he took command of his old company, leaving the post in Company I temporarily vacant. That particular company was one of those on picket duty, so when Brown joined its members on the march toward Pennsylvania, it was an unpleasant surprise. If anyone in the company even knew about his previous service, no one cared. They considered him a civilian in uniform, an untried interloper who had yet to share the hardships of the march or the dangers of the battlefield. The men of Company I would have much preferred that one of their own sergeants or an officer from another company be chosen to command them. Brown's reception by the men in the ranks was icy to say the least. It was noted by Captain Charles Weygant that, had Brown dropped dead by the side of the road, not a man would have paused to bury him.

The young officer, not so unfamiliar with the military as those in his company thought, knew what he was up against. He had to prove himself to a hostile group of soldiers who had seen their ranks thinned by disease, disability, and enemy fire. He set out to make an impression on them, not leaving his post at the head of the company throughout one of the most demanding marches they had yet endured. The men in Company I knew he was suffering terribly but he said not a word of complaint and asked no one for help. That night they watched as he silently pulled off his shoes and socks, then pierced and drained the "live blisters" covering his feet. When he put his shoes back on without comment and walked off with no sign of pain, their opinion of him began to change.[39]

On June 26, the regiment started early. "We got up this morning," wrote Henry Howell,

after a poor nights rest on account of its raining so with scarcely time for breakfast we had to pack up our wet things and march along through the mud. We crossed the Monocacy River on the canal Acquaduct where it flows in the Potomac. The artillery forded it. We passed over some good grain land. Corn and wheat was growing in abundance. It looked well. We stopped about two oclock and put up our tents. Point of Rocks is half a mile from us. I went there and got a wheatcake. I came across a cherry tree on my way there and got a good lot of them to eat. We have come about 10 miles to day and we are all footsore and weary.[40]

William Howell, who was again feeling the effects of the march, got a pass to march at the rear of the column.[41]

On June 27, William wrote that they marched through Jefferson, Maryland, to the sounds of music. It was "a fine country," he noted. "We started on the morning, his brother noted, "crossing a chain of hills and passing through a section of country that is devoted to the raising of wheat. We stopped a while for dinner and then the journey was renewed. We passed through a fine little village named Jefferson." For dramatic effect, and to raise the spirits of the residents who had seen the Confederate army pass this way, the regiment formed into a column of companies "with the bands playing and flags floating to the breeze." This was probably done by each regiment as it passed through the town. "We marched until night having traveled something like eighteen miles. After we got settled on a hill I was detailed for to go on brigade Guard. We are in what is supposed to be a loyal state and the orders are severe against plundering and straggling."[42]

June 28, the regiment made eleven miles, marching through Middletown, again with flags flying, then it was on to Frederick, Maryland. It will be remembered that Maryland was a slave state and assumed by many to be hostile to the Union. But such was not the case in western Maryland. "In no southern town or city, during our three years wanderings up and down through Virginia and Maryland, did we find half so many outspoken loyal women as we that day met with in Frederick. It was very warm and at nearly every second garden gate, or doorway, there stood loyal, smiling mothers not unfrequently accompanied by comely daughters, all eagerly passing to our thirsty soldiers pure cold water, and it is beyond belief how thirsty our young men were, and the quantity they drank." As Captain Weygant's company passed a "Quaker-dressed, grey-haired matron" and her two good-looking granddaughters, the three ladies were dipping water from a pail with cut glass goblets and pouring it into the men's coffee cups. One very thirsty Newburgh boy stepped up and prepared to dip the water himself using his filthy tin cup which had seen action over hundreds of camp fires without a proper cleaning. "Lizzie! Lizzie!" the old lady screamed, catching hold of the unfortunate soldier's arm. "Don't let that man spoil your pail of nice clean water with that horrid, nasty black cup." The embarrassed soldier skedaddled as if under fire for the first time, to the hoots and howls of laughter of his comrades.[43]

Sergeant Daniel Crotty of the 3rd Michigan wrote, "General Lee seems to think after he is in Maryland he can recruit up his ranks from the sons of that state, but wherever he goes the cold shoulder is turned to him, for the loyal State of Maryland is true to the Union and its people testify to their loyalty by giving us everything they can to help us on our way to drive the invader from their soil."[44] Corporal William Howell succinctly described the march: "On to Frederick. Hard roads, sore feet ... not a morsel to eat. Go to sleep. Draw 3 days rations in night."[45]

His brother paused long enough to write home on June 28,

Dear Mother,

I do not know as I shall have five minutes time to write but I will improve it if I do. Here we are safe and sound within five miles of the Pennsylvanian line and a fair prospect of being in that state before night.... There is a vast difference between the country here and in Virginia. Maryland looks almost like a garden after coming from the barren soil of Virginia. We marched 12 miles this day ... with flags floating and bands playing ... passing through Middleton, & Frederick City. This is a very loyal place about the size of Newburgh I should think. General Sickles arrived at this place and resumed his command. The boys were not very sorry to see him for we think he will see about giving us a little more GRUB. We had fun on short rations for several days before, but at the present writing I am glad to say that we have our haversacks well filled with pork & crackers.... My feet were so sore last night that I could scarcely get along. I washed them, and they feel pretty well this morning. Our mail came up a day or two ago but we have been traveling along so that we have not got it all yet on account that there was no one had any time to divide it out to the different Regiments but by the looks of it we will have a little more of it in a few minutes.... We have marched about 90 miles in the last five days. Some of the boys say we will soon be in Orange County. I think if the Rebs stay up in Penn. a few days longer we will give them such a flogging that will crush this rebellion. Our army is marching in such a shape that we will surely meet them at some point, and if the Militia is good for anything we will give it to them. We scarcely get time to wash ourselves without washing our clothes. I wish we could stop one day side of a good creek and wash up once more....

Well I am your affectionate son, Henry[46]

Finishing his letter, Henry took up his diary.

We started early in the morning marched two miles to a village called Middletown which we passed through and turned to the right crossing the mountain on the way to Frederick City nine miles distant. We marched through the city with our colors floating proudly to the breeze about two oclock. The inhabitants of this place are very loyal. They had the streets lined with flags and waving handkerchiefs. We turned down on the Harrisburg pike crossing the Monocacy and halting near Walkersville. We have traveled something like eighteen miles today. Gen Sickles has returned and took charge of the Corps & Gen's Birney and Ward go back to their respective commands.[47]

The regiment halted for the night about four miles beyond Frederick, but was on the move again early on the morning of June 29.[48] Ahead lay another grueling march in the rain, twenty five miles to Taneytown. "Start quite early," William Howell wrote in his diary. "Pass through Woodborough road miday. Go through Several small villages. Go through Tanneytown where we received a hearty welcome. Stop for the night most tired out."[49] His brother Henry penciled into his diary for the same day,

> We are called up in the middle of the night last night for to draw three days rations. We started early in the morning and marched through Walkersville. Woodborough, Mechanicstown, Middleburg & Taneyville. We marched all day except a noon spell for dinner. We traveled about 20 miles and halted in a piece of woods for the night. My boots rubbed my feet so sore that I had to fall to the rear. I stopped at a creek and gave them a good wash which made them feel a good deal better. I soon catched up to the regt again. We got a mail last night. There was so much of it at headquarters that they did not have time to divide it all out.[50]

The regiment finally halted for the night north of Taneytown.[51]

On Tuesday, June 30, the 124th New York was mustered for inspection of arms. When they left Falmouth for Brandy Station on June 6, about three hundred men were present and ready for duty. Another fifty men had returned from the hospitals or detached duty but the losses at Brandy Station and the losses along the march left but two hundred sixty-four men in line for inspection that day. The Ordnance Report for that date showed that the regiment was armed with "Enfield Rifles and U.S. Regulation Accouterments" but also listed "35 Springfield Rifled Muskets," which had probably been picked up on the field at Chancellorsville.[52]

After the muster, an order was read informing the troops that General Hooker was no longer in command of the army but instead Major General George Meade, late commander of the 5th Corps, was now in charge. This caused a considerable amount of speculation among the troops, who expected that a battle would take place in the near future; some wondered aloud why the government would do such a thing at this time. Finally a man from Company F shouted for everyone's attention and, taking an exaggerated stage posture, launched into a humorous rendition of how these events had come to pass. He ended with a prophetic statement: "The next battle is on the free soil of old Pennsylvania, and Lee is whipped, no matter who commands us."[53]

That day, General Meade sent a dispatch to General Sickles critical of the slow progress made by the 3rd Corps the day before, noting the "good condition of the road and the favorable state of the weather."[54] It is interesting that Henry Howell and Captain Weygant, both of whom actually made the march, described it as from twenty to twenty-five miles respectively, and Weygant wrote that for part of the march it was "raining quite hard."[55] Perhaps the sun had been shining at Meade's headquarters, but where the 124th marched that day, the conditions were less than ideal.

At 12:45 P.M. Sickles received an order from Meade's headquarters.

> The major-general commanding directs that you move your corps up to Emmitsburg. You will take three days' rations in haversacks, 60 rounds of ammunition, and your ambulances. Your trains will remain parked here until further orders. General Reynolds' First Corps, and General Howard's Eleventh Corps, are between Emmitsburg and Gettysburg. General Reynolds will command the left wing, consisting of the First, Eleventh, and Third Corps. The enemy are reported to be in force in Gettysburg. You will move without delay. You will report to General Reynolds, and throw out strong pickets on the roads from Emmitsburg to Greencastle and Chambersburg. Mechanicstown, on your left, is occupied by a brigade of cavalry, with whom you will communicate.[56]

The 3rd Corps got underway, but was intercepted by Meade, who gave Sickles "verbal orders to halt his corps where it then was."[57] Enemy troops had been spotted near Fairfield, Pennsylvania, and Meade wanted the 3rd Corps close at hand to deal with them if the need arose. A bit later, Sickles received an order from Reynolds telling him to move to Emmitsburg. Sickles realized that this was in "conflict with the verbal order given me by the general commanding while on the march." He dutifully sent a courier to Meade. "Shall I move forward? My First Division is about a mile this side of Emmitsburg." He received a reply from Reynolds ordering him to camp at

Cat Tail Branch and telling him to send a staff officer to Reynolds's headquarters.[58] Sickles replied at 7:45 P.M. "By direction of the general commanding, I have gone into camp here, countermanding a previous order to go to Emmitsburg, and I am to await here further orders from headquarters Army of the Potomac. When these orders were received, I sent Captain Crocker, of my staff, to communicate them to Major-General Reynolds, and to inform him of my position. My First Division and two batteries are farther toward Emmitsburg (across Middle Creek)."[59]

On the night of June 30, William Howell noted in his diary and in a letter home that he and Henry were able to get an amiable farmer to give them some straw to cushion the damp ground, quite a luxury on this march. Henry also mentioned the straw stack in a letter home and added that they had the permission of the owner to use it. The fact that both brothers mentioned the kindness of the farmer and the value they placed on a dry place to sleep is a good indication of how hard the march up from Virginia had been. They also wanted to reassure their mother that they had secured permission first and did not steal the straw.[60]

Henry even mentioned the straw in his diary entry for June 30.

> We laid in the woods resting until about noon. Then we were off again. We turned to the left from the road we had been marching on. It rained a very heavy shower in the afternoon which made it slippery traveling, we kept going all afternoon stopping near a large stack of straw which we soon had scattered around for to lay on. We traveled about 10 miles to day. This makes about 100 miles that we have marched in the last six days. There are quite a number of convalescents came back from the hospital to the Third Corps today.[61]

While he rested, Captain Weygant wrote in his diary, "The men of our regiment are in tolerably good spirits but have lost considerable flesh during the last week, and complain bitterly whenever we start on a march, of the pain in their swollen, blistered feet." He remarked again on the fact that the country side of Maryland contained prosperous farms, fertile and well cultivated. "The villages contain many fine cottages, and the people generally appear to be strongly Union in sentiment."[62]

North of Emmitsburg lay south central Pennsylvania where events were nearing a crisis. Lee's brigades, though scattered, were deep into Pennsylvania, bringing mayhem to the peaceful towns in their path. Confederate troops reached the south bank of the Susquehanna River near Harrisburg and were as far east as Wrightsville, where they came close to capturing a bridge across the broad river. It would be difficult to overstate the panic this invading army spread as the Confederates swept up huge amounts of supplies and livestock to be used by the army or sent south. The exultant rebels, though weary from the long march, enjoyed the plenty they found along the way and were confident of victory.

Lee was somewhat surprised to discover that the Army of the Potomac was coming north at a brisk, un–McClellan-like rate. He ordered his scattered units to converge on Gettysburg, an important communication and transportation hub where eight major roads converged. Meade was not sure of the enemy's intentions and he did not wish to take the offensive just yet. In fact, he issued the Pipe Creek Circular in which he outlined plans to fall back on a position just south of the Pennsylvania/Maryland state line if circumstances warranted, the better to defend Washington and Baltimore.

On the last day in June, Union troopers rode into Gettysburg led by Brigadier General John Buford, who had done well at Brandy Station and who was about to win himself a place in the pantheon of Gettysburg heroes. Approaching from the west came the lead units of the Army of Northern Virginia. Lee had cautioned his commanders not to bring on a general engagement until his army was concentrated and until he knew what enemy force was in front of him.

On Wednesday, July 1, Union cavalry northwest of Gettysburg performed consistent with their newfound élan. They took up positions on the ridge lines across the main road from Chambersburg and made ready to contest Lee's advance. Fighting dismounted with breech loading carbines and horse artillery support, the troopers forced Lee's men to leave the roads, deploy into line, and fight for the ridges. This was an uneven match, to be sure, since the weight of Confederate infantry supported by their own artillery would eventually win the field. The point, however, was that the Yankee cavalry, no longer afraid to mix it up with rebel cavalry, or rebel infantry for that matter, delayed Lee's brigades long enough for the Union 1st Corps to reach the last of the ridges and form into line of battle.

In the end, Union infantry fighting northwest of the town and two divisions of the 11th Corps fighting in the broad open fields north of the town, were pushed back. But these units rallied on the high ground south of the town in strong defensive positions that would come to define the Battle of Gettysburg. Most important of these defensive positions was Cemetery Hill, quickly recognized by both Lee and Meade as key to victory. What is more, the Yankee lines of supply, communication, and, if need be, retreat, were wide open to the rear. Striding up those open roads came thousands of troops from five uncommitted Yankee infantry corps.

Henry Howell wrote to his mother on July 1 that "after another soaking shower" the regiment marched through Emmitsburg where the men were halted.[63] General Birney posted his division beyond Emmitsburg in such a manner as to cover the roads to Fairfield and Gettysburg while General Ward began preparations to have his brigade bivouac in place for the night.[64] Private Peter Ayars of the 99th Pennsylvania, Ward's Brigade, told of how his men "engaged in making coffee — which, by the way, was all they had, and precious few of them had that."[65]

Sickles had orders to remain at Emmitsburg but he sent an aide to open up communication with General Reynolds, who commanded the left wing of the army. Sickles's aide, Major Henry Tremain, spoke to the general, who said, "Tell General Sickles I think he had better come up."[66] This contradicted Meade's orders, so another aide was sent galloping to Reynolds, but just then a message arrived from General Howard of the 11th Corps requesting that Sickles come to Gettysburg. This further complicated things for the 3rd Corps commander. If he moved north, the Confederates might cut the lines of communication with Washington and quite possibly cut off a line of retreat outlined by Meade in the Pipe Creek Circular. Sickles made what historian Richard Sauers called "a critical decision." He ordered his men onto the road to Gettysburg but left two brigades behind to guard Emmitsburg and the lines to the rear.[67]

At about 2 P.M., General Birney was ordered to "proceed immediately" to Gettysburg. Captain Weygant wrote, "A few minutes later sharp bugle blasts from every direction called us into line. Our brigade then moved through Emmitsburg, and filed off into a green field just beyond the village, where we remained until several other brigades had moved past."[68] Even before the orders were given, the men lying in the fields along the main road about two miles from the state line could hear the distant yet distinct rumble of artillery off to the north. Ward's Brigade fell in with a new urgency and started off after the brigades that had just passed "at quick time on a forced march for Gettysburg."[69]

Henry Howell wrote in his diary, "We did not move until the afternoon & then we were tried pretty severely the rest of the day. It had been raining nearly all the Forenoon and the artillery had cut the roads up very bad. We started and went through Emmitsburg turned to the right and kept on."[70] The weather cleared and became quite humid. Weygant remembered, "Soon, strong men began to stagger from the ranks and fall fainting by the wayside, but our pace was not slackened. Louder and fiercer boomed the yet distant guns, and, 'Forward, men Forward!' shouted the officers."[71]

When the 3rd Corps was well on its way, Sickles received an order from Meade that he remain in Emmitsburg until he heard otherwise from General Hancock who was now commanding the troops already at Gettysburg. Sickles ignored the order and pressed on.[72]

The roadside was littered with discarded clothing, knapsacks, tents, and weapons. To lighten the loads of the men, some officers dismounted, took rifles and accoutrements from those about to collapse, and piled the equipment on the backs of their horses. Birney described his men as "marching with enthusiasm and alacrity over the road, rendered almost impassable by mud and the passage over it of the First and Eleventh Corps through the rain." General Ward described the road to Gettysburg as simply "horrible."[73]

> Now began one of the hardest marches it was ever our lot to be engaged in — all the way from Emmittsburg to Gettysburg, 12 miles, with the thermometer certainly up among the nineties, with only one stop, a breathing spell of about 15 minutes. Men fell by the roadside by the score from the effects of the terrible heat. The water in the canteens was almost steaming hot, and I only remember of having passed one small stream in all that march. We reached Gettysburg ... just after dark, and immediately went into line of battle, facing south and east, from the Peach Orchard down through the edge of the woods towards Devil's Den. Here we rested all night, as completely "played out" a lot of soldiers as I ever saw.[74]

Henry Howell added, "The roads were ankle deep with water & mud. We were soon in the State of Pennsylvania. After we got in the state we heard that there had been a battle near Gettysburg in which we lost one of our Corps commanders (Gen Reynolds) and captured 1000 prisoners. We got in the vicinity of the battle-field before we halted having marched about 12 miles. The day was lost in the fight but tomorrow we expect to regain everything."[75]

Exhausted by the march, the Orange Blossoms reached the Gettysburg area after the first day's battle was over. At a crossroads near a peach orchard they turned right onto a rutted wagon road and marched several hundred yards before turning left onto the Weikert farm, halting just north of the farmhouse.[76] A sergeant in the 124th estimated their arrival time at 8:30 P.M.[77]

Sergeant Harvey Hanford, Company B, and his wife. When the regiment formed up on Houck's Ridge at Gettysburg, he was the last man on the left of the line (Robert Cammaroto collection).

Here the regiment waited for the stragglers to catch up. Soaked with sweat and covered with dust, the tired men were ordered not to remove their belts, cartridge boxes, haversacks, or knapsacks but to sleep with all their gear in place as they were in the presence of the enemy. "We marched up at quick time," Henry Howell wrote to his mother, "but did not arrive in time to save the battlefield where General Reynolds had been fighting during the day. We were posted that night near the battlefield."[78] Second Sergeant Harvey Hanford described the scene: "We lay down in an open field, with orders to sleep on our arms, and not to take off an article of clothing or any of our accoutrements. This was hard sauce after such a march as we had had; but soldier-like, we had to take it out in grumbling."[79]

At 9:30 P.M., after the 3rd Corps went into bivouac, Sickles sent a message to headquarters. He described the position of the four brigades of his corps and asked that the two left behind rejoin him as soon as conditions allowed. He was fully aware that the left and rear were "not sufficiently guarded" and assured Meade that nothing but the "earnest and frequent appeals of General Howard ... could have induced me to move from the position assigned to men in general orders; but I believed the emergency justified the movement." He ended his message with his opinion of the position. "This is a good battle-field."[80]

CHAPTER 8

"We stood there like veterans without giving an inch"
July 2–5, 1863

At dawn on Thursday, July 2, the second day of the battle, Graham's Brigade and Ward's Brigade, both of Birney's Division, were camped at the south end of Cemetery Ridge near the George Weikert house. They faced west, with Ward and the 124th just to the north and slightly west of the farm buildings.[1] Henry Howell wrote, "The next morning we were taken forward a short distance and our skirmishers went out to find the position of the enemy."[2] Looking south from this position, the young private and his comrades would have seen two hills, one wooded, the other clearcut on the western face. A ridgeline lay to the west of the hills with a sluggish creek in the valley between. That morning, the men in blue thought them as common as the wheat field and peach orchard they'd passed on the march in the night before. These landmarks — the Peach Orchard, the Wheatfield, the Slaughter Pen, Bloody Run — anonymous as the thousand other hills, creeks, orchards, and fields they had seen on the long march up from Virginia, would, by sundown, be among of the most celebrated locations in American military history.

Sergeant Hanford noted, "Early the next morning of the 2d we got our breakfast, and were then formed in line of battle behind a stone wall — an excellent position we thought."[3] Private A.W. Tucker of Hanford's company also remembered the stone wall. "In the morning of the 2d we began making preparations for a fight by fortifying our position; which was in the woods and along a stone wall."[4]

The ammunition wagons arrived while the men were in position along the stone wall. Each man already carried sixty cartridges but "were ordered to take at least 80 rounds of ammunition, of which there was a generous supply. I do not believe any of the boys took less than 100 rounds, and many took twice that amount, putting the extra cartridges in their empty haversacks in lieu of rations."[5]

General Birney received orders from General Sickles to have his division take up a position along Cemetery Ridge to their rear. Birney wrote, "I relieved Geary's division, and formed a line, resting its left on the Sugar Loaf Mountain and the right thrown in a direct line toward the cemetery, connection on the right with the Second Division of this corps. My picket line was in the Emmitsburg road, with sharpshooters some 300 yards in advance."[6] The 2nd Division, commanded by General A.A. Humphries, was to connect to the 2nd Corps farther north on the ridge line toward Cemetery Hill.

So it was, that as early as 7 A.M., General Sickles had his men in roughly the position General Meade had assigned to him: two divisions on Cemetery Ridge, the right of the corps connected

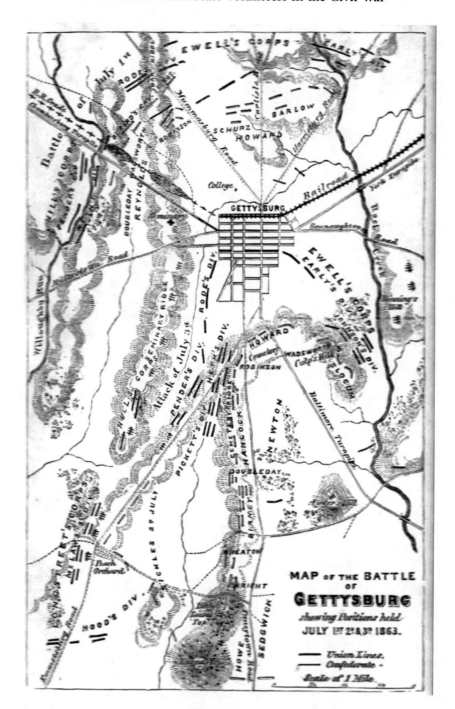

Harper's Gettysburg

to the left of Hancock's Corps to the north, the left of the corps on or near the rocky hill — Sugar Loaf Mountain, Birney called it. As a precaution, Birney advanced pickets and sharpshooters well in front of the main line to warn of the approach of the enemy.

But General Sickles had some serious concerns about his position at the southern end of the line. First there was the question of control of the Emmitsburg Road to his front. Sickles was worried that the Confederates might seize the road and prevent de Trobriand's Brigade and the 3rd Corps wagon trains from rejoining him. Then there was the issue of the high ground to his front. A peach orchard up near the road was about forty feet higher than the ground held by the 3rd Corps. If the Confederates massed artillery there, they would pose a serious threat to Sickles's line. There was high ground to his left as well, Houck's Ridge, an ideal position for the enemy to post artillery with a commanding view of the left of Sickles's line. Two months before, almost to the day, the 3rd Corps had been subjected to a concentrated artillery crossfire from enemy guns at Hazel Grove and from along the Plank Road at Chancellorsville. Sickles, with the experience of Sunday, May 3, still fresh on his mind, did not want his Corps exposed to such destructive fire again.

And then there was the Pipe Creek Circular issued July 1 from Taneytown by General Meade. It stated in part that "If the enemy assume the offensive, and attack, it is his [Meade's] intention after holding them in check sufficiently long, to withdraw the trains and other impedimenta; to Withdraw the army from its present position, and form line of battle with the left resting in the neighborhood of Middleburg, and the right at Manchester, the general direction being that of Pipe Creek." The document went on to detail where each of the Union infantry corps would be posted south of the state line along Big Pipe Creek in Maryland should the Gettysburg position become untenable. "The time for falling back can only be developed by circumstances" Meade concluded.

Any good commander would make such provisions and, as it turned out, circumstances led to the circular being countermanded almost as soon as it was written. The Confederate advance on Gettysburg and the determination of Buford and Reynolds to fight there rendered the order moot. But it sounded all too familiar to Dan Sickles. At Chancellorsville, Hooker had given up Hazel Grove, a key position on the field. Then, with victory within his grasp, he'd pulled back across the Rappahannock. In later years, Sickles would say that on July 2, he was concerned that Meade might have had something similar in mind.

Sometime Thursday morning, Sickles became convinced that the main Confederate attack would take place on his front, which, as things turned out, it did. He also felt that Meade was ignoring the left of the line where Sickles's Corps was located, in favor of the right, an idea that historian Richard Sauers and author David Downs have convincingly disputed.[7]

But in Dan Sickles's defense, there *were* disquieting events taking place at his end of the line. General Geary's 12th Corps division, which had spent the night on or near Little Round Top, had been pulled out early in the morning of July 2 and marched to the far right of the line to rejoin the 12th Corps. Then, around noon, most of the cavalry screen to the left of Sickles's line disappeared when General Buford moved his troopers to Westminster to refit. Buford's men were tired from the spirited defense they'd put up along the ridgelines northwest of town the day before, but surely no more so than foot soldiers tramping the roads leading to Gettysburg. General Pleasanton, the federal cavalry commander, was supposed to send more horse soldiers to replace Buford, something Meade ordered and assumed had been done. But it had not been done and as the day wore on, only a single Yankee cavalry brigade prowled the roads and fields south and west of Sickles's line. "Had Buford's men remained in place," author Peter C. Vermilyea argues, "it is likely they would have detected the preparations for Longstreet's July 2 assault."[8]

So, what exactly did General Lee have in mind for the Army of the Potomac on the second day of the battle? After sending out scouting parties and conferring with his subordinates, the Confederate commander decided to demonstrate against the Union right on Culp's Hill to draw attention, and perhaps Union troops, in that direction while he launched an attack with two of his best divisions against the Union left flank. Lee planned to use the cover of ridgelines and woods to get Hood's Division and McLaw's Division of General James Longstreet's Corps into position on the west side of the Emmitsburg Road opposite and below the extreme left of the

Union line. An overwhelming attack on the Yankees' exposed flank was becoming Lee's stock in trade and if the Confederates made headway in their feint against Meade's right, so much the better. It was essential to get Longstreet's divisions into position undetected, coordinate the attacks against the left and right flanks of the Union army, and get the attack underway early enough to exploit the breakthrough before it got dark. If all went according to plan, the result might be a victory to rival even that at Chancellorsville.

The Confederate attack on the left was to be "up the Emmitsburg Road," a phrase that demonstrated that Lee had incorrectly assumed that the Union line stretched south along that road from the area around Cemetery Hill. In actuality, the Union line on the morning of July 2, stretched south along Cemetery Ridge, well to the east of where Lee thought it would be. "Indeed," wrote Daniel M. Laney, "the Yankee line had never been where Lee thought it was."[9] And what was Lee's ultimate goal if his brigades successfully began to roll up the Union flank? That goal was certainly not Little Round Top or the Peach Orchard but, as historian Troy D. Harman argues, Cemetery Hill, the all-important jugular that dominated the Baltimore Pike, Meade's lifeline to the rear.[10]

As Lee planned, there was a lot of activity along the Union lines. Between 6 and 7 A.M., General Meade sent his son and aide, Captain George Meade, to check out the southern end of the line. He found Sickles's headquarters in a grove of trees, the place deceptively quiet. Captain Meade was surprised to be told that the 3rd Corps was not where it was supposed to be. In addition, he was told that there was some question as where exactly it was to be deployed. The young captain returned to headquarters to tell his father, the general, of the situation. General Meade sent his son back with specific instructions as to where he wanted the 3rd Corps to be placed. When Captain Meade arrived, Sickles told him that he was deploying his corps as they spoke but was still unsure where his left flank was supposed to be — all this despite the fact that the 3rd Corps was even then in place along Cemetery Ridge.[11]

At about 10 A.M., Sickles himself arrived at headquarters. He found Meade, who stepped outside, pointed south toward Little Round Top, and told Sickles in no uncertain terms that this was where he wanted the left flank of the 3rd Corps to be. However, the two generals later disagreed as to what was said. Dan Sickles asked his commanding officer if he would like to come to the southern end of the line to personally inspect his dispositions. Meade, fearing an attack near Culp's Hill on the right, declined. When Sickles asked if General Henry Hunt, Meade's chief of artillery, could help him post the corps' artillery, Meade readily agreed.[12]

Hunt and Sickles toured the area along the Emmitsburg Road near the peach orchard. As the two men rode, Hunt realized Sickles wanted to move his corps forward to this new, advanced position. Hunt made some observations and offered advice but he would not approve the move forward simply because he had no authority to do so. As the two officers talked, heavy cannon fire could be heard from the direction of Cemetery Hill. Hunt took his leave and rode north to find out what was happening but he stopped off at headquarters to talk to Meade of Sickles's plans.[13] "After finishing my examination I returned to headquarters and briefly reported to General Meade that the proposed line was a good one in itself, that it offered favorable positions for artillery, but that its relations to other lines were such that I could not advise it, and suggested that he examine it himself before ordering its occupation. He nodded assent, and I proceeded to Cemetery Hill."[14]

Meade did not immediately go to the left but instead stayed at his headquarters well into the afternoon awaiting the arrival of Union reinforcements.

General Birney wrote,

> At 12 m., believing from the constant fire of the enemy that a movement was being made toward the left, I received permission from Major-General Sickles to send 100 of Berdan's Sharpshooters, with the Third Maine Regiment as a support, and feel the enemy's right. I sent Capt. J.C. Briscoe, of my staff,

with the reconnaissance, which was under Colonel Berdan's command. They advanced from the peach orchard out the Millerstown road, and entered the woods in order to flank the enemy. The skirmishers of the enemy were driven in, but three columns of their forces were found marching to our left. The force sent by me was driven back by overwhelming numbers, with the loss of about 60, killed and wounded.[15]

In later years, Colonel Berdan would claim that he had located Longstreet's two divisions making their way to turn the Union left flank. Berdan also would claim that his sharpshooters engaged Longstreet's men and delayed the Confederate advance long enough for the 3rd Corps to get into position. Neither assertion was true. Berdan had stumbled upon the three Alabama regiments of General Cadmus Wilcox's Brigade, troops not part of Longstreet's Corps at all.

Nevertheless, Berdan got the word back to Birney, who wrote, "Communicating this important information to Major-General Sickles, I was ordered by that officer to change my front to meet the attack. I did this by advancing my left 500 yards, and swinging around the right so as to rest on the Emmitsburg road at the peach orchard. He also informed me that a division from the Second and one from the Fifth Corps had been ordered to be in readiness to support me."[16]

So there it was: enemy troops *were* moving on Sickles's front, just as he had suspected. The irony should not be lost on any student of the battle. Berdan, who had a reputation for being somewhat flighty, and Sickles, who once took target practice on his wife's boyfriend, used faulty information to draw the correct conclusion. There were indeed masses of enemy troops headed their way but they were not the troops Berdan had seen. Longstreet's men were in the woods behind Wilcox, well out of sight of anyone on the Union side. Sickles seized upon Berdan's report and took matters into his own hands. He ordered his corps forward to take up the advanced line on the high ground to his front that he had been thinking about all morning. It should be mentioned that one of the reasons Sickles later gave for this advance was that he did not have enough men in the 3rd Corps to defend the line assigned to him by Meade. One might wonder how he intended to defend an even longer line with the same number of men.

All this was unknown to the men in the ranks of the 124th New York who would have been delighted just to get some rest and hot food. At roll call that morning, two hundred forty men were present. "The majority of those who had given out and fallen behind during our forced march from Emmetsburg, answered to their names."[17]

One of those men was Private A.W. Tucker, who wrote,

> It must have been nearly noon when we were ordered to fall in and began to maneuver to form a line of battle. A general quietude prevailed except an occasional picket shot. After changing position several times we came to the historic Wheatfield. At that time it was in its golden ripeness. Our regiment was the first troops to despoil its beauty. We marched battalion front to the middle of it and rested, perhaps, half an hour. We then moved by the left flank through a narrow piece of woods and took position on an open, rocky ridge, called Houck's Ridge, which we supposed at the time was Little Round Top. There we lay quiet perhaps two hours, or till 2:30 P.M.[18]

Second Sergeant J. Harvey Hanford of Company B recalled that he would have been content to remain behind his fortified stone wall back near Cemetery Ridge when the order "forward, march" was given. Once through the wheat field the regiment marched by the left flank, moving from a line of battle to a column four men abreast. Hanford wrote, "When halt was sounded, I being the extreme left man in the regiment, I found myself on the rocks at Devil's Den."[19] Historian Kathleen Georg Harrison of the Gettysburg National Military Park has argued that the much heralded Devil's Den has achieved fame far beyond its value as a place of military importance in the battle. The rocks were "not an asset to either Union or Confederate armies of Gettysburg. The tide of battle flowed around this bulwark, and any who stood on its huge boulders too long became an eventual target."[20]

Along this rock-strewn landscape, wooded in some places and with open fields in others, General Birney positioned his three brigades to cover the Union line from Devil's Den in the south to a peach orchard up on the Emmitsburg Road to the northwest. Ward's Brigade formed the left of the line along Houck's Ridge, de Trobriand's Brigade held the center near a wheat field, and Graham's Brigade took position on the right near the peach orchard. From that point, Sickles positioned General Andrew A. Humphrey's Division along the Emmitsburg Road north toward Gettysburg. Sickles's line from Devil's Den to the rightmost regiment of Humphrey's Division stretched for about a mile and a half and was manned by 11,924 infantry and artillerymen of the 3rd Corps.[21]

Sickles's decision to move forward upset Meade's plans for July 2 but it also disrupted Lee's plans, perhaps to the point of preventing another Chancellorsville-like flank attack. At least Dan Sickles and his defenders thought so and they would argue the point until the last of the proud veterans of the 3rd Corps was in his grave. In the fight to come Sickles would lose a leg and gain a Medal of Honor instead of the court martial many, now as then, thought he deserved.

Once the 3rd Corps was moving forward, it was up to subordinate officers to position their men. Birney wanted Captain James Smith's 4th New York Independent Battery where it could "command the gorge at the base of the Sugar Loaf Mountain."[22] At about 1 P.M., Captain G.E. Randolph, 3rd Corps chief of artillery, personally led Smith to the southern end of Houck's Ridge, ordering him to position his guns as he saw fit.[23]

Smith's battery consisted of six rifled Parrott cannons, easily recognizable by the extra wrap of reinforcing iron at the rear of the tube. The guns had been cast at the West Point Foundry at Cold Spring, New York, just across the Hudson River from the military academy. These were powerful weapons, capable of firing a ten pound solid shot well over a mile. Standard procedure for artillery placement called for fourteen yards between each gun and a quick look at the proposed location told Smith he had room for only four guns. "In rear of this ridge," he wrote, "the ground descended sharply to the east, leaving no room for the limbers on the crest, therefore they were posted as near to the guns as the nature of the declivity permitted."[24] The placement of the limbers below the crest protected them from enemy fire but required that each round would have to be carried up and over the steep hill to the gunners.

Thomas Bradley, recently promoted from corporal to 2nd sergeant of Company H, watched as Smith's Battery approached. "I saw the Battery come down Rock Run Glen. The guns were unlimbered at the foot of Rock Ridge and hauled up the steep acclivity into position amid the rocks on its crest."[25] The four guns on Houck's Ridge easily had the range of the Emmitsburg Road, but if the enemy advanced into the valley created by Rose Run, at the foot of the ridge, the cannon barrels could not be depressed sufficiently to hit them. Thus the enemy would be sheltered from the fire of Smith's guns just when he could do them the most damage. The remaining section of two guns was placed in the rear of the ridge pointing south to cover any Confederate advance into the Plum Run gorge between Big Round Top and Devil's Den.

General Ward arranged his regiments left to right along the ridge line: 124th New York, 86th New York, 20th Indiana, and 99th Pennsylvania. Major Stoughton of the 2nd U.S. Sharpshooters, back from its fight with Wilcox's

Sergeant Thomas W. Bradley as he looked at the Battle of Gettysburg. "What a mad act it was," he said of the charge into the Weikert Field (Marcus Millspaugh collection).

troops, reported to Ward who sent the elite regiment forward about half a mile to "await further orders."[26] The 4th Maine, doing picket duty out in front of the 1st Corps, arrived on the field and was placed to the left of Smith's guns near Devil's Den. But it should be remembered, argues Kathleen Harrison, that it was Houck's Ridge itself, not Devil's Den, that "was the anchor of the Federal defense by the 3rd Corps. The position of Smith's New York Battery, and of those infantrymen ... should be heralded as the defensive rock and not relegated to a supporting role for the granitic rock beneath them to their left."[27]

The troops nearest the battery were the 4th Maine and the 124th New York, "formed so as to cover the open space between the woods and base of Round Top; the former being on the extreme left, while the latter, the 'Orange Blossoms,' were directly in rear of the four guns."[28] The 86th New York was posted to the right of the 124th in a piece of woods; between the two regiments was a gap of about 100 yards which Captain Weygant plugged with several men from his company.[29] In front of the regiment was an open field in the shape of a triangle owned by George Weikert. The field formed part of the western slope of the ridge that terminated at a branch of Plum Run known locally as Rose Run.

By mid-afternoon, Smith's guns were in place, as were the infantry regiments assigned to protect the battery. The men of the 4th Maine "were hungry, having drank water for supper, breakfast, and dinner. Fires were kindled, a heifer was found nearby and slaughtered, coffee was steeped and beef impaled on sticks and warmed over the blaze. We drank our coffee and ate the very rare and thoroughly smoked meat, sprinkling it with salt, of which condiment every soldier carried a little in his pocket."[30]

Captain Weygant remembered, "We had not yet learned by bitter experience the inestimable value of breastworks, and instead of spending our leisure time in rolling together the loose stones and throwing over them such a quantity of earth as would have formed a bullet proof line, we lounged about on the grass and rocks, quietly awaiting the coming shock, which many declared themselves ready and anxious to receive."[31]

Weygant's comments notwithstanding, the 124th certainly did have experience fighting from cover, enough experience to know the benefits of a stout breastworks. At Chancellorsville just two months prior, the regiment took a position near Hazel Grove in rifle pits and behind a fence, repelling several Confederate probing attacks after dark. They fought from behind artillery earthworks the next day and were put to work digging rifle pits on the days following that battle. At Brandy Station they fought in the woods, knowing enough to take cover behind trees and in thick brush.

By the time they reached Devil's Den on the afternoon of July 2, they had already changed positions several times. The veterans themselves, including Weygant, wrote years later that they boiled coffee, rested, or foraged for something to eat instead of building earthworks near Devil's Den. Having been marched about all morning, including one move that took them away from a position they had made the effort to fortify, they probably thought they would move again.

Since early morning, according to Captain Weygant, it was widely held among the rank and file that Lee was present with all his troops but was hesitant to attack. The men attributed this to the absence of Stonewall Jackson, who died of wounds received at Chancellorsville. It was further held, and by late afternoon probably taken as gospel, that Lee preferred to allow the Yankees to attack *him*. While this was wildly optimistic and belied the fact that Lee had done plenty of attacking the day before, it nonetheless may well have accounted for the lack of activity among the troops that afternoon. "During all this time an ominous silence prevailed, broken only by the occasional exchange of rifle shots by skirmishers or sharpshooters."[32]

At about this time, General Meade decided to take a look at his left flank. He rode south along the line to supervise the placement of the 5th Corps and to inspect the 3rd Corps positions when he discovered that Sickles's new line was well in advance of where the army commander wanted it to be. Meade told Sickles that he had placed his men beyond supporting distance of the rest of the army and that this move forced him to fight on ground not of his own choosing. Sickles apologized and offered to pull his men back, but the opening guns of the Confederate attack cancelled any plans of withdrawal.[33]

Private Josiah Dawson of Company H was "resting upon a rock, thinking of home, with the skirmish line out. All at once our pickets were driven in and the battle was on." Sergeant Harvey Hanford noted, "Presently a shell came shrieking, and bursting near us, we needed no order or invitation to get behind the rocks, but did so at once."[34]

Captain William A. Jackson described the scene. "The next morning we were placed in position on the left wing and had a rather quiet time until between 3 & 4 o'clock when a sharp artillery fire commenced. The previous silence was then explained the rebs had been massing their troops to force our left wing. About 4 P.M. or a little later we saw them coming in three lines while as yet we had but one to oppose them but we determined to give them a hot reception."[35]

"Why I remember well the first shot fired at Gettysburg," Private John T. LaRue of Company I told a reporter sixty-six years later.

> We had been formed in echelon, a battle wedge, between Longstreet's Johnnies and our own back lines. We were all lying down behind the rocks, and natural formations on the hill. My old school teacher was on my right and we were talking when all of a sudden the man on the other side of me dug me a hefty wallop in the ribs and pointed to some rebs placing a battery directly in front of us. "In a minute she'll fire," he said, and the word was no sooner out of his mouth when "boom" she went, and the shell flew over our heads.[36]

General Hunt, who had returned to the left of the line, was concerned that Captain Smith had not engaged the Confederates with his battery and he sought out Smith to determine the reason. "The difficulty in getting these guns up the height had caused the delay in Smith's opening his fire," Hunt observed, but once he got the guns in place "his fire was very effective." Hunt saw that Smith's position "commanded that of the enemy and enfiladed their line."[37]

General Ward wrote that the 2nd U.S. Sharpshooters, the regiment he had sent out in front of the brigade, "had scarcely obtained the position designated before the skirmishers of the enemy issued from a wood in front, followed by heavy lines of infantry. Captain Smith's battery of rifled guns, posted on the eminence to my left, opened on the advancing enemy, as well as Captain Winslow's battery on my right, the enemy replying from a battery near the Emmitsburg road."[38]

The artillery duel at the south end of the line now began in earnest. From their position to the right of the battery, the men of the 124th New York were about to witness "a trial of skill between artillerists" they would remember for years to come. Smith's battery first engaged "several guns" on his right front. Twenty minutes later he "discovered the enemy was endeavoring to get a section of twelve-pounder guns in position on my left and front, in order to enfilade this part of our line; but I succeeded in driving them off before they had an opportunity to open fire." Smith had no sooner dealt with the two-gun section when he noticed a battery of twelve-pound Napoleons emerge from the woods in a field about fourteen hundred yards distant. "A spirited duel immediately began between this battery and my own, lasting nearly twenty minutes."[39]

Private A.W. Tucker of Company B put the position of Smith's Battery at about thirty feet to the left and in front of his company, so close that enemy shells, directed at Smith's guns, fell uncomfortably close to the Orange Blossoms.

> Our Colonel [Ellis] moved us by the right-flank into the woods on which our right rested. I judge he thought after he had got us in there that instead of the woods being a protection they made our new position more hazardous than the one we had just abandoned. We were soon moved by the left flank back to our old position, Company B resting within a few feet of Smith's battery. During all this time the cannonading was going on incessantly from 100 pieces along the lines on each side. It lasted for about an hour. There were several casualties in our regiment from the enemy's shells.[40]

According to Tucker, the firing ended at about 3 P.M., both sides stopping "as by mutual consent, as though for a breathing spell; but it was of short duration."[41] Tucker and those on the left of the regiment saw the reason for the breathing spell: Confederate skirmishers began to move across the Emmittsburg Road in large numbers, but what followed the skirmish line caught everyone's attention. "Within supporting distance was a long line of battle extending in either direction as far as the eye could reach. It was followed by a second and third line, each in supporting distance."[42] The Confederate batteries ceased firing to allow the infantry formations to pass through them. "It was at this particular time that Smith's battery did splendid service. The guns were worked to their utmost. The heroic Captain gave every order in a clear, distinct tone, that could be heard above the tumult. I heard him tell his gunners to give them five and six second fuse, and when the gunners told him the case shot and shrapnel were all gone, he said, 'Give them shell; give the solid shot; d — n them, give them anything!'"[43]

From his position near the center of the line, Sergeant Bradley saw the Confederates advance.

> The battery changed from shell to canister and working as I never saw gunners work before or since, tore gap after gap through the ranks of the advancing foe. All this time the gallant Captain and his men were exposed to the direct fire of Longstreet's sharpshooters and his front line. Every round of ammunition had to be carried from the foot of the ridge. Man after man went down, but still the exhausting work went steadily on, the officers tirelessly falling in to fill out a working detail for the guns, and keeping up a well-directed fire until the enemy was at the base of the heights and the guns could no longer be depressed to reach him.[44]

Sergeant Hanford had an even better view from the far left of the line. "Then shone out the bravery of Capt. Smith. When he had not men enough left to man the guns, he would come to us and ask and beg of us to help him fire them. Then he would run back to the guns, do what he could, and then back to us, and, with tears in his eyes, would say: 'For God's sake, men, don't let them take my guns away from me!'" Even as he wrote this remembrance twenty-two years after the event, Sergeant Hanford could still see the look on Smith's face and hear his voice. "O, how I would like to see him and thank him for what he then did, and if this meets his eye I would like to have him write to me."[45] The effect of Smith's fire and that of the other Union batteries in the wheat field and the peach orchard did much to break up the Confederate attack. But it was the plan of attack itself and the unexpected placement of the 3rd Corps that caused the Confederates even more trouble.

The Confederates were under the impression that the Union line ran south along the Emmitsburg Road from Cemetery Hill to just north of a crossroads near the John Sherfy Farm. Lee's plan called for Hood's Division of Longstreet's Corps to cross the Emmitsburg Road, out of sight of the Yankees to the north, then advance in a northeasterly direction through the relatively open farmland east of the road. McLaws's Division, positioned to the left of Hood, would do the same. Together the two powerful divisions would hit the Yankee flank somewhere to the north. As far as they knew, there would be no enemy troops anywhere near the peach orchard to challenge their progress. They would "roll up the flank" as they had done at Chancellorsville.

Once on the scene, General Hood quickly recognized the problem with the plan of attack: Yankee infantry and artillery were on a ridgeline to his front where they were not supposed to be. He was looking at Houck's Ridge with Smith's Battery and Ward's Brigade in place and waiting. If he moved as ordered, his right flank would be exposed to their fire. He also saw that McLaws would be attacking the high ground around the peach orchard, a place unexpectedly studded with guns and packed with Union infantry. Whatever else may be said about Dan Sickles and his move forward, it certainly put a crimp in Lee's plan for the second day of the battle.

As the first brigades of Hood's Division moved out, the plan of attack was customized on the spot. Brigadier General Evander Law's Alabama Brigade crossed the Emmittsburg Road and headed east, not northeast, toward the gorge between Devil's Den and Big Round Top. Law had settled the point about the direction of the attack by simply going straight at the Yankees. To Law's left came Brigadier General Jerome B. Robertson's Brigade. His rightmost regiments, the 4th and 5th Texas, kept hold of Law's left while the 3rd Arkansas and 1st Texas tried to keep aligned with the Emmittsburg Road. It quickly became clear to General Robertson that he could not do both, as the gap between his two right regiments and two left regiments grew wider with each step. Colonel Manning of the 3rd Arkansas wrote, "I decided to keep my line on a prolongation of the line formed by the troops on my right," and headed toward Houck's Ridge and Smith's Battery, which had been sending shot and shell among them since the Confederate batteries had opened fire.[46] "Like a magnet," wrote Daniel Laney, "the deadly fire of these guns had brought the Southerners to this place."[47]

Behind the lead brigades came Brigadier General Henry L. Benning's four Georgia regiments, also headed for the gorge, then came Brigadier General George T. Anderson's Brigade marching toward the Rose woods and the northern end of Houck's Ridge. No one was targeting Devil's Den itself although the 44th and 48th Alabama of Law's Brigade cut loose from the others who were headed for Big Round Top, and, once past the Slyder homestead, turned north to deal with that annoying Yankee battery.

Smith and his men were keeping up a deadly fire on the advancing southern infantry, demonstrating what well-trained gunners firing superior weaponry could do. General Robertson wrote "As we advanced through this field, for half a mile, we were exposed to a heavy and destructive fire of canister, grape, and shell ...·and from the enemy's sharpshooters from behind the numerous rocks, fences and houses in the field."[48] These were members of the 2nd U.S. Sharpshooters operating around the John Slyder homestead, using natural cover and taking a toll on the advancing enemy, one well-aimed shot at a time. Major J.P. Bane of the 4th Texas wrote, "Advancing at the double-quick, we soon met the enemy's skirmishers, who occupied a skirt of thick undergrowth about one-quarter of a mile from the base of the cliffs, upon which the enemy had a battery playing upon us with most deadly effect."[49]

Private James O. Bradfield, Company E, 1st Texas, wrote of the advance, "We were in direct range of the enemy's guns on the mountain beyond. As our artillery began feeling for their batteries, the answering shells struck our lines with cruel effect. The Fourth Texas suffered most severely. As they were passing this zone of fire, one shell killed and wounded fifteen men. It certainly tries a man's nerve to have to stand still and receive such a fire without being able to return it."[50]

Thomas M. Ries of Company A, 2nd U.S. Sharpshooters, wrote, "Our Sharpshooters were about ½ a mile in advance of our main line — checked the advance of the enemy — twice throwing their line into confusion — being out of ammunition fell back — until we reach the 124 N.Y. Regt posted on the rocky knoll near our left — then the fighting became general."[51]

About twenty minutes into the advance, one of Sickles's begrimed artillerymen unknowingly performed a routine task that may well have doomed the enemy attack just as it was getting underway. He cut the timed fuse on a shell so that it exploded at a critical point — right above division commander General John B. Hood. The general was nearly knocked from the saddle by a shell fragment that tore into his left arm. As he was being carried to the rear, he felt "deep distress of mind and heart at the thought of the inevitable fate of my brave fellow-soldiers," and well he might.[52] The attack was going in without his strong guiding hand. Hood's men pressed relentlessly ahead, subordinate officers taking the initiative and making decisions on their own. Chief among them was the decision to silence the battery atop Houck's Ridge and destroy any Federal infantry in support.

Early in the fight one of Smith's guns was disabled by an enemy shell. It was hauled to the rear, leaving three Parrott's still in action. Now, as Hood's men drew near, Captain Smith assessed his options. The enemy was closing with his battery in front and on the left. He was fully aware that once the Confederates were on the low ground at the base of Houck's Ridge and in the gorge between Devil's Den and Big Round Top, he could do them little damage. He also knew that just two small regiments protected his three remaining guns, the 4th Maine to his left, which at his suggestion had moved into the valley below Devil's Den, and the 124th New York to the right and rear. He still had time to withdraw, pull the three guns back over the hill, and place them next to the section he had in the rear. But to do so would spur the enemy forward and demoralize his Union infantry supports on his right and left. It did not take Captain Smith long to make his decision: he would stand by his guns and use them against the enemy as long as possible.

Smith's gunners grimly kept up their fire. "I never saw the men do better work; every shot told; the pieces were discharged as rapidly as they could be with regard to effectiveness, while the conduct of the men was superb."[53] Now the enemy was but three hundred yards off and coming fast. Smith called out the order to switch to canister, each round packed with iron balls that tore great holes in the enemy lines. To increase the rate of fire and rain yet more destruction, Smith ordered that the charges be rammed home without taking the precaution of first swabbing the hot bore with a wet sponge to extinguish any sparks left behind from the previous round. This was extremely dangerous as the new round could ignite in the tube while the gunner was still in the act of ramming home the charge. Hood's men were now close enough to bring the battery under rifle fire but Smith's men stood by their guns

"Our position i.e. of the 124th was on a knoll with a wood on our right (the 86th N.Y. were on our right)," Captain Jackson wrote. "In fact the ground was much broken, very uneven. The 4th Me. on our left. The rebs advanced to the foot of the knoll or hill on which we were and were protected by it."[54] The "rebs" referred to by Captain Jackson were the 1st Texas, commanded by Lieutenant Colonel P.A. Work, and 3rd Arkansas, commanded by Colonel Van Manning, both of General J.B. Robertson's "Texas Brigade."

When the two regiments approached the low ground near Rose Run, their skirmishers engaged and drove off the Yankee skirmishers posted behind the stone wall at the base of Weikert's triangular field.[55] They had reached the relative safety at the base of Houck's Ridge, where Smith's guns could do them little damage.

The two regiments moved forward together, the 3rd Arkansas into the Rose Woods and the 1st Texas into the Weikert Field. Having advanced about one hundred fifty yards, Manning found that his regiment "was suffering from a fire to my left and rear," as the 17th Maine of de Trobriand's Brigade opened up on them from behind a stone wall at a range of about one hundred yards. He halted his regiment, then drew back his leftmost company to deal with the threat. Manning was again able to advance, "the enemy fighting stubbornly, but retiring," until his left was again threatened. The 3rd Arkansas, which moved forward with about four hundred seventy men, found itself facing four Yankee regiments with a combined strength of well over one thousand men, not to mention Winslow's six-gun battery firing on their flank from the Wheatfield.[56] Manning was forced to halt, then fell back "fifty to seventy five yards, to meet the contingency."[57] Private Bradfield of the 1st Texas recalled the halt and wrote, "It cost us dearly."[58]

This exposed the left flank of the 1st Texas to enemy fire so, within about one hundred twenty five yards of the enemy guns, Colonel Work also called a halt and sent forty men from Company G to help. They "soon engaged the enemy and drove them from their threatening position to the left and the front of the Third Arkansas."[59]

General Ward had prepared his brigade to meet the advance of Hood's men. "The supports of the first two lines of the enemy were now-coming up in columns *en masse*, while we had but a single line of battle to receive the shock.... My line awaited the clash. To the regiments on the right, who were sheltered in the wood, I gave directions not to fire until they could plainly see the enemy; to those who were on the left, not to fire at a longer distance than 200 yards."[60] The regiments on Ward's right were the 99th Pennsylvania, 20th Indiana, and the 86th New York;

Gettysburg, July 2, 1863

Late in the afternoon, General Longstreet launched his attack against the left of the Union line. Two regiments of Robertson's Brigade and two from Law's Brigade moved against the units of General J.H.H. Ward's Union brigade atop Houck's Ridge. The 1st Texas, in attempting to capture the three remaining guns of Captain James Smith's 4th New York Battery, advanced toward the 124th New York. Colonel Ellis had his men positioned behind and to the right of Smith's guns. The men lay on the ground with loaded weapons, bayonets fixed. When Ellis gave the order, they rose up and fired two devastating volleys into the Texans, then charged.

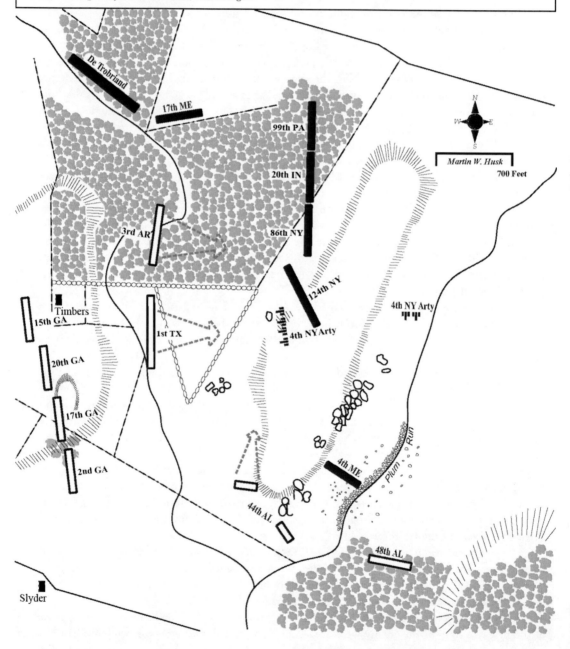

De Trobriand

17th ME

99th PA

20th IN

3rd AR

86th NY

124th NY

Timbers

15th GA

1st TX

4th NY Arty

4th NY Arty

20th GA

17th GA

2nd GA

4th ME

Plum Run

44th AL

48th AL

Slyder

Martin W. Husk

700 Feet

N
W   E
S

all were "sheltered in the wood." Those on the left were the 124th New York and the 4th Maine, the former partially in the Rose Woods, the latter in position well to the left of Smith's guns. "The enemy had now approached to within 200 yards of my position ... yelling and shouting."[61]

Private Tucker saw three rebel lines advancing against one thin line of Union blue. The 3rd Arkansas was in the woods moving to engage the right of Ward's line while the 1st Texas began its advance up through the Weikert Field toward Smith's guns. What Tucker did not see was the 44th Alabama making its way up the south face of Houck's Ridge preparing to attack the battery from the left. The 44th and the 48th Alabama had been detached from Law's Brigade early in the advance and ordered to move through the area between Devil's Den and Big Round Top to silence Smith's Battery.[62]

The advance of the 1st Texas now resumed but it was steady and deliberate rather than a charge.[63] Henry Howell wrote later that the Texans were "creeping up the hill" and although the Southerners described exchanging rifle fire with the infantry regiment near Smith's guns, Howell maintained that the "Union infantry was kept under cover while the artillery duel was fought."[64]

Colonel Ellis had made his own preparations for his Orange Blossoms to meet the Texans. He had his men load, then lie down, the left of the 124th New York just fifty feet behind Smith's guns. The 1st Texas moved steadily up the triangular field, every man's eyes on the three smoking Parrott Rifles clearly visible on the hill. When the Texans were just one hundred yards off, Ellis ordered his men to fix bayonets, but not to rise or fire until he ordered them to do so. "The order was obeyed to the letter. It was a trying position, the bullets pattering around and amongst us without our being privileged to return the compliment."[65] Every Orange Blossom did as ordered — the wrath of their colonel was as terrifying as any Rebel charge. Ellis had enough battle experience to know that he needed to do more than just stop the Texans. He must drive them from the field to regain the initiative and turn the tide of battle on his front.

When the enemy was within pistol range, Smith's beleaguered artillerymen grabbed rammers, primers, and anything else they could carry and headed for the rear, rendering the Parrotts useless. Private Tucker looked toward Captain Smith, "when I saw him sheath his sword as he said the infantry must support him. No man ever commanded a battery more bravely than did Capt. J.E. Smith at Gettysburg."[66]

The Texans surged up the last few yards and were among Smith's guns when Ellis gave the order to rise up and fire. "There was never a more destructive volley fired. It seemed to paralyze their whole line." Ellis gave the order to load and fire again and then prepared to charge the stunned Texans.[67]

"My command did not fire a shot until the enemy came within the distance prescribed," wrote General Ward, "when the whole command fired a volley. This checked the enemy's advance suddenly, which gave our men an opportunity to reload, when another volley was fired into them."[68]

In the short time between the first and second volley, a celebrated moment in the history of the 124th New York played itself out. Colonel Ellis was in his proper position at the rear center of the regiment, his arms folded, calm and determined. Earlier, Major James Cromwell, whose post was at the center of the left wing, had urged the colonel to order the charge, "but the Colonel shakes his head and tells the Major to go back to his place again." Captain Silliman, who chronicled the scene, implied that this was not Cromwell's first request to charge.[69]

Now, as the men reloaded, Cromwell again hurried toward Ellis, and this time Lieutenant Henry Ramsdell accompanied him to press the case. Again both men are told to return to their places. But now the horses were brought up, probably at the direction of Ellis himself, who knew what he wanted to do. According to Silliman, Ellis and Cromwell "had their horses brought up," implying that each man called for his mount separately.[70] It is highly unlikely that Colonel Ellis would have permitted two junior officers to ride while he remained on foot. Against the remonstrations of their comrades, the three officers, Ellis, Cromwell, and Ramsdell, mounted. Captain Silliman warned the major, a longtime friend from Cornwall, that he would make too inviting a target. Cromwell's reply became legend: "The men must see us to-day."[71] The major then told the company officers nearest him to "have their men ready for a charge."[72]

Lieutenant James Finnegan of Company K approached Ellis with the same warning. Finnegan "advised him to dismount, as he would not present, on foot, quite so prominent a mark for the rebel sharpshooters." The colonel's reply, made while astride his iron-gray horse, was not as dramatic as was the major's, but it was just as striking: "If I am fated to fall to-day, dismounting will not save me."[73]

There is some disagreement as to what happened next. Captain Weygant, who was at the far right end of the line, remembered that after Cromwell's comment to Silliman, the major rode to the left center of this regiment. He then drew his sword, fixed his eyes on Ellis, and "impatiently" waited for the command. In short order, the colonel looked in Cromwell's direction, and "by a simple nod gives the desired permission."[74] Silliman wrote that the "enemy, with fierce yells, commenced to ascend the hill in front" and, with the Texans but fifty paces off, Ellis gave the order to rise up and fire "and as the volley was poured in he simply nodded his head to the Major as an order to charge them." Silliman made no mention of the second volley nor is mention made of Ellis giving any orders to his men.[75]

"Now Cromwell waved his sword twice above his head," Weygant wrote, "makes a lunge forward, shouts the charge, and putting spurs to his horse, dashes forward through the lines. The men cease firing for a minute and with ready bayonets rush after him. Ellis sits still in his saddle and looks on as if in proud admiration of both his loved Major and gallant sons of Orange, until the regiment is fairly under way, and then rushes with them into the thickest of the fray."[76] Sergeant Hanford, in his usual succinct manner, remembered, "we were ordered to charge, and charge we did, driving the enemy back to the foot of the hill."[77]

General Ward saw the destructive effect of the volleys he had ordered. "The enemy now exhibited much disorder, and, taking advantage of this circumstance, I advanced my right and center with a view of obtaining a position behind a stone wall, about 160 yards in advance, and which the enemy was endeavoring to reach."[78] At this point the three regiments in the woods and on the right advanced at Ward's command in an attempt to drive the 3rd Arkansas from the Rose Woods. All three regiments to the right of the 124th New York reported some kind of advance after the enemy appeared on their front and after they had commenced firing.

By some accounts Colonel Ellis seemed indecisive and hesitant after the second volley. It was almost as if Major Cromwell had to goad him on to make the charge. Quite the opposite appears to be the case. When General Ward gave the order to fire, "the whole command fired a volley." Ward did not write that part of his command or the right wing of his command fired, he wrote that they *all* fired so it is likely that Ellis awaited the order to fire from his brigade commander before he gave that order to the regiment. Likewise, Ellis was not agonizing over whether to charge, he was awaiting the order from General Ward. "I advanced my right and center," Ward noted, leaving little doubt that he included the 124th New York in the advance. It may well be that Ellis did not hear the order or that he waited until he saw the regiments on his right advancing into the Rose Woods before he gave the order to charge but then, to borrow a phrase from Sergeant Hanford, charge he did.

Private Tucker made no mention of the exchange between Ellis and Cromwell but he did remember that after the second volley, Colonel Ellis gave the command "Charge bayonets! Forward; double-quick—March!"[79] He saw Cromwell ride around the left of his company to the front of the regiment. Then the Orange Blossoms let loose a "defiant cheer, and made as gallant and heroic a dash as the pages of history record." The Texans, halted by the first volley, shaken by the second, "withered" when the 124th came through the guns and started down the hill.

"They ran like frightened sheep," Tucker wrote, noting that the Texans did not stop until they reached two supporting lines coming up near the base of the hill, where they were halted and rallied by their officers. Some of Major Cromwell's left wing charged 200 yards to a rail fence at the foot of the Weikert Field and within 100 feet of this new force of Confederates.

"The enemy's line, unable to withstand our fierce onset, broke and fled," wrote Weygant. Major Cromwell, "his noble face flushed with victory," waved his sword and shouted in triumph but almost immediately a second line of the enemy "poured into us a terrible fire which seemed in an instant to bring down a full quarter of our number." Just as the major waved his sword and cried, "The day is ours!" a bullet struck him in the chest near his collar bone, severing an artery.[80] Henry Howell wrote, "The Major's horse carried him at least four rods in front of our lines after he was shot and four or five of us dashed out and brought in his body."[81]

Private Bradfield of the 1st Texas left a description of an officer, who may well have been Major Cromwell, "who won our admiration by his courage and gallantry."

> He was a very handsome man, and rode a beautiful, high-spirited horse. The animal seemed to partake of the spirit of the rider, and as he came on with a free, graceful stride into that hell of death and carnage, head erect and ears pointed, horse and man offered a picture as is seldom seen.... As the withering, scathing volleys from behind the rocks cut into the ranks of the regiment the major led, and his gallant men went down like grain before a scythe, he followed close as their heels, and when, time and again, they stopped and would have fled the merciless fire, each time he rallied them as if his puissant arm alone could stay the storm.

The Texans were so impressed that they began to shout "Don't shoot at him!" but horse and rider were cut down in the next instant.[82]

Colonel Ellis was still on horseback, riding among his men when he saw Cromwell fall. "My God! My God, men!" Weygant heard him shout, "Your Major's down; save him! save him." Through the din of battle, others heard something slightly different. Crediting these as the "last words Ellis was heard to say," an unknown witness heard, "My God boys the Major is down boys save your Major."[83] In either case, the colonel's words had the desired effect. Those men still on their feet obeyed without hesitation and in charging forward to rescue Cromwell, drove the Texans back again. Ellis, sensing a change in the battle, rose in the stirrups to get a better view through the smoke. Waving his sword, he cried, "Come on boys, it's a grand victory!" A bullet smashed into his forehead and he pitched from the saddle into the rock strewn field. His horse, rearing and plunging, ran toward the ranks of the enemy. "Colonel Ellis was struck through the brain," wrote Silliman, "and the men bore their bodys sadly from the field. Thus dying as best becomes a man, fell side by side two as brave as ever wore a sword."[84]

Thirty three years after the battle, in documents supporting an effort to award Medals of Honor to members of the 124th New York, Captain Charles Wood of Company A and Captain Lewis Wisner of Company K offered their view of what happened in those first minutes in the Weikert Field. Captain Wood wrote that

> we were stationed on a Rock Hill guarding the approach to Little Round Top and supporting Smith's Battery.... It was then to save the Battery, we had been ordered to support that Colonel Ellis ordered a charge of his little Regiment, numbering at that time but eighteen Officers and two hundred and twenty enlisted men. At the command to charge the gallant Maj. Cromwell spurred his horse through the ranks and with the shout, "Come on boys," rode straight at the Confederate lines, far in advance of the Regiment. A moment later he was shot through the heart, but his feet caught in the stirrups and his horse was swiftly bearing him into the Confederate lines. Under the concentrated fire of the Confederate batteries and their swiftly advancing lines the charge of the 124th N.Y. Vols., had been temporarily checked. When Maj. Cromwell fell ... Colonel Ellis himself rode through the lines and putting his horse at a gallop, started to head off the Major's horse nearly to the Confederate lines. It was then that the men of Co's E and K above mentioned at the call of Colonel Ellis, "to save your Major," voluntarily sprang to the front to rescue their loved Major. In the meantime Colonel Ellis had also fallen near the Major (the Major's horse having been shot by one of the men). James H. Conklin, Wood. T. Ogden and Louis S. Wisner

bore back to the lines, Colonel Ellis—Henry M. Howell, his brother William H. Howell, George Brown and James A. Beakes the body of the Major.[85]

At this crucial moment the Orange Blossoms were halted by the "deadly fire" from the front and by a new, unexpected threat from the left. Enemy troops heading through the gorge between Devil's Den and Big Round Top moved toward the south end of Houck's Ridge and Smith's guns. The 44th Alabama hit the 124th in the flank just as the New Yorkers were advancing down the hill. The Alabamans had been ordered by General Law to take the battery and Colonel Perry of the 44th ordered his men forward to do just that. As they advanced up the south end of Houck's Ridge headed for Smith's guns, the regiment split, the left wing firing into the left flank of the Orange Blossoms, the right wing engaging the 4th Maine on the other side of Devil's Den.[86]

"No troops could withstand such a storm," Tucker wrote. "At the rate the men were being shot down it would have been the work of but a few minutes to have annihilated the 124th N.Y.... I don't think the 124th was supported on either flank, but made the charge independently and alone."[87] Private Tucker's position in the leftmost company meant he probably did not see Ward's men advancing into the Rose Woods to do battle with the 3rd Arkansas, but his assessment about their left was entirely correct; there were only Confederates in that direction.

"We then advance to within 40 yds. Cheering," wrote Capt. Jackson, "and then followed a terrible fight. Both sides were partially protected by rocks. Sometime they & sometimes we have the best. Our Col. & Maj. were killed almost at the first of the action. Finally they got a cross fire on us and we had to fall back but fresh troops came up and drove them far back."[88]

The momentum of the charge had the intended effect: the enemy in front at least was forced back, firing as they went. But the lower end of the Weikert field was swarming with Texans who were trying desperately to reform. Behind them came rank upon rank of Benning's Georgia Brigade approaching from the west. Weygant knew that they were too few to press the charge, especially with the developing threat from the 44th Alabama on the flank. The surviving Orange Blossoms quickly gathered up as many of the wounded as they could and fell back. The body of their colonel was carried up the hill through the lines and placed on a rock next to Major Cromwell. "Three times we have beaten them back, but now we are exhausted," Weygant wrote.[89]

"I remember well how we fought," wrote Confederate Private Richard Cyrus Yarbrough, Company F, 20th Georgia, of Benning's Brigade.

> When we got up to the 1st Texas they raised a yell and wee all charged together and some of the Union Soldiers stood our charge untill wee ware very clost to them I do not remember but I think Was General Laws Alabama Brigade that was to our right doing the cross fireing.... I know when wee charged and the Union army fell back about 2 hundred yards thare was an oficer with his Sword in his hand trying to Ralley the union Soldiers and myself and James Manning got behind a big rock. Jim Manning sed Dick I am going to kill that oficer but he never did hit that officer. Those was some of the Bravest men thare I ever saw on both sides.[90]

The left wing of the 44th Alabama attacking from the south was not to be denied its prize. The rapidly advancing Confederates overran and captured most of the men of Company F, 4th Maine, and then went on to take the three guns of Smith's Battery. Corporal James L. Forte of the 44th raced forward with the colors, climbed up on one of Smith's guns, and defiantly waved the flag until a Yankee gunner knocked him from the piece with a rammer. But the victory was short lived. The guns were useless without ammunition or implements to load them and the Confederates were in such an exposed position that Colonel Perry quickly ordered them off the crest.[91]

General Ward wrote that "while advancing, the rear columns of the enemy pressed forward to the support of the advance, who rallied and again advanced. This time our single line was forced back a short distance by the heavy columns of the enemy. In this manner for the space of one and a half hours did we advance and retire, both parties endeavoring to gain possession of the stone wall."[92]

With the 124th New York reforming in the woods and the left wing of the 44th Alabama falling back, the 1st Texas had another go at capturing the guns. Advancing to the crest, they became the second regiment to take Smith's guns, a Texan this time mounting one of the Parrott Rifles to shout a cry of victory. General Robertson immediately ordered Lieutenant Colonel Work to hold the position at the crest with two companies and send the rest of the 1st Texas into the Rose Woods to support Colonel Manning's 3rd Arkansas, whose regiment was being roughly handled by a hard-fighting combination of the 17th Maine, 20th Indiana, and 86th New York.[93]

From the reverse side of Houck's Ridge in what would become known as the Valley of Death, Colonel Walker of the 4th Maine looked up to see the Texans among Smith's guns. On his own initiative, he broke off the fight with the other half of Perry's 44th Alabama, fell back about 100 yards, and regrouped for a charge. He had his men fix bayonets and advance at the right oblique, each man facing half right. Up the steep rear slope they went, taking the Texans by surprise and driving them from the guns.[94]

From his position in the Rose Woods, Captain Weygant saw what was happening and moved the 124th forward to link up with the right flank of the 4th Maine. Both regiments were now facing west, looking down hill into the Weikert's field. Colonel Walker's left flank, just to the south of the guns, came under attack again from the 44th Alabama. The fighting quickly became a hand-to-hand struggle for control of the southern end of the ridge line. A rebel soldier grabbed the colonel's sword and took it from him. The men from Maine and New York fought desperately to hold the ground and the guns at the top of the ridge. There could have been no more welcome sight than the 99th Pennsylvania charging across the ridge to their aid. With the battle at its height, Ward could see that his left, beyond Smith's guns, needed reinforcements. He found Major John Moore of the 99th Pennsylvania, who remembered, "I was now ordered by General Ward to march my regiment double-quick from the right to the left of the brigade." The 99th faced to the left, forming a column four men abreast, and raced south along the rocky, wooded ridgeline. "This movement, rapidly executed, placed my command on the brow of a hill, overlooking a deep ravine interspersed with large bowlders of rock." Major Moore deployed his regiment on Walker's exposed left flank, standing ready to defend the crest and the battery.[95]

Private Tucker wrote that

> once back to the top of the hill our colors were stuck in the ground and we were ordered to "rally on those colors; not a man to leave them." The order was cheerfully obeyed. Once more on the line of battle, with the 86th N.Y. on our right in the woods, and the 4th Maine and 99th Pa. on our left, we had no fear of being flanked from either direction. The enemy, encouraged by our falling back to our old position, advanced on us in force. But we had taken a position we were determined to hold as long as there were enough of the 124th left to hold the ground, or to stay until ordered back by our officers.[96]

Though outnumbered, the Union troops atop Houck's Ridge were in a strong position. But at this critical moment, Brigadier General Henry Benning's brigade of four Georgia regiments, fourteen hundred men strong, arrived to tip the balance. Together with the remnants of the Texas Brigade and Law's Brigade, the southerners steadily pushed Ward's men north along Houck's Ridge. Ward called for reinforcements and Birney sent the 6th New Jersey and the 40th New York, both regiments advancing south into the Plum Run Valley to temporarily stabilize the left of the line.

But the numbers were against them. To the north, Confederate units were surging around the Peach Orchard threatening Ward's right near the Wheatfield. To the south, Benning and Law were steadily advancing. "The enemy was pretty thick and well concealed," wrote one member of the 4th Texas. "It was more like Indian fighting than anything that I experienced during the war. They had sharpshooters in the trees and on high places that made it exceedingly dangerous to appear in any open place."[97] Word was passed among Ward's men that Union reinforcements were coming up and many of the men on Houck's Ridge thought they were being relieved, not retreating.

The Orange Blossoms had laid down such a heavy volume of fire that some of their rifle muskets were beginning to foul to the point that they could not be reloaded while others became too hot to handle. The soldiers threw these weapons aside, cautioned their comrades that they were going after more serviceable weapons, and ran out between the lines to pick up those dropped by the dead or wounded. Henry Howell noted, "We held our position until 4 o'clock."[98]

"Our company officers bravely did their duty. They were everywhere amongst the men with cheering words, telling them we had them on our own ground, where we wanted them, and to 'give it to them.'"[99] Sergeant Hanford took cover behind a rock after the regiment pulled back, concentrating his fire toward a gap in the stone wall at the bottom of the field where the Texans were seeking cover. There were so many of them that even the open space was "crowded full of men."[100] Lieutenant James Denniston of Company G picked up a rifle and jumped over Hanford to take cover behind a rock on his left. Denniston caught his toe on the sergeant's ramrod, bending it so that it could no longer be used. Hanford "scolded" the lieutenant, no doubt telling him the officers should let the enlisted men do the shooting or at least stay out of the way. Once behind cover, Denniston made ready to fire when he was hit in the leg by a bullet. "I've got it, I've got it," he shouted and started for the rear when he was hit again. Denniston survived but his wounds were so serious that he had to be carried to the rear, "never to return to duty with the regiment."[101]

Hanford kept shooting until he used all his ammunition, then fell back over the hill where he saw reinforcements coming up at last. These men were reported by David Dewitt of Company G to be a "brigade with Maltese crosses, the regulars." Dewitt added that they were just over the hill boiling coffee while the 124th New York was fighting for its life. Writing about it more than ten years later, Weygant still rankled at their tardy advance.[102]

During the second charge, nineteen-year-old Sergeant Thomas Bradley, Company H, was hit in the groin by a piece of artillery shell and fell into the arms of his comrade, Private Dawson. Bradley pleaded not to be left behind. He knew that he would surely bleed to death without medical care. Dawson ran for help and returned with Charles Tyndel and Jesse Camp, both of Company H, but just as they made ready to carry Bradley to the rear, the Rebels swept through Devils Den. Tyndel and Camp were shot, leaving Dawson alone once more. He found three more Orange Blossoms and together they placed Bradley in a blanket and carried him away.[103]

Private John LaRue was wounded by "an ounce ball through his left shoulder in the battle, and was ordered to leave the field. 'The medics weren't very big talkers,' he said. 'The first one I met took a look at my shoulder when I thought I was bleeding to death and said 'A nice wound, a very nice wound.' Can you beat that? And then the surgeon in the hospital took another look and said, 'A half inch more.' That's all he did. But I'm here—and I'm lucky," he remembered years later. Not so lucky was his old school teacher, Charles Edwards, who stood next to LaRue in line of battle and who had been with him at the start of the fight. The forty-year-old private from Newburgh was reported missing and presumed dead. Private Edwards most likely did not leave Houck's Ridge alive and was probably buried in an unmarked grave where he fell. The newspaper reporter who interviewed the old soldier added, "Colonel Ellis was killed within a rod of Mr. Larue's stand and the Middletown Orange Blossom himself was wounded on approximately the present site of the Gettysburg monument."[104]

As with the Confederates, there were casualties among the Union high command. Near the Trostle Farm, a cannon ball crushed General Sickles's leg as he observed the battle going on at the Peach Orchard. Legend has it that as he was carried to the rear, he wanted his men to see him and know that he still lived so he propped himself up on the stretcher, jauntily smoking a cigar for effect. General Birney took over command of the 3rd Corps, General Ward took Birney's Division, and Colonel Berdan took charge of Ward's Brigade. Lieutenant Colonel Cummins of the 124th had also been wounded just as the regiment charged. He was trying to get the artillery pieces dragged to the rear when an enemy shell exploded near a gun, rocking it into him. With all three field grade officers out of action, command of the 124th New York fell to the senior company commander, Captain Charles Weygant.

Once the regiment was safely out of the Weikert's field, Weygant got his men into a semblance of a battle line and took stock. "Our immediate foes keep up a brisk fire but do not again attempt to ascend the hill in front of us," he wrote. He guessed he had about a hundred men with him, "gathered together in little squads like picket posts along the front." The enemy was so thick at the bottom of the hill that the young captain was sure every shot was finding a mark. He passed up and down the much reduced regimental line, asking about casualties and checking the condition of his men. He saw there was no officer in charge of what was left of Company I and asked for the "plucky new Lieutenant" Milnor Brown. "You will find him lying down yonder with four or five of I, beside him," was the reply. Brown had been coolly received by the veterans he was sent to command but he earned their respect fighting at the head of his company until he was shot dead leading them forward.

Weygant heard that Lieutenant Finnegan of Company K had been carried to rear, wounded twice and now out of action. He came upon Company G, the largest in the regiment at the start of the battle, now but "a corporal's guard in charge of a corporal." He asked after Captain Isaac Nicoll, only to be told that he lay dead, wedged between two rocks at the farthest point of the advance. The men who tried to retrieve Nicoll's body lay dead or wounded beside him. "The slope in front was strewn with our dead, and not a few of our severely wounded lay beyond the reach of their unscathed comrades, bleeding, helpless, and some of them dying."[105] Near Captain Nicoll lay Corporal James Scott of Company B, wounded by bullets and shell fragments so many times that no one thought he could possibly be alive. But alive he was, his blood-covered hand could be seen waving through the smoke of battle. Scott had been among the first to follow Major Cromwell in the charge and when the major fell the enraged corporal fought on though "wounded in the arm and his hand and face were covered with blood, but he did not seem to know anything about it, and kept on fighting until a ball hit him in the breast, and went clear through and came out his back."[106]

The bodies of Colonel Ellis and Major Cromwell had been carried to the top of the field and placed on a large rock in the rear of the regiment, clearly visible to those men still in the fight. Captain Weygant noticed the small round hole through Ellis's forehead through which a piece of his brain protruded. He also noticed the gold locket pinned on the major's jacket which he knew contained a miniature portrait of his wife and a lock of hair from the newborn daughter he had never seen. One veteran later wrote that this was the same rock where the 124th New York's monument now stands.

Captain Weygant, seeing that the men in the valley behind them were being driven from the field and that the 99th Pennsylvania was being outflanked and giving ground, knew it was time to pull back. As he prepared to go in search of the men he'd placed in the gap on the right at the start of the battle, an aide rode up to him "with orders to fall back without a moment's delay. He told Captain Silliman, the next senior officer, to see to it that the order was executed and went in search of his men. Once he had them together, Weygant started for the rear but realized that the enemy was now on the crest, or "ledge" as he called it, where the regiment had stood just moments before. It was, he said, "by mere chance" that they were not all captured.[107]

William Howell wrote,

> I was completely exhausted after carrying or helping Major Cromwell back behind a rock. We took his valuables and gave them to Lieutenant Colonel Cummings and he said carry him farther back. So I

divested myself of everything and went a little farther but my ability to help was then gone and I quit helping. Leon and Lieutenant Wood with the assistance of two men carried his body back as far as the 3rd Corps hospital and we staid there that night. The next morning they took him on to where the Colonel's body was. They were to be sent home. The major died where we first halted with him."[108]

Henry Howell sent a letter to his mother that bore the heading "Battlefield, July 5, 1863," that found its way into the *Whig Press*. In it he wrote,

> We had to yield at last, which we did slowly and in good order taking nearly all the wounded with us. We had not fallen back more than twenty or thirty rods, when the 2nd corps and part of the 5th came up to our assistance and speedily retook the ground we had lost and quite a number of prisoners.... When we got where we could rest for the night Co E had only three men with the colors, the others having gone to the rear with the wounded. George Godfrey, Adam Miller and myself were the three, and we felt as though we were alone in the world, for we did not know what had become of the rest; but towards noon the next day the men began to come in, but I am sorry to say that Wheat, Wood, and Hirst are among the missing, but we know they are unhurt.[109]

As the Orange County boys fell back, stunned at the loss of their position as well as the loss of so many comrades, they were called to a halt in front of General Ward. Their brigade commander spoke to them in a most animated manner, "saying that he expected almost impossible things of his old troops, but that such heroic, noble resistance as we had made, was beyond any thing he had ever dared to hope for, even from them." These words, Charles Weygant later wrote, were "sweet indeed."[110]

Lieutenant William Mapes, who led Company B into the battle, wrote that "Gen Ward told us we had earned the Kearney Cross & red patch & shall have it."[111] This was about as great a tribute as could be given to the regiment and the incident was mentioned by several Orange Blossoms. To hear General Ward tell them, in such a dramatic manner as they left the field of battle, that they were worthy to wear the red diamond badge — the Kearny Badge — meant that they would to be numbered among the greatest fighting regiments of the war. The red badge would figure prominently in their reunion medals, ribbons, and other devices worn by members of the 124th until the last of them was gone.[112]

Captain Weygant moved his regiment farther to the rear and allowed his men some much-needed rest. "The active part the 124th was to play in this great three days' battle, had now been performed. Moving to a piece of woods about a mile in the rear of the Union battle line, we prepared, and with saddened hearts and gloomy thought, quietly partook our evening meal."[113] The regiment pulled back to a position beyond the Weikert Farm, closer to the center of the Union line and prepared for the renewal of the battle they knew would come. Fortunately, they were not called upon to fight again that day because in Sergeant Hanford's opinion, "we were so badly cut up as to be hardly a show of a regiment."[114]

Private Jeremiah Hartnett wrote home the next day.

> Our regiment lost heavily, according to its number — twenty-two killed and fifty-nine wounded. We lost all our field officers — Colonel Ellis and Major Cromwell killed, and Lieutenant-Colonel Cummings wounded. Ellis is a sore loss to us; while he was with us, I consider we had a father, but now he is gone. A braver man never lived. He and the Major both got killed while leading the little regiment on a charge. The last words he was heard to say were, "Give it to them, my tulips!" This, and "my Orange blossoms," were favorite names he always called us by. But now he is gone, no more to be seen at the head of our little regiment that he took so much pride in. His and the Major's bodies were sent home in charge of Lieutenant Ramsdell. Orange County cannot do to their remains too much honor.[115]

The fighting over, Henry Howell took pencil in hand and filled in the pages in his diary for this momentous day.

> The 3rd Corps again won fresh laurels. We were on the extreme left & the enemy massed their forces and tried to flank us but we stood there like veterans without giving an inch for 2 hours and 40 minutes. We only had one line while they had three and we broke two of them several times when we would

charge through them. The sharpshooters say that they saw them forming at least ten times and advance upon us, again to be driven back. At the time we made the farthest charge our Major was shot dead and the Col. was shot so that he died in a few hours after. Capt. Nichols and Lieut Brown fell about the same time and a great many others. Some of our cowardly artillerymen left one of their pieces and ran away. At length over come by numbers and being worn out we were compelled to yield which we did in good order. But the 5th Corps arrived just then and the tide was turned. Forming as they went up they advanced in three columns and reoccupied our old position. The 3rd Corps was taken to the rear after we were relieved and as the day was about gone we rested there for the night. The loss from the 124th as near as we have learned so far is 20 killed and 54 wounded. We had 209 muskets when we went in. Lieut. Col. Cummings is among the wounded. Major General Dan Sickles lost his right leg but is doing very well. The command will devolve upon General Birney for the present.[116]

During the night, artillery and small arms fire continued sporadically until just before dawn, when it reached "considerable fury" and continued until about 9 o'clock in the morning. Following the spirited exchange of artillery and picket firing in the morning of July 3, an "ominous silence" came over the field. All the while, Union troops changed positions "plainly indicating that the lines were being strengthened in anticipation of another determined onset of the now most desperate foe." Henry Howell noted in a July 3 diary entry, "We moved up near the front in a piece of woods and staid there until near night. We were shelled considerable during the day but no casualties occurred. We drew three days rations and we were greatly in need of them for our rations had run out the night before."[117] William Howell's diary entry for the same day read, "We go to the rear draw rations & rest. I am sick but prefer not to go to the hospital with the wounded."[118] He elaborated on the events of July 3 in a letter home. "Cannonading and musketry firing was very brisk. A great many prisoners were taken. They gave me a pass to go to the hospital but I knew that was no place for a man that was not wounded."[119]

From their position south of the Union center the regiment witnessed the final act in the pivotal battle. "About two o'clock the enemy opened a most furious cannonade with a hundred and twenty guns," Weygant wrote. "The Union batteries soon began to reply, and for over two hours the earth seemed to tremble beneath us, and the air was filled with fire and smoke and iron. The enemy's infantry kept concealed, and our troops with loaded weapons hugged the ground, impatiently awaiting the opening of the less noisy but more deadly contest with small arms which they all knew was sure to follow. At four o'clock it came, grand, desperate, terrible. But the 124th were not called to participate in it, and I will not therefore attempt to describe it." But the captain could not resist describing the outcome as a "great and undisputed" Union victory in which the opposing forces were about equal in number.[120] The regiment's position behind the front lines during Pickett's Charge was hardly a safe place. Corporal William Howell noted the "solid shot came crashing through all around us."[121]

Once Pickett's men had been repulsed, the regiment was ordered forward to act as a reserve just behind the main lines. Henry Howell wrote home to his mother telling her, "We were shelled a little during the 3d, but our corps were not otherwise engaged. At night we moved up near the front to support the picket line, which we did all day the 4th. The battlefield was in our possession—we went out and picked up the guns that were strewn over the field. Our pioneers were fired upon while engaging in burying the dead."[122]

Henry confided more to his diary than he did to his mother.

We did not move during the day. We were sent out over the field to pick up the guns that had been scattered around during the action. We brought in several hundred. Our pioneers were sent out to bury the dead but were fired upon. There are great many from each side all scattered around amongst each other. How great a difference between the way I passed the 4th of July this year from the way I passed the last one. I hope I will never have to spend another 4th in the army. It is said that the enemy are in full retreat and I think it is true for we whipped them too bad on the 2nd & 3rd for them to stay here long.[123]

Corporal William Howell wrote home from the battlefield:

We have been engaged in a bloody battle again and have thus far escaped death. That is, Henry and I have, though many of our regiment have not been so lucky. You will hear through the papers of our losses. John Scott (of Goshen), and James B Moore (of Newburgh) are wounded and Hezekiah Harris (of Wallkill) was killed. A few are missing but I think they are all to the rear with the wounded. Colonel Ellis and Major Cromwell were killed as they charged at the advancing foe. They were rash but done it to save a batery. I received a bullet hole through my coat and shirt sleeve between my wrist and elbow. It bruised my arm and it swelled up and was quite painful but it does not hurt but very little now. We were engaged at close range when we received our loss which was on the 2nd of July, but we were under their shell all day supporting the 4th New York batery. I cannot have time to write now and give the particulars. Henry and I left our knapsacks when we came off the field and lost everything. We have had hard work to bring them here and do not expect to carry anything except our accourtrements till we get stronger than we are now. We are pretty well used up.... You should not expect us to write while we are in the field for no matter how great our inclination to write we cannot do it while things are in the state they are now with us.... The 2nd Corps came up in time to save our lines but too late to save the 124th or 2nd Brigade of the 3rd Corps from fearful loss. Henry and George Godfrey and Adam Miller were all that were with the regiment from Company E."[124]

Henry Howell penciled into his diary:

July 3rd/63
We moved up near the front in a piece of woods and staid there until near night. We were shelled considerable during the day but no casualties occurred. We drew three days rations and we were greatly in need of them for our rations had run out the night before. The news of the great battle from other parts of the field came in. We captured four Rebel Generals Longstreet among the number & ten stand of Colors with several hundred prisoners. In the afternoon we were moved up behind our skirmishers as a support in case we were attacked during the night. The cannonading had been terrible to day. When we first came out the 86th planted their flag which immediately brought on a shower of shells which wounded some of their men.[125]

Captain James Benedict who led Company D at Gettysburg wrote home on July 6, "We have gained at least one victory for the Army of the Potomac, but a dearly bought one, I assure you, and a most disastrous one to the enemy. They are retreating.... We have as many prisoners as we know what to do with. Company D had no skedadlers this time.... Capt Weygant is in command."[126]

"We lost heavy," wrote Captain William Jackson, "so did they. The ground in front of us was piled with them. Our reg. as usual fought very bravely and only came out when ordered. In Company K. we lost 4 killed & 3 wounded Lieut Finnegan among the latter. We took no part in the action on the 3rd. On the 4th we lay still. Our men went over the field and picked up guns etc.... I have time to write no more."[127]

Sergeant J.J. Crawford of Company K took the time to write a letter to the parents of Ambrose S. Holbert of his company. Holbert had been the first recruit to join Company K and did so much to fill up the ranks that he was promoted to corporal.

Mr. A.S. Holbert — Sir:
It is my painful duty to inform you of the fate of your son Ambrose, whom we all suppose to be dead, as the last that was seem of him he was very badly wounded, having one leg broken, and it is supposed that he had other wounds, as blood was foaming from his mouth. We were in the fight Thursday, and the dead were buried on Sunday in that part of the field. It was impossible to recognize many of our dead when we went to bury them, so I have not the least hope of his being alive. We had been on detached duty for some time past and had returned to the company only a few days before the battle in which he fell a brave and noble soldier doing his duty to his country and his country's cause.[128]

In later years, Captain Weygant would address the heated controversy with regard to Sickles's move to the forward line.

That Sickles erred in advancing beyond the position assigned him, no student of the art of war denies. That his entire corps fought most nobly; and that Ward's brigade was left unsupported and held its own for over an hour in a most deadly contest with a force of the enemy which outnumbered it four to one—until its line of battle was reduced to a mere skeleton and then with the exception of one regiment was not driven, but withdrew because there was no force at hand to prevent the enemy's moving past its flank, must be acknowledged by all honest writers who are acquainted with the facts.[129]

Sergeant Thomas Bradley, Company H, seriously wounded at Gettysburg, dearly wished that Colonel Ellis had not moved off the crest of Houck's Ridge. Bradley was a frequent visitor to the battlefield well into the next century and had plenty of time to consider the actions of the regiment on that fateful day. "Without that charge and the work of Smith's Battery, our left would have been more seriously turned; but now, in the light of after experience, as I think of it, what a mad act it was. Our regiment—a mere handful, at that—with no order back of its Colonel, charging from its base in line of battle to lock arms with Longstreet."[130]

Thomas Rodman, Company C, had no such misgivings. In his copy of Weygant's regimental history, in the chapter dealing with the battle, he wrote his opinion in the margin in a bold hand. "Time has proven that Sickles *did not err* in advancing his line, both our *own* and confederate officers uphold him. TR."[131]

Fifty years after the battle, Richard Yarbourgh, the private from the 20th Georgia who witnessed an officer trying to rally the 124th in Weikert's Field, took pencil in hand to answer a circular sent out by Henry Howell of the 124th. Howell was trying to reach veterans, North and South, who had fought in the Devil's Den area. His goal was to get them to attend the anniversary celebration of the battle scheduled for July 1913. Howell hoped the old combatants would meet

Reunion at the Ellis Monument, Gettysburg. Sergeant Chase of the 86th New York wrote that the veterans of the 124th New York erected "a beautiful monument on the very spot where Colonel Ellis fell and he stands in stone upon it, the very picture of a soldier." Henry Howell is seated fourth from the right in the second row. Historical Society of Middletown and the Wallkill Precinct.

and shake hands where they'd fought fifty years before. On June 15, Yarbrough wrote from Gateswood, Georgia,

> Dear Brother Howell
>   I received your kind answer to my first letter I wrote to you. You wrote to me to send you some names of the 20th Georgia Regiment. I can send you a plenty of names of our regiment but I expect thare is not but a few left on this Earth.... I am the only one left living of Company F.... I would like verry much to be up thare on the auld Hills of Gettysburg whare the boys in blue and the gray showed thare Bravery before each other and I am glad to know that meeting of the boys is for Peace and forgiveness. I am not in good Health and able to do good work now wee want to Raise the Banners High at Gettysburgh and let thar be inscribed on that Banner love for God and man and when we all get to our great Commander on High all Wars will stop forever.... I expect you have got the right name for that place, Devils Den.
>   Your Brother
>   Richard Cyrus Yarbrough[132]

Two years later, Sergeant Stephen Chase of the 86th New York wrote a series of articles for his hometown newspaper in upstate New York. In the Gettysburg article he wrote that the Orange Blossoms very much wanted to be allowed to wear the red diamond badge of the 1st Division, Third Corps but they were told that they could not just presume to wear it, "they must win it." In the Weikert Field at Gettysburg, "they settled the question of heroism once and forever. No one ever asked the 86th or 124th N.Y. regiments what right they had to the red diamond. This 124th N.Y. was on our left near the 'Devil's Den' and our regiment was on their right and in the woods while they were in the open field. I looked several times to see how this regiment was doing and happened to be looking in that direction when Colonel Ellis was shot and fell dead from his horse."

Chase added that the regiment had since constructed "a beautiful monument on the very spot where Colonel Ellis fell and he stands in stone upon it, the very picture of a soldier."[133]

CHAPTER 9

"Tell them my voice is still for war"
July 4–October 10, 1863

"The wounded Rebs are sadled off on us as usual," Lieutenant William Mapes wrote to his brother soon after the battle at Gettysburg. "I had a talk with some wounded a col maj & capt & many privates. They are tired of the war but say it will never be settled by fighting. I can't see it, they are a vicious ignorant people & God will never prosper there. I firmly believe this Union will be reconstructed again. The Rebs took shoes canteens & haversacks off our dead soldiers."[1]

Lieutenant Mapes described the battle and was quick to inform his brother that Corporal James Scott had been wounded six times but still lived.

> They massed all their force at one point. I think they have had enough of Pa. or will before they get out of it.... You would be surprised to hear & see a battle, men facing the canons mouth &c. I escaped unharmed my sword was hit with a minnie when I was raising it defiantly.... We all rallied round the flag of the Free fought under it & brought if off rent with balls. We are proud of it and will bring it home but weather beaten and battle worn.... Tell my good friends that I think of them often, which inspires me to go forward in the performance of duty & with my sword hew out my way to distinction. I hope they may never have reason to regret that they advanced me.... The Rebs are discouraged some threw down their arms & came in. We took 10 stands of colors & many prisoners.... Remember me to all.... Tell them my voice is still for war until the stars & stripes float again over every inch of American soil.[2]

William Howell felt so poorly the evening of July 3 that he did not join the regiment until the next day. "I started for them in the morning and found them on the front center," he wrote home to his family. "The rebs had fallen back. Some skirmishers firing ahead of us."[3] Then he took up his diary. "We hold the 4th at the front. Skirmishing. Large quantities of arms brought in. Heavy Showers."[4]

Enemy mounted scouts were nowhere to be seen but when the skirmish line was pushed forward, they soon ran into Confederates in a line of rifle pits. At about noon, Weygant walked out in front of the battle line into "that harvest field of death." What he saw shocked him. "Scores of blackened, distorted human faces lay in front of me, turn which way I would. The bodies of many of these had been torn most frightfully by pieces of shell. Interspersed among them lay the bloated carcasses of dead horses. The ground in all directions was strewn with the broken engines and paraphernalia of war, and here and there upon the grass could be seen dark crimson spots which told of pools of blood."[5]

The regiment held this position on the national holiday in support of the picket line through a rainstorm Saturday night. Sunday morning, two men from each company were detailed to return to the Weikert Field to bury the dead.[6] Private Henry Howell drew that duty, describing it in a letter home dated July 5.

I went, but I hope I may never have an opportunity to do so again. We buried all the dead from our regiment, and about half a dozen rebs. John Drake was killed, but his death was amply avenged; for within three rods of where he lay were thirteen dead rebs. In one place ten rebs lay so close that they touched one another. Last night the enemy fell back about a mile, and while I am writing there is cannonading going on that sounds as though our side was driving them farther. Our gallant Sickles lost his leg, and it is reported to day that he is dead; I hope not. Our loss in the 124th is 24 dead, 55 wounded, and 7 missing — as far as we know at present. We went in with 204 muskets and 17 officers. There were 4 officers killed and 3 wounded. Hoping this battle will end the war.[7]

Henry's diary was more graphic than his letters home.

It rained nearly all night. There were 20 men from the 124th detailed to go out and bury the dead. I went but I hope it will never fall to my lot to have another opportunity for it is a great deal more sickening than it is during the battle for we do not have any chance to see the way they are cut to pieces then but now we can examine them. We buried all of our own regiment's dead and 12 or 13 of the rebs. We all began to feel sick being around in such a bad smell so long, so we were taken back but the regiment had moved a little piece from where they were in to the woods. So we took our things and went on. We staid there during the remainder of the day and that night.[8]

The body of Captain Isaac Nicoll, who led Company G into the Weikert Field, was found wedged between the rocks at the farthest point of the regiment's advance. Several men had been killed trying to retrieve the body during the fight; now his comrades dug his grave and prepared to bury him. First Lieutenant Charles Wood, Company E, who had charge of the burial detail, could not bring himself to throw dirt on the young Captain. He placed his own cap over Nicoll's face to protect it from the clods that were shoveled in on top of him. This detail buried seventy five Union men and a few of the enemy.[9]

After the battle, friends from home came to Gettysburg to retrieve Nicoll's body. "It was, unlike many thousands of other victims on that field, readily found, from the fact that a board

Dead at the edge of the Rose Woods at Gettysburg (Library of Congress, Prints & Photographs Division).

was placed at the head of the grave, bearing his name, the No. of his regiment, and a Masonic symbol. On removing the earth above the body, evergreens were found deposited in the grave." No one in the group recognized the significance until they returned home to find a letter from "a rebel officer" stating that when the body was examined immediately after the fight, a small

Captain Isaac Nicoll was killed in action leading Company G at Gettysburg on July 2, 1863. A fellow Mason in the Confederate army saw to it that he was buried on the field according to Masonic rites (Michael J. McAfee collection).

Bible was found with Nicoll's name, directions in case he was killed, and the Masonic symbol. The officer, presumed to be from Georgia, was also a Mason. "True to the obligations of the brotherhood, though they had met in hostile array on the battle field, the rebels stopped to give decent rites of sepulture, and left directions with a resident in the vicinity to have the Testament forwarded to the friends of the deceased."[10]

From the conflicting accounts, it's not clear who buried Captain Nicoll with Masonic rites but in any case, the rites were observed.

Meanwhile, Lee had an important decision to make. He was deep in Pennsylvania with his precarious line of retreat in danger of being cut. He did not know what other Yankee troops — militia regiments or units from the defenses of Washington — might be brought to bear against him. When the Yankees did not follow up their victory on July 3 with an attack of their own, Lee decided that he could not remain in enemy territory. His quickest route of withdrawal was through the Fairfield Gap and on to Waynesboro. From there it was a short march to Hagerstown, Maryland, and then to Williamsport on the Potomac River. The speed with which Lee disengaged, and the route he took, pretty much guaranteed that he would reach the river crossing ahead of Meade.

By July 6 the bulk of the Army of the Potomac had moved away from Gettysburg to begin the pursuit, but the 3rd Corps remained on the field. The Orange County farm boys looked to the sky and saw a storm brewing so they put up their shelter tents and "crowded under them, intent on a good rest and sound sleep ere they started off on, what all believed was to be a long and rapid march."[11] Henry Howell wrote,

We are still in the woods that we came in yesterday. We had orders to march & get out on the road and were countermarched to our old position where we remained during the day. There is 10 or 12 prisoners up at headquarters who came in and gave themselves up. They say there are more watching for a good opportunity to come. Our army have nearly all been sent in pursuit of the retreating foe who left his position on the 4th with our forces close at his heels. They left some 50 pieces of spiked cannon behind them so great was their haste to get away.[12]

After midnight, Captain Weygant received orders to have his men pack up their gear, get something to eat, and be ready to move "at a moment's notice"[13] Nothing happened for several hours, just long enough for the storm to arrive and drench the men who had, as ordered, taken down their tents, rolled them up, and strapped on their knapsacks. "Rains again," wrote Corporal Howell. "Strike tents but do not get away."[14]

Weygant had with him about one hundred fifty armed men and nine officers. He noted that "a considerable number" of the able-bodied men and officers were absent, helping out at the 3rd

Corps hospital. One of them was Thomas Rodman of Company C, who sent three letters home from Gettysburg during the month of July. On July 17 he wrote to his parents telling them that he had not heard from them since he marched from winter camp more than a month before. He asked after his mother's health and said that it was safe to send him a letter because communication with the North had opened up again. "When you write I wish you would send me some money say $5.00. Write just as soon as you get this. Never mind getting the letter registered for it takes to long for it to get here." He noted that they should address letters to him via "Co C 124th Regt NYSV, 3rd Corpse Hospital, Gettysburg Pa," an unfortunate lapse in spelling if there ever was one.[15]

   When Rodman did not receive an answer after ten days he wrote again, giving his address as "Field Hospital near Gettysburg Pa."

> Dear Father and Mother
>   I take my pencil in hand again (for I have no pen) to let you know that I am well and I hope these few lines will find you both the same. I am still remaining at the Hospital taking care of the sick. I suppose I will remain there some time yet for there is a great many that are not able to be removed away yet. I am having a good time now to what I have been having for some time back. Plenty to eat nothing much to do except at night.... The Wounded are getting along quite well although there is a great many deaths. As fast as they get able they are sent to Baltimore and Phila to the General Hospital where they are more comfortable.
>   Well Father what do you think of the War by this time. For my part I think the thing is getting played out. Almost all of the wounded Rebs think that it will end this summer.
>   I hope you have received my 2 letters I sent you from here. If you have not I wish you to answer this one immediately and send me 5 Dollars.[16]

   Two days later he wrote again to his father that he was "still in the land of the living and am enjoying good health and hope you and Mother the same." He told his father that he had that day received the long-awaited letter from home dated just two days earlier. He noted that he received the money he'd asked for and some local newspapers. He had a bit of good news, "The Doctor says that I am such a good nurse he will not let me go to my Regt and I am not sorry for I have good times here. I should like to see you and mother. But if we move to Philad. and I stay with the boys, I will write and you can come down if you like and see me, and maybe I can get a furlough."[17]

   While Rodman remained behind in Gettysburg nursing the wounded, his comrades began their pursuit of Lee's army. It was just at dawn and raining when the regiment finally moved south toward Emmitsburg, a route that took them over the battlefield, "a horrible sight," Corporal William Howell wrote. They made it to Mechanicstown that day, a total of twenty miles. Before dawn the next day they were heading south over a road that, though macadamized part of the way, was deep in gooey mud where it was not. Some of the men lost a shoe, their feet coming right out of the government-issued brogans. Those who did threw away the other one, rolled up their trousers and declared they would "wade it through bare-footed, sink or swim."[18]

   The regiment marched twenty-three miles through Frederick, Maryland, a town it had passed on the way to Gettysburg. Captain Weygant reflected on all the men had experienced.

> Ten days before we had marched through that village with clothes brushed, banners flying, and polished arms reflecting the rays of the sun; intent on keeping between the invading victorious and most mighty army the confederacy ever put in the field, and our threatened capitol, which we were resolved to defend to the last extremity. Since then we had met that grand southern army even handed, and defeated it in the most ably managed, desperate, and deadly battle ever fought on American soil; and were now pursuing its depleted legions in their inglorious flight back to the forests of Virginia.

But he was willing to admit that they were now a sorry looking bunch, wet and filthy from marching two days in the rainstorm. "Our guns and swords were covered with rust; our pockets were filled with dirt; muddy water oozed from the toes of the footmen's government shoes at every step, ran out of the tops of the horsemans boots."[19]

On July 9, the column changed direction west onto the Hagerstown Road, over Catoctin Mountain, and through Middletown, reaching the summit of South Mountain. "This day's march was decidedly severe, though the distance traveled was but twelve miles," Captain Weygant wrote.[20] William Howell, who was starting to feel the exertions of the march and the effects of the weather, noted that as they passed through Middletown, the farmers were harvesting their crops, a scene that reminded the boys of home. They drew rations and continued on "up a pass in South Mountain."[21]

The same day, General William French assumed command of the 3rd Corps. A native of Maryland, French graduated from West Point, class of 1837. He'd served in the Creek-Seminole wars and in Mexico where he was brevetted for "gallantry and meritorious conduct." When the Civil War began, French rose quickly to brigade and division command and, a week after Sickles was wounded at Gettysburg, he took over the 3rd Corps. He had with him eight thousand men, bringing the 3rd Corps back to a three division configuration. In his after-action report, French maintained that during the advance of July 10–14, his corps was held in reserve should there be a major battle near Williamsport, where Lee was attempting to cross the rain-swollen Potomac River.[22]

On July 10 the regiment made another twelve-mile march, halting for a time in Keedeysville, then continued on to Millpoint. "Start early descend into the valley," wrote William Howell. Heavy artillery fire was heard in the distance and a detachment of the 1st New York Cavalry was sent to investigate. "Cros at Antietam bridges. Start on in the night go 5 miles more," the corporal wrote as the heat of mid–July finally put him out of action. He fell victim to a fever and then diarrhea which made him so weak that he began to straggle at the rear of the column. He slept alone on the road. His diary entries for the next few days were brief: "sick no chance to go to an ambulance. Remain in the same place.... Went a mile & stopped at a house where several sick of our division had been left. No Doctor. No medicine." He spent another night at the home of a Mr. Smith at Roxbury Mills. The next day a Sanitary Commission wagon found him and took him and the other sick and wounded to Boonsboro, where they slept in the Odd Fellows Hall. Finally, Corporal Howell reached the General Hospital in Frederick, Maryland, where he would remain for about two weeks.[23]

By July 11, as the 124th New York neared Roxbury Mills, rumors spread that the Confederates were near at hand. The Orange County boys moved two miles farther, spending the night resting on their arms, expecting to make contact with the enemy at any moment. That night, Lieutenant Ramsdell returned from his melancholy journey to New York, where he delivered the bodies of Colonel Ellis and Major Cromwell to their families.[24]

Saturday, July 12, there was considerable activity and plenty of indications that the long-awaited battle with Lee's retreating army was about to begin. Artillery batteries moved to commanding positions and made preparations to engage the enemy while a column of infantry quickly passed the 124th New York and deployed for battle just a few hundred yards in front of them. Birney's Division, 3rd Corps, moved about half a mile to the left. The ammunition train came up and fresh cartridges were issued. Those who had been carrying loaded weapons during the wet weather were told to draw out the old rounds and reload to insure that the powder was dry. A light rain had been falling all morning but in the afternoon the sun came out, fueling new rumors that the advance was imminent. As so often happened, no orders arrived so "the men set to work with a will, putting up their muslin shelters, for it was raining again."[25]

The enemy was indeed close at hand, dug in behind strong earthworks stretching for miles from Hagerstown to the Potomac. The Confederates dearly wished the Yankees would attack them so that they might avenge the defeat suffered at Gettysburg. All the rainy weather over the past few days made the Potomac River too deep to ford where Lee expected to cross. With the escape route blocked, Lee's scouts feverishly looked for another place to ford as his engineers tried to figure out how they might bridge the Potomac.

While Meade contemplated his options and called a counsel of his corps commanders, the river fell enough to ford at one place and a rudimentary bridge was thrown across at another. Lee set the rear guard to stoking campfires to make it look like the whole army was in place, ready to fight. Then, in a legendary feat of engineering skill and pure bluff, the Confederates slipped away.[26]

On Monday morning Union scouts reported that "the enemy had actually recrossed the swollen *impassable* Potomac, 'bag and baggage.'" The news was received with some disgust by the men in the ranks but also with a good measure of relief to be sure. When the men got a close look at the earthworks, which Weygant noted were of "considerable strength," most were happy they had not been called upon to make an assault.[27]

The smoldering campfires of Lee's rear guard were quickly rekindled "under the tin cups of our always dry — no matter how wet they are — boys in blue." At about mid-afternoon the brigade commissary wagons came up "with the usual clatter and shouts of "hi! Ho! — grub, grub, here's your grub," and the familiar reply, "Turn out for our salt 'hoss,' sugar, coffee and hard-tack," echoing along the line. The commissary sergeant of the 124th New York was the "exceedingly jolly" Ellis Post, later promoted to quartermaster of the regiment. It was noted that as his duties increased, so did his girth and he "had been growing fatter and fatter ever since the date of his enlistment."[28] He and those detailed with him were usually "good natured fellows" always the source of the latest joke or a humorous tale but this day their mood was somber. The regiment had lost half its number at Gettysburg so only half the rations were needed. Here was a dramatic reminder of what the fight on Houck's Ridge had cost Orange County. A newly appointed sergeant pointed out that Post was doling out too much. He threw a piece of salt pork at the man with a few choice words to add insult to injury, then went right back to handing out double rations to the survivors of the great battle.[29]

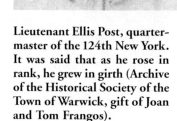

Lieutenant Ellis Post, quartermaster of the 124th New York. It was said that as he rose in rank, he grew in girth (Archive of the Historical Society of the Town of Warwick, gift of Joan and Tom Frangos).

When the news of Lee's escape reached President Lincoln, he was distraught. "We had them within our grasp," he told his secretary. "We had only to stretch forth our hands and they were ours. And nothing I could say or do could make the army move." He spoke to one of his cabinet members of "bad faith somewhere" and wondered aloud why his generals would not simply "pounce on Lee" to end the war.[30]

General-in-Chief Henry Halleck expressed the president's displeasure in a telegram to General Meade. "I need hardly say to you that the escape of Lee's army without another battle has created great dissatisfaction in the mind of the President, and it will require an active and energetic pursuit on your part to remove the impression that it has not been sufficiently active heretofore."[31] Meade wrote to his wife that this was exactly what he expected from the administration. Just as he had ignored the "senseless adulation of the public & press," so would he ignore the unjust criticism of those who expected the impossible of him. He *said* he would ignore it, but he did not. For the second time in less than a month, a commander of the Army of the Potomac offered to resign his command.

Unlike with Hooker, Lincoln moved quickly to smooth things over with Meade. The president, ever the perceptive student of military matters, wanted nothing to get in the way of overtaking the Army of Northern Virginia before it reached safe haven south of the Rapidan River in Virginia. To that end, Meade too crossed the Potomac in a pursuit that took a course east of the Blue Ridge Mountains, while Lee's men marched south behind the mountain shield. As with

McClellan the year before, Lincoln hoped that Meade could get south of Lee, turn west, and push through a gap to isolate part of the enemy and break it up piecemeal. Despite his conciliatory words to Meade and pledges of support, the president was about to be disappointed again.

The Army of the Potomac began moving toward the river crossings, French's 3rd Corps in the lead. Birney's Division was on the road at dawn July 15 reaching the Frederick City Pike near Fairplay, then marched four miles before changing direction until they "passed over the battlefield and through the bullet-scarred forests of Antietam. We reached Sharpsburg about noon, bivouacked on the outskirts of the village three hours, then moved on down the Harper's Ferry road four miles and pitched tents for the night."[32]

Early on July 17, near Harpers Ferry, Henry Howell wrote to his mother,

> I am in the best of health but I cannot say the same for Will, his strength has been failing for some time but he has managed to keep up until last Saturday when we started to march on that day he went on ahead of the regiment so he is able to go slow and I have not seen him since. He has not complained of anything except a poor appetite. I think if he can lay still and rest a few days he will be alright & come on & catch us. There are a great many that have marched until they are "worried" out. These stop for a few days rest that sets them upon their pins again & they come on.... All Superflurous flesh is gone which leaves me my fighting weight 142 pounds. That is more than I ever weighed (at this time of year) before. Now about the war. Old Lee has got out of Maryland but if what we heard yesterday is true, he has jumped out of the frying pan in to the fire.

The camp rumors had it that reinforcements were on the way from Fortress Monroe and North Carolina and that the Union army held a strong blocking position at Winchester. None of it was true. In Henry Howell's opinion, the army could have attacked when Lee was dug in north of the Potomac River, but would have suffered an "awful sacrifice of life." When he heard the news of the Draft Riot in New York City, Henry was outraged. "What dreadful news we hear from N.Y. city. It is a shame & disgrace to the whole country. Most especially the army. Here we are fighting to keep the enemy from coming north to destroy our cities & the very ones we have been fighting for turn against us. Every soldier that I have heard speak about it say they would shoot them quicker than they would a Reb if they had a chance. Last Monday was my 20th birthday & if Louisa was alive she would be six years old today."[33]

Later in the day, the regiment crossed the Potomac on the pontoon bridge at Harpers Ferry. On July 18, the men marched an additional eight miles, and halted to spend the night at Hillsborough, where Captain William Jackson wrote that the 124th New York was "now again on sacred soil hunting up or following Lee's army. We are disappointed in not having wiped out Lee in Md. We had a rough march last night in the mud and dark.... New York city is now reaping the fruit sown by Wood & Company. I wish the 124th could have a hand in putting down the riot."[34]

The same day, Henry Howell wrote home.

> We crossed the Shenandoah upon the wire suspension bridge which was not destroyed. It was so dark and muddy that we could hardly get along but when we turned on the Leesburg road we found it better travelling. We got up on the Bolivar Heights and halted for the remainder of the night.... This morning we were called up at 3 oclock so we could get our breakfasts & be ready to start at daylight.... Where we stopped to day was the greatest place for running blackberries that I ever saw in my life. The 3rd Corps was soon deployed picking them. I wish you could have seen us. It would make a nice picture for an artist. I soon had my tin cup full of them and then what a dinner we did have. Tholf & I went out yesterday morning to a farm house and bought five loaves of bread. We gave Leon one of them. I have just bought six sheets of writing paper that a soldier had received in a package from home but could get no envelopes. I don't think I ever enjoyed better health in my life.[35]

The next morning well before dawn, the soldiers had their breakfasts of hardtack and salt pork and were on the road, making eighteen miles before stopping to camp in a piece of woods near Upperville. Here they remained until noon on July 21, when orders were received to prepare to move up to the picket line. "Blankets and tents were soon strapped, and a staff officer — who had brought the order and remained in camp while we were packing up — conducted us to the picket line which had been established about two miles beyond where our division was lying." A quiet night was spent on the line, the same was true for the following morning which "was passed very pleasantly." The men were eating their dinner when bugle calls were heard signaling action. Captain Weygant received orders to withdraw his men from the picket line and to rejoin the division which was marching south on the Warrentown Pike. "An hour later we came up with the rear of our brigade and took position in the moving column. About three P.M. we changed direction to the right and it became very apparent that the ground on which we were to bivouac, lay in Manassas gap."[36]

On July 22 General French received orders to move into the Gap to reinforce General Buford, whose cavalry was patrolling the area. French's plan was to mass two divisions at Piedmont, east of the mountains, while the First Division, commanded by General Ward in Birney's absence, moved into the Gap to support the cavalry. When this was accomplished, French planned to move the rest of the 3rd Corps into and through Manassas Gap, drive the enemy, and attack whatever portion of Lee's army he could find near Front Royal.[37] It should have been obvious that the faster French moved, the greater chance he would have of success.

Upon reaching Piedmont, Ward received his orders and quickly put his division in motion toward the gap with two batteries of artillery. Ward sent one of his staff officers riding forward to find Buford and ask about the situation but when the officer returned he brought news that Buford was no longer in the area. General Merritt was on the scene with one brigade of cavalry holding the gap but he fully expected to be attacked at dawn. Needless to say, Merritt was "anxious for the arrival of supports." Merritt added that he was under orders to move to another position so Ward lost no time in pushing forward, halting near Linden Station a little before midnight within supporting distance of the cavalry. His infantry relieved the cavalry on the picket line while he placed his batteries so as to command the gap. Ward sent scouts beyond the pickets to ascertain where the enemy was located, then he waited for orders from General French to advance.[38] The speed with which Ward marched was chronicled by Captain Weygant who wrote that they made fourteen miles that afternoon before filing into the very same field where they had spent a bitterly cold night the previous November, "hungry and blanketless, shivered the dark hours away."[39]

Captain Weygant and those men not exhausted by the march contemplated the past nine months.

> But few tents were pitched that evening and not a few of our number lay awake for hours, rolled in their warm blankets, looking off toward that dark steep mountain side which had been the scene of our regiment's first skirmish — thinking of the then and now and of events that had intervened. Then the regiment numbered for duty over seven hundred rank and file, and had a full field and staff, and twenty-five line officers — now ... there were present in the battalion less than two hundred.

Many lay awake long into the night listening to the picket firing in the distance.[40]

Dawn found the 3rd Corps a day's march ahead of the other infantry corps, with Ward's Division several miles ahead of French's other two divisions. Success in this "bold and apparently hazardous undertaking," Weygant wrote, "evidently depended on its being commenced immediately and prosecuted with the utmost vigor." Four hours of daylight burned away and no orders came from General French to attack. As the Orange County men were eating breakfast, the "attention" was sounded from brigade headquarters and the "124th was soon in line but after standing at arms ten or fifteen minutes without noticing any further indications of an immediate movement, I ordered them to stack arms and break ranks, at which not a few of the boys hurried back to their camp fires, bent on having another cup of coffee before they started."[41]

French began the march from Piedmont with the remaining two divisions at "early daylight," and wrote that he arrived at Linden by 9 A.M. Both Ward and Weygant placed the arrival of the balance of the 3rd Corps a full hour later. General Ward had just planted his division flag near the rifle stacks and ordered that his horse be brought up when another witness, Captain William Jackson of Company K, took out his pocket watch and noted the time aloud, "It is five minutes past ten."[42]

Finally, General French ordered that a "small battalion of skirmishers" be sent out to "feel the enemy and to compel him to show his pickets on the heights as well as in the revines." He deployed a skirmish line covering the whole area to the front, ordered up artillery and more infantry, and sent out troops to cover his flanks and rear. "These dispositions were followed by the massing of the Second and Third Divisions to follow the First Division, deployed in line of battle, when the advance was ordered of my entire force."[43]

"Let my old brigade take the lead — tell Colonel Berdan to move forward immediately," General Ward ordered.[44] His old brigade, of course, included the 124th New York, which quickly formed up and moved forward, driving back a thin line of skirmishers. The advance was cautious but steady until, after two hours, heavy rifle fire could be heard about three hundred yards ahead. A halt was ordered while the 1st and 2nd U.S. Sharpshooters, supported by the 3rd and 4th Maine, 63rd Pennsylvania, and 20th Indiana, were formed in a heavy skirmish line across the road and up both sides of the gap. The 124th New York, 86th New York and 99th Pennsylvania formed in column and moved forward as support. The going was extremely difficult, the ground covered with thick brush on the mountain sides.

The Second Division, commanded by General Prince, was now within supporting distance of Ward's men. The Union forces were nearing the western end of the gap where the Confederates were making a stand, holding the Union troops back while long "columns of cavalry, infantry, artillery, and baggage-wagons were seen during the day moving from the direction of Winchester toward Strasburg, Luray, and Front Royal, the force in front of us being evidently a large flank guard to delay our advance."[45]

The Union push continued until the brigade reached a place where the road took a sharp turn to the right. The skirmish line halted when a "solid battle line of the foe had been discovered on the top of a lofty ridge which loomed up directly in front of us," Weygant wrote.[46] Now General Ward came forward to personally direct his brigade. The two regiments of Sharpshooters formed the right of the skirmish line while the 20th Indiana and the 63rd Pennsylvania formed the left, each group moving high up the mountain sides on either side of the gap, so high that when the halt was ordered, they could clearly see the enemy's battle line. They moved forward, engaging the flanks of the enemy battle line "causing no little consternation in his ranks."[47]

Among the Sharpshooters was Chaplain Barbour, "one of the best shots in our army" Weygant wrote. Private Henry Dill took note of Barbour and compared him to their own Chaplain Bradner, "our Chaplan is the Laseyest man that god Ever Let Live He Has not Preched in six months And Does Nothing But guard the mess Chest the sharpshooters Have A Buly Chaplan He takes His Rifel And goes in Ever Fight With the Boys And if He gets sight on A Rebel it is shure Deth to Him Fore He is as good A shot as they Have."[48] At Manassas Gap, Chaplain Barbour, "trusty rifle in hand" spotted a rebel marksman perched in a distant treetop. A couple of well placed shots "so demoralized the poor fellow that he dropped his own gun, descended to the ground begging for mercy and ran into our lines declaring that the first bullet had taken off his hat and the next two had singed his hair." Neither Weygant nor Dill commented on the whereabouts of their own Chaplain Bradner during the advance.[49]

As this action was taking place, the 3rd and 4th Maine formed a line of battle and began to move slowly up the steep ridge to the front, preparing to get into position opposite the center of the enemy position. General Ward took personal command of the supporting column which included the 124th New York. They moved forward quickly through the thick woods, formed in a column of four men abreast instead of a line of battle, and came to an open field where, without even halting the column, Ward ordered, "Forward into line" in a "gruff undertone." The 99th Pennsylvania and 86th New York were ahead of the Orange County regiment and as they formed into line of battle, the 124th New York had to double quick to make up the distance. The first company quickly went into line, the second moving up and forming on its left and so on until the entire regiment was in line. Weygant watched the men deploy as the enemy fire increased, bullets whistling around them all the while. He needed someone to run out and post himself where the left of the regiment should be so that the line could be formed in the proper manner as the companies came up. He spotted Private David W. Dewitt, who had once served as a general guide and who was familiar with what needed to be done. Just as Weygant was about to tell Dewitt where he was to post himself, the private was shot dead right in front of him.

The 124th had moved up quite close to the two Maine regiments which were stalled by the increasing enemy fire. General Ward, obviously perturbed by the delay, shouted to the commander of one of the regiments, "Move forward and clear that hill or I will send the 86th and 124th through your ranks to do it for you." This was quite a challenge to men who had fought under Phil Kearny, and it must have hit a nerve because as Weygant noted, "With one of the wildest and most determined shouts I ever heard, they rushed forward." With Yankees firing from mountain sides into their flanks, Yankees charging up the hill in front of them, and a cleric dropping them from trees, the Confederates broke and ran down the back side of the hill. The Maine troops "gained the summit, poured a volley point blank into the ranks of the foe, charged forward through the smoke and cleared the hill."[50]

The road to Front Royal and the flank of Lee's retreating army now lay open. General Ward wrote, "The enemy retreated, and took position in the valley beyond, on the road leading from the Gap to Front Royal. I ordered a portion of the First and Third Brigades forward, to support the skirmishers and drive the enemy out."[51] Ward's advance, however, was ordered to halt and he was to await the arrival of the Second Brigade, the Excelsior Brigade, which for reasons known only to French was to carry the last ridge line held by the enemy.

Another hour passed before the brigade got into position. Commanding these four New York regiments was General S.B. Spinola, described by Weygant as a newly appointed general officer, "thirsting for glory." It was said that Spinola brought his own press corps with him of "two or three newspaper reporters" to insure that he received proper credit for his exploits.[52]

The attack was made while Ward's men watched from Wapping Heights, the hill they had just carried. Ward, French, and even Weygant were lavish in their praise as the Excelsiors "most gallantly" charged down the slope, across the valley, and up the hill on the other side. They hit the enemy head on and although the Union losses were described as "quite severe," the hill was taken. Shouts of victory, the "manly deep throated Hurrah!" as Weygant described it, could be heard again and again in the distance, leaving little doubt who had won the battle. Spinola himself was carried to the rear bleeding from two wounds and "covered with glory."

It was now late in the afternoon. Word was received that a large enemy force had turned north and was now on the way back toward Front Royal. The Union advance was halted and the troops in the gap made ready to receive the enemy attack that never came. "By dusk, the poorly coordinated Union attacks were abandoned. During the night, Confederate forces withdrew into the Luray Valley."[53]

French praised Ward and made much of the courage and gallantry of his men in the battle. There can be no doubt that the soldiers who pushed through the Gap did behave splendidly. However, the point of the whole operation was to snare a portion of Lee's retreating army, not capture, and then abandon, a piece of real estate. In the end it was to be the latter, not the former that would mark the operation. Weygant did not directly blame French for his lackluster behavior at Manassas Gap or Wapping Heights, as the battle was known, and neither did Ward. But each man knew that delay had cost them the opportunity to deal a blow to Lee's army. The 124th New York lost but one man killed, Private Dewitt. A number were hit by spent bullets but only one man, Corporal Harrison Bull, was hurt seriously. His wound sent him to the Veteran Reserve Corps for the remainder of the war.

Corporal John. W. Pitts, Company K, wrote home of the battle, "When the rebs retreated we followed them up, and at Manassas Gap we supported the skirmish line and had one man killed and one wounded. We drove the rebs out of the Gap, and then marched to Warrenton and from thence to White Sulpher Springs, about 7 miles from Warrenton, where we still lay, ready when the order comes to shoulder our rifles and again do our part in the War for the Union.[54] Historian Stephen Sears summed up the battle this way: "While Lee moved slowly up the Shenandoah, Meade kept pace east of the Blue Ridge. On the 23rd he took the aggressive, sending William French and the 3rd Corps as a spearhead through Manassas Gap in the Blue Ridge to attempt to cut off a sizable portion of Dick Ewell's command. But it was too much of a challenge for the bumbling French. Ewell slipped away and followed the rest of the Army of Northern Virginia to safer ground."[55]

In a rapid series of marches, the 3rd Corps headed east out of Manassas Gap toward Warrenton on the north bank of the Rappahannock River, where General Meade resolved to halt his army, rest, and refit. In the meantime, Lee's army had reached safety and was dug in near Culpeper south of the Rappahannock River.[56]

Union and Confederate pickets appeared along the river banks and despite their officers' best efforts, quickly established an unofficial truce. Young men in blue and gray agreed not to shoot at each other, then set up a brisk trade in coffee, tobacco, and newspapers while the generals tried to figure out what to do next. By the end of July, the regiment moved three miles more to Sulphur Springs and a few days later was moved again to the campground about a mile and a half away, to a pine grove near Great Run where it would spend the next six weeks. Here the "warm days of August slipped quietly by without bringing to us any news, or even rumors of importance, so far as that portion of the army to which we belonged was concerned."[57]

William Howell's health had deteriorated during the pursuit of Lee's army and he ended up in Baltimore at the Patterson Park Hospital. On August 5 he wrote his mother,

I left Frederck & came here to Baltimore on the afternoon of the 3rd. This is a sort of convalescent camp & you need not direct any mail to me here.... All classes of people are to be found though they are all under military regulations. At Frederick they were bringing in the reb prisoners that they had picked up at Hagerstown & Williamsport and the vicinity of whom some were wounded & others were sick at the time they were left behind. It was getting to be a rebel prison & any one with any regard of his honor would feel greatly insulted to be placed among them at the mess room. I was inclined to leave the place but not so soon as I did. I said that I would get well sooner at the regt.... The nurse had my name handed in when a list of those that wanted to go to their regts were taken & so I was called upon to get ready which I did & I was off at short notice. As I before told you I found myself much weaker and unable for duty than I anticipated when I came to march a little.

There is a light duty & drill department attached to this place & as the food is suitable for those that are on light duty they will improve in health and strength.

I will get with them on the light duty department quite likely & if able to do anything will improve but my constitution seems so much broken down that I don't expect to get fit for the field again this summer.[58]

Henry Howell was still with the regiment at Sulphur Springs and feeling fine. The men set up camp with company streets, a regular camp guard, and a guard house. There was squad drill, company drill, battalion drill and brigade drill with regulation dress parade in the evening.

Near the end of July, Captain Weygant was ordered to choose three officers and six enlisted men to return home to Orange County to act as recruiters for the regiment. At that time in the war, regiments in the field could not count on the government to send replacements, they had to recruit on their own. The effective strength of the 124th was only two hundred men and Weygant wanted to augment that number. Captain William Silliman was chosen to lead the group. He had extensive experience as a recruiter but there was another reason for sending him: Weygant knew that Silliman was physically exhausted and recommended that he go, at least in part, to regain his strength.

On July 29, the nine men departed the camp, but their mission was a failure. They secured no recruits and, according to Weygant, only one of the recruiters returned to active duty with the regiment. Of the three officers, Silliman resigned his commission in the 124th and secured a colonel's commission in the 26th U.S. Colored Troops, Lieutenant Charles Crissey died in an army hospital a year later, and Lieutenant James Grier was promoted to captain and mustered out in 1865 but is not shown on the rolls in the regimental history after his departure for recruiting duty. Of the six sergeants sent home, only Sergeant Mead of Company C returned in January 1865, almost a year and a half after he left for home. In fact, two of the sergeants, James Beakes and John J. Crawford, were reduced in rank and mustered out with the regiment. The record shows no evidence of transfer to the Invalid Corps or to another regiment so it can be assumed that they returned to the 124th New York.

The failure of the effort to secure additional volunteers to the 124th New York had everything to do with its fighting reputation. Word had spread in Orange County that to serve in the field with the 124th New York was to see active service where the risk of death or injury was greater than in regiments serving elsewhere. Men of military age weighed their options and many chose to take their chances with the draft or join a nine-month regiment. The likelihood of getting shot, they calculated, would be less somewhere other than in a fighting regiment of the 3rd Corps, Army of the Potomac.

Six weeks passed while the army camped at Sulphur Springs, a delay that must have caused President Lincoln a great deal of anxiety. The boys took advantage of the stay to partake of the health-giving spring nearby, to "drink of the nauseous water" as Weygant put it. The captain caustically noted that the waters "*may have had* a beneficial effect on the health of many of those who partook of it *unadulterated.*"[59]

Captain Jackson wrote that he had been suffering from chronic diarrhea and feeling poorly as a result. "Still I stuck to the regiment and company all through until the last few days march in the last of July when I gave up. As long as there was a prospect of fight I was counted in though it was hard work." He reported that his company had present for duty, aside from himself, just "1 sergt. 1 corp. 10 privates, 1 teamster, 7 present sick total 20.... This is about an average for the regiment." Lewis Wisner of Jackson's company would soon be promoted to 2nd Lieutenant.

> He deserves well a commission. We ought to fill our vacancies for there is not an officer for each company here on duty. The 124th has had a rough time scince it came out but it stands high *here* and I *think* that it is looked on with favor at *home*. If all had fought so stubbornly the rebellion would have been at an end. If we are filled up with men and all vacancies of officers filled, it will relieve us old chaps who are somewhat tired and put new life in the regiment. There will be a chance for our two senior Capts. Weygant and Murray, the first to be Lieutenant Colonel and the other Maj. The only effect these promotions will have on me will be to raise me from 10th Captain in rank to 5th. Now if I only had been smart enough when recruiting to have come in among the first companies I might have had a lift, but I am well satisfied as it is. I don't care to be any where else than with Company K.

Mapes too had been watching for a promotion; if Murray became the major, he would be the captain of Company B.[60]

On August 10, Lieutenant Mapes wrote from Sulphur Springs "CSA." He asked his brother to put together a box for him to include "some of Story's Whiskey." The long marches had made the men weary but "excitement kept us up." He'd been down to the springs to bathe "which is as good as a go down here.... Come Hurry up that draft & send some more men here my company wants to be filled up." He asked his mother to get someone to dry me about ½ Bushell corn to eat with beans it will be bully. Remember me to Sheriff H one more thing. I want your opinion whether my acts and services to my country will be appreciated enough should I get killed for Florida to erect some lasting monument or tablet for "Copperheads" to look at in all ages to come that is until they are extinct & as they looked at it could feel the burnings of reproach & regret that they were ever traitors & my opposers. It would ever put them in mind of it but I hope I will live to be their scourage. Don't fail to answer this question.[61]

On August 13 he wrote again noting that Governor Seymour was asking the president to delay the draft so that some irregularities might be investigated. "But Abe won't. Bully for him." Mapes reminisced that it was "just one year ago since I took the first obligation to serve my country & at night I was called up at about 11 o'clock to go to Goshen. I walked back that night after 1 o'clock & sober too." He bathed every night at a nearby creek which was often frequented by some local women. "But I am nowhere with them," he assured his brother, because they preferred the staff officers from headquarters.[62]

In the middle of August, Private Henry Dill once more tortured the rules of spelling and punctuation to write to his friend Will back in Orange County. The heading on his letter read "White Sulfer Springs Virginy" and he started by telling Will the obvious: the cold spring water had a strong taste of sulfur. "Wel," he wrote, "the Wether is Warm and Plesent," adding that they had plenty to eat and not much to do. As for military matters, "Had orders on sunday to be Redy to march At A minutes Notice the Enemy Atacked our Cavelery But Was Drove Back so We Had to go on Picket to Day." He added the interesting news that "Thar is A man to be shot in our Division Fore Deserting on the First of the month." He told Will he had seen his cousin William White who was a sergeant major in the 68th "Penselvany," of Graham's Brigade, Humphreys' Division, Sickles' 3rd Corps which had been posted on the Emmitsburg Road near the Peach Orchard at Gettysburg and suffered accordingly. As for the recruiting effort of Captain Silliman and the others sent home "thar is some conscripts come to some of the Regiments But None to ours yet." He wrote that a mutual friend, Lester Genung, was a lieutenant in the 19th New York State Militia, commenting, "He Would Hold His Comision About one Day in our Riegement."

Since the New York City draft riots and the prospects of a new callup were on everyone's mind, he had some advice for his friend. "I supose if you are Drafted you Will Have to stand it and Leve Saly and All the Rest." That led him to a discussion of the local diversions available to the soldiers. "Thar is some Fancy girls Hear But you know I Never Would Bother them At Home so Do not Hear." Then he wrote on a subject that had nothing to do with the woodpile, "You Can get Plenty of Black oake to split Down Hear But it smels very Bad in Hot Wether."

Dill had high regard for his corps commander Dan Sickles, who lost a leg at Gettysburg. "Every man in the Riegement give one Days Worke to Buy A Carige And Horses Fore general sickels and We Will Have Him Back in a Few Days. He is A Buly man." As with most others in the 124th New York, Dill thought highly of Lieutenant Colonel Cummins, who had just returned to the regiment, having recovered from his Gettysburg wound. "Coloenel Cumings Has Comand of the Regement He is good to the Boys And Thay All Like Him First Rate He Likes His Whiskey very Well." Finally, he had some advice for a lady he and Will obviously knew, "Tell Thon to Looke out Fore Joe Bell And tell Her if she Has a Christen spirit to Come Down Hear And Lernn the young nigers How to read the Bibel." He concluded with "give my Love to All inquring Friends."[63]

"We were paid on the 20th for four months," Henry Howell wrote to his mother.

> We were out on picket when the paymaster came. He sent the rolls out and we signed them so that when we went back to camp the next morning he went right to work and paid us off. He agreed to take the checks & money that the men wanted to send home & post them in Washington. I thought perhaps I would have a better chance in a few days & so did not send mine. The reason I have not more time to write is because I am on guard & it will soon be time to for me to go on post. I suppose Ramsdell will start for home early in the morning. Enclosed you will find my check for $32. Out of this take $9 and

put it with the $116 already sent will make $125. From the remaining $23 I will make you a present of 10 dollars to pay you for the box last winter & the papers & letters you have sent me. The other 13 is to remain in your care subject to my call. I do not want to be without money again the way I was all along the march. Tom Clearwater owes me a couple of dollars & I shall write to him to hand it over to you. If he has got a $100 to bet on the war he must be able to pay his debts. We have drills quite regular now days. We had a brigade drill day before yesterday. It was awful hot. Ward could not stand it so he did not put us through many maneuvers. Yesterday there was a Division Review by General Birney Colonel Cummins is not doing as well as he was. He was so drunk out on review that he made himself ridiculous in the eyes of his men & Officers. It is to bad that he should act so. He was field Officer of the day.[64]

Early in September, William Howell, who had returned to the regiment after his stay in the hospital, wrote to his mother, "As for health I am doing well at present. I have been troubled with the diahraea more or less since I left Baltimore, was worse than usual a few days ago but am considerable the better off the complaint at present. Henry is troubled with his bowels the last two or three days so much so that he is unfit for duty. He thinks he has the piles or something of that sort."

Then he told her that he had been "promoted to the ranks," meaning he'd lost his corporal's stripes.

My gun has been laying idle so long while I was sick that the rust had eaten it so that it did not look very bright on the outside & as Henry was excused from inspection. I took his gun as it looked better outside than mine but lo when the inspector inserted the ramrod and rubbed up and down he brought out some rust on it. Henry had not cleaned his gun out much since he came off picket the same morning & there I missed it by taking his gun for mine I had cleaned out well.

I went down to the Col. to tell him how the matter was but he was in a bad humor & would not hear a word of excuse. It was a very light offense even if the gun had been my own & perhaps the order will not be carried into effect after all. At any rate I shall have the proud consciousness that I have done nothing that merits such sentence & will not feel at all disgraced.

He went on to write about the recent promotions and demotions in the company. "There is considerable jealousy in the regt about promotions but I am unconcerned now free & independent & no care or responsibility that is unless the Col. reconsiders his order. Today makes just a year that we have been mustered in the U.S. Army & a year to morrow Since we left Goshen."[65]

A few weeks later, William Howell wrote, "I am doing duty as a private and find it just as easy about as anything else but it is a shame the way promotions are given in the reg't to those that have never done their duty in times of hardship and peril. Those that can drink, smoke, cheer, and swear seem to be popular and get all the easy 'berths.'"[66]

Mid-September, Private William Howell wrote to his sister Emily, "The warm days of August slipped quietly by." He told her that he and Henry were in good health, had plenty of rations, and that their time was taken up with such mundane activities as drill, camp guard, and picket duty. In fact he noted that they "drill considerable." The week prior, the 3rd Corps had been reviewed by General Meade and his staff. "Everything passed off well as usual. It was a warm day; we started at half past six in the morning and as we are in the 1st Division now we got through in better season for we started for camp soon as we were reviewed and were back by the middle of the afternoon.... The 40th N.Y. came out with their white gloves at the review and the word is that we are to have white gloves and state jackets." William wrote that the two Maine regiments had recently been reinforced with three or four hundred men and asked for news of the recruiting party sent home the month before. "By the way we don't hear anything yet about our men with the conscripts. I suppose Mt. Hope will have to turn out some men to meet the requirements of the draft." This was a reference to the fact that the more volunteers sent from the town, the fewer would be called in the next draft.

"The weather has been cloudy," he wrote, "with ever appearance of a storm but our signs don't seem to be of much account in a Southern climate. The fences in this section have been used for firewood and the fields are all in one. The land has been in a good state of cultivation but it is all trampled down now and over run with weeds and briers. The surface is rolling and numerous hillocks are to be found far as we can observe on all sides of us; the north branch of the rapahanock or hedgemans river as it is called up here is but ¼ of a mile west of us and the village of the Springs which has been burnt so that the chief portion is now a mass of ruins is just to our right." They were camped on a two thousand–acre farm owned by a man who was serving in the rebel army, William told his sister. "There are but a few inhabitants left here and they consist principally of women and children with a few aged darkies. They fetch in milk and green corn to sell or exchange for coffee or pork."

William knew that the peaceful interlude could not last much longer. "We drew blankets yesterday and are fitted out for a move. We are to have a division drill this afternoon." He was sure that they would soon "hear that the wheel is in motion and then we will pack up our world of possessions shoulder our muskets and be off at short notice. The opinions seem prevalent that we will have another campaign and then settle the war and bid adieu to the strifes of the battlefield."[67]

Captain James Benedict, Company D wrote two letters home at about the same time. "We have had six new officers commissioned lately and still have ten vacancies you see one year has used up officers as well as men." He wrote of a package that was delivered to the officers of the regiment.

> I have received a photograph of Major Cromwell, which I wish you to put with the others and take special care of as he was to my mind the Noblest, Bravest, Best Young Man I ever Knew and one I am proud to be able to call friend. Oh! That he might have been spared to us for none felt or took so much interest in the welfare of the Reg't as he, while the Colonel was constantly working to advance the regiment in Military Matters, the Major at the same time assisting in that branch was continually working for the sick and for the health of the whole. Last spring as soon as the ground was dry enough he went to work with his whole soul to work the boys into fit condition for marching by getting them to play Ball and in every way to get them to work themselves down knowing they were fat and soft after lying idle for so long a time and no one played with more spirit than he did and in various ways he contributed to health and comfort and pleasures of us all. If an officer or man wanted a favor they went to him in perfect confidence that if it was proper and he could accommodate them he was anxious to do it. His memory will ever be cherished by us all, could you have seen and heard the officers when the package came and was distributed you would certainly have thought his memory was precious."[68]

In the second letter he expressed his opinion that the much-anticipated fall of Charleston would do more to hurt the South than the capture of any other city.

> They have considered that port as impregnable and if we succeed in taking it, it seems to me they have but one more source of hope, and that source the Copperheads, what a shame that the people of the North should encourage the Rebels in their rebellion against the Government and in Killing their neighbors. I sometimes think I can never live among them again in anything like friendship. Why should I? Do they not hold out inducements to the enemy to take my life and the life of every one that has taken up arms for their country?[69]

During the second week of September, General Meade learned that Lee's army had pulled back from Culpeper. He ordered the cavalry to push the rebels across the Rapidan River. He sent the infantry across the Rappahannock and took up position between the rivers. The 124th New York moved south on September 15, crossing the Rappahannock at Freedman's Ford the next day. By September 17, the troops were within a few miles of Culpeper, where they halted and set up camp. Five days' marching rations were issued on September 21, which set the rumor mill to work. On September 26 the paymaster arrived and "dealt out a considerable quantity of greenbacks."[70]

Captain Jackson wrote home from Culpeper Court House that they were now on the south side of the Rapidan River. "On the morning of the 17th we move a short distance to the right of the town on the main pike to Gordonville." The 6th Corps was on their right, the rest of the army to their front. In Jackson's opinion, they were not strong enough to "drive" the enemy but they wanted to keep in close contact to prevent reinforcements being sent to help the western Confederates. "Our boys have good times, living on secesh turkies, ducks, chickens, and live stock generally. The day we marched it was a caution to hear the ducks quack, and the next day in our company alone I counted more than a dozen turkies beside other plunder. This is all very nice while it lasts but we soon rid quite a section of country of all such game. Even corn and all kinds of vegetables soon disappear. White folks are very scarce. What are left are miserably destitute, even those of the F.F.V.'s."

Artillery fire could be heard every day as the cavalry probed and skirmished with the enemy. "These cavalry fights make a great noise but don't amount to much after all. I should like very much to see you down here and show you how an army lives, moves, and has its being, but I could not recommend the whiskey they have down here. It is all the rifled kind that will kill at 500 yds."[71]

A few days later Henry Dill took up his pencil once more to write to his friend Will. The letter, dated "September the 18, 1863, Virginy," brought his friend up to date on the recent move toward Culpeper.

> Our Cavelry Had A Fight Hear on sunday And Drove the Rebels into Gordonville twenty miles From Hear.... We marched twenty miles From sulpher springs and Had to Ford too Rivers the Watere Was Warm and I Did Not take Any cold We Have A good Place to Camp Plenty of sharp Chickens and Corn And Wee Consfistacate All We Can Find the Paymaster is Hear And We Will soon Be Payed the sutler sels Ale For Fifty scents A Botel thayr is one good Drinke in A Botel Buter Fifty scentes A Pound Cheese Forty scentes A Pound And Every thing in Proportion.[72]

Five days later, on September 23, Corporal George Godfrey of Company E also wrote a letter home to Will.

> I recieved your letter of the 13th and was glad to hear that you were all well. It is as you say that nothing does a soldier any more good than a letter and I should like to have heard from you before. I am well again and doing duty. I was not very sick anytime though but only tired and worn out marching up into Pa and back I tell you it was pretty hard business and no mistake but we gave them what they did not go after and they were very well satisfied to get back on their old grounds and now I think they are getting back farther yet. Our Cavalry are beyond Gordonville and Gen Kilpatrick has his Head Quarters in the place. We expect to march from here at any moment we are called on and i think it wont be but a short while before we are. I should advise you to pay your $300 sooner than come down here and carry your knapsack and all the load that a soldier has to carry for I tell you it is no fun to travel all day and sometimes a good part of the night through mud dust and everything else. And besides you will find the Grub not quite like what you get home and that you would not like it as well. It is quite cold down here now nights and not very warm daytimes but we will have hot enough wether yet to roast us before we get through this falls campaign I think. I hope it is as the People up there think that this is about played out but I don't know.[73]

The paymaster visited the 124th New York on September 25 and Henry Howell wrote home the next day.

> Will received the full amount for six months but I was docked $1.13 for the two months they owed me. I got the full payment of my allotment which I will enclose herewith. Most all of the boys got cut short on their pocket change for with most of them the extra amount of clothing and their allotments cheque overrun the two months wages. A very few of them had to give Uncle Sam their two months pay entire. It is a *shame* the way some of the contractors speculate on "poor" Soldiers. We get shoes sometimes that will not last more than two or three weeks on a march for which we have to pay $2.05 and the socks last about the same length of time & cost us 32 cents. We have not drawn overcoats yet nor would not care to for two or three weeks if we were sure of being on a march. The boxes of clothing that we have packed up in camp last spring may come on after a while.... We have very good water and a good supply of hard bread, pork, coffee, sugar and some of the time soft bread and fresh beef. The Sutlers are getting so much afraid of the Guerrillas that they have not ventured back to Washington with their teams but are waiting for to get government transportation for their goods. They have boots for which they ask from $8 to $10.

I was lucky enough to get me a secondhand pair for which I paid $3.50. Parrot of Company K bought them off one of the conscripts (for almost nothing I suppose) but they were too small for him, they are worth $7. They are calfskin with very heavy bottoms & top plates.... Most all the white inhabitants have left this part of the country. Those that are left are secesh to the backbone. I was talking with one girl who said that she was just as sure that the south would gain their independence as she could be. There was a nice yearling calf there so we captured it, brought to camp and divided it around amongst Company E. It was fat and good. Secesh "live stock" stands a far sight here. It is too near dress parade time for me to start another sheet.[74]

On September 27, Lieutenant Mapes wrote again about the draft. "I read Seymour's Speech. It is a splendid thing. He ought to be shot." Mapes may have been referring to Governor Seymour's July speech to the New York City draft rioters in which he told them that he was attempting to get the draft suspended for the present and eventually stopped altogether.[75] He asked if Wesley Storms of his company, who was wounded at Gettysburg, was home yet. "If not I will try & get him home. He is a good Boy." A friend had sent Mapes copies of a New York newspaper which he did not like. "Gene sent me some of the *Dailey News.* I wrote him to send no more but send some religious ones that would teach me the duty I owe to my God & country, not treason." As usual, he asked for the latest about the local girls in Florida and Warwick. He'd received a letter from a friend who must have gone on in great detail about the ladies. "Norm is Cunt Struck I guess by the way he talks about them."[76]

At the end of the month, the brigade was assembled to watch a "humiliating sentence" carried out on a deserter from the 124th New York named George Babcock of Company B. In the presence of his comrades, he had the hair shaved from one side of his head and his buttons torn from his uniform coat. He was marched at bayonet point from the camp while the drum corps beat the rogue's march and the men hooted and insulted him. In Weygant's opinion the soldiers in the ranks would "rather death a thousand times, than such a disgrace."[77] Captain Jackson thought the punishment too light but there may have been "mitigating circumstances."[78]

On October 2, Weygant reported that Colonel Cummins received a five day pass and took the train for Orange County. Cummins had a pass all right, but he was headed to Gettysburg with two men from Company I to locate the body of Lieutenant Milnor Brown, who had been killed on July 2 in the Weikert Field. The family was very influential and wanted his remains brought home. The pass was secured through the offices of "the secretary," which meant William Seward, secretary of state. The two men who accompanied the colonel had carried Brown off the field and presumably buried him.[79] With the colonel absent, Captain Weygant was in charge of the regiment. Military business in camp went as usual with a couple of scares on the picket line to liven things up. The Confederates stampeded a small herd of "glandered" mules into the Union lines, probably to spread the disease among the cavalry horses and mayhem among the pickets.[80]

Lieutenant Mapes was on the picket line when it happened. Rebel cavalry had been seen prowling around looking to capture any unwary sentinels.

I was detached with 15 picked men to go & bring them in if I saw them "Dead or alive." I started out & scouted the country out saw but 2 or 3 riding in the distance out of range so I had no sport. I was going to try my Generalship if I had met them but they were more to observe than fight. At night we had strict orders that if a man came in sight not to let him get away alive. It was very dark at one at night I heard one of the boys cry "Halt" & fired. I jumped up & rushed to the spot I heard "halt" at the next post & a report also I thought we would have some sport soon but when I got there I heard the Boys laughing at them shooting a mule they brought him low I tell you.[81]

Repeated false alarms over the next few days and nights, distant artillery fire, and Union troop movements convinced the men that something was up. That opinion was reinforced when five days' rations were issued on October 8, the day after Colonel Cummins returned from his trip. At noon on October 10 the rumble of artillery could again be heard and the division was called into line and ordered to be ready to move at the obligatory "moment's notice." At dusk the men gathered wood for fires. "As soon as these were started we lay down beside them and tried to sleep."[82]

While the men rested by their fires, the next campaign was already underway.

CHAPTER 10

"The poor boys ... have suffered as I could not describe to you"

October 10–December 3, 1863

The Confederate leadership knew that, with the defeat at Gettysburg and the long retreat that followed, they must regain the initiative if their rebellion was to survive. But where to attempt it? In the West, General Ulysses S. Grant's capture of Vicksburg and General William Rosecrans's move into northwestern Georgia were causes of great concern. After considerable debate, it was decided to send General Longstreet with two of his divisions to halt the Yankee advance on Atlanta. General Lee and President Jefferson Davis were gambling that the seasoned brigades from the east, used to victory and with a fighting spirit some thought lacking among western Confederates, might do the trick. Longstreet moved out on September 5. It did not take long for that news to reach Washington. Sensing an opportunity, Meade advanced on Culpeper, forcing Lee to fall back to the south side of the Rapidan River.

The Confederate gamble paid off handsomely. Rosecrans was so badly whipped at Chickamauga that both the 11th Corps and the 12th Corps were detached from Meade's army and rushed west to shore up the situation. Now it was Lee's turn to get some valuable intelligence. When he learned that the Army of the Potomac was weaker by two corps, he decided he would try again what he had so successfully done the year before: move around the right flank of the Union army and beat it in a foot race to Centreville, Virginia. This would put the Army of Northern Virginia squarely between the Army of the Potomac and the Yankee capital, a thought that terrified the president, General Halleck, and every government clerk in town.

The move did not come as much of a surprise to Meade because his scouts had noticed unusual activity along the Rapidan River. At first Meade thought Lee might be headed for the Shenandoah Valley, but by Saturday, October 10, he was convinced Lee was moving on his right flank. He responded by ordering a withdrawal across the Rappahannock River. By Sunday it became clear that Lee was not just maneuvering against Meade's flank, but was trying to get his army in Meade's rear.

So began what Weygant called the Centreville Campaign, which, together with the Mine Run Campaign in November, was the last great military effort of 1863 in the East. The coming week would be characterized by grueling marches and sharp skirmishing as Meade skillfully pulled his men back toward the fortifications at Centreville where he could best protect Washington. Although Meade outnumbered the Confederates, he realized that it would be too dangerous to fight Lee on his own terms and, on October 11 put his men in motion for Centreville.[1]

Captain Ira Bush, Company F, was wounded in action and discharged for wounds, June 21, 1864 (archive of the Historical Society of the Town of Warwick, gift of Joan and Tom Frangos).

The 124th New York was camped near Culpeper when the orders came to pack up and be ready to march. Captain Ira Bush, who led Company F, wrote to a friend,

> I have often thought of writing to you in refference to the progress made, and now making, to put down Rebellion, and cause the dear old flag again the waive in triumph over our Entire land ... on Saturday the 10th of October the larger portion of the Potomac Army ocupied Culpepper and Vicinity. Our Corps the 3rd lay aboute 3 miles south of the town, the move in was fine, and while we were congratulating ourselves uppon the pleasantrys of Our
>
> camp the Bugle called the Commanders of Cos to Head Quarters, where we was informed that We would strike tents in half an hour and that to secure our Earthly Effects. Greate dispatch was requisite, but as we had little and the little kept constantly in readiness to depart aney hour Day or night it only Excited a Smile and we were ready.[2]

Ready or not, the men were soon on the march, but to where they did not know. "We formed line of Battle some half Mile from Our Camp," Captain Bush wrote, "and awaited the foe, then changed front giving us to understand that the Enemy was trieing to flank us, and during the day we changed Position frequently and lay on our arms all night."[3]

These movements were in accordance with orders from General French to his division commanders. General Birney wrote, "My division remained on the extreme right until the 10th of October when by the command of Major-General French, I formed line of battle, connecting on my left with Carr's division and on the right with the Second Corps, in a position a mile nearer Culpeper than my previous camp."[4]

The army remained near Culpeper until Sunday morning to allow the ambulances and ammunition wagons to get ahead, and then marched north. "We now began to realize," wrote Chaplain Bradner, "that we were pulling back to Sulphur Springs and perhaps Washington, a terrible march for the poor men. Sixty rounds of cartridges, eight days' rations, with clothing and blankets, will give you some conception of what was to be borne in a rapid march. We came back on the same road we went down until we were in sight of the estate of John Miner Botts, when we turned to the left, making for Freeman's Ford, eight miles below Sulphur Springs."[5]

General Birney described the march north.

> I prepared to bring up the rear of corps in its march to Freeman's Ford.... During the march the cavalry of the enemy hung upon and threatened the left flank of the column and at one time made an attack upon my flankers forcing me to form a brigade in line of battle and place a battery in position. The First U.S. Sharpshooters, Lieutenant-Colonel Trepp, were deployed as skirmishers, and speedily drove away the enemy. Near Welford's house, I saw the attack on Pleasonton's cavalry near Brandy Station and, forming Ward's brigade in line of battle, made a demonstration of force and artillery to protect Pleasonton's right, and sending Captain J. B. Fassitt aide-de-camp, to Major-General Pleasonton, offered him any assistance that he might desire. He declined the assistance.... My division crossed Freeman's Ford at midnight and bivouacked near Freeman's house.[6]

Captain Bush wrote that "it became apparent that the Enemy was trieing to cut us off from Crossing the several fords it was then that the Muscle of the Northern troops triumphed over the FFVs. Many of their force were Mounted, but Our Cavalry harrassed them untill 3 O'clock P.M. when a Cavalry fight of some moment took place, we sent word to know if the 3rd Corps was wanted, and word came back to Make for the ford as quick as possible, as they could hold them, again we moved forward and 3 times were drawn up in line of Battle."[7]

Chaplain Bradner heard the artillery fire as the regiment approached and formed into a line of battle. Couriers riding back and forth convinced him that "we were in for a fight." He had a ringside seat as the Union and Confederate troops went after each other. "We could see the shells fly and our cavalry wheel on the plain and charge, but could not tell the result." After about an hour they were off again, marching until nightfall when "we halted, stacked arms, and the men ran for rails and water." But before the farm fences could bring the coffee to a boil "the bugles blew 'fall in' and now began a terrible march. Robbed of sleep the previous night, cold, hungry and tired, the night dark" they pushed on, crossing Hazel River, a branch of the Rappahannock, on a pontoon bridge, then marched on a good dry road toward the next river crossing.[8]

About an hour later numerous camp fires could be seen on a bluff in the distance and men could be heard yelling in the darkness. "It was our troops fording the Rappahannock, and it brought relief, for we felt an assurance that we could now rest. The river was neither deep nor wide; officers and men, started in with a yell, a laugh and a joke, then out, and through the camp fires, winding among the hills about a mile, when we halted for the night, made fires, had a cup of coffee, and at 2 o'clock laid down upon the ground to sleep."[9]

The river was waist deep, according to Captain Bush, who wrote, "went aboute a Mile and Bivoucked for two hours without tents and Clothes Wet, and yet the joking propensity of the Soldier predominated amidst all these drawbacks, again took position in Woods commanding Raccoon ford, being the one we forded."[10]

The regiment was off again at daylight Monday morning without having time to boil coffee but was halted after just a short march and spent the rest of the day on a wooded hill. Throughout the day and into the evening artillery fire could be heard in the distance from the direction of Brandy Station. It was rumored that the enemy was trying to cross the river at Sulphur Springs and that the Union cavalry could not hold them.[11] General Birney was ordered "to mass my division in front of Freeman's Ford, and to picket my front" in order to prevent the enemy from using the ford. Captain Bush wrote that "as night approached there was a call for two of the best Regt in our Brigade to act as Videtts, when the 124th and 86 N.Y. Vols were chosen by General Ward; Occupied a critical position, and aboute 4 oclock A.M. Our Corps passed, and we were ordered to again fetch up the men as usual when the Enemy is in that quarter."[12]

Chaplain Bradner remained awake during the tense night until, at daylight, the 3rd Corps moved past the pickets and the two New York regiments rejoined the brigade. The march continued until they reached Three Mile Station on the Warrenton Branch Railroad, at which point the 3rd Corps was deployed in line of battle to await the Confederate attack which did not come. Mid-afternoon, they moved out again, heading for the village of Auburn, where the enemy was waiting for them. The head of the column was fired upon by dismounted cavalry and artillery. "At 4 o'clock we were startled with the boom of cannon ahead of us and, as our brigade was second from the front, we could see the fire of our guns two fields beyond. General French took personal command of Sleeper's Battery and ordered the gunners to load with canister and not to fire as the enemy closed in on them. He waited until they were within close range and gave the order to fire himself. Then the First Brigade charged and the Rebs took to their heels."[13]

"We were attacked Sunday south of the Rap by cavalry but lost none, yesterday we had a brisk little fight with Dismounted cavalry & artillery our loss about one killed & 25 wounded. The 124th had Capt. Jackson hit in the Stomach with a spent Ball & a man in co F also, it will not amount to much."[14] The bullet hit the buckle on Jackson's sword belt which "doubled him over a little while, but he was not badly hurt."[15] As the 3rd Corps resumed the march toward Greenwich, General Warren's 2nd Corps came up and moved into the woods where the Confederates had been and, as Bradner wrote, began making supper. What they were making was not just salt pork and coffee but a trap for the pursuing enemy. Captain Bush wrote of the rest of the day, "Made another forced march traveling over thirty miles, and participating in one fight and at Nine P.M. Bivoucked near Greenwich a small town with some fifteen Houses which with a creditable Church in appearance made up the town and to day the least it was not improved by us for we left it looking very much like unto a flock of Geese newly Picked."[16]

Chaplain Bradner wrote that the 3rd Corps "had hardly commenced moving on Wednesday morning the 14th, before heavy firing was heard in our rear, apparently just where the Second corps had staid all night."[17] What the chaplain heard was firing from a sharp engagement with the pursuing rebels in which "A.P. Hill finally overtook the Union rear guard, under Warren, near Bristoe Station, just south of Manassas Junction. Hill attacked with headlong fury, only to thrust his leading division into a clever trap where it was shattered. The check took the remaining drive out of Lee's pursuit."[18]

Lieutenant Mapes agreed. "To day the 2nd Corps has given the Rebs rats. Meade is a Napoleon never was a retreat more ably conducted & without loss of property. Lee could not flank him as he did Pope. The army is in fine spirits & not demoralized. My 'Gunsharps' are true. I have them all yesterday we double quicked about a mile it made our 'colb kick.' I am well & in good spirits but jaded all most out. I am confident of success here in we all are determined to if possible wipe out this Rebellion on the field."[19]

Captain Bush described how the regiment "again at daylight took up the march, went with incredible Volocity for troops loaded as we were with some eight days Rations when we started, forded the Two Runs, among which was the Bull Run Creek, and aboute 3 P.M. took Position in CenterVille fortifications, then could be distinctly heard the Battle Raging with the 2nd Corps, who done so nobly on that occashion and of which the papers kept you fully advised, lay at Centervile all night and next day Marched to fairfax Station, lay there for four days."[20]

"We passed on over Bull Run at Blackburn's Ford," wrote the chaplain, "and halted at Centreville about 6 P.M. devoutly thankful to the Great Deliverer for his preserving care. We felt our fare to be sumptuous, although it was but boiled beans and pork."[21]

Military historian Colonel Vincent Esposito wrote of the movement, "Meade's withdrawal proceeded in good order. He refused to halt at any position where there was any chance of his west flank being enveloped (as had happened to Pope and Hooker), but he kept his army well together and gave Lee no opportunity for a successful attack."[22] William Howell agreed, saying, "I think a skedaddle was never made quicker nor in better order by any body of troops in the world than was made by us."[23]

"Well," Henry Howell wrote, "I will give you a few particulars and incidents of the march commencing at Centerville from which place Will wrote a sheet. The day he wrote we marched to Fairfax Station and encamped behind the earthworks. Before night General D.E. Sickles came out to visit us. We all turned out and gave him a 'welcome.' It was so late when he got up to Headquarters that he could not make us a speech. He looked very well. A report soon got in circulation that he was to take command of the Old 3rd around the defenses at Washington, but that is 'played out.'[24]

"Our division moved about two miles to the left of where we had spent the night and encamped near Fairfax Station, wrote. During the day our old commander, Genreal Sickles, paid us a visit and was received with shouts of welcome which must have convinced him that he was held in high regard by the officers and men who had fought under him at Chancellorsville and Gettysburg. Toward evening our division was called upon to witness the shooting of a deserter from the 5th Michigan." Bradner wrote that this was "a scene so terrible that I will not attempt to describe it."[25]

Henry Howell did describe the scene.

The next day there was a deserter shot in the presence of the whole Division. He belonged to the 5th Michigan 3rd Brig. He was marched along the whole line with the band playing the "Death March" and four men carrying his coffin in front of him. They took him right up to his grave, which was already dug when the Chaplain offered prayer after which he sat down on his coffin for the rest of his sentence to be fulfilled. The Provost Guards were the executioners and they done their duty well every gun was discharged at once and the man fell dead. Oh! What a fate for an American soldier. But it was just.[26]

Thomas Rodman simply referred to the execution as "a sad sight."[27]

"Since writing you last I have had a pretty hard march," Thomas Rodman wrote to his parents.

Last Saturday 1 week ago we were at Culpepper and took up the line of March and we have marched and skirmished all the way here to within ten miles of Alaxandria. I never enjoyed better health than I now do. I think we will soon go into Winter quarters by the looks of things.... We are encamped within ½ mile of the Depot and I expect we will live pretty good soon. This is the last sheet of paper I have and no money to buy any more. I want a little. We have not been paid off. I have received all your letters that you sent me and Mothers likeness but not yours. You must send it. When we get settled I am going to send for a box and I want a good one. I wish you would send me a pair of Gloves such as you sent me last winter right away by mail. I hope you and Mother is well. Write immediately and let me know how the draft is going on. I want you to get me a pair of Boots made about 8½ and not very heavy nor light and have them ready to send when I send for the Box. (Double sole high tops.)[28]

Meade won the foot race to protect Washington and he quickly entrenched his army in strong defensive positions. Lee's "grand turning movement" had failed and now he weighed his options. He could assault the Yankees in their strongly held position or fall back the way he had come. Since his lines of supply and communication were stretched and exposed, he decided to do the latter, "destroying the railroad as he went. Meade, thoroughly nagged by Hallock, followed promptly; but it took month to re-lay the railroad track behind his army."[29] The President, who likened Meade's pursuit of Lee after Gettysburg to "an old woman shooing geese across a creek," now had a telegram sent to him saying, "Lee is unquestionably bullying you." The general took it in stride although he once more offered to resign if his actions did not meet with Lincoln's approval.[30]

Lee began the march south on Sunday, October 18, with the Union army right behind him. "Early Monday morning, October 19th," Weygant wrote, "our division struck tents and moved southward again, following in the wake of a portion of our cavalry corps which came up with and engaged the enemy's rear guard at Bristoe Station."[31] On October 20 "we started forward with the rising sun," crossed Broad Run and the cavalry battlefield of the day before, halting at Greenwich where they went into camp. The next day they resumed the march "at a rapid gait for ten miles," halting at Catlett's Station. They were told to set up their tents in regular company streets because the commanding general "had resolved to give over his pursuit of Lee, and encamp in that vicinity until he could rebuild some twenty miles of the Orange and Alexandria Railroad, which Lee's army had destroyed; for it was over that road that our supplies were sent to us."[32]

"Well we remained at Fairfax until Monday morning when we started on the counter march," Henry wrote to his mother from Catlett Station.

We came back by way of Union Mills crossing the Bull Run Creek on the Railroad bridge. We marched back as far as Bristoe that night. The Rebs have made a complete destruction of the Railroad from that station to the Rappahannock. The ties were piled up and the rails laid across and the whole burned. The bridges are all blown up but the Government has taken prompt measures to replace everything. The bridges are all framed and brought out by railroad to where they are wanted. Where there are so many hands they soon do up a job. Tuesday we took a circle up around towards the Bull Run mountains & put up for the night near Greenwich. Yesterday we marched to this place passing through Auburn near which place we had the little skirmish. Capt Jackson was lucky in not getting hurt there. Something like I was at Chancellorsville only the ball must have been nearly spent this time. We are encamped on the plains along the railroad and from appearance we will stay here until the track is repaired so our supplies can come up. There is to be an inspection but perhaps I will get time to write more.[33]

From Catlett's Station, William Howell wrote to his sister Emily,

I will write you a brief note this afternoon if my fingers do not get too cold before I get through for it is very chilly today & yesterday & were told we were under marching orders. We began to think we would not move but as we were eating supper the bugle sounded strike tents & we packed up immediately. We moved scarcely half a mile & were drawn up in line & told to spread our blankets & turn in which we did but the biting north wind did not allow us to sleep very sound & made us think of winter quarters. Today we have put up our tents & we do not see any cause for our moving last night.... I need my boots now I have bought me a pair of knit gloves for 75 cts. We went to a house out on the picket line & got our breakfast & dinner. We got bread butter honey & milk, we got pancakes & fresh pork for breakfast. It was a great rarity but nothing like what you can make home. The folks out here are very scant for provisions. Ewell corps retreated back past the house where we breakfasted. It is call the Jersey Settlement because the people are from that State. Some of them have gone north to avoid the rebel conscription.... We had an inspection yesterday & condemned some of our wormy hard tack & gave us better. We get fresh beef every two or three days. We break our crackers up in a cup & soak with water fry our meat & put the crackers in the gravy & fry them up which with a cup of coffee makes our principle meals. We are anxious for the railroad to get up here so we can get bread A gang of men have just come up here with their tools to put up a bridge. They bring along their stoves & every thing looks as though they mean to stay till every thing is repaired up. Our officers baggage has come in as though we were like to stay here for a few days.[34]

Thomas Rodman was impressed at how the enemy

tore up the Rail Road from the Rapahanock to Manassas Plains. They completely spoiled the Rails and burned the ties. The way they took to do it, was, First they piled the ties up in a heap and then laid the Rails across them and then set Fire to the ties and the heat bent the Rails so as to spoil them, some of the Rails we found wound around the trees. But it does not take Uncle Sam long to rebuild it, for it is almost rebuilt to the River and they did not touch it this side of it and then we will be able to get Boxes and things from home and Soft Bread from Alexandria.[35]

Once the army halted, the routine of putting out pickets began again. This was a duty that grew more uncomfortable as the weather turned colder. It was "wonderful to what an extent our sick list would be suddenly lengthened on the slightest rumor that an order detailing the 124th for picket had reached camp."[36]

After three days shivering on the picket line, the regiment returned to camp and immediately set about cutting fresh pine boughs for their beds, looking forward to a warm night's sleep. Shortly after the sun set, just as the men began to settle in for the night, orders came to strike tents and form into line. "When this was done we stacked arms, and after shivering about the stacks for an hour or more, formed line again and in obedience to orders from brigade head-quarters advanced about twenty rods, to a muddy flat where we were directed to form a column of division and make ourselves comfortable." The men spent another cold damp night in the open air, teeth chattering and limbs shaking. When morning came all were tired and sore except for a few officers who had gotten themselves "gloriously happy" on a bottle of whiskey they had on hand. The sun warmed them a bit and some men rolled themselves in their blankets to get a little sleep just as reveille sounded. After breakfast, the regiment was marched back to the old campground and told to put up its tents again. The men knew enough not to ask why they had been moved in the first place.[37]

The Orange Blossoms turned in early that night, exhausted from their twenty rod (about 320 feet) march to the mud flat and back. After a few hours' sleep the regiment was ordered up again and into line. Just before midnight the men moved out at a "rapid gait" for points south, but were halted for the night after just a few hours. On October 27 they moved a half mile farther, camping in an oak grove, when they learned that their division was serving as a grand reserve for the picket line, which had been slowly advancing south and was, at that point, about a quarter mile ahead of them. By October 30, the 124th was near Bealton Station where it remained for a week. By November 7, the railroad had been repaired to that point and General Meade was ready to advance on the enemy.[38]

In the meantime, Lee had moved south of the Rappahannock River into his old defensive positions, but he maintained a "fortified bridgehead" on the north bank at Rappahannock Station, where the Orange & Alexandria Railroad bridge once stood. On the north bank, earthwork forts were constructed with artillery positions and rifle pits. A pontoon bridge connected the north and south banks so that troops could be quickly moved to reinforce the admittedly exposed bridgehead. Lee reasoned that if Meade tried to cross the Rappahannock he would do it at Kelly's Ford. High ground on the north bank and flat open land on the south bank made this place very difficult to defend, so Lee devised a clever plan. If Meade moved against Kelly's Ford, he would send reinforcements to the bridgehead at Rappahannock Station to threaten Meade's right and rear. This would force Meade to split his army to defend his lines of supply, right flank, and communications, thus weakening any attack he might make.

Meade, meanwhile, was making plans of his own. Despite a reputation for caution that irritated the administration in Washington, he offered Lincoln a plan that called for a change of base, the rapid movement of the army downstream where he might have an opportunity to cross the Rappahannock and turn the enemy's right flank. Now it was Lincoln's turn to be cautious. He rejected the plan in part because of memories of the debacle at Fredericksburg the year before and no doubt because he wanted to have Meade move against Lee in his present position. Historians Graham and Skoch argue that Meade was not afraid to attack Lee. "He desired, however, to dictate to Lee the terms of the engagement, both time and place, instead of permitting the crafty Confederate commander to have things all his own way. Meade realized that the latter was the major factor in the downfall of his predecessors."[39]

So Meade came up with a new plan that split his army into two wings, just as Lee thought he would be compelled to do. The right wing was made up of the 5th and 6th Corps and was commanded by Major General John Sedgwick, who would lead it against the bridgehead at Rappahannock Station. The left wing, consisting of the 1st, 2nd, and 3rd Corps under Major General William French, would attack at the all-important Kelly's Ford. "Both wings were ordered to travel light, leaving unnecessary wagons and equipment behind, for the strength of Meade's plan lay in his army's ability to move quickly, giving the enemy little time to strengthen the points of attack."[40] Meade thought French's attack at Kelly's Ford offered the best chance of success so he ordered French to move quickly to Sedgwick's aid once across the river. Together they could reduce the bridgehead at Rappahannock Station, reunite the army and push on to Brandy Station. There was a danger inherent in Meade's plan: if either of the attacking wings was delayed, Lee might be able to concentrate against the other wing and destroy it.

Meade got his force underway early on November 7, with General French, acting as wing commander, moving out from Warrenton Junction at 5 A.M. General Birney commanded the 3rd Corps and General Ward the First Division, which marched at the head of the column. Weygant put the time of their departure from Bealton at about 8 A.M., noting that "at 2 P.M. the head of the column was halted under cover of a piece of woods that skirted the north-eastern bank of the Rappahannock at Kellys Ford."[41] Captain Ira Bush wrote that "on Saturday Morning the 6th instant we Broke Camp and from all appearances the Move as it has proved was a general one we arrived much jaded aboute high twelve at Kellys Ford when our Regt was chosen to support a Battery, we went a little to the left of the ford, the guns were run in Position by hand and Concealed by Engineers until the time of use."[42] As expected, French took advantage of the high ground north of the river, bringing three batteries to bear on the enemy. It was only when the cannons rolled into place that the enemy became aware of their presence.

Weygant described the position as one with "a commanding point" from which they could clearly see the enemy's picket line and everything along the opposite shore. "They seemed greatly surprised at our sudden appearance" but once aware that Yankees were nearby the men opened fire, wounding a gunner and hitting two battery horses. French chose to send de Trobriand's Brigade of Ward's Division, 3rd Corps, to lead the assault, reinforcing it with the 20th Indiana and the 2nd U.S. Sharpshooters, a total of seven regiments. The Confederates on the other side of the river had orders to stall the Yankees just long enough for Rodes's Division to get in position on the high ground south of the ford.

The 124th New York was deployed in support of Captain J. Henry Sleeper's 10th Massachusetts Battery of 3-inch ordnance rifles. The regiment was about three hundred yards from the breastworks and rifle pits occupied by the 2nd North Carolina. When the enemy began to fire, Weygant noted, "Some of our best shots crept out to the edge of the bluff, and with deliberate and effective aim opened a counter fire." The three Yankee batteries commanded the ford and the level ground beyond, sweeping the field and preventing reinforcements from coming up to the support of the 2nd North Carolina.

The first Federal troops to advance were two regiments of U.S. Sharpshooters, posted just to the right of Sleeper's Battery and the 124th New York. They took cover among the trees and rocks on the north bank, opening a destructive fire on the North Carolina troops on the opposite shore. General Birney sent the 1st U.S. Sharpshooters to cross the river to capture the rifle pits, which they did in the face of stiff resistance. The rest of de Trobriand's Brigade crossed the ford and charged a second line of rifle pits; the enemy soldiers not killed or wounded were quickly made prisoners. By 3 P.M. Ward's whole division was across the river and deployed in line of battle.

"Our lines did not fire on theirs," noted Captain Bush,

> untill within a hundred yards of our line when they Commenced and our Battery opened with 9 guns throwing Shot and Shell right in there midst. They broke and ran like Sheep, when our line advanced & took their Rifle Pitts, when we took some (300) prisoners, & again they showed a front and the Battle kept up untill 4 oclock P.M. the Rebel Dead and Wounded falling into our hands we lost in Killed and Wounded in our Division some two hundred and took some seven hundred Rebs Prisoners what there loss in Killed & Wounded was I cannot state accurately but it was great.[43]

After Ward's men waded the river, a pontoon bridge was floated across "which all night long weaved and creaked beneath the roll of the huge clattering wheels of battery after battery, and the 'tramp — tramp — tramp' of an almost unbroken column of rapidly moving troops." After dark, the 10th Massachusetts Battery which the 124th had been supporting, withdrew and the regiment crossed the bridge and camped near Kellysville just beyond the ford.[44]

The news from Rappahannock Station was good as well. Sedgwick's men overran the earthworks on the north side of the river, shattering two of Lee's best brigades in the process. It is interesting to note that as night fell, Lee was under the impression that his two brigades north of the river had held back Sedgwick's massive force and that the bridgehead was secure. So confident was he that he began to conjure up in his mind the very pleasant prospect of massing his men against the 3rd Corps and crushing it on the south side of the river. The news that his two brigades of crack troops had not only lost the bridgehead but had suffered severely in the process put an end to any plans Lee had for the offensive.

The next morning Meade took up the advance, with the 3rd Corps in the lead. "Our brigade led the division, and moved in battle line through the fields toward Brandy Station." He noted that at about noon they halted to eat, after which the Third Division moved ahead. "At dusk the 'halt' was sounded and we bivouacked in the woods at Brandy Station."[45]

Captain Bush wrote, "when the Collum Moved forward we took our position as flankers, and arrived at the place some two miles South of Brandy Station we change position frequently and what the next move will be we know not but are all in good Spirits and glad to know that our friends are for the Glorious old Union, and determined to aid in Putting down the Rebellion. All My Men are quite well Pvt. John J. Harrison wished me to say that after we give the Johneys one more good thrashing he would write you."[46]

Meade's victories at Rappahannock Station and Kelly's Ford came at a time when his stock was low with the administration. Any euphoria felt in Washington was quickly dampened by

Meade's hesitation. Although he had his men across the river and had inflicted far more casualties on the enemy than his own men suffered, he was again slow and cautious in the pursuit. Secretary of War Stanton, no friend of the general, was so angry that he refused to receive the honor guard sent to present him with the Confederate battle flags captured at Rappahannock Station.[47]

On Monday, November 9, the 124th did not move until almost 5 in the afternoon and then only about two miles beyond the railroad station into some woods. The next day the men were ordered to begin construction of winter quarters. "The brush was soon cleared away and the men set to work building log walls for their muslin shelters, but there were only three or four axes in each regiment, and as no more could be either drawn from the quartermaster or borrowed from the engineers or supply trains, the work progressed but slowly."[48] Captain Jackson gave the reason for not advancing. "Even if the weather should prove favorable we will not likely advance until railroad communication can be opened."[49]

William Howell wrote that on November 16 there was a corps review "by Gen'l French and Sedgwick. We noticed a couple officers with fancy colored caps and see by the papers they belonged to the Royal british guards of England. Mr. Botts was also present. He had a large drove of cattle and sheep and nothing but his well known loyalty could save them from the slaughter. The road between this and Culpepper is strewn with the carcasses of dead horses slain in the recent cavalry engagements. There are rumors that we will go home and recruit this winter. I think it is rather doubtful."[50] The next day, half the regiment went out on three days' picket duty. The picket line ran near the estate of the aforementioned John Minor Botts, a Virginia Congressman who had opposed the secessionist movement. This was too fine a distinction for the Orange County boys to grasp; they plundered his livestock just the same as they would have done had the farm been owned by a rank Secessionist. As Captain Weygant patrolled the picket line on horseback, he noted that chicken feathers floated thick in the air near where one of the Newburgh companies was posted.[51]

Lieutenant Mapes was delighted to hear the results of the recent elections in Orange County and he felt that certain of his relatives had not written to him lately "either because the Copperhds got whipped or because the Unionists were victors." He was, however, not happy with his commanding officer, Colonel Francis Cummins. "Col. C is a perfect old Cuss a drunken Old SOB. This is the first I ever spoke on this Subject. I am entirely disgusted with him. I am entitled to be a Captain & there are 2 others & he has not sent a single name to Seymour who will probably substitute some one. I spoke to him on the subject he gave me an evasive answer & there it rests." There was a rumor going around that Mapes would be home in December and that he'd asked a friend to introduce him to some ladies. "Tell 'Jeemis Rumsey' my axehandle is all right. Who are you planning to get me. Old Mrs. Bennet or some such. I want none but a handsome Rich gall young &c. now who is it. So I can judge. I should like to have Seen the 'Klam.'"[52]

William Howell and Archibald Freeman decided they would like to go to Culpeper, which was within walking distance, to do some "reconnoitering on our own hook, there was nothing but calvery stationed there but the provost guards were armed and we had no pass. We did not explore the town very closely We found considerable amusement in reading script of the Southern papers amongst the old camps. I will enclose a piece of a revenue stamp or curincy, I don't know which."[53] As winter approached, Meade had to decide if he would attack or go into winter quarters. He realized that to do the latter might mean his dismissal as commander of the Army of the Potomac, but he was reluctant to attack Lee's army head on. South of the Rapidan, the enemy had built imposing earthworks, but Confederate deserters as well as his own scouts told him that Lee had neglected to adequately protect his right flank where the lower fords of the Rapidan were unguarded. Better yet, the two roads that ran behind the Confederate lines, the Orange Plank Road and the Orange Turnpike, both accessible from the lower fords, were wide open with no earthworks to stop Meade from striking at the rear of his wily adversary. This would allow him to flank Lee out of the imposing earthworks. Success would hinge on surprise and the ability of Meade to get his men across the river and onto the improved roads before Lee realized what was happening.[54]

Meade planned to march on November 24. He called a meeting of his corps commanders the night before to give them their orders. They would be entering the Wilderness again and maps were drawn to help the generals find their way. Ten days' rations were to be issued to the men. Then, as always seemed to happened when the Army of the Potomac planned to move, it began to rain. Rivers and creeks rose and dirt roads turned to muddy quagmires. Reluctantly, Meade was forced to postpone the advance for two days. Meade kept the planned move so quiet that the men quite logically assumed they would be going into winter quarters. Bonfires were built to keep them warm as they worked. Many cabins were up, the roofs on, and the mud coating on the wooden chimneys was just about dry when orders were received to prepare to march. Then the storm came up thoroughly soaking and chilling all concerned. As the men stood around in the rain, the order came postponing the march.[55]

Two days later, November 26, Thanksgiving Day, the army moved south at last. Meade's plan called for the 3rd Corps supported by the 6th Corps to cross the Rapidan at Jacob's Ford, close to the enemy's lines. The rest of the army would cross down river at two other fords and the whole force would reunite at or near Robinson's Tavern, an important crossroads in the Wilderness near Locust Grove, just four miles southeast of the Confederate right flank. Warren's 5th Corps would take up positions at the center near Robinson's Tavern with the rest of the army closing on Warren's left and right.

Reveille was sounded in the camp of the 124th at dawn but it was 9 A.M. before Ward's Brigade was underway. Everything started out just fine. General Birney was back in charge of the division and the men were pleased that for once they were not leading the way. Prince's Third Division moved out first followed by Carr's Second Division. By placing his least able division commander at the front of the 3rd Corps, French was asking for trouble and he got it right away. "Once started we marched at quick time for over two hours without a halt," Weygant wrote. "After that we moved by jerks, over a narrow road, cut through a dense forest." By the time they reached the Rapidan it was dark and they were hours behind schedule.[56]

The reasons for the delay were many, but most of the blame could be laid at the feet of Brigadier General Henry Prince, West Point class of 1835. He started from camp that morning an hour late and was soon stalled on the north bank of the Rapidan at Jacob's Ford. Prince was sure he saw enemy cavalry and infantry on the opposite shore. As he was contemplating the situation, General French rode up somewhat perplexed at the delay. He helped Prince deploy the artillery and get the pontoon train to the front. One wonders why the pontoons were not near the front of the column to start with, but this was just the beginning of a long and unfortunate chain of events.

Volunteers from the 11th New Jersey floated some of the pontoons across, expecting to face terrific fire but to everyone's relief there were no enemy soldiers to be found. This good news was quickly outweighed by bad news. The river was over its banks from all the rain, making it wider than expected. The engineers did not have enough pontoons to span the Rapidan and had to construct a trestle on the spot to complete the bridge. Not until 4 P.M., far behind schedule, did Prince's Division get over the Rapidan.[57]

"Just before dark we were ordered to file in among the trees, and eat our dinner," Weygant wrote, "but the men had barely time to start fires, and boil and drink their coffee, before the 'forward' was sounded again." It was not until 10 P.M. that Ward's Brigade reached the pontoon bridge and crossed the Rapidan. They were now back in the Wilderness of Virginia, just a few miles west of where they had fought during the Battle of Chancellorsville the previous May.[58]

The other troops reached their crossing points downriver on time, but Meade held them back until French's command could cross for fear that Lee had some trap laid for him on the south side of the Rapidan. It was well after dark before all were across but they were able to advance only about two miles before nightfall when Meade called a halt. The general was no doubt frustrated at how his campaign started and was well aware that it was critical that he make up the lost time. On the evening of November 26 he told his commanders that they must reunite at Robinson's Tavern in the morning and then push on six miles to Old Verdiersville, which would still put them well behind enemy lines. Again, everything depended upon speed.

Lee knew pretty quickly that the Yankees were on the south side of the Rapidan but he was unsure what Meade intended. He could be trying to turn the Confederate right flank or perhaps this was just a feint. If Lee took the bait and pulled back into a defensive posture, Meade might turn and head for Richmond. Whatever Meade's objective might be, Lee's right or the Confederate capital, Lee needed to be ready to deal with it.

Before daylight on the morning of November 27, the Orange County men ate their breakfasts and by 7 A.M. the 3rd Corps was in motion with Birney's Division at the rear and Ward's Brigade last in line. Meanwhile, Warren's 2nd Corps had moved rapidly to the center of the line, occupying the high ground west of Robinson's Tavern and was preparing to advance. Meade, who had been following the corps, rode up and told Warren to stay put until the rest of the army was on the field. Meade could not understand why, with the lead units of French's 3rd Corps less than five miles away, he had, by 11 A.M., heard nothing from French. Still apprehensive about Lee's ability to deliver a knockout blow from nowhere, Meade sent dispatches ordering French to move in support of Warren at once.

An unsigned letter printed in the *Goshen Democrat*, described the march.

> We had, the morning we started on the march after crossing the river, proceeded but a short distance before skirmishing commenced, but it did not become very active till in the afternoon. The enemy's line of skirmishers receded till they reached the ground, where it was no doubt determined to offer us battle. About 3 o'clock in the afternoon the battle commenced in earnest. The Third Division of our corps was sent ahead in the march, and so first encountered the enemy. The Second and First Division in the order mentioned followed in supporting distance. It was almost exclusively an infantry engagement. The wilderness character of the ground, on which the battle was fought, and the country adjacent prevented the maneuvering of artillery. On either side the guns were used at short range and fired grape and canister upon charges made to take the pieces. It was emphatically an action at close range. The thick forest compelled the combatants to approach with unusual nearness to each other, in order respectively to be seen. Fighting in such close proximity tested the courage of either foe, and the character of the charges reciprocally made, evidenced the most determined resistance of both. I have excellent reason for believing the ground chosen had been selected for its advantages in respect to position by the enemy in his intended interception, and check to our advance. I am of the opinion, the enemy had a strong force available but did not use in the action only a portion of it.[59]

Prince's Division, still leading the 3rd Corps, started out at daybreak but halted after a mile near the Widow Morris farm. Here the road split, one fork heading southwest, the other southeast. When Prince consulted the map issued to him by the commanding general, he saw that either fork would take him to Robinson's Tavern where the army was to concentrate, one route was just a bit longer than the other. Instead of picking one, he did nothing and waited for French to tell him what to do. The commander of the 3rd Corps, meanwhile, established his headquarters a short distance to the rear at the Morris place and did nothing as well, except get drunk, if the rumors were to be believed. The men in the ranks, always good judges as to the sobriety of their officers, called out to French as he rode by using the pejorative nicknames "old Blinky" and "old gin barrel." It was observed that French "had plied himself with a large amount of stimulant to ward off the chill and damp." In the words of a soldier in the 17th Maine, their general was "fuller'n a goat."[60]

French ordered Prince to take the right fork which he did in his own good time, sending out skirmishers to clear the way. By mid-afternoon he had made little progress and was stalled again when he received a message from French informing him that the left fork was the correct one. Prince rode the couple hundred yards to French's headquarters to tell him that now there were lots of enemy troops in his front. French ordered him to continue the advance and to call on Carr's Division, the next one in line, for support. The lengthy exchange between these two general officers, one drunk, the other inept, would have been comical but for the fact that the consequence of their inaction was about to take a deadly serious turn.

When it finally moved, the 3rd Corps line was deployed with Prince on the right, Carr on the left, and Birney in reserve. Here is how General Birney, whose division should have been in the front, described the movement:

> I marched my division parallel to Carr, through a thick wood, some 200 paces to the rear, moving by the flank. Carr soon became hotly engaged, and formed in line of battle. I deployed the Third Brigade (Egan) in his rear as my first line, massing the Second Brigade (Ward) in the rear of its right, and the First Brigade (Collis) in rear of its left. Before the formation was completed, say within twenty minutes, General Carr informed me that the right of his line was hardly pressed, and ammunition nearly expended. I immediately ordered the Second Brigade, General Ward, to move up and relieve Carr's right, connecting with Prince's left. He did so, however, without pressing the enemy.[61]

As the 3rd Corps deployed, it ran into skirmishers from General Edward Johnson's Division of Ewell's Corps along the Raccoon Ford Road. "The leading Union brigade was soon deployed and a brisk skirmish fire was opened." Weygant wrote. "The column quickened its pace, and as brigade after brigade came up, they hurried to the right and left through the brush and trees; for we were again in the weird region of Virginia, known as the Wilderness. As the line lengthened, the firing increased. Presently every brigade of the Third corps except ours had been thrown in, and General Ward, in obedience to orders, formed his command in column of regiments, and moved up to within thirty rods of the centre of the main line, and held himself in readiness to hasten to any point where assistance was needed."[62]

The men of the regiment lay flat on the ground listening to the battle develop around them. Skirmish firing spread across the whole front as each side probed the other's lines to find a weakness. Soon the firing became general, the shouts of officers, bugle calls, artillery, and volleys of rifle fire adding to the din. The firing spread "until it seemed to come from all around us — front, flanks and rear." But still Ward's Brigade was not called into action.[63]

Coming into line in front of the 3rd Corps was an aggressive, decisive, and sober Confederate officer, Major General Edward Johnson, West Point class of 1838. What was more, he rode at the head of Stonewall Jackson's old division, one of the great fighting units of the Army of Northern Virginia. As Carr was deploying, Johnson seized the initiative and ordered his 5,300 men forward. Because of the thick underbrush, he could not know that he faced two full Yankee divisions in front with another in support, not to mention the 6th Corps in reserve just a short distance back up the road, 32,000 men in all.

By now the fighting had been going on for some time. Carr's men fired the forty rounds from their cartridge boxes and were calling for ammunition when, as if on cue, Johnson struck the Union line and routed some of Carr's men. The other end of the line was also in trouble. The enemy was seen to be massing to charge a battery in a gap on the right near Prince's line. General Ward was ordered to move to the right, across a small creek and form up to support the battery. Just as the brigade got into position behind the guns, "the enemy made a most furious charge, driving back the Union line on both sides of us; but our battery was handled in a masterly manner — its rapid discharges of grape told with fearful effect on that portion of the enemy's charging line in our immediate front, which soon broke and fled." As the enemy troops fell back, the Union troops who had abandoned the battery, probably some of the hapless Prince's command, took heart "and with a shout started forward on a counter-charge, and all that portion of the Confederate line in front of the Union right, fell back a considerable distance and took shelter behind a line of rifle pits, whither General French did not care to follow."[64] It should be mentioned that Prince led three brigades long known for bravery and with a fighting spirit displayed on many battlefields. What was lacking at the division level was leadership at the top, not resolve in the ranks.

In Birney's after-action report, he said that Ward moved to the right but did not press the enemy. The tone is rather peevish, which was one of his more unpleasant traits. Weygant maintained, however, that it was French who did not wish to press the enemy rather than Ward.

For the rest of the afternoon a quiet settled in, punctuated by sporadic skirmishing along the front. But just after sundown, "the battle opened again and the crash of musketry, and thunder of artillery from either side of us soon became most terrific." The men of the 124th New York threw themselves to the ground and could do little to determine which way the battle was going. Out of the gathering darkness one of Birney's staff officers galloped up, shouting, "A portion of the 1st brigade has been forced back, and the General wishes you to send your two best regiments to fill the gap." General Ward did not hesitate. "Take the 124th and 86th New York," he said, at which the two regiments "filed from the column, and were hastening forward at a double quick, to re-occupy a position from which the 17th Maine — one of the largest and best regiments in the army — had just been driven." There was no doubt in the ranks of the two New York regiments that if the 17th Maine had been driven back, they were headed for a very dangerous place.[65]

The staff officer led the way from their position in an open field into a dense woods. Weygant wrote that "the gloom became most intense" and they were guided by the muzzle flashes of the Union lines on either side of the gap they were called on to fill. Up ahead a Confederate battery sent solid shot ripping through the trees, bringing limbs crashing down and sending wood splinters flying. Stumbling over the bodies of the dead and wounded, the 124th moved ahead and connected with the troops on the right. The 86th New York came up and formed on the left of the Orange County regiment and "the Union line was again intact." Weygant had been wondering why the enemy battery was firing high, assuming the gunners had lost the range but he was in for an unpleasant surprise — the battery had been firing over the heads of its own infantry, who could be heard but not seen right in front of the 124th New York. "We opened fire on our unseen foes, by sending such a volley down through the woods, as not only brought that advancing line to the ground, but drove the artillerymen from their guns."[66]

For a moment it seemed to Weygant as if the woods in front were full of fireflies. The hiss of bullets told him that the enemy had not been driven off after all. "Our men either sprang behind the trees, or threw themselves on the ground, but kept on firing as rapidly as they could." The enemy rifle flashes seemed to recede but then the battery opened again sending three or four rounds screeching through the trees, killing and wounding several men of the 86th New York. The concentrated rifle fire of the two New York regiments drove the gunners from their pieces again, but with night closing in and nothing to guide their aim, the Union soldiers lost their targets in the dark. This gave the enemy artillerymen an opportunity to reload and fire a couple of rounds before being driven to ground again. Thus the battle continued until after dark, when quiet settled over the battlefield.

The anonymous correspondent, possibly Surgeon Thompson, described the action in a letter to the *Goshen Democrat*.

> In position, and numbers, the rebels fought as though they possessed both. The only clearing of any extent, they attempted with great audacity to charge across, and in this instance of reckless bravery, they were as could be seen, repulsed with singular and dreadful loss. I do not compliment the defiant manner and courage with which the rebels fought because I like to, but because I *have* to — yet I can assure you with the most liberal consessions to them, they were *over matched* in the resistless, and dauntless bravery displayed in the fighting of our corps.... Our loss in killed and wounded was small considering the fierce-

ness of the battle. I doubt whether it will reach five hundred. The wounded I know is less than four hundred that have been treated in hospitals. An unusually few had severe wounds, and the greater number were insignificant in character. The rebels gave up the field leaving the killed and some of their wounded, and it is certain they sustained the severest loss. I am thankful at so small a number wounded of our Regiment. There was only one man had any considerable wound and his was only a flesh one of the scalp. Several, however were slightly bruised, by falling limbs of trees, caused by the enemy's artillery.[67]

After the Battle of Locust Grove, as this engagement was named, the 124th and 86th lay in the woods on picket duty near the enemy when, at 4 A.M. November 29, General Birney received orders to withdraw his division about a mile to the rear and mass it near the Widow Morris's house. Before they fell back, his ordinance officer collected or destroyed all the discarded weapons so that they would not fall into the hands of the enemy. In the meantime, Federal skirmishers advanced to find that the enemy was no longer in their front, at which point the two New York regiments also fell back and rejoined the brigade.

At 8 A.M., Birney received his orders and moved out toward Robertson's Tavern. "On reaching the left of the Sixth Corps, I massed my division. Thence I marched to a point near Muddy Run, in rear of the left of the First Corps, and again massed. Under orders from Major-General French, I bridged Muddy Run, and pushed forward a strong reconnaissance to the heights, connecting on the right with the First Corps, my line forming almost a right angle with the line of that corps, occupying the position indicated by Major Duane, chief engineer. During the 29th my division was held in readiness for the expected assault."[68]

The "expected assault" was to be against one of the strongest positions seen by the Union army to date. "The Confederate line was drawn along a prominent ridge or series of heights, extending north and south for six or eight miles. This series of hills formed all the angles of a complete fortification, and comprised the essential elements of a fortress." The unnamed soldier who wrote this description went on in great detail to describe the strength of the earthworks as well as the natural barriers incorporated. He ended his assessment with these words, "The position was, in fact, exceedingly formidable."[69]

The anonymous letter to the *Goshen Democrat* described the morning of November 29, "The whole manovering of the enemy, evidently during our presence previously upon the other side of the Rapidan, has been to reach and secure that position, and prevent our gaining it. To even an unmilitary observer, it could readily be discovered the well chosen character of the defensive battle line."[70]

It was Sunday morning when the Orange Blossoms at last formed up at the center of the Union line, the point they were supposed to reach two days before. Emerging from the woods they came upon an open area about a thousand yards from Mine Run, a marshy creek that was not very wide, but due to the nature of the ground, a formidable obstacle nonetheless. Beyond the run the ground rose to the enemy works. The Confederates had used the past two days to turn this naturally strong position into a fortress. The Orange County boys, who by now could judge the strength of an enemy position with the best of them, silently gazed at the line of freshly turned earth that marked the Confederate position left and right as far as the eye could see. They studied the position for at least a half-hour and grew more uneasy by the minute. In the distance they were sure they heard church bells tolling, calling some small community to prayer — a somber omen lost on none of them.

As they moved into a belt of woods and stacked arms, orders arrived "to hold ourselves in readiness to form line of battle and move against the enemy's works. Then, suddenly, there settled down upon all a cloud of gloom; and a marked dread of what was to come, hitherto unknown in the 124th, seemed to take possession of every officer and man in our brigade. Laughing and even social conversation entirely ceased and the men sat and lay around under the trees in silent serious meditation. Presently prayer meetings were started here and there in all the regiments."[71]

At noon a rumor circulated that the army would attack the works en mass and that a signal would be given to begin the attack sometime between 1 P.M. and 3 P.M. Now the men had more time to think. "One after another walked to the edge of the woods and looked off at the frowning heights covered with massive earth-works which completely concealed the foe from their view, many a brave, intelligent face turned pale." At 2 P.M., when the order to fall in and take arms was given, "the Sons of Orange County sprang to their places, and there was a man for every rifle" and when the order was given to march, "something in the precise, resolute movement of our line ... said to me plainer than it could have been expressed by words, 'Let come what may, you will have no occasion to blush because of the conduct of any member of the 124th to-day.'"[72]

The regiment advanced about thirty rods and stacked arms again, the wait continuing until dark while the generals tried to formulate a plan to take the imposing works. Then the brigade fell back into the same woods from which it had advanced and tried to get some rest. The weather turned bitter cold. After midnight, several regiments, including the 124th New York, were roused out of their blankets and ordered to relieve the picket line, which was now within two hundred fifty yards of the enemy's entrenchments. The men moved out across the open ground in the darkness, waded Mine Run, and slogged up the marshy bank until they reached the picket line, where they lay down on the partially frozen ground.[73]

William Howell wrote, "Sunday afternoon we got word that we would charge the enemy works. We piled our knapsacks & held ourselves in readiness to start but the movement was postponed. We went out on picket after midnight. We were on a range of hills & the rebs were on another range opposite. Our cannon were nearly a mile apart & our picket lines about a third. At dawn we could see them as they relieved their pickets. The Col came along & said we were to move & the ball would open at seven oclock. He said we must knock over everything we come to."[74]

General Birney prepared his men to attack the Mine Run position.

Before daylight on the 30th, Prince's and Carr's divisions were withdrawn to the support of the movement by General Warren, and I received orders from General French to be prepared to assault the enemy in my front crossing Mine Run. Detaching the Third Michigan, One hundred and twenty-fourth New York, First and Second U.S. Sharpshooters, all under command of Colonel B.R. Pierce, Third Michigan (I relieved my entire picket line), and deploying the regiments named as an advanced line of skirmishers, connected with First Corps on the right and General Warren on the left, and driving the enemy's pickets from the bank of Mine Run, made crossings of rails and logs, and two bridges for artillery, so that the run would be no obstacle to a rapid advance in line of battle. I deployed the second Brigade (Ward) as the second skirmish line in open order, with four companies from each regiment as supports, with orders to follow the advanced line at 200 paces. The First and Third Brigades were formed in line of battle, excepting the regiments detached for the support of the batteries.[75]

"It was near eight oclock when we were told to advance as skirmishers," William Howell wrote.

At the same moment I saw a cannon wheel into position just opposite & a shell was dropped right in front of us not two rods short. We deployed five paces apart & advanced while the artillery opened on both sides. They nearly all burst before they reached us and ours also fell short. The 124th was on the left with the 99th Pa as a second line to follow us & the Sharpshooters on the right with the 86th behind them while the rest of the brigade & division were to follow in line of battle. About mid way between us was a brook & after we crossed that there was a thicket & a knoll covered with pine trees. Soon as we showed ourselves there the minnies would whistle by us from their outposts. We were ordered to fall back the third time as far as the brook when they opened a heavy cannonading on our line as well as on the line of battle. They fell back but we fell to the ground & hugged it close too. I'll assure you. The shell intended for the line of battle mostly burst over us. The pieces flew in every direction one struck just in front of us plowed up the earth & passed over us another threw dirt all over us. But what is the use of particularizing.[76]

The rising sun was at their backs and clearly showed the strong earthworks and artillery emplacements that crowned the enemy position. At 7 A.M., the Union battle lines emerged from the woods and began to cross the open ground. At the same time the 124th received orders to bring up their reserves, form a skirmish line, and move forward. "Again men's faces grew pale, but no one faltered." Colonel Cummins took charge of the right wing, Weygant the left, the colonel shouting, "Forward men, forward."[77] At 8 A.M. the Union guns on the right and center opened on the enemy while the picket line, including the 124th New York, "gallantly pushed forward the advanced line, driving the first line of the enemy out of the advanced rifle-pits, capturing a few prisoners."[78]

Enemy artillery immediately opened fire, but they were aiming at the massed troops on the other side of Mine Run, not at the skirmish line. A number of the shells passed right above the Orange County soldiers. Weygant had his hat knocked from his head by a passing shell. He recovered the hat and found no hole in it so he thought the "sudden rising of my hair" may have caused it to fly off his head. Although the Confederate infantry was as yet not firing, Lieutenant Ramsdell was hit by a musket ball. Weygant credited this to a sharpshooter who obviously was trying to single out the officers. The ball hit Ramsdell's belt buckle, just as had happened to Captain William Jackson a couple of weeks prior, raising a painful bruise but sparing the young lieutenant a mortal wound to the midsection.

The skirmish line had advanced about fifty yards when the order came to halt. Exposed in the open, the men threw themselves to the ground again. "Suffice it to say they shelled us from several batteries as fast as they could work for upwards of fifteen minutes. And would send a shot occasionally till we got back to our old picket line. After they stopped shelling we advanced for the fourth time but we soon got the order to march in retreat & we willingly turned our backs from the frowning cannon. We had looked in the muzzle so long & fell back with the line in perfect order." The assault had been called off and by 9 A.M. the skirmish line was back near Mine Run. The hillside in front of the troops began to smolder, probably the result of exploding shells, and within a short time the underbrush caught fire near the ground where the 124th had advanced. During that move forward, Private Charles McGregor of Company H had been hit by a shell fragment near where the fires were now springing up. He was carried a short distance to the rear but his comrades were sure the wound was mortal and left him for dead. Now it was reported to Weygant that the pickets could hear him calling for someone to save him before the fire reached him. Volunteers were called for and three or four men stepped forward including Corporal Duncan Boyd of Company C, who said he was willing to risk his life to save a wounded soldier from burning to death, whether friend or foe. Although fired upon by the enemy they safely returned to the Union lines carrying McGregor in a blanket. The soldier had regained consciousness but had been too weak to move as he watched the fire draw near. The flames were within ten feet when he was rescued but his wound required amputation — an enemy shell had shattered his thigh — and by morning he was dead.[79]

That afternoon, Weygant was witness to a conversation between Generals French and Warren as they surveyed the enemy position from the picket reserve. He did not catch the whole exchange but at one point, in response to something Warren said, French "turned his face toward the enemy's works, raised in his stirrups, and with his eyes blinking furiously, replied 'Thunder! Warren, it would be throwing your purse before swine,'" at which they wheeled their horses and rode off in opposite directions. The momentous was soon overshadowed by the mundane when a steer came running out of the woods and stopped right where the generals had been talking. In a matter of minutes the animal was "cut in several hundred strips and fastened to as many forked sticks" over little fires that flared along the line.

"We took up our old picket line till night then went on the reserve." Monday evening, the regiment was relieved by Vermont troops from the 1st Corps and moved a short distance to the left where it was posted as part of the grand reserve behind Colonel Berdan's two regiments of sharpshooters on the outer picket line.

"That night (Monday)," wrote William Howell,

ice froze nearly an inch thick in a gully by the grove of pines where we slept. Tuesday we went back to
the brigade. At night we commenced to evacuate. We did not get fairly underway till nine oclock & then
we marched very fast till daylight when we recrossed the Rapidan at Ely's ford.... We came to the Plank
road through Wilderness to within a few miles of Chancellorsville & then turned to the left making an
angle where the Elys ford road joined it. A cavalryman said we came 27 miles that night but I guess he
put it too light. It was rather amusing to hear our brass band strike up "Oh aint I glad to get out the
Wilderness" Yesterday morning after we had got the pontoons up & we were preparing to leave. We
marched till night got our coffee & a rest then started for our old camps. The roads were badly cut up.
The hub of the cannon were on the ground. We are pretty well "played out" but well & in good spirits.
We don't want any more such again very soon though. We went to Orange County but our reception was
such that a seven days furlough sufficed & we were glad to return to Brandy Station again.[80]

Thursday morning, December 3, the regiment finally reached winter camp. There "among
the roofless log huts" of the "Old Camp Ground" the men tossed off their knapsacks and went
to work refurbishing their winter quarters at Brandy Station.[81]

Weygant suggested that Meade never really intended a direct assault on the Mine Run earthworks, but if he ever entertained thoughts of doing it, he changed his mind and "wisely decided
to abandon it." The anonymous correspondent agreed. "The Object of Gen. Mead in crossing
the river was not intended I believe, to attack the enemy where ever found, but only under favorable circumstances. His purpose mainly was to hold Lee's army I suppose, and prevent reinforcements from it being sent to Bragg. Some demonstrations was made upon the enemy in our front,
and their first line of rifle pits were taken in doing which our own Regiment shared the perils
and glory of the achievement."[82]

Once back in camp, the anonymous correspondent finished his letter to the Goshen newspaper.

I omitted to mention the name also of Theron Bodine, Company H, who was wounded in the right
fore arm, with Minnie ball, the ball passing between the bones of arm without fracturing either.... Along
with myself the poor boys of the Regiment have suffered as I could not describe to you.... I may be
allowed to observe that no troops ever stood firmer than did every man of our Regiment, so far as I
know; or did better service on a battle field than did the 124th. I am confident of one fact, and that is,
the Regiment has a reputation in the army, if it has not in Orange County, that it may well be proud
of.[83]

Of the Mine Run Campaign, William Howell wrote, "We have had a severe trial of our
courage & power of endurance & have nobly done all that was required of us."[84]

The Army of the Potomac settled into winter quarters on the north bank of the Rapidan
River at Brandy Station, Virginia. The Army of Northern Virginia, as resolute as ever, was camped
just south of the Rapidan. The previous December, the two armies camped for the winter a few
miles downstream at Falmouth on opposite banks of the Rappahannock River. The brutal fighting
of 1863 cost thousands of men killed or crippled, hundreds of millions of dollars spent, and large
areas of the American landscape laid waste, yet the war went on much as before. The only change
in the situation seemed to be that now, a year later, Union and Confederate soldiers "frowned at
each other" across a different Virginia river.[85]

CHAPTER 11

"I am spared to enjoy the pleasure of life another winter in my log cabin"

December 3, 1863–May 1, 1864

Following the Mine Run Campaign, the men returned to the same camp at Brandy Station, Virginia, they'd left just a week before. They set to work "repairing and fitting up the log cabins in which we now expected to spend the winter, we took up again the routine duties of camp life, and barring the unusual number of bitter cold days spent on the picket line, the winter passed more pleasantly than we had any reason to expect it would."[1]

Lieutenant Charles Stewart wrote on December 3, "Reached our old camp at daybreak, foot-sore and tired out. Went to bed early, but about 9 o'clock the bugle sounded 'strike tents' and we had to get up and tear down our houses." The men pulled down the canvas, unbuttoned the pieces, and strapped them on their knapsacks. "After forming on the color line and waiting there an hour, the order was countermanded and we lay down again but without fixing up tents."[2]

At about noon December 4, the regiment was formed up to witness the execution of a deserter by firing squad identified by Captain Jackson as a conscript from the 3rd Maine. William Reeder of the 20th Indiana of Ward's Brigade wrote in great detail of how the condemned man was marched behind his coffin in full view of the entire division before being executed. Private Brice Birdsall of Company B was also scheduled to be shot for desertion but the president interceded and pardoned him.[3]

On December 5, "that confounded strike tents sounded again." The brigade was marched to an open field where the men stacked arms and waited until after dark, when they were told to make themselves comfortable. "The night was bitter cold and as we had no tents up we *could not be* comfortable — was glad when daylight came." The men moved back to the recently vacated log huts, replaced the canvas roofs, and started their fires. The wind came up so strong that the smoke backed up in the chimneys and the fires had to be extinguished. No one had any idea why the brigade was forced to spend a cold night in the open.[4]

"When I wrote you last we were all packing up & have for 4 or 5 successive days pulled down our tents & got ready for a move & have not gone yet & do not know when we will. Everything is lively." As winter approached, Lieutenant Mapes asked his brother Jesse to send him a number of items. He wanted three half gross boxes of three cent cigars — "Leilenthalls fine cut." He planned to resell the cigars to pay for the entire contents of the box. He reported to Jesse that the box and its contents arrived safe and sound the first week in December.[5]

When a shipment of boxes from home arrived in camp, Thomas Rodman wrote to his parents that it was safe to send him one. He'd previously asked for boots, some handkerchiefs, and a butcher's knife; now he added

> some paper and Envelopes and 1 checked shirt and what ever little eatables Mother thinks best. Nothing that you think will spoil 2 Pocket Hdks and one of those little silver spoons you used to have when I was home and the letter C and Fig 124 to put on my Cap and a pair of suspenders and a 1 qt tin pail with butter in it. Some candies and whatever you think best. I send you a Rattle of a Rattle Snake that I got where we fought our last Battle near Mine Run.

As an afterthought and on the reverse side of the paper he added, "And a Pound Cake."[6]

"No drills to-day to disturb the plans of any body" Lieutenant Stewart wrote on December 10th. "The weather is fine and the boys are busy fixing up their winter quarters. We have made some improvements on ours to-day. It is reported that General Thomas has succeeded Meade and is now in command of this army. All hands are keeping a sharp lookout for the paymaster." Of course, General George H. Thomas, the "Rock of Chicamauga," did not replace Meade, but it is interesting that such a rumor was current among the men. It was obvious to them that the "Old Snapping Turtle" had few fans in Washington. The next day at dress parade, an order was read granting furloughs to officers and men. No more than three line officers and five enlisted men could be absent from the regiment at one time. This was welcome news indeed as most of the men had not been back to Orange County in more than a year. That night half the men in Stewart's company applied to go home.[7]

"Last night we signed the pay roll," Thomas Rodman wrote to his parents, "and I expect we will get paid off soon. The weather here is quite cool looks like snow now. We have gone into Winter Quarters and I think we will remain here some time. You can send the Box as soon as you have a mind to." Two days later he finished the letter adding that he had been paid and was sending a check home in the full amount. He instructed his father to send him ten dollars by return mail so that he could buy tobacco, presumably in bulk, and then resell it at a profit. "I can make enough with that to keep me in spending money a long while." He did not mention the source of tobacco for his business venture but it must have been a local one.[8]

The weather turned bitter, with high winds and heavy frost. "The regiment ordered out for inspection at 1 P.M. This was a cold job, but did not last long."[9] During the cold spell the men kept indoors, their only outside activity being the daily dress parade. On December 21 the bad news came that they would be detailed to picket duty no matter the cold. Captain Travis was the field officer of the day but Stewart was the lucky one, as he was detailed to the camp guard and got to stay close to his cabin and warm hearth. Two days before Christmas, Travis received a box from home "with a good assortment of delicacies to pass the Christmas with." On December 25 he wrote, "Spent a pretty good Christmas. The Colonel and Captains Benedict and Jackson, returned from furlough — a whiskey ration was issued to the regiment and a number of the boys feel good." They felt so good, in fact, that most of them needed the next day to sleep it off.[10]

"The same old camp Sabbath," Stewart wrote the following Sunday, "no inspection — no drill — no work, but in other respects the same as other days." The weather continued to be "wet and disagreeable," forcing the men to "hug the fire very close to keep at all comfortable." At the end of the month, another batch of officers took the train for Orange County, including Major Weygant, Captains Travis and Wood, Adjutant Van Houten, and Chaplain Bradner. The weather was so bad that the men were mustered by companies in front of Colonel Cummins' tent, using it for shelter. Stewart turned in early on New Years' Eve but was awakened from his bed by the portly Quartermaster Post who hustled him off to his own tent where a party was underway, the officers "waiting to see the old year out and the new year in."[11]

"We have been out on picket (from Saturday until Yesterday) and we found it pretty cold but there were plenty of rails & we kept up rousing fires all the while," Henry Howell wrote.

Members of Division Court Martial, ca. 1863. Left to right: (seated) Captain James Benedict, Company D, 124th New York; Captain William H. Warner, 40th New York; Captain John Phinney, 86th New York; (standing) Captain Joseph H. Hurst, Company A, 141st Pennsylvania; Captain George A. Nye, 3rd Maine (archive of the Historical Society of the Town of Warwick, gift of Joan and Tom Frangos).

There was a crossroad near where our post was, there was a sign board up which said it was 6 miles to Brandy Station 3 miles to Culpepper C. H. Eldorado Culpepper 3½ miles, Thompsonville 8 miles & Chestnut Fork 1½ miles The last named place was on the direct road to our camp. There were cross roads & a brick Church. (or has been one) but while we were out our soldiers had torn it down and drawn the brick to camp to build their fireplaces out of. The Rebs will have it printed in their papers soon in Capital letters. The Yankees Tearing Down Churches To Build Winter Quarters. Well it is too bad I suppose but I would like to have had a load of the brick.... The dried fruit, sugar & tea lasts yet, but we have made way with the sausage. We have been fatting up lately. We both weigh between 160 & 165. I saw a record of the 124th in the Democrat from Col. Cummins, It was Official I suppose. Those Officers that had been recommended for promotion have received the appointment but do not take their new commands yet. Lieut Sayer is the Captain of Co E.[12]

For the first month and a half of 1864, the rain gave way to freezing cold. Sgt Thomas Taft, Company C, celebrated the New Year with a pudding made of "flour, dried apples, and molasses" but it did little to warm things up. The night before the regiment started for picket duty was the coldest to date, freezing the puddles near the camp "thick enough to bear a man's weight." The road was rough and icy, the march so difficult that it took three hours to cover the five miles to the picket line located about two miles from Culpeper Courthouse. "It snowed all last night and there were two inches of snow on the ground this morning. The commissary sergeant brought us our two days' rations of soft bread, sugar coffee and fresh meat. We captured a contraband trying to run the picket line. He says we can do anything we have in mind to with him, if we will only let him live. The poor 'dark' has evidently been taught to believe that we are all cannibals."[13]

On Tuesday, the men were relieved on the picket line by the 86th New York and the Sharp-shooters. "The march back to camp over the frozen ground was very severe and about used me up." Once back to the routine of camp, Sergeant Taft spent a day getting the company books in order. "Very cold. Ground still covered with snow. We have to carry our firewood about a mile." On Saturday, which was wash day, the men were issued "three days' rations of salt pork and fresh beef, coffee and sugar." The division was ordered to prepare to move camp two miles closer to Culpeper, partly because the local firewood supply was exhausted.[14]

"It is very provoking to move after we have our quarters so comfortable and the weather so cold but that is 'military,'" wrote Captain Jackson.

> We all think that John M. Botts is at the bottom of this change. As it is now, we are encamped on his place and his wood goes fast. Of this he has complained to Gen. Meade so we have to move. Now this don't suit us more especially as Mr. B. gets well paid for all losses sustained on account of the Union soldiers. We never did think much of his loyalty and now think still less. Quite a large number of old soldiers in our Division have reenlisted and gone home. It is very encouraging to know that so many veterans are willing to stick it out. The 35 days at home is a great inducement, more so than the liberal bounties. After all the army contains the larger part of the patriotism of our country.[15]

Monday, January 11, one hundred twenty five men headed out for picket duty again while Sergeant Taft spent the day working on the company ordnance returns. "The regiment now has mostly Springfield rifled muskets cal .58 in all companies and each company has a few Enfields."[16]

Mid-January, the regiment began moving camp, using wagons to transport the equipment and personal items, officers' gear first, of course. Sergeant Taft wrote that he had some of his tent logs loaded on the wagons and, with the now plentiful wood supply, he was able to make his quarters seven logs high. He cut and split the logs, setting them in place smooth side in with mud chinking to keep out the cold. The next morning the men were up at daylight and at it again, "up to our eyes in mud and dirt." A tent was placed on top of the log walls to complete the shelter and a chimney was added made of wood heavily plastered with mud. Taft noted that the camp was located on a well wooded hill with plenty of hickory and oak nearby. On Sunday, January 17, Taft and his tentmates installed bunks off the ground and were pretty much set for the winter.[17]

The same day, Private Horace D. Paret, Company K, wrote a letter to the *Whig Press*:

> Some of our boys have their cabins up, and expect to put up one for Captain Jackson, Company K, to-morrow. Company K are all right. The boys enjoy themselves first best, are getting fat and not one in the Company sick, I believe.—The Captain looks well; he is in the best of health, and a very nice Captain he is. He is very good to his men. The 124th is No. 1 in battle, and stand right to their post. The men think a great deal of our Colonel. A man by the name of Bullock, in Philadelphia, has sent on to the First Division woolen mittens for every man. They are distributing them out to the men who are much pleased with so useful a present.[18]

The regiment was now situated closer to the picket line and near a plentiful supply of firewood and water. "We had a first rate time on picket," William Howell wrote to his sister Emily. "There is a house not twenty rods from our post outside the lines. We traded coffee for pies with the folks. The family consisted of Mr. Brown his wife and two children and his sister and two sisters in law were staying with him. They were all young ladies tolerably good looking intelligent and agreeable." William noted that he was at the house "all the time" along with some other soldiers and thought the ladies enjoyed the visits as much as the young men did. "The girls sang all manner of songs for us. Some of the Secesh songs were fine and it can hardly be wondered at that the Southern youth thus appealed to should rush to arms & prove a traitor to the country. One song was about the death of the Gallent Ashby whom you will recollect was a noted guerilla chief of the Shenandoah. Another was called Potomac, one Virginia, &c. They sang several Union songs too. They had the red white & blue adapted to the Southern cause & the girl in the Home-spun dress."[19]

William's mother had asked about their clothing, how they kept warm at night, and about their military service to date. "We each have a woolen and rubber blanket which with our dress coats and overcoats makes us a warm bed. We have tall dry grass for bedding and sleep first rate. As for clothing we have aplenty and a chance to draw more at least once a month. Our last winters clothing was destroyed last spring at Aquia Creek and we do not expect to get renumerated for it but we were not charged any thing for clothing from the battle of Chancellorsville to Gettysburg on account of the books being lost we are told." He went on to detail their battles and stays in the hospital since Fredericksburg, summarizing their service at Brandy Station and other battles with the words, "We upheld the honor of Old Orange well."[20]

Private William Edgar, Company I, decided to write a letter from camp to the editor of the Newburgh *Daily Journal* describing his new quarters.

Our camp is situated on a slight eminence, with a beautiful brook running at its base. Our company streets are laid out with the strictest care, while our shanties, comparing our present ones with those of last winter, show a decided improvement. But why should they not, since experience is truly allowed to be our best teacher, and we have not lacked its advantages? My present house is the fourth one that I have helped build in Dixie.

Now, in order that you may understand what kind of a house it is that I with three other persons occupy, it will be necessary for me to describe it, so you can judge how much comfort the soldier can take if left alone. It is built up with logs about four feet high, twelve feet long, and seven feet wide, with a bunk in each end sufficiently large to hold two persons, and under which we pile wood and our cooking utensils, &c. Between the two bunks is a space of about five feet, in the centre of which is a fireplace, and directly opposite a door of about the dimensions of those you have often seen in a pig pen. This, covered with our shelter tent, affords a better protection from storm than a person unused to them would suppose. Being situated on an elevated piece of ground renders the health of the regiment generally good.[21]

"We have a very fine location as regards fuel and water," wrote Captain Jackson,

but are most too far from the station, being about 4½ miles from Brandy Station. We are some 2½ miles from Culpepper and north of it, but trains do not run to that place i.e. the most important ones. Guerrillas lately have been very daring and have gobbled up stray parties even within our picket lines and the orders now are that no wagons shall leave the station after 6 P.M. with out a strong escort. This is a disgrace to our army. These scoundrels ought to be hunted down and every white citizen within the limits of the army sent out to Dixie; yes and the women too for all that I have seen about here are regular she devils, fed by Uncle Sam and yet all the time acting as spys for the Rebs.

It irked him that anytime there was to be a move, "these confounded women" had to go beyond the lines to visit a sick relative or some such excuse. Since they usually had a pass from provost marshal General Marsena Patrick, "I had to let them go sorely against my will. The worst of it they are all as homely 'as a brush fence.' Now there might be some fun in halting a pretty girl but these old hags I hate the sight of."[22]

December 26, the pickets returned to camp just in time for a "big thing" as the soldiers liked to say. "Received our new flag" wrote Sergeant Taft. "Had dress parade at 3 o'clock — both colors out, the old and new, side by side. We saluted them, and then gave three cheers, first for the old and then for the new."[23]

The need for a new battle flag was raised by Chaplain Bradner to his sister as far back as September 30, when the regiment was camped near Culpeper. The chaplain hinted broadly that the officers of the regiment did not want to ask outright for such a thing but it would be "very acceptable" if the patriotic citizens, the Daughters of Orange specifically, might consider it. "Our present colors, *as they represent to men*, besides being pierced with bullets and ragged on the edges from the severe service it has seen, is also worn to such a degree that there is danger that it may tear from the staff, in a strong wind, or sudden struggle. Not to mention the fact that from the beginning there was some difficulty in the material by which the colors ran together." He told her that other regiments were replacing battle torn flags with new ones sent from home. "It is hardly possible for anyone to imagine the degree of pride & interest which a Regt takes in its colors, more than one of our number has fallen on the battle field rather than suffer them to go down. They are unfurled & saluted at the dress parade every day."

He put the matter squarely to his sister, "I leave you to act your pleasure about it. It was thought that with your probably extensive correspondence through the County, you could soon learn how the public pulse felt on the matter." Obviously confident that she would agree and be able to gain support for the request he went on to tell her what the regiment wanted. The new flag would be the same as the old one with one exception, "an Orange blossom be worked in a corner of the blue ground in memory not only of our locality, but also of our brave Col. Ellis, who fell at Gettysburg in their defense and who was accustomed to call his boys Orange blossoms, a ribbon of that color being also now on our breasts."[24]

The *Goshen Democrat* reported on January 6, "A new stand of colors is about to be forwarded to the 124th Regt., N.Y.S.V., by the Daughters of Orange. The flag is precisely like the one presented at their organization in September, '62, with the addition of a cluster of Orange blossoms and fruit on the blue ground, added as a memento of the lamented Col. Ellis, who called his 'boys' his 'Orange Blossoms,' and a ribbon of that color is now universally worn by the regiment." The flag was ordered November 15 and was ready by the end of December. Letters were sent out to all the towns in Orange County asking for a contribution toward the purchase and each town offered to pay the whole expense, but the Daughters of Orange "deemed best to be impartial and allow all a share." Each donation was accompanied by "kind wishes for the welfare of their favorite regiment."[25]

With the new flag came a letter.

> The Daughters of Orange, having heard that the colors they presented to you at the time of your organization have been impaired in battle, take great pleasure in substituting new ones. Please regard them as renewed tokens of their high appreciation of your services as a regiment, and as a pledge of their desire to have their interests in this contest identified with your own.... You have already won a name for courage.... Your diminished numbers tell eloquently what you have already suffered since you left us under the leadership of the able and bold Colonel Ellis. Send us back the old and revered flag that it may be placed with the cherished mementoes of your lamented commander and his immortal braves.

The letter, read to the regiment at Dress Parade, was received with "vociferous applause."[26]

Cummins wrote to the president of the Ladies Society of Orange County with heartfelt thanks to the donors of the new flag and his thoughts on what should be done with the old flag. "We trust that, after it has served its part at the Sanitary Fairs of the County, in awakening an interest in the Soldier by reminding of a soldiers' work, it may be thought worthy to form part of a new collection to be placed in Washington's Head Quarters at Newburgh, side by side with the relics and trophies that are now there. The one Collection, to speak eloquently of Liberty gained in the Revolutionary struggle the other, of Liberty defended against the Great Rebellion."[27]

At the end of January, Corporal Ben Dutcher of Company H wrote home to tell his parents that his box had come "with everything all safe and sound." Boxes of enlisted men were opened and inspected, and none too carefully either, as his had been split open. Officers' boxes were not inspected "but we poor miserable privates must have our boxes torn open to satisfy the curiosity of some government grog shop with shoulder straps on who is in search of liquor. Well if they did not get any rum until they got it in my Boxes they would go dry. Til this war is over any way."

Dutcher thanked them for sending the items he had asked for as well as those they had added on their own. "Mother, your mince pie was luscious. They were just as nice as when you put them up. I tell you I was not long in getting my Bill in one of them ... please remember me to Mrs. Capson for the jar of Jelly. also thank Mrs. Marshall for me, for the pies." Then he launched into a complaint about the high prices charged by the sutler.

Flag of the 124th Reg't N. Y. Vols.,

PRESENTED BY

THE LADIES OF ORANGE, MARCH, 1864.

ITS BATTLES:

Manassas Gap, Wilderness, Po River, Spottsylvania, North
Anna, Cold Harbor, Petersburgh, Deep Bottom, Strawberry
Plains, Boydton Road, Hatchers' Run, 25th of March, Sailors'
Creek.

FOR SALE AT REMILLARD'S,
82 Water St., and at the Newburgh Bookstores.

We cant get any thing here unless we give double or even triple what it is worth. For instance butter 60 cents per pound cheese 40 cents can of milk 60 cents apples little nerly ones 25 cts. it dont pay to get any thing here, if we say anything to an officer about Sutlers high prices the consolation we get is if you dont like the prices dont buy ... the weather is now & has been for several days as warm & pleasant as May. I have been part of the time to day without either coat or vest. & tonight it is very warm. Well I will close. I will enclose $ in this & in my next I will send some more. I don't like to send too much at once.[28]

On the third day in February, Captain Silliman, who commanded Company C, received his commission as colonel of the 26th U.S. Colored Regiment. As was the custom, black regiments were commanded by white officers and in most cases that included the company grade officers as well. The next day Silliman gave a farewell dinner for the officers of the regiment. They assembled at Captain Jackson's tent that evening "and had a jovial time ... from the noise they made." The next morning, Silliman asked Sergeant Taft to assemble the company without arms so that he might address them before he departed. He then shook hands with each man and bid them good-by. He had not been well liked at the start of his service but the men must have grown to respect him because as he turned to walk away they "gave three hearty cheers for Colonel Silliman" in recognition of his new rank.[29]

"We have no commissioned officers with our Company." Thomas Rodman wrote, "Capt Silliman has just received an appointment as Col of a negro Regt, but I hear that Lieut Finnegan of Co K is to be our Capt."[30]

The same day, Private Horace D. Paret of Company D wrote home to "Friend Hasbrouck," the editor of the *Whig Press* in Middletown. He told of a party hosted by General Ward to which the officers of the 124th New York were invited and of a ball hosted by General Birney which featured a band and female guests as well as male.

I see in Tuesday's Washington *Chronicle* that Gabriel Colby of Company K, 124th regiment, was arrested among the deserters. He left the regiment December, 1862, I think. I see Father Abraham has called for half a million of men, to be drafted the 19th of March. I wish it had been for a million of men. I want to see some of the stiffest Copperheads sent down here now. Only send men enough, and we will wipe out this rebellion by the 4th of July. Then we can get home to vote for Uncle Abe for the next President.[31]

During the first week in February, Union General Benjamin Franklin Butler, commander of the Department of Virginia and North Carolina, learned that the defenses of Richmond had been stripped of men to support operations elsewhere. Butler, another of those colorful generals Lincoln kept on because they were also powerful politicians, thought he might take a stab at capturing the Confederate capital. The enterprise would be undertaken by a strong column of cavalry striking from the east. By the fourth day of February, it was decided by the powers in Washington that the Army of the Potomac should make a "diversion in favor of Butler's enterprise" by crossing the Rapidan and pinning Lee's men in place so that reinforcements could not be sent to defend Richmond.[32]

The feint, which quickly turned into another "mud march," would be made by the army's mounted arm and by the infantry of the 3rd Corps. Saturday, February 6, the infantry prepared to move out but, as always, the march was delayed until mid-afternoon by the rain. As the men stood around, they were startled by the boom of artillery. Private William Edgar, Company I,

Opposite: **Second Battle Flag of the 124th New York. At the request of the regiment, the Daughters of Orange supplied a replacement for the battle-worn regimental colors. "The flag is precisely like the one presented at their organization in September, '62, with the addition of a cluster of Orange blossoms and fruit on the blue ground, added as a memento of the lamented Col. Ellis, who called his 'boys' his Orange Blossoms, and a ribbon of that color is now universally worn by the regiment"** (archive of the Historical Society of the Town of Warwick, gift of Joan and Tom Frangos).

wrote to a Newburgh newspaper about the expedition. "But time wore on, and still no further orders till four o'clock P.M. when an orderly came hastily into camp, and the next minute the bugle sounded strike tents, and half past four o'clock found us tramping through Virginia mud, for it continued to rain all day, and you know at this season a little rain makes a great deal of mud."[33]

Corporal William Howell described the march to his mother. "We got word that our cavalry supported by the Second Corps were on a reconnaissance & we were to be ready to go & help if they got into any mess. Birney had command of the corps. We went through Culpepper & did not halt till we came to Pony Mountain where we stopped for the night. The roads were muddy & slippery and we were quite tired so we rolled ourselves up on our blankets & went to sleep a gentle rain falling at the time."[34] Quite a few men straggled, some not reaching the 124th until well after nightfall. Early the next morning they fell in and got on the road to Raccoon Ford on the Rapidan River. Private Edgar wrote, "After marching about two miles we were halted in a miserable wet swamp, where we staid about five hours, during which time all was quiet except an occasional gun."[35]

Major Weygant wrote of Sunday morning, February 7, "It had stormed hard all night and the rain was yet falling, but at daybreak we started forward again. The mud was so deep we could scarcely wade through it, and when at mid-day we halted for dinner, we had made but four miles."[36] Corporal Howell wrote, "In the morning we started early went three miles & stopped all day within a couple of miles of the Rapidan. Some cannonading was heard along the river."[37] Up ahead, the Yankee cavalry ran into resistance, putting up a "terrible racket, with both artillery and small arms, until about 1 P.M., when the din of the battle died away." So concluded the Battle of Morton's Ford, but the 124th New York did not take part. Private Edgar wrote, "We were ordered back a short distance to a beautiful pine grove, and as Sol was now pouring forth his rays, we took a much needed repose in this place. We remained till near sundown, when we were ordered back to our old quarters."[38] By William Howell's account, "At night we started for camp and traveled 'right smart' when we got to Pony mountain I concluded to 'gang my own gait.' I stopped to rest just then a rocket went shrieking up from the signal station." Weygant wrote, "Then hour after hour, we plodded on through mud almost knee deep, and just after midnight reached our tents again, all covered with dirt and completely worn out."[39]

As if being soaked to the skin and covered with mud on a useless enterprise was not enough, William Howell returned to find that the box from home, left in his quarters while on the march, had been rummaged through and many of the goodies sent by the family were missing.[40]

Weygant joined the men on picket duty as "brigade officer of the pickets" and noted the following in his diary regarding the unpleasant tour of duty:

> Wednesday, Feb. 10th — The dividing of the reserve into reliefs last night, so that a part might sleep while the balance remained ready for duty, was a useless task, for it was so damp and cold that no one was able to sleep.
> Thursday, Feb. 11th — I lay down quite early under my little tent at the picket reserve last evening, but the cold was so intense I could not sleep, and soon got up and spent the night sitting on a cracker box by a smoking log fire, around which I kept moving, first one way and then the other, to keep out of range of the strong pine smoke which almost eats one's eyes out.

He then noted with obvious joy, "This was my last three days picket tour." A few days later Francis Cummins was promoted to full colonel of the regiment and Weygant was mustered as lieutenant colonel, removing his name from the list of picket officers and adding it to the list of those who would do duty as "division officers of the day." The latter duty offered far more comfortable accommodations, indoors, with a roof over one's head and a fireplace.[41]

Thomas Rodman had a few things to say about recent events in a letter to his mother. "We have just returned from a Reconoiscence in force across or rather to the Rapidan. Our Corps strange to say did not get engaged, but we were within rifle shot of where the 2nd Corps were Fighting. We have just returned from off Picket today. Our Regt is filled up at last 200 of the 40 N.Y. Vols came into camp yesterday." This last-mentioned event, the arrival of the 40th New York, had more to do with mustering Francis Cummins as colonel and Charles Weygant as lieutenant colonel than any other reason. "You must not worry because I am situated as I am, concidering all things I am getting along first rate. No sickness or wounds troubling me but enjoying good health and thanks be to the maker of all things I have never been wounded as many of my brave Regt have but am spared to enjoy the pleasure of life another winter in my log cabin."

He reminded his mother of the warning she had given him upon his departure for the army.

> I have not forgotten your request you wished me to never forget, that was the vices of Gambling and drinking. Thanks be to the Lord I have been capable of resisting them. I have never played a game of Cards or dice or any other species of Gambling nor drank more than ½ pint of liquor since I left home nor do I with the help of God intend to. I have seen a great deal of such work going on even on the Battlefield, but as a general thing when there is any signs of a fight you might see the road literaly strewn with Cards as though they intended to cheat the Devil out of his dues.[42]

A few days later, February 22, President Washington's birthday, Rodman wrote home again, this time to his father. They had just signed the payroll that morning and expected to get two months pay in a day or so.

> We have got quite a large Regt now, about 250 of the 40th NY who could not reenlist and about 80 or 100 of the 86th. I think we will number 800 men now. The 40th has just arrived from home this morning. Some of them quite sick of their bargain. 52 days at home for 3 long years in the Army. I think 3 yrs is long enough to stay out here. The report is that the men of the 40th in our Regt are going back to their own Regt again. I hope it is so and also the 86 for they are mostly all deserters or Bounty jumpers. Such men for fighting I do not like. Let me fight alone rather than with a deserter. My health continues the very best so far this Winter. I think the coming summer will be a cutter on the Rebs. I think I shall see Richmond this summer. If I have good luck not as a prisoner but hunting Rebs.

He told his father that he had a horse and "he is just the thing for me for I like to go all over the Country and you know it is easier than to walk. I would like to be in the Cavilry a short time.

"There is some talk of our regt going to do guard duty at Washington this Summer but I can't see it, it is to good a fighting Regt for that, the Regt that runs the fastest when they get into a fight is the one to do guard duty, I think I shall try running some time and see if I cannot get an easy job. I received the $1.00 and I thank you for it."

A little while later Rodman added several postscripts. "And may the Lord give you Peace and Comfort in your latter days and years" and "Good Bye A kiss for you and Mother" among them. Then, at about four thirty in the afternoon, he added, "Quite a change has taken place today in the Regt since I commenced this letter. We have been paid off and all the members of the 40th that were with us have gone back to their own Regt. You will find my check for $24.00 and I wish you to send me back $10.00. I want to get my boots fixed and some other things and oblige." After signing his name he joked, "Remember I do not spend any money at card playing and the like."[43]

Henry Howell added a bit more to the story of the consolidation of the regiments. "There are nearly 300 men of the 40th to be sent to the 124th to serve out the remainder of their time. They do not appear to like it very well. I heard some of them say if they were sent there they would not go in another battle. I should not think that would make any difference about what regt. they were in about their fighting. We heard that the veterans of the 40th & 86th are to be consolidated in one."[44] This confirmed the speculation that this was done so that the regiment would have enough men to justify mustering Cummins as colonel and Weygant as lieutenant colonel, because shortly thereafter, the members of the two regiments were separated from the 124th New York.

Private Henry Howell had things on his mind other than promotion: he and his friend George Brown had been arrested and both were being held at headquarters awaiting a court martial. Of course he wanted to assuage his mother's concern so he started off by assuring her that all "they can do is to take our pay for a couple of months. It will not be so bad on us as it would if we had families to support." Then he went on to tell his version of events.

"Monday, February 1st we went out on picket. At the post I was on there was a Sergt, a Corp, & nine men. We stood an hour apiece. then B. and I went to a shoemakers he wanted to get his boots mended. The house was just inside of the picket line." After the boots were fixed, they decided they would go out beyond the picket line to "see the girls," presumably the same girls in the house mentioned by William Howell in a letter home a month earlier. "The house where they lived was about ten rods outside of the line. Our boys had often been there & we met a commissioned officer on his way back from the house & of course we thought we had as good a right out there as he had. But we did not get away so easy. We were there about an hour & one of the girls was writing us a song when a Captain and 8 or 10 men surrounded the house. Our Major was in command of the reserve where we were taken & we thought he would let us go. On the contrary he reported us to the Officer of the day who ordered us to be sent here."[45]

At the time Henry wrote this letter, it was two weeks after the fact and the court had yet to sit. In the meantime he wanted his mother to know that they had talked to Colonel Cummins just recently and that "Old Shiloh" had assured them he had just sent the major who arrested them to talk to General Ward "to see if he could not get us out." Howell also wanted to let his mother know that although under arrest, this was not like jail back home in New York. "We are comfortably established in an old barn with plenty of hay to lay on. There are over 30 here under arrest, most of them for desertion. We can go where we please but are expected to be here most of the time."

He mentioned that he was wearing the "number 8 boots" sent in the last box and wrote as if other pairs of boots had been sent from home to be sold in camp. He said that "those big nails" hurt the sale, probably referring to hobnails on the soles. Again complaining that their quarters had been pilfered while he was away he wrote, "We did not get quite as much good from our box on account of that reconnaissance as we would it had not been made." He concluded with, "It is snowing now but we expect it will turn to rain before morning. St. Valentines day is passed but I did not see any Valentines. There were 16 or 18 men for our regt. arrived from Elmira a day or two ago most of them were for Co. D. I am in good spirits and hope this will find you all well."[46]

Early in March, William Howell decided he might like to send a letter home to the editor of the *Whig Press*, his hometown newspaper. Dated "March 3d 1864," it began, "Perhaps it would not be uninteresting to hear from the 'Orange Blossoms.' So I guess I will give you a brief account of our doings of late." He wrote about the "quiet times" along the picket line until the morning of February 26, when

orders came around for the 2nd Brigade to go and relieve the 6th Corps pickets, as they were to start out on a reconnoisance the next morning. The remainder of the 124th, about forty of us, had to go along. We started about three o'clock, and went to the line of the 6th Corps, which runs from our line to the Rappahannock river. I had to go about seven miles before I got on post, and then it was nine o'clock. We were on the north side of the Hezel river, which empties into the Rappahannock. The weather was cold and windy, and it had a fair sweep at us, as the line ran along a range of hills at the base of the Blue Ridge. In the morning about four o'clock we heard the 6th Corps bugles calling, "Tear out! pack up!" &c. We passed the day very comfortably, as the weather was milder. The officer of the line was along, and stopped at a post where there were some conscripts. He accosted them with the usual inquiry, "How many men have you on this post?" The befuddled conscript replied, "Three men and a 'non-commissioned corporal.'"

The joke, of course, being that corporals don't receive a commission.

That night at about ten o'clock, the men were awakened to the sound of troops moving toward them and

> presently they came up and informed us that we were to be relieved by the 2d Division, as the 1st was to go out to the support of the 6th Corps. The 1st Division was to move at daylight. We thought we would get lost if we tried to reach camp in the night, so we did not start till morning. We went in camp the next morning, drew five days' rations, and prepared to start on after the division. Our detachment fell in the rear of the 20th Indiana, and we proceeded on the march at three o'clock. We marched steadily through Culpepper in a southwesterly direction for ten miles, before we bivouacked for the night. We were aroused early in the morning, ate our breakfast, and proceeded on our way. After marching some five miles, we came up with the division near an insignificant hamlet by the name of James City. The division had arrived there before our party left camp. We got there just in time to be mustered for pay with our company. We are mustered on the last day of every second month. We were in the vicinity of Slaughter Mountain, eight miles from Madison Court House, which was four miles the other side of Robinson river, a branch of the Rapidan. The boys were engaged in all kinds of sport during the day. They all appeared to be in the best spirits, and eager for a "flight," as the word goes.[47]

The veteran regiments were returning from their furloughs home and the army was quickly filling up again. William Howell noted that many in the 124th New York had been disappointed at not being able to go home for even a short visit during the winter months. Then he addressed the issue of replacements.

> Why is it that volunteers from our section prefer cavalry and artillery to joining the 124th? Do they think they can uphold the honor of Old Orange better there than with us, or is it true that they prefer that because with us, judging from the past, the future will bring them to a post of danger! I fear they prefer garrisoning forts, and guarding towns to meeting the foe in the open field, amid the roar of cannon and the smoke of battle. I understand the county has filled her quota and there will be no draft. That is well, and now *we all* hope that the coming campaign will forever end this "cruel war" and then if God spares us we will return once more to our happy homes and peaceful avocations.

His Company E had been without officers for almost a year. What he meant was that the three original officers who recruited the company were gone and they were now led by Lieutenant Charles Wood of Company A and Captain Daniel Sayer of Company D, "and we were somewhat in the condition of the lost children but we are all right now, as far as that was concerned." He concluded by saying that the health of the regiment was excellent and that Colonel Cummins and Surgeon Thompson both had their wives visiting them in winter camp. His opinion on having ladies in the camp? "I think it is an excellent idea and it would go far toward preventing vice and demoralization in the army, if officers and men could have the benefit of female society."[48]

Early in March, Thomas Rodman wrote to his father about the raid against Richmond mentioned by William Howell. "The weather here is beginning to get quite stormy now. We have just returned from another expedition toward Gordansville. We had very stormy weather all the time we were gone, but I do not mind that for Genrl Killpatrick is doing a great thing just now. The report came to Headquarters last night that he was within 3 miles of Richmond. If he gets into the City this time he will liberate all our prisoners and hold the City, but if I was in his place I would burn it to the Ground. The War is knocked in the head and the Fighting will be done by next fall." He noted that exactly a year and a half had passed since he was mustered into service for three years and added, "18 months from today if I am alive and well I expect to be home for good."[49]

The incident both Howell and Rodman wrote about was the famous Kilpatrick-Dahlgren Raid against Richmond. The raid had two objectives. The first was to enter the city and release up to 15,000 Union prisoners of war held there. The second was political. President Lincoln had issued the Declaration of Amnesty and Reconstruction, allowing those Southerners who swore loyalty to the United States and promised to uphold the Emancipation Proclamation to regain full civil liberties. He also set down a very lenient plan to allow seceded states to re-enter the

Union if just 10 percent of the voters swore loyalty to the Union. The president hoped that a successful raid would help Unionists in the South push for an end to the war under these better terms. Lincoln, usually the masterful politician, was overly optimistic in both his assessment of the strength of Unionist sentiment in the South and the ability of General Kilpatrick to get the job done. As with all such attempts to capture the enemy capital with a swift, bold strike, this one failed.

At about the same time, a soldier's letter, an "Indignant Protest," was published in the *Newburgh Daily Journal*. At issue was a special election in New York slated for March 8 to ratify an amendment to the state constitution allowing soldiers to cast absentee ballots from the field in the coming presidential election.[50] Democrats in New York, including Governor Horatio Seymour, opposed the idea but dared not oppose it too much lest they be labeled Copperheads. It was estimated that as many as eighteen thousand soldiers from regiments raised in Republican areas of the state were furloughed home specifically so that they might vote in this special election. Whether this charge was true or not, the fact that Orange County voted against Lincoln in 1860 and elected a Democrat to the House of Representatives in 1862 may explain why so few Orange Blossoms made it home that winter.

The Democrats in Cornwall, it seems, were challenging this soldier's right to vote on the grounds that he was not a resident of the town. "I am quite surprised," the soldier from Cornwall began,

> to learn that it was necessary for father to go out to Middletown to satisfy those mean, filthy, vile, detestable, damnable Copperheads, traitors, and tories, that my home was in Canterbury [a part of the town of Cornwall] and at his house, and that I had perfect right to my vote there.
>
> If I had no right to vote there, where did I have a right to vote? It is the only place that I ever voted in my life; is the place I have lived and called home for a portion of six years, and now I have no right to vote there, according to their opinion. It is not my home aye? Well, just show them the multitude of letters I have sent home, and proudly headed "Dear Father and Mother." Show them where I have spoken of home in letters penned by the light of the campfire in the far off camp, in letters penned upon the battle-field, and the hospital when suffering from wounds received in battle and sickness contracted in the service of the United States; fighting for the best government under the canopy of heaven; fighting to maintain that Government which has always protected them, and which in the past three years has saved them from ruin.
>
> Do they wish the war brought to their doors? — their buildings burned down, their fields made barren and unproductive wastes? Do they wish a cruel, heartless enemy to invade their country and sleep beneath their roofs, and destroy everything that comes in their path?
>
> They know nothing of the ravages of war. Just let them take a trip down to the depopulated, deserted and desolate country of Virginia; let them gaze upon the realities of war and be thankful that it is so far from their homes. If they love their brother traitors so well, why do they not go and fight with them? Let them go, oh the cowards, they know too well what their fate would be. My young heart would again overflow with patriot pride; I would rush to the field of battle and in the thickest of the fight, I would level my musket with deadly aim and would pray God to direct the bullet to the centre of their wicked hearts, and as the gore streamed from their deadly wounds, I would not have half the pity and sympathy for them that I would for the vilest rebel in the so-called "Confederacy."[51]

Later the same week, William Howell wrote home to his sister with some good news. "Henry has received his court martial at last. The Sentence has gone to headquarters when it returns he will return to the company. He had a first rate counsel and made an excellent defence, I apprehend his sentence will be very light if he is not acquitted altogether."[52] By March 11, Henry himself was able to report to his mother,

> I have been returned to my company at last. I have not heard what my punishment is to be. If it was not for the cost of all the whiskey that was drank during the trial I would think that I was not to be fined any but it would not hardly do for us to take up the time of the court for four days without having to pay for part of the liquor that would be consumed in that time. The worst crime a man can commit here appears to have the lightest sentence. A man that will desert go home and jump a couple of bountys will

be sent to his regiment and receive pay for all the time he is away. But I will not say any more about it. I consider that I am able to stand anything they can put upon me.[53]

Mid-March, another letter went home to the *Whig Press*, this one from a private in Company B named William H. Luckey. What he had to say about the cause and the life of a soldier may have moved a few at home to reconsider their viewpoints on the war and the coming presidential election.

> Editor of the Press: Being a reader of your valuable paper, I thought I would pen you a few lines, and as I see you are kept pretty well posted concerning the affairs of the regiment, I will express a few of my thoughts, which may perhaps amuse you for a moment.
>
> It is all well enough to talk about the hardships of a soldier's life, of the hard work, hard marches, and long, wearisome hours of guard, and harder yet the hard tack, but after all the hardest work of all is when we have nothing to do. When we are on the march, things and sights are always changing. Although there is not much variety about this part of Virginia, still there is something to occupy our minds, while if we are laying still, with nothing to do even for a day, we begin to think of home and those we have left there, and wonder when if ever we will see them again, and whether this war will ever end; and then we have our dark hours, our doubts and fears, and almost wish it would end any way so that we were out of it, but that passes away, and we feel assured that this unholy rebellion will soon be put down, and that glorious old flag under which we are fighting will float over an undivided nation.
>
> I sometime think the people at home do not have the same feeling for that flag, and when I say that flag, I not only mean the flag, but all that it represents — our country and our homes. I say they do not appear to have the same feeling for it as we soldiers do. Perhaps it is because they have not been through the hardships for it that we have. I seldom see it (and I see it every day) but I remember the oath we have taken to defend it, and my resolution grows stronger to fight for it as long as it is in any danger.
>
> I must close my letter, but I suppose the people, that is the political part of them, are about as much interested about the next Presidential election as they are about the war, and I will say, as far as I can judge, the soldiers would like to see nominated not a Copperhead, but either Abraham Lincoln or a man after his own heart.[54]

At about the same time these letters were being mailed home, General Grant arrived in Washington to meet with President Lincoln. The next day he was commissioned lieutenant general in a White House ceremony and then met privately with the president to discuss his plans. The day after that Grant visited the Army of the Potomac. "The generals discussed the position, condition, and future of the army, and worked out their relationship to each other, for Grant expected to be in the field with his army commander."[55] Weygant wrote that at the middle of March, Grant announced his headquarters would be in the field with the Army of the Potomac, a clear signal to nearly every soldier in the army that "a severer campaign than it had yet known" was about to begin in earnest.[56]

Near the end of March, Henry Howell wrote to his mother to bring her up to date on his court martial.

> Well they did not get much the best of us on the Courtmartial business. The only verdict brought in was fifteen days fatigue duty and the Colonel sent us to do duty in the company so we do not have to fulfill the sentence. The Major is quite crest fallen. The 40th was out on picket the same time we were. Their officers got spreeing it pretty well. It was 5 of them at the house, but the folks would not have anything to do with them preferring the society of the soldiers who know enough not to get drunk. The theater is all the go around here now I have not been up yet. I think I shall go up tomorrow night if it is pleasant I believe they act one thing over and over every second night. Whiskey appears to be quite plenty around here now days. Some of our noncommissioned chaps are using the article quite free to day but the Officers are willing to countenance such things and do them themselves so it is all right (or all wrong rather) Murray was here a few days but has gone away again. I guess they did not get him mustered as Major. It was a "big thing" putting those men of the 40th in here long enough to muster in Cummins & Weygant one step higher. We heard that we had exchanged places with the 40th for the purpose of getting the Colonel of that regiment out of the 3rd Brigade while they made a Brigadier out the Colonel of the 3rd Michigan and then we are to return to our old place again unless they finally conclude to smash up the 3rd Corps.... I guess I will have to get you to send me a pair of suspenders as they cost so much here. This storm will put a stop to all drilling for a few days.[57]

March 29 was Thomas Rodman's twentieth birthday. He wrote to his parents telling them that the men were to be reviewed by General Grant but that the rainstorm that had moved in postponed it.

> I suppose we will be on the road to Richmond in a few weeks more. Gen Grant is reorganizing the Army now and making a great many important changes. Our Corps has been broken up and put in the 2nd 5th & 6th. Our division has been put into the 2nd Corps and the 3rd in the 6th where they will have some fighting to do which they have not done before. And they are sending some troops from around Washington to help us. We will go to Richmond this summer but not without a great deal of fighting for it will be a hard job to go there this way.

He hoped that his parents' health was good and speculated on their moving to a farm in the spring. "I hope you may have good luck and that I may be spared to come home and enjoy the remainder of my life with you. But as the Lord said not my will but thine be done."[58]

During the last weeks of March, the 124th spent the usual amount of time on the picket line. In camp, large shipments of ammunition arrived by rail and wagon "and many an hour hitherto given to recreation, were by special orders expended in target practice and shooting at imaginary foes; and drills, inspections, and reviews, became so frequent as to leave us but few leisure hours."[59] Short furloughs were still being granted "on a more liberal scale than usual" and a number of company grade officers and NCOs were sent to Orange County to take another stab at recruiting—and perhaps to vote. On March 12, Captain William Jackson of Company K, Lieutenant Charles Stewart of Company I, and a group of NCOs were sent home to recruit. In a month, Jackson was so discouraged that he asked to be recalled to duty with the regiment; he brought with him but twelve recruits.

Jackson echoed William Howell's assertion that to serve with the 124th was a dangerous proposition. He had gone home fully expecting to find plenty of young men eager to join "but our record, it would appear, was already too bloody. Our long list of killed and wounded, when contrasted with the comparatively small number lost in battle by Congressman Van Wyck's regiment, the 10th Legion, which had entered the service nearly a year before the 124th, told most seriously to our disadvantage, so far as procuring recruits was concerned." What Jackson found in Orange County was a population very proud of its regiment and eager to sing its praises but "every man, woman, and child in the county entertains a superstition that the placing of one's name on the rolls of the 124th is equivalent to signing his death warrant."[60]

On March 17 a bombshell was dropped on the 124th New York. In order to equalize the size of his brigades, General Birney ordered that the 124th New York be transferred to the third brigade, while the 40th New York, one of the largest in Birney's Division, would replace the Orange Blossoms in the second brigade. Almost immediately the officers of the 124th protested the transfer primarily because it would take them away from the 86th New York, considered their brother regiment. General Ward, the brigade commander, added his endorsement. "The officers and men are very melancholy in regard to the transfer. The esprit-du-corps is great; it is with regiments as with brigades.... There is no better fighting regiment in the division than the 124th New York. They feel proud of their brigade and division. I sincerely hope it, in the judgment of the Major General commanding, the service will not be injured thereby, that the petition of the officers may be granted."[61]

General Birney replied the same day that the "exigencies of the service demanded a transfer now, it may not be necessary to make it a permanent transfer." He went on to say that he would try to grant their request. Nonetheless, the regiment was ordered to prepare to move its camp on the next day. However, on March 18 orders were issued to send all reports to the Third Brigade but to remain in the old camp. After about ten days, the 124th was officially transferred back to Ward's Brigade, having never actually moved anywhere.[62]

The last week in March, it snowed eight inches, "a very unusual thing for the sunny south,"

Sergeant Taft wrote. The always resourceful Quartermaster Post found a sled "and he and several of our line officers who remained in camp are riding about in high glee." The often prickly General Birney, not to be outdone, had an ambulance body fitted with runners and joined in the fun. "It must have been very severe on our boys out on picket last night," Taft wrote.[63]

As March turned to April, Private Horace D. Paret, Company K, wrote home to Editor Hasbrouck of the *Whig Press.* Paret noted that there would be a draft in the North and urged the government to "send on some of those at home who are having easy times, while we are down here traveling with our knapsacks and six or eight days' rations. But the boys are cheerful over it—always in good spirits. If it rains, or the mud is deep, or it is cold, you will see the 124th at their post, and as lively as if all was fine and pleasant. They go along as if they were going home from a day's work in the North."

He turned his attention to two topics on the minds of the soldiers: General Grant and the presidential election. He spoke first about Lincoln. "Our boys say Uncle Abe must settle this war; he is the man for President. Again, there are many that voted against him before who say he is their choice now." As for the general, "Lee has Grant to face now, and if he is not careful, Grant will serve him worse than he did Pemberton at Vicksburg. You can look for stirring times down here next month. Then onward to Richmond, and we will go in then, too." The unusual early spring storms continued with the mountain tops in the distance "white with snow," although the temperatures had been moderate. "The 124th is all right, and ready for action, but I hope we won't have to go in any more battles. We have done our part, I think. The boys are afraid up North to come in the 124th, I believe, because we have been in so many battles."[64]

Thomas Rodman's mother must have asked her son why he had yet to be promoted. This prompted Thomas to write a scathing account of that situation in the regiment.

> You speak about promotions. You think it is those that have suffered the most that are promoted, but you are mistaken. Those men that have stayed away from the Reg the longest, and drank the most Rum are the one that get promoted. Then there is another class that get promotions, and they are the ones that hang around the officers and suck around and get on their knees and tell lies about their comrades. I would not give a snap to get promoted by doing that. More than that there is men promoted to Sergents in my Co that can hardly rite there names. Never mind my time is to come, If I get out of this service all right I would not give a pin for a pair of shoulder straps even if they contained an Eagle or Star.

He finished with a "kiss for you and Father" and a request for postage stamps.[65]

He followed up on April 13 with a letter to his father.

> We have just been paid off today and I suppose that we will be off the Rapidan and from thence to Richmond. You will find my check for $10.85 enclosed, they took $15.15 off for Clothing which I have had over my allowance since I enlisted. The clothes are so poor that it takes all a man can make to clothe him. You may get this cashed and send it right back.... We had a Division Review today. We were reviewed by Gen Hancock commanding 2nd Corps of which we are a part and Gen Meade & Gen Birney our Div Gen. We are now in the 1st Brigade 3rd Div 2nd Corps but we still retain our old Badge. We had on white Gloves something new for the old 1st Div.[66]

Rodman's mention of "our old badge" was a reference to the red diamond, the Kearny Badge. As part of the Third Division, 2nd Corps, the proper corps badge would have been a blue trefoil but the soldiers who had served under Kearny and Birney were very proud of the red badge and refused to remove it. An officer on Meade's staff wrote, "Some of the 3d Corps (among which are to be found shoals of bowery boys) have made a fuss about going in the 2d Corps, and the merry Excelsiors have sewed the trefoil to the seats of their trousers!"[67] The brigade of New York troops mentioned had been the one raised by General Sickles at the start of the war and obviously remained loyal to its colorful founder. There was even talk in Congress of placing Dan Sickles at the head of the Army of the Potomac, once his Gettysburg wound had healed. It has been speculated that the consolidation of the eastern army into three infantry corps and the elimination

of Sickles' command precluded his return and may have been the motivating factor in reorganizing the army in the first place. In any case, the army was reorganized and Grant, not Sickles, would lead it to battle in 1864.

The 86th New York was camped next to the 124th, sharing the chapel and the guard duty. The congregations met together with the chaplains of the two regiments preaching on alternate Sundays. As spring approached, "the fact that our long period of comparative repose was drawing rapidly to a close became daily more and more apparent." On April 12 orders were received to pack up all extra clothing in cracker boxes and send them to Washington for storage; four days later the sutlers were ordered to leave the army. On April 21, the regimental hospitals were emptied and the sick were sent to Washington by train. The next day there was a grand review by General Grant and General Meade in company with all the corps commanders, and on April 26 the army moved out of winter quarters and "pitched its canvas and muslin shelters in the open fields." It was understood by all that the long-awaited spring campaign was about to begin.

Weygant took the opportunity to assess the losses and gains since the army went into winter quarters at Brandy Station. The 124th added sixty-eight men, volunteers from Orange County, some of whom had seen service in other regiments. Weygant noted that a dozen men were added to the "Death List" of the regiment from the usual camp diseases contracted that winter. An additional eighty-two men left the regiment due to physical disability or battle wounds, to be transferred to the Veteran Reserve Corps. Another sixty four were mustered out and sent home due to disease or battle wounds. Among them were Private William Wirt Bailey, Captain Leander Clark, and Lieutenant James Denniston, who ran afoul of Sergeant Hanford's ramrod at Gettysburg and who was about to bring charges against Colonel Cummins for being drunk on duty. Finally, Weygant added six more names to the list of losses under the category deserter. Among them was Private Jeremiah Hartnett, who had arrived late to Gettysburg but managed to pen a detailed letter home about the great battle.[68]

As the army made ready for the spring campaign, a flurry of letters and orders passed through headquarters dealing with the sobriety of Colonel Cummins. A letter sent by "James Otis Denniston, late Captain Company G. 124 NYSV" to General Hancock, accused Cummins of "being a habitual drunkard." Denniston mentioned that Cummins was dismissed for drunkenness at Shiloh and added, "All the officers of the regiment who I have seen say he is drunk nearly all the time and is therefor unfit for command. There are many noble men in my old company whom I should be unwilling to see sacrificed in battle under the command of a drunken regimental officer. I am out of the service and cannot prefer charges formally, I therefore write you hoping he may be removed."

General Birney acted quickly that very same day. "Respectfully returned to Major Duff who will call the attention of Brigade Inspector to Par. 472 Army Regulations and call for a report as to the case. As this malicious report has been sent to all the Comdg Generals, it is due to the Inspector's Dept. and Col. Cummins that it should be properly branded if untrue as it is supposed to be."

Opposite: **Company H, 124th New York, image taken April, 1864, at Camp Brandy Station, Virginia. The company is at "parade rest" with winter quarters in the background. The men in the rear rank have stepped up between the men in the front rank so that their faces can be seen. In 1910, Lt. John R. Hays identified the members of his company. Excluding the men in the right background who are not part of the company, they are, right to left: Captain David Crist, 1st Sgt. Thomas Bradley, Corp. William McVey, E. Dexter Van Keuren, Corp. Abram Rapelje, Gouveneer Legg, Sgt. George Butters, Josiah Dawson, William Buchanan, John Rediker, unknown (possibly John E. Kidd), Corp. William Henry Brown, unknown, Chester Judson, unknown, Milton Crist, Jesse Camp, unknown, James Crist, Francis S. Brown, Corp. Andrew Armstrong, Grandison Judson, John Buckley (musician), Arthur Haigh (musician), Charles Whitehead (musician), Lieutenant John R. Hays (Historical Society of Walden and Wallkill Valley).**

Major Levi Bird Duff of the 105th Pennsylvania, then serving as division inspector, set about the work of getting to the bottom of the charges. He ran into a wall of silence from the officers of the regiment. "I have the honor to respectfully report that I have not been able to get any information concerning the character of Col. Cummins. The company commanders of the regiment, on being asked by me the question, 'What is Col. Cummins character for sobriety?' declined to answer on the ground that I had not authority to ask such questions. Having no authority to compel an answer and knowing of no other source of information I am obliged to return the letter without a report in the case."

With no serving officer willing to substantiate the charges against Cummins it was up to Captain Edwin J. Houghton, 17th Maine Regiment and brigade inspector, to investigate. Just two days later he rendered his finding:

> I have been acting Brigade Inspector of the Brigade since April 12th 1864 during which time I have seen Col. Cummins, while on duty with his Regiment, at his own tent or at these Head Quarters nearly every day. I have never seen him intoxicated, or when I supposed he was under the influence of intoxicating liquors since I have been in this Brigade.
>
> His reputation for sobriety among the Field Officers, of the Brigade with whom he has been associated as I have ascertained by personal inquiry is *good*.
>
> I find that the author of the within communication was never a Captain in the 124th Regt NYSV but was discharged as 1st Lieut. by S. O. 448 1863 War Dept having been absent from his command for more than sixty days.
>
> From personal observation since I have been connected with the Inspectors Dept of this Brigade and from what information I have been able to gather I have no hesitation in pronouncing the within communication malicious and untrue.[69]

Expecting to move south before too long, Corporal Ben Dutcher, Company H, wrote that he was concerned to hear that his mother had been sick. "I hope and pray that ere this reaches you, you may be enjoying your usual good health. Thank God I can say that I enjoy very good health ... we all expect some hard fighting in the coming campaigns we also think that if we are victorious on the start that the rebs wouldnt fight so hard after a while. you must not forget us in your prayers as we all know that thousands of us must fall when the conflict begins."[70]

Less than a month from the day he wrote this letter home, Corporal Dutcher was dead, an early casualty of the brutal slugging match that was the Battle of the Wilderness.

The Howell brothers wrote home in late April, sure that they would not have time to do so once Grant's campaign got underway. William wrote from the picket line.

> We are on the reserve in the vicinity of Stephensburg this time. We were never on this part of the line before. Pony mountain is to our left. The picket line is a mile out in front of the reserve and the men go out from there every 12 hours and relieve the pickets. I believe they call it Butterfields plan but we think the plan that we have been acting on previously is far superior to this. We have had considerable rain while we have been out and taking all into reckoning we have had a rather disagreeable time of it. Part of us have packed and sent away our over coats. Henry did not send his & he thinks he is lucky in keeping it. He will have to throw it away soon as we begin to march and we expect to have ours come back next fall when we may need them more. Last week we had a division review by Gens Birney, Hancock, & Meade. We were told that Grant would probably be there too but he was not. The rains done considerable damage to the railroad and bridges but it was soon repaired.
>
> Gen Custars headquarters are but a short distance from here. The cavalry corps are encamped around Stevensburg & we saw them drill friday in the afternoon. they had a horse race near our reserve. Shoulder Straps were predominant and bet heavily on the race. Solid shot and shell lay scattered all along here I believe there was a cavalry fight here last summer. Mountain run is quite high & the bridges are swept away. Men are very busy repairing them now.... The snow still covers the peaks of the Blue ridge while the plains to the east are spred with a mantle of green. We will probably move as soon as the roads and weather will allow. And when we do move Grant means to hold all he gains I think.

Upon his return from picket duty the next day, William added a postscript, "We have a rumor that our communications with Washington are to be closed for 90 days from May 1st." Here was the best indication he could ask for that the march south would soon begin.[71]

Henry Howell wrote home a week later to his mother,

I will try to write you a sheet this afternoon and send by the mail to night unless we have to drill again. We drill quite regular now. I suppose it is done to get us in order for the campaign that must certainly open very soon. We have been training for the grand review that has been talked of so long & which did come off yesterday. Generals Grant Meade and Hancock were on hand. We got a good look at Grant. He is a very common looking & was very plainly dressed. He wears a full beard which is black. We were fixed up in our best with white gloves to lead. He was the 3rd Div of the 2 Corps & I think we passed as well as any of them. We went out to Stephensburg in sight of the 4th Artillery camp. I suppose they were out but we could not see them among so many. It would have been a grand sight to anyone that never seen an army, but with us it has got to be an old story. Grant did not make any fuss about the matter not even allowing the salute to be fired. We are drilling in target practice now days which I think will be very beneficial to the recruits. It is getting so late in the spring that it does not take us long for a storm to dry up. The sun and wind together dried it. The roads are quite passible now and we will not be surprised to be ordered out at any time. Grant moves so mysterious that no one can tell where he will strike until the army gets in motion. There are all sorts of rumors afloat but I will not repeat any of them for you will be likely to learn the truth as soon as we do.... Col. Weygant has got Capt. Wood under arrest for disobeying orders....

There has been a Sergeant from the 2nd Shaprshooters promoted to the 1st Lieut in Co G, 124th NY. It was some of Gen Wards doings. I do not see any thing very prepassentsing in his appearance to say the least. It has given great dissatisfaction here and some of the officers are quite inclined to give him the cold shoulder.[72]

This was a reference to 1st Lieutenant Edward Carmick, who was put in charge of Company F, not G as Howell said, when William Mapes was promoted and sent to command Company A. The "cold shoulder" reception, much like that given to Lieutenant Milnor Brown the previous year, is a good indication of how the men felt about outsiders sent to command them.

At the end of the month Henry wrote again, this time to his cousin Helen. For all he knew, this might be the last chance he had to do so before the campaign started.

I expect that my time will be occupied in a very different way from writing letters in a very few days. The machinery is being put in working order every day. I believe it only lacks a little motion. We are quite confident that when we do start there is to be (no) backward movements.

Meades Army with the cooperation of Burnsides and Butlers forces all under the immediate command of the never failing Grant will be likely to produce a different effect upon Richmond from any it has yet seen. There is no way to find out the plans of our commanders that we have found so far. We have had all sorts of reports about the mail being detained in Washington for a certain number of days but we can discover no truth in the affairs so far. I would be very sorry for to have such a thing happen but of course we would have to acquiesce in any thing that our commanders think necessary for to help end this war which is so much to be deplored....

The 2nd Corps was reviewed by Gen's Grant, Meade, and Hancock a couple of weeks ago. Everything passed off well and the Generals expressed themselves satisfied with our appearance. I like Grants looks. The weather has been very favorable for military opperations for some little time back but now it has every appearance of a storm soon. I believe they have a new minister at Howells but I never heard his name. Well Cousin I will bring this to a close. Wishing to hear from you soon.[73]

Thomas Rodman wrote what he knew might be his last letter home before the shooting started. He was happy to hear that his mother was feeling better and hoped his parents would continue in good health. "I am well as usual having been blessed with remarkably good health for the past six months and I hope through the goodness of God to remain so." He told them that they might not hear from him, "this privelge of writing to you," would stop once campaigning began, and he noted the latest camp rumor. "The report is now that the Rebs are moving up the Shanandoah Valley, and if that is so we will not stay here long."

He began to assess the situation and what might happen.

The weather is getting quite warm down here and the roads are good so there is nothing to hinder us from moving just now. Hard Fighting is to be our lot this summer, but it makes little difference to those that are prepared to die. We are fighting in a good cause and it is an honor to die for ones Country. But for all that there is no use for ones throwing away his life foolishly if he can in any way help it. As for me I am going to save myself as much as I can this summer and if I am spared to live till next winter I shall begin to think there is some hopes of my getting out of it.

But life is uncertain. The Lord's will, not mine, be done. So Good Bye.[74]

CHAPTER 12

"All at once we heard that cussed Rebel yell"
May 3–6, 1864

In the spring of 1864, great changes were in the wind. The Union victories at Gettysburg and Vicksburg had pretty much ended any chance of European recognition of the South as an independent nation. War weariness gripped both sections, but the North's wealth in manpower, finance, and machines could see it through to the end if the people's resolve did not falter. The South, on the other hand, was running short of everything but resolve. Most important of all, there was a change of leadership at the top in the Army of the Potomac. The vestiges of "McClellanism" would soon be purged from the officer corps by Lieutenant General Ulysses S. Grant, a westerner who had made his mistakes far away from second-guessing Washington politicians and the glare of the press corps. He would bring to the Army of the Potomac a bold leadership style that would be tested by Lee, but not broken.

The constant was Lincoln himself. He steadfastly refused to recognize the conflict as anything more than a rebellion of individuals and would not consider an end to hostilities unless it left the Union intact. At the same time, he moved ahead in tapping and committing to battle resources ignored in the first two years of war: the runaway slaves of the South and the free negroes of the North. In addition, he called on those veterans in the ranks and at home to reenlist by offering federal bounties and other inducements. At the same time he threatened to draft those who had, so far, not been willing to join the fight.

Lincoln and Grant would together set in motion an engine of destruction that would beat out the fires of secession once and for all. But not before many more sons of Orange County were consumed.

Through late April and early May, last-minute preparations for the start of the spring campaign in the east reached fever pitch. On hand were one hundred fifty rounds per infantryman, fifty of which were kept by the soldiers in their cartridge boxes. Medical supplies, rations, ammunition for the artillery, almost two weeks' supply of beef on the hoof, forage for the horses, and all manner of stores were stockpiled and made ready to move.

General Grant reviewed the troops, giving the men a chance to see him as well as an opportunity for him to see them. While reviewing the 6th Corps, he created a minor flap by receiving General Sedgwick's salute with a cigar stuck in his teeth. The blame for this lapse, recounted by the priggish Boston blueblood, Lieutenant-Colonel Theodore Lyman of Meade's staff, was laid at the feet of General Meade himself who supposedly told his commander "there was no harm in it." Lyman went on, in an aloof manner, to say of Meade, "The good General has the failing of nine tenths of our officers, a disregard of formal details that brings more trouble than one would think."[1]

The last week in April, Meade and Lyman had lunch with Grant at Culpeper. Lyman described the meal, then he described the man.

> It was plain but good; soup, fish, 2 meats, 3 vegetables & a pudding with coffee. There were the staff at table, including Capt. Parker the Indian, who is chief of his tribe. Grant drinks no wine or spirit; the moment the last man was through, he rose. He is a very still, steady man, but evidently enjoyed a pleasant joke. He also makes quiet, sarcastic remarks, without moving a line of his face. He said (referring to Bank's late fight on the Red River, where he lost 20 guns and some thousands of prisoners, though he at last drove the enemy back) that "Bank's victories were of a kind that three of four of them would ruin anybody." He added that "there were some Generals who had not enough patriotism to resign."[2]

Such comments, had they not been chronicled as Grant's own, might just as easily have come from President Lincoln.

The Army of the Potomac, while nominally led by General Meade, was really at the command of General Grant, who would be directing all Union armies in the field. Grant was not interested in capturing real estate because he knew that only the destruction of the Army of Northern Virginia would bring an end to the rebellion. Grant gave as his reason for placing his headquarters with the Army of the Potomac his desire to deflect interference from Washington, which had been the bane of all previous commanders. But his presence blurred the chain of command. The fact that General Burnside would be in the field at the head of the 9th Corps as an independent command not accountable to Meade would lead to problems in the coming battle that demonstrated the weakness of this most unusual arrangement.

The 2nd Corps, to which Birney's Division (and the 124th New York) was sent, was led by Major General Winfield Scott Hancock, a hero of Gettysburg. His ability to inspire confidence in his men was best described by a member of his own staff, who wrote, "One felt safe when near him." A native of Montgomery Square, Pennsylvania, Hancock graduated from West Point in 1844. His varied military career included a brevet for gallantry in the war with Mexico and service in the Seminole War, the civil war in Kansas, and the expedition against the Mormons. He was stationed in California at the start of the Civil War, coming east after things were well underway. Once Hancock was on the scene, General McClellan had him appointed brigadier general in command of a brigade composed of one regiment each from Maine, New York, Pennsylvania, and Wisconsin. He moved up steadily, taking over a division after Antietam and the 2nd Corps after Chancellorsville.

Hancock's "crowded hour of glory" came at Gettysburg when he took charge of the situation in the afternoon of July 1 and then went on to be instrumental in defeating Lee's attempt to break the Union center on July 3. He was so badly wounded during Pickett's Charge that he did not return to command for almost six months.[3] The reinforced 2nd Corps consisted of four divisions: the First led by Brigadier General Francis Barlow, the Second led by Brigadier General John Gibbon, the Third by Major General David Birney, and the Fourth led by Brigadier General Gershom Mott.

Birney's Division was made up of two brigades. The First Brigade, led by Brigadier General J.H. Hobart Ward, was one of the largest in the army. It included the 99th Pennsylvania, 110th Pennsylvania, 141st Pennsylvania, 40th New York, 86th New York, 124th New York, 3rd Maine, 20th Indiana, and 2nd U.S. Sharpshooters, totaling about twenty seven hundred men present for duty.[4] The Second Brigade was led by Brigadier General Alexander Hays, West Point class of 1844.

The 5th and 6th corps were also enlarged and led by veterans of the hard fighting of the Army of the Potomac. Major General Gouverneur Warren, a native of Cold Spring, New York, commanded the 5th Corps. Warren, who graduated in 1850, had been appointed to West Point

Officers of the 124th New York at Brandy Station, May 1864. The three officers seated at the center are, left to right, Col. Cummins, Surgeon Thompson, and Lt. Col. Weygant.

when he was just sixteen.[5] The 6th Corps was commanded by Major General John Sedgewick, an 1837 graduate of West Point known to the men in the ranks as "Uncle John." When Sedgewick led his men across the Rapidan on May 4, he had but six days to live.[6]

Grant had a two-to-one advantage in numbers over Lee. While this might look to be overwhelming, it should be kept in mind that Lee and his men knew every inch of the Wilderness, the ground on which he would fight Grant. The dense woods, tangled paths, and lack of clear ground all but neutralized the advantage held by Grant in men and artillery.

"The first and second days of May were devoted by the subordinate commanders to making of a final inspection of their respective commands."[7] On May 3, six days' rations and fifty rounds of ammunition were distributed and marching orders issued. The 124th New York would be led to battle by Colonel Francis M. Cummins and Lieutenant Colonel Charles H. Weygant. Captain Henry Murray would have to settle for the rank of "acting major" for the time being. The regiment was still composed of ten companies, but their order in line of battle had been changed in part to place the largest companies on the left and right flanks. Company D, commanded by Captain James Benedict, was on the left and Company B, commanded by Captain William Mapes, was on the right. Company F was now the color company and stood at the center of the regiment. The Color Guard was incorporated at the left of the company where Color Bearer George Washington Edwards stood with the new national flag.

There were new faces in the line on May 3. Company B mustered forty-eight men, twenty-two of whom were new recruits. At the other end of the line, Company D mustered forty-six men, also with twenty-two new men. A smattering of "fresh fish" could be found in one or two of the other companies but most had no new recruits. Of those on detached duty, Norman Augustus Sly of D and John R. Post of H were both at General Ward's brigade headquarters. Sly was listed as brigade color bearer and Post as clerk when in fact both would serve as couriers for Ward in the coming battle.[8]

Private Norman Augustus Sly, Company D. He was wounded in action May 5, 1864, at the Wilderness, and again at Spotsylvania Court House, May 13, 1864. A courier for General Ward, he was transferred to the 152nd New York Volunteers for promotion to 2nd lieutenant in February 1865 (archive of the Historical Society of the Town of Warwick, gift of Joan and Tom Frangos).

Grant knew that it would be dangerous to attack Lee head-on in his entrenchments at Mine Run on the far side of the Rapidan River, "a position so well fortified that a direct attack was out of the question."[9] Grant also knew that it made little sense to allow the Army of Northern Virginia to fall back into the defenses of Richmond, something Lincoln himself had observed months before. "If our army cannot fall upon the enemy and hurt him where he is," the President said, "it is plain to me it can gain nothing by attempting to follow him over a succession of intrenched lines into a fortified city."[10]

Grant considered his options and decided that he would cross the Rapidan downriver, east of Lee's army, then turn west against the enemy's right flank. Grant chose this route because it would put him below the dreaded Mine Run defenses and in a position to threaten Lee's communications with Richmond. The route would also shield Washington from attack, make secure Grant's own lines of supply, and get him closer to the Army of the James, which might support him against Lee. That army of 33,000 men, larger than any single corps in the Army of the Potomac, was commanded by General Benjamin Butler, who was to move against Richmond when Grant crossed the Rapidan. As it turned out, little would come of Butler's efforts, or lack thereof.

The problem with this plan, and it would prove to be a big problem, was that the route took Grant into the Wilderness, the same forest that had entangled Hooker at Chancellorsville and Meade at Mine Run. "It is a region of gloom, and the shadow of death," wrote one of General Ward's men.[11] "The key to maneuvering past Lee's downriver flank," wrote historian Gordon Rhea, "was getting through the Wilderness as quickly as possible."[12]

The broad plan in place, General A.A. Humphreys, Meade's chief of staff, was given the task of working out the details. Humphreys was well aware of the dangers inherent in trying to move through the Wilderness. This capable officer quickly set in place the minutia of which corps marched where, their departure time, and the route to be used as well as what supplies would be needed, where they would be stored, and so on. His plan called for the army to be divided into two columns, one to use Germanna Ford, the other to use Ely's Ford. Both were very familiar to the engineers who had planned river crossings at each place before. The left wing, including the 124th New York, would cross at Ely's Ford.[13]

Once across the river, the right wing would reach the Orange Turnpike at Wilderness Tavern, the left wing would strike it at Chancellorsville. The Orange Blossoms knew the east-west thoroughfare, having marched and fought along it just one year before. South of the Turnpike and running parallel to it was the Orange Plank Road and yet farther south, at the edge of the Wilderness, were the Catharpin and Pamunkey roads; these lower roads led west around the flank of the Mine Run earthworks. Humphreys's plan called for the right wing to move all the way south to the Catharpin Road with the left wing marching through Chancellorsville south until it could turn west and join the right wing below the enemy's positions. Grant was sure that if the army got underway before midnight on May 3, and if it met no opposition, the two wings would be reunited late on May 4, facing west and threatening Lee's army. Speed, of course, was critical to success.[14]

While it may have occurred to some that this plan repeated the mistakes of Chancellorsville and Mine Run, there were factors that may have lulled Yankee headquarters into a sense of security. First was an erroneous assumption that Lee would react slowly to Grant's advance. This was based in part on Lee's deliberate pace the previous November when he checked Meade long enough for his army to get into the Mine Run earthworks. Second, no one expected that Lee might actually launch an attack on Grant's flank as he moved his brigades through the Wilderness. Finally, just below the surface, there was an as yet unstated arrogance among the men from the west, a feeling that the eastern officers were not aggressive enough and were intimidated by the very name of Lee.

Overconfidence, assuming Lee would do this or that, and the need to keep huge amounts of supplies close at hand led to a fateful decision: the army would halt on the afternoon of May 4 to allow the supply wagons to catch up. This was clearly inconsistent with the need to get through the Wilderness quickly and would prove to be a major impediment to the success Grant was hoping for.[15] Another problem, according to historian-mapmaker Colonel Vincent Esposito, was the dispersion of Union cavalry. Each column would be led by a division of cavalry, General Wilson ahead of the right wing and General Gregg ahead of the left. General Alfred Tolbert, an infantry officer recently moved to cavalry command, was left behind with his division to guard the wagon train which stretched miles to the rear and might prove to be an inviting target for Jeb Stuart's raiders. "Therefore," reasoned Esposito, "no cavalry was available to screen the exposed Federal right flank during the move through the Wilderness."[16]

Private Norman Augustus Sly was serving as a "Mounted Orderly to Genl J.H.H. Ward." He saw his duty as simple: "to ride out with the Genl and carry his private letters wich at times were quite numerous."[17] Years later he wrote of the start of the campaign: "On Tuesday morning the 3rd day of May 1864 the looked for Order came to break camp and move against the enemy at midnight.... Then the orders began to come thick and fast, I can jest call to mind now all most the first order that came in the Brigadere Genl commanding will see at once that troops in his command have the required amt of ammunition namely 80 rounds per man." The orders had to be quickly copied and sent to the regimental commanders "then one right after annorther have all your arms and accountrments all inspected and then annorther have the required rations bin isued and cooked and then annorther have all your sick removed to the Hospital ... every order had a spur tacked to it to bee done at once it was a hard day on the Orderly I can tell."[18]

At dark on May 3, marching orders reached the 124th New York setting 11 P.M. as the start time for Birney's Division. At 9 P.M. the same night, the regiment was drawn up in front of Colonel Cummins's quarters to hear Adjutant Van Houten read an address from the commanding general. "Soldiers!" Meade's orders began. "Again you are called upon to advance on the enemies of your country." He assured them that this was a coordinated effort of several armies under the command of General Grant who had the confidence of the administration, the people of the north, and the men who marched with him. "Soldiers! the eyes of the whole country are looking with anxious hope to the blow you are about to strike in the most sacred cause that ever called men to arms." They had heard it all before: the reminder of home and hearth, of family and forefathers, the call to sacrifice. If any phrase served to motivate them it was probably the observation that "if true to ourselves, victory, under god's blessing, must and will attend our efforts."[19]

This was a change from Hooker's blasphemous bombast before Chancellorsville or Meade's own threats to shoot the deserters at Gettysburg. The veterans listened with quiet indifference, while the "fresh fish" trembled in their stiff, new army brogans.

Right on time, the men pulled down their tents, formed up, and moved off into the darkness. Private Sly remembered, "Our Brigade was first — Hays 2nd followed.... I never saw the troops in such a jolly mood as they were that morning on the start cracking jokes such as how would my sweet heart like to see me harnessed up as I am and singing but that soon died out for wee had a clear road and fast time from the time shortly after we started."[20]

Lieutenant Colonel Weygant wrote, "Hour after hour we plodded on. Daylight came, the sun appeared, and at length, after a march of full twenty miles, we reached the Rapidan at Ely's Ford, and crossed on pontoons to the southern shore." A member of the 141st Pennsylvania wrote that the roads were good and the weather warm. "All were lame and footsore, but there were very few stragglers, although the roads were strewn with overcoats and blankets."[21]

"About a mile beyond the river an aide met us with the order, 'File to the right and eat your breakfast without delay.' It was now ten o'clock. At eleven we were moving forward again toward Chancellorsville, and at two P.M. bivouacked on the old battle field." The supply and ammunition train, said to be four thousand wagons long, would follow the 2nd Corps over the pontoon bridge at Ely's Ford. Colonel Weygant took this as an indication that, once across the Rapidan, Grant had no intention of turning back.[22]

General Ward and his staff dismounted and sat under a tree by the side of the road. It was not until all the troops had passed that Sly realized why Ward had chosen that particular spot. The general pointed out that there were graves near the tree. "They were sunken in and partly filled with leaves but the bones of one hand and arm with some of the sleeve uncovered." According to Sly, "That is what brought the Genl down by me." He and his staff were shielding from view the graves of the dead for "wee were then on the same ground that wee fought at Chancellorsville."[23]

Ward's Brigade came to a halt at Fairview, a melancholy place to spend the afternoon to say the least. "A quarter of a mile to our right ran that little stream, at the edge of the woods, the shores of which, just a year and a day before, were moistened with the warm blood of nearly two hundred Sons of Orange, about fifty of whom, with their wounds healed to honorable scars, were again on duty with the regiment."[24] Some of the men started down toward the stream to fill their canteens but stopped short. The way was barred by the "bleached bones of their dead comrades." Shallow graves, a year of rain and flood, and the sheer number of casualties made decent interment impossible. Bones and skulls were scattered about all over the place, the last earthly remains of "many a comrade who ... seemed to have so quietly waited our coming to bury them."[25] The Wilderness, just as foreboding and gloomy as the year before, would soon have new horrors to repel the visitor. Mighty armies were again on the march; when they found each other, the woods would be home to thousands more soldiers' graves.

Stephen Crane, in *The Red Badge of Courage*, expressed what must have been a common sentiment among the Orange Blossoms as they looked around this haunted place. In a scene from the novel, Private Henry Fleming awoke on this very ground — for the novel was set at Chancellorsville — and mistook his sleeping comrades for the dead.

> The gaunt, careworn features and dusty figures were made plain by this quaint light at the dawning but it dressed the skin of the men in corpselike hues and made the tangled limbs appear pulseless and dead. The youth started up with a little cry when his eyes first swept over this motionless mass of men, thick-spread upon the ground, pallid, and in strange postures. His disordered mind interpreted the hall of the forest as a charnel place. He believed for an instant that he was in the house of the dead.... In a second, however, he achieved his proper mind. He saw that this somber picture was not a fact of the present, but a mere prophecy.[26]

Captain Murray wrote to his father, "I have been over the old field — seen the place where I was wounded, the identical bog on which I was kneeling when I fell and the place I was carried to by our boys. Our dead were but partially buried, and skulls and bones lay about in great profusion. I found a skull where Shawcross fell with a hole in the forehead just where he was shot. Captain Crist found an India rubber blanket marked with the name of the first man who fell in his Co. It made my heart sick to look over the ground." Murray picked some wildflowers and found a few weather-worn pages from a Bible on the ground where Company B stood during the battle; he enclosed the mementos in the letter home.[27]

After supper, orders came for the next day's march. General Ward was "to have the troops awakened at 3 am cook and get breakfast and ready to move at 430 am." At about midnight, the adjutant general rode up with additional orders which he read to Ward. Sly was nearby and heard that "Hancocks corps the 2nd to move down the Brock Road to Tods Tavern and their throw out his right connect with Warrens left at Parkers Store and our left to the Po River it was about 8 miles from where wee lay to the tavern."[28]

This would put them near the southern verge of the worst of the entangling forest. The right of Warren's 5th Corps was to connect to the north with Sedgwick's 6th Corps then forming at Old Wilderness Tavern. According to Weygant, had Grant been able to move to this position unmolested, he would have been facing Lee's line at Mine Run and would be in control of the Brock Road which led to Spotsylvania Court House and out of the Wilderness. The men of the 124th were "directed to prepare and eat their breakfast, buckle on their accoutrements, and remain in readiness to move at a moment's notice — every armed man in the ranks."[29]

But the carefully laid plans of Humphreys, Meade, and Grant were about to come unhinged. To the west, Lee intended neither to allow the enemy to move leisurely around his flank nor to take cover behind the Mine Run defenses. He would instead launch his three corps directly at Grant's exposed right flank as the Yankee army moved into position. Why did he choose to attack? The answer was quite simply that he had no other choice. To take the defensive against this new Yankee commander must ultimately lead to defeat. Just as in other battles, Lee's boldness was borne of desperation, something well understood by Stonewall Jackson exactly one year before and but a few miles to the east at Chancellorsville. Then as now, it would not be enough to drive the Yankees back across the river; they would simply call up more men and supplies and be ready to fight again. Only the annihilation of this Federal army would save the Confederacy and Lee knew it.

Especially vulnerable was the Union 5th Corps, which was in the path of two Confederate corps. If Lee could break up Warren's divisions and seize an important crossroads nearby, he would isolate Hancock's Corps before it could reach the field. And if he could get General James Longstreet up quickly enough and onto the Yankee flank, the result might be a truly decisive victory.

By five o'clock on the morning of May 5, Hancock's Corps was on the road. "We moved forward at a moderate gait, and with occasional short halts, past the ruins of the old Chancellor mansion and along the Fredericksburg plank for about two miles; when we reached, and changing direction to the right and quickening our pace, pushed forward along the Catharine Furnace road." The charismatic leader of the Union 2nd Corps was in his element. The wound he'd suffered at Gettysburg had not completely healed, but it did not keep him out of the saddle. He rode among his men, a "stirring figure."[30] Despite Hancock's shining demeanor, the pace was reduced to an "agonizing crawl" as the morning heat began to take its toll. "The sun's rays were exceedingly warm, and before eight o'clock men began to stagger from the ranks and sink down by the roadside overcome by the heat."[31]

An hour or two earlier, off to the west, General Warren was surprised to learn that Confederates were advancing along the Orange Turnpike against his picket line. At first he thought it was just a feint to distract him or an overreaction by jumpy skirmishers. Just to be cautious, he sent a dispatch off to Meade. Within a short time it was clear that this was no mere distraction. Large numbers of enemy soldiers could be seen filing into the woods on either side of the turnpike, deploying for battle. When Meade heard that the enemy was "in some force" just two miles west of Wilderness Tavern, he ordered Warren to halt the march south and attack. As soon as Grant got news of the developments along the Turnpike, he endorsed Meade's order with the words, "If any opportunity presents itself of pitching into a part of Lee's army, do so without giving time for disposition."[32]

Meanwhile, Hancock's Corps made steady progress. Ward's Brigade reached Todd's Tavern at about 9 A.M. with the head of the 2nd Corps about a mile beyond. Birney's Division was ordered to mass in an open field just south of the tavern with a "strong picket line" thrown out to the front. "As soon as the pickets were posted we stacked arms; and while the majority threw themselves down by the gun stacks, not a few old soldiers scouted the idea of lying down to rest until they had first fortified themselves against the scorching rays of the sun by 'getting outside of a pint cup of piping hot Old Java.'"[33]

During the morning and early afternoon, the 5th Corps engaged elements of Ewell's Corps on the Turnpike and Hill's Corps on the Plank Road. Warren's men got into exactly the kind of fighting General Humphreys's plan was designed to avoid: close quarters shootouts where the enemy could not be seen and where numbers of men and artillery mattered little. Precisely because Warren could not see what was in front of him, his attacks were disjointed, flanks were uncovered to raking enemy fire, and a coordinated effort seemed beyond his grasp. Some eyewitnesses described the region not as a forest or even as a wilderness but as a jungle. Units like the Iron Brigade fell back under the pressure for the first time in its history. If the soldiers of storied Iron Brigade could be routed in the Wilderness, what chance for success had lesser men?[34]

The bloodletting achieved little except the entanglement of more and more Union soldiers who should have been marching south. To relieve the crisis, General Sedgwick's 6th Corps reinforced Warren from the north while Hancock was ordered to cancel his march west and head up the Brock Road to reinforce Warren from the south.

The Federal command realized that the intersection of the Brock Road and the Orange Plank Road was a key point on the battlefield. If the Confederates seized it, the Union army would be split; if the Yankees got there first, their lines of communication would be secure and they could launch attacks from that location.

At about 10:30 A.M., General George Getty was detached from the 6th Corps and ordered to march his division to the crossroads, there to hold on until Hancock's Corps arrived. But the messages between Meade and Hancock were delayed. Earlier, Meade sent an order to the 2nd Corps commander to halt at Todd's Tavern, but the message took over two hours in transit. By the time it arrived, the head of the 2nd Corps was well beyond the tavern on the Catharpin Road. At the same time Getty was ordered to march, another message went to Hancock ordering him to countermarch to Todd's Tavern and head north on the Brock Road. The order was over an hour in transit.[35] In the meantime, Getty and his staff arrived at the crossroads quite literally as enemy skirmishers were moving in to seize the prize. The Union officers and their aides stood fast until the first of Getty's brigades, winded and dusty, moved into line of battle and began sending volleys at the enemy. Everything now depended on Getty's three brigades holding until Hancock and the 2nd Corps arrived.[36]

Back near Todd's Tavern, Private Sly watched as "a mounted staff officer came riding along enquiring for Genl Hancock." Off in the distance to the right could be heard the low rumble of heavy firing as Warren's men clashed with the lead Confederate units pushing along the Orange Turnpike toward the crucial Brock Road intersection. While the Orange County men rested, some eating and others trying to sleep, they heard a commotion. Up galloped another staff officer, "his horse white with foam," asking the whereabouts of General Hancock. "Wee knew what that meant," Sly wrote. Hancock called for his staff and ordered a countermarch quick time back to Todd's Tavern and up the Brock Road.[37] Birney's Division had been at the rear of the column. When the countermarch was ordered, everyone simply executed an about face, placing Birney's Division at the head of the column as it started up the Brock Road to battle.[38]

Colonel Weygant wrote, "As we hurried forward the artillery firing became more and yet more distinct, but it was irregular and not very heavy. We were of the opinion that our column was marching toward the scene of a brisk cavalry skirmish, but ere long there was borne back to us a dull, heavy, and continuous roar, which told of something more serious and deadly."[39]

General Hays's Brigade led Birney's Division with Ward's Brigade right behind. "Then is when the fun commenced," wrote Sly, "on a narrow road through thick wood and brush and all of our corps artillery strung along that road at times hard for a singel horsman to get by."[40] At about noon Meade sent another message to Hancock ordering him: "Move out the plank road toward Parker's Store, and, supporting Getty, drive the enemy beyond Parker's Store, and occupy the place and unite with Warren on the right of it." The order showed that Meade did not fully understand where Hancock was or how long it would take him to get untangled, countermarch, and up the Brock Road to Getty's position. To make matters worse, the order went astray and did not reach Hancock until mid-afternoon.[41]

"Proceeding ahead of my command to the junction of the Brock road and Orange plank road," Hancock wrote, "I there met Brigadier-General Getty, commanding Second Division, Sixth Corps, who, with a part of his division, had encountered the enemy's advance at that point, and after a sharp contest had taken possession of the crossroad."[42]

Birney's Division marched "with closed ranks and without slackening its pace, for an hour and a half, it reached, and was formed in line at right angles with, and on the east side of, the Orange plank road." According to Hancock, his lead units moved into position at about 2 P.M., forming two lines of battle along the Brock Road to the left of Getty's Division. In the woods to the front, Union soldiers were skirmishing with Hill's Confederates. "As soon as our line was completed we stacked arms, and in a few moments, notwithstanding the occasional whistle of a passing bullet and the scorching rays of the sun, scores of the Orange Blossoms were lying fast asleep by their gun-stacks."[43]

Colonel Weygant watched as Mott's Division came up and

> moved on past us and formed line in the woods west of the plank road. Presently a detachment of engineers, accompanied by a strong body of pioneers, advanced a short distance through the brush on the west side of the Brock road, and began throwing up a line of breastworks. Those of us who were awake looked on in momentary expectation of an order to move forward and "lend a hand"; but there was other and more perilous work awaiting us. About four o'clock a most terrific crashing of riflery in the woods in front, and so near that the enemy's bullets whistled over our heads, caused our men to spring to their feet with such alacrity that in less than a minute Birney's entire command had taken arms and was ready for action.[44]

"Mott's and Gibbon's divisions, coming up rapidly, took their position on Birney's left in the same formation." Thus Hancock deployed his men from the crossroads covered by Getty, south along the Brock Road, ending his line with artillery posed "on some high, clear ground in front of the Brock road. This elevated ground commanded the country for some distance to the right and left covering the Fredericksburg and Orange Court-House Railroad in front." Orders had been issued to the division commanders to start building earthworks as soon as they arrived — works that would play a critical role in the battle to come. "This was accomplished without delay. Commencing at the point where my right joined General Getty's left, a substantial line of breastworks was constructed of earth and logs the whole length of my line of battle, running along the Brock road until the line diverged to the right."[45]

Thus began a pattern of digging, described by historian Earl J. Hess as "a virtual explosion in the use of fieldworks" that would continue on both sides until the last days of the war.[46] Field fortifications were nothing new to the eastern armies but it would be different after May 5, 1864. Hess argues that it would be Grant's decision to keep his army in close contact with enemy that would bring about the change. To compensate for his lack of numbers, Lee would need strong fortifications to stem the Yankee tide. Grant would need earthworks to hold key positions with fewer men so that he could hit his enemy's works with massive, concentrated strength or maneuver around them.[47]

The regimental historian of the 141st Pennsylvania of Ward's Brigade, Chaplain David Craft, wrote that "Birney's Division was on the left of Getty, the line facing westward with Ward's Brigade on the right, and Hays' on the left of it." He strongly asserted in his history — so strongly that other accounts must have conflicted with his — that the right of the 141st rested on the Plank Road at the start of battle on May 5 and, when the battle ended at dark, his regiment still had its flank on the Plank Road, occupying the same position at dawn the next morning. He further stated that Ward's Brigade was formed in two lines, the 141st at the right of the rear line. "The front line was about fifty rods [275 yards] west of the Brock road, and the second line about eight rods [44 yards] back of it." Craft noted that a creek, most likely Poplar Run, was "midway between the two lines of battle."[48] The location of the 124th New York, in all likelihood, was in the front line.

The fighting done by Warren's 5th Corps to the north earlier in the day had accomplished little. Grant and Meade called upon Hancock to advance against the Confederates posted along the Plank Road. In preparation for this attack, Birney was ordered to move his division north of Getty, connecting with Getty's right just as Mott's Division moved up to connect with Getty's left. This dangerous "double shift" maneuver was to be attempted while under fire. To complicate matters further, Getty received orders to advance before Birney could get fairly underway.[49]

Within thirty minutes of receiving his orders, and against his better judgment, Getty had his brigades moving west along the Orange Plank Road, two to the north of the road and one to the south. "About 4 P.M. Getty's skirmishers disappeared into the woods and aroused sharp fire from Heth's restless pickets."[50] Waiting beyond the pickets, dug in and hiding in the forest, were four brigades of General Heth's Division, 6,500 men in all. It did not take them long to shred the Yankee advance. Hancock wrote,

> Finding that General Getty had met the enemy in great force, I ordered General Birney to advance his command (his own and Mott's divisions) to support the movement of Getty at once, although the formation I had directed to be made before carrying out my instructions to advance was not yet completed. General Birney immediately moved forward on General Getty's right and left, one section of Ricketts' battery (Co. F, First Pennsylvania Artillery) moving down the plank road just in rear of the infantry. The fight became very fierce at once. The lines of battle were exceedingly close, the musketry continuous and deadly along the entire line.[51]

The nature of the ground, confusing orders at the start of the advance, and plenty of Confederates, all led to a "scattered formation, thereby inviting severe retaliation." The fighting was so heavy that Getty came to the conclusion that he had taken on all three divisions of Hill's Corps and that they were pressing hard to turn the left of his line. Getty's brigade commanders called on him for help but there were no reserves at hand. Getty in turn called for reinforcements from Birney, who advanced Hays's Brigade behind Getty and to his right. Hays's disciplined regiments survived the initial shock of contact with Heth's men, then settled into a brutal slugging match.[52] Private Sly had watched as Ward and Hays deployed their men. At about 5 P.M. Hays was ordered forward, his left resting on the Plank Road, his right extending as far as possible. Hays led a large brigade made up of veteran 3rd Corps units, some of which had served under Birney at Gettysburg.

Sly wrote,

> Genl Ward and his staff got up the Plank road before Hays went in for when Gen Hays started to go to the front he called to Ward "good bye Ward." That was the last wee ever saw Genl Hays alive.... While our Brig was being formed Genl Ward and myself were dismounted along the Brock Road near the Plank when Lieut Doughty came in and reported that Capt Nash and Lieut Lee of our staff had bin captured they had run right in the Rebbel line for the saplings and brush was so thick in places you could scarcely see ten feet ahead of you nor could hardly walk.[53]

With the capture of these two aides, Ward had but two others, Captain Doughty and Lieutenant Wells. They immediately went to work placing the brigade's regiments into line. When this was done, they reported to the general who ordered the skirmish line to advance. "They very quickly ran in a Hornets nest." Ward mounted and said to Sly, "You stay here with the collors and if orders come tell them I am at the front." The courier from Orange County hesitated. "Gen'l I want to go with you." Ward smiled saying, "All right, give the flag to one of the other orderlies." They spurred their horses up the Brock Road and turned onto the Orange Plank Road toward where the fighting was "warming up finely at the front. It was then that wee met the four men carrying the dead body of Genl Hays. Wee all got off the road and took off our Hats as they

Wilderness, May 5, 1864

During the afternoon, the 2nd Corps marched north on the Brock Road to the important junction with the Plank Road. As Hancock's brigades arrived on the field, they formed facing west and moved forward into the heavy underbrush. The Union attacks were difficult to coordinate under such conditions, and were made piecemeal, frittering away their advantage in numbers. While difficult to confirm, the 124th New York was probably in the front rank of Ward's Brigade.

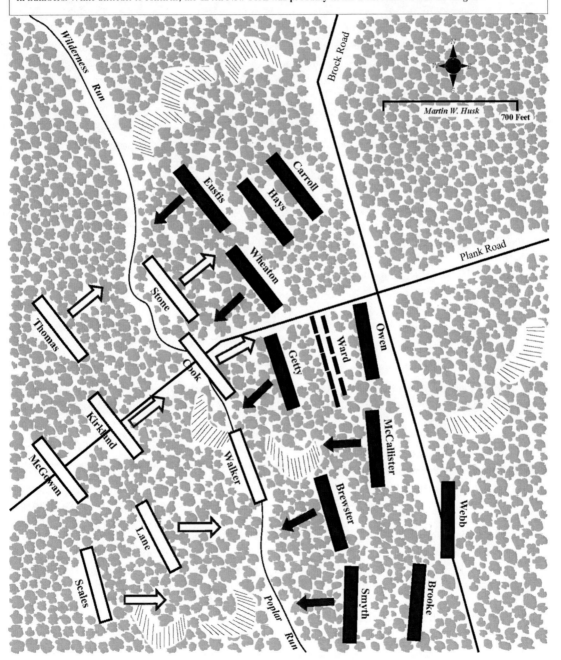

carried him by the Genl felt verry bad." Captain Doughty dropped back and rode beside Sly. All who had seen the body of General Hays carried to the rear on a stretcher, the corner of an army blanket covering his face, had been affected by his death, but Captain Doughty told Sly he felt Ward had been "unnerved" by it. "They were great friends also Genl Sedgwick the whole three of them served togather in one regt in the Mexican War."[54]

Meanwhile, Colonel Lewis A. Grant's Brigade of Getty's Division, composed of five Vermont regiments, moved out just south of the Plank Road and, like so many others, used the road as an anchor for the right flank. Grant's men stumbled into a buzz saw of Confederate fire. "With a skill and promptitude that equals the finest feats of troop leadership on the Wilderness field," Grant sorted out his men, established a line in the tangle of brush and trees, and sent frantic appeals to the rear for help.[55]

Birney, who had just been delegated command of Mott's Division as well as his own, acted quickly. The "double shift" as historian Edward Steere called it, was already underway — Mott was moving his two brigades to the right to connect with Getty's left and one of Birney's own brigades was already fighting on Getty's right. The other of Birney's brigades, that of Hobart Ward, was halted and formed up in two lines of battle facing west. Then Birney sent what must have been Ward's second line forward to help Grant. The 141st Pennsylvania, 40th New York, and 20th Indiana moved into position behind Grant and prepared to advance. The 141st moved to the right of Grant's line to support the 2nd and 4th Vermont, while the 40th New York and the 20th Indiana moved in behind the 5th Vermont on the precariously held left to help stabilize the line.[56] Ward still held a sizable force of six regiments in reserve: 3rd Maine, 86th New York, 124th New York, 99th Pennsylvania, 110th Pennsylvania, and 2nd U.S. Sharpshooters.

Craft wrote that Ward's Brigade moved to the attack.

> After having gone a mile on the "double quick" the brigade got into position and the front line commenced the attack, while the second line began to throw up breastworks of logs and dirt. The second line was then ordered to lie down, but the bullets flew like hail among them, killing and wounding a number of men. A half an hour later there was a slight lull in the firing and the second line moved to the front, relieved the first line, and the battle was renewed with great fury.[57]

On both sides of the Plank Road, Getty's men were getting support from Hays' Brigade on the right and a portion of Ward's Brigade on the left. Now the two veteran brigades of Mott's Division moved off the Brock Road, advancing into the woods beyond. Historian Edward Steere noted that Mott's advance posed a lethal threat to Heth's men, a threat that might have turned the battle against Lee. Instead, Mott's regiments became entangled not with just the brambles and underbrush, but also with Union troops already in position to their front. The rightmost regiment in Mott's right brigade found itself behind the leftmost regiment of Grant's Brigade and the same was true on Mott's left and center. Regiments lost their alignment with each other just as they were hit with heavy volleys seeming to come from nowhere. Stacked up as they were, they could not effectively return fire.[58]

Steere called this "fatal crowding" and it points to the need for regiments to be proficient at drill and to be able to bring that proficiency to the battlefield. Mott's regiments advanced "by right of companies to the front" which put each of ten companies into column of fours marching forward, all ten parallel with each other. The maneuver is a good one for crossing rough terrain or passing through a line of skirmishers, just as Mott's men were about to attempt. To achieve the desired result, the heads of each column must stay abreast of each other and the columns must not crowd together. When the regiment reaches the point at which the colonel wants to reform the line of battle, he orders "by companies into line."[59] If the intervals have been kept, the regimental battle line will deploy in a matter of seconds. Steere postulates that as the columns moved forward, there was "an inevitable tendency of parallel company columns, advancing in a general right oblique [forty five degrees to the right], to converge on the direction held by the right element of the formation."[60] When the men were ordered into line of battle there was not room enough to do so and an orderly formation quickly became a mob of men who did not know which way to go.

Just at that crucial point,

the unseen enemy opened a double volley, which sent thousands of bullets crashing through the woods into their faces. This fire, so sudden, so unexpected, and so deadly, was returned in but a feeble and scattering manner, because the men were so generally separated from their officers and so far apart from each other, besides being perplexed in forcing their way through the tangled forest, that they were comparatively without organization. The enemy answered with another terrific volley, which told with deadly effect upon the foremost groups struggling along to get into some sort of fighting array, killing and wounding a large number and straightway forcing the rest to fall back.[61]

One officer described it as a rolling wave, falling back toward the Brock Road. "All efforts to rally them short of the breastworks were in vain," he wrote.[62] The dramatic retreat opened a gap between Getty's left and Mott's right. There was but one unit on the scene that could fill that gap: the remaining regiments of Ward's Brigade. They were still back near the earthworks so they had to "double quick down the Brock road for half a mile, and then changing direction by the left flank, sprang over some rifle pits on the west side of the road, and plunged into the woods" to help stiffen the line.[63] Steere mistakenly identified the "144th New York" as being on the left of the line. There can be no doubt that it was the 124th New York that held the front line of Ward's Brigade as they advanced into the fight.[64]

"The emergency was critical," wrote Steere, "but Ward's reserve proved equal to the occasion. Its line moved off by the left flank to get into position. It was a difficult maneuver, similar to the one which Mott had attempted and failed to accomplish. Scores of Mott's men hastening back through the woods broke through the line of the 124th New York." Ward was moving his men forward "by the left of companies to the front" the same as Mott had done but with the left of the company leading the way instead of the right.[65]

"We were none too soon," wrote Lieutenant Colonel Weygant. Union wounded were streaming to the rear, among them unwounded members of Mott's Division "falling back in disorder." They were easily identified by the white diamond corps badges, the mark of the Second Division, 3rd Corps which they still wore on their caps. One could hardly blame them for their actions as behind them came a "wild storm of bullets, which rattled through the brush, pattered against the trees, and hissed and whistled through the air." The Orange Blossoms halted, the ten company commanders hustling their men forward into line just as they had been taught to do by Colonel Ellis. They quickly dressed the line, pulled in some of Mott's men, and moved forward again, "opening a counter fire as we went, which soon turned the tide of battle at that point."[66]

Colonel Lyman, of Meade's staff, was with Hancock when an officer rode up bearing the news. "Sir! Gen. Mott's division has broken and is coming back!" Hancock bellowed, "Tell him to stop them!" but then, as was typical of his leadership style, he rode forward to rally the troops himself.[67]

Lyman put his finger on one reason for what he called the "disgraceful" behavior of Mott's men: demoralization due to poor leadership and the breakup of the 3rd Corps. Since the departure of Sickles, charismatic and a good leader despite his many faults, the 3rd Corps seemed to have lost its way. What was needed was a general who could call up the old days and use the pride felt by the men who had marched under the diamond corps badge to inspire them. Birney might well have done it had he been given the chance. Instead the 3rd Corps got French and Prince, a drunk and a dullard, who symbolized a good part of the problem in the Army of the Potomac. The final blow was to disband one of the great fighting organizations of that army. Regiments and brigades used to fighting alongside each other were shuffled off to different commands. Hooker, Sickles, Butterfield, and others have been excoriated by historians for their political intrigue, but the breakup of the 3rd Corps in the name of organizational efficiency was a mistake that bore bitter fruit in the Wilderness.

The Union line near the intersection of the Plank Road and Brock Road was at this critical juncture reinforced by three brigades of Gibbons's Division, Hancock's Corps. General Joshua Owen's Brigade of mostly Pennsylvania troops, coming up to relieve Grant's Vermonters, was stalled by a vigorous enemy counterattack just below the Plank Road. "Ward's reserve line (five volunteer regiments and the 2d U.S. Sharpshooters), which had moved into the gap between Mott and Getty, probably lent material support to Owen's left." This reserve line would have included the 124th New York.[68] Again the attacks were uncoordinated but served to tip the balance. Now the Confederates were falling back. "Slowly but steadily they retired before our fresh and withering fire, contesting every foot of ground. We soon began to pass over their dead and wounded, but we left the ground strewn with not a few of our own men. A little farther on we began to take prisoners, sometimes singly, and sometimes in squads of two and three. We could seldom see the enemy's battle-line because of the denseness of the foliage; but powder flashes from the opposing lines often told that they were but a few yards apart."[69]

After advancing about a mile into the woods, pushing the enemy before them all the way, Ward's men halted at the edge of a swale. The low ground in front of them was covered with a dense growth of trees.

> The trunks were not larger than one's wrist. They were from eight to fifteen feet high, with no limbs or foliage except a small tuft of leaves on their extreme tops, and stood so closely together that it was only by pushing them apart that a man could make his way through them. The men of the 124th now caught sight of the enemy's battle-line along their entire front; and in the midst of this — as they at the time appropriately named it — hoop-pole forest, poured into that line such a destructive fire that a considerable number threw themselves on the ground and cried for quarter; whereupon a volunteer skirmish line was ordered out, and brought in upwards of twenty prisoners.[70]

General Ward and his staff, riding west along the Plank Road, turned off to the left, plunging into the forest. "Then the fun was in to get through the brush mounted but we worked our way to the front and down in a hollow by a brook their wee halted."[71] In the slight depression they found cover from the stray bullets zipping past. Ward's Brigade was posted beyond a creek on high ground. To the right, Sly could see Colonel Egan and the 40th New York lying a few feet back from the main line for protection. General Ward told Sly to go to Egan and tell him to move up and open immediately on the enemy. As Sly got ready to go, Captain Doughty warned him to dismount as he made an inviting target on horseback but Sly, a superb horseman, chose to stay in the saddle. He rode up to Colonel Egan and delivered the order. Writing years later, Sly could still hear the "sharp quick commands. 'Attention 40th New York! Forward march! Halt! On the center dress! Ready! Aim! Fire!' and they were back at us I tell you in quick time." It was then that Sly was hit in the head by an enemy round that "took off some of my scalp and it made me feel funny.... I tell you it hurt, seemed as though some one hit me on the head with a Hammer." Sly would have fallen from his horse but for Colonel Egan and some of the men from the 40th New York who grabbed him and eased him to the ground.

With their help Sly got himself to the rear "in quick time for it was a warm place" and back to where Ward was waiting. All who saw him thought he was gravely wounded and the general ordered him to the hospital. The blood ran down his face nearly blinding him but he ignored the order and made ready to continue his duties. "I bled like a trouper," he recalled.[72]

The battle continued on the right and left of the 124th New York; the skirmishers in front kept up a brisk fire until well after dark. Finally both armies stopped shooting "as by mutual consent" and lay down to get some rest for the battle.

> Full twelve thousand men lay dead, dying, or seriously wounded in those most dismal woods, and yet this was but the first scene of the first act of that bloody drama, called the Campaign of the Wilderness.

The 124th had taken thirty-two prisoners, including one commissioned officer. It had suffered no loss in prisoners captured or in men killed outright, but twenty-three of the best and bravest in its ranks had been severely wounded, a number of them mortally.[73]

"It was sickening to see the Wounded come back that could walk with some help," wrote Sly, "and stop at that brook and bath their wounds they were a bloody lot and I was glad when the Genl called for his horse and rode out of that place. I mounted and went with him." The two riders headed for Birney's headquarters near the intersection where they remained until sundown.[74] The pickets on both sides were alert all night but neither side fired on those who moved up to fill their canteens from the sluggish stream that ran between the lines.[75]

Battered as the Union troops were, the Confederates were just as battle-worn. Their attacks late in the day were made in a desperate attempt to hold back the Yankee tide. General Hill's men still held the high ground, such as it was, and were dug in, but the sheer weight of Union troops made a breakthrough all but inevitable unless reinforcements arrived soon. Their only hope was Longstreet, who was coming up from the southwest, but as yet he was nowhere in sight.

Long after the sun set, Sly, minus a piece of his scalp, was at Birney's headquarters, still on duty with General Ward. Captain Doughty came in to tell Ward that he had put in every man in the brigade except the 2nd U.S. Sharpshooters, a regiment the general had been determined to hold back for an emergency. Uneasy at the report, Ward sent Lieutenant Wells to General Birney asking for a regiment to fill in the lines. Sly remembered that "he got what he asked for and with them came Capt Briscoe of Birney's staff. The Genl brightened up as soon as he saw Briscoe. He wanted to know the whole situation. Briscoe says 'Genl they hold us fast and they seem heavier than we are' and from what he could learn from prisoners that Hills corps was all up and if that was the case and they made a dash they would break through here a sure as Hell."[76]

Captain Briscoe told Ward he was going back to headquarters to report. The dark and quiet settled in over the field, broken only by sporadic firing from jumpy pickets who hadn't heard of the unofficial truce. After what had been a harrowing day, Sly saw the general visibly relax. Then, without warning, "the heaviest volley we heard yet" filled the night. Ward called for his horse and together he and Sly made for the front. They found Birney who was sure the enemy was about to make a dash at the crossroads. "They got quite some troops their in quick time as that was the key to the whole line, the Brock Plank road, and Lee wanted it as will bee seen how hard he worked for it next day. Then every thing was quiet that was about 9 P.M."[77]

As he lay on the ground, Sly's scalp wound began to bother him. "Then the darkeys came up with supper for the Genl and staff. Then is when I felt hungry had nothing to eat since 4 am in the morning but a couple of sandwiches had put in my saddle bag." All of Sly's other rations were back with the wagon train and there was no way he was going to find them that night. "When the darkey brought Genl his plate and a tin cup of coffee he told him to bring Sly some and then called Stinson his foot orderly to bring a Bottle of whiskey. He took a drink and told him to give me some, that was the first drink I saw the Genl take that day. What a feast, cold boiled ham potatoes with the skins on cup of good coffee with sugar and condensed milk. I ate with the Genl every day after that untill 12th then the Genl left."[78]

When Capt. Briscoe returned to Ward's headquarters, he told them there would be "hard work" tomorrow because Longstreet would surely be on the field by then. He noted that Burnside was not yet up to support the three Federal corps that had been "handled rough" and "well pounded" as he said in a jovial tone. As he listened to the exchange, Sly rolled up in his blanket, letting the whiskey ease the pain in his scalp. At about midnight General Birney came over to Ward's camp asking about casualties. Three regiments had not delivered their reports to brigade headquarters as yet and Sly, head wound or not, was sent out into the darkness to find them.

He felt his way west along the Orange Plank Road, fearing he would run into the enemy picket line at any moment. Up ahead, he spotted some stretcher bearers carrying their grim loads to the rear. They told him to keep on going over a ridge then down into a hollow by a stream. "I soon found them ... and got the returns and started back." Sly handed the paperwork to the brigade adjutant, who tallied up the numbers. The officer said of the 3,400 men in the brigade at the start of the fight, only 2,000 were now fit for duty. As the brutal statistics were sinking in, an order arrived from 2nd Corps headquarters. Each brigade was to send an officer to the Plank Road/Brock Road junction to round up all the skulkers and deadbeats they could find and return them to duty on the line. This was soon followed by an order from army headquarters to wake the men at 3:30 A.M., have them eat breakfast, and be ready to move against the enemy one hour later. Grant intended to press the attack.[79]

At headquarters, the talk was of tomorrow's battle. General Grant expressed no criticism of the performance of the army and issued orders to mass Union troops against Hill, who was dug in on the Orange Plank Road. Grant would hit him from the north with Warren's 5th Corps and from the south with Hancock's 2nd Corps. Burnside's 9th Corps was ordered forward to close the gap between the two and to surge to crush Hill before Longstreet could arrive. As Sly earlier noted, officers were sent to the rear to gather up any man who could carry a rifle—including artillery crews whose guns were useless in the heavy undergrowth.[80]

General Hancock wrote, "During the night of the 5th, I received orders to move upon the enemy again at 5 A.M. on the 6th." General Birney, who had done well in the fighting on May 5, would again command the right wing of the 2nd Corps line, leading his own men as well as those of Mott and Getty. "Before the hour at which the attack was directed to commence had arrived I was informed that Longstreet's corps was passing up the Catharpin road to attack my left flank." Hancock made ready to block any attack on his left by placing General Gibbon in command on the flank and by posting "a strong skirmish line" and artillery to cover the road.[81]

Up near the Orange Plank Road, General Hancock's men waited for the signal to advance. In the front line with its right on the Orange Plank Road was Ward's Brigade and the 124th New York. To Ward's left was posted Hays' Brigade, now commanded by Colonel Walker of the 4th Maine, and beyond Walker was McAlister's Brigade. Behind those two brigades were four more stretching from McAllister's left to beyond the road on the right. A third line of three brigades was on or near the Plank Road stretching back nearly to the Brock Road. To the north were four brigades under the command of General Wadsworth. This powerful formation was perfectly positioned to smash into Hill's front and flank.

Lieutenant Colonel Weygant remembered that the army commander "directed that a general advance be made at five A.M.,—each corps attacking vigorously whatever it found in its front.... Just what was before us no one in the Union army knew; and many of our brigadiers if questioned as to where their own commands were, could have but pointed toward the front and answered 'yonder.'" Lack of information aside, Grant's orders were clear: "Attack along the whole line at five o'clock."[82]

Sly was at headquarters "waiting for the signall gun but she did not come until 5 when our line was all in motion in 5 min and bye half past 6:00 wee had driven the enemy over one mile [and] had got out of the Wilderness when we come to their works and wee come to a halt."[83]

The dawn attack took most Confederate units by surprise. Exhausted by the fighting on May 5, few of Hill's men dug in but simply dropped where they found themselves and went to sleep. Many did not take the time to clean their weapons, which were fouled and could not be fired at the advancing Yankees. Others, out of ammunition and expecting to be relieved at first light, were in no condition for the wave of blue that rolled toward them. When it hit, Lee's men fell back in disorder, piling up against each other until the retreat south of the Plank Road became a rout. The hasty withdrawal exposed units on the other side of the road to attack from the front by Hancock's men and the flank by Wadsworth's men advancing from the north.[84]

Colonel Weygant remembered the advance. "Hancock started a few minutes ahead of the prescribed time.... The 124th formed part of his advance line, which soon came up to, attacked, and, in the words of the Confederate historian Pollard, 'threw Heth's and Wilcox's divisions of Hill's corps in confusion, and pushed them back.'" The Orange Blossoms took fourteen prisoners, among them a captain who was trying to rally his men. The lines were so close together that Private Henry R. Turner, who stood in the front rank of Company I, was able to grab the officer by the collar and jerk him into the ranks of the 124th New York "with such force that when his captor loosened his hold he fell to the ground in a sitting posture striking so hard that his hat bounced from his head and his hair seemed to stand on end."[85]

As the fight progressed, Sly and Ward rode back along the Plank Road until they met General Birney and together they rode on to the junction with the Brock Road where they found General Hancock "all afire." Hancock called out, "Birney how is things on your front?" "Doing fine," came Birney's reply.[86]

Sly recognized Lieutenant Colonel Lyman of Meade's staff, who had "jest started to go," but as they rode up Lyman waited to hear the latest news from the front. "Hancock and Birney talked a minute when Hancock said 'Lyman tell Genl Mead wee are doing Handsome.' This was not latter than 7 A.M. then Hancock started back to the front very slowly."[87] As they drew near the brigade line, Sly was ordered to ride back up the road, find the 2nd U.S. Sharpshooters, and bring them forward. They were to form in a clear area in skirmish order "and stop all men not wounded" from going to the rear. Ward told Sly he "would find the regiment near the Plank Road ... for he had asked them to have their collers near the road so would be easy seen and after they had bin formed in rear for me to stay with them."[88]

Sly rode through the woods to the Brock Road. Just as he was about to turn at the junction with the Plank Road an officer hailed him saying a wounded Union colonel was asking for him. Sly rode a short distance back up the road where he found his regimental commander, Colonel Cummins. He dismounted and went to Cummins, who was wounded in the thigh, "suffering untold agony and crying." Cummins took him in a "death grip" and held him for a couple of minutes, "when they come to put him an ambulance ... every minute then seemed like a hour to me I tell you." Sly quickly mounted and raced down the Plank Road until he found the Sharp-shooters' colors planted near the road. "Told the Major my orders the regt was got out of their in quick time and doubled quick up the road and in the woods in rear of our line and staid their with them untill about 9 A.M." as ordered.[89]

Weygant claimed the 124th advanced about a mile and half, the enemy giving ground all the way. The regiment passed over twenty dead Confederates but lost about a dozen killed or wounded among their own men. "We did not cease firing when the halt was ordered, but kept a continuous shower of lead raining through the woods toward where we supposed the battle-line of the foe to be; for we could see nothing of it, though we were kept aware of its presence by the returning bullets, which continually sang about our ears, and occasionally felled to the ground one of our number."[90] The 124th must have drifted to the left, away from the Plank Road, because they did not see the large clearing to the right—the Widow Tapp farm, dominated by high ground on which were placed Confederate cannon. The clearing was so large that Sly, who was not with the 124th at that time, thought they had reached the edge of the Wilderness.

Hancock's advance had been stopped just short of the Tapp farm by units of Longstreet's Corps coming into the fight and by Hill's men rallying at the sight of reinforcements. Confederate prisoners being led to the rear identified themselves as members of Longstreet's Corps, answering the question as to his whereabouts and sending a chill through the Federal command.

Longstreet began planning his attack as soon as he came onto the field. He held the Federals in place east of the Tapp farm by attacking and creating the impression that he was pushing up the Plank Road. Meanwhile he sent scouting parties to find a way around the Yankee flank.

Wilderness, May 6, 1864

At 5:00 A.M. a massive Union attack was launched along the Plank Road. Ward's Brigade was at the front and drove the Confederates all the way to the Tapp Farm clearing. Just as success seemed within grasp, Longstreet launched a counterattack against the Union left. "All at once we heard that cussed Rebel yell," wrote Norman Sly as Confederate forces drove the Union forces all the way back to the Brock Road earthworks.

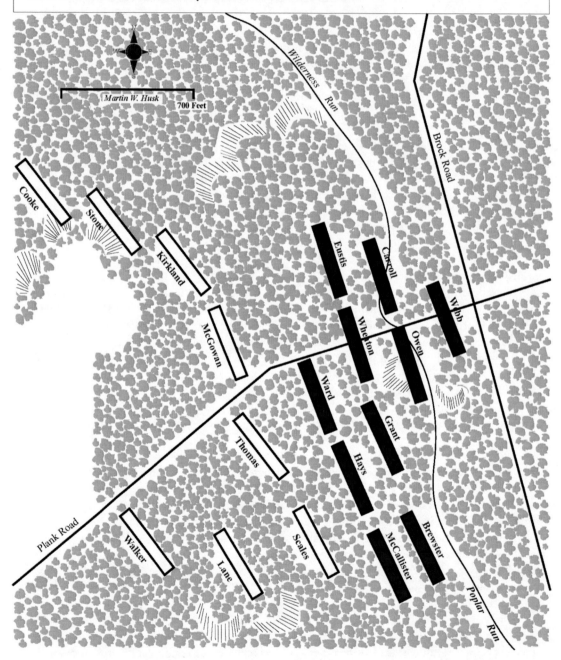

Martin W. Husk   700 Feet

As often happened in this kind of fighting, the advancing soldiers became as disorganized as those in retreat.

> The Union columns had become terribly mixed and disordered in their forward movement, under the excitement and bewilderment of battle, through woods so dense that at the best no body of troops could possibly preserve their alignment. In some cases they were heaped up in unnecessary strength; elsewhere great gaps appeared; men, and even officers, had lost their regiments in the jungles; the advance had not been, could not have been, made uniformly from right to left, and the line of battle ran here forward, and there backward, through the forest; thousands had fallen in the furious struggle; the men in front were largely out of ammunition.[91]

Pressing the attack became all but impossible. After an hour of heavy fighting and an advance of over a mile, the Union troops were stalled by exhaustion and enemy resistance. The Yankees were content to stop at the edge of the large clearing.

At about 9 A.M., Captain Daniel Sayer of Company E reported to Weygant that his men would soon be out of ammunition. Weygant told him to go to Colonel Cummins with the information, to which Sayer replied, "Why, Colonel Cummins was carried to the rear fifteen minutes ago seriously, and I am afraid, mortally wounded." Weygant was thunderstruck. He could not believe that Cummins had been wounded just a few feet from him and carried to the rear without his knowledge. He also realized that he was now the commanding officer of the 124th New York.[92]

The lull in the fighting was deceptive as it signaled not an end to the battle but another flanking movement against the Union line. Longstreet, his corps now massed at the Tapp farm, got the news he'd hoped to hear. His scouts had found a railroad right of way that had been cleared and graded but not further improved. The cut was known to the Yankees who had crossed it earlier in the day but they had not thought to use it themselves as an avenue of advance against the enemy. Longstreet seized upon it and sent four brigades around the Union left undetected. A little after ten o'clock these four brigades smashed into the exposed Union flank and quite literally rolled it up. So swift was the advance that the Yankees had not time to orient their lines to the left and as a consequence they could not bring fire to bear on Longstreet's men. Blue regiments collapsed in succession and made for the rear, exposing the flanks of the regiments to their right, which quickly dissolved in turn.

Sly remembered the moment when this took place. "All at once we heard that cussed Rebel yell off to our left. The first word was My God Longstreet is up and at us. That yell gave us the horrers. Back come the Genl ordering the sharpshooters up to the front line." The enemy to their front kept up a heavy fire but did not advance. Sly figured it out later on: they "only wanted to hold us all their from sending any troops to the left."[93]

Just before the flank attack started, a supporting line of Gibbon's men came up behind the 124th. The men quickly set to work kindling small fires to boil coffee. Weygant's men asked if they might do the same but the colonel would not let them leave the ranks for fear that they might be attacked at any moment. After the men to the rear finished breakfast, their commander agreed to exchange places with the 124th New York for a few minutes so that the Orange Blossoms might cook some breakfast.

> But before we had finished the meal a terrific racket broke out in the woods to our left, and bullets began to fly thick and fast above and among us, passing lengthwise of the Union line. The grand assault which Lee had intended to make at an early hour in the morning had come at last, and was led by Lieutenant General Longstreet in person. Six lines deep they come, striking first Frank's brigade on its exposed left flank, and hurling it back in disorder against the left of Mott's command, which was soon doubled up and disorganized; and the men of the various brigades, regiments and companies became so inseparably mixed, that all efforts to re-form them there among the trees and brush, in face of Longstreet's impetuous advance, proved unavailing.[94]

Private Sly thought it to be about 10 A.M. when he and General Ward met General Hancock back near the Brock Road. Hancock told them that his left had been smashed but that he still

held the Brock Road. "I tell you wee were anxious about the outcome." Ward called for reinforcements to stiffen his line but there were none to spare. Ward and Sly went back up to the
line, dismounted, and walked along the front of the brigade "where in places was not more than
a skirmish line. The Gen'l I don't recollect of saying a word and when wee got back to our horses
on this wood road and mounted he told the orderly to go back and find Doughty and tell him
he was here at the front."[95]

They were in a hollow and when they rode up a low rise to their front they saw the brigade
just below them, the left of the line stretching beyond a narrow wood road. Just then a staff
officer rode up asking for General Ward. "Here I am. What do you want?" came the brusque
reply. The rider said that General Hancock had sent him to find out where the left of the line
was located. Ward told Sly to take the officer out and show him. As the two men rode out between
the lines, the staff officer told Sly that the enemy was on the Brock Road and "was coming in line
of battle. I tell you I did not feel good at that news."

They rode out to where the left of the brigade line should have been and it became clear
why Hancock wanted the information: the enemy line was in sight. The officer instructed Sly
that the brigade was to be brought up to this point. "I started right back on a good run and
before I got to the Genl I thought and will say it — all Hell seemed to let loose."[96]

Weygant rushed his men back into line and had them change their front to the left, toward
the advancing enemy, no easy job while under fire in the tangled Wilderness. He did all he could
to stem the disaster but, as he later wrote,

> I might as well have tried to stop the flight of a cannon ball, by interposing the lid of a cracker box.
> Back pell-mell came the ever swelling crowd of fugitives, and the next moment the Sons of Orange were
> caught up as by a whirlwind, and broken to fragments; and the terrible tempest of disaster swept on
> down the Union line, beating back brigade after brigade, and tearing to pieces regiment after regiment,
> until upwards of twenty thousand veterans were fleeing, every man for himself, through the disorganizing
> and already blood-stained woods, toward the Union rear.[97]

Sly made no mention as to what happened to the staff officer but when he rode up to Ward,
the general wanted to know "what was up down their." He told Sly to "to go right back on a
good run with loose rein the way wee allways rode" and as the private approached the sharp bend
in the road he "run all most right in a fresh rebbel battle line." Sly tried to spin his mount around
to avoid what was surely death or capture. "Well sir, no time for thought then and if their was
ever a horse and rider turned a summersault in the air it was right their and then and when he
landed he went on his nose." It's not clear if Sly's horse had been shot or lost its footing. "I think
I gave him a yank in the bit but no moove in him but I tell you I mooved and run well." He
sprinted up to where he'd left General Ward just a couple of minutes before but he was gone.
"That was the first time that I ever heard so manny bullets and they were all fired low. I did not
stop to wait to see the Genl."[98]

Weygant and those men still with him halted about a mile to the rear. They turned about and
cobbled together a mixed force to halt the Confederate advance. He had Corporal Edwards unfurl
the colors, "but almost the next moment a heavy volley coming from the woods to our rear and
left, told that a fresh and unexpected body of the foe was close upon us, and away went our men
again in an instant. I now became thoroughly disheartened, and, abandoning all hopes of gathering
my command south of the Rapidan, sheathed my sword, and moved back with the rabble."[99]

Sly ran as fast as he could, "going all the time" he said, until he came up on a squad of men
with their colors and an officer. As Sly approached, about a hundred men came out of the woods
preparing to make a stand with the first group "when they poured in annother volley — that was
enough for me, back I got." If this group had been members of the 124th, Sly would surely have
identified them as such. All along the disorganized line, small groups of men and officers were
attempting to rally but were being quickly overrun by Longstreet's men.[100]

"The enemy, when he had forced us back full two miles, suddenly ceased firing. Our understanding of this fact at the time was, that the Confederate lines had become so broken and disorganized their commander deemed it expedient to halt and re-form them."[101] What actually happened was far more dramatic. A Confederate regiment, upon seeing Longstreet and his mounted headquarters staff through the haze of smoke and brush, mistook them for a group of Union officers and opened fire. Longstreet was shot through the neck, a wound assumed to be fatal, and reported as such throughout the rest of the day.[102]

"Press the enemy," urged Longstreet as he was carried to the rear, but it was not that easy. His coordinated attack on the front and flank of Hancock's men had been a wonderful success, but just as with the Union attacks, his men had become disorganized and intermingled. It would take hours to sort things out and renew the attack—and Lee had every intention of renewing the attack. In the meantime, Hancock was able to pull his men back to the protection of the Brock Road earthworks.[103] The wounding of Longstreet, in Weygant's opinion, was "an undisguised blessing to Grant's army."[104]

Weygant and his men continued on until they emerged from the woods into an area of "slashing," where the trees and brush had been cut to open up fields of fire. "Across this there suddenly loomed up a strong line of log breastworks, from the top of which several Union flags could be seen waving in the breeze, whereupon an old sailor in our ranks fitly expressed the feelings of all by shouting, 'Ship ahoy, land ahead, boys, land ahead!'"

The works did not look heavily manned but Weygant saw mounted aides and officers galloping up and down the Brock Road trying to position men as they came across the slashing. "Quickening our pace, we soon passed in through an opening, and found ourselves again on the Brock road. Along the south-western side of this, there stretched as far as the eye could penetrate in either direction, one of the strongest lines of temporary works it had ever been my fortune to stand behind." Staff officers directed the men to their units "so that in an incredibly short space of time Hancock's command was substantially re-formed, re-supplied with ammunition, and ready for action."[105]

After his brush with the enemy, Sly was moving in the same direction as everyone else when he came upon General Ward "trying to stop the men but nary stop. I told the Genl I had lost my horse. He said 'Sly I never expected to see you again.'" He took a horse from one of the orderlies and rode with Ward back toward the road junction where they found "officers begging of the men to fall in behind our works along the Brock road but they all seemed blind to their appeals." Finally the men began to rally and return to the earthworks. Sly wrote, "Bye 12 wee had our works all maned and about 1 P.M. wee began to get our troops in their propper places and buy 2 P.M. wee were eating our dinner and after dinner wee were lying around when an Orderly came about half past 2 P.M. to get our troops in their propper Positions and was going to charge the Enemy at 6 P.M. Sharp but at about 3 P.M. or little later they saved us that trouble for they charged us."[106]

The renewed Confederate advance drove in the pickets who barely had time to escape to the earthworks "ere their pursuers appeared in solid battle line, and the combat was re-opened with a terrific crash of riflery all along the lines; but so impetuous and persistent was the advance of the victorious foe, they were half-way through the slashing and within thirty yards of our works before we could bring them to a stand."[107] The rapid fire of the enemy had but little effect on the men behind the earthworks or "bullet-proof cover" as Weygant called it. The Yankees were able to take deliberate aim from behind their works, firing "into their exposed but unwavering line an incessant and most deadly fire. Again and yet again did their shattered regiments in our front close on their colors, while fresh troops from the rear moved up and filled the gaps."[108]

Finally, the enemy began to waver. Just as a Union force was being gathered to charge, the earthworks caught fire to the left of Ward's men. Weygant wrote that "a strong wind suddenly sprang up, and carried the fire to our log breastworks, along which the flames spread with wonderful rapidity. Several regiments to the left of the 124th, unable to withstand the heat and smoke, abandoned the works, though several individual members of these commands remained until their hair was singed, for the smoke and flames were blown directly into their faces. Presently huge clouds of strong black pine smoke, such as almost eats one's eyes out, rolled over and completely enveloped our regiment."[109]

The Confederates to their front rallied and advanced over the burning works. Union troops to the rear of the 124th New York, assuming the works had been abandoned and, unable to clearly see who was in front of them, opened fire. A volley sailed over the heads of the men still at the breastworks but no one was hit. "General Ward had, for half an hour or more, been sitting on a log or pacing to and fro, about ten paces behind the centre of our regiment, and had not yet left us, Up to that moment he had not spoken a word to anyone, but when he heard these bullets from the rear whistling so close to his ears, he turned to me with the order, 'Take your regiment to the rear of those — —' and walked rapidly away."[110] Weygant did as ordered and pulled his men back behind the strong second line of rifle pits.

He looked back to where his regimental flag had been posted just moments before, to see a Confederate battle flag in its place just as he heard Union artillery open up. Weygant glanced to the right and saw that a cannon had been pushed through an opening in the works on the far side of the road and turned to the left. It was in perfect position to do maximum damage to the Confederates milling around the earthworks. Ramming double loads of canister, the gunners tore apart the Confederate flank. The Union rear line, seeing an opportunity, charged back across the Brock Road, opening "a most deadly fire into the very faces of the bleeding foe on the opposite side." Clubbing and bayoneting their way forward, the Yankees, with a mighty Hurrah! to announce their coming, drove the enemy, "who broke for the rear, and fled in the wildest disorder across the slashing and down through the woods again; and, so we were informed by prisoners captured the next day, did not halt to re-form their lines until they were back on the very ground they started from in the morning."[111]

Sly admitted that some in Ward's Brigade ran, but not until those to their left fell back exposing their flank to enemy fire. "They captured our line," he wrote, " but could not hold it as their was annother line in rear Equally as strong as ours and they hald them when our Brig soon reformed and drove them out. That ended our fighting in the wilderness."[112]

Francis Walker, serving as an adjutant to General Hancock, described the Confederate attack on the Brock Road as "a real one, but was not made with great spirit," an observation that would have surprised the members of the 124th who bore the brunt of the attack. "Nor, it must be confessed, was the response from our side as hearty as it was wont to be."[113] One can only imagine how the members of the 124th New York would have responded to that insulting remark. "Most unexpected and unnecessary" is how Walker went on to describe the break in the line. "Some of Mott's troops in the second line gave way, without the slightest cause other than excitement and the strain, the labors and losses of the morning; and a portion of General J.H. Hobart Ward's brigade, of Birney's division, rushed pell-mell to the rear, their commander jumping upon a caisson, which was driven rapidly off."[114]

Walker's observations notwithstanding, General Ward had the presence of mind to order his men to the rear after being fired upon by confused troops posted behind them. Perhaps if Hancock's adjutant had been in the thick of the fighting, he might have been able to prevent what happened. "It was a critical moment, rather from the generally strained and tired condition of our troops, than from the actual number of the Confederates who had thus gained entrance."[115] Walker's observations were insulting to the brave men on both sides who fought along the Brock Road earthworks that day. Private Henry Howell wrote home two days later and mentioned nothing about running away, but instead told of how he and his comrades stood at their posts.

The regimental historians of the 8th Georgia noted that the "Federals had dug in behind breastworks along the Brock Road and fought fiercely. Confederate losses were heavy. Anderson's brigade, in the forefront of the assault of Field's division, was able to drive the defenders back briefly on its front, but the advantage was short lived. The Federals quickly rallied and counter-attacked, driving the Georgians back and, according to one account, capturing the flag of the Eighth Georgia."[116] The account of the loss of the flag may have been incorrect but there is no doubt that the struggle along the earthworks did not lack for spirit on either side.

Historian Earl Hess, in arguing that Hancock had a "newfound respect for field fortifications," offers another opinion on the nature of the attack. "The Brock Road Line proved its worth as a defensive-offensive feature. From it, Hancock launched his ineffective advance on May 5 and his very effective attack on May 6. This line saved the Federals from a near disaster in the afternoon, when Lee personally directed a heavy attack against it."[117]

The 124th New York spent that night in place on the Brock Road, "our weapons close beside us, ready to spring to our feet and man the works in front at a moment's notice." Some expected the fight to continue on May 7 but that was not to be the case. "The dread contest was not to be renewed on that weird field," Weygant wrote. He also noted that this was the first time Lee and Grant had fought against each other. Both were graduates of the same military school, but each "misunderstood the character and under-estimated the fighting qualities of the other."[118]

In two days of fighting, the 124th lost 60 men killed or wounded, Colonel Cummins among them. He survived the wound but did not return to command the regiment. Dead also was Corporal Ben Dutcher, who had written his last letter to his parents in mid–April in which he told them that "we all know that thousands of us must fall when the conflict begins."

Captain Henry Travis, who led Company I into the Wilderness, wrote to his father that he had eight men wounded and wanted their names published in the local press so that their families would know the fate of their loved ones. Travis told his father that "we had just been out to the front picking up all the arms the dead lay around thick."[119]

Two days later Henry Howell took the opportunity to write home about the two day battle in the Wilderness.

> I do not know as I can get any chance to send any word home but I will try and see what I can do about it. We are all right so far. We lost 55 in wounded and 2 killed. I cannot give you the number missing but should think there would be a dozen. Jo Johnson of our Co. was the only one hurt and he was very badly wounded in the hip. W.W. Parsons had his right leg amputated. The Colonel is wounded again in the hip. He was the only officer hurt. Our Div. has had the honor to capture several stand of colors and a great quantity of prisoners. We have fought for three days and whipped them so far. They are working off but we try to keep up with them. We done the first fighting we ever done in breastworks day before yesterday. The Johnnys tried to charge us out. We could not see the point though so we just let them come up close and then give it to them. Some fell some run and the rest surrendered. We almost wiped the 8th Georgia out of existence.
>
> Well I have not got time to give you any particulars. Lin Wheat is all right. Tholf wants me to ask you to tell his folks that he has not been hurt so far. I saw Henry Tuthill and all the Heavy Artillery boys this morning. They have heard the noise but have been in no action themselves.
>
> The weather is clear and warm. It is rather dusty traveling. The water is none of the best. We have plenty of rations. Longstreet is said to be wounded and another reb General was killed at the same time. All the prisoners seem to agree in the opinion of the war being soon over if we whip them this time. We have got the road. It is a complete wilderness all around us. Our heavy fighting was where a road leading south crossed the plank road. There is where they tried to drive us out. We have possession of Spotsylvania Court House and the inside road to Richmond. I can not tell anything about how heavy our army lost. Gen. Hays was killed. We heard a report that General Wadsworth was also. Well good bye for the present If Will and I remain as lucky as we have so far we will try and write again soon.[120]

The Jo Johnson mentioned in Henry's letter was the same soldier whose sister Hannah wrote the letter urging him to live as a Christian and avoid the temptations of army life. "Josey," as he

1st Lieutenant Ebenezer Holbert, Company D. He was wounded in action May 6, 1864, at the Wilderness, and again at Boydton Road, Virginia. He mustered out with the regiment (archive of the Historical Society of the Town of Warwick, gift of Joan and Tom Frangos).

liked to be called, suffered throughout the summer in the hospital near Washington before being sent home to die of his wounds in November.

Of course, Henry was incorrect. The Yankees did not have possession of Spotsylvania Court House but they did hold the crossroads and a portion of the Brock Road. But what they did have was a tenacious commander who was determined to maneuver his way around Lee's army in such a manner as to avoid another bloodletting as had just happened in the Wilderness — "a scientific 'bushwack' of 200,000 men" as Lieutenant Colonel Lyman termed it.[121] Senator Elihu Washburn, who accompanied the army as a personal friend of Grant, had come along to watch his protégé "swallow and annihilate Lee; but he wears another face now!" wrote Lyman. He went on to say that Grant told Meade that General Joseph Johnston, who commanded rebel armies in the West, "would have retreated after two such days' punishment." After three days in the field against the eastern Confederates, Grant "recognizes the difference."[122]

Meanwhile, back in Washington, no word had been received from Grant on the progress of the battle. At one point, Lincoln told a congressman, "Grant has gone to the Wilderness, crawled in, drawn up the ladder, and pulled in the hole after him, and I guess we'll have to wait until he comes out before we know just what he's up to."[123]
The president joked, but he was frantic with worry that the battle in the Wilderness might be just the latest in a long string of military disasters.

At Grant's headquarters early on the morning of May 6, Henry Wing, a young newspaper reporter with the *New York Tribune*, volunteered to try to reach the capital with news of the fighting so that his paper might "scoop" the others. This would be a trip filled with danger and with slim prospects of success. But the reporter not only made it safely to Washington, he sat with Lincoln and his cabinet to tell them how things were going — after he was allowed to telegraph his story to the *Tribune*, of course.

At the end of the meeting, when Wing was alone with the president, he told him that he had a personal message from General Grant. "Something from Grant to me?" Lincoln asked. "He told me I was to tell you, Mr. President, that there would be no turning back."[124]

Officers of the 124th New York. Front row left to right: Henry Ramsdell and Lt. James Grier. Rear row left to right: Captain Charles B. Wood and Captain Henry Travis.

CHAPTER 13

"There was no such thing as fail"
May 7–12, 1864

"On Friday May the 6th bye 430 P.M. all of our fighting in the Wilderness was over but were all looking for annother moove and after wee got our lines all straigent out it was nearly dark wee held the same front that wee had but back on the Brock Road wee all turned in quiet early."[1]

Private Sly had good reason to turn in early. He had been shot in the head, thrown from his horse, nearly captured by the enemy, and seen men cut down by the thousands, his own colonel among them. All in two days of the toughest fighting the Army of the Potomac had yet experienced. And this was just the beginning. The coming weeks would see continuous, deadly contact with an enemy who knew that defeat here, south of the Rapidan River, would mean the end of their dream of an independent Confederacy.

"When we rose this morn," wrote Lieutenant Colonel Lyman on Saturday, May 7, "we were pretty uncertain what the enemy was about, whether working on our flanks, or fallen back, or stationary.—All quiet."[2] Lyman described the troops of Hancock's Corps along the Brock Road that morning. "It was a picturesque sight the infantry closely huddled asleep, under the breastwork that followed the road. On top it and outside were sentries with their muskets ready. The officers paced up and down; all were prepared for instant action."[3]

Lyman noted the army's exhausted state at this early stage of the Overland Campaign, "the sudden transition from a long winter's rest to hard marching, sleepless nights, and protracted fighting, with no prospect of cessation, produced a powerful effect on the nervous system of the whole army. And never, perhaps, were officers and men more jaded and prostrated than on this very Sunday."[4] Throughout the North, newspapers reported that a huge offensive was underway, but specifics were scarce. Families anxiously awaited news, but the men had no time to write letters and no way to mail them.

In his assessment of the Battle of the Wilderness, British military historian James Marshall-Cornwall wrote that tactically it was a draw, "but strategically it ended in Grant's favour, for he had succeeded in outflanking Lee in the attempt to get between him and his base at Richmond." On the morning of May 7, neither Grant nor Lee appeared eager to renew the fight. "The morning mist, mingled with the smoke from the smouldering forest fires, obscured the landscape, but reconnaissances showed that the Confederates had withdrawn from their forward breastworks. Grant, who had risen at dawn, decided to push on to Richmond, and at 6:30 A.M. issued orders for the army to march to Spottsylvania Court House, ten miles to the south-east, as soon as it was dark."[5]

In his *Memoirs*, Grant gave his reasons for choosing this path. "My object in moving to

Spottslyvania was twofold: first, I did not want Lee to get back to Richmond in time to attempt to crush Butler before I could get there; second I wanted to get between his army and Richmond if possible; and if not, to draw him into the open field."[6] The essence of Grant's plan was to quickly march Union troops to Spotsylvania, where they would take up a blocking position. If this could be accomplished by the morning of May 8, his army would hold that "inside road to Richmond" Henry Howell had written about to his mother.[7] The general's reasoning showed that he planned a campaign of maneuver that would allow him to use his superior numbers to the best advantage. He was looking for a flaw in Lee's position. The bitter lesson he had yet to learn was that the elusive weak point was hard to find, and the men who led the Army of Northern Virginia were adept at shifting their forces to that point with speed and dexterity.

According to Lieutenant Colonel Weygant, Grant made plans on the morning of May 7 to "extricate his army from the dense Wilderness into which his wily antagonist had entangled it."[8] For his part, Lee tried to determine what Grant's next move would be. It was reported to him that Union cavalry was active on the Brock Road south of the Trigg farm. Federal troopers had previously abandoned that sector but were now back in strength, clearing the road all the way southeast to Todd's Tavern. After sending out his own reconnaissance, Lee correctly concluded that Grant was about to move, but he was not sure whether the objective would be Spotsylvania or Fredericksburg.[9]

Grant knew that once underway, his army would be vulnerable to attack by an enemy assumed to be lurking somewhere to the west. To counter this threat, he ordered General Hancock to hold the 2nd Corps in place until elements of the army on the march to Spotsylvania passed behind him. He also ordered that the units from other corps detached to Hancock during the fighting on May 6 be returned to their original commands.[10]

On the afternoon of May 7, Hancock rode the line held by Ward's Brigade. He ordered that the weapons lying about in front of the works be gathered up. The 124th New York was selected for the job and within an hour they picked up fifteen hundred rifles and muskets, some of them pried from the hands of the dead.[11] Most of these weapons lay outside the Union works, dropped by the attacking Confederates. Here was a clear indication of the ferocity of their unsuccessful attempt to break the Brock Road line the day before.

At five o'clock, Weygant with two officers and forty men moved forward to take up picket duty "amid the putrid bodies of friends and foes — for only those who had fallen nearest the works had been buried — listening to every unusual sound and watching the movements of every shadow, not knowing at what moment a body of the foe might be discovered stealing toward them."[12]

From his position at brigade headquarters, Private Sly knew the details of Grant's plan. "*Hancock* was to hold fast to our front the 6th corps wich was on our Extreem right was to march down the Plank Road to Spotsvalia as soon as the trains could bee got out of their way and then the 9th corps to follow the 6th nothing to start untill dark and then the 5th corp that connected with our right was to moove out and down the Brock Road they the head of their collum got down to our rear about 10 P.M."[13]

An hour later, Ward's Brigade was ordered to "fall in line quick." The men marched about two miles "when wee turned off to the left in the woods and went about a mile when wee halted in colum and lay down." The men hardly had time to get comfortable before they were called back into line and countermarched "right back to the same works they had taken us from." Confederate cavalry was probing the line and Ward's men were countermarched to hold them at arm's length.[14]

Well before dawn the next day, Weygant was awakened to read and sign a circular from brigade headquarters. It required his men, who had but two hours' sleep, to eat breakfast, and be ready to march "at any moment." Fires were kindled, blankets rolled, and soon "the air was freighted with the aroma of boiling coffee." Right after breakfast, they fell in and "started off, following the direction the Fifth Corps had taken."[15]

Lee, anticipating Grant's move, ordered General Richard Anderson, now in command of Longstreet's Corps, to also march for Spotslyvania Court House. Anderson used a country road that paralleled the Brock Road but was clear of traffic, Union or Confederate. He took the initiative and started early, in part to escape the stench of the dead on the Wilderness battlefield. He headed south and east, crossed the Po River, and marched to Laurel Hill where he reinforced a division of southern cavalry that was desperately trying to prevent Warren's Corps from breaking through to Spotsylvania. Anderson moved his brigades into position and ordered his men to dig in.[16]

Warren arrived on the field under the mistaken impression that he faced only Confederate cavalry. The 5th Corps commander fully expected to brush them aside and then quickly move on to Spotsylvania. Private Sly scoffed at the slow progress of the 5th Corps, "all the troops they had to oppose *Warren* was some dismounted calvalry as their Infantry were all hurrying to Spotsylvania to head off *Grant*."[17] Grant, Warren, and Sly were soon to discover that the enemy in front of the 5th Corps consisted of a lot more than a few dismounted "calvalry."

As Warren's brigades came up, he fed them into the battle piecemeal instead of waiting to build his forces for a massed attack. He pressed the battle all day at Laurel Hill to little effect, other than to lengthen the casualty lists. Warren's men did not reach Spotsylvania that day or the next day or the day after that. Poor planning and even worse execution doomed thousands of Union men, who would have to fight their way to Spotsylvania over the next five days.

In the opinion of historian Gordon Rhea, the operation was a miserable failure. He compared it with the Mud March and placed part of the blame on Grant for expecting a coordinated march in the dark over long distances. But Meade was also to blame as he did not "communicate urgency to his subordinates" nor did he monitor the progress of the cavalry. His staff did not effectively clear the roads of wagons to speed up the infantry, bringing Warren's column to a halt while General Anderson, with an open road before him, covered the ground quickly.[18]

Meanwhile, Hancock's Corps headed down the Brock Road toward the sound of the fighting. The young commander of the 124th New York wrote that May 8 "was exceedingly warm," and a number of his men fell victim to sunstroke. After a march of about two miles, the column halted and Ward's Brigade filed into "an open field near an old frame house, and remained there about an hour." They again took up the march and after another two miles reached Todd's Tavern at about 11 A.M., where Ward's men halted, "the left resting on the Spotsylvania Court-House road, and the right connecting with Second Brigade."[19] This put the 2nd Corps on the extreme right of the Union army and in a position to guard against a thrust by Lee against that flank. "Presently a refreshing breeze sprang up, which, while it cooled our heated brows, brought to our ears the thunder of distant battle." Some men were sent out on picket duty while the rest began building breastworks.[20]

The work went on until four in the afternoon, "when we rested from our labors, very tired and hungry too, for we had not eaten anything since morning." After a "late dinner" of standard army fare, they began to gather "pine feathers ... in anticipation of a comfortable night's rest." But as evening approached, Confederate dismounted cavalry attacked their picket line. The regiment formed up in an instant and opened fire on them, killing some, taking twenty prisoners, and driving off the rest. Once the excitement was over, the men continued making their beds in the woods and "lay down on them well content; and the night passed without further disturbance."[21]

By now it was clear that Lee had beaten Grant to Spotsylvania. Warren was making no headway at Laurel Hill, the southwestern end of Lee's line, and the enemy earthworks to Warren's left were growing stronger by the hour. Grant decided to turn Lee's victory in the foot race to

Spotsylvania to his advantage. He would demonstrate against Lee to hold him in place at Laurel Hill, while the 2nd Corps marched from its position near Todd's Tavern, crossed the Po River, and hit the Confederate left in an attempt to turn Anderson's line. On May 9, Hancock was ordered to move from Todd's Tavern with three divisions, skirmishers in front, leaving Mott's Division to guard the rear.[22]

In less than three hours, the skirmish line covered eight miles "during which we occasionally exchanged a few shots with the enemy's rear guard, but encountered no serious opposition. We did not see any considerable numbers of the foe until we began to descend into the valley through which the Po ran."[23]

Ward's men marched at about 3 P.M. "The 20th Ind. and 124th N. Y Vols. were, by direction of Major General Birney, thrown out as skirmishers for the division, and the 99th Pa. Vols. was dispatched toward the ford of Po River, to intercept the crossing of the enemy, who it was supposed was retreating in that direction, from our skirmishers. In the meantime the brigade was massed under cover of the hill, preparatory to crossing the river." Needless to say, Lee would not sit still while all this unfolded in front of him.[24]

"At noon," Hancock reported, "Birney and Barlow moved down the Spotsylvania road about 1 mile. Then taking a wood road leading to the right, to the height of open ground overlooking the Po River, they joined General Gibbon, who had previously moved to the left. Here line of battle was formed by the three divisions along the crest commanding the valley of the Po. Thorough reconnaissances of the ground between our position and the river were made."[25] The three divisions of the 2nd Corps were on the north bank of the Po River by about 4:30 P.M., preparing to "force a passage over the stream." Birney deployed his two brigades, Ward on the left and that of Colonel John S. Crocker, now in command of Hays's Brigade, on the right.[26]

Weygant noted that the river in front of Ward's Brigade was only about twenty feet wide and no more than eighteen inches deep. The 124th New York, still deployed in a skirmish line, moved ahead, coming under a lively but inaccurate artillery fire from two Confederate cannon on the other side.[27] The enemy guns limbered up and headed for the rear as the skirmish line splashed across the Po River and advanced in their direction. Once all three divisions had crossed, the 2nd Corps moved to the east along the Block House Road, but in order to advance upon Anderson's position, the Yankees needed to cross the Po a second time as its course turned sharply south. However, a halt was called at dusk and Hancock would have to wait until morning to cross.[28] Weygant noted that the regiment camped in the woods about two miles beyond the place where it had forded the Po River.

Private Sly was at General Ward's headquarters when, at about midnight, a familiar member of Birney's staff rode up. It was Captain Joseph C. Briscoe, who asked that Sly accompany him to scout the enemy position. General Ward left the matter up to the private, who readily agreed to go. "I knew or thought did what his business was for had heard so much talk about *Briscoe* was allways thrashing around in the front when the troops were asleep examining the ground and it was generally talked that *Briscoe* was the man that fought *Birney's* Division and I guess he was a big factor in it."[29]

Sly wrote that he was "very chummy" with Briscoe and was thrilled to have the opportunity to be "thrashing about" on a dangerous mission. Briscoe, a colorful native of Kilkenny, Ireland, came to America in 1854 at the age of twenty. He had enlisted at the start of the war and quickly caught the eye of General Phil Kearny, who brought him to headquarters. He'd later served as a staff officer for generals Stoneman, Hancock, and French and was now working for Sly's division commander, General Birney.[30]

The two rode out until they located Colonel Egan of the 40th New York, who was the brigade officer in charge of the picket line that night. Briscoe told Egan that he wanted to make a little survey that could not verry well do in daylight and wanted the Pickets to know wee were out in their front all the arrangements made wee started for the line left our Horses with an Orderly that was with us and wee started. Now the Ground between the Picket lines was a little lower than the ground on wich the Pickets were. The spot that the *Capt* wanted to inspect was some high ground across this low ground right opisite the High ground our brig was on now I dont beleive their was a rebel picket in front of us at that time for wee thrashed around quite some time on this high ground and then started back and it was quite a distance to our line got our Horses and went back to where the *Col* was the *Capt* told the *Col* he did not think their was anything in our front."[31]

Meanwhile, Sly figured out the purpose of Briscoe's mission: "*Grant* wanted to break their lines somewhere. The 5th and 6th had bin pounding all day around Spotsailvana and could not make a break." Briscoe thought this a "fine opportunity to carry their lines in our front." As Egan and Briscoe talked, "it was then jest getting daylight and wee had started to mount when right in our front they made *a bold dash* at our pickets." The fighting that followed was described by Sly as a "hot time" before "wee got them on the run." He was able to identify the attackers as troops from Heth's Division, Hill's Corps.[32]

All this activity on his left flank had not gone unnoticed by General Lee. He knew he must send reinforcements, but from where should he draw them? Union General Ambrose Burnside's 9th Corps was opposite the eastern end of the Confederate earthworks. Lee correctly saw Burnside as no threat and moved two divisions of Early's Corps from that sector and sent them west to deal with the new threat to his left. Elements of Mahone's Division arrived at about 7 P.M., and began to throw up earthworks just as the Union troops were approaching along the Block House Road. But Lee saw more: there might be an opportunity to turn a threat to his advantage. Hancock's three divisions were moving on his flank, it was true, but once below the Po River, they were isolated from the rest of the Union army. General E. Porter Alexander, always, a keen observer, noted,

> It was a great, an immense piece of luck for us, that Hancock had made his move across the Po late in the afternoon, giving us the night to make preparation to meet him. Early on the 10th Gen. Lee had Heth's division brought back from Spottsylvania & taken down the road past the Blockhouse, by the old court house, across the Po & then turned to the right to go up & take Hancock in flank. It was a very bold proposition to send this lone division to meet so large a force, & one so easily reinforced, but for-tune favors the brave & luck was still with us.[33]

As the sun rose on May 10, Hancock saw that the enemy entrenchments on the opposite shore of the Po were too strong to attack head on. In order to find a way around the enemy, he sent out scouting parties to find another crossing. One regiment was able to locate a ford about a half mile below the Block House Bridge, and promptly stormed across the river, driving back the enemy. This was the breakthrough Hancock was looking for and he made ready to send rein-forcements to exploit the crossing, but Grant had other plans. He mistakenly thought Lee had shifted men away from Laurel Hill to confront the 2nd Corps and he was "determined to take advantage of it." He ordered Hancock to pull two divisions, those of Birney and Gibbon, back to the north side of the Po, and move them east to link up with the 5th and 6th corps. Hancock would then personally coordinate a 5 P.M. attack against the supposedly vulnerable earthworks at Laurel Hill. Barlow Division remained south of the Po with skirmishers to his front.[34]

Had Grant left Hancock's troops in place, Heth's single division would have faced three Yankee divisions below the Po River with another in supporting distance. Instead, Grant withdrew two thirds of his force. "This is what saved us west of the Po," wrote Porter Alexander.[35]

As General Hancock marched Gibbon and Birney to the north side of the Po, Barlow's skir-mishers became hotly engaged with Heth's skirmishers. Right behind came heavy lines of Con-federate infantry bent on destroying Barlow before he could be reinforced or withdrawn.[36]

"As we moved to our left," wrote Sergeant Stephen Chase of the 86th New York, "the enemy moved to their right. At first, we could see them moving, but soon both sides were in the woods and we could not see each others army, but knew in all reason that there was soon to be a hard fight. So we stood in line, moving a little way and halting, sometimes leaning on our guns a few minutes and then moving on a few rods ... and went into a breastworks which some of our army had left and gone on farther to the left."[37]

Weygant wrote that after crossing the Po, the brigade marched about a mile, "and relieved a brigade of Warren's men, whom we found posted behind light earthworks which had evidently been erected during the night. We now formed part of a new main line, which we soon learned had been posted there to confront Lee's army."[38]

Meanwhile, the situation below the Po River on Hancock's right grew progressively worse. Barlow's men were sorely pressed and it looked as if they might be overrun. Meade ordered Hancock to get Barlow back on the north side of the Po and told him to take care of it personally. "I immediately joined General Barlow and instructed him to prepare his command to recross the river on the bridges we had laid in the morning. The enemy was then driving in his skirmishers."[39]

Hancock ordered Birney to bring his division back to the Po River bridges and take up a position on the heights to aid in Barlow's crossing if needed. General de Trobriand put the time of this move to the right at noon when "the brigade was double-quicked back to the Po River to cover the crossing of the First Division, they being heavily pressed by the enemy."[40]

Private Sly wrote that Barlow was positioned on a "fine Plain and verry soon Heths Rebbel Division crossed and pitched right in to *Barlow* who soon began to call for help and our Brig being in reserve our troops where the ones he borrowed." By noon, according to Sly, Birney's Division was in position north of the river to support Barlow. Ward's Brigade was not ordered to re-cross the Po, but both Ward and Sly did cross to watch as Barlow's men put up a fight that became legend in the history of the 2nd Corps.

"On both sides of the river," noted Sly,

> were high banks and when wee got over and up on the Plain wee turned a little too our right and went to where their war two big chimnies standing the house was all torn down or burnt I don't know and wee had bin their but a short time when Genl Birney and his Orderly rode up and wee were watching Barlow his front should think was not more than a half a mile from where wee were and both Barlow and Heth were warming up finely that was the first time I ever saw two distinct lines of Battle at least a half a mile long and could see the whole length of both lines Warming up together what a grand sight, I had no head hurt then.[41]

In preparation to withdrawing the division, the two leftmost brigades were pulled back to cover the bridges over the river, then the two remaining brigades fell back as well.[42] Sly and General Ward watched as the enemy "advancing in line of battle supported by columns" seized the abandoned breastworks and attempted to push the Yankees into the river. They were met by "heavy and destructive fire" and the battle became general.

As they watched the fight, Sly got his first close look at General Barlow. Sly wrote,

> Soon *Genl Hancock* joined us he had no one with him but an Orderly the three *Genls* were thier in a bunch and us Orderlies right with them all mounted when down come *Genl Barlow* coat and hat off on a dead run reined up quick bye the side of the *Genls* the first word he said *Genl Hancock let me have a Battery. Hancock* never spoke but shook his head (No) Genl let me have a Battery and I will give you my check for it and that is good for a doz Batteries but no and back *Barlow* went to his front as fast as his Horse could carry him that was the first time I ever saw *Genl Barlow* to know him and never forgot him ... he was only about my age wich I learned some time latter and a *Major Genl* and verry rich but a fighter."[43]

Barlow's men successfully held the enemy at bay long enough to extricate themselves from a potentially disastrous situation. As soon as the crossing was seen to be successful, Ward's Brigade marched back to the position held prior to the move west. Weygant put the time at about 4:30 P.M. "After proceeding in that direction about a mile, we were halted at the base of a thickly wooded hill, and there formed for the assault. Vast bodies of troops could be seen going into position on either side of us."[44]

As Ward and Sly rode toward their new position near Warren's line, Sly looked back across the enemy lines and saw a hill lined with Confederate artillery. "This is the Hill that Briscoe and I were on, but it was diferent now than when wee were their." The difference was that now it was full of enemy guns.

Ward had another hazardous detail for Sly. Earlier he had detached two regiments to General Barlow's Division and now he wanted them back. Sly rode about three quarters of a mile over an area cut by ravines, under heavy enemy artillery fire. "I went and right over the hill in rear of our guns well sir to tell you the truth when got up on that Hill it did look dusty but I got across to the other side then had to go down and through a ravineen." He was challenged by an officer who demanded to know his mission. When Sly told him where he was headed, the officer shouted above the thundering Union guns, "No man can live to get through their, jest as he said that down he went and on I went and got through all safe and found the regts and told my Orders from Genl Ward and wee soon started."[45]

Sly had to retrace his steps with two infantry regiments and a major in tow "and when wee got to this crossing the Major leading the troops said he would not go over that Hill." Sly told the major not to worry as he had come over this same ground saying it was "a hot place but I think you will find a hotter one in the rear." The major wanted to go farther to the rear of the guns not realizing enemy rounds that overshot the batteries would land right among his men. Sly remembered, "Wee went his way and found it so before wee got through. As a general thing," he observed, "the nearer you are to a Battery that is working the safer you are." As for the major, "he found it out and will bet he profitted by it if he ever was called on to move in rear of a line of guns but wee got back had some men hit but guess not many." He reflected much later in life that the loss of three or four hundred men in those days did not amount to anything and that "them days ... wee had bin used to loosing 10,000 or 12000 that was quiet some fighting." Sly brought the regiments back as Ward was gathering his brigade for an assault on the Confederate line.[46]

Grant continued in the belief that Lee had weakened his line at Laurel Hill, and, eager to retain the initiative, he stuck to his plan for a late afternoon attack all along the enemy position. Birney and Gibbon of Hancock's Corps, now positioned in support of Warren's troops, would join in the effort. The 6th Corps would attack farther up the western face of the line supported by Mott's Division which would hit the tip of the heavily defended works. At the same time, Burnside's 9th Corps would attack the eastern face of the enemy line. It was expected that all four attacks would be launched at 5 P.M. Grant hoped that massive blows on all fronts, east, north, and west would surely find the weak spot and punch a hole somewhere. But even this early in his tenure, Grant should have realized that coordinated movement of large bodies of men over such distances, and in the face of the Army of Northern Virginia, was just about impossible.[47]

With Hancock called away to deal with the crisis on the right, Grant's plan began to unravel when Warren convinced Meade to let him attack at 4 P.M., one hour early, with his corps and Gibbon's Division of the 2nd Corps in support. The 5th Corps commander saw a chance to redeem himself and save his reputation. With Hancock gone, he would lead the charge that might finally break the line at Laurel Hill.[48]

General Gibbon personally scouted the position to be attacked and came to the conclusion that no line of battle could approach the enemy earthworks, let alone break through. He stated his objections to General Meade who "seemed to rely wholly upon Warren's judgment in the matter." It was Gibbon's opinion that Warren "seemed bent upon the attack with some idea that the occasion was a crisis in the battle of which advantage must be taken."[49] Gibbon clearly saw a disaster in the making.

So, one hour before Grant had initially planned, four divisions advanced into a shower of lead and iron. Confederate artillery swept the ground from well-placed batteries, knocking down dozens of men at a time. When the Yankees were within rifle range, their counterparts in gray opened fire from behind their earth and log works. Once again, the destructive power of the rifle musket, when used by men firing from behind strong defenses, was plain to anyone who cared to look. Fortunately for the 124th New York, Birney's Division, initially scheduled to be part of the attack, was held back. But their turn to attack Laurel Hill would come soon enough.

On the left of the Confederate position an officer from the Texas Brigade watched the action. "Enemy attacked our line. Batteries in front, and enfilading fire on our left played on them famously; attack repulsed with about an hour's fighting ... the enemy handsomely mown down by our men."[50]

Hancock, who was back from his mission to help extract Barlow's Division on the right, arrived just in time to see the attack fail.

At 5.30 P.M., when I returned to General Warren's front, I found the Fifth Corps and Gibbon's division, of the Second Corps, engaged in an assault on the enemy's line in front of Alsop's house. The

Confederate dead at Spotsylvania Court House near the Alsop House where the 124th New York fought on May 10, 1864 (Library of Congress, Prints & Photographs Division).

enemy held the crest of a densely wooded hill, crowned by earth-works, his artillery and musketry sweeping his front. The approach to this position was rendered more difficult and hazardous by a heavy growth of low cedar trees, most of them dead, whose long, bayonet-like branches interlaced and pointing in all directions presented an almost impassable barrier to the advance of our lines. Here, as in the Wilderness, the woods prevented me from observing the conduct of the troops, although close to the point of attack; but it was soon evident that we had failed. The men struggled on bravely for a time and even entered the enemy's breast-works at one or two points, but soon wavered and fell.... Gibbon's division reformed on the ground from which it had advanced to the attack. It lost heavily on this occasion.[51]

The initial attack of Grant's overall plan went in early and was repulsed. Despite the setback, the army commander was determined to go ahead with the rest of his plan anyway. The next attack would be made by twelve handpicked regiments of the 6th Corps. It was rescheduled for 6 P.M. but nobody told General Mott. His regiments, positioned opposite the tip of the Confederate works, went in right on time at 5 P.M. and were summarily repulsed. This left two final efforts against the western face of the enemy earthworks: yet another attempt against the Laurel Hill line and a charge by a group of 6th Corps regiments farther up the line to the left.[52]

The latter attack was the brainchild of Colonel Emory Upton, three years out of West Point and the self-proclaimed originator of a new style of warfare. He proposed to get his men as close as possible to the enemy works, then advance at the run, bayonets fixed. His soldiers had orders not to fire their weapons as it would slow the momentum of the charge. Upton had under his command twelve well-disciplined regiments with able commanders. They would make the charge across a narrow front, three regiments wide and four deep.[53]

In his new theory of the attack, Upton advocated that reinforcements be close at hand to exploit any break in the enemy's lines. The attacking regiments would immediately become disorganized once they breached the works and battled the defenders hand-to-hand inside the enemy position. Only fresh troops would have their organization still intact and be able to move left and right to secure the shoulders of the breakthrough. Yet more reinforcements would be needed to come in behind them to push forward into the interior of the enemy position. This is where Upton's charge fell apart; no provision was made for reinforcements to exploit a successful breakthrough. Like the others, this attack was scheduled to go in at 5 P.M., but because of the continued threats to Hancock's right by Heth's Confederates, it was postponed until 6:35, near sundown.

When Upton finally ordered his men forward, they caught the Confederates by surprise. The handpicked Yankee regiments were into the earthworks before they could be stopped; hundreds of Confederate were captured and sent streaming to the rear. But this success was doomed as no Union reinforcements were on the way. Mott, who was to support the attack from the north, had been repulsed an hour and a half earlier. Inside the salient the stunned enemy soldiers quickly regained their balance. Confederate brigades rushed to seal the breach and threw back Upton's men. As darkness fell over the field, it was the same story repeated: courage and desperate fighting by the men in the ranks lost by the ineptitude of those in high command.[54]

Now everything in Grant's ill-conceived and poorly executed plan depended on the final attack. About thirty minutes after Upton's men moved forward, seven Yankee brigades prepared to assail Confederate General Charles Field's formidable earthworks at pretty much the same spot where Warren had failed just two and half hours earlier. Warren's battered 5th Corps contributed four brigades, Hancock's 2nd Corps contributed three. Two of these were Gibbons's men who'd already had about enough fighting for one day. As might be expected, the attacks were disjointed, some men advancing while others refused to move. Some units simply decided on their own to head for the rear. Most of the regiments involved in the charge had failed to break this same position earlier in the day and now, as historian Gordon Rhea noted, "They had little stomach for it."[55] The only added weight was General Ward's Brigade, including the 124th New York.

Hancock had been ordered to send in this last attack at 6:30 so as to coordinate with Colonel Upton. Just as Hancock was ready to go, he received orders from Meade "to defer my advance if the troops were not already in motion, and to move a strong force to the right of Barlow's position to oppose a heavy column of the enemy, which was reported to have crossed the Po, and to be advancing on our right flank." Hancock had just given orders to execute the move to the right as directed, when the order was countermanded. Now he was to turn his attention again to the assault on the Laurel Hill earthworks. Because of the mixup, any hope of exploiting a distracted enemy was squandered.[56]

The delay did nothing to raise the men's spirits but instead gave them more time to dwell upon what they knew awaited them. As dusk approached, some began to think that the whole thing might be postponed, but that hope evaporated when the order to advance was given.

Only Ward's Brigade on the right flank of the attack made progress. The general had his men massed in column "so close together that the field officers were obliged to take position on the flanks of their respective command," much as Upton had done. Ward's men were to advance in the same manner, across a narrow front at the double quick. They were to hold their fire until they reached the enemy, then carry the position with the bayonet and pour through. Ward would advance with eight regiments formed one behind the other, as opposed to Upton's three regiments abreast formation. Ward's Brigade was "massed in column" front to rear in the following order: 86th New York, 3rd Maine, 124th New York, 99th Pennsylvania, 141st Pennsylvania, 20th Indiana, 110th Pennsylvania, and 40th New York.[57]

Sergeant Stephen D. Chase of the 86th New York wrote, "When we had position, we could look over our works and see the enemy bringing their artillery into position. Before we had gone into these works, we had descended a slight decline in the lay of the land, and anyone a few rods to the rear could see the enemy over the breastworks without standing up." Before advancing, some of the men left their knapsacks in the rear, one with a six quart coffee pail strapped to it. "'Look at them bringing that cannon into position. That means us,'" an officer warned.

> Again he said: "Look, I can see right down the whole length of that piece, and we want to get down when that cannon discharges." We all kept watch until she belched forth and sent her missle of death after us. The cannon ball had just killed the top of our works and went through the pail which Brown had strapped on his knapsack. The open end of the pail being towards the enemy, the shot had entered it and of course took out the bottom and went on bounding through the trees and brush ... and it was quite a cause of jollification among the boys.[58]

Ward's massed column of regiments, the 86th New York in front, were behind a double line of works, the stacked regiments stretching uphill into the woods. In front of the entrenchments, clear ground fell away for about two hundred yards with the Jones farmhouse to the right. A thin belt of trees near a creek opened to clear ground that sloped uphill to the enemy works which "still smoldered from fires set during the earlier combat. Farther on, behind Laurel Hill's frowning works, Charles Field's Confederates cleaned their muskets and stashed their ammunition close at hand."[59]

Just as the men were formed up, General Crawford of Warren's Corps came walking along the line with his staff, wringing his hands. "I tell you this is sheer madness," he said, "and can only end in wanton slaughter and certain repulse."[60] One can easily imagine the impact such words would have on men preparing to make the difficult assault.

Ahead in the earthworks lay an old enemy, the very same Texas Brigade Ward's men had fought at Gettysburg: the 3rd Arkansas, 1st Texas, 4th Texas, and 5th Texas, now led by General John Gregg. The brigade had been in place since early on May 8 improving its defenses and fretting that it might not get a chance to fight the Yankees from behind its earthworks. "For many hours of the 8th, and all day of the 9th, the dull but incessant roar of small arms and the wicked boom of artillery told of repeated assaults on Ewell's lines on its right, and behind breastworks for the first time and anxious to learn what execution it could do from them, it felt slighted." Finally, with darkness approaching, the enemy would try one more time. "Their heaviest blow was directed against the Texas Brigade."[61]

Gregg's Brigade occupied earthworks on the left of Anderson's line which projected slightly forward to form a salient. To strengthen the position, four batteries were positioned inside the works. When the Yankees advanced, they would be protected for a time by a belt of trees, but once they marched into the open they would have to cross three hundred yards of cleared ground before they reached the enemy position. Canister rounds were made for this kind of work and the gunners, well protected by earthworks, would have an opportunity to use it to maximum effect. As with all the attacks this day, Grant had made little attempt to reconnoiter the ground to be crossed or the position to be assaulted. Historian Gordon Rhea wrote, "Ward unwittingly funneled his troops into a deathtrap."[62]

Shortly before the attack stepped off, General Ward was hit on the right side of the head near his temple by a shell fragment. The wound was serious enough to need cleaning and wrapping with a handkerchief. Colonel Egan of the 40th New York did the job himself.[63] General de Trobriand wrote that Ward was wounded during the attack but in either case, the brigadier was determined to lead his brigade.

Weygant wrote that "at length the order 'move forward' was given, and off, up the hill, at a rapid gait we started, tearing our way through the brush, leaping across ditches, and clambering over felled trees."[64] Ward's men went through the belt of woods, then emerged into the open, moving ahead at the double quick. They approached the earthworks at an angle, which exposed their left to fire from Anderson's Georgia Brigade.

Weygant made a point of saying that the three lead regiments, the 86th New York, 3rd Maine, and 124th New York, became so intermingled that they were "handled as one body." The enemy picket line was quickly overrun, but not before a number of them scampered to the rear, firing shots to warn their comrades of the Yankee onslaught. Alerted, the Confederates inside the works grabbed their rifles and opened a "storm of battle" with a "horrid crash and roar" from the right and left. Then the attackers were hit by fire from straight ahead where the 4th and 5th Texas held the line. Ward's men came on at a steady pace "tumbling into ditches, tripped by tangling vines, lacerated by springing branches and pierced and torn by the dry pointed cedars,— onward, right onward through the gathering gloom, filled with whizzing, whistling bullets, we forced our way."[65]

A "heavy earthen breastworks" protected by a wide, water-filled ditch stood between the attackers and the enemy. The commanders of the three lead regiments were at the front shouting the charge, which, according to de Trobriand, was "promptly obeyed." Now the men broke into a run, covering the last few yards in a matter of seconds. Confederate riflemen, too late realizing that the Yankees were right on top of them, rose above the protection of the log works to take aim but were swept away by a volley.[66]

Quite a few of the Southerners behind the earthworks were convinced that the fighting was over for the day and had started cooking the evening meal. "It must be confessed," one of them wrote, "they took us by surprise. Giving no notice of their intentions, five of their brigades, under cover of the heavy timber, crawled close up to the breastworks. Then, with loud huzzas they sprang forward in a seemingly reckless charge. Having made up their minds that they would not be attacked at all that day, the Texas regiments were not as ready as they should have been, and for a few seconds it looked as if the enemy would win the breastworks."[67]

"The First Texas was not as successful as its comrade regiments in repelling the enemy" wrote one of the Texans. There was a forty foot gap in the middle of the earthworks occupied by his regiment. Whether this gap was by design or had been opened by artillery fire he did not say, but the lead regiments, 86th New York in front, headed straight for it. To the right of the

1st Texas stood the 4th Texas, and at the same time "a storming column" struck both their lines. The Yankees were over the works at one point and surging through a gap at another.[68]

The 86th New York and the 3rd Maine planted their colors atop the earthworks as the fighting around them became a wild melee. Chase of the 86th saw two of his comrades use their bayonets to kill an enemy soldier, a very rare occurrence in the Civil War and evidence of the close in nature of the fight.[69] On either flank, artillery pieces were turned to fire at the Yankees inside the works while other guns continued to send blasts of canister at those attempting to make it through or over the barricade. "Two Napoleons from the 1st Richmond Howitzers swung around and fired down the trench with double canister."[70] At this point Weygant and most of the 124th New York were still outside the works, but they could clearly hear from within "the sound of voices of artillery officers, giving commands which told of the coming shower we had no desire to breast, and could not then escape by flight."[71]

The only thing to do was hit the dirt. "The order *lie down* was obeyed with alacrity." Weygant wrote. He did not say who gave the order but it can be assumed that he did not. The men were on their bellies when the order to fire came and "out leaped the powder flames; and over us passed a volley of canister which made the very earth beneath us seem to shiver, and sent to their last home a score or more of men from the regiments behind us, which had been halted to re-form their lines at the lower end of the abitis, some fifty yards away."[72] The commanders of those rear five regiments quickly had their men face about and head for cover.

The 1st Texas was "taken more by surprise than the other regiments, being habitually more careless, and driven from their works," but the famed regiment rallied and rushed back into the hand-to-hand fight. The rest of the brigade, as well as those from nearby regiments, ran toward the threatened area, first checking the Federal advance and then pushing it back.[73]

When the artillery fire fell off, Weygant knew the reason: the gunners were depressing the pieces to fire at them. With prospects of canister at point blank range, Weygant and his men "sprang up and retraced our steps to the base of the hill."[74] General de Trobriand wrote, "Owing to the superior position of the enemy to our own and the rough ground over which the brigade had to charge, support could not advance in time to hold the position, and the charge was unsuccessful. The Eighty-sixth New York and Third Maine Volunteers lost quite heavily in this assault, but fell back to our works in good order, bringing their colors with them."[75]

A Confederate wrote of the enemy troops who attacked the earthworks, "Those who entered, with very few exceptions, were either killed, wounded or captured."[76] Another wrote of the enemy, "When his hope was strongest, a sheet of flame and a yell of defiance burst from the intrenchments, the bullets mowing the assailants down by the hundreds, and in front of the Fourth and Fifth Texas and the Third Arkansas the onset was soon checked."[77] It had to be admitted that at one point things "looked ugly to the Confederates, and troops were hurried to the reinforcement of the Texas Brigade. By the time they arrived, though, the part of the line seized was recaptured, and the Union troops in its front were on the run."[78]

Hancock's report on the attack was hardly laudatory. "The assault as formerly directed was then made by the Fifth Corps and portions of Gibbon's and Birney's divisions of the Second Corps. The troops encountered the same obstacle which had forced them to retire when they had assaulted this point at 5 P.M.... They were again repulsed with considerable loss. Ward's brigade retired in disorder until rallied by my own staff and that of General Birney. The heavy firing did not cease until 7.30 P.M."[79]

Historian Earl Hess was more complimentary in his assessment of Ward's attack on the west face of the Confederate salient. "Ward managed to get his men into a section of Field's trench on the far Confederate left, held by Brig. Gen. John Gregg's Texas and Arkansas brigade. Gregg's Line bulged forward in a semicircle, creating a mini-salient. Some of Ward's men crawled through the tangled trees and caught Gregg by surprise, but they had to give up their foothold as no Federals came to support them. The key to Ward's minor success was that he pushed his men as quickly possible, without pause, to the objective. The key to his failure was lack of help to exploit his gains."[80]

Historian Gordon Rhea, in his appraisal of the day's events, wrote,

> Ward's and Upton's charges bore striking similarities. Each had overrun the rebel entrenchments by attacking without pausing to fire. And each had failed because Grant and Meade had neglected to provide proper support.... Ward's men had performed as gallantly as Upton's and were as deserving of praise. Upton's attack, however, received accolades, while Ward's was quickly forgotten. Developments during the remainder of the war were responsible. Ward was to be drummed out of the army for drunkenness on May 12, while Upton emerged from the war a hero.[81]

It is interesting to note that the historian of the 2nd Corps hardly mentioned Ward's attack even though they were 2nd Corps troops, but made much of Upton's temporary success leading 6th Corps troops.[82]

Weygant made no claim that the colors of the 124th New York were on the barricade with those of the 86th New York and the 3rd Maine, nor did he claim that he or anyone else from the 124th New York made it inside the earthworks. In fact his report that he lost but four men wounded makes it clear that they did not. Perhaps if the rear regiments of Ward's Brigade had come on or had one or two other brigades been on hand for ready support, the breakthrough in front of the 1st Texas might have been exploited. Colonel Weygant noted that the other attacks "were even less successful than Ward's brigade, and their losses were infinitely greater." He gave the losses as "fully five thousand men" for the Union, doubting if the rebels lost even five hundred. The young commander of the 124th described the defeat at Laurel Hill as "complete and most disastrous."[83]

The charges of Ward's Brigade and Upton's regiments on May 10, however, were not total failures. Grant learned something from them: the enemy line *could* be broken and now he knew how to do it. He would let his men rest for a day before he launched another attack against Lee's Spotsylvania position. Next time, he would use the entire 2nd Corps, 20,000 men, massed on a narrow front.

It was nearly daylight on May 11 by the time General Ward got his brigade in place beyond the range of the rebel guns. He and Norman Sly were resting under a large pine when they were joined by Major Fitzhugh Birney, the division commander's brother, who served on his staff. The officer sat down beside Ward "wanting to know if he was all safe and if he knew his losses in the Brig the *Genl* said he did not but thought slight." Birney told Ward of the move to the left planned for after dark. "Hancock to moove the whole corp down to the Brown House and Mass their for a charge on the Confederate works at day light the whole corp to charge and that wee must moove would bee quite close to the enemy's lines all commands given in a wisper and all tin utensils used by the soldiers to bee carried in their haversacks and sabers to bee muffeld and was going to let the troops rest that day and draw their rations and all to be ready to moove as soon as was dark."[84]

The Union troops in the earthworks did get a chance to rest most of the day and some even drew rations. But for Ward's Brigade, May 11 was "the hardest days work yet." There was still a real danger that the enemy might attack the Union right and spoil Grant's plans. Sly wrote that Ward's men were out of the trenches and that "they kept us on the jump all day as Genl Heth was on the other side of the River and it did appear that he was going to keep Hancock from making the moove but our Brig did have a hard day off and never drew any rations untill dark and then started."[85]

"Nothing of importance occurred on the 11th, except in preparation for the morrow, General Meade having decided to attack the enemy on the 12th near the point where Mott's division had made its ineffectual assault."[86] The historian of the 2nd Corps made it sound as if the decision to attack the Spotsylvania salient was Meade's idea when in fact Grant issued specific orders on May 11 to Meade:

> Move three divisions of the 2d corps by the rear of the 5th and 6th corps, under cover of night, so as to join the 9th corps in a vigorous assault on the enemy at four o'clock A.M. to-morrow. I will send one or two staff officers over to-night to stay with Burnside, and impress him with the importance of a prompt and vigorous attack.... There is but little doubt in my mind that the assault last evening would have proved entirely successful if it had commenced one hour earlier and had been heartily entered into by Mott's division and the 9th corps.[87]

In this assessment of the attacks on Laurel Hill, it was almost as if Grant were speaking of an entirely different battle.

As the generals planned, the men in the ranks busied themselves with the more immediate matters of food, water, and rest. William Howell took a moment to write a short letter to his sister. It bore no date but was almost certainly written sometime on May 11 before the 2nd Corps marched out for the left of the line.

> Dear Sister
>
> I take a hasty pencil to inform you that Henry & I are all right yet. It rains now. Muskets are poping occasionally. Yesterday we fought hard all day. We are near the Po river we are told. Henry started a few lines the 8th & perhaps you have got now. Hardships have made us quite weak but we hope to be victorious this time. We charged a rebel breastworks last night but were repulsed. Our Co is still lucky as no One but Jo Johnston has been seriously wounded so far. The Qr master will try to forward a few letters so I will try this. It rains harder & I will now bid you all good bye.
> Yours Sincerely
> Wm H. Howell[88]

The target for the upcoming attack, and the feature in the Confederate line that filled the thoughts of the Yankee high command, was an unusual bulge that pointed straight north from the eastern end of the three-mile long line of earthworks. A relatively straight line would have been easier to defend, but Confederate engineers saw that the high ground just beyond the McCoull house would make an ideal position from which Union artillery could be used against any earthworks they might construct. It was decided to deny this piece of real estate to Grant and instead include it within the Confederate defensive line. The resulting fortified position was shaped like an inverted horse shoe and came to be known ever after as the Mule Shoe Salient.

In military terms, a salient is a line that projects into enemy territory. By its nature, a salient can be difficult to defend.[89] Lee, an engineer himself, compensated by ordering traverses built inside the works at right angles to it. Should the enemy break through, the defenders could retire to the protection of the traverses to fire on the attackers. Head logs were placed atop the works to protect the riflemen. Abatis made of felled trees with sharpened limbs pointing toward the enemy lined the outside of the works, and inside the salient were stationed veteran troops and artillery — lots of artillery. The ground outside the works was cleared of trees as much as possible so the guns had open fields of fire, and so that the infantry crouched under the head logs could take advantage of the impressive range of the rifle musket. But it was the artillery that gave this particular salient its strength.

A soldier in Ward's Brigade wrote after seeing them, "The works at this point were very strong, consisting of a double line of intrenchments of oak logs, banked up with dirt from six to eight feet in height, and connected at short intervals with traverse sections well protected with artillery.[90]

Across the line, Lee tried to calculate his enemy's next move. The Union army was still intact after a week of tough fighting and heavy casualties. Lee knew that one mistake might well prove fatal, and late in the afternoon of May 11 he made just such a mistake. Lee concluded that Grant was about to fall back to Fredericksburg, so, with his fondness for the attack, he ordered his men to prepare to strike the Yankees while they were on the move. He directed that the guns at the tip of the Mule Shoe and on the eastern face of the earthworks limber up and pull back so that nothing would impede their joining in the anticipated pursuit of Grant's retreating army. In doing so he fatally weakened the very point where Grant was planning to attack. Lee's instincts failed him now and in failing him, doomed his soldiers packed into the tip of the salient.

Out along the Union lines, the men of the 2nd Corps made ready to begin the march to the left, but first they piled more wood on the campfires to make the enemy think they were settling in for the night.[91] Hancock's goal was the relatively open area just west of the Brown House, a little over a half mile north of the tip of the salient. The 2nd Corps began to move after dark through an intermittent drizzle. "We crept along, a step at a time, hour after hour," Weygant wrote. Since he had taken command of the regiment in the Wilderness, he and his men had but little sleep. They had been kept under arms for several nights and now at each stop along the march, the men dropped and were instantly asleep. "And yet their sense of hearing was in no wise blunted, even in the midst of their fitful slumbers." As soon as the march continued the men were back on their feet until the column again halted. "Our horses even, were seized with the same irresistible desire to close their weary eyes; and with their noses almost touching the ground, would weave to and fro like drunken men."[92]

A soldier in the 141st Pennsylvania observed, "The line of march was in the rear of the Fifth and Sixth Corps in nearly an easterly direction, without regard to roads, through open fields, through heavy forests, fording streams and floundering through swamps guided only by the compass, so dark that often one could not see the man in front of him."[93]

"I had never before suffered such acute agony from any cause; my eyes would close, do what I would to prevent it." Weygant tried to rest by leaning forward, holding on to his horse's neck, but he had to take care lest he slide right off. The animal weaved and trembled with exhaustion. He finally dismounted and attempted to keep himself upright by gripping the saddle, but he slid to the ground every time.[94]

It was well after midnight when Adjutant Van Houten rode up to Weygant and handed him a canteen of "very poor commissary whiskey." The colonel, a well known abstainer, resorted to splashing the "vile stuff" in his eyes but "even that did not keep me awake more than ten minutes." At one of the numerous halts, a member of the 86th New York sat on a fence rail and fell asleep. He tumbled off and broke his neck. "In less than ten minutes from the time the unfortunate man sat down on the fence his comrades were digging his grave."[95]

Sly was at his post, riding beside General Ward, "when at last an officer in the road says Genl Ward turn the head of your collum in to the right." Ward directed two of his aides to place the regiments and told Sly to stay put until the entire brigade was turned and was moving in the right direction, then he was to rejoin the general. The two men took shelter under a tree where the ground was relatively firm to await the dawn. "I droped under that tree in jest about one minnute and was dead to the World."[96]

Weygant reckoned that it took them seven hours to cover the three and half miles to the field where they were now deployed. Every soldier was soaked to the skin, covered with mud, and exhausted. It was three o'clock in the morning, the rain had stopped but a dense, chilling fog descended over the fields. Those with blankets lay on the wet ground and took what comfort they could, but many just sat down in place or huddled together for warmth. The entire regiment was asleep on the ground save two members of the color guard who stood with the flag. Though it was mid–May in Virginia, Weygant had been wearing his wool overcoat in addition to his wool officer's jacket. Now he retrieved his rubber rain coat and put that on over everything else "for it was damp and very chilly." To stay awake he'd taken to biting his tongue "so that the blood flowed from it quite freely."[97]

As he stood shivering in the mist, Weygant gazed out toward the enemy works he could not yet see, and marveled at how effective chewing his tongue had been in keeping him awake. A hand upon his shoulder startled him. He found himself "confronted by General Ward" who was alone and in a "gloomy mood." Ward, wrapped in his cloak, seemed to rise right out of the fog, which did nothing to lighten the scene. He spoke to Weygant first of the repulse of his brigade just a day and a half before, the burden of responsibility heavy in his voice. Years later, Weygant could recall what the general said: "Colonel, you have been assigned a post of honor. I expect you to take your regiment over the works this time or die in the attempt." His use of "this time" must have hit Weygant like a slap across the face, although the young officer made no mention of his reaction. Ward's inference was clear to the commander of the 124th New York: at Laurel Hill you failed to lead your regiment into the works behind the 86th New York, your sister regiment. Now you have an opportunity to redeem that failure.

There was no ambiguity in the general's statement and no room for half measures. At last, someone at the top of the chain of command had successfully communicated the urgency of the moment to those who would actually carry out the attack. Everyone understood that this was the day, Thursday, May 12, 1864, to break the enemy line that had held them at bay through a week of brutal fighting.

"Give your orders in a whisper," the general continued, "preserve strict silence in your ranks when you advance and do not fire a shot this side of the enemy's works. You will take direction from the 20th Indiana, the second regiment to your left." Without waiting for comment, Ward turned and strode away to give similar orders to the other regimental commanders of his brigade.[98]

There had been no thorough reconnaissance of the enemy position. It was known that the ground ascended to the enemy's works and that a stream flowed across their front. There was open ground ahead on the left and woods on the right. "The direction in which our troops should advance was ascertained by a line determined by a compass on the map from the Brown house toward a large white house known to be inside the enemy's works, near the point we wished to strike."[99]

The 2nd Corps would be massed for the attack, Barlow's Division on the left, Birney on the right, Gibbon and Mott coming up behind. On Birney's front, Ward's Brigade was formed in two lines of regiments, Crocker's Brigade behind formed up the same way. Ward positioned his regiments left to right in the front rank: 20th Indiana, 86th New York, 124th New York, and 99th Pennsylvania. In the second rank, left to right were the 141st Pennsylvania, 40th New York, 110th Pennsylvania, 2nd U.S. Sharpshooters, and 3rd Maine. Hancock wrote that a "heavy fog decided me to delay the order for the assault to commence for a short time, until we should have sufficient light. I therefore waited until 4.35 A.M., when the order was given to advance."[100]

William Howell stood in the front rank of Company E, his brother Henry in the rear rank and to the left. Both men were dangerously close to Color Bearer G.W. Edwards. Experience had taught them that the Confederates would be aiming to knock down the battle flag and anyone nearby.[101]

As Ward had instructed Weygant, so all the troops of Hancock's Corps were instructed — no bugle calls, no drums, no cheering, weapons loaded but no firing until the works were carried. Bayonets were to be fixed, the men were to go forward at a steady pace keeping their alignment and unit cohesion as long as possible.

Inside the earthworks, the Confederates knew something was afoot. For hours they had heard ominous noises from somewhere out in the fog. Brigadier General George H. Steuart, whose regiments occupied the right side of the salient, sent a written warning to his division commander stating in no uncertain terms that Yankees were massing on his front and that he expected to be attacked at dawn. He begged to have the artillery returned to the salient at once.[102] The warning went to Lee, who agreed. However, it was not until 3:30 A.M. that the battery commanders got their orders and by then it was too late to have the guns back in place by dawn. The artillery left behind in the salient and the riflemen crouching behind the earthworks would have to handle whatever came out of the fog.

Weygant noticed that the sky to the east was lightening. Word was passed in a whisper that the men were to form up. Many rose from their sleep, found their places in the ranks and sank again to the ground. "Since the opening of the campaign we had been facing death so much of the time, our sensibilities may have become somewhat blunted" Weygant remembered. Everyone knew this would be "one of most desperate undertakings they had ever known," but that did not stop them from trying to get just a few moments more of rest.[103] Sly slept soundly until someone shook him and said, "'Sly get up!' and I did." Ward and his staff prepared to move out on foot. Sly chose to lead his horse by the reins over the open ground and mount later.[104]

By 4:30 A.M., the fog had cleared enough to satisfy Hancock who gave the order: "Forward, guide left, march!" Weygant thought the men looked "taller than was their want. There was that too in their handling of their weapons and in the unordered but continual quickening of their pace until I was forced to spur my horse to a lively trot to keep ahead of them, which thrilled me with a feeling of confidence, in both them and myself, such as I had never experienced before."[105]

The battle line moved resolutely forward, ranks of men elbow to elbow, until they reached the woods. The difficult ground and thick underbrush did little to slow them as twenty thousand men strode through the chilly dawn. Orders for silence notwithstanding, this dawn was filled with sound: the rustle of clothing and squeak of leather, the snapping of twigs, the slap of thousands of brogans against the soggy ground, the strained breathing of the men, all magnified in the damp morning air. Sly wrote, "the troops seemed to march so fast could not lead the horse and keep up and then I mounted I dont think I ever seen troops march so fast and walk as strait as they did that morning"[106] A soldier in the 17th Maine of Crocker's Brigade, remembered, "All orders were given in whispers.... There was something terribly weird ... in the hooting of owls as the dark figures of men moved through the pines, in the sobbing of the wind through the wet trees."[107]

Keeping ranks closed with Barlow's Division to their left was no easy job for Birney's men. The terrain to their front was wooded and swampy while Barlow's men crossed open ground. The 124th New York came out of the woods, crossed a low a ridge line along which ran an east-west farm lane, and advanced into a swale. By now the Orange Blossoms were close enough to see what they had come to dread: another ridge of freshly dug earthworks with cannon and riflemen aiming right at them.

The exhausted enemy pickets were sleeping at their posts when the blue wave broke over them. A few did get off a shot or two before they were bayoneted, captured, or fled toward the safety of their earthworks to raise the alarm. The shots served to spur the Yankees' pace until the enemy earthworks rose up in front of them. It was then that they knew that they had successfully crossed the killing ground unscathed and they raised a "wild ringing shout" in celebration. Tearing through the abitis in front of the enemy works, they surged forward.[108]

Opposite Ward's men were two brigades of battle-hardened Confederate veterans: five Louisiana regiments of Stafford's Brigade commanded by Colonel Zebulon York and five Virginia regiments of the legendary Stonewall Brigade commanded by Brigadier General James A. Walker. Like the Union brigades coming toward them, they were exhausted and their ranks thinned by continuous fighting, but having been alerted, many were at their posts. The Confederates took aim at the blue mass coming at them, each man confident that he could not miss at such close range. But instead of the flash and roar of musketry, all that was heard was the hollow popping of hundreds of percussion caps. The rain had dampened their powder charges and the weapons misfired. When they heard the tinny bangs, the Union men knew exactly what was happening; with renewed strength they tore away the obstructions and broke into the open.[109]

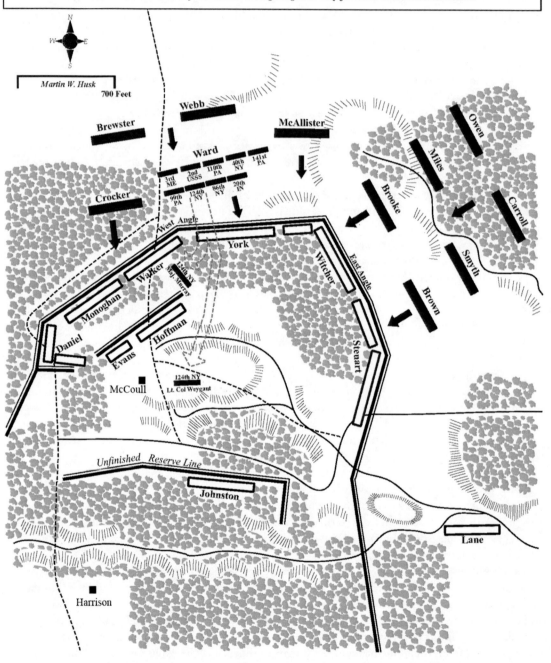

Spotsylvania Court House, May 12, 1864

The 124th New York, along with the rest of Ward's Brigade, assault the Confederates along the West Angle. After overrunning York's Brigade, the regiment divided into two sections. The right-most section, commanded by Major Murray, swung to the Southwest. The left-most section, commanded by Lt. Col. Weygant and including members of the 141st PA, continued to push Southwest, fighting their way just East of the McCoull house.

The Orange Blossoms had been advancing at the right shoulder shift, rifle butt cradled in the palm, elbow bent, lock high up on the shoulder. Now they threw their weapons forward, tightly held, bayonets at eye level pointing directly at the enemy, and broke into a run. No one gave the order, but a cheer, the mighty "hurrah!" of the Union, followed by a sustained roar told the Confederates all they needed to know: The Yankees were upon them.

"Here they tore away the abitis with their hands and poured over the works in an irresistible mass," wrote a soldier in the 141st Pennsylvania. "The men were in great confusion. The several commands mixed in great disorder, but such was the enthusiasm inspired that every one seemed bent on doing his best to make the dash successful."[110]

On the outside of the earthworks, Weygant's horse was crowded into a ditch and he was forced to dismount "to clamber over the earthen barrier, lest his regiment should lead him instead of his leading them. Several of our number, while straightening themselves up on the top of the works, were pierced by bullets fired by the rallying foe, but a moment later we bore down on their half-formed line with a force that could not be resisted."[111]

Henry Howell wrote of their steely determination: "At daylight we formed and double-quicked a quarter of a mile and went right over their works without once stopping to breathe. We commenced cheering before we got in sight of the works. It seemed as though every one was borne irresistibly forward. There was no such thing as fail."[112]

General Hancock wrote that the men raced forward

> up the slope about half way to the enemy's line, when the men broke into a tremendous cheer, and spontaneously taking the double-quick, they rolled like an irresistible wave into the enemy's works, tearing away what abatis there was in front of the entrenchments with their hands and carrying the line at all points in a few moments, although it was desperately defended. Barlow's and Birney's divisions entered almost at the same moment, striking the enemy's line at a sharp salient immediately in front of the Landrum house. A fierce and bloody fight ensued in the works with bayonets and clubbed muskets.[113]

Covering the very tip of the salient and its eastern face was Jones's Brigade, now commanded by Colonel William Witcher. His five Virginia regiments had the dubious distinction of being the first to crumble under the onslaught and in doing so they uncovered the right flank of York's Brigade on the western side of the salient's tip. In truth, no brigade, Federal or Confederate, could have held that ill-fated position.

Birney's two brigades, Ward's and Crocker's, struck the earthworks just below the East Angle. The right regiments of Ward's Brigade, the 99th Pennsylvania and the 124th New York, hit the enemy line at the Angle itself. The men from Orange County saw at once that they were again at the critical point on the battlefield. Some bore straight ahead to get into the interior of the works, while others headed to the right to hit the flank of the nearest enemy soldiers. The Louisiana regiments opposite them commanded by Colonel York were "scooped" with many prisoners taken. Two Confederate batteries suffered the same fate, thus securing the tip of the salient and the East Angle for the Yankees, at least for the moment.[114]

Weygant was now inside the works trying to keep the regiment together in the swirling chaos. He had to look to his own safety as well. A colonel of the Stonewall Brigade, who had just fired the last shot from his revolver, presumably at Weygant, "gracefully" reversed the weapon and handed it to the New Yorker. "I ask as a favor to be sent off the field under guard, for I do not care to be considered one of that flock of sheep" he said pointing to his former command, now prisoners and heading back into Union lines.[115]

Coming in behind Birney were two brigades of Mott's Division and one of Gibbon's Division. As they struck the northwestern face of the salient, the Confederates were hit from the east by four brigades of Barlow's Division with two more brigades of Gibbon's Division coming on in support. Contemporary accounts likened the attack to a wave crashing against the shore — a wave of 20,000 Union soldiers.

Hancock wrote that his men overran the tip of the salient quickly, which

resulted in the capture of nearly 4,000 prisoners of Johnson's division, of Ewell's corps, 20 pieces of artillery, with horse, caissons, and material complete, several thousand stand of small-arms, and upward of 30 colors. Among the prisoners were Major General Edward Johnson and Brigadier General George H. Steuart, of the Confederate service. The enemy fled in great confusion and disorder. Their loss in killed and wounded was unusually great. The interior of the entrenchments presented a terrible and ghastly spectacle of dead, most of whom were killed by our men with the bayonet when they penetrated the works. So thickly lay the dead at this point, that at many places the bodies were touching and piled upon each other.[116]

Sly wrote that Ward's men went right over the top of the defending Confederates and found some of them asleep inside the works, "but we had them." He listed the captured as "one Major Genl Johnson and one Brigadear Stewart over 3000 men and 36 guns but wee only got 22 of them off." Some of the men thought they had captured Jeb Stuart. Sly went on to detail the problems already clear even in victory:

all Formation of our troops was lost wee were nothing more than mobs then and the men all seemed drunk with Delight I was up this time ahead of the Genl and staff I had my Horse and they were afoot but they were soon their and their Horses soon came when they mounted and went over the works then the Genl tried to form our Brig wee got them partly formed but it was impossible to hold them as Hancock was their saying wee had captured Johnson and his whole Division now he was goine in to Early.[117]

The two rebel generals were not happy at being taken in the assault. According to Colonel Lyman, Johnson shook hands all around but said to a Union general, "Doubtless you have gained an advantage, but you are much mistaken if you think we are beaten yet!" Johnson was then taken for some breakfast. Steuart refused to shake hands with Hancock, who sent the prisoner off to Fredericksburg on foot through the ankle deep mud.[118]

Early in the action, a Louisiana color bearer planted his regiment's flag on the earthworks in an effort to rally the men. Not three feet away, Color Bearer George Washington Edwards drove his flagstaff into the ground, letting loose the brand new battle flag of the 124th New York. For just a moment "the two flags floated together on the earthworks," when Corporal Archibald Freeman of Company E, "sprang on the works and quick as a flash jerked up the traitor rag and was back in his place without getting a scratch." When Freeman took the flag "well now, you just ought to have heard our boys yell." This bravado enraged the Confederates who "tried to get even by coming the same dodge on us and capturing our flag; but they ought to have known better than to attempt such a job, for we tumbled them back, completely riddled with bullets every time they came near it."[119]

In Freeman's Medal of Honor citation, and in subsequent secondary accounts, the flag is identified as that of the 17th Louisiana. Even Colonel Weygant, in his regimental history, quoted a wounded Orange Blossom of Freeman's company as naming that regiment.[120] The Confederate Order of Battle lists no 17th Louisiana regiment as being on the line that day. The 17th fought at Shiloh and later was captured at Vicksburg, paroled, and exchanged. The regiment spent most of the rest of the war in its home state. York's Brigade did, however, contain the 15th Louisiana and in a letter home written two days after the event, Henry Howell listed the wounded of his company including Archibald Freeman. "The last named captured the flag of the 15th Louisiana," he wrote. It may be that the 17th and 15th were consolidated under the banner of the 15th but it is more likely that in the confusion, the regimental number was incorrectly recorded. In the end it didn't matter. Freeman got his Medal of Honor and men on each side of the line had the opportunity to witness the extraordinary bravery, both of the Confederate soldier who boldly planted his colors in the face of the enemy, and of the Union soldier who took them.[121]

The second line of Ward's Brigade came over the works right behind the first—141st Pennsylvania, 40th New York, 110th Pennsylvania, 2nd U.S. Sharpshooters, and 3rd Maine. Most of

Ward's men, including a good number of Orange Blossoms who'd become separated from their colonel, turned right once they were beyond the earthworks. They pitched into the few remaining Louisiana troops and Walker's Stonewall Brigade which already had its hands full dealing with Crocker's Brigade piling over the works in front of it. Before the rebels knew what was happening, Ward's men were rolling up their flank. A member of the 86th New York who had come over the works just to the left of the Orange Blossoms wrote that Ward's regiments became completely intermingled almost immediately.[122]

For these Union troops moving west along the earthworks, success was a mixed blessing. They were taking so many prisoners that their progress slowed. This gave Confederate Brigadier General Junius Daniel time to pivot his rightmost regiment to the rear to form a line of battle perpendicular to the earthworks. Daniel then rolled two batteries into position facing right, lending artillery support to his beleaguered riflemen and slowing the Yankees still more.

Weygant wrote that "Ward's second line came up while we were yet engaged in the contest over the enemy's guns and had entered into the pursuit with such a spirit as to lose their organization at the very outset."[123] In their exuberance to run down the fleeing enemy, a number of "Orange Blossoms," including the colonel, headed south. They chased the enemy a third of a mile into the interior of the salient, by one account. Weygant and a small group of men halted in the vicinity of the McCoull House, joined up with members of the 141st Pennsylvania, and moved forward to a line of rifle pits. Minnie balls began zipping past them, fired from the woods in the distance. Ahead about one hundred and fifty yards was a line of unfinished earthworks, beyond which Weygant saw a heavy line of gray infantry advancing, firing as it came. "Our further success depended on our reaching these works first, and in sufficient force to hold them."[124]

Their chances were slim but they tried it anyway. Two members of the color guard of the 141st were wounded in the process, as was Weygant. He personally planted the flag on the works before being shot in the leg, and now the whole group risked capture. But first he tore the colors of the Pennsylvania regiment from the staff and stuffed the flag inside his coat. As the large enemy force advanced, eight Confederates who had taken refuge on the opposite side of the works, jumped over to the Union side, not to capture the Yankees but to surrender. Weygant drew his revolver and ordered the group to use his rubber raincoat as a stretcher to carry him to the rear. They made their way, prisoners and all, back across the battlefield to a point where the Confederates could be turned over to the provost and the colonel could have his wound treated. Later on, he returned the flag of the 141st to a corporal of the color guard.

Sly corroborated Weygant's claim that they had penetrated quite a distance before they were stopped. "Wee got as far as the Mccool House when they mooved out their Main works with a strong Battle line that brought us to a halt then wee were ordered back and Man the works wee had captured."[125]

This all happened within the first hour of the battle. Through the efforts of Confederate units still intact and fighting, but mostly due to the confused situation in the salient, the Yankee attack was stalled. Lee was now on the scene and he knew he had but one option to restore the situation: he must launch a counterattack to stabilize the line and buy time so that a second strong line of earthworks, about half a mile beyond the one Weygant had tried to secure, could be manned.

When Weygant had become separated from the main body of the 124th New York, command fell to Major Murray, who led his men against the enemy troops in the area defended by General Daniel's Confederates. The 124th fought alongside the 86th and the rest of the brigade, all intermingled of course, pushing the enemy along the inner face of the earthworks. But the Confederates still held a reserve line of works to the rear of the main line and running parallel to it for about a third of a mile. It was early, the field still shrouded in fog and powder smoke, when General Stephen D. Ramseur led his four North Carolina regiments forward to prevent the line from being further rolled up by the Yankees. Under heavy fire, Ramseur's men carried the reserve line. Seeing nothing but blue uniforms between them and the main works, they charged the disorganized Federals who took refuge on the outer side of the works at the salient, while the rebels did the same on the inside. With Yankees on one side of the six- to eight-foot high barricade and rebels on the inside, there began an all-day seesaw struggle that came to define May 12, 1864.

The fight along this section of the works was close and brutal. Captain James Benedict of Company D was wounded and taken to the rear, but a good many more lay where they fell and could not be moved, that day or the next. "Horible to think of," remembered Sly, "but such is war."[126]

The men under Murray's command were falling back but brought with them "two of the captured brass guns, and a quantity of fixed ammunition," solid shot or shell with the powder

Captain Henry Travis. He and Captain Wood had artillery experience and turned the enemy's guns back on them at Spotsylvania (Michael J. McAfee collection).

charge attached ready to be rammed into the gun and fired. Captains Wood and Travis, both of whom had served with Colonel Ellis' howitzer section at Bull Run, took charge of the guns and "used them most effectually" against the enemy until they ran out of ammunition.[127]

The early Confederate counterattacks had been delaying actions. The main effort, led by General John Gordon, one of the most capable of Lee's division commanders, came just before 6:00 A.M. Lee's presence on the field inspired his men but, fearing he would be killed, they shouted, "Lee to the rear!" until someone led the horse and rider away. Then Gordon's men hit the Yankees hard. Union troops south or east of the McCoull House were pushed back to the main line of earthworks. Reinforcements coming up and those driven back massed along the outer edge of the works, packed together rank upon rank.[128]

General Birney was attempting to sort out the confusion back at the tip of the salient when he saw General Ward heading for the rear. Ward was obviously excited, saying he was looking for his horse, so Birney had an aide give him one. Then Ward insisted on making a charge. Birney suspected the general was drunk and informed Hancock who went to see for himself. After speaking with Ward, the 2nd Corps commander concluded that he "had been drinking more than proper," and informed Birney, who "immediately rode to the rifle pits, where Ward was, to satisfy myself as to the correctness of Major General Hancock's opinion." Birney wrote, "Watching his movements, I felt it my duty to order him to the rear under arrest. I believed him to be grossly intoxicated." Messengers were sent to find Colonel Thomas W. Egan of the 40th New York to inform him that he was now in command of the brigade.[129]

Weygant was puzzled as to why the general was relieved. He wrote that the brigade was "now under command of Colonel Eagen, of the 40th N.Y. (General Ward having been, for some cause unknown to those under him, relieved from command)."

Sly was more than just puzzled, he was upset. Here was a soldier who saw Ward every day during the campaign and often slept near his headquarters. He made no mention of Ward being drunk or even taking a drink on May 12. Sly wrote, "Now about noon should think Genl Ward with his staff rode down in rear of our line it was then wee lost Liet Wells wounded ... and our

Brig Bugler killed most every horse hit mine twice I tell you was mighty glad when wee got down out of range of their Bullets then soon after wee got back the Genel left us took Luit Doughty with him I wanted to go with him bad and cried like a big booby." As the party turned to ride away, Lieutenant Doughty, no doubt seeing how this had affected Sly, rode back and said that he thought the general would be back soon. "He never got back," Sly wrote. "I was there all alone not another man with the collors."[130]

Not long after the general left, an aide from Birney's headquarters galloped up asking for Colonel Egan. When Sly told the aid he had not seen him, he was handed a letter and told to give it to Egan when he showed up. "This was Capt. Wineburner of Genl Birney staff he told me Col. Egan was going to command the Brig I asking him about Genl Ward he told he thought he would bee back soon but he never did."[131]

Meanwhile, the Confederate counterattack on the west side of the salient shoved Birney's men back toward the apex, the Yankees hugging the outside wall of the earthworks. With some of Mott's troops, they wrapped themselves around the tip of the East Angle, where they spent the rest of the day in a vicious stalemate in which many more were to die in the rain and mud. Grant shifted his troops and brought up fresh reinforcements. Lee did the same but neither general could wrest the grip of the other from the sections they held by 7 A.M. All the while Lee was bolstering the line of earthworks to the rear so that he could straighten out his line.

Both commanding generals thought the West Angle, the "Bloody Angle," was the key to the battlefield and for the rest of the day the slaughter at that section of the line went on unabated. By mid afternoon both sides recognized that stalemate had been reached. Grant hoped for another breakthrough on the flanks but neither Warren nor Burnside was up to the task.

Lieutenant Lewis Wisner of Company K was on detached duty, serving as an engineer officer on General Ward's staff. At about 9 A.M. he received a written order to proceed with a detail of men to the earthworks near the Bloody Angle where a Union battery was busy raking the treetops with canister to dislodge enemy snipers. Wisner's order was to "lower the breastworks," which meant remove the head log at the top of the works so that the artillery piece might depress its barrel enough to fire into the Confederates on the other side of the works. When Wisner presented his order to the battery commander his reply was, "I'll train my gun upon the man, and blow him to 'Kingdom Come,' who dares touch the works." There were Confederates on the opposite side who might get a clean shot at the gun crew if the log was removed.

"Here are my orders, sir. They will be obeyed, guns or no guns." Wisner put two men at each end of the log. They attempted to heave it aside but it had been wired into place and would not budge. Wisner grabbed an axe, leaped up on the works, and  "with one well-directed blow, severed one end of the log. He ran quickly to the other end and cut the log at that point." In those few seconds, his clothes were riddled but he jumped down unhurt. The battery commander was duly impressed. "You have accomplished the most heroic act I ever witnessed, Captain," he said, and shook his hand. When the "folly of this order was revealed"—which probably meant that the gunners were exposed—the battery commander asked that the head log be replaced. Wisner complied, again exposing himself to enemy fire. For this action he was awarded a Medal of Honor.[132]

The battle raged all day along the earthworks, and many Union

Lieutenant Lewis Wisner. "Here are my orders, sir. They will be obeyed," said the lieutenant to the battery commander at Spotsylvania. For his actions he was awarded a Medal of Honor (Michael J. McAfee collection).

men claimed to have fired over two hundred rounds. Plenty of ammunition was close at hand, one thousand rounds per wooden box. Officers collected the boxes in the rear of their men, broke them open, and passed the cartridge packages forward. An ordinance officer noted, "The only way to keep the men there is to let them fire."[133]

It was about 4 P.M. when Colonel Egan rode up and, with a laugh and a salute, "reported" to Private Sly for duty. Egan, who seemed to think the whole affair with Ward ridiculous, read the order promoting him to brigade command. He said, "Sly you can say you have commanded a Brigade for two Hours under the hardest fighting I ever saw."

The field inside the works was one huge smoking sea of mud and casualties. Sly wrote that the "men lay their all day and night and never saw it rain harder than it did that day and the heaviest fighting that wee ever knew to hold them works but wee held them no let up untill dark when they drew off their troops to their main line."[134]

After a brutal day of fighting, during which Lee completed the second line of earthworks and manned it as best he could, the situation remained at a stalemate. After dark, Colonel Egan sent out a skirmish line as far as the McCoull House. He told Sly to stay with the picket reserve and report if anything happened, but it was quiet all night.

Colonel Lyman assessed the day's fighting, but he also commented on the western attitude at Grant's headquarters.

> The great historical fight of this day extended over a front of only 1,000 to 1,500 yards, along the faces of the salient, or the "Death-angle" as it was afterwards called. Within that narrow field two corps were piled up to assault and in support. Indeed we had too many troops, as the generals justly said. The lines got mixed and jammed together and were hard to handle. For 14 hours the troops were at close quarters, and the amount of bullets fired may be known from the fact, that a red oak, 23 inches in diameterr was reduced, about 6 feet from the ground, to a fibrous structure and blew down that night! Bodies that lay between the lines were shot to pieces and could only be raised in blankets! The result was damaging to the enemy — very — but the army of Lee was not cut in two, an issue clearly looked for by Rawlins and some others of Grant's staff, but not so confidently assumed by those who knew a little more.[135]

A few days later Captain William A. Jackson of Company K wrote to his friend Alsop Purdy that he had "not a scratch" from the battle. "Up to this time the regt has lost about 15 killed 110 wounded and 25 missing, names will be soon sent on." Jackson asked Purdy to contact editor Hasbrouck of the *Whig Press*

> to make these facts public. John Scott is most likely killed. Our charge on the 12th inst. was very daring and a decided success. In Co. K Parsons is wounded bad in the leg Ogden not bad. Vermilya bad in the leg. Crans ditto. Kanoff bad in face. Studar slight in arm. Faulkner missing. About half our regt. are gone but they fought well. No off. Killed but six wounded. Murray commands the regt. Some of our wounded are in Fredericksburgh and some in Washington. How we did cut the rebs after taking their works when they tried to get them back. We have as yet got no mail. My paper & envelopes are gone. Please send me some. We have done no hard fighting scince 12th but under fire and skirmish.... We hope to flank the rebs out this summer but must go careful for they fight desperate.

He finished his letter with a postscript saying that Corp. D.U. Quick, who had been reported missing, was present with the regiment. He then added the names of officers present, which included but five company commanders — Murray, Crist, Sayre, Travis, and Jackson — and three lieutenants — Robinson, Van Houten, and Wisner.[136]

Writing to his mother soon after the battle, Henry Howell noted,

> That morning we made the most magnificent and successful charge of the war. Birney's Division captured very near as many prisoners as there were men in the Division. We also claim over twenty pieces of artillery and a dozen stand of colors, & three Generals. We lost quite heavy in wounded and I was hit with the rest. I have a flesh wound in my left leg below the knee. Comparatively Slight. We had not been engaged more than an hour that morning before I was hit. I went to the rear at once.... They had the strongest position I ever seen carried by assault since I have known anything about military."

But there was bad news.

My Dear Mother, It gives me pain to think of the sad news which it is my duty to communicate to you. William fell wounded in the breast on the morning of the 12th inst. Those who saw him thought it was so bad that he could not live. He gave his pocket book and watch to Lieut. Mapes, who passed them over to Lieut. Robinson. Mother he may be living, but if not let us console ourselves with the thought that he died when a patriot would have been proud to die.... Lieut. Mapes came in wounded in the afternoon and he told me about William. He said the last he seen of him three or four of the boys were carrying him off the field. Dora will send his things home as soon as they get where they can send out a mail.

Henry went on to detail the killed and wounded of the regiment.

Tholf received a bruise from a shell. It glanced by his side breaking his bayonet, and bruising his hip ... it did not break the skin. Simeon Wheat was hit in the hand, two fingers being quite badly injured. Adam Miller was wounded so bad that he died the next day. H. Wheeler, L. Baxter, & A. Freeman were wounded in my Company.... Col. Weygant, Captains Wood, Benedict, Lieuts Mapes & Cormick are wounded. The 12th was the 8th days fighting. For about two hours in the forenoon of the second day they got the best of us but all the rest of the 8 days has been in our favor. We kept flanking them out of their intrenchments all the while. Our Army charged their works in several places with indifferent results until the morning we tried it.

This would be Henry Howell's last letter from the front lines. He downplayed the leg wound to his mother as "comparatively slight," but he would never return to the ranks of the 124th New York. The young private was taken to the field hospital where his wound was given a perfunctory examination and probably bandaged. Then he was sent on his way to Fredericksburg with thousands of other wounded men. He wrote on May 14 from that town where he and other wounded men were housed in an "unused Church," adding that they expected to be sent north from there and would write as soon as he could. He finished his letter with, "The latest news from the front says that Grant is still victorious."[137]

Three days later he wrote to his sister Emily from Lincoln Hospital after what the wounded soldier described as a "very tedious journey" by army wagon to Belle Plain and then on to Washington by steamboat. He slept on board the steamer before being loaded into an ambulance to be taken to the hospital. Rumor had it that the wounded would be sent north because the hospitals in the capital were overwhelmed by the two great battles.

Each state is to take care of their own wounded I suppose. There is not a man in this ward that I ever saw or heard tell of before.... My leg feels pretty well now. I have got it washed up and clean clothes on again.... Everything is kept very nice around here but I do not think there is as much attention shown to the wounded as there should be that is on dressing the wounds. I am able to help myself so I get along better than some of the others.... In other respects I believe our wants are attended to. I had the best nights rest last night of any night since we left camp.

He was referring to their winter camp at Brandy Station, from which the regiment marched on the third of May.

He mentioned that Captain Wood and Lieutenant Mapes were both in the same hospital but as yet he had not seen either of them. Colonel Cummins was still at Fredericksburg, the thigh wound making it too dangerous to move him. "I believe he frets considerably," Howell said of the popular old officer who always showed concern for his men. Captain Travis had written home earlier that Cummins's wound was serious and

Captain Charles B. Wood, Company A. He was wounded in action May 12, 1864, at Spotsylvania Court House, and discharged for wounds September 21, 1864. He had prior service as private, Company I, 71st NYSM. He used his artillery experience to turn the enemy's guns back on them at Spotsylvania (archive of the Historical Society of the Town of Warwick, gift of Joan and Tom Frangos).

he feared that things would go hard for him. Major Murray wrote to his father that "Col Cummins is wounded in the leg by bullet & has gone to Washington. He will have a hard time as his blood is in a terrible condition, & they can't find the ball."

Then Howell turned to the painful subject of his brother's death. "I have learned that William became insensible of anything that was going on around him before he died. He would talk at random but he kept saying. 'Tell the general to bring them men up on this line by my order.'" He told his sister that he had just mailed a letter to Adam Miller's parents telling them of the death of their son and enclosing his personal effects. "I guess you need not write until you hear from me again for I do not think I will be here long enough to receive one. I have a little money left yet."

Howell then gave his sister his opinion of the war to date. He spoke not as a high-ranking officer with his eye on promotion, but as a soldier in the ranks with a wealth of experience behind him.

> I met considerable reinforcements for Grant on my way up here. I think the way he is doing the thing up he intends to annihilate Lee before he gets through with him for our army instead of getting smaller on account of the killed wounded and missing it is kept about the same size all the while. Lee cannot do that certainly. This battle beats any one that has taken place since the war broke out. We had used more ammunition in the regt before I was wounded than we ever did in all the fights that we had ere been in before. I hope this will certainly finish up the war.[138]

CHAPTER 14

"I think that we will whip them very bad with the help of God"
May 13–June 14, 1864

Friday morning, May 13, 1864, Colonel Lyman of Meade's staff wrote, "6 A.M. The enemy has abandoned the salient and fallen back, some hundreds of yards, to its base, and straightened his line.... Officers in from the salient described its awful aspect ... the bodies piled, one on another in heaps and rows!"[1] Private Sly was still out on the picket line gathering information for Colonel Egan. Later that morning he rode back to headquarters. "It had all cleared off and the sun was shining bright when reported all quiet." The colonel obviously knew and appreciated Sly's value as an aide. "He says Sly go up to the road and get your Breakfast I told him to save it for you." Sly was very pleased to hear that piece of news. "I got around that very quick for about all a soldier cares for is the grub and when that dont come things dont prove right."[2]

After breakfast, Colonel Egan sent a detail to bury the dead on the inside of the earthworks. Although they buried men in blue and gray without discrimination, rebel snipers fired on the burial detail, killing one and wounding several more. Egan and Sly went to where the men were working and the colonel ordered the detail brought in at once. "It was their I looked over the works," wrote Sly, "and that was the most Horrible sight that I ever saw they laid in piles and their own shells had torn some of them all to pieces I tell you. Made a short look at them. It was their own men that wee went out to burry when they commenced firing on us."

At noon Colonel Egan sent Sly back to the supply train to exchange his wounded horse for another. "It was a butiafull day the sun bright and warm that was about two miles to the rear." He stopped in at Division Hospital for news of the wounded. As he rode up, a hospital steward named Morell called out to him wanting to know how things were at the front. After Sly gave him what news he had, the steward ducked into his tent and brought out a bottle of brandy and put it into Sly's saddle bag.

He'd gone but a short distance farther when he was approached. "Little Annie of the 4th Michigan in our other Brig wanted to know if I knew anything about her regt." Anne Etheridge was well known in the Army of the Potomac as "the angel of the 3rd Corps" and had been appointed to the rank of sergeant by none other than General Phil Kearny. She was a "daughter of the regiment" who shared the danger and hardship of the campaign and ministered to the needs of the sick and wounded. She was an expert, fearless rider who often carried the wounded men to the rear under fire. Annie told Sly that after he got his new horse, she would accompany him back to the line to help the boys in need.

Sly made his way to the supply train "and what a reception I got." The captain in charge "said I should have the best Horse he had or anything else that I wanted and had a splendid dinner fixed for mee and he gave me as good a Horse as I lost in the Wilderness and got filled up with good Eatables and started back. Found Little Annie ready to mount her Black Roan wich she rode and wee started up the road."[3]

As they passed by the hospital, the steward called out that the doctor in charge wanted to see the young courier from Orange County. He told Sly to carry his compliments to Colonel Egan as well as a bottle of brandy and a bottle of whiskey. "So you see I was well provided with the Old Stuff." When Sly got to brigade headquarters, Egan thanked him for the message and the bottles then handed him a small pocket flask. The colonel told him to fill the flask with brandy and keep the rest for himself while he congratulated him on "what a fine Horse they let me have."

Sly rode to where the 124th New York was positioned on the earthworks to look for his friend, Captain Daniel Sayer. Sly had not seen the captain since the campaign opened and thought he might appreciate one of the bottles he carried in his saddle bag. Sly was shocked when he found him. "He sayed he was all played out and he looked it now to think what that Dear good Man had gone through the last ten days fought two of the Bloodiest Battles of the War and in fact fighting every day and marching all night do you wonder that this man looked and felt all used up." It was then that Sly first heard of the losses among the officers of the 124th New York. Captain Benedict and Lieutenant Houston, both of Company D, were thought to be mortally wounded, a report that turned out to be false. Captain Wood and Colonel Weygant were wounded but no one knew how seriously. "Wee chatted their untill after dark when I bid the Capt good bye and how little did wee think that the next morning the Capt would be sending word Home that I was Killed."[4]

Captain Daniel Sayer was the 43-year-old commander of Company E at the end of the war. Wounded at Chancellorsville, he mustered out with company June 3, 1865, near Washington, D.C. (archive of the Historical Society of the Town of Warwick, gift of Joan and Tom Frangos).

General Grant was not one to remain idle, and he began looking for another way to strike the enemy. He was of the opinion that the rebels' heavy losses of May 12 must have weakened them to the point of collapse. He sent infantry into the Mule Shoe, probing for some weakness, but they found the new line of earthworks at the base of the salient to be well defended. Instead, Grant decided to send two of his infantry corps, the 5th and 6th, from the right of his line to the left, west to east, marching them behind Hancock and Burnside to where they could threaten Lee's line. Once in position, Grant thought that his men could gain the enemy's flank by a swift coordinated movement. The plan had a chance of success, assuming Lee didn't react first and assuming that the 5th and 6th Corps could get into position by dawn on May 14, after a night march in the rain over roads clogged with men, supply wagons, artillery, and wounded Yankees.[5]

The orders came late and the march was behind schedule almost before it started. The roads were poor even by rural Virginia standards. Much of the march was through open fields cut by streams over their banks from all the rain. As it turned out, only a few brigades were able to get into position at the appointed time and the dawn attack against Lee's vulnerable right was cancelled. More federal troops came into line later that morning and might have succeeded against the lightly held earthworks, but Grant failed to seize the opportunity. The skirmish lines sparred with each other throughout the day while Grant tried to come up with some other way to break Lee's strong position.[6]

Hancock's men were in place along the Mule Shoe that morning, ready to attack if Grant's turning movement succeeded. Egan's Brigade still lay on the north side of the earthworks with the pickets out some distance toward the enemy. Sly was back at the front and watched a member of the 124th calmly "eating his Breakfast with his face toward the Enemy when he went to take a Mouthfull of food his Mouth open a Bullet went in with The food and came out in the back off his neck ... he thought he was killed but he was not and I think he soon got over it."[7]

Sly mounted up and rode toward brigade headquarters "wich then were behind the works and I think were very near the Death Angle." He did not feel a thing when a sharpshooter's bullet pierced his shoulder and exited through his neck. He glanced down, puzzled to see blood all over his horse's neck and for an instant he assumed that his mount had been hit. He tried to raise his arm but could not. Only then did he realize that the blood he saw on the animal was spurting out of *him*. "I don't think I fell off the Horse but Jimmy Erwin of my Old Company said he saw me when I was hit as the regt lay right near and he thought I fell off but I dont know how I got off."

Sly was gravely wounded. "I bled jest like sticking a Hog," he recalled. Colonel Egan was nearby and immediately summoned the regimental surgeon of the 40th New York. In the doctor's opinion, the wound was mortal. It would serve no purpose to move the courier to the rear. The colonel emphatically disagreed and ordered that Sly be taken to the division hospital at once. Sly was administered two doses of "White Powder" on the blade of a knife that knocked him out. He "waked up along side of the road troops were going bye up to the front and they looked all so clean and fresh when they had bin marching bye me quite some time they came to a halt and an officer came up and spoke to me." Rousing himself from his stupor, Sly wanted to know what regiment was marching past. "He told me 1st Connitcut Heavy Artillery and they were 2000 strong."

Sly drifted in and out of consciousness. He had no idea of the time of day or how long he lay near the road. He remembered the sun warming his body, but loss of blood and the effects of the opiate knocked him out again. When he awoke, he lay in an old barn, rain pounding on the roof. Someone raised him up a bit and insisted that he drink a "milk Punch made with condensed milk and plenty of whiskey for it did smart my throat but he wanted me to drink plenty of it and then their stood a man at my feet with a rubber coat and hat on with a lantern Book and Pencil taking our names Co and Regt when I gave him mine he told the man bye me to step out and he steped in and lifted me up asking me if I came from Warwick told I did he said he was Doctor Vanderweer." Dr. Albert Vander Veer would shortly become one of the operating surgeons of the 2nd Corps and serve in that capacity until the end of the war. Sly could not have wished for a more capable doctor at his side. The courier was examined and told he would live to see "the Little Girls of Orange County" again. He went to sleep with this welcome news. "The next thing remember they were caring me in a House a big fire in the fire Place that is all can recollect."[8]

Private James Irwin, the soldier who saw Sly fall from his horse penciled into this diary, "We went to the right and put some breast works up and then lay behind them so the sharp shooters could not hit us. Sly wounded by one at headqrts and died in a few days afterward."[9] Some time later, Irwin crossed out the last six words.

The same day that Sly was wounded, Birney's Division was finally pulled out of the line and moved about 200 yards to the rear where they set about digging a new line of earthworks. A "small observing force," of Confederates watched the activity from a safe distance. The 86th New York and 124th New York, under the command of Colonel Lansing of the 86th, charged and drove them away. The little foray cost the Orange Blossoms one man killed and another wounded.[10]

On the afternoon of May 14, Birney's men were moved still farther back to the extreme right wing of the Union army. They faced southwest, taking a position near the Shelton House. Colonel Egan sent three of his regiments forward on picket duty—the 141st Pennsylvania in the woods on the right, 124th New York in the open fields, and 86th New York in the woods on the left. To their front, Brigadier General Pierce Young's cavalry brigade of Wade Hampton's fabled division prowled the wood roads and thickets, proof to the men on the picket line that the Confederates were still capable to taking the offensive.[11]

The 124th had suffered so many casualties since the start of the campaign that the regiment was consolidated into just three companies instead of the normal ten. A few days later, the 124th and 86th were further consolidated into a single regiment under the command of the senior officers of the 86th New York. "This union, which lasted until they settled down in camp in front of Petersburg, strengthened the already strong ties existing between the two commands; and the bond of fellowship formed in camp and on the march, was sealed amid the smoke and thunder of battle where their valiant dead fell side by side."[12]

On Sunday, Sly was fit enough for travel to better medical facilities in Fredericksburg. The ambulance ride to that town was remembered by any wounded man who survived it. The road was rough and muddy, every jarring bump threw the wounded about. His companion in the vehicle was a captain from Michigan with a dangerous thigh wound, "and every move he made all most took his life and if ever a Driver got a Daming it was that one." The captain swore that if he had a pistol he would shoot the driver but once out on the main road it was a relatively smooth ride into Fredericksburg.[13]

The ambulance arrived in the city late in the afternoon on Sunday. "They put us in an Old Tobacco Ware House on the 1st floor then an Elderly Lady came in from the Christian Commission to see what wee could Eat. I had not had any thing from saturday morning untill Sunday 5 P.M. to eat was Hungery and my throt was sore she gave me a big dish of fresh pudding and I dont think I ever eat as good a Pudding as that in my life." Wounded friends from the regiment found Sly and brought him to share a room in a private residence with Captain Briscoe, who'd also been wounded.

"I tell you was glad to get with Briscoe he told as soon as he got his Leave of absence he would take me on to Washington." They received but little treatment for their wounds in Fredericksburg and pretty much took care of themselves. By May 21, Briscoc's leave was granted and that afternoon the two men boarded the mail boat for Washington and home.[14]

So ended Norman Augustus Sly's "Ramblings" on the opening battles of the Overland Campaign of 1864. His writings are a glimpse into life at the brigade level and a recollection of the danger he faced whether on a scout with Captain Briscoe, carrying messages for General Ward, or checking the picket line for Colonel Egan. General Ward said of him, "I have sent that man many times when I never expected him to return." His candid observations on General Barlow ("he was only about my age ... and a *Major Genl* and verry rich but a fighter"), his feelings toward General Ward ("I wanted to go with him bad and cried like a big booby"), and his opinion of Colonel Charles Weygant ("a more truthfull or Braver officer never went to the front the only thing he was a little flighty"), are unique insights. Sly did return to active duty, but not with the 124th New York. While recuperating at home he secured a commission in the 152nd New York and served with that regiment until the end of the war.

Grant's campaign brought with it a terrible attrition to the Orange Blossoms, whose letters illuminated their day-to-day lives. In addition to Norman Sly, both Howell brothers, William and Henry, had been casualties in the great charge of May 12, putting an end to their letters from the field. Joseph Johnston suffered a mortal wound on May 5 in the Wilderness that took months to kill him. Among the enlisted men, only Thomas Rodman, James Irwin, and John Z. Drake kept up a correspondence with their families at home. Of the officers, Captains Travis and Murray were still on duty with the regiment. Captain Mapes was wounded in the eye on May 12 and Captain Benedict was wounded in the leg the same day. Both would return, but as the regiment dwindled, the letters home slowed to a trickle.

Grant was determined to keep the pressure on Lee by launching yet another attack. Once the rain let up, the 6th Corps was marched back to the Mule Shoe to participate in an assault on the new Confederate line. Grant suspected that Lee, in shifting his men to meet the threat posed to his right flank, must have weakened his left. The attack, when it came on the morning of May 18, was no surprise to the Confederates. Elements of the 6th Corps and two divisions of the 2nd Corps charged across the same ground as in the attack of May 12, but this time against the reinforced earthworks at the base of the salient. Massed enemy artillery and riflemen behind improved battlements made short work of the attackers, most of whom did not advance through the abitis. The ill-conceived attack resulted in an additional 1,500 dead and wounded Union soldiers and reinforced the nickname already applied to the Mule Shoe Salient: "Hell's Half Acre."[15]

Fortunately for the 124th, Birney's Division, now reorganized into four brigades, was not called forward, but instead watched the debacle unfold before it. Just one man of the regiment was wounded by a stray bullet.[16] Private Irwin wrote of May 18, "We retook our old pits with some loss quite heavy cannonading. We stayed in the pits until 10 P.M. when we were ordered to get ready to march as quiet as possible. We move a short distance and halted for a few hours."[17] At daylight, the regiment moved farther east, halting to go into camp near the Anderson House in preparation for Grant's next move.[18]

Grant did not let the latest repulse slow him down in the least. He wasted no time in issuing orders for the next move in the campaign, another "grand turning movement" to the left. The goal was to be the same: get Lee out of his entrenchments and catch him in open country. This time he would send Hancock's 2nd Corps, his best and most dependable fighting unit, across the Ni River on a march south toward the North Anna River, twenty miles away as the crow flies and more yet for soldiers traveling back roads. This, Grant thought, would offer Lee something he could not resist—an isolated federal corps that he could attack and crush. If Lee took the bait, left his trenches and went south after Hancock, Grant might be able to swoop down and attack him on the march.

Meanwhile, Lee wanted to know what the Yankees were planning. Just as the 2nd Corps was about to get underway, he directed General Ewell to send out a reconnaissance along the main road to Fredericksburg. Ewell decided to take his entire corps on this patrol which, after the fighting of the past two weeks, was down to just six thousand men. He was heading, whether he knew it or not, toward a huge federal wagon train that stretched for miles along the Fredericksburg Road.

The men of the 124th New York were resting when, late in the afternoon, "they were aroused by the sound of heavy firing, off to their rear—in the direction of the Fredericksburg road, on which it was known the trains were parked."[19]

Grant ordered a staff officer to ride to the sound of the guns, find the nearest unit, and pitch into the enemy. Closest to Ewell's attacking force was a true novelty in the battle-worn Army of the Potomac: five regiments of heavy artillery made up of men who'd spent their enlistment thus far manning the big guns in the forts around the capital. Grant ordered them to leave the cannon behind, saw to it that they were issued rifle muskets like regular infantry, and brought them to the front to fight. Eighty-eight hundred men strong and consisting of one regiment each from Maine and Massachusetts and three from New York, they were quite a spectacle with their clean uniforms and gleaming weapons. Their commander, Brigadier General Robert Tyler, was no stranger to combat. An 1853 graduate of West Point, he'd commanded artillery for McClellan, Burnside, Hooker, and Meade.[20]

The "heavies" as they were called, may have been untried in battle but they were well disciplined and put up a determined fight. Meanwhile, other troops raced to their assistance. "Hancock, galloping to the front, sent word to Birney to come forward with his division at the double-quick."[21] Egan's Brigade fell in and, "grasping their guns, canteens, and haversacks, and leaving tents standing and knapsacks strewn about, they hurried into line, which was scarcely formed ere the brigade bugler *tooted* the forward, and the column started on a double-quick toward the scene of action."[22] As the brigade moved out, it was joined by a 5th Corps brigade, the two marching side by side toward the sound of the firing.

By the time they reached the wagon park, both brigades were at the run. Tyler's men, cut up and exhausted, had just repulsed and scattered the latest attack and held the field. Egan's Brigade deployed in line of battle "and moving over Tyler's exhausted command, rushed forward with wild shouts after the flying foe, whom they pursued several miles. And when at length darkness put an end to the wild chase, the pursuers about faced and retraced their steps, bringing in with them upwards of five hundred prisoners." The 124th New York captured two officers and thirty-five enlisted men during the Battle of Harris Farm, as the engagement was called, suffering but one man wounded, Private Joseph Vradenburg of Company G.[23]

Egan's men camped on the battlefield that night, returning on May 20 to the Anderson Plantation, where they cleaned their weapons and "spent the day very pleasantly lounging about on the grass, writing letters home, and talking over the many changes and never to be forgotten events of the preceding sixteen days." Among those writing home was Thomas Rodman, whose letter bore the heading,

> In Camp about 15 Miles South east of Fredericksburg May 20th 1864 —
>
> I have been spared again to write and let you know that I am still well and hope these few lines will find you the same. We have had a very hard time for the last 15 days without even being relieved while the rest of the troops were in camp having a fine time. Besides we have been marching every night fighting all day and marching by night. We have participated in 2 Charges and came out victorious in only one. The last one we captured 15 pieces of artilery and 3 or 4 thousand prisoners our division alone. Gen Grant handles the army quite different from what it was ever done before. We build more breast works and rifle pits than we used to. I have just returned from an expedition which started last night in which we captured in our brigade over 600 prisoners and driving the enemy like sheep. We lost quite heavy not our Regt but mostly the heavy Artilery used as infantry. Truly the lord has been on our side this spring and I think that we will whip them very bad with the help of God. I for one have been very lucky and I thank the Lord for the Preserving care that he has exerscized over me since the fight began hoping that he will continue to do so in future and also so unto you.... Your Affectionate Son Thos Rodman Good Bye and the Lord be with you both[24]

After dark on May 20, Grant resumed his march. The movement took Hancock's men east, then southeast in a wide arc around the right of the Confederate army. After a few miles the 2nd Corps roughly followed the Richmond, Fredericksburg & Potomac Railroad south to Milford Station, where it crossed the Mattapony River and halted about two miles beyond for the night. In the lead, Union cavalry scouted the way, brushing aside any troops found opposing it.[25] "On the morning of the 22nd moved out with the brigade and built works near the Coleman house, which we occupied until near dark, when with other regiments of the brigade was sent out on a reconnaissance toward Pole Cat Station, returning without finding the enemy."[26] James Irwin wrote that once across the river, they built earth works but were sent out on picket duty until five in the afternoon when they were called back in. "Went inside the breastworks, and drew rations and slept all night without disturbance."[27]

Hancock was now just far enough out to entice the Confederate commander to attack him. Grant became concerned at the speed with which Lee reacted to the movement of the 2nd Corps.

Enemy troops appeared to be in the process of blocking the route he planned to use to send reinforcements to Hancock, but, true to form, Lee refused to be enticed. He saw the move for what it was — the beginning of another turning movement around his flank by the entire Army of the Potomac. However, he had yet to determine just where Grant was headed. Lee ordered his army to march south to keep pace with Grant, but he had no intention of attacking Hancock. "For the next thirty-six hours," wrote historian Mark Grimsley, "the two armies marched along roughly parallel routes. The Army of the Potomac followed the II Corps in a march that carried it generally southeast.... The Army of Northern Virginia headed directly for the North Anna River, equidistant between Spotsylvania and Richmond."[28] From this new position, Lee could block Grant from crossing the North Anna but he would also have room to maneuver if Grant should try to attack Richmond by crossing the Pamunkey River farther to the east.

Grant decided to move the Army of the Potomac south in hopes of springing the trap he planned for Lee. But the Confederate commander was already on his way to the North Anna River.[29]

Lee arrived below the North Anna on May 22 and quickly sized up the situation. He became convinced that Grant would move east rather than try to attack across the river. South of the river, the Confederate troops remained in their camps instead of preparing earthworks. When Union and Confederate cavalry got into a tussle north of the river, Lee thought it just another feint to distract him from Grant's real intention, which was to turn his right flank again. In this, says historian Gordon Rhea, "Lee was dangerously mistaken. Grant's juggernaut was feeling its way toward the North Anna."[30]

By nightfall of May 22, Grant's army was concentrating. The 5th, 6th, and 9th corps "were all well abreast of Hancock, or in position to support him. Lee had nearly concentrated his army at Hanover Junction, fifteen to eighteen miles away. Grant had determined to move directly to the North Anna River, to force its passage."[31] Just as Lee was incorrect that Grant would attack farther east, Grant was incorrect in his assumption that Lee would not fight along the banks of the North Anna River, but would instead fall back below the South Anna.

On the morning of May 23, the 2nd Corps continued the march with Birney's Division in the lead. James Irwin wrote, "We left the Mattapony at 7 A.M. March all the forenoon and 2 P.M. We throwed out in line of battle under heavy shelling...."[32] Hancock and Warren were marching south, closing the distance with the North Anna, hampered only slightly by maps that proved to

Chesterfield Bridge on the North Anna River, captured by 2nd Corps units, May 23, 1864. Here the flag staff of the 124th New York was shot in two (Library of Congress, Prints & Photographs Division).

be woefully inaccurate. Grant's intention was to have his two lead infantry corps cross the North Anna, Warren at Jericho Mills and Hancock downstream at Chesterfield Bridge.[33]

Grant's advance had taken two days and now his men approached the North Anna along a wide front. Warren's 5th Corps arrived first and waded the waist deep river at Jericho Ford. By 5:00 P.M., a pontoon bridge strong enough to bear the weight of artillery spanned the river and in short order the entire 5th Corps was on the south side of the North Anna. At about the same time a Confederate prisoner told Warren that a division lay in wait behind a railroad embankment about two miles off. Warren took that to mean the Confederates posed no immediate threat.[34]

But Warren was attacked late in the afternoon by a division of infantry and cavalry at Jericho Mills. Although it was touch and go for a while, Warren, who seemed to have recovered in grand style from his poor performance in the Wilderness, drove the enemy and secured his position.[35]

Meanwhile, about five miles downstream, Hancock, too, was advancing toward the North Anna. His orders were clear: "The Second Corps will proceed to suitable camping-grounds on the banks of the North Anna, near the New Bridge, which is the crossing of the Telegraph road.... If possible, the bridge and crossing will be secured. This corps will also extend east to hold the railroad bridge."[36] As the 2nd Corps approached the North Anna, Gibbon and Barlow moved their divisions to the east side of the main road toward the railroad bridge. Two of Birney's brigades, Brewster and Pierce, deployed to the west of the road while Egan's Brigade straddled the road, the 110th Pennsylvania, 3rd Maine, and 20th Indiana to the west, and the combined 124th New York/86th New York, 40th New York, and 2nd U.S. Sharpshooters to the east. The Orange Blossoms had their right flank on the Telegraph Road.[37]

Hancock wrote to Meade at 2:35 P.M., "The enemy appear to be in force, although I do not think he can prevent a crossing. I can hear the whistle of locomotives frequently on the Virginia Central. A good many troops have been seen across the river, yet they appear to be marching down; therefore I have extended my left. I have no doubt a respectable force is holding my front, on account of the epaulements, &c., there, but whether they expect to remain long enough to dispute the passage strongly I do not know yet.... Shall I force a crossing?" The note went from Meade to Grant bearing the endorsement, "Shall Hancock force a crossing?" Grant replied at 3:00 P.M., "By all means."[38]

On the north side of the river, the Confederates had constructed a tete-de-pont, a bridgehead on the side of the river closest to the enemy. Historian Earl Hess described the works, built in 1863, as "well suited to defend against cavalry raids" but totally inadequate against the Yankee infantry bearing down.[39] It is hard to imagine why Lee held onto the earthworks, now known as "Henagan's Redoubt," which was described as "on a bluff about fifteen feet high, facing north," and unenclosed. Three South Carolina regiments manned the works and the trenches on either side.[40]

Historian William Swinton described the defenses as "an extended redan with a wet ditch in front, the gorge being commanded by rifle trenches in the rear. On the Southern bank, which dominates the Northern, was a similar work." He described the ground in front of the Union regiments as "a bare and barren plain several hundred yards in width." To support the assault, Colonel Tidball, chief of artillery for the 2nd Corps, called up six guns to engage the enemy artillery.[41]

"Our advance steadily pushed the enemy backward until their skirmishers were all driven across, though the bridge-head was held by troops from Kershaw's division. This, accordingly, Hancock determined to carry. Two of Birney's brigades, now under Colonel Thomas W. Egan, Fortieth New York, and Colonel Byron R. Pierce, Third Michigan, were formed for attack...."[42] The two brigades had a combined strength of about 3,000 men.[43] Captain Henry Travis of Company I wrote,

Earthworks at the Chesterfield Bridge. This is the interior of Henagan's Redoubt captured by units of Hancock's 2nd Corps, including the 124th New York, on May 23, 1864 (Library of Congress, Prints & Photographs Division).

About a quarter of a mile ahead of us ran the North Anna. From and at right angles with our line, as it was formed for the charge, ran a road straight down to the river. The right of our consolidated regiment (the 86th and 124th, now commanded by Major Stafford) rested on this road. On our right were the Maine regiments; and we were joined on the left by the 40 N.Y. At the bridge were two redoubts, each containing two guns, and heavily manned with infantry. In front of these ran a well filled line of rifle trenches. The advance of our regiment and the 40th N.Y. was directed against the trenches and redoubts on the left of the bridge.[44]

The Confederate position was about to be assaulted by an overwhelming force approaching from three directions.

Sergeant Stephen D. Chase of the 86th New York noted that the two regiments together "were not larger than one or two full companies"—probably no more than one hundred fifty men total—and there were not enough officers left to lead one regiment. Chase carried the colors of the 86th and placed himself at the left of his regiment while the color bearer of the 124th—presumably Corporal George Washington Edwards of Company A—stood at the right of his regiment. Both flags were at the center of the combined regiments in line of battle. By mutual agreement, the acting colonel of the 86th had overall command of the group while the officers of the 124th took charge of their left wing.[45] Across the field they were to assault, Chase saw one twelve pounder on the bridge and six or eight more guns on the south shore of the river. "From where we formed our line of battle to the enemy's line was a large field, I should think one half mile across it, with not a shrub nor stone nor ditch, but about as level and smooth as a city park." He could see enemy soldiers, their heads just visible above the earthworks. "We were now soon ready for the charge across this field and the enemy were ready to receive us.... They were just waiting and I suppose wishing us on.... I was looking over the situation and dreading the order which I knew was about to be given, but we only had to wait a minute and the orders came, 'Battalion, quick time, guide center, march!'"[46]

Captain Travis wrote, "About half past five the order to start was given and we rushed down the slope, and over the plain, on the run; encountering as we went one of the most savage fires of shell and bullets I had ever experienced. But the men only rushed on all the faster. We were only a few moments crossing the flats but left strewn along our route nearly one-fifth of the charging line."[47]

Chase thought that they were within forty rods of the earthworks before the first enemy gun was fired. "Then the artillery belched forth her death and havoc and a roll of musketry followed." As the two color bearers raced forward, a piece of shell struck the flagstaff of the 124th colors, "turning the color bearer two or three times over and taking he and the colors several feet to the rear." Seeing this, both regiments faltered for just a moment as if not sure what to do. Chase knew he must move the men forward or be swept from the field by the enemy fire. "I gave the flag a whirl and shouted: 'Come on boys.' Both regiments rallied as one man and were in the enemies works in less than two minutes and took one hundred prisoners and the cannon which was on the bridge."[48]

"Just before we reached the redoubts the rebels became satisfied they could not hold us back," Travis wrote, "and hurried their guns over the bridge; and a moment later their entire force broke and fled. But leaping the ditch and scaling the works, we managed to reach this bridge in time to cut off and capture a considerable number of the hindermost. Of these the boys of the 124th scooped in eight, but we left not a few of our number stretched on the plain."[49]

Walker wrote that at 6:30 P.M., Egan and Pierce charged "from nearly opposite directions converging upon the earthworks. The two brigades advanced in splendid style over open ground, vying with each other in gallantry of bearing, rapidity of movement, and carrying the intrenchments without a halt." In recognition of their action at the redoubt, both Egan and Pierce were rewarded with promotion to brigadier general.[50]

That evening Sergeant Chase was summoned to headquarters, where he found present the officers of both regiments. There he "never had so much praise said over me in all my life put together, and I had not the true courage to tell them why I went forward; that it was because I was afraid to go to the rear."[51]

Chase wrote that when the staff was hit and Edwards knocked backward, *both* regiments faltered. The only way he got the 124th and 86th moving again was to wave the colors of his regiment and call upon them to move forward. The sight of the national flag of the 86th, which most likely looked much like the flag of the 124th, waving in front of them served as a rallying point and an inspiration to the soldiers. Chase and Edwards had been chosen to carry the colors precisely because they knew the powerful attachment soldiers had for the flag of the Union they were fighting to preserve.

The attack on Henagan's Redoubt cost the 124th New York six men wounded and one killed outright, nineteen-year-old Private Samuel Potter of Company A. He had escaped injury in all the big battles only to fall in an all but forgotten charge. Forty-five-year-old Private Daniel Ackerman, also of Company A, was listed as wounded but died two weeks later in a Washington hospital.[52]

The troops settled in on the north side of the river and improved the earthworks. Hancock did not immediately follow up this success with a charge across the bridge because he knew he could cross the next morning without much trouble.[53]

At dawn, it was discovered that the enemy had abandoned the works on the south side of the river, leaving only a line of pickets behind. Hancock ordered his 2nd Corps to cross with the 86th and 124th in the lead. The combined regiments deployed in skirmish order and advanced, driving the Confederate pickets before them. Hancock's men "occupied the abandoned works around the Fox House, after driving away the enemy's skirmishers. Two pontoon bridges were thrown over, below the railroad bridge, on which Barlow's and Gibbon's divisions crossed."[54]

Colonel Egan wrote that the brigade massed near the Fox house, where the men built breastworks under a severe artillery fire.[55] One of the men from the 124th wrote, "We lay in our works until 1 P.M. under very hard shelling and then cross the river. Advance in their works and stack arms. Stop here but short time. Went out to support the skirmish line. We stop a little while and then deployed out and advanced lay there all day under some shelling. Quite a number of wounded. Relieved about 10 P.M."[56] Hancock kept pushing his skirmishers south hoping to locate a weak spot in the enemy's position. The Confederates skirmished aggressively to keep the Yankees back as far as possible, but Hancock's men got close enough to see formidable earthworks flanked by swampy ground.[57]

The Union forces were across the North Anna River at two places — Jericho Mills and the Chesterfield Bridge — but Lee was prepared for them. He could not defend the river up close, so Lee decided to set up his defenses in the shape of an inverted "V" farther back from the river. The point faced north and touched the river at Ox Ford, one of the few places where the southern bank was higher and thus more easily defended. Lee's lines then stretched back from the river, each leg of the "V" heavily fortified with earthworks. This not only split Grant's army in two, but gave Lee the advantage of interior lines — his troops inside the inverted "V" could support each other far easier than Grant's separated wings.

The Confederate position was scouted by Union troops but no weakness could be found. "To have attacked the army of Northern Virginia across intrenchments of the character found here, would have involved a useless slaughter," wrote the historian of the 2nd Corps.[58] "We were ordered to get all the rest we could," James Irwin wrote, "as we had to be under arms at 3 o'clock A.M. but did not get up until daylight. We put up short breastworks to protect us from shells as we expected to be shelled but everything was still all day. At 5 o'clock P.M. we were put on the line to support the 12th N.Y. Bat."[59]

Grant's advance so far had been impressive, but once across the North Anna, he found that Lee had him in a precarious position. The nature of Lee's defensive line afforded the Confederate commander the opportunity to concentrate his forces quickly against any part of Grant's army and crush it. But at this crucial moment, Lee was floored by a bout of chronic diarrhea. At the same time, two of his trusted lieutenants were also incapacitated, Ewell from exhaustion, and A.P. Hill with a mysterious recurring disease that plagued him until his death. With no leader healthy enough to exploit Grant's weak position, the opportunity slipped away.

"Finding himself thus held, as in a vice, on the North Anna, Grant determined on a yet farther movement to the left."[60] Weygant wrote of the enemy earthworks that Grant "wisely concluded it would be easier to go around than over them." Grant sent cavalry west to threaten the Confederate left and create the impression that his next move would be in that direction. Meanwhile he prepared to withdraw the army from the North Anna line "and attempt his entrance into the Confederate capital by another route."[61]

The regimental historian of the 141st Pennsylvania of Egan's Brigade wrote that the move to the east was done for three reasons: to get Grant's army nearer to Richmond, to force Lee to give up the North Anna line, and to cross the Pamunkey River, which was formed by the confluence of the North and South Anna rivers. Doing so would "bring the army into communication with a new and excellent water base, and secure fresh supplies of provision and ammunition, the want of which began to be felt."[62]

On the night of May 26, Grant began his withdrawal. The 5th and 6th corps got away without incident, crossing the pontoons before the Confederates were aware of their movement. They marched north, then east, then southeast, roughly paralleling the river but well back from it. Burnside's 9th Corps and Hancock's 2nd Corps remained in place to cover the withdrawal, Burnside above the river, Hancock below it.[63]

"Still in the front line," James Irwin wrote on May 26. "Everything is quiet. The boys out of rations. Ordered to be ready to move at dark. We drew rations and prepared ourselves for a march which commenced about 11 P.M."[64] Pulling the 2nd Corps back to the north bank of the river unnoticed would require some delicacy. At about 9:00 P.M. Hancock's men began the move. "The command remained in the breast-works in front of the Fox house until the evening of the 26th, when we recrossed the North Anna River and massed about 2 miles from the crossing."[65] A member of the Egan's Brigade wrote that once across the North Anna, they went into bivouac about a mile back from the river, taking up the march again at about noon on Friday, May 27 and traveling until midnight "without incident."[66]

Thirty miles downstream, Union cavalry crossed the Pamunkey River, then moved west looking to seize the crossroads that the infantry would need in its search for the enemy. Lee got word of the crossing almost as soon as the Yankees set foot on the near bank of the river and concluded that, unlike the cavalry move to his left, this was no feint. He decided to concentrate his army near Atlee's Station on the Virginia Central Railroad, where he had a better chance to block Grant's advance from behind another line of strong earthworks.[67] Here again, Lee had the advantage of interior lines and a shorter march. His engineers told him that the ground near Totopotomoy Creek, northeast of Atlee's Station, would be an excellent defensive position once earthworks were constructed.

Surgeon Thompson described the march east. "Saturday, May 28 Slept at the road side during last night, about three hours. Marched about ten miles to-day. Crossed the Pamunkey river at evening. Camped for the night about a mile and a half on the south side of the river."[68]

Along the road, Thompson caught sight of the 124th and he was shocked by what he saw. "On the first days march after leaving the North Anna River, I saw the remnant of our fine Regiment. I think in a short time I never saw such a change as has occurred in the few officers and men left. They appear to be only shadows of what they were when I parted with them at the first fighting. Maj. Murray seemed in better flesh than any officer, but greatly fatigued. Capt. Jackson and the Adjutant look changed, Captain is greatly reduced in flesh and has marvelously escaped harm thus far, being continually at the front."[69] "The column commenced to move at 6 A.M.," Irwin wrote. "It is very warm. We march about 15 miles. We cross the Pamunkey River at 5 P.M. Marched a few miles and halted for the night about 6 P.M. we commenced to throw up breast-works."[70]

As the Union infantry corps came across the river, Grant put them in line facing west with the Pamunkey to the rear and Totopotomoy Creek to the front. Wright's 6th Corps held the northernmost position with its right anchored on the river. Historian Earl Hess described the Union position on the morning of May 29 as "a continuous line of trench south of the Pamunkey River." He noted that Meade had specifically instructed that the men under his command be in position, dug in, and ready to move at once should the need arise.[71]

By forced marches, Lee had been able to interpose himself between Grant and Richmond before dark on May 28. His defensive position along Totopotomoy Creek took advantage of the natural features of high ground fronting a low, swampy area across which the Union troops would have to advance. The position was described as "rather more favorable than otherwise" to Lee —

quite an understatement as the line was as strong as any yet placed in front of the Army of the Potomac.[72]

Grant was not sure where the Army of Northern Virginia was located. He was not about to advance blindly and run the risk being attacked from out of nowhere. To rectify this, as Grant described it, "a reconnaissance was made in force, to find the position of Lee."[73] Late in the morning of May 29, units from the 6th Corps were sent northwest toward Hanover Court House, Barlow's Division of Hancock's Corps was sent west along the Richmond-Hanovertown Road (also known as Atlee Station Road) to Totopotomoy Creek, and a division of the 5th Corps was to probe south and then west across Totopotomoy Creek.

Hancock had been at work aligning his 2nd Corps with those to his left and right. "These dispositions were hardly completed," he wrote, "when I was directed to make a reconnaissance with a division of infantry, accompanied by artillery, supported, if necessary, by the remainder of my corps, on the road from Haw's Shop to Hanover Junction.... Barlow's division moved at 12 m. [*sic*], meeting with no opposition, except from the enemy's cavalry vedettes."[74]

"Barlow advanced about two miles until he arrived at the crossing of the Totopotomoy, as laid down on the map, or of Swift Run, a branch of the Totopotomoy, as stated by the negroes in the vicinity. The enemy was found in force, entrenched on the opposite bank, and a brisk skirmish ensued, General Barlow attempting to dislodge him."[75] When it became clear that Barlow could advance no farther, he sent a message to the rear calling for support. At about 5 P.M. orders were issued "for all the corps to move up, form line of battle, and close in on the enemy."[76]

When Barlow's Division marched out, the rest of Hancock's men remained in place. "The surrounding country was beautiful," wrote a member of Egan's Brigade.

> The magnolias were in full bloom. Cherries were ripe, but the army was short of rations both salt and fresh was exhausted, and the hard tack nearly consumed. Sunday morning dawned beautiful and bright. For once the army lay comparatively still on the Sabbath, and as the forenoon advanced the bands began to play, mostly sacred music, occasionally interspersed with patriotic and sentimental airs like "Star Spangled Banner" and "Home Sweet Home".... It seems more like Sunday than anything I have seen for a long while, but not as much as I would like to see it. How I wish I were at home. I would go to church and feel much more happy than here.[77]

The men were ordered to clean their weapons which they took to mean they would sit tight for the rest of the day. However, orders came at noon for them to be ready to move. At 3:00 P.M., the 124th marched forward about three miles then stopped for the night. James Irwin wrote that the men had still not been issued rations and grumbled that they would do no more marching until they got something to eat.[78]

Sergeant Chase wrote, "Sunday, the 29th, we moved into our new works and in the afternoon the Chaplain came up into the works to preach and he got well into his sermon when the bugle sounded: 'Fall in,' and down we came again to earth with a thud, for we were carried high into the spiritual realm by his eloquence and spirit. We soon had a realizing sense that we were mortals on this wicked earth, and close to the very opposite of Heaven. The closing of the service was very much like an explosion."[79]

As Birney brought his Division up to reinforce Barlow, he deployed his men to the right of the Atlee Station Road near the Shelton House, a colonial era mansion with a rich history — Patrick Henry had married Sarah Shelton in the parlor. But now the house had the dubious honor of being at the center of the Union line. Egan's Brigade changed position several times during the day and ended up camped in a stand of pine woods nearby.[80] Toward evening, Union troops advanced on some rifle pits and drove the enemy back into the main works on the other side of the Totopotomoy. Weygant wrote that Egan's men then set to digging a line of entrenchments opposite those of the enemy. "This occupied their attention for two days — meantime, though neither side advanced, a large amount of ammunition was expended." Sergeant Chase of the 86th New York wrote that the men "worked like heroes all night making breastworks" at this new position near the Shelton House.[81]

As darkness settled over the field on May 29, both armies were moving to confront each other in a piece of Virginia that was, in its own way, every bit as dismal as The Wilderness. The trackless forest was replaced by mosquito-infested swampy lowlands and ridgelines ideal for defense. Lee had taken position along the south bank of the Totopotomoy, described as "a substantial barrier astride the route to Richmond." Egan's men could see very little through the foliage beyond the creek but what they could see was not encouraging. Over the next few days, the 124th was stuck in front of a position that could not be breached by direct assault. The fighting degenerated into a series of disjointed advances that accomplished little other than capturing the enemy's advance line of rifle pits.

Colonel Watkins of the 141st Pennsylvania wrote that the "sharpshooters are entertaining each other" and that neither officers nor men had hardtack or sugar. "I do not know what we shall do if we do not get bread soon," he wrote. "The water here is also very bad."[82]

Along this new line, pickets kept up a steady fire which occasionally flared into heated exchanges of artillery and rifle volleys. "Worse and most dreaded than all else," noted Colonel Weygant, "were the sharpshooters' bullets which kept picking off a man, first here and then there, all over the camp. They were bloody days in which, though no general engagement took place, many names were added to the death rolls of the Second Corps."[83]

Monday, May 30 dawned "precious hot."[84] Hancock brought Gibbon's Division forward, and moved it into line on Barlow's left. Now the entire 2nd Corps was deployed from the Overton Farm at Oak Forest in the north to the Shelton House and beyond in the south. Hancock was instructed to keep up the pressure and to serve as the anchor of the Union line while Wright to the north and Warren to the south probed, searching for a way around or through the strong Confederate line.

By mid-afternoon, Wright's 6th Corps, feeling its way around the Union right, moved into position near the Overton Farm next to Birney, extending the Union line north. "The enemy were very advantageously posted, their line being protected by the creek and a marsh. The skirmishing was incessant during the day in endeavoring to develop the enemy's line."[85] Meanwhile, Warren's 5th Corps moved south in the direction of the Confederate right flank. The whole Union line seemed to be shifting position and the Confederate commander took all the activity to mean that Grant intended to attack. Lee correctly surmised that his right was the most likely target and ordered elements of Early's Corps to attack Warren's 5th Corps to stop the Yankees.

The Union commander described it this way: "There was some skirmishing along the centre, and in the evening Early attacked Warren with some vigor, driving him back at first, and threatening to turn our left flank. As the best means of reinforcing the left, Hancock was ordered to attack in his front. He carried and held the rifle-pits. While this was going on Warren got his men up, repulsed Early, and drove him more than a mile."[86] The resulting Battle of Bethesda Church failed to drive the Federals back but did serve to add two thousand more names to the Union and Confederate casualty lists.

Hancock's attacks in support of Warren were not as successful as Grant made them out to be. Two brigades, those of Egan and Mott, were chosen to make the advance. Skirmishers were sent forward but within half an hour, the attack was called off.[87]

The 141st Pennsylvania of Egan's brigade "was advanced until within about sixty yards of the enemy's lines, where they were sheltered in a ravine until evening, when they received intrenching tools and threw up works of considerable strength."[88] James Irwin wrote, "The regt drew rations for four days. We lay in the place we went in the night until 12 A.M. and then we fell in to go out and build works about 900 yards in front of the enemy. Last of the brigade out.... We move in our works about dark then the ART opened and mortars. It was the first mortar shell that I ever saw. They done the work well."[89]

Earlier in the day, it was "decided that, after dark, a new line of earthworks would be constructed "several hundred feet in front of that portion of the line where the 124th was lying."[90] Major Murray, who commanded what was left of the regiment, received orders to immediately send two or three men with an officer to stake out the position of the new line. Headquarters should have been aware that Confederate marksmen were posted all along the line and had been active, and lethal, all day. To send a construction party out into the open in daylight was tantamount to lining the men up in front of a firing squad.

Murray gave the job to forty-nine-year-old Captain David Crist, the much-beloved leader of Company H from Montgomery. Crist must have known his chances of survival were slim but "the brave old Captain moved resolutely forward in plain sight of the deadly sharpshooters, and with unusual coolness began the task assigned him." Murray was watching the group, admiring the "noble example" Crist set for the men under obvious mortal danger. Murray was about to turn away to other matters when he saw Crist fall, "his dead body instead of a stake marked the prolongation of the line on which the contemplated works were to be erected."[91]

Murray reported that Crist was "shot through the breast and died immediately," but it was not until ten o'clock at night that the body was recovered. It was simply too risky to expose any more men during daylight hours. That night, the men from his company, most of whom were much younger and who had known Crist all their lives, made a coffin for him using boards from empty hardtack boxes. They gathered around a grave they'd dug and placed his body in it. Captain Travis wrote, "It was the most solemn thing I ever witnessed, and was done amid the thunder of artillery and rattle of musketry — a fit burial for so noble a man. We miss him in the regiment, for he was a kind friend, a noble soldier, and a man whose whole soul was wrapped up in his country's cause." As the captain was being laid to rest, a sudden flare-up of musket fire along the picket line swelled into a roar as every artillery piece on both sides joined in, drowning out the prayer offered up by Sergeant Shultz of Company G, and wounding Private Matthew Babcock of Company B in the hand.[92]

Captain Travis' letter was quoted in part by Weygant in his regimental history. But the original copy of the letter added a little more about the sad event. "Capt. Crist was killed the 1st of June building breastworks by a Sharp Shooter. We buried him as good as we could, put up a head stone had a prayer offered."[93]

The loss of Captain Crist was deeply felt by the men in the regiment and was mentioned in a number of letters home. A *New York Herald* reporter carried Surgeon Thompson's letter to the *Goshen Independent Republican*, where it was soon published. In it the doctor wrote, "It is now evening, no general engagement has happened to-day as we expected would. I am pained to tell you in all probability Capt. Crist is killed. He was sent in front of our skirmish line to mark out a line of rifle pits and was shot. His body has

Captain David Crist, Company H. He was wounded in action, May 3, 1863, at Chancellorsville, Virginia; and killed in action, May 30, 1864, at Totopotomy Creek, Virginia. "He was a fine officer and one of the old Capts," and was highly thought of by his men (archive of the Historical Society of the Town of Warwick, Gift of Joan and Tom Frangos).

not been recovered yet. He may possibly be alive.... Have heard of no other casualties in our Regiment. Several wounded of the Division have come in to the Hospital. I have a horror of the events of tomorrow, as a terrible battle is expected."[94]

Before darkness settled in near the Shelton House, Captain William Jackson wrote to his friend Alsop Purdy. The letter bore the heading "South of the Pamunkey River P.M. May 30th 1864." "I have just come in from the rifle pits and am sitting in a ravine. My friend Capt. Crist of Co. H. was killed an hour or so ago. We had eaten dinner together but an hour before. He was pointing out a place to drive stakes for a breastworks when a rebel sharpshooter shot him through the breast. He was a fine officer and one of the old Capts. I am now the only original Capt. left unhurt."

Jackson thanked his friend for sending a package of writing paper and other things he did not enumerate.

> We crossed the Pamunkey on Saturday last and we are now forcing our way slowly south. We are now under fire.... Since the 18th three of Co. K. have been wounded. Colby, Mayette & Point all slight. I hope that some of these fine days you will hear of our knocking at the door of Richmond, but it will take time. All of us are about played out and *must* have rest if we fight. We have confidence in Grant, Meade and Hancock and believe the 2nd corps is about X. Give my regards to inquiring friends. By the way it is said that Anna Robertson is soon to change her state of single blessedness. But I must close. Remember me to Mr. & Mrs. Roberts Mr. Dent, etc.[95]

In his history, Colonel Weygant referred to these as "bloody days" but they were also days of "privation and great suffering" among the men in the ranks. Major Murray, who had once been a prisoner of the Confederates, wrote, "This is the first time in my life that I have ever really suffered from Hunger. We had drawn nothing for seven days and I was almost used up. Roast corn, and coffee without sugar had been our daily meals for two days, until this evening, when the train that went to Port Royal for supplies came up. I never relished anything better than some boiled beef, hardtack and coffee we had to-night."[96]

The day's activities accomplished little to change the overall situation except to bring the armies into close proximity to each other. Both sides dug in where they had not done so already and improved their earthworks where they had. Meanwhile, Lee had received information that Union Major General William F. Smith's 18th Corps had been peeled away from Butler's inert Army of the James and was on its way by boat to reinforce Grant. Smith's 16,000 men were to come ashore at White House Landing and Lee guessed that they would march against his southern flank. He felt that this large body of fresh troops would surely tip the balance in favor of the Union. A glance at the map showed Smith's probable approach route to be through Old Cold Harbor, where five roads came together. Lee dispatched cavalry to hold the vital crossroads until infantry could be brought up.[97]

Grant's plan for the last day of May was to sit tight and keep up the pressure on the enemy until Smith's men arrived. Mott's Brigade, at the north end of Birney's line, again advanced across Totopotomoy Creek and again drove the enemy pickets from their rifle pits. They could proceed no farther so they dug in and held on. A battery was brought up and began shelling the enemy position. At about 8 A.M., Egan's Brigade moved forward from its position just to the north of the Atlee Station Road. Soldiers advanced alongside Miles's Brigade of Barlow's Division with the 2nd U.S. Sharpshooters ahead in skirmish order. Some abandoned rifle pits were seized and then began a deadly exchange of fire with the enemy. "The Berdan Sharp Shooters advance and carried the enemy work," wrote Private Irwin. "We followed up in short time and lay in there works all day under cross fire ... and after dark we advance out — to build breast works most all night and fell back to our old work. The regt right and left wings could not advance with us."[98] At dark, they moved forward and began a new line of earthworks. "A portion of the time the men were exposed to a pretty severe fire and lost two severely wounded."[99]

The men worked on this new line of earthworks "in advance of the line captured from the enemy," but the end result was the same: no weakness could be found in their main lines. General de Trobriand wrote that the enemy had been "routed" but that after dark, the brigade withdrew to the earthworks held on the night of May 29 and remained there until June 1. The general noted that at this time the 17th Maine was transferred into Egan's Brigade thus adding a regiment with a well-known fighting reputation.[100] Hancock summed it up in his after-action report. "Birney moved forward across Swift Run and carried the enemy's advanced line on the right of the Richmond road. Generals Barlow and Gibbon pushed up close to the enemy's line, but owing to the unfavorable nature of the ground could effect nothing more. The artillery was engaged often and with great credit. General Wright was ready to support me with his whole corps, if necessary, but I had no occasion to call on him."[101]

Blocked along the Totopotomoy Creek line, Grant now turned his attention to Old Cold Harbor and to the reinforcements headed his way. Once the 18th Corps was ashore, Smith was to march up the south bank of the Pamunkey and head directly for the important crossroads, but "by some blunder" the orders sent Smith north instead of west. Sheridan brought two cavalry divisions to Cold Harbor with orders to dig in and hold on until relieved by the infantry. When the Confederate attack came, dismounted Union cavalry beat it back.

Next, Grant ordered the 6th Corps to shift from the far right of the line to the far left at Cold Harbor to reinforce Smith and Sheridan. It was a difficult march but by late in the afternoon of June 1, both the 6th and 18th Corps were in position. They launched an attack but the Confederates had constructed earthworks in record time and no permanent breakthrough was possible. Both Lee and Grant now began concentrating their men at Cold Harbor.

Hancock wrote, "Early on the morning of the 1st of June Wright's corps was withdrawn to Cold Harbor, and I therefore drew Birney's division back from the south side of the run, his pickets remaining in the advanced line."[102] A member of Egan's Brigade wrote that the "enemy held a position enfilading our advanced line of works, consequently at three o'clock of the morning of a June 1st the regiment had orders to fall back to a more sheltered place."[103] With the withdrawal of Wright's 6th Corps, Birney's Division of the 2nd Corps became the right of the Union line.

During the rest of the day, the Confederates made attempts to discover what was happening on Hancock's front. Just before noon, Hancock was ordered to prepare to support the anticipated attack by Union troops to the south by pinning the enemy troops to his front in place. "I immediately gave orders for a careful examination of the enemy's position in my front with a view to an assault. The reports from division commanders were quite unfavorable, the enemy's position being, as heretofore mentioned, one of great natural strength, and his works fully manned. My skirmish line was sharply engaged during the day, and about 2 o'clock the enemy, apparently anticipating an attack, was discovered re-enforcing his line, and no further attempt was made to force the position."[104] Irwin wrote that the brigade was resting when, in the middle of the afternoon, the enemy attacked the picket line. "Then we had to go to the front. The Regt was sent out to support the skirmish line until dark when one half of it had to go on picket. Our men were posted and lay there. About 12 P.M. we were called in."[105]

Grant realized that the 2nd Corps, still his best fighting unit, was being wasted on picket duty far from the impending battle around Old Cold Harbor. At 3:30 P.M., Hancock was ordered to be ready to move after dark. At about the same time, the enemy began to probe the 2nd Corps front as if it was going to attempt to turn Hancock's right. A series of attacks on both sides settled into desultory skirmishing until nightfall when the 2nd Corps began the move south. The plan, overly optimistic in the extreme, was to have Hancock's men in position at Old Cold Harbor in time for an early morning attack.

Hancock pulled his divisions out one at a time, with Birney being the last to get started at about midnight. The Confederates on the other side of the creek heard the sounds of troops on the move and aggressively probed the Union line, now held by a thin line of skirmishers left behind to act as a rearguard. Among them was "Lieutenant Charles Stewart of Co. I, with a detail of ten enlisted men from the 124th and an equal number from the 86th.... The pickets were of necessity left for a time to cover the movement. And before they could be withdrawn, the enemy discovered what had taken place, threw a force around their rear; closed in on them and captured a considerable number; including Lieutenant Stewart and six enlisted men of the regiment."[106]

The 124th was one of the last regiments to withdraw and its members did not catch up with the rest of the brigade until 2:00 A.M. The march to Old Cold Harbor was as miserable as any of the campaign. "The route was necessarily circuitous, the night pitchy dark, the roads were unknown, while the heat and dust were oppressive."[107] Meade had ordered "every exertion to move promptly," but a guide sent by headquarters lost his way. "In the darkness much confusion arose throughout the column, and the troops became mixed to a degree which made it difficult to straighten them out again. The night had been intensely hot and breathless, and the march through roads deep with dust, which rose in suffocating clouds as it was stirred by thousands of feet of men and horses and by the wheels of the artillery, had been exceedingly trying." When the 2nd Corps finally stumbled into Old Cold Harbor, the men were exhausted, hungry, and in no condition to participate in an attack scheduled for that morning. Meade recognized this and postponed the attack to give Hancock's men time to rest.[108]

Colonel Egan put the time of arrival at 9 A.M., "and then we marched in the rear of our line of battle about all the forenoon but little time given for to eat our breakfast."[109] The 2nd Corps was massed south of Cold Harbor Road facing a combination of enemy troops that included those of Generals Mahone and Breckinridge, the very same Confederate soldiers they thought they left behind at Totopotomoy Creek. The enemy was dug in and waiting, its line anchored on the Chickahominy River. Birney's Division came up at about 2:00 P.M., but about forty minutes later an order was issued postponing the attack until early the next morning.[110] James Irwin wrote, "We march near the left of the line and halted until 4 P.M., when we went to the front to support the First Division and mass. Stayed all night very heavy musketry."[111]

Grant's attack on the Confederate works got underway at about 4:30 A.M. June 3 with disappointing results. "Barlow advanced at the time indicated and found the enemy strongly posted in a sunken road in front of his works, from which they were driven after a severe struggle and followed into their works under a very heavy artillery and musketry fire."[112] Prisoners and colors were taken but no adequate reserves were close at hand to exploit the breakthrough. In the end, Barlow was driven back. Gibbon's Division met with less success, which was repeated all the way up the line by other units. The deadly combination of experienced troops behind well prepared earthworks, enfilading artillery fire, and open fields of fire again proved too much for the 2nd Corps soldiers. At 8:45 A.M., a message was sent to Hancock from Meade to the effect that the other army corps commanders were willing to try another attack unless Hancock thought it "hopeless." This odd message left the decision to the 2nd Corps commander, who declined accepting the responsibility for renewing an attack that never should have happened in the first place.[113]

Birney's Division was directly behind Barlow and Gibbon and within easy supporting distance, but no order was issued for it to join the attack. James Irwin left his own brief account of the battle. "The Brigade moved farther to the front and lay under cover (as we were shell) for an hour and then we fell in and move to the right a little ways. Stop here a short time." No fires were permitted so Irwin and another soldier he identified as "WHD," possibly William H. Dill of Irwin's Company, decided to go to the rear to boil some coffee. While they were gone, the brigade moved up in support and the two men quickly rejoined the regiment. "Very heavy firing on our left by the 2nd Corps. The enemy tried to take our works. An order issued no more advance of our army at present."[114]

Craft of the 141st Pennsylvania wrote that Birney's Division was sent about half a mile north of Cold Harbor to support the 18th Corps "but in the afternoon our brigade went into bivouac in a piece of wood on Woody's farm, where they remained all night. This afternoon a very welcome shower fell and the rain continued late in the evening." The Union troops held their positions, extending their left to the Chickahominy. "Offensive operations were now suspended," wrote Colonel Weygant, "and for several days the Union army was armed with picks and shovels, instead of rifles and muskets." Earthworks, trenches, and rifle pits covered the land while sharpshooters continued to pick off the unwary on both sides. "Siege operations were conducted for several days.... The daily skirmishing was sharp and caused us some loss. The nights were characterized by heavy artillery firing and sometimes heavy musketry, the close proximity of our lines causing unusual nervousness."[115]

Hancock wrote, "The first report of casualties after the action, which was unusually short, hardly an hour in duration, showed a loss of 3,024. Among officers the loss had been without precedent. I had to mourn the loss of those who had hitherto been foremost and most daring and brilliant in action."[116] When Lieutenant Colonel Francis Walker published his *History of the Second Corps*, he revised the figures upward. He listed 3,510 casualties, June 2 through 12 inclusive, the vast majority occurring on June 3. Birney's Division, which was not engaged on that day, suffered only 220 of that number.[117] The casualties for the Army of the Potomac stood in stark contrast to those suffered by the Confederates, who lost about 700 killed and wounded.[118]

The charge on June 3 has come to symbolize the folly of attacking earthworks head on and has been cited by his critics as proof of Grant's inability to attack any other way. "I have always regretted," he wrote, "that the last assault at Cold Harbor was ever made."[119] But a message sent to Meade at 7:00 A.M. on the morning of the charge revealed his intent: "The moment it becomes certain that an assault cannot succeed, suspend the offensive; but when one does succeed, push it vigorously and if necessary pile in troops at the successful point from wherever they can be taken."[120]

The entries in James Irwin's diary for the next three days reflect the stalemate following the assault. "June 4 All quiet this forenoon. About 3 P.M. orders to pack up and about 5 P.M. we were relieved by Burnside's Corps and the division join the corps again." "June 5 Everything quiet. Order to clean up behind our work. About 3 P.M. we moved to the left of Gen. Barlow's division and put up works in the night." "June 6 A good deal of firing along the line. The first time that I have had chance to wash my shirt in this campaign."[121]

A member of the 141st Pennsylvania, Egan's Brigade, wrote, "On Sunday, the 5th, everything was quiet most of the day, but in the evening the brigade was moved to the front and to the extreme left of the line where they intrenched and remained until morning, when the works were completed."[122] Sergeant Chase of the 86th New York wrote that the troops spent most of the day improving their earthworks,

and while working on them, the Johnnies made it very disagreeable for us for they had a jackass battery of mortars which threw about a twelve pound shell and they had dead range on us.... We could hear the report of each mortar as it was discharged and shortly after we could hear the shell coming down over our heads and could determine nearly where it would strike and we all tried to get on the opposite side of a tree from where it was to come down and in that way protect us from flying pieces as the shell would explode. They sent them fast enough so it kept us busy dodging all day, and they continued it well along in the evening.[123]

The two armies faced each other, stuck in place until one side or the other made a move. With no marching to do, the men wrote home to let their families know they were still among the living. But as they wrote, the deadly business of the pickets and sharpshooters continued on both sides.

Thomas Rodman wrote his parents a letter which bore the heading, "In the Trenches about

4 miles from Coal Harbor Va, June 6th/64." He began with the news that he was well and hoped that they were the same. "I have passed safely through all the battles and not got a scratch. I think that the hardest fighting is over for the Infantry. I think the most will be Cannon aiding." He told his parents of an order recently read to the troops stating that there would be "no more charging but that we would advance by regular approaches and fortify as we went along. We have to work at night. The way we advance a position is, we form a picket line tonight, and support them all day untill night again, and then we advance a line of battle up to the picket line very still and fortify ourselves." The main works were within 150 yards of the enemy, but the pickets were closer still. The enlisted men on each side carried on conversations, each side agreeing by mutual consent not to shoot at each other. A regular commerce was established: Confederate tobacco traded for Yankee coffee. Newspapers, Northern and Southern, were exchanged for war news. The Confederates, he wrote, "acknowledge Grant to be a tough one." When it came to the Union commander, Rodman freely expressed his confidence. "I think Grant is going to wind this thing up." He concluded his letter by telling them that the days were warm in eastern Virginia but the nights cold. "The Lord spare and Guide us in this life and at last bring us to a happy home."[124]

"June 7 Still in our works," wrote James Irwin, "yet not anything happen through the day of importance. Drew 4 days rations — some talk of moving further out. A flag of truce went out to bury the dead in front of the first division."[125]

As the army rested, twenty-year-old Sergeant George L. Brewster wrote an optimistic letter home to this father who forwarded it on to the *Whig Press* for publication. Editor Hasbrouck, always a supporter of the war and the Lincoln administration, prefaced the letter with the comment, "It evinces the spirit of Grant's army — a spirit that augurs of success."

In the Field, Va., June 8, 1864

We are enjoying ourselves in the usual way. We have FIGHT for breakfast, dinner, and supper, twice between meals, and three times during the night — in short, it has become a second nature. It is said a man that will leave his meals to fight, loves it; in that case the Yankees must love to fight, for it is an every day occurrence to jump up from coffee and hard tack, and give the Rebs a round or two.

Our regiment has been under fire twenty-three days in succession, fighting more or less every day. It is whittled down pretty close. We have about eighty men left. We have nine men in Company C, now in the front, fighting like heroes. We have lost thousands of men, but more men come in daily than we lose. I saw two Wisconsin regiments yesterday, the 37th and 38th, enlisted for 100 days to do garrison duty. Grant has brought them to the front, to do GARRISON DUTY BEFORE RICHMOND.

Grant makes the band-box soldiers fight. White collars and patent leather boots are "played out." He fights his men for what they are worth. He has the full confidence of the men; all orders, charges, marches, and all, are cheerfully obeyed.

Our troops can see the spires in Richmond, the glorious fruits of 34 days hard fighting, and we are bound to take it, take a look all around, and go on through Dixie on a double quick. January 1st, 1865, will see the Flag floating all over the United States, its 34 Stars and 13 Stripes frowning on secession as it slumbers in the grave.[126]

During the respite, Captain William Jackson wrote what was his last letter to Alsop Purdy. The heading read, "June 8th 1864 Place where I don't know but In Rifle Pits north of the Chick-ahominy with the rebs Between it and us." He thanked Purdy for the writing paper he'd sent and told him there was not much news from the front.

Our army is holding up a little, resting the men supplying them with shoes clothing etc. Officers had a day or so ago the first chance to change under clothing scince we broke camp. Until yesterday the 2nd Corps was on the left but now the 5th Corps has gone on our left and last night opened some big guns. I suppose now we must dig and siege for a while as charging is about played out on both sides. The rebs tried one on us commencing with the evening of the 3rd but every time were sent back double quick. We are taking it a little easy just now but are ready, for we don't know when we may have to 'pitch in' or get 'pitched into.' The 18th army corps (Baldy's) are here and are on our right. It is reported that the 56th are coming. I hope so it will take off a little of the shine. We have lost no men the last few days. Though we are under fire of pickets skirmishers etc. we are tolerably well posted. Rations are now plenty. At one time the boys were a little hard up and growled considerably. The way they came short was this. When they started from camp they had three days in their knapsacks which they "chucked" on the first days fight. Yesterday Meade issued an order to have the loss made up. The weather is fine and cool.

If this reaches you before the "moon changes" or if it don't you have my best wishes for happiness and prosperity.[127]

James Irwin wrote, "June 8 All quiet along the lines. About 3 P.M. the wagons came up with one days rations of beans potatoes, dried apples & pickled cabbage. The Col Commanding brigade ordered them all to be sold but the beans." The next day a detail was sent out to build earthworks in advance of those held by the 124th. In no time, the whole regiment was at work on them. "It is very wet place to build works. Joseph Wood and Sergt. Robert Connelly return to the regt." Irwin noted very little firing along the line on June 10 but strict order was being kept, which probably meant that the officers prevented them from trading with their Confederate counterparts.[128]

On June 10, Private John Drake took advantage of the lull in the fighting to write his sister Minerva, with whom he had not corresponded since the start of the campaign. The letter bore the heading "Camp in the Swamp near Cold Harbor." He told her that he would have written sooner

but I wanted to rest for I am pretty well worn out. Yesterday I was on picket. The Rebel pickets and us made a bargain not to fire at one another unless one side or the other tried to advance their line. It has been very quiet for the last three days but I don't know how long it will last. I have come pretty near being taken prisoner twice when I was on picket. The Corps would move to the right or left of the line. Then we would have to skedaddle. But I guess I have said enough of this at present. There is no use telling you about the Battles for I cant think of half of them. If you read the papers you will know nearly as much as I do.

Drake continued, "We belong to the first Brigade of Birney's Division. I think you hear a great deal about him in the papers. I don't think there is a man in the whole Division that likes him for he wants to have this Division in the front lines all the while. Gen. Ward used to have command of the Brigade but he is under arrest now so Colonel Egan of the 40th NY has the command. And he dont know as much as he might. But I guess I have said enough about war for this time." He asked her to send him two or three dollars and a local newspaper from time to time. In the envelope he included a "Rebel Postage stamp" as a souvenir.[129]

Stalled at Cold Harbor, Grant turned his attention south. The railroad line that fed Richmond, and Lee's army, ran through Petersburg, a city thirty miles directly south of the Confederate capital. If he could cut the lines entering Petersburg from the south and west, Richmond would have to be evacuated and the long sought-after dream of getting Lee's army into the open might be realized. But first he would have to get clear of the entrenched enemy at Cold Harbor. If Grant could safely pull back and get his army away before Lee realized it, he could, by swift marches, cross first the Chickahominy River and then the James River to attack the lightly defended city of Petersburg from the east.

The Yankees gave the Confederates every indication that they would remain in place. They busily strengthened earthworks and kept up a brisk exchange of rifle fire, all the while opening roads to the rear. "June 12 We are still behind our works. Quiet and some firing along the line. About 8 o'clock we had orders to be ready to march at 9 P.M. by the left flank."[130] After dark, the pickets remained in place while both the 2nd and 6th corps pulled back into a new line of defenses built in case Lee discovered the move and launched a sudden attack. The 18th Corps marched first, heading for White House Landing where the men boarded steamers for the 140 mile journey to rejoin Butler's army at Bermuda Hundred. Wilson's cavalry division, followed by the 5th Corps, crossed the Chickahominy and then marched west toward Riddell's Shop. They were to prevent attacks from that quarter while the rest of the army marched south and to make Lee think that Grant intended to attack Richmond along that line.[131] By 11:00 P.M., the remaining three army corps — those of Hancock, Wright, and Burnside — were on the move south to Long Bridge on the Chickahominy.

The Confederates still manning the trenches at Cold Harbor awoke on the morning of June 13 to find the earthworks opposite them empty. As Lee considered where Grant had gone, he got reports that large formations of the enemy, horse and foot, were pushing toward New Market to his south, equidistant between Richmond and Petersburg. "Thereupon, Grant's new movement became perfectly clear to Robert E. Lee (or so he thought). This was merely another one of those short-range attempts to envelop his right flank that the Federal command had been trying ever since the Wilderness."[132] Lee mistakenly thought that Wilson and Warren made up the main effort so he shifted reinforcements south and dug in along a line that stretched from White Oak Swamp Creek in the north to Malvern Hill in the south. As he did so, Wilson's cavalry kept up the deception while Warren's Corps pulled back and headed for the James River crossings. The key to success, wrote historian Robert E.L. Krick, was the effectiveness with which Grant screened his movements.[133]

James Irwin noted that the march was slow but steady all night. Once across the Chickahominy, the regiment massed in a clover field and started to build small fires to cook rations when the order came to fall in, form a line, and build earthworks. But before the work could begin the men took up the march for the James River. "June 14... About 12 A.M. we got on the boat at Akman landing and cross over to Wilcox Landing."[134] Weygant wrote that it was a march of fifty-five miles from Cold Harbor to the James where the 124th "was speedily transferred by steamboats in waiting."[135] Upon reaching the far shore, the men "move up the river a short distance and halted for the night in line of battle."[136]

As the Army of the Potomac was crossing the James River, General Charles H. Morgan, Hancock's chief of staff, wrote an assessment of the Overland Campaign just coming to a close. "The Second Corps here received a mortal blow, and never again was the same body of men." In the thirty days of fighting between the crossing of the Rapidan in early May and the crossing of the Chickahominy, the corps lost an average of over four hundred men a day. Morgan cited the Chickahominy instead of the James because nearly two years before, the 2nd Corps had crossed that river on the retreat from the Peninsula in 1862. During that long-ago campaign, General Edwin Sumner led the 2nd Corps and the legendary Phil Kearny yet rode at the head of the First Division. But now, both were gone, and many more. Of the recent campaign Morgan wrote, "It was not in numbers only that the loss was so grievously felt. Between those rivers the corps had lost terribly in its leaders; the men whose presence and example were worth many thousand men."[137]

Two years prior, the boats took the Army of the Potomac down the river and back to Washington in defeat. Now the boats carried the army to the southern shore of the James to pursue the war to its conclusion. If the Orange County men realized the import, none wrote of it. But the old soldiers of the 2nd Corps, who had passed this way once before, certainly did know the importance of the James River crossing and the cost in men that it had taken to get there. Colonel Francis Walker, 2nd Corps historian, as he finished the chapter on the Overland Campaign and Cold Harbor, noted that he felt as if he had written the epitaph of the 2nd Corps.[138]

CHAPTER 15

"I think Grant is going to wind the thing up"

Petersburg to Appomattox
June 14, 1864–April 9, 1865

Late in the afternoon of June 14, the 2nd Corps began disembarking on the south side of the James River. General Hancock was informed that 60,000 rations, three days' each for 20,000 men, would be delivered to him. Once the rations were distributed, he was to hold his troops "in readiness to move."[1] But no rations were to be found. Hancock waited until 10:30 A.M. the following morning before deciding to move on without them. The men foraged for what they could find, the countryside being "of great beauty and fertility." They were exhausted by the long march from Cold Harbor but in good spirits, "and every man looked forward to what he believed would be the speedy downfall of the rebellion."[2]

Hancock's goal was Petersburg, a rail hub on the Appomattox River which was, at that point, virtually undefended. The overall Confederate commander in the area was the able but temperamental General Pierre T.G. Beauregard, a man not known for his ability to work well with others. His instincts told him that Petersburg, not Richmond, was Grant's next target. Beauregard had already stopped one attempt to capture Petersburg launched the week before by the hapless General Butler, but he wasted no time in celebration. The Confederate general telegraphed Richmond and General Lee asking that reinforcements be sent to Petersburg at once as the Yankee army seemed to be concentrating in front of the city. He got no reply.[3]

The city's small garrison stood behind a ten-mile string of redans — V shaped artillery positions that projected toward the enemy. Christened the "Dimmock Line" in honor of Captain Charles H. Dimmock, who designed it, the line looped completely around the city with each flank securely anchored on the Appomattox River. But there was a key weakness to the line: Petersburg's defenses had been stripped of men to reinforce Lee's army during the fighting at Cold Harbor. To hold the city, Beauregard had but 2,200 men concentrated mainly along the eastern face of the line.[4]

General Smith's 18th Corps, recently arrived from Cold Harbor and 14,000 strong, was ordered across the Appomattox River to take up positions opposite the northeastern section of the Dimmock Line where it met the river. Grant's plan was to have the 2nd Corps move up and form on Smith's left. The two corps would then assault the city from the east while a division of Butler's cavalry threatened from the south. Grant had every expectation that Petersburg would fall by noon on June 15. The plan might have worked had someone bothered to tell Hancock that the 2nd Corps was to be part of the attack. Had he been privy to this critical piece of information, he would certainly have made haste and not waited around for rations that never came.[5]

James Irwin wrote in his diary for June 15, "We lay in line until about 10½ /A.M., We were ordered to fall in to march. We had a very hard march to Petersburg but ordered to go to City

Point. We got within 3 miles of City Point but the order was countermanded."[6] After fourteen miles of hard marching, it was discovered that Hancock's men had taken a wrong turn and were heading away from Petersburg, not toward it. Another two hours were wasted before Hancock received a message from Grant "directing all haste to be made in getting up to the assistance of General Smith, who," it stated, "had attacked Petersburg, and carried the outer works in front of that city." This constituted the first indication to Hancock that his men were expected to support the 18th Corps in the attack. With clear orders in hand, Hancock reversed the 2nd Corps, with Birney's Division in the lead, and headed it toward Petersburg.[7]

Along the Dimmock Line, Smith conducted a careful but time-consuming reconnaissance while his men skirmished with the enemy. "Very little infantry could be seen in the works ... and it did not seem probable to him that the number of guns at work against him would be there without support." That, of course, was exactly the case. Beauregard had plenty of artillery but very few infantry. When the 18th Corps finally did attack at about 7 P.M., Smith's men overran a surprisingly large section of the Dimmock Line, capturing two hundred fifty of the defenders,

Sgt. James Irwin as he appeared when he was writing his diary entries at Petersburg in 1864 (Robert Cammaroto collection).

four cannon, and five of the thirteen redans in front of him. Smith had no way of knowing what lay beyond the earthworks he had captured, and, wary of plunging ahead, he called a halt.[8]

While he pondered his next move, night closed in and an opportunity to capture Petersburg — and possibly end the war — quietly slipped away. A soldier in Egan's Brigade wrote, "The old 2nd Corps was pushed to the front as lively as could be. Early in the evening we were within gunshot of the rebel lines and lay on our arms all night to participate in some hard fighting on the 16th of June, 1864."[9] The 2nd Corp divisions went into line with orders to reconnoiter the position, identify the strong points, and attack at dawn.[10]

Across the line, the Confederates were busy constructing a new line of entrenchments behind the Dimmock Line. Once completed, this new line of earthworks would connect the redans in the north still in Confederate hands with those to the south. The position was strong, on high ground, and had clear fields of fire.[11] There was still great danger because Lee was unsure of Grant's ultimate target and found it hard to believe that the Union army was across the James River. Lee agreed to send some reinforcements to Beauregard but he would not commit the entire Army of Northern Virginia. Beauregard pulled troops in where ever he could find them but his earthworks were thinly manned. On both sides of the line, men dug in and waited.

At daylight, June 16, the entire 2nd Corps was on the field, covering a two-mile front from where it joined Smith's left flank to the Norfolk and Petersburg Railroad in the south.[12] As the 9th Corps arrived during the morning, exhausted by its long march, Burnside moved into position south of Hancock. Since the Union 5th and 6th corps were still some distance to the rear, Meade and Grant decided to attack with the troops already on the scene.

The men of the 124th New York and the 86th New York, still operating as a single unit,

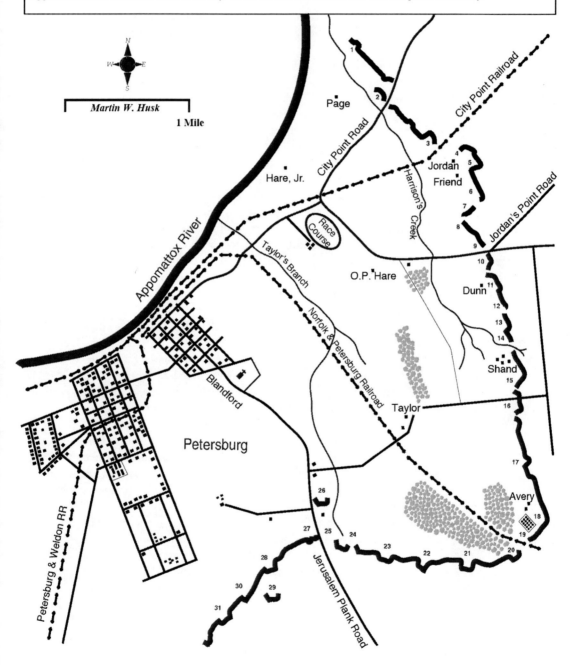

Petersburg, Virginia

This is the situation faced by the 124th New York as the regiment approached the defenses of Petersburg on June 15, 1864. A line of earthen forts and artillery positions, known as the Dimmock Line, ringed the city and connected to the Appomattox River north and south of the city. In all, the defenses bristled with over 350 pieces of artillery.

slept on their arms "within a close gun range of the enemy. Their artillery was in plain sight and we could see their troops maneuvering."[13] Early on the morning of June 16, Birney and Gibbon started their examination of the enemy works. Historian Thomas J. Howe noted that while the exact location is hard to determine, Egan's men probably formed up "among the fallen timber to the left (southeast) of the Prince George Court House Road. This belt of cut timber fronted the area from the Dunn House to the Avery House." To the south lay the portion of the original line of works still in enemy hands including Battery No. 12.[14] A soldier in Egan's Brigade wrote that they formed up at about 6 A.M., in front of the Confederate works, "near where the Rebel works covered the Petersburg and Norfolk Railroad."[15] James Irwin noted that the regiment was on the right of the brigade. He was in the process of getting something to eat when "the first thing we new the rebs open on us with Artillery." The order came to fall in and "we move off to the left under very heavy shelling."[16]

The enemy works had been only lightly manned until early in the morning, when Confederate reinforcements could be seen filing into position just as Egan's men moved to the attack. "On the morning of the 16th instant, at daylight, the enemy opened upon us with their batteries, killing and wounding a considerable number of the brigade."[17] The 17th Maine and 20th Indiana made up the attacking column although the 40th New York and 99th Pennsylvania may have been involved as well. "An advance was made, but the position being one of great strength and held by a large force, it was found impossible to carry it. The line was reformed, and a second attempt, with a larger force, was unsuccessful. The enemy were too strong and their position impregnable to the small force brought against it. The gallantry of the charging party was not equal to taking a position which a whole division afterward failed to carry. The brigade then formed a line at right angles to the line deserted by the enemy."[18]

"Tommy Egan is a third rate idiot," one of the men in the ranks wrote, critical of his brigade commander for even attempting the first charge. Then the "gallant Tommy," as a soldier mockingly referred to him, ordered a second charge, but the result was the same.[19] Hancock wrote that Battery 12 was "carried by Egan in his usual intrepid manner," but some of his men considered the whole affair a big mistake. Later in the day, Egan was wounded and carried to the rear. "If any tears were shed, they were tears of joy, mingled with the hope that his wound will keep him away till our terms end."[20] In Egan's absence, Colonel Henry J. Madill of the 141st Pennsylvania took command of the brigade.

In its supporting position, the 124th New York suffered only one man wounded, Lieutenant William H. Benjamin of Company G. Later in the evening Private Judson P. Lupton of Company H was wounded in the arm by a stray musket ball. "During the afternoon the brigade changed position several times, but did not become actually engaged, though heavy fighting was continually going on all about them."[21] The brigade held its position until late in the afternoon when it was relieved and moved to the right in support of an attacking column. Meanwhile, Generals Meade and Grant conferred while they examined the works captured the day before. Meade was to take direct command of the units in the field and, as the 5th Corps arrived later in the day, he was to have that corps form on the left of the line to protect the flank. Grant was pleased with the progress made so far. "Smith has taken a line of works stronger than anything we have seen this campaign," he

Lieutenant William H. Benjamin, Company E. He enlisted as 1st sergeant of Company G and was promoted. He was wounded in action June 16, 1864, in front of Petersburg, Virginia (archive of the Historical Society of the Town of Warwick, gift of Joan and Tom Frangos).

said. "If it is a possible thing, I want an assault made at six o'clock this evening." Grant felt that with the arrival of Burnside's 9th Corps and Warren's 5th Corps, he would have the strength he needed to break the Confederate line. But as the day progressed, the temperature steadily rose and the men crouching behind the earthworks suffered from the dust, heat, and lack of drinking water. By the time Burnside's men got into position, they were "physically spent."[22]

By 4 P.M., Meade decided that the attack would be made by Hancock's Corps against the earthworks near the Hare Farm, west of the Prince George Road. Smith's 18th Corps on the right would demonstrate to keep the enemy occupied in that quarter and to stop them from firing on the attackers. Gibbon's Division would advance in support on Birney's right. Barlow, with support from the 9th Corps, would attack on Birney's left.[23]

Right on time, the Union guns opened on the Confederate earthworks. After the requisite bombardment, the gunners slackened their fire, signaling the infantry that it was time to advance. Confederate artillery, supported by growing numbers of infantry, cut the attackers down. Advancing as far as they dared, the men threw themselves flat on the ground and furiously dug into the soft soil for protection — they were simply too exhausted to press the attack. The 2nd Corps divisions drove the Confederate skirmishers back into their earthworks and did manage to capture three redans, but they were not able to breach the enemy earthworks. It was becoming increasingly clear that any advantage Grant had gained by his brilliant march from Cold Harbor to the very gates of Petersburg, had evaporated in the summer heat. The army was physically drained on the march that got it there and now had not the strength to press the advantage.[24]

Meade reported to Grant, "The attack was made at 6 P.M. yesterday, as ordered, on the whole of the front of the Second Corps and by that corps. Birney made considerable progress, taking some of the advanced works of the enemy and one of their main works of their first line.... There has been continuous fighting all along the line since the attack commenced at 6 P.M. yesterday. Advantage was taken of the fine moonlight to press the enemy all night. The loss has not been great. A rough estimate would make it under 2,000 killed and wounded."[25]

Grant's efforts on June 16 had been frustrated by oppressive heat, exhausted troops, and poor coordination. The good news for Grant was that by midnight the lead units of the 5th Corps were taking up positions on the left of the line where they might, at last, tip the balance in his favor.[26]

At dawn June 17, an assault on the left did indeed break through the enemy earthworks, but there was no support to exploit the success. In the center, Birney advanced his division along the Prince George Court House Road to occupy Hare House Hill. The Confederates had moved back to their earthworks, but Birney saw no Union forces advancing to his right or left so he halted. Ahead lay open ground leading up to the enemy earthworks held in unknown strength. Madill's Brigade, including the 124th New York, lay in support of the division. All the while, the men were subjected to deadly sniper fire.[27] The 124th drew three days' rations "and then we went to the front to relieve another brigade," wrote Private Irwin. "Quite a good deal of firing a long the line. At 3 P.M. the musketry commenced to increase until 5 P.M. when the 9 & 5 corps made a charge on the left of the division and the enemy flank. Very heavy musketry."[28]

Meade called upon his commanders to prepare for a massive attack the next morning at 4 A.M. In anticipation of heavy fighting, Hancock asked his division commanders to assess the readiness of their men. "There are scarcely any officers in the brigades," Barlow told him, and he had no idea how they would do if called upon to assault the enemy position again. Gibbon reported he might be able to muster 2500 men but noted that his division had suffered so many casualties that the new heavy artillery regiments were larger than his veteran brigades. Notwithstanding the losses, Meade was determined to try again.[29]

At this moment of crisis, the 2nd Corps suffered its most important casualty of the war. On the march south from Cold Harbor, General Hancock's Gettysburg wound began to bother him.

Nearly a year before, as he directed the repulse of Pickett's Charge, a musket ball that shattered the pommel of his saddle drove into his upper right thigh near the groin, bringing with it wood fragments and a nail or two. The wound, which never properly healed, reopened and became enflamed as shards of bone worked their way to the surface. Over time, his discomfort turned to pain so severe that he could not sit on a horse. There are those who would argue that the wound hampered his ability to command the corps and was a factor in the failure of the Union troops to capture Petersburg. During the early hours of June 18, Hancock turned command of the 2nd Corps over to General Birney, who in turn gave command of his division to General Gershom Mott.

Meanwhile, the Confederates were busy building another line of earthworks closer to the city. During the night, the front line troops did all they could to convince the Yankees that they held the line, then quietly fell back to their new positions. Beauregard posted fifty-one artillery pieces along the new line where they could do the most damage. Eight of his guns were on a height on the opposite side of the Appomattox north of the city where they could fire into the flank of any Union troops sweeping across the open ground in front of the Confederate works.[30]

Lee, at last convinced that all of Grant's army was now before Petersburg, began shifting the Army of Northern Virginia south. Before dawn June 18, the lead brigades were filing into the trenches south of Petersburg, relieving Beauregard's exhausted men in some places and extending the line in others. But with the arrival of the Union 5th Corps, Grant had a better than three-to-one advantage over the defenders. Unless the entire Army of Northern Virginia could concentrate rapidly, the Yankees might yet take the city.

Late on the night of June 17, Meade issued the following order to his corps commanders: "A vigorous assault on the enemy's works will be made to-morrow morning at 4 o'clock by the whole force of the Fifth, Ninth, and Second Corps. Corps commanders will make all needful arrangements in time to have the assault simultaneous, and are directed to make it in strong columns, well supported, so that, if successful, it can be followed up."[31]

As the hour of attack approached, those not asleep on the Union side of the line were exhausted and edgy. General Meade, never known to be of sunny disposition, was in a "tearing humor."[32] At 4 A.M., the 2nd Corps artillery opened on the enemy earthworks and the city itself. Skirmishers from the 141st Pennsylvania moved forward in front of Madill's Brigade. All along the 2nd Corps line, massed formations of Union regiments followed the skirmishers, dreading the moment when the enemy batteries opened on them. Mott's Division headed for the Hare House and the enemy works beyond. Where the day before they had been greeted with shot and shell, the only sound heard now was that of their own movement. They followed the line of the Prince George Court House Road west, Gibbon to the north, Mott to the south, until the road took a sharp turn to the right.[33]

Enemy picket lines were quickly overrun and prisoners taken. The rebel soldiers freely told the Yankees that the line had been abandoned and that reinforcements from Lee's army were on the way. At 6:30 A.M., Birney forwarded to Meade an order found in the enemy rifle pits which "indicates a new line. I am getting the troops in hand, and advancing my skirmishers rapidly. We find a skirmish line in front." Meade replied at 7 A.M. that he thought the enemy had no fortified line between the one recently abandoned and the city. "If the time is given them they will make one," he said. "If we can engage them before they are fortified we ought to whip them."[34] Weygant wrote that "when the skirmish line advanced it was discovered that the enemy had withdrawn to an inner and stronger line, and the main assault was deferred. But a portion of Madill's brigade consisting in part of the 124th, advanced to within two hundred yards of the enemy's new line and entrenched themselves. Here Edward Hunter of H was mortally wounded."[35]

"I have ordered the whole army forward, and directed the commanding officers on your right and left to communicate with you," Meade telegraphed Birney. "It is of great importance the enemy should be pressed, and, if possible, forced across the Appomattox."[36] To the south, the earthworks in front of Warren and Burnside, hotly contested the day before, were empty as well. Skirmishers cautiously moved forward until the outline of the new enemy works began to appear. When Meade got the news, he urged his commanders to push forward at once but all along the line units were having trouble keeping their alignment with each other. The ground was difficult to cross, the heat rising fast, and the natural caution of the men, not to mention their exhaustion, made for slow going. As Birney's men felt their way forward, more units of Lee's long-awaited reinforcements were marching through Petersburg, heading out to take up positions in the earthworks.

At 10 A.M. Meade wanted to know the situation on the 2nd Corps front. Within half an hour Birney told him that he'd located the enemy earthworks and they looked to be as strong as any he'd seen. Further, due to the nature of the ground, Birney's units were having trouble moving forward together. Meade, no doubt exasperated, ordered that a general assault step off at noon. He gave specific instructions that the attacks be made by troops in column, which presumably could move against the earthworks faster and hit the line in a more compact formation.[37]

As soon as the enemy pickets had been driven away from Hare House, Union artillery was brought up and gun emplacements dug. Gibbon's Division attacked at about noon. "The assault was not a spirited one," Birney reported, "but the enemy's position was strong. I will seek another front. I hold advanced ground and have gained a good crest for artillery, which is in position." A flurry of telegraph messages went out from Meade to his corps commanders desperately trying to organize a concerted attack. Birney decided that Mott's Division would make the assault, but he told Meade that it would take time to mass the nine brigades he intended to use. He would have Gibbon attack on the right and Barlow on the left to draw off fire and attack "in columns, covered by a heavy skirmish line." Meade urged him to "hasten matters as much as possible."[38] Up and down the Union line, the story was the same. Advances could not be coordinated and attacks went in piecemeal. Meade tried desperately to coordinate the five infantry corps he had at his disposal, but distance and the nature of the terrain hampered his every effort.

A little after 4 P.M., Birney telegraphed Meade that "General Mott is forming as rapidly as possible, and every exertion will be made to hurry up the attack. It will be made in columns, covered by a heavy skirmish line, and will be sustained by an advance all along my line. Even where I have but one line I shall put in all the troops I can. The attack would probably be successful had I enough good officers left to lead the attacking columns. This is the difficulty."[39] Birney knew the attack would fail even before the men left their earthworks.

Mott's Division "was in front and to the right of the Hare house, on the left of the Prince George Court House road, supported by one of Gibbon's brigades, and Barlow's Division on his left."[40] Madill's Brigade, including the 124th, was "massed in column of regiments for the charge" behind the Hare House, the 141st Pennsylvania being the rearmost regiment. The men had been under artillery and sniper fire all day and had been standing in the sun for hours while the division formed. Chaplin's Brigade was north of the Hare House, alongside the Prince George Court House Road. Colonel Daniel Chaplin of the 1st Maine Heavy Artillery, brand new to what had been Mott's Brigade, now had command of the brigade. Chaplin's regiment, at the front of the column, was so large that it would attack in three lines of about three hundred men each. The 1st Maine "heavies" dwarfed the rest of the brigade and probably had more than three times the number of men present in the 124th and 86th combined. By 4:30, Mott's Division was as ready as it was going to be.[41]

Madill and Chaplin would lead the division forward with Mott's other two brigades, those of McAllister and Brewster, massed in column ready to support the attack. Between them and the enemy works, a distance of about 500 yards, there was "a rise of ground which, while it sheltered and concealed the movements of the brigade, was found ... to be swept by a terrible fire of shot, shell and musketry."[42]

Soon after Madill and the regimental commanders returned from viewing the enemy position from atop this rise, the order came to advance. "Our Regiment with fixed bayonets pressing forward and keeping the lines before them solid. In passing over the ridge to reach the enemy's works they as well as the regiments in front of them, suffering fearfully."[43] Not every regiment advanced. The 16th Massachusetts refused to move and the 7th New Jersey, feeling it was not properly supported, did not go beyond the rise. From the rearmost brigades came shouts of "Played out! Let the 1st Maine go!"[44]

Color Sergeant Chase of the 86th New York thought the plan of attack was to advance slowly up an "inclined plane to some buildings, there to take a rest and organize for the charge," but no sooner did they get near the top than "the enemy opened fire it seemed to me with every piece of cannon in the Southern Confederacy." The 86th and the 124th took cover behind an old barn but the enemy had the range and put shot and shell through it sending a shower of boards and wood splinters among the men. Chase stepped out from behind the cover and looked back at the regiment for orders when a Minnie ball hit him "going through the lower part of my left ear and lodging in the back of my head just above my neck joint." He fell to the ground but kept a "death grip" on the colors until they were taken from him.[45]

Coming over the rise, the tightly packed columns of men were immediately under enemy artillery fire. Shell exploded over and among them but the real killing began when the gunners switched to canister. As the blue columns came on, each deadly round tore a hole where men had stood but a moment before. From across the Appomattox River, long-range artillery slammed shell and solid shot into their flank and as the 2nd Corps soldiers drew near the earthworks, Confederate riflemen joined in the fight. The charge had been vigorous enough at the start but it didn't take the long for things to fall apart. The troops who had been through this before faltered, then either fell to the ground or headed to the rear. A participant wrote, "The bullets whistled like rain." Officers urged their men forward but the impossibility of the task was evident to all but the 1st Maine Heavies, who kept going forward until even their ranks were too shredded to continue. In the ten minutes it took the Confederates to blast the attack apart, the 1st Maine Heavy Artillery lost 632 men, more than any regiment, blue or gray, in any battle of the Civil War.[46]

A Union soldier wrote, "I doubt if a man on the Union side saw a Confederate during the charge. They were completely sheltered by a strong earthwork. It is a positive fact that wounded men lay in the open field in front of their works throughout the remainder of the day under a burning sun, dying for want of water."[47] In Color Sergeant Chase's opinion they were "the strongest breastworks I ever saw." On top of the works the Confederate soldiers had arranged two parallel poles across which to rest their rifles. A man could load, slide the rifle into place overhead, and pull the trigger without showing himself.[48] Against such positions and firepower, no Union attack had any chance of success.

At 5 P.M. Birney telegraphed Meade. "I have just made an assault with nine brigades and have been repulsed with considerable loss." Meade replied almost immediately, "Sorry to hear you could not carry the works. Get the best line you can and be prepared to hold it. I suppose you cannot make any more attacks, and I feel satisfied all has been done that can be done."[49]

"In this last assault Madill's command suffered terribly," Weygant wrote, "losing nearly two hundred men in killed and wounded. The 124th which advanced with but eighty-two muskets, lost one of its best officers, the gallant Captain William A. Jackson killed, and had eight enlisted men, wounded — several of them mortally." The surviving members of Company K, nine in number, carried Jackson's body to the rear and buried him at the base of a tree. They wrote his name, regiment, and date of death on a plank, nailing it to the tree so that his body might be recovered later and sent north.[50]

As Captain Jackson had noted in a letter home just days before his death, he was the last of the original ten company commanders still serving in that capacity. Weygant and Murray had been promoted within the regiment. Silliman had been promoted outside and left the regiment. Benedict, McBirney, Bush, and Clark had been disabled and were no longer with the regiment. Nicoll, Crist, and now Jackson had been killed in battle. His death was announced in the *Goshen Democrat* five days later, just below the banner headline announcing the nomination on the Union ticket of Abraham Lincoln for president. The paper had few details of the action of June 18 but expressed its high regard for Captain Jackson and the Orange Blossoms. "In view of the terrible losses which this Regiment has suffered since entering the service, we can hardly repress the thought so often recurring in our mind, will any of the brave men composing this Regiment survive to return to us at the end of their three year's service?"[51]

Lieutenant Lewis Wisner of Company K wrote a brief letter to the *Whig Press*, intending that it be published. It bore the heading "One Mile From Petersburg, Va., Sabbath Morn, June 19th, 1864."

> Friends—It is my painful duty to announce to you the death of our beloved Captain Jackson. He fell yesterday afternoon, June 18th, while gallantly urging on his men to the charge. His death was painless: he was shot with a Minnie ball just above the heart. He never spoke, for the enemy who wished his life did his work but too well. We buried him by a white house, and plainly marked his grave. All his effects we saved for his friends, which will be delivered as soon as possible.
>
> His death has cast a gloom over the officers and men of the whole Regiment, for he was a favorite with all. To me it is a sad blow, for I loved him as a brother. It does not become me to speak of his merits, for you know them all. But while we mourn his death, we must remember that it was the will of Him "who doeth all things well," and that he died to save the sacred cause of Liberty.[52]

Sergeant Ben Hull had been writing to Henry Howell, who was recovering in the hospital from his Spotsylvania wound, to keep him abreast of news from the regiment. A month after Jackson had been killed and just after his body was disinterred he wrote,

> But Henry we lost our best officer, Capt Jackson, he was taken up yesterday and sent home he was hit with a ball while trying to drive some men out from behind some Breastworks we were going to make a charge or we had tried it once the Brigade was closed in mass they got quite close to the Enemy's works they got behind a barn our Regt was third in line you never saw such a time we lost a great many men more than we would if we had went into the Enemy's works but our comp was very lucky not a man hurt not many out of our Regt there is 9 of us here now for duty.[53]

Sergeant Ben Hull, Company K, corresponded with Henry Howell, updating him on the news from the regiment. Historical Society of Middletown and the Wallkill Precinct.

When compared with Chase's account, it seems that he and Jackson were shot at the same location. The outbuildings of the Hare farm served as a shelter once it became clear that the attack was doomed and few troops, other than the 1st Maine Heavy Artillery, were going forward. Historian Earl Hess referred to June 18 as "one of the most dismal days" ever suffered by the Army of the Potomac. Exhausted by the long marches, the intense heat, and heavy fighting with little success, veterans of many battles refused to advance. "We have had enough of assaulting earthworks," one Union soldier said.[54]

The next day Thomas Rodman wrote a letter home bearing the heading, "In the Breastworks near Petersburg Va, June 19th 1864." After asking about their health, he gave his parents a brief summary of the military situation at Petersburg. He did not mention Jackson's death or the events of the past few days but a tone of anger and a wish for revenge came through loud and clear.

"We are now within ½ mile from Petersburg. We can see the steeples quite plain from where we are and we keep advancing inch by inch and I think that we will soon be there, then, how are you Richmond, having all their R Roads cut off they starve to death or surrender or run and be slaughtered like sheep."[55]

After dark, the brigade was put to work building earthworks very close to the enemy's position. Near midnight, the men were relieved and moved about a mile and a half to the rear to rest. The next morning Madill's men moved to the left to a new position on the Jerusalem Plank Road. They rested for two hours, then advanced to relieve a brigade in the front line. On the morning of June 22, the picket line advanced, followed by a line of battle. "The enemy's pickets fell back as we advanced for a short distance," wrote John E. Kidd of Company H, "when suddenly a heavy body of Confederate infantry appeared charging at a double-quick around our flank. They soon routed our battle line taking a large number of prisoners. The only 124th man captured was John Tompkins, of Co. C."[56] Over the course of the next week, the brigade moved about quite a bit but did not engage the enemy. On June 30, the regiment established a camp and put up tents a few yards behind the main line of Union earthworks.[57]

While on picket duty, Corporal David Quick of Company K wrote home to William Wirt Bailey that he was in "good health and spirits, but nearly worn out with the fatigue of an active campaign of fifty days duration. Since the 7th of May last, the Army of the Potomac has scarcely seen a moment's rest or peace, it either being on the march, engaged with the enemy in battle, or working like beavers at rifle pits."

On the march from Cold Harbor, Quick had a chance to examine some of the earthworks put up by McClellan two years before and pronounced them not nearly as strong as those being dug now.

> In ours the troops are advanced and dressed up near enough to the line for practical purposes, stack arms, and go to work, the line of guns serving as a guide for the line of works. Every private is well conversant with the most approved and quickest way of building them, viz; first, a line of stout stakes, firmly driven in the earth and braced from the rear — next a layer of stout logs about four feet high, and lastly against the logs we throw up a bank of dirt about eight feet thick at the bottom, and from three to four feet at the top. This makes a work that no field battery can demolish, or even make any impression upon, even at short range. The men used to grumble whenever called upon to work a little in the trenches, always saying it signified retreat, but Grant, in this as in nearly everything else, has inaugurated a different system, and now every man (officers and all) works with a will, and as a consequence the work is soon done, and in some instances many lives saved as well as a victory gained ... when taking a new position, no one thinks of sleep until there is a moderately strong work betwixt him and the "chivalrous sons of the South." It is scarcely two hundred yards from our "vidette posts" to those of the enemy, and the "videttes" often hallo at each other. There is no firing in our immediate front, there being a sort of truce established by the pickets, to the effect that they will not fire upon each other unless either side attempt an advance.
>
> The line of our corps is about two miles south of the city, while the right, at present held by Smith and Burnside, is in less than one mile. The city lies at our mercy, as our batteries could raze it to the ground in one hour's time were the order given, but that is not the apparent policy of our commander. The possession of the railroads leading from it to the south, is the objective for which they are working. Three of these roads are now held by our forces — the City Point, Petersburg and Norfolk, and the Roanoke River Railroad. Hunter is before Lynchburg, and should he succeed in its reduction, the last one will be destroyed, and Richmond cut off from the rest of the Confederacy. After which its capture will be simply a work of time for "General Starvation" when he commands, generally advocates a speedy surrender or evacuation of a place, and those under him generally come to the same conclusion.[58]

Meanwhile, Colonel Weygant had recovered from his Spotsylvania wound to the point that he could return to the regiment. He departed Newburgh on July 1 with his baggage: "a regulation sabre, a contraband, a valise, and an overcoat." He made his way south from Newburgh to City Point, Virginia, but had to wait around until a Sanitary Commission wagon took him to the division field hospital, where he visited the sick and wounded of the regiment. When he reached the regiment, he found it "quite pleasantly situated in the shade of a grove of pines where they had been lying for several days." He'd arrived just as Captain Travis was about to begin the first dress parade they'd had in more than two months. The last parade had been in Culpeper at the start of the Overland Campaign and on that occasion three hundred and fifty men were present for duty. Now less than a hundred "ragged, dirty, tired looking veterans, that was my regiment— all that was left fit for duty of the fighting men of the Orange Blossoms."[59] At the center of the line was the flag sent by the Daughters of Orange the previous winter. The flag was still in good shape but torn by bullets and shell. The staff splintered at the North Anna crossing had been repaired with twine. "Yes, the men were ragged, and dirty too, but they were a band of battle-tried veterans."[60]

During the next three weeks, the regiment spent every third day on the picket line or working on the fortifications. There were no real engagements but plenty of fatigue duty.[61]

Thomas Rodman assured his parents that he was in "first rate health" and hoped they were as well.

> We are having easy times here at present but I do not know how long it will last. We have gone into camp and are doing picket duty which is the most we have to do. We have no firing in front of our Brigade Pickett while on the right and left it is nothing but shoot all the time. Our boys make an agreement with them not to fire on them if they will not fire on us. They are about 30 yds apart in little holes dug in the ground but we never have any use for them. We talk to them and trade coffee for tobacco. The weather is very warm down here and no rain at all. Very dusty. Water scarce... I think Grant is going to wind the thing up before he gives up. But he has got his hands full. He is not taking Vicksburg now. We are so close to the city that we can hear the church bells ring when a stray shell sets the city on fire which it sometimes does. There is a Reb bridge that crosses the River at Petersburg to Pocahontis within reach of our serge Guns and it sometimes happens that they start across with a train and get it knocked off like mice.[62]

A few days later, he wrote again.

> We are yet in Camp and I think we will soon be able to go and give the Rebs another turn.... It is all quiet along the lines except an occasional shot from some Big Gun or Mortar trying the range.... This Virginia is a great Country. One dense mass of Woods and Swamps. But there is some splendid Plantations on the James River. Splendid buildings and some very nice houses. No livestock of any kind except once in a while a poor mule or cow and very few people except the nig. Some of them look to be about 300 years old or more. De Lord bress de Union soger. They make out to feed us pretty good now. Soft bread, pickles onions cucumbers plenty of fresh beef and good pork although the sugar and coffee is rather short.

In a postscript, he wrote that he was now paid $18 a month, which is what a corporal earned. "When you think it would be safe I wish you would send me a watch. I lost mine in the Wilderness. A cheep one will do."[63]

Sergeant Ben Hull wrote home to "Miss Annie" during this period of inactivity. He told her that the mail had been delayed but attributed that to a raid into Maryland by Confederate Jubal Early that had Washington in a panic. He mentioned that the camp was a mile from the front but

> not out of hearing of their big guns, nor have missed not a day since we left our winter quarters but what we have heard that all dreaded sound that echoes from a cannon and we know its meaning full well. But we are having a good rest now, which our whole army needs, never was men so much in need of rest, both us and our enemy. They are coming into our lines very fast. They say their rations are getting short and they are tired of fighting. The men in the ranks say, if shaking hands with us would end this war, they would be willing to do it.... Is it not to bad to make men fight so against their will? ... We have been out two nights all night to the front tareing down the old works of the Enemy wich the black troops took from them, the day we got in front of Petersburgh. They are of the strongest kind and made a great deal more so by being on high ground. If I thought you up their could understand, I would write more about our lines in front of Petersburgh, but one that never saw any such thing can form but a small idea of how a war is carried on."[64]

During the first week in July, General Jubal Early launched an attack into Maryland that threatened Washington, D.C., to the degree that Grant was compelled to send the 6th Corps to meet it. Until that threat was gone, he could launch no major attacks against Petersburg.

On July 17, Captain William Mapes wrote home to his brother that companies B and H had been combined and he now commanded them with commensurate rank. He proudly wrote that he was now drawing the pay of a captain, $130 a month.

> This Reg't numbers 400 all told & 200 present Co. B most 30. H about 15... We are detached from the A of P & are now about ½ way from City Point & Petersburg. Out of Range & we have no picket duty to do but have had some fatigue tearing down Some Forts of the rebs the niggers captured. I tell you they are bricks & excel the white troops in Discipline & fight well. I am proud of them & not one of the Soldiers found fault with their assaulting and carrying the forts &c for us to occupy.... Write often & give me the news Destroy this.[65]

An enlisted man wrote in his diary for July 24 that they did fatigue duty from before dawn until after dark.

> We are getting very tired of the pick and shovel business. It is said that since we came here Hancock's men have torn down over twenty miles of old works. And we have built the Lord only knows how many miles of new. During the past month, our old division commander Major General D.B. Birney has been assigned to the command of the Tenth Corps. The veterans of the "Old Third " have been consolidated into one division under General Mott, and our brigade which has lost the 3d Maine, and 141st Pa., but to which the 73d N.Y. and 17th Me. have been added, has received a new and permanent commander in the person of General de Trobriand.[66]

While the Orange Blossoms were digging trenches, some Schuylkill County coal miners from the 48th Pennsylvania were busy digging a shaft under the Confederate earthworks. They figured that if the men could not go over the works, they would fill an underground chamber with barrels of gunpowder, touch it off, and blow a hole in the enemy line. Army engineers told them the task was impossible but the miners went ahead anyway. As the date scheduled for the explosion neared, the Union high command decided to send troops to the north side of the James River to distract the Confederates into thinking a big attack was planned on their flanks. Hancock's command was ordered to move to Deep Bottom to be part of the diversion.

At 5:00 P.M. July 25, Hancock's men marched to City Point and bivouacked for the night. Captain Henry Travis wrote, "On the 26th we marched across the Appomattox river, crossed Bermuda Hundred the same day and at night crossed the James River at Turkeys Bend and as soon as daylight appeared we advanced but had not gone far before we was getting shell thrown into us fast but that did not keep us from going. The 1st div. of our Corps captured four heavy guns and ours a few prisoners. The 124th was on the skirmish line but fortunately no one was hurt."[67] The 2nd Corps pushed on, driving the enemy across open country known locally as Strawberry Plains. The presence of a large body of troops threatening the Confederate right worked just as Grant had hoped. Fearing that his left flank would be turned, Lee dispatched a division from the defenses of Petersburg north to meet the supposed threat.[68]

By July 28, Hancock's Corps was back on the line at Petersburg, having accomplished its goal of distracting the enemy while the miners were busy stuffing the end of the shaft with explosives. Then Madill's Brigade moved up to the front line, relieving a federal division and "occupying the rifle pits on the picket line in front, with its left resting at a point about a quarter of a mile to the right of the doomed Confederate fort."[69]

When the powder was touched off, at about 5 A.M. on July 30, the Orange Blossoms heard a dull boom and saw a huge mass of earth tossed into the air. The Pennsylvania miners knew their craft well, for when the smoke cleared, a gaping hole had replaced the once formidable Confederate earthworks. This was followed by a sustained Union artillery barrage and a mass attack of infantry. While the mine itself was brilliantly executed, the attack was an abject failure. It did not take long for the Confederates to recover from their initial shock. Reinforcements and artillery were quickly brought forward to seal the breach in their lines and shells began falling among the 124th New York, wounding three of their number. Colonel Weygant referred to it as the "Burnside Fiasco" and Grant said it was "a stupendous failure" that cost the army four thousand men.[70]

That night, Captain Henry Travis wrote to his father describing the feint to the north and their return to the line in time to see the mine explosion. "Now about the Charge.... The storming party was composed of Negro soldiers supported by the white troops of the 18th and 10th Corps."[71] Travis was incorrect, the "storming party" was made up of 9th Corps white troops who were poorly led and, for the most part, did not advance much past the gigantic hole created by the explosion. Travis praised the colored regiments, as they were called, and was critical of the white troops when, in fact, the blame for the failure lay with Burnside, some of his division commanders, and with Meade as well.[72] When the troops, white and black, came streaming back, Travis commented, "I was in a position where I could see a good deal of the fighting and I felt bad enough when seeing our men coming back in a rabble to turn our own guns on them.... The troops that was fighting was none of the old Army of the Potomac or you would never have seen them come back."[73]

At 9:00 P.M. on July 30, the 124th New York pulled back from the rifle pits and moved to the rear, where it found the brigade "in column awaiting our arrival." The regiment fell in and headed back to its old camp. For the next ten days, the men rested and welcomed back to the regiment a number of men who had been on detached service or convalescing in the hospital. "Our morning report of August 11th showed that there were four hundred and twenty names remaining on the rolls of the regiment, and twelve officers, and one hundred and forty-two enlisted men present for duty."[74]

A soldier who signed himself "P." sent a letter to the editor of the *Whig Press* bearing the heading "Camp Before Petersburgh, Va., Sunday, Aug; 7th, 1864." He was a member of Company K, who was on detached duty with the ambulance train.

> Gen. Meade and Gen. Hancock told our Division Commander (Lieut. Pancoast, of the 110th P.V.) that he had the best train not only in the corps, but the best in the army; that his men, wagons and horses, looked the best on inspection, and that they were proud of the Division. Lieut. Pancoast read an order to that effect, and told the boys that he was proud of them for taking pains to keep things up so nice. We have an inspection every Sunday, and every man in our Division (now Mott's) has to come out on inspection in full uniform, and everything military style. The whole Division of troops are laying in camp in the woods, and I hope may lay there until it gets cooler. We have had but little rain for a long time. The 124th is in a nice grove, but it is now a small regiment. Col. Weygant and Major Murray are in good health. We lost one of the best men in the regiment when Capt. Jackson got killed. Woe to the Rebel that killed him. Lieut. Wisner has got his discharge for disability. Co. K will miss Wisner very much; they put great confidence in having him for their leader after Jackson fell. But he was not able to stay with us. W.T. Ogden will now be 1st Lieutenant, I suppose. He came out private. He has been through some pretty hard places, and been wounded two or three times battling for his country. Company K has lost some of its best men: the Captain, Lieut. Denton, Isaac Decker, Daniel Webb, W.W. Parsons, W.W. Ritch, beside many others. The 124th has

Left: Woodward T. Ogden enlisted as a corporal and rose through the ranks. He was such an "efficient orderly" that Colonel Weygant secured him a commission as 2nd lieutenant. *Right:* Sergeant Watson Ritch, Company K, was killed at Petersburg. "Company K has lost some of its best men ... W.W. Ritch, besides many others" (both photographs from the Michael J. McAfee collection).

lost many very smart and useful men since it left Orange County two years ago, and still the accursed traitors are not subdued, but I hope the time is not far distant when the rebellion will effectively be put down.

The soldier went on to describe the fighting of the previous few weeks and said he felt confident of ultimate victory of the army. "Grant will conquer the Rebs yet, and drive them like the wind. One word for the 124th. Won't Middletown rally and send us volunteers enough to fill up the 124th to its maximum? If there is a regiment in the field that has won any praise, it is the 124th, the Ellis Guards, Orange Blossoms. We yet have good men at the helm so send us recruits."[75]

The very next day, an unsigned letter from the regiment was sent to *The Daily Journal* in Newburgh. The author wrote that he had read of plans in Orange County to raise a new regiment which would satisfy the quota of men for Newburgh under the new draft. He asked if it did not make more sense to ask the male population of the county to enlist in the 124th New York? The author may have inadvertently undermined his own argument by mentioning that of the original 960 enlisted men and 30 officers who departed Goshen nearly two years before, only 140 men and 12 officers were present for duty on the day he wrote. Joining a new regiment that might never see action might seem a lot safer than joining a regiment already in the field that seemed to always be in the thick of the battle.[76]

August 12, Grant decided to go on the offensive again. He did so in part to prevent Lee from sending reinforcements from Petersburg to General Jubal Early in the Shenandoah Valley. Early had, at the end of July, burned Chambersburg, Pennsylvania, and was threatening Washington, D.C. Grant thought that the enemy lines north of the James River guarding the approaches to Richmond must be lightly held. He also wanted to cut the all-important Weldon Railroad southwest of Petersburg. He decided to coordinate his next attack against Lee's left at Deep Bottom with an attack against the enemy's right near the Weldon Railroad. Grant chose Hancock's Corps to lead the attack on the Confederate works along the approaches to Richmond at Deep Bottom. Hancock was to coordinate operations with General Birney's 10th Corps.[77]

The 2nd Corps marched from Petersburg at 4 P.M. and went into bivouac four hours later at City Point. The movement was observed by the enemy, so in order to mask their real intentions, a rumor was put out that the 2nd Corps was headed for Washington, D.C. The men boarded transports and got underway, but once out of sight, the transports halted. A tug came up carrying Generals Mott and de Trobriand to lead the convoy back toward Deep Bottom.[78] At daybreak on August 13, de Trobriand's Brigade, including the 124th, began to disembark at Tilghman's Wharf. The men secured the landing area with a strong picket line and awaited the arrival of the rest of the corps. As the troops assembled, General Birney's 10th Corps took up a position on the left of the line closest to the James River, Mott's Division held the center, and General Barlow, in command of Gibbon's Division, held the right. Union Cavalry patrolled the far right looking for an opportunity to break through and press on to Richmond.

At 9 A.M., de Trobriand's regiments deployed as skirmishers and advanced into the woods about a mile before they engaged and drove the enemy into its earthworks "on the brow of a commanding ridge." The position was very strong and loaded with artillery. The Union skirmishers picketed the woods while the main body marched up to join them. The 124th advanced in support of the 4th Maine Artillery, which was hotly engaged with a Confederate battery.[79]

The Maine gun crew was very accurate, each round bringing cheers from the infantry. Captain Mapes could not get a good enough view of the action from the rear of his company so he moved up to the rear of one of the field pieces. Just as the gun fired, Mapes was hit in the thigh by a sharpshooter's ball, or, as Weygant called it, a "call to the hospital." The bone was shattered, "a piece of which, about the size of a minnie ball, was carried through the wound and clung to his pants just below the hole made in them by the exit of the bullet." Two more men were hit, but for Mapes, this was the wound that would end his military career.[80]

The news was quickly reported in the local newspapers of Orange County. "We are sorry to learn that Capt. Mapes, of Co. B, 124th Regt., N.Y.S.V., was again wounded in the recent engagement at Deep Bottom, Va., and the wound is of a very serious nature. He was struck by a Minnie Ball, in his right thigh, which shattered the bone so that it was found necessary to amputate the limb about four inches above the knee. The operation was successfully performed by Dr. Thompson, surgeon of the Regiment, and at last accounts he was doing well, although it will be a long time before he can be removed to his home."

At noon, the Maine battery was withdrawn and the 124th moved back into the shelter of the trees where members spent the remainder of the day and the following night. Units from the 2nd Corps tried to flank the enemy position but it proved to be too strong. The Union troops were forced to withdraw after "considerable loss." The regiment was on picket duty on the morning of August 15 and watched as Union gunboats approached and opened fire with "monstrous shells" as big as nail kegs. "Fortunately no member of 124th was killed, or permanently injured by them, but several had their feelings badly wounded."[81]

Grant's estimate of the enemy strength north of the James had been overly optimistic: there were a lot more Confederates present on the battlefield than he'd expected. The tangled underbrush and swampy ground made maneuvering difficult and it soon became clear that Hancock didn't have enough men to break the enemy's lines. But the Union commander was not in the least upset. He told Hancock to remain where he was and continue to skirmish with the enemy and threaten, but not to launch any major attack. It was now time to move two Union corps against the Weldon Railroad south of Petersburg.[82]

On August 16, the 124th moved to the left to take up picket duty in some woods where they were protected from enemy artillery fire. To the front was a field of grain. "Presently a small body of Confederates crept forward through this grain and opened on our men, who, standing in the open field, became conspicuous targets, the foe meantime remaining entirely concealed." Weygant selected a dozen men from Companies G and K to advance, firing as they went. Two of the enemy were hit and the rest quickly retreated to the breastworks. Weygant cited Sergeant Lewis T. Shultz of Company G and Corporal David U. Quick of Company K for "conspicuous gallantry." Although both had been wounded early in the fight, neither man went to the rear until the enemy retreated.[83]

That ended the action in front of General Mott's Division, but heavy cannonading told of General Birney's 10th Corps assaulting the enemy's earthworks. They took three battle flags and three hundred prisoners but could not make a breakthrough. The same was true for Barlow's Division of the 2nd Corps and Gregg's mounted troops. On the night of August 18, Hancock's Corps began the return march to Petersburg which they reached two days later.[84] The men of the 2nd Corps had no sooner settled into life in the trenches when two divisions were pulled out and sent to join Warren's Corps in their destruction of the Weldon Railroad. Fortunately for the 124th New York, Mott's Division remained in place.

Weygant wrote that from the "20th of August to the 9th of September very little of general interest transpired in Mott's division, the troops which were as usual kept busy building earthworks and doing picket duty."[85] The picket lines were very close and, as neither side was interested in overrunning the other, a sort of truce went into effect. The officers, even the usually fastidious Colonel Weygant, overlooked the trading that went on.

The men kept themselves busy constructing bomb proofs, or "gopher holes" as they were called. A soldier in the 124th New York described how they were built. Pits were dug and covered with heavy logs and earth. The men did not live in the shelters but kept them up because "we can't tell how soon we may have occasion to use them." The soldier attempted to describe how the trenches and earthworks covered the landscape.

Earthworks at Petersburg. Note the openings for artillery along the wall and sharpened logs outside the works. Open fields of fire prevented enemy troops from getting close to the works before the defenders could fire on them. Bombproofs inside the works protected the soldier from enemy artillery fire (Library of Congress, Prints & Photographs Division).

Immense furrows follow each other over a strip of ground nearly a mile wide, and the principle ones are about fifteen miles in length.... This belt of earthworks is fringed with road pits which run back toward the rear, and are built zig-zag fashion, like rail fences at the north, with dirt thrown upon the side toward the enemy. They have been made for the protection of all the trains, but more particularly for that of the ammunition wagons which are sometimes obliged to come up to the works under fire.[86]

Thomas Rodman wrote home from the "Bomb Proofs near Petersburg" to tell his parents that the shelters were really "quite comfortable" and that

we do not stay in them all the time. We have tents pitched behind them to sleep in. The weather is getting quite cold down here at night. We have some rain just now. Our picket line is about 300 yds from the Rebs, we do a good share of trading with them. We trade coffee and sugar for tobacco and sometimes we get the Greenbacks for things they want such as hats shoes and other things. It has almost ceased now quite a number of our side having deserted and gone over to them. We have had only one such case in our Regt and that was a foreigner from England.

He told his parents that he had recently been promoted to 2nd sergeant but he had no access to the appropriate stripes so he asked them to send him a pair. He'd also not received his pocket watch and asked again about their sending it to him.[87]

Colonel Weygant was always eager to bring new recruits into the regiment. When he heard that Robert A. Malone and John S. King, both of Middletown, had enrolled sixty-eight men, he

Captain Robert Malone joined the regiment in August 1864 and was named to command Company K when Captain Mapes was wounded. He had prior service in the 18th New York Volunteers (archive of the Historical Society of the Town of Warwick, gift of Joan and Tom Frangos).

quickly wrote the governor of New York, Horatio Seymour, asking for commissions for the two men that they might bring their volunteers into the 124th. Nearly all of the men had prior service, as did Malone and King, who were both officers in Company D of the 18th New York Volunteers, a two-year regiment which had been mustered out of federal service. Since the death of Captain Jackson, Company K had no officers. Malone became the captain of that company and King the 1st lieutenant. Weygant reserved the 2nd lieutenant slot for the "efficient orderly" Woodward T. Ogden. The colonel also secured commissions for sergeants Jonathan Birdsall, Thomas Taft, and Ebenezer Holbert, and each was given command of a company.[88]

On the night of September 9, Weygant was ordered to have the regiment ready to move out in support of the 20th Indiana, 99th Pennsylvania, and 2nd U.S. Sharpshooters, who would attempt to capture some forward enemy rifle pits. The night attack was a success that overran the position and took over a hundred prisoners back into Federal lines. The Confederates made three attempts to recapture the line of rifle pits without success, which quickly escalated into three days of artillery barrages and infantry attacks. During one of the battles, the colonel of the 20th Indiana was wounded. Private George G. King of the 124th New York, who was serving with the ambulance train, rushed forward to help him. The courageous private ran into a hail of bullets and was killed. The next morning, Weygant sent out a detachment to retrieve King's body for burial.[89]

During this time, Captain Mapes, wounded at Deep Bottom, sent home the last letters of his military career. He wrote cheerfully to his brother Jesse from the army hospital at Fort Monroe, Virginia,

> You need not fear about my toes. I am bully. I have some pain. They all pronounce my case as a Miracle getting healed up so soon it is all healed but on the sides where the ball come out. It runs some out of there but not more than a table spoon full. I sit up in a chair & in bed. Apitite good & Bowels regular. I also stand up on my foot & take my stump in my hand & got over beds the whole length of the room.... I wish to stay in the service as long as I can & if my coming home would put me out I would not come. I would stay here. I can stay undoubtedly 6 months here but if Col. Weygant would put me on recruiting service at home I would come. I am able to come home now if someone would come for me.... I cannot go to the Bosses House & will have to go to yours. I will be some trouble but will pay my loan. I will finish tomorrow.

The next day, Mapes took up his pencil and finished his letter. "My stump is quite painful this morning as it looks like rain. I had some fish this morning. I got 2 mos pay yesterday $214.00 & the Gov owes me 2 more as Capt $250, which I will get soon. Remember me to all." He then added a postscript. "I have just walked 100 feet between 2 chairs will be on cruches in a week."[90]

Captain Mapes wrote his final letter on September 18, 1864. Defiant as ever, he refused to ask the "boss" for lodging.

> I claim to be a man of honor & have nothing to yield. I scorn any attempt to bring me home until he asks me. I have the same plan as Maj. Murray & will adhere to it. I will not be able to get my leave before the week after next. The D — m Doctors are such pimps & besides the Surg. in charge runs the

machine by contract & keeps all here to get our Dollar per day but as I told the Doctor today if Dr. Mc Lellan did not forward my request I would rely upon my own influence to get it.... I will accept your kind offer to make my home with you until I get a bird (If I can catch one) & cage of my own.[91]

Sergeant Rodman wrote home again on September 20. "I have received your letter of the 13th and was sorry to hear that Mother had been sick. But I hope that she is better by this time." His father said they had not heard anything from him since mid–August but Rodman replied that he'd written four times since then.

> We are still laying in the front line doing pickett duty and fatigue. We have the Rail Road within ¼ of a mile from us. It was fun to see the Rebs begin shelling the train when they first began to run. But our old 32 lb Parrott Guns began to shell them and the City. We have had 2 men killed in the last week on pickett by sharpshooters. Pickett firing has began again since we made a charge on them and captured 100 of them which they call a mean Yankee trick. We expect they will try the same thing on us one of these dark nights. But we are ready for them.... I want you to send me a check shirt and a pair of Shevrons for a sergeant \/ 3 stripes and a couple of pockett handkerchiefs.[92]

On September 26, the paymaster arrived in camp, which did wonders to raise morale, but the regiment was soon called to action again. On October 1 most of Mott's Division was marched to a railroad station near the Jerusalem Plank Road where the men boarded the cars and were taken to the left of the Union line. Warren's 5th Corps had cut the Weldon Railroad and was fending off concerted efforts by the enemy to retake it. The 124th New York and six other regiments of de Trobriand's Brigade set to work clearing "drive ways" through the woods and constructing earthworks near the Clement House. After working for three days, the division was relieved and "moved leisurely back to the Jerusalem plank road, and encamped in the second line near Fort Sedgewick."[93]

Although not in the front line, the men were still in danger, as enemy sharpshooters were active. Private Grant Benjamin was killed as he was relieved from the picket line, a bullet hitting him in the head as he folded his blanket. A few days later, as the regiment prepared for inspection, newly commissioned Lieutenant Birdsall was shot through the forehead while resting in his tent. He was described as a "thorough gentleman as well as Christian, and of course had the respect of those under him and the esteem of his superiors." His fellow officers had his body embalmed and sent home in a metallic coffin.

Early in October, a soldier of Company K who signed himself "J.H.W." wrote home to the Middletown *Whig Press*. "There has been a great change in the Army, politically speaking, as well as otherwise, within the last few days. Lincoln will carry the vote of nearly the whole army — and our Regiment is all right. We are on the move, and everything works to a charm. We are sure of victory, and defeat can't come. We are all in the best of spirits, and hope soon to close this war without McClellan Armistace — but by a humble submission on the part of the rebels to law and order."[94]

On October 20, Sergeant Rodman wrote to his father, acknowledging the death of his mother.

> I received a letter from Pannie which bore such sad tidings to me and I tell you it was sad news to me.... I am almost ashamed to answer your letter, it having been 3 weeks almost since I got it. But you must excuse me for we have been moving since I got it and we now have to hold ourselves in readiness to go at a moments warning. I received the stripes but have not got the shirts yet. You must try and enjoy yourself as best you can. I will be home in ten months if the lord is willing and then I hope to stay with you forever. That likeness that you speak of of Mothers is gone. It got wet and faded all off but I hung to it but it got lost. I do not see what you were at that you did not get her likeness taken long ago. I send a lock of her hair which I want you to take to Mr Haights and get it put into the top of a gold ring. Never mind what it costs and oblige me and send it to me. Keep a part of the hair for yourself.[95]

At the end of October, the 124th could muster sixteen officers and about two hundred thirty enlisted men. With Weygant as colonel, Murray as lieutenant colonel, and Benedict as major, the regiment had its full complement of field grade officers. What is more, with the addition of Lieutenant Carmick to Company F and Lieutenant Bradley to Company B, the regiment had an experienced officer at the head of each of its companies. Weygant commented that he was confident

Captain Thomas Bradley as he appeared at the end of the war.

that the regiment could perform whatever duty was assigned. As it turned out, the men would soon have the opportunity to do so, as Grant was not going into winter quarters without trying at least once more to break the stalemate at Petersburg.

On the night of October 24, selected troops were pulled back from the line and massed out of sight of the enemy. Two days later, the 2nd Corps was moved left as far as the Weldon Road. At 4:00 A.M. on the cold, rainy morning of October 27, the 5th and 9th Corps began the advance while Mott's Division moved southwest along the Vaughan Road until the Union forces ran into enemy skirmishers within half a mile of Hatcher's Run. Gibbon's Division, now commanded by General Egan, drove the enemy from its rifle pits. Mott's men followed along after Egan, the cannonading to the north growing louder as they advanced. De Trobriand's Brigade was ordered to move up to the left of Egan's line and relieve one of the brigades which had fallen behind. De Trobriand's men, including the 124th New York formed a line of battle with two regiments thrown forward in a skirmish line.

The brigade steadily drove the enemy pickets into the woods behind an old steam mill, where they reconnected with Egan's Division. The whole line moved forward until it reached the Boydton Road, where General Meade called a halt. General de Trobriand's Brigade was now the extreme left of the line and arranged in order from right to left: 99th Pennsylvania, 110th Pennsylvania, 20th Indiana, 40th New York, 1st Maine Heavy Artillery, and 17th Maine. The 73rd New York, 86th New York and cavalry pickets were pushed forward about a third of a mile to cover the front and flank. The 124th was in advance of the main line on the right and was deployed in a "rather extended battle line at the outer edge of a piece of woods, across a road down which it was expected the enemy would attempt to advance." In front of the regiment was an open field with woods twenty rods in the distance.[96]

After moving forward, Hancock's line was to connect on the right with Crawford's Division of the 5th Corps, but the link up had not been made, leaving a dangerous gap in the Union line. While the 5th and 9th Corps were to keep the Confederates busy along their front, the 2nd Corps was to follow Hatcher's Run northwest until it led the men to the target of the operation: the South Side Railroad, Lee's last supply route into Petersburg. Hancock moved forward, easily brushing aside enemy pickets until he reached the Boydton Plank Road. At that point the gap between the 2nd Corps and the 5th Corps was a mile wide. Crawford tried to close up but the dense woods and heavy underbrush made that impossible. It was all his men could do to keep from stumbling into the unseen Confederates.[97]

At about 4:00 P.M., Pierce's Brigade of Mott's Division was routed by a surprise attack, but Egan was nearby and led a counterattack that rolled the enemy force back. At about the same time, dismounted cavalry charged down the road held by the 124th New York but were brought to a halt by the accurate fire of the Orange Blossoms. The Confederates brought up a battery of rifled guns and a furious exchange took place. A short while later, an aide from General de Trobriand rode up and asked Weygant if the regiment might be able to capture the battery. The colonel said he would try but asked for a regiment to support the attack. Moments later the aide returned with the Sharpshooters. As their commander greeted Weygant, he was shot from the saddle. The Sharpshooters immediately tore into the enemy and drove them back. As Weygant turned in his saddle to call upon the 86th New York for help, he was shot through the side and fell from his horse. The fighting continued in a pouring rain as Weygant made his way to the rear.

In what became known as the Battle of Boydton Plank Road, the Confederates came close to crushing Hancock's Corps. General Lee saw an opportunity to strike the isolated 2nd Corps and ordered A.P. Hill's men to advance against Hancock's center while Wade Hampton's cavalry advanced on the left and Mahone flanked him on the right. But Hancock and Egan were up to the challenge. Attacked from behind, Egan fought his way out of the trap. Hancock redeployed his men to meet Mahone's attack while Egan hit the enemy in the flank and the Union cavalry fought off Hampton's best efforts. After dark Hancock withdrew to his original line.[98]

In the chaotic battle, the under-strength 124th lost twenty men killed, wounded, or captured. Incredibly, six of that number were officers. Captain James Finnigan, who had just returned from the same hospital where Captain Mapes was recuperating, was killed. Major Henry Murray was wounded and captured again, while Colonel Weygant and Lieutenants Carmick, Holbert, and Bradley were all wounded.

Sergeant Rodman wrote home when the regiment reached camp.

> Since I wrote you last we have had a very hard march and one day of pretty hard fighting. We marched about 13 miles down towards the Danville Rail Road and encountered the Rebs which were ready for us and we had a pretty hard fight all day and at night we fell back and started for Camp next morning where we arrived near night. We lost in our Company our Captain Finnegan, he was shot through the bowells and died the next morning. Robt Foley was also wounded and I expect he is dead or a prisoner for he was left on the field. Our Major was wounded in the foot and taken prisoner. Our Colonel wounded and I suppose he is home now. When you write let me know if you received my check for $72.00 some time ago and how the election went. And let me know if you are going to have that ring fixxed that I sent the lock of hair to put into it. We have got quite a large number of recruits in the Regt, and we have 15 in our Company, but they have to be watched for they desert whenever they can from off Pickett. I wish you would send me some paper or other, send me a coppy of the Frank Leslies and Oblige.[99]

The Battle of First Hatcher's Run, also known as the Battle of the Boydton Plank Road, was a defeat for the Union that cost seventeen hundred casualties. The Confederates lost about one thousand men but they turned back Grant's attempt to cut the last remaining rail line that brought food and military supplies into Richmond. President Lincoln regarded it as an unmitigated disaster that threatened his chances with the presidential election just a week away. He need not have worried. Lincoln won every state still in the Union except New Jersey, Delaware, and Kentucky. He defeated General McClellan 55 percent to 45 percent in the popular vote and carried the all important electoral vote two hundred twelve to twenty one.

As for the regiment, the 124th New York remained on the field until 10:00 P.M., then marched back the way it came to the Vaughan Road where the men camped until the next day, when they took up the march again. By 6:00 P.M., the men were back in the camp they had left on October 24.[100]

There was one officer in the regiment, however, for whom the battle went on. Major John Thompson, the regimental surgeon, was accused of cowardice and was subject to a court martial. During the battle, he was at the rear with the other medical staff and ambulances. Late in the afternoon, when the Confederates launched their counterattack in the rain, the 124th held its ground. So did Surgeon Thompson. At about 9:00 P.M., when the Union forces began to leave the field, Thompson became separated and wandered around in the night looking for his regiment.

At dawn, he came to the edge of a clearing where he saw a group of Union and Confederate soldiers questioning a woman who was standing in the doorway of her house. The surgeon rode up and heard them asking about the locations of the Union and Confederate lines. Thompson asked if any were officers and was told that all were enlisted men. Just then, another body of mounted Confederates approached, one of whom carried a white flag which Thompson took to be flag of truce.[101] As this group also appeared to be lost, Thompson suggested that they all take a course to the right and whichever line they came to first would take control of the whole group. According to Thompson, he thought the direction he suggested would take them to the Union lines. He further proposed that whichever force they came upon, no firing should take place as just a few of the men were armed. He tied a towel to his riding whip. "I did this on my own notion and for the purpose of protection from being fired upon," Thompson wrote. They proceeded on, presumably in the direction suggested by the doctor, until they met a Federal officer who took charge of the group and led them into the Union lines. Major Thompson left them and found his way back to the regiment.[102]

In early November, four soldiers of the 7th Wisconsin brought charges against Thompson. One of the soldiers maintained that they had control of the rebels who were their prisoners and the doctor, though a noncombatant, took charge of the situation. Three other Union soldiers concurred with the assertions of the fourth. Thompson was summoned to 2nd Corps headquarters and formally charged with "cowardice and treachery." He did not insist that his accusers be forced to testify and called three character witnesses on his own behalf. In doing so he sealed his own fate. All three testified to his loyalty but none to his bravery. When Assistant Surgeon M.V.K. Montfort of the 124th testified, he volunteered that in battle, the doctor always assumed as safe a position as possible to perform his duties. While one might assume that to be the proper position for a doctor to take, Montfort was asked another question about Thompson's reputation among the men of the 124th as to bravery. "It is not good," replied Montfort.[103]

On November 25, the court absolved him of the charge of disloyalty but said his actions in taking charge of the situation caused him to lose his noncombatant status. He was found guilty of all the other charges and was sentenced to be dismissed from the service with loss of pay and allowances. Surgeon Thompson returned to Orange County, but his case was soon taken up by the officers of the regiment, who willingly testified to his loyalty if not to his bravery. Secretary of State William Seward used his influence to have the matter brought before President Lincoln, who pardoned Thompson by executive order on January 25, 1865. He had the option of reenlisting in February but failed to respond.[104]

Colonel Weygant, who had been wounded at the Boydton Plank Road, obtained a furlough so that he could return to Newburgh to recuperate, but he kept in contact with the officers of the regiment. Captain Benedict, who now commanded the regiment, wrote that Captain Malone and Lieutenant King had arrived with eighty-seven men, most of whom went to Companies K and E. Captain Travis also wrote and mentioned the new additions. "The old regiment looks big

Top: Assistant Surgeon Robert V. K. Montfort, appointed surgeon near the end of the war. His testimony led to Surgeon Thompson's dismissal from the service. *Bottom:* Lieutenant John S. King, joined the regiment in October 1864, and served in Company K. He was wounded in action at Hatcher's Run, Virginia. He had prior service in the 18th New York (both photographs from the archive of the Historical Society of the Town of Warwick, gift of Joan and Tom Frangos).

again." They both mentioned that Captain Finnigan's body had been disinterred and Travis added, "If any of his friends speak to you in regard to refunding the money it cost us, it is $133, and you are authorized to receive it for us. Do not mention it to them unless they speak first about it to you."[105] Weygant noted that by the end of November the regiment numbered nineteen officers and three hundred sixty two enlisted men, more men than they'd had in the ranks since the Battle of Chancellorsville.[106]

A rumor was going around the camp that Hancock was leaving the 2nd Corps and that General John Gibbon would take command. Still suffering from the effects of his Gettysburg wound, Hancock could no longer remain in the field. Command of the 2nd Corps went to Major General Andrew A. Humphreys, Meade's able chief of staff.[107]

"Dear Father," wrote Thomas Rodman.

> I take my pencil in hand to let you know that I am quite well but I am not at the Division. A little under the weather with the complaint so frequent called the Diareah but I am not at all bad being able to travil about and I think I will go to the Regt in a few days. Things are going on prosperous down here since election. The Rebs are coming in daily or rather nightly in large numbers. They are tired of the war and do not like the looks of things. They think they will have to serve 4 years more and they think it is better to come in now than suffer all Winter with cold and hunger. The weather is quite cold here at night, but in the middle of the day it is quite warm.... Since beginning this letter yestoday I have been transferred to the Genrl Hospt at City Point where I arrived last night at 10 O Clock and I am quite at home this morning. You must not write again until you hear from me. It began to rain here last night and rains quite smart just now. The Army is again under marching orders with 8 days rations.[108]

On November 21, Private Charles O. Goodyear of Company I wrote to the local press. He and three other men from upstate New York had enlisted in August 1864 for one year's service. "There are only four in this Regiment that come from old Seneca, that I know of. None of us enlisted for this regiment, but for some unknown reason we were sent here. We are all suited, though, as well as if we had went to the regiments that we enlisted for. We have a very good lot of officers." The opposing lines of the armies near Fort Sedgwick, where Goodyear was doing picket duty, were about two hundred fifty yards apart, but where he was stationed the lines were but twenty-five yards apart.

Where the 40th and 86th N.Y. are doing picket duty, our men talk to the Rebs, and some times they exchange papers with them, at the same time keeping their heads below the bank of dirt. The way they do it is by tying a piece of dirt up in the paper and then throwing it over, and they are generally honest enough to do the same. I have been told that before I came here and before we advanced our picket line, that the pickets were on very good terms. Our men would go half way to meet the Rebs, and trade coffee for tobacco, and one thing for another, and talk for an hour or two at a time; but since we advanced our picket in and captured about two hundred and fifty of them, there has been a constant firing on both sides, so much so that it is not safe for a man to show any part of his body above the works. Our pits are in an awful condition, now we are having so much rain, that it makes the mud about a foot deep in them. When a man goes on picket here, he does not expect much sleep. If he does sleep, he will have to do it standing up. It is not very agreeable standing there in the mud for twenty-four hours, I can assure you, for I tried it yesterday and night before last, and it must have been a great deal worse last night, for it has been raining for the past three days. I have been lucky so far in dodging the balls....[109]

As winter approached, the men were eager to begin construction of winter quarters. At the end of November it was rumored that Mott's Division would soon march to a new camp some-where in the rear. The next day they set out for Poplar Grove Church where de Trobriand's Brigade made camp between Fort Cummings and Fort Siebert. But instead of winter camp, the regiment marched to make another attack against Lee's supply line into Petersburg. The Weldon Railroad had already been cut at Globe Tavern, but the ever-resourceful Confederates simply used horse-drawn wagons to carry supplies to where the railroad was still under their control. Grant wanted to destroy the tracks farther south, which would effectively deny the enemy use of the Weldon Railroad. He chose as his target Stony Creek Station, nineteen miles south of Petersburg. He planned to send General Warren's 5th Corps and Mott's Division to do as much damage to the rail line as possible. After a long and cold march, the men reached Jarrett's Station, ten miles south of Stony Creek Station, where they began their work. Rails and ties were pulled up, the ties set ablaze, and the rails heated until they could be bent. Bridges and culverts were destroyed as was anything else that might impede rail traffic.

In an attempt to protect his lifeline, Lee sent General A.P. Hill to put a stop to Warren's marauding. But Hill was not able to bring him to battle, as Warren had done as much damage as he thought feasible and withdrew, heading north to the safety of his own lines. Along the way, slaves crowded around the Union column and showed the soldiers the bodies of their comrades who appeared to have been murdered. Enraged at the sight, the Union column destroyed private property as well as military stores on the march back to Petersburg. Mott's Division arrived in camp on December 12 and, although the line they destroyed was up and running again in the spring, their work did considerable damage to Lee's supply line during the winter.

Colonel Weygant returned from his furlough to find a package containing the official documents relating to Private, now Sergeant, Archibald Freeman's Medal of Honor. The presentation ceremony was scheduled for December 15 and "Archibald Freeman became for the time being the envied hero of de Trobriand's command."[110]

As Christmas neared, the colonel received a large box from F.H. Reevs of Goshen and a letter which read, "I have this day packed and shipped to you per express, by order of the ladies, one box containing five hundred and thirty sleeping caps for your regiment. While the ladies of the different towns have worked with a hearty good will, you may attribute a large share of your indebtedness to Mrs. Dr. Jane., of Florida, who has evidently been the moving power."[111]

As 1864 came to a close, the men were as anxious as ever to start building their winter quarters. The weather was cold and rainy and, for the most part, the men still relied on their shelter halves to keep them warm and dry. A good deal of time was devoted to preparing for the spring campaign. Drills, inspections, and reviews became more frequent while digging trenches and building earthworks came to a halt. The new governor of New York, Reuben Fenton, issued commissions to Charles Weygant as colonel, Henry S. Murray as lieutenant colonel, and James Benedict as major. However, Murray was still a prisoner of war, which meant that Major Benedict served as acting lieutenant colonel in his place.

On February 4, orders were received for yet another try at turning Lee's right flank. The attacking force would be comprised of the 5th Corps, 2nd Corps, and Gregg's Cavalry Division. The next day at 7:00 A.M., de Trobriand's brigade formed up and marched two miles to the left, where it halted to form a line of battle with the 124th New York on the right. The brigade moved forward, encountering and driving the enemy's picket line until it came to Hatcher's Run, where the men found the Confederates on the other side of the creek. The Federal troops continued the advance, driving the enemy into a formidable line of earthworks, about three quarters of a mile from the creek. General de Trobriand ordered his men to put up earthworks and while they were at the job, they heard the low rumble of artillery off to the left. The plan had been for the 2nd Corps to assault the enemy line head on while the 5th Corps tried to turn their right flank.[112]

Warren's flanking move proved unsuccessful. The elated Confederates now turned their attention to the 2nd Corps in an effort to drive the Yankees back. Their efforts led to nothing but a heavy loss among the Confederates. At 3:00 A.M., the brigade was relieved by units of the 5th Corps, and moved about a half mile to the rear. The men expected to be able to start their winter quarters but were ordered to build earthworks instead. That night, they slept on the

Winter Quarters, City Point, Virginia. This late war photograph shows soldiers' cabins arranged in neat company streets. Most had canvas roofs and were home to four soldiers (Library of Congress, Prints & Photographs Division).

ground under muslin shelter tents through a cold winter rainstorm. Finally, on February 12 the order was rescinded and the men were allowed to put up real shelters.[113]

At the beginning of March, the 124th received another batch of reinforcements, this time from the 1st U.S. Sharpshooters. The regiment's term of enlistment had expired but some men wanted to remain in the army and they were allowed to choose their new regiment. Twenty-one of the sharpshooters chose the 124th New York. They included a lieutenant, four corporals, and sixteen privates, all of whom were assigned to Company H, Captain Theodore M. Roberson commanding.[114]

By the end of the month, the collapse of the Petersburg line was eagerly anticipated by the Orange Blossoms. Confederate deserters came over to the Union lines on a regular basis and the newspapers were full of stories of Union successes. Daily drill ceased as the men prepared for one last campaign. Grant planned to start the attack on March 29 but Lee beat him to the punch by attacking Fort Stedman on March 25. General Gordon, as able a commander as Lee had, led four divisions forward at dawn and caught the 14th New York Heavy Artillery by surprise. Those who did not flee the fort were captured and the fort's artillery was turned on the nearest Yankee strongholds. But Gordon failed to take the two adjacent forts and did not seize the high ground behind Fort Stedman. Union troops nearby rallied, counterattacked, recaptured Fort Stedman and inflicted heavy losses on Gordon's men. Meade was sure the enemy had stripped its earthworks to make the attack, so he ordered the 2nd and 6th Corps to find the weak spot and break through.[115]

The 124th New York was not part of the battle at Fort Stedman, but de Trobriand had turned out the brigade with orders to strike tents and prepare to march. By 5:00 A.M., the men had buckled on their accoutrements and stood in line, ready to move out. The 1st Division of the 2nd Corps on the right of the 124th New York advanced and drove the enemy from a line of rifle pits. The Confederates counterattacked with such ferocity that the 1st Division called for help. Weygant was ordered to move forward to a house near the picket line where he would receive orders. But when the regiment arrived at the house, no officer was present. Just ahead, the 5th New Hampshire moved forward, leaving a strong position unoccupied. Weygant took it upon himself to move the regiment to the top of the slope and to occupy the rifle pits vacated by the 5th New Hampshire. He immediately ordered his men to improve the position with light breastworks. When the works were strong enough, he had his men lie down under cover while he moved forward into the gathering dusk to examine his ridgeline and another crest in the distance.[116]

Lee was hoping to recapture sections of the picket line lost during the day's fighting. Across the line from the 124th was the 59th Alabama, commanded by Lieutenant Colonel Daniel S. Troy, and the 43rd Alabama, led by Major William J. Mims. They had been ordered to make an attack over rough terrain against a Union line of unknown strength. "We all felt very blue," wrote Col. Troy, "at least I did, and the other officers and men looked so, for there was hardly a doubt we would find the enemy in large force supporting their pickets who held the new line we were to recapture. But I gave the order to the regiment, mounted the breastworks and over we all went." The Alabamans advanced into a low swampy area of standing water, tree stumps, fallen timber, and darkness.[117]

Using his field glasses, Weygant spotted what he was sure was a moving column of the enemy coming down the road his regiment lay across. He told his pickets to fire and fall back when the Confederates got close and informed his company officers as to what was coming their way. As the enemy soldiers approached, they quickly deployed in line of battle "as if they had been on drill" not knowing that a Union regiment awaited them. Captain Thomas Taft of Company C wrote that their earthworks were hardly complete when "the Johnnies came down on us driving in our skirmishers, and advancing in two lines on a double-quick, bayonets fixed, and with a yell that would have made your hair stand on end." The Orange Blossoms on the picket line opened a terrific fire before they retired. Among the first Confederate casualties was Captain Zach Daniel, who shouted "Go to it boys, they'll run like turkeys." He was struck in the forehead and fell dead right in front of Colonel Troy.[118]

The Alabamans reached the contested picket line only to discover that they had captured just a small portion of the earthworks. At that moment, Weygant shouted "commence firing" and his men "opened the most telling and terrific fire I have ever witnessed, instantly breaking and completely demoralizing the charging line, the troops of which either threw themselves flat on the ground or rushed pell mell for shelter into the picket pits until they were literally piled on top of each other." Then Weygant ordered the 124th New York to charge.

Colonel Troy wanted his men to move right and left so that they would not be flanked and called upon four officers nearby to move the men as he'd ordered. Each rose and was immediately shot down. Troy then sent two runners to the rear for reinforcements just as Major Mims brought the 43rd Alabama up at the run. When he reached Colonel Troy, he asked, "'What do you think we had better do?' ... He was somewhat excited, as I was myself, and said, 'Don't you think we had better charge?'" Troy and Mims each took a large chew of tobacco when one of the men called out, "Colonel, they're flanking us on the right, yonder goes their flag!"

Colonel Troy turned to see the men of the 124th charging through a depression to cut the Confederates off from their breastworks. He grabbed the colors of the 59th Alabama and began to wave the flag to rally his men, but only a handful responded before Private John Tompkins, Company F, 124th New York, shot him through the left lung. "Major, I am a dead man," the colonel said, still standing. Mims replied, "No, I hope it is not as bad as that!" The bullet had passed through his body just inches from his spine. In a flash, the colonel thought of his wife and wanted to make sure the ring she had given him was returned. He said a quick prayer then fell face first to the ground. Although he could hear voices around him, Colonel Troy was sure he was dead.[119]

Someone rolled him over and began searching his pockets. The colonel heard one of the Orange Blossoms call out, "Here's one of their officers." There were more voices asking "Is he dead?" Yes, came the reply, "dead as Julius Caesar." For some reason, that caused Colonel Troy to think that perhaps he had not been killed after all and he summoned all his strength to move his foot. The first soldier called out, "No, he ain't dead yet!" Several of the Orange County men gathered around him and began the process of saving his life. First they turned him over and then tried to give him some water but Troy realized that if he swallowed his chew of tobacco he would choke. Troy clamped his lips tight and the water ran down his chin. "He is goner, he can't swallow!" observed one of the soldiers. With great effort, Troy pushed the chew out of his mouth with his tongue. "That's what's the matter, give him some water!" After he drank another asked, "Don't you want some whiskey?" Again, with great effort, Colonel Troy let them know that he did. "Then, more water was given me and after a little while another drink of whiskey and more water and soon I was able to converse with them freely."[120]

The Orange Blossoms tried to make Colonel Troy as comfortable as possible. No one, not even the colonel himself, expected that he would survive. A fire was started to warm his feet and some boards and a blanket were used as a pillow. Troy was kept supplied with water and whiskey, which may well have staved off the effects of shock. Captain Thomas Taft rearranged his blanket and pillow while preparations were made to have him taken to the hospital in the rear. Troy asked that he be taken instead across the lines so that he might die among friends but that request was denied and with the denial, his life was probably saved once again by the same men who tried to kill him. He was taken to a Union field hospital where a member of the Sanitary Commission gave him hot milk punch, a mix of hot milk, sugar, and yet more whiskey to combat the chills developed from loss of blood. The attendant asked if he could pray for the colonel, to which Troy readily agreed. Among those prayers, which the man must have recited out loud, was one beseeching that Colonel Troy's "sins of rebellion" be forgiven. "The thought passed through my mind that his hot milk punch had done me more good than his prayers ever would!"[121]

Not one Orange Blossom received so much as a scratch in the battle but Weygant sent for Surgeon Montfort to minister to the Confederate wounded.[122] The 124th had captured six officers and one hundred sixty-four men. They also gathered up two hundred enemy weapons before being relieved by a "heavy picket force." When General Mott heard that a flag had been taken, he immediately sent an aide to get it. Later that evening, General de Trobriand arrived in camp to personally congratulate the men for their action on the picket line. Then the general took Weygant aside and chastised him for not sending the flag to him before Mott got wind of it.[123] As if that wasn't enough, the New York City newspapers reported that the colors were taken by the 124th *Pennsylvania*.

Grant made ready his plan of attack for March 29. The earthworks from the Appomattox River in the northeast to Hatcher's Run were turned over to the 6th Corps and three divisions of the Army of the James commanded by General Ord. At dawn, Sheridan's horsemen, along with the infantry of the 5th and 2nd Corps took up the march for the Union left. When they bedded down for the night, the 2nd Corps and Warren's 5th Corps faced the Confederate earthworks at White Oak Road, while Sheridan's riders were farther west near Dinwiddie Court House. They were after the South Side Rail Road again and Lee was forced to strip troops from his earthworks to counter the mortal threat to his supply line.[124]

On March 31, the 2nd Corps was unsuccessful in taking the earthworks to the front. The 124th New York and the rest of the brigade were being held in reserve until, at about 2:00 P.M., the regiment was ordered forward to occupy some recently vacated earthworks. Colonel Weygant led his men at the run just as Grant and his staff "went galloping slowly past." The Orange Blos-

Captain Edward J. Carmick had prior military service with the 1st U.S. Sharpshooters before joining the 124th New York as a 1st Lieutenant of Company F. He was wounded at Spotsylvania Court House and the Boydton Plank Road before being killed on April 1, 1865, near Petersburg, Virginia (West Point Museum's United States Military Academy collection).

soms suffered a few casualties getting into place but were moved a mile to the left where they put up a new line of breastworks and spent the night.[125]

The first day of April, Sheridan and Warren fought and won a decisive victory at Five Forks, which doomed Petersburg by opening the way to at last cut the South Side Rail Road. At 11:45 P.M., an order arrived directing Colonel Weygant to move the regiment forward to within two hundred fifty feet of the enemy's works and to open a vigorous fire but to advance no farther. The colonel referred to the order as "apparently suicidal" but the men moved out nonetheless. The night was quite dark but when the regiment moved through some woods it seemed to become darker yet. To add to its misery, the regiment was forced to wade through a swamp to get as close as ordered. The enemy discovered the men and opened fire with rifles and artillery. The brigade commander rushed two regiments forward to reinforce the Orange Blossoms, but after fifteen minutes recalled all three to the main line. The only man killed from the regiment was Captain Edward Carmick of Company F. At dawn his comrades buried him at the junction of the Boydton and Quaker roads and carved a headboard so that his grave could be easily found.[126]

At first Colonel Weygant wondered if the advance that took Captain Carmick's life was necessary. He later found that it was not only necessary but very successful. His was not the only regiment sent forward in the night to fire but not vigorously attack. Several others had done the same and they achieved their purpose: the enemy was pinned for several hours in his works on the Boydton Plank Road. This delayed the march south to attack Warren's 5th Corps so that when Grant's big attack began the next morning, the seventeen thousand Confederates sent to stop Warren were on the march and not in place to do any real damage.[127]

Grant's final assault began on April 2 and achieved breakthroughs in several places. The 124th moved at the double quick right up one of the main roads leading to Petersburg. "Ahead of us was a demoralized fleeing body of Confederates.... With wild huzzas, we pushed rapidly on and did not halt until the enemy had been driven behind his inner line of works immediately surrounding the city."[128] Mott's Division was in the advance and by dusk, both flanks of the Army of the Potomac were on the Appomattox River. Petersburg was encircled and the only escape route lay across the river.

By the night of April 2, both Richmond and Petersburg had been evacuated and the Army of Northern Virginia was in full retreat west toward Amelia Court House, where Lee hoped to be resupplied. His next move would be south to link up with General Joseph Johnston's army, then making its way north through the Carolinas. The two armies might be able to use their combined strength to crush first Grant then Sherman. If that failed, they might yet escape into the mountainous terrain to the west and safety.

The 124th New York had been foraging liberally from the countryside as it marched in pursuit of Lee's retreating army. Early on the morning of April 5 the supply train caught up and three days' rations of hardtack, coffee, and sugar were issued. Later the same day, they linked up with Sheridan's cavalry which had taken up a position at Jetersville, blocking the all important Danville Railroad. Lee's supply line and escape route were now in Union hands.

The next morning the pursuit began anew. The 2nd Corps followed the route Lee had taken with the 5th and 6th Corps moving on either flank. General de Trobriand's Brigade was in the lead of the 2nd Corps when they came upon Lee's rear guard at Sayler's Creek. The 20th Indiana "was deployed in a heavy skirmish line and soon became hotly engaged." As the other regiments arrived, they went into lines of battle. General Mott rode forward to assess the situation and a few minutes later Captain Bradley, who was serving on General Mott's staff, came riding back with orders for General de Trobriand to send the 124th at once. Weygant led the regiment forward at the run. General Mott pointed ahead and told the colonel to cross the creek at once and capture the enemy wagon train up ahead. Weygant dismounted and ran forward to get a better look. Then he ran back to his horse and was about to mount when a bullet whistled past his head and hit the general in the thigh. In the few minutes it took for de Trobriand to take command of the division and Colonel Shepherd of the 1st Maine Heavy Artillery to take charge of the brigade, the wagon train made its escape.[129]

The division moved ahead quickly and the 124th was ordered to relieve the 20th Indiana, which was out of ammunition. Once deployed, the regiment moved forward and caught sight of the same wagon train that had previously eluded it. The men opened an effective fire that caused the drivers to abandon twenty wagons and two cannon. Skirmishers from the 124th moved so quickly that Weygant had to spur his horse to a trot to keep up. As the wagon train tried to outrun them, Weygant's men shot the horses and more wagons were captured. Each time the Confederate rear guard halted to fire on the skirmish line, it only served to drive the Orange Blossoms forward until at last they saw in front of them a "solid battle line of the foe" and enemy cavalry on the flank. The regiment opened a brisk and accurate fire which eventually drove the enemy from his works.[130]

Once the prisoners were gathered up, the pursuit continued until it was halted before what appeared to be the main body of Lee's army. "The works which were manned by a solid battle line, studded at intervals with artillery and gaily decked with Confederate battle flags, ran from a point almost opposite the right of my skirmish line along our front, and extended into the woods to our left as far as I could see." In short order, the entire division moved up and prepared to make "its last general charge against its brave old adversaries; and we soon swept up to and over the enemy's works in our front, capturing several hundred prisoners together with a number of battle flags and five or six pieces of artillery."[131]

Meanwhile, Sheridan and the 6th Corps were fighting off to the left where they encountered much heavier resistance and suffered over two thousand casualties. In the process, they captured a large number of Ewell's Corps, including the general himself. The pursuit continued on April 7 with the 2nd Corps in the lead. At 8:00 A.M., they reached High Bridge, six miles east of Farmville, a place where two bridges crossed the Appomattox River. The Confederate rear guard fired both bridges but troops from Barlow's Division managed to extinguish the blaze on one of them and Union soldiers crossed and routed the defenders.

Barlow's men headed for Farmville while the other two divisions of the 2nd Corps moved out on the old stage road to Appomattox Court House. They'd marched about five miles when they came upon the main body of Lee's army behind another stout line of earthworks. Couriers were sent to recall Barlow and the 2nd Corps settled in to wait for reinforcements to arrive before launching the assault. As the day wore on, Union troops probed the line and found it to be very strong. Barlow arrived too late in the day to make the attack so it was decided to wait until morning. By dawn, Lee's army had slipped away and the 2nd Corps took up the pursuit again.

As the 2nd Corps was pressuring the rear of Lee's column, Sheridan's cavalry and the 5th

Corps had moved ahead of the Confederate army to Appomattox Station, severing the rail line that was to carry Lee to safety and ending any hope he had to be resupplied or to escape.

Weygant wrote that on the morning of April 9, "the air seemed filled with wild rumors indicating very plainly that the end for which we had sacrificed and endured so much — for which we had so long been marching, fighting, and suffering, — was close at hand." The 2nd Corps moved slowly forward for about four hours when, at about noon, the men were called to a halt to rest. News was passed among the men that Grant and Lee were even then arranging for the surrender of the Confederate army, but no one dared believe it. Then an aide from headquarters rode the lines confirming the news. "As strange as it may seem, no one shouted, but instead many a stalwart fellow turned pale." Then Meade and his staff rode by. When the men saw that the general was smiling, a very rare occurrence, they knew that the war had finally ended. Only then did the Union line erupt into thunderous cheers.[132]

"This Regiment of Heroes"

On Wednesday, April 12, the fourth anniversary of the firing on Fort Sumter, the soldiers of the Army of Northern Virginia surrendered their arms and colors in a ceremony at Appomattox Court House. Within days, thousands of Confederate soldiers were paroled and began to make their way home. At the same time, the Union soldiers started their march toward Richmond. Relations between the victors and the vanquished were pleasant enough until the shocking news reached them of the assassination of the president. Then, "these paroled prisoners disappeared as if by magical agency, and were seen no more." The early reports were that Secretary of State Seward and General Grant had also been murdered, but these rumors were quickly dispelled. The effect on the men was immediate. They gathered in small groups around campfires "with heavy hearts and speechless tongues" awaiting further news.[1]

"Long ere this you have heard of the death of our noble President," Henry Howell wrote from his Washington hospital. "The greatest gloom is spread over our Country that it ever was my lot to witness. Even the greatest disaster our army has had in the field did not seem to depress the feelings of the people as much as the death of one man has in the present instance." He reported that Booth had been caught, which, of course, was incorrect. "What a daring act it was for the murderer to show himself on the Stage after committing the terrible deed. It seems to me as though some of the other actors upon the stage must have known that he was up to something of the sort or Booth could not have got away in the first place."[2]

Henry told his mother that the dreadful news reached the hospital at about 2:00 A.M. on April 15. After hearing it, he could not sleep, as "cold chills fairly took possession of me for a short time." A man in the hospital made the mistake of voicing his opinion that he was delighted that Lincoln had been killed. "The boys pitched upon him and would have torn him to pieces had not the guard took possession of him. He is now in the Central Guardhouse." As for the defeated Confederates, Henry took a hard line. He thought the Confederate leadership should pay a stiff price. "I have been very much opposed to allowing Lee to go to Europe all along but now I want him hung."

He hoped that Vice President Andrew Johnson, who was inaugurated that day, was capable of performing his new job but expressed his doubts that the new president had "the ruling qualities by which Lincoln was governed."

The night before the assassination, Howell had been to the city and seen "the best illumination that ever took place here." But things were very different a few days later when every house and building was hung in black mourning crepe. The streets were filled with people but no one spoke. Howell walked among them until he made himself ill from exertion. He knew no other way to express his grief.[3]

On May 1, the Army of the Potomac took up the march for Washington, where the men bivouacked on the south side of the Potomac River. Their camp was near Minor's Hill, just two miles from old Camp Cromwell, where many soldiers began their military careers two and one-half years before. They were about seven miles from Howell's hospital and he considered trying to pay them a visit but his heath was still poor. In the end, he decided to wait until they were a little closer.

On May 23, the Army of the Potomac marched in the Grand Review in the capital. Before an immense crowd of spectators, the cavalry passed in review first, then the provost marshal and engineer battalions. The 9th Corps led the infantry units followed by the 5th Corps and finally the 2nd Corps bringing up the rear. The following day, Sherman's men paraded but the 6th Corps remained at Appomattox and would march on June 8. Henry Howell did not write home that he watched the parade but it would be hard to believe that, if he were still in the city, he did not find some way to be in the crowd.

Then the Orange County men prepared for their journey home. After bidding farewell to General de Trobriand, they boarded trains for New York City, where they spent nearly a week at Hart's Island, a dismal place located at the western end of Long Island Sound. Their thoughts were of home and they looked forward to being greeted by a few friends and family members. They had no idea of the reception that awaited them.

The regiment departed Hart's Island at 8:00 A.M., Tuesday morning, June 13, and was transported to Desbrosses Pier on the island of Manhattan. There the men boarded the *Mary Powell*, a swift and stately Hudson River steamer, for the trip to Orange County — free of charge, thanks to ship's pilot, Captain Anderson.

Their destination was Newburgh, about sixty miles up the Hudson River. The morning editions of the Newburgh newspapers announced that the regiment was expected to arrive shortly after 6:30 P.M. All businesses were urged to close, and a spirited welcome was being planned. The parade route was published in the *Newburgh Daily Journal* with the following admonition: "Citizens of Newburgh! Laying aside for the time all our usual business avocations, let us greet the returning veterans with a spirit, an enthusiasm, and an outpouring of numbers which shall show to them that they are indeed, 'Welcome Home again.'"[4]

Not to be outdone, a rival newspaper, *The Daily Union*, wrote of the Orange Blossoms' anticipated return: "This regiment of heroes, for such they have proved themselves to be, are expected home soon. They have made as noble a record as any regiment in the field. They have poured out their blood on dozens of historic fields and have a roll of heroic dead whose memory should be precious to Old Orange forever."[5]

Before they reached Newburgh, the *Mary Powell* put in at Cozzens' Dock in Highland Falls to take on passengers, one of whom was covering the story for the *Newburgh Daily Journal*. He noticed that most of the men were on the forward deck "pointing out to each other the familiar features of the scenery along the river," which many had not seen in nearly three years. Amid the revelry, the reporter noticed that some of the soldiers could not help but have an occasional look of sadness in remembrance of those comrades who would never make this trip.[6]

The steamer got underway again, passing the military academy at the west point of the Hudson River. A few miles farther on, it docked briefly at Cornwall, the home of Captain William Silliman and Major James Cromwell, both of whom had fallen in the line of duty. Again the *Mary Powell* got underway for the short trip to Newburgh, just a couple of miles to the north past Plum Point, where Colonel Ellis had once lived. By 5:00 P.M., the streets of the city were packed. One half-hour later, every bell in every church tower began to peal and continued to do so until 6:45, when the *Mary Powell* was spotted making her way up the broad river. As the ship approached, cannon fire from the wharf greeted the soldiers' return and the men in turn raised a shout that left no doubt that they were happy to be home.

"The sight that greeted the eyes of those who were on the *Powell* as she neared our village can hardly ever be forgotten by them. Every place which commanded a view of the river seemed to be crowded with eager spectators. Flags were flying, bells ringing, cannon booming, innumerable handkerchiefs waving, and the whole village seemed bent on making itself seen and heard."[7]

About two-thirds of the men had decided to purchase their rifle muskets for six dollars each, nearly half a month's pay for a private. Arrangements had been made with the local militia company to provide arms for the rest. As the Orange Blossoms disembarked, they moved between ranks of city firemen and members of the Union League who stood with heads uncovered to honor them. Water Street, the riverfront business district, was packed with men, women, and children who waved handkerchiefs and cheered. But there were those who were quiet as they scanned the faces of the soldiers. A father, brother, husband, or son expected home was not among the men in blue and their worst fears were confirmed: he lay wounded or sick in the hospital or was gone forever.[8]

The procession formed quickly. The firemen would lead the parade, then the trustees of the city and local dignitaries. These were followed by members of the Union League, and Eastman's famous marching band from Poughkeepsie. And then came the 124th New York State Volunteers. The men marching that evening in Newburgh were all that remained of more than nine hundred men and boys who had volunteered to be mustered into federal service at the county seat at Goshen in early September 1862. Now, two and one-half years and a lifetime later, just one hundred thirty of that original number came up from the Newburgh docks to the cheers of their grateful countrymen.

The parade started up the steep, narrow streets from the old part of the city to Grand Street,

more open and airy. A young soldier and his father marched side by side, the father insisting that he carry his son's haversack, while "tears of joy were rolling down his cheeks at receiving his boy back again alive and well." They followed Grand to Western Avenue, a broad and majestic thoroughfare from which the Hudson River and the mountains beyond formed a breathtaking backdrop.[9]

But it was the soldiers themselves who "lit up the hearts of the multitude ... and round after round of cheers went before, around and behind them as they passed. Signs, flags, and wreaths of welcome lined the streets. Every spot, from roof to curbstone, even to the outer edges of the passing regiment, was densely packed. The ladies bloomed out of the buildings wherever a window opening could be found, they poured a grateful tribute of flowers on the regiment."[10] Cheering crowds along the route stopped the soldiers so that the ladies might place tiny bouquets of flowers in the muzzle of each rifle musket, a symbolic gesture that their duty was done and that these weapons need never again be fired in defense of their beloved Union. Their much diminished ranks, lean bronzed faces, and faded blue uniforms

Sergeant James A. Beakes, Company E, was promoted to sergeant prior to April 10, 1863; he returned to the ranks, November 1, 1864, and mustered out June 15, 1865, at Hart's Island, New York Harbor (archive of the Historical Society of the Town of Warwick, gift of Joan and Tom Frangos).

spoke of their ordeal. Their steady tread recalled a determination borne of many far more trying marches. It was obvious to all who saw them that these were veterans, not just in name, but in fact. In its proper place at the center of the moving column of men came the national colors, a thirty-four star flag shredded by enemy fire just as their ranks had been shredded on so many battlefields.

At their head rode Colonel Charles H. Weygant, a twenty-four-year-old former livery stable

owner who, in the summer of 1862, had raised a company in Newburgh and who now, with the loss of those officers senior to him, commanded the regiment. As the colonel and his men turned onto Liberty Street, they neared their destination — the Hasbrouck House, where General George Washington had his headquarters during a particularly difficult period of the Revolutionary War. At this hallowed place, and in the presence of their fellow citizens, they would form up one last time as soldiers of the Union.

As the parade came onto the grounds, the firemen and Union League members formed a hollow square, into which the regiment marched and came to a halt. "The crowd on the ground was immense, entirely covering the lawn from the house to the eastern limits." By one estimate, more than ten thousand people were present to witness the ceremony.

Eastman's Band serenaded them until all were in their places, at which time Judge James W. Taylor rose to officially welcome them home. He spoke of pride in the regiment and sadness at the loss of so many of their number. He reminded them that on this very spot, the Continental Army had been disbanded and that, just as Washington's army had saved the republic, so had they.

Colonel Charles H. Weygant. He led the Orange Blossoms from The Wilderness to their last march up Western Avenue in Newburgh (Michael J. McAfee collection).

But beyond preserving to us the institutions which our fathers left us, you have presented to us anew our glorious Union, more pure, more elevated, more perfect than before. You will have enabled us, on the ensuing Fourth of July — the anniversary of our national independence — to celebrate the absolute fact that "all men are born free and equal"; that the contradiction which has existed for the last three-quarters of a century, that four millions of bondmen were held under the starry flag, no longer exists, but that all, of whatever color, birth, or nationality, when they come upon the soil of the United States, under the shadow of that glorious banner, are freemen, and entitled to its protection under all circumstance.[11]

Colonel Weygant "fittingly responded" with a few remarks of thanks and the ceremony ended with rousing cheers. The regiment then marched to the People's Hall where a "sumptuous entertainment" awaited them in the form of a supper catered by the same Mr. B.B. Odell who provided their meals while encamped at Goshen nearly three years before. There were biscuit sandwiches, a "profusion of cold meats," pickles, and "other dainties." Mr. Odell's immense tables were "literally *loaded* with the luxuries and substantials of life." The affair was concluded with dishes of strawberries and cream and "smoking cups of coffee."

Many of the soldiers spent the night in the People's Hall and were reasonably well behaved, although there was a quite a bit of good-natured horsing around while the men were entertained by the Glee Club well into the night.

On June 15, the *Newburgh Daily Journal* ran an article that contradicted a story published in the rival local newspaper the day before. The *Union* claimed that some of the soldiers got drunk and, declaring that they had "fought for the country but not for the negro," grabbed a local black man and began to toss him in a blanket. The *Union* must have reported that the

Monument in Memory of 124th, N.Y.Vol.Ins.
— (orange Blossoms) —
Erected By Hon.Thomas W.Bradley M.C.
Goshen, N.Y.
Thos.Alice Ruggles Kitson, Sculptor.
Copyright 1907   Chas.A.Ketcham.   182

blanket toss got out of hand and the soldiers let the man hit the pavement a number of times. The *Journal* branded this as "characteristic coinage of the spurious print on the dock." It was all just so much innocent fun, the *Journal* article reported. "The men said nothing of the kind, but while tossing the negro up, they kept wishing that he was a Copperhead, so they could let him drop to the pavement occasionally. To a man almost these returned soldiers are bitter in denouncing the Copperheads. They may not have much sympathy for the negro, but they have less respect for the Copps."[12]

One last administrative detail had to be addressed: the men needed to be "paid off." The government discharge forms were delivered by the *Mary Powell* on the evening of June 15 and three companies settled up with the paymaster that night. On the morning of June 16, the rest of the men received their back pay. Most were owed for four months but a few were recently released prisoners of war who received as much as eighteen months' back pay. In addition, each enlisted man was paid a seventy-five dollar bounty. The officers were not eligible for the bounty but instead got "a bonus of three months 'pay proper'" for having stayed on and seen the war to its conclusion. "The amount paid out to this regiment to-day and yesterday, is about seventy thousand dollars," the press reported.[13]

Remillard, the local photographer, took out an ad in the newspapers announcing that he had "photographed the colors of the One Hundred and Twenty-Fourth. Cards containing the photograph can be bought at Salmon's." In fact, several hundred copies were quickly produced to take advantage of the intense interest in the flag by the returning soldiers and civilians alike. "The flag will probably be deposited in Washington's Headquarters, where, it will be remembered, their first battle-flag is resting on its laurels."

The local railroad lines and private vehicles carried the new civilians to Middletown, Chester, Warwick, Port Jervis, and Montgomery, where there was more celebrating to be done. Company H, raised primarily in the Town of Montgomery, was welcomed back with a parade through Walden, the home of Captain Thomas Bradley who would receive a Medal of Honor for his actions at Chancellorsville and of Captain David Crist who had been killed in action at Totopotomoy Creek. The company marched through the village to Schofield Hall where patriotic addresses were given by the Reverend Mr. Stewart, Reverend Mr. McNulty and H.B. Bull, Esq., of Montgomery. Following the speeches, the company "made a charge on a splendid supper which had been prepared for them."

In the days and weeks that followed, the celebrations slowly gave way to the routine of civilian life. But the Orange Blossoms, like soldiers everywhere, wanted their sacrifices to be remembered and those lost in the war to save the Union to be honored. In years to come, veterans' groups were organized, ceremonies and reunions held, monuments erected, and remembrances and regimental histories were written well into the twentieth century.

In 1868, General John Alexander Logan issued General Order 11, calling upon the nation to observe May 30 of each year as a day to place flowers on the graves of the Union dead. It became known as Decoration Day, now called Memorial Day. He wrote, "Let no vandalism of avarice or neglect, no ravages of time testify to the present or to the coming generations that we have forgotten ... the cost of a free and undivided republic."

The Orange Blossoms who survived the war were determined not to forget. They had fought as part of the Army of the Potomac, *the* major Federal army in the field; their opponents were the best soldiers that the South could send against them led by the already deified Robert E. Lee. The long casualty lists that appeared in the local Orange County newspapers after the battles at Chancellorsville, Gettysburg, the Wilderness, Spotsylvania Court House, the Siege at Petersburg, and many smaller but no less deadly encounters with the enemy testified to their usual place

Opposite: "The Standard Bearer" monument to the 124th New York located in Goshen, New York.

where the fighting was the toughest. As part of so mighty an army, and against so formidable an opponent, they had forged a reputation in fire and blood.

During the war, the soldiers knew that everything depended on their force of arms. Only victory on the battlefield would insure that the Union, created by their grandfathers and defended by their fathers, would endure. Their steadfast loyalty to the cause and steely determination to see it through to victory, no matter the cost, was most eloquently put into words by Private Henry Howell, Company E, 124th New York State Volunteers. As he lay wounded, he described the charge that broke the Confederate line at Spotsylvania, but he might just as well have been describing the spirit that characterized the Orange Blossoms throughout their service — "everyone," he wrote, "was borne irresistibly forward. There was no such thing as fail."

Regimental Roster

Source: *Annual Report of the Adjutant-General for the State of New York for the Year 1903*, No. 36 (Albany: Oliver Quayle, 1904), pp. 500–666.* For a complete listing of information on the 124th New York, visit Kenneth J. Wooster's website on the regiment at Skaneateles. org/124_inf/124.

ACKER, CHARLES H.—Age, 18 years. Enlisted, August 11, 1862, at Goshen, to serve three years; mustered in as private, Co. D, September 5, 1862; discharged for hernia, October 4, 1862.

ACKER, JONATHAN.—Age, 30 years. Enlisted, August 20, 1862, at Newburgh, to serve three years; mustered in as private, Co. K, September 5, 1862; discharged for disability, April 16, 1863, at Falmouth, Va.

ACKERMAN, DANIEL.—Age, 44 years. Enlisted, August 7, 1862, at Goshen, to serve three years; mustered in as private, Co. A, September 5, 1862; wounded in action, June 9, 1863, at Beverly Ford, Va., and May 23 or 24, 1864, at North Anna, Va.; died of his wounds, June 4, 1864, at hospital, Washington, D.C.

ACKERMAN, JOHN H.—Age, 19 years. Enlisted, August 11, 1862, at Goshen, to serve three years; mustered in as private, Co. D, September 5, 1862; mustered out with company, June 3, 1865, near Washington, D.C.

ADAMS, GEORGE W.—Age, 32 years. Enlisted. August 11, 1862, at Port Jervis, to serve three years; mustered in as private, Co. F, September 5, 1862; wounded in action, May 3, 1863, at Chancellorsville, Va.; discharged for disability, caused from wounds, October 28, 1863, from hospital at West Philadelphia, Pa.

ADAMS, JUDSON P.—Age, 25 years. Enlisted, August 12, 1862, at Port Jervis, to serve three years; mustered in as private, Co. F, September 5, 1862; transferred to Third Co., Second Battalion, Veteran Reserve Corps, April 25, 1865; mustered out, August 9, 1865, at Washington, D.C.

ADAMS, LEWIS D.—Age, 23 years. Enlisted, August 13, 1862, at Port Jervis, to serve three years; mustered in as private, Co. F, September 5, 1862; transferred to Third Co., Second Battalion, Veteran Reserve Corps, April 25, 1865; mustered out, August 9, 1865, at Washington, D.C.

AISALE, CASPER.—Age, 37 years. Enlisted, at Goshen, to serve one year, and mustered in as private, Co. C, September 10, 1864; mustered out with company, June 3, 1865, near Washington, D.C.

AKERMAN, CURTIS.—Age, 30 years. Enlisted, August 8, 1862, at Otisville, to serve three years; mustered in as private, Co. E, September 5, 1862; mustered out with detachment, June 2, 1865, at Washington, D.C.

ALINGTON, THOMAS R.—Age, 25 years. Enlisted, August 12, 1862, at Port Jervis, to serve three years; mustered in as private, Co. F, September 5, 1862; promoted corporal, October 9, 1862; returned to ranks, November 1, 1863; mustered out with company, June 3, 1865, near Washington, D.C.

ALLEN, CORNELIUS S.—Age, 27 years. Enlisted, August 15, 1862, at Newburgh, to serve three years; mustered in as private, Co. I, September 5, 1862; killed in action, July 2, 1863, at Gettysburg, Pa.

ALLEN, EDMUND F.—Age, 20 years. Enlisted, August 11, 1862, at Goshen, to serve three years; mustered in as corporal, Co. D, September 5, 1862; discharged for hernia, January 12, 1863.

ALLINSON, CORNELIUS.—Age, 41 years. Enlisted, August 6, 1862, at Goshen, to serve three years; mustered in as private, Co. D, September 5, 1862. Died of phthisis pulmonalis, December 10, 1862, at Baltimore, Md.

ALLWOOD, JOSEPH S.—Age, 30 years. Enlisted, August 20, 1862, at Newburgh, to serve three years; mustered in as corporal, Co. I, September 5, 1862; promoted sergeant, November 1, 1863, first sergeant, December 1, 1864; mustered out with company, June 3, 1865, near Washington, D.C.

AMMERMAN, WILLIAM W.—Age, 18 years. Enlisted, August 11, 1862, at Newburgh, to serve three years; mustered in as private, Co. C, September 5, 1862; promoted corporal, January 1, 1865; mustered out with company, June 3, 1865, near Washington, D.C.

ANDERSON, CLEMENT B.—Age, 18 years. Enlisted, August 25, 1862, at Port Jervis, to serve three years; mustered in as private, Co. F, September 5, 1862; wounded in action, May 3, 1863, at Chancellorsville, Va.; transferred to Veteran Reserve Corps, March 31, 1864.

Corrections have been made to alphabetical order.

ANDERSON, JOHN.—Age, 18 years. Enlisted at Auburn, to serve one year, and mustered in as private, Co. I, August 22, 1864; wounded in action, December 7, 1864, at Berryville, Va.; mustered out, June 23, 1865, from Armory Square Hospital, at Washington, D.C.

APPELMAN, HENRY B.—Age, 32 years. Enlisted, August 12, 1862, at Port Jervis, to serve three years; mustered in as private, Co. F, September 5, 1862; died of chronic diarrhea, February 24, 1864, at Brandy Station, Va.

ARCULARIUS, HENRY.—Age, 21 years. Enlisted, August 6, 1862, at Chester, to serve three years. Mustered in as private, Co. A, September 5, 1862; wounded in action, May 3, 1863, at Chancellorsville, Va.; promoted corporal, prior to May 1, 1864; absent, missing in action, May 12, 1864, at Spotsylvania Court House, Va., and at muster-out of company.

ARDEN, GEORGE DE PEYSTER.—Age, — years. Enrolled, August 20, 1862, at Goshen, to serve three years; mustered in as first lieutenant and adjutant, September 5, 1862; mustered out January 14, 1863, for promotion to major, Tenth Artillery.

ARMSTRONG ANDREW.—Age. 17 years. Enlisted, August 13, 1862, at Walden, to serve three years; mustered in as private, Co. H, September 5, 1862; promoted corporal, July 16, 1863, sergeant, prior to October, 1864, sergeant major, November 15, 1864; mustered out with regiment June 3, 1865, near Washington, D.C.

ASHLEY, JOSEPH.—Age, 18 years. Enlisted, August 7, 1862, at Goshen, to serve three years; mustered in as private Co. D, September 5, 1862; mustered out with company, June 3, 1865, near Washington, D.C.

ASHMAN, ROBERT.—Age, 18 years. Enlisted, August 4, 1862 at Goshen, to serve three years; mustered in as private, Co. ?, September 5, 1862; wounded in action, May 12, 1864, Spotsylvania Court House, Va.; mustered out, June 21, 1864, from Harewood Hospital, at Washington, D.C.

Lieutenant George De Peyster Arden served as adjutant. He was mustered out in January 1863 for promotion to major in the 10th Artillery (Archive of the Historical Society of the Town of Warwick, gift of Joan and Tom Frangos).

AVERY, CHARLES A.—Age, 22 years. Enlisted, August 13, 1862, at Goshen, to serve three years; mustered in as corporal Co. A, September 5, 1862; returned to ranks, no date; discharged, September 2, 1862, at St. Aloysius Hospital, Washington, D.C.

BABCOCK, CHARLES.—Age, 31 years. Enlisted at Goshen, to serve three years, and mustered in as private, Co. B, January 19, 1864; wounded in action, May 6, 1864, at the Wilderness, Va.; transferred to Co. C, Ninety-third Infantry, June 1, 1865.

BABCOCK, DANIEL.—Age, 19 years. Enlisted, August 4, 1862, at Goshen, to serve three years; mustered in as private, Co. B, September 5, 1862; discharged, April 17, 1863; again enlisted, January 4, 1864; wounded in action, May 26, 1864, at North Anna River, Va.; died of his wounds, June 12, 1864, at Washington, D.C.

BABCOCK, DAVID.—Age, 22 years. Enlisted, August 8, 1862; at Warwick, to serve three years; mustered in as private, Co. B, September 5, 1862; discharged, October 4, 1862; again enlisted, to serve one year, as private, Co. K, August 23, 1864; mustered out with company June 3, 1865, near Washington, D.C.

BABCOCK, GEORGE.—Age, 38 years. Enlisted, August 8, 1862, at Florida, to serve three years; mustered in as private, Co. B, September 5, 1862; deserted, January 7, 1863, from hospital at Philadelphia, Pa; dishonorably discharged, October 1, 1863, per sentence G. C. M.

BABCOCK, JONAS.—Age, 42 years. Enlisted, August 7, 1862, at Goshen, to serve three years; mustered in as private, Co. B, September 5, 1862; deserted, October 19, 1862, at Knoxville, Md.

BABCOCK, MATHEW.—Age, 39 years. Enlisted at Goshen, to serve three years; mustered in as private, Co. B, January 19, 1864; wounded in action, May 30, 1864, at Totopotomoy, Va.; mustered out, May 13, 1865, at Rochester, N.Y.

BABCOCK, WILLIAM.—Age, 18 years. Enlisted, August 13, 1862, at Cornwall, to serve three years; mustered in as private, Co. C, September 5, 1862; deserted, no date.

BABCOCK, WILLIAM H.—Age, 39 years. Enlisted at Goshen, to serve one year; mustered in as private, unassigned, August 22, 1864; mustered out with detachment, May 10, 1865, at Hart's Island, New York Harbor.

BAHRMANN, E. MORRIS.—Age, 23 years. Enlisted, August 7, 1862, at Goshen, to serve three years; mustered in as corporal, Co. D, September 5, 1862; transferred to Veteran Reserve Corps, June 9, 1863.

BAILEY, HENRY A.—Age, 18 years. Enlisted, August 14, 1862, at Newburgh, to serve three years; mustered in as private, Co. I, September 5, 1862; deserted, same date, from Goshen, N.Y.

BAILEY, WILLIAM W.—Age, 18 years. Enlisted, August 15, 1862, at Wallkill, to serve three years; mustered in as sergeant, Co. K, September 5, 1862; returned to ranks, January 1, 1863; wounded in action, May 3, 1863, at Chancellorsville, Va.; discharged, for wounds, March 28, 1864.

BAIRD, JOHN E.—Age, 39 years. Enlisted, August 12, 1862, at Goshen, to serve three years; mustered in as private, Co. B, September 5, 1862; deserted, October 19, 1862, at Knoxville, Md.

BAIRD, JOHN E.— Age, 18 years. Enlisted at Goshen, to serve one year, and mustered in as private, Co. K, August 20, 1864; mustered out with company, June 3,1865, near Washington, D.C.

BAIRD, STEPHEN E.— Age, 28 years. Enlisted, August 12, 1862, at Goshen, to serve three years; mustered in as private, Co. B, September 5, 1862; deserted, October 19, 1862, at Knoxville, Md.

BAIRD, THOMAS E.— Age, 22 years. Enlisted, August 15, 1862, at Port Jervis, to serve three years; mustered in as private, Co. F, September 5, 1862; deserted, October 19, 1862, near Knoxville, Md.

BAKER, DANIEL W.— Age, 21 years. Enlisted, August 23, 1862, at Goshen, to serve three years; mustered in as private, Co. H, September 5, 1862; mustered out with company, June 3, 1865, near Washington, D.C.

BAKER, HENRY C.— Age, 21 years. Enlisted, August 21, 1862, at Goshen, to serve three years; mustered in as private, Co. E, September 5, 1862; promoted corporal, October 1, 1864; mustered out with company, June 3, 1865, near Washington, D.C

BAKER, JAMES J.— Age, 40 years. Enlisted, August 11, 1862, at Port Jervis, to serve three years; mustered in as private, Co. F, September 5, 1862; deserted, February 28, 1863, on expiration of furlough.

BAKER, THOMAS H.— Age, 18 years. Enlisted, August 23 1862, at Goshen, to serve three years; mustered in as private, Co. H, September 5, 1862; wounded in action, May 3, 1863, at Chancellorsville, Va.; transferred to Veteran Reserve Corps, March 7, 1864.

BALLARD, LEVI P.— Age, 19 years. Enlisted, August 9, 1862, at Florida, to serve three years; mustered in as private, Co. B, September 5, 1862; deserted, October 26, 1862, at Berlin, Md.

BANEER, PETER F.— Age, 44 years. Enlisted, August 12, 1862, at Washingtonville, to serve three years; mustered in as private, Co. G, September 5, 1862; transferred to Co. C, Seventh Regiment, Veteran Reserve Corps, September 26, 1863; mustered out with detachment, June 28, 1865, as of Veteran Reserve Corps, at Washington, D.C.

BANKER, FRANCIS.— Age, 21 years. Enlisted, August 2, 1862, at Florida, to serve three years; mustered in as private, Co. B, August 9, 1862; discharged, August 23, 1862; also borne as Bunker.

BANKER, JOHN R.— Age, 24 years. Enlisted, August 11, 1862, at Otisville, to serve three years; mustered in as sergeant, Co. E, September 5, 1862; discharged, November 22, 1862, at Washington, D.C.

BARKLY, ALFRED S.— Age, 20 years. Enlisted, August 15, 1862, at Port Jervis, to serve three years; mustered in as private, Co. F, September 5, 1862; promoted corporal, prior to April 1863; wounded in action, May 3, 1863, at Chancellorsville, Va.; died of his wounds, May 20, 1863, at Potomac Creek Hospital, Va.

BARNES, DAVID P.— Age, 19 years. Enlisted, August 9, 1862, at Florida, to serve three years; mustered in as private, Co. B, September 5, 1862; mustered out with company, June 3, 1865, near Washington, D.C.

BARNES, JAMES H.— Age, 20 years. Enlisted, August 9, 1862, at Monroe, to serve three years; mustered in as private, Co. C, September 5, 1862; killed in action, May 3, 1863, at Chancellorsville, Va.

BARNHART, IRA.— Age, 19 years. Enlisted, August 12, 1862, at Newburgh, to serve three years; mustered in as private, Co. I, September 5, 1862; discharged, February 7, 1863.

BARRETT, JR., DAVID.— Age, 30 years. Enlisted at Warwick, to serve three years and mustered in as private, Co. D, January 26, 1864; transferred to Co. H, Ninety-third Infantry, June 1, 1865.

BARRETT, DAVID A.— Age, 21 years. Enlisted at Warwick, to serve three years, and mustered in as private, Co. D, January 26, 1864; killed in action, May 13, 1864, at Spotsylvania Court House, Va.

BARRETT, JAMES S.— Age, 18 years. Enlisted, August 11, 1862, at Newburgh, to serve three years; mustered in as private, Co. I, September 5, 1862; wounded in action, May 3, 1863, at Chancellorsville, Va.; mustered out with company, June 3, 1865, near Washington, D.C.

BARTLESON, CHARLES.— Age, 18 years. Enlisted at Poughkeepsie, to serve one year, and mustered in as private, Co. D, September 21, 1864; mustered out with company, June 3, 1865, near Washington, D.C.

BARTLEY, DAVID.— Age, 37 years. Enlisted, August 14, 1862, at Goshen, to serve three years, as private, Co. E, and deserted, August 15, 1862, from Goshen, N.Y.; also borne as Barkley.

BARTON, ALANSON H.— Age, 25 years. Enlisted, August 11, 1862, at Newburgh, to serve three years; mustered in as corporal, Co. C, September 5, 1862; returned to ranks, no date; discharged for disability, January 9, 1863, at Falmouth, Va.

BARTON, WALTER.— Age, 22 years. Enlisted, August 11, 1862, at Washingtonville, to serve three years; mustered in as private, Co. G, September 5, 1862; killed in action, July 2, 1863, at Gettysburg, Pa.

BATEMAN, EMANUEL.— Age, 19 years. Enlisted, September 3, 1864, at Romulus, to serve one year; mustered in as private, Co. I, September 5, 1864; mustered out with company, June 3, 1865, near Washington, D.C.

BAXTER, LEWIS.— Age, 22 years. Enlisted, August 15, 1862, at Goshen, to serve three years; mustered in as private, Co. E, September 5, 1862; killed in action, May 12, 1864, at Spotsylvania Court House, Va., as Lewis W.

BAXTER, WHITMORE.— Age, 35 years. Enlisted, August 16, 1862, at Newburgh, to serve three years; mustered in as private, Co. I, September 5, 1862; transferred to Fifty-eighth Company, Second Battalion, Veteran Reserve Corps, October 10, 1863; mustered out with detachment, August 8, 1865, at Washington, D.C.

BAYST, WILLIAM.— Age, 32 years. Enlisted, August 13, 1862, at Port Jervis, to serve three years; mustered in as private, Co. F, September 5, 1862; discharged for disability, February 7, 1863, at convalescent camp, Barnard, Va.

BEAKES, ADAM W.— Age, 18 years. Enlisted, August 9, 1862, at Wallkill, to serve three years; mustered in as private, Co. E, September 5, 1862; wounded in action, May 3, 1863, at Chancellorsville, Va.; discharged for disability, October 12, 1863, at hospital, Philadelphia, Pa.

BEAKES, JAMES A.— Age, 21 years. Enlisted, August 7, 1862, at Goshen, to serve three years; mustered in as corporal, Co. E, September 5, 1862; promoted sergeant, prior to April 10, 1863; returned to ranks, November 1, 1864; mustered out, June 15, 1865, at Hart's Island, New York Harbor.

BEARD, RANSLER D.—Age, 39 years. Enlisted, August 12, 1862, at Newburgh, to serve three years; mustered in as private, Co. I, September 5, 1862; wounded in action, May 3, 1863, at Chancellorsville, Va.; wounded and captured in action, May 6, 1864, at the Wilderness, Va.; paroled prior to October 1864; mustered out, June 13, 1865, from hospital at Annapolis, Md., as Baird.

BECK, JACOB.—Age, place, date of enlistment and muster in as private, Co. C, not stated; transferred to Co. A, Ninety-third Infantry, June 1, 1865.

BECRAFT, WILLIAM L.—Age, 21 years. Enlisted, August 11, 1862, at Goshen, to serve three years; mustered in as private, Co. D, September 5, 1862; wounded in action, May 3, 1863, at Chancellorsville, Va.; discharged for disability, September, 1863.

BELLES, SIMON.—Age, 24 years. Enlisted, August 11, 1862, at Goshen, to serve three years; mustered in as private, Co. B, September 5, 1862; wounded in action, May 6, 1864, at the Wilderness, Va.; promoted corporal, prior to October 1864; mustered out with company, June 3, 1865, near Washington, D.C.; also borne as Bellis.

BELLOWS, ABRAHAM.—Age, 23 years. Enlisted, July 28, 1862, at Newburgh, to serve three years; mustered in as corporal, Co. A, September 5, 1862; returned to ranks, December 10, 1862; wounded in action, May 3, 1863, at Chancellorsville, Va.; transferred to Co. E, Twentieth Regiment, Veteran Reserve Corps, no date; mustered out, July 1, 1865, at Camp Cadwallader, Philadelphia, Pa.

BENEDICT, CHARLES E.—Age, 24 years. Enlisted, August 12, 1862, at Goshen, to serve three years; mustered in as private, Co. D, September 5, 1862; died of typhoid fever, November 2, 1862, at Warwick, N.Y.

BENEDICT, FRANCIS A.—Age, 21 years. Enlisted, August 11, 1862, at Goshen, to serve three years; mustered in as corporal, Co. D, September 5, 1862; killed in action, May 3, 1863, at Chancellorsville, Va.

BENEDICT, JAMES W.—Age, 32 years. Enrolled at Goshen to serve three years, and mustered in as captain, Co. D, August 16, 1862; wounded in action, May 12, 1864, at Spotsylvania, Va.; mustered out with company, June 3, 1865, near Washington, D.C. Commissioned captain, September 10, 1862, with rank from August 16, 1862, original; major, not mustered, January 11, 1865, with rank from September 19, 1864, vice H. S. Murray promoted.

BENETT, GARRETT H.—Age, 18 years. Enlisted, August 20, 1862, at Washingtonville, to serve three years; mustered in as private, Co. G, September 5, 1862; wounded in action, July 2, 1863, at Gettysburg Pa.; died of pneumonia, January 17, 1865, near Petersburg, Va.

BENJAMIN, CHARLES.—Age, 21 years. Enlisted, August 18, 1862, at Goshen, to serve three years; mustered in as private, Co. G, September 5, 1862; wounded in action, July 2, 1863, at Gettysburg, Pa.; mustered out with company, June 3, 1865, near Washington, D.C.

BENJAMIN, ELISHA B.—Age, 21 years. Enlisted, August 11, 1862, at Goshen, to serve three years; mustered in as private, Co. B, September 5, 1862; promoted corporal, October 1, 1863; died of smallpox, January 28, 1864, at Kalorama Hospital, Washington, D.C.

BENJAMIN, GRANT B.—Age, 29 years. Enlisted, August 12, 1862, at Blooming Grove, to serve three years; mustered in as private, Co. G, September 5, 1862; captured in action, May 3, 1863, at Chancellorsville, Va.; paroled, May 4, 1863, at Confederate Hospital, Chancellorsville, Va.; killed in action, October 9, 1864, before Petersburg, Va.

BENJAMIN, WELLS.—Age, 20 years. Enlisted, August 11, 1862, at Goshen to serve three years; mustered in as private, Co. D, September 5, 1862; mustered out with company, June 3, 1865, near Washington, D.C.

BENJAMIN, WILLIAM H.—Age, 30 years. Enrolled, August 4, 1862, at Blooming Grove, to serve three years; mustered in as first sergeant, Co. G, September 5, 1862; as second lieutenant, February 26, 1863; wounded in action, June 16, 1864, in front of Petersburg, Va.; mustered in as first lieutenant, Co. E, January 1, 1865; mustered out with company, June 3, 1865, near Washington, D.C.

BENNETT, JOHN W.—Age, 45 years. Enlisted, August 8, 1862, at Little Britain, to serve three years; mustered in as private, Co. G, September 5, 1862; captured in action, May 3, 1863, at Chancellorsville, Va.; paroled, May 1863; deserted, June 1863, at Annapolis, Md.

BENNETT, WILLIAM.—Age, 20 years. Enlisted at Utica, to serve three years, and mustered in as private, Co. K, September 8, 1864; transferred to Co. F, Ninety-third Infantry, June 1, 1865.

BENTON, JAMES A.—Age, 18 years. Enlisted at Great Valley, to serve one year, and mustered in as private, Co. I, September 28, 1864; wounded in action, April 6, 1865; died of his wounds, April 7, 1865, at Deatonsville Road, Va.

BERNER, CHARLES.—private, Co. K. First U.S. Sharpshooters; transferred to Co. H, this regiment. March 1, 1865; mustered out with company, June 3, 1865, near Washington, D.C.

BERTHOLF, GILLIAM.—Age, 26 years. Enlisted, August 15, 1862, at Goshen, to serve three years; mustered in as private, Co. B, September 5, 1862; deserted, August, 1863, at Rikers Island, New York Harbor.

BERTHOLF, JAMES H.—Age, 29 years. Enlisted, August 11, 1862, at Goshen, to serve three years; mustered in as private, Co. B, September 5, 1862; died of typhoid fever, December 8, 1862, at Falmouth, Va.

BETEKER, WILLIAM.—Age, 40 years. Enlisted at Wheatfield, to serve one year, and mustered in as private, Co. C, September 23, 1864; mustered out with company, June 3, 1865, near Washington D.C.

BIGLER, ALFRED.—Age, 24 years. Enlisted at Brooklyn to serve three years, and mustered in as private, Co. D, November 12, 1864; wounded in action, April 6, 1865, at Deatonsville Road, Va.; transferred to Co. H, Ninety-third Infantry, June 1, 1865.

BILLINGS, ALLEN R.—Age, 18 years. Enlisted at Ontario to serve one year, and mustered in as private, Co. I, August 25, 1864; mustered out with company, June 3, 1865, near Washington, D.C., as Allen P.

BIRDSALL, BRICE E.—Age, 21 years. Enlisted, August 5, 1862, at Goshen, to serve three years; mustered in as private, Co. B, September 5, 1862; deserted, January 7, 1863; sentenced to death; pardoned by the President, and sent to Dry Tortugas, Fla.; released and returned to company, January 11, 1865; mustered out with company June 3, 1865, near Washington, D.C., as Birdsill.

BIRDSALL, JAMES H.— Age, 30 years. Enlisted, August 5, 1862, at Goshen, to serve three years; mustered in as sergeant, Co. B, September 5, 1862; returned to ranks, prior to April 10, 1863; wounded in action, May 12, 1864, at Spotsylvania Court House, Va.; transferred to Seventy-fifth Company, Second Battalion Veteran Reserve Corps April 7, 1865; mustered out with detachment as corporal, July 1, 1865, at Washington, D.C., as Birdsill.

BIRDSALL, JONATHAN T.— Age, 20 years. Enrolled August 4, 1862, at Goshen to serve three years; mustered in as corporal, Co. A, September 5, 1862; promoted sergeant February 14, 1863; mustered in as second lieutenant, August 17, 1864; killed, October 22, 1864, in camp near Petersburg, Va.

BIRDSLEY, SMITH.— Age, 21 years. Enlisted, August 20, 1862, at Newburgh to serve three years; mustered in as private, Co. I, September 5, 1862; mustered out with company, June 3, 1865, near Washington, D.C.

BISBEE, WINSLOW.— Age, 20 years. Enlisted at Goshen, to serve one year, and mustered in as private, Co. K, August 20, 1864; mustered out with detachment, May 17, 1865, from Satterlee Hospital, West Philadelphia, Pa.

BISHOP, JOHN.— Age, 29 years. Enlisted at Goshen, to serve one year, and mustered in as private, Co. K, October 6, 1864; transferred to Co. F, Ninety-third Infantry, June 1, 1865.

BLACKMAN, CYRUS I.— Age, 23 years. Enlisted at Plattsburgh, to serve one year, and mustered in as private, Co. E, September 12, 1864; captured, November 7, 1864, on Weldon Railroad raid, Va.; paroled, prior to April 1865; mustered out with company, June 3, 1865, near Washington, D.C.

BLAIR, JOHN H.— Age, 29 years. Enlisted, August 13, 1862, at Newburgh, to serve three years; mustered in as private, Co. C, September 5, 1862; wounded in action, May 5, 1864, at the Wilderness, Va.; discharged for wounds, February 6, 1865, from McClellan Hospital, at Philadelphia, Pa.

BLAKE, EDWARD J.— Age, 25 years. Enlisted, August 8, 1862, at Goshen, to serve three years; mustered in as private, Co. I, September 5, 1862; mustered out with detachment, June 15, 1865, at Whitehall Hospital, Philadelphia, Pa.

BLIVEN, JOSEPH A.— Age, 17 years. Enlisted, August 8, 1862, at Otisville, to serve three years; mustered in as private, Co. E, September 5, 1862; absent, sick at Washington, D.C., since October 16, 1862, and at muster-out of company.

BLUNT, RICHARD.— Age, 25 years. Enlisted at Livingston, to serve one year, and mustered in as private, Co. C, September 26, 1864; mustered out with company, June 3, 1865, near Washington, D.C.

BODINE, CORTLAND.— Age, 36 years. Enlisted, August 16, 1862, at Newburgh, to serve three years; mustered in as private, Co. I, September 5, 1862; killed in action, May 3, 1863, at Chancellorsville, Va.

BODINE, THERON.— Age, 29 years. Enlisted, August 13, 1862, at Walden, to serve three years; mustered in as corporal, Co. A, September 5, 1862; wounded in action, May 3,1863, at Chancellorsville. Va.; again November 27, 1863 at Locust Grove, Va.; returned to ranks, prior to October 1864; transferred to Veteran Reserve Corps, January 9, 1865.

BODLE, CHARLES W.— Age, 16 years. Enlisted, August 11, 1862, at Chester, to serve three years; mustered in as musician, Co. A, September 5, 1862; wounded in action, June 16, 1864, before Petersburg, Va.; mustered out, June 28, 1865, from Lovell Hospital, at Portsmouth Grove, R.I.

BODY, WILLIAM.— Age, 22 years. Enlisted at Rochester, to serve three years, and mustered in as private, Co. I, October 3, 1864; deserted, October 19, 1864, as Boddy.

BOLLMOS, WILLIAM.— Age, 20 years. Enlisted, August 9, 1862, at Port Jervis, to serve three years; mustered in as private, Co. F, September 5, 1862; promoted corporal, December 29, 1864; mustered out with company, June 3, 1865, near Washington, D.C.

BONNELL, WILLIAM L.— Age, 19 years. Enlisted at Syracuse, to serve one year, and mustered in as private, Co. C, September 4, 1864; mustered out with company, June 3, 1865, near Washington, D.C.

BOON, GEORGE.— Age, 24 years. Enlisted at Fifth Congressional District, to serve three years, and mustered in as private, Co. B, December 10, 1863; killed in action, May 12, 1864, at Spotsylvania, Va.; also borne as Boone.

BOOZ, ISAIAH.— Age, 29 years. Enlisted at Plattsburgh, to serve one year, and mustered in as private, Co. E, September 15, 1864; mustered out with company, June 3, 1865, near Washington, D.C.; also borne as Boaz.

BORDENSTEIN, WILLIAM.— Age, 22 years. Enlisted, August 8, 1862, at Cornwall to serve three years; mustered in as private, Co. C, September 5, 1862; wounded in action, May 3, 1863, at Chancellorsville, Va.; transferred to Veteran Reserve Corps, October 28, 1863; also borne as Bodenstein.

BOUNE, BENJAMIN F.— Age, 32 years. Enlisted, August 2, 1862, at Newburgh, to serve three years; mustered in as corporal, Co. A, September 5, 1862; deserted, October 23, 1862, at South Mountain, Md.; also borne as Bowen.

BOUTON, LEANDER S.— Age, 32 years. Enlisted, August 11, 1862, at Goshen, to serve three years; mustered in as private, Co. B, September 5, 1862; deserted, October 25, 1862, from South Mountain, Md.

BOVELL, JAMES.— Age, 44 years. Enlisted, August 18, 1862, at Newburgh, to serve three years; mustered in as private, Co. I, September 5, 1862; wounded in action, May 3, 1863, at Chancellorsville, Va.; transferred to Fiftieth Company, Second Battalion, Veteran Reserve Corps, September 3, 1863; mustered out, September 5, 1865, at Satterlee Hospital, West Philadelphia, Pa.

BOWEN, DAVID.— Age, 33 years. Enlisted, August 21, 1862, at Goshen, to serve three years; mustered in as private, Co. C, September 5, 1862; deserted, November 17, 1862, at Warrenton, Va.

BOWERY, WILLIAM.— Age, 30 years. Enlisted at Goshen, to serve one year, and mustered in as private, Co. K, September 3, 1864; mustered out with detachment, June 5, 1865, at Lincoln Hospital, Washington, D.C.

BOWMAN, ANDREW.— Age, 30 years. Enlisted, August 13, 1862, at Walden, to serve three years; mustered in as private, Co. H, September 5, 1862; wounded in action, May 3, 1863, at Chancellorsville, Va.; transferred to Company I, Twenty-first Regiment, VRC, April 10, 1864; discharged, July 14, 1865, at Trenton, N.J.

BOYCE, WALTER D.— Age, 37 years. Enlisted at Wheatfield, to serve one year, and mustered in as private, Co. I, September 30, 1864; wounded in action, October 27, 1864, at Boydton Road, Va.; discharged for disability, April 13, 1865, at Carver Hospital, Washington, D.C.

BOYD, ANDREW M.— Age, 32 years. Enlisted, August 14, 1862, at Newburgh, to serve three years; mustered in as private, Co. C, September 5, 1862; wounded in action, May 3, 1863, at Chancellorsville, Va.; killed in action, May 6, 1864, at the Wilderness, Va.

BOYD, DUNCAN W.— Age, 41 years. Enlisted, August 18, 1862, at Newburgh, to serve three years; mustered in as private, Co. C, September 5, 1862; promoted sergeant, prior to June 1864; wounded and captured in action, June 1, 1864, at Totopotomoy Creek, Va.; paroled, no date; mustered out, July 14, 1865, at New York City.

BRADENBURGH, SAMUEL.— Age, 26 years. Enlisted, August 13, 1862, at Newburgh, to serve three years; mustered in as private, Co. C, September 5, 1862; absent, sick since April 6, 1863, in hospital at Philadelphia, Pa., and at muster-out of company; also borne as Bredenburgh.

BRADLEY, ALBERT.— Age, 18 years. Enlisted at Goshen, to serve three years, and mustered in as private, Co. K, August 29, 1864; no further record.

BRADLEY, THOMAS W.— Age, 18 years. Enrolled, August 14, 1862, at Walden, to serve three years; mustered in as private, Co. H, September 5, 1862; promoted corporal, September 15, 1862; sergeant, November 1, 1862; first sergeant, June 22, 1863; wounded in action, July 2, 1863, at Gettysburg, Pa., and May 6, 1864, at the Wilderness, Va.; mustered in as first lieutenant, Co. B, September 1, 1864; wounded in action, October 27, 1864, at Boydton Road, Va.; mustered in as captain, November 16, 1864; mustered out with company, June 3, 1865, near Washington, D.C.; awarded *medal of honor*. Commissioned first lieutenant, September 27, 1864, with rank from August 1, 1864, vice J. R. Hayes resigned; captain, November 15, 1864, with rank from August 2, 1864, vice L. S. Wisner resigned.

BRADNER, THOMAS SCOTT.— Age, — years. Enrolled, August 23, 1862, at Goshen, to serve three years; mustered in as chaplain, September 5, 1862; mustered out with regiment, June 3, 1865, near Washington, D.C. Commissioned chaplain, October 21, 1862, with rank from August 23, 1862, original.

BRADY, JOHN F.— Age, 21 years. Enlisted, August 15, 1862 at Goshen, to serve three years; mustered in as private, Co. C, September 5, 1862; deserted, no date.

BRAISTED, JAMES R.— Age, 24 years. Enlisted at Goshen to serve one year, and mustered in as private, Co. K, August 29, 1864; mustered out with company, June 3, 1865, near Washington, D.C.; also borne as Brasted.

BRENNAN, MARTIN.— Age, 23 years. Enlisted at Goshen, to serve three years, and mustered in as private, Co. I, April 15, 1864; deserted, August 27, 1864.

BREWSTER, GEORGE L.— Age, 19 years. Enlisted, August 11, 1862, at Cornwall, to serve three years; mustered in as corporal, Co. C, September 5, 1862; promoted sergeant, March 1, 1863, and first sergeant, prior to October 1864; mustered out with company, June 3, 1865, near Washington, D.C.

BRICKEY, PETER.— Age, 44 years. Enlisted at Plattsburgh to serve one year, and mustered in as private, Co. B, September 15, 1864; mustered out with company, June 3, 1865, near Washington, D.C.

BRIGGS, GEORGE.— Age, 26 years. Enlisted, August 14, 1862 at Newburgh, to serve three years; mustered in as private, Co. C, September 5, 1862; promoted corporal, prior to August 1863; returned to ranks, no date; transferred to the Navy, March 29, 1864.

BROCK, HARVEY.— Age, 30 years. Enlisted, August 22, 1862, at Goshen, to serve three years; mustered in as private, Co. G, September 5, 1862; wounded in action, May 5, 1864, at the Wilderness, Va.; absent, at Carver Hospital, Washington, D.C., since October 1864, and at muster-out of company.

BROCK, SELAH.— Age, 35 years. Enlisted, August 26, 1862, at New Windsor, to serve three years; mustered in as private, Co. G, September 5, 1862; wounded in action, July 2, 1863, at Gettysburg, Pa.; discharged, February 2, 1864, at Culpepper, Va.

BRODHEAD, HARRY R.— Age, 18 years. Enlisted, August 15, 1862, at Port Jervis, to serve three years; mustered in as private, Co. F, September 5, 1862; wounded in action, May 3, 1863, at Chancellorsville, Va.; killed in action, October 27, 1864, at Boydton Road, Va.

BROOKS, HENRY.— Age, 18 years. Enlisted, August 11, 1862 at Washingtonville, to serve three years; mustered in as private, Co. G, September 5, 1862; mustered out with company June 3, 1865, near Washington, D.C.

BROOKS, JOHN H.— Age, 29 years. Enlisted; August 19, 1862 at Newburgh, to serve three years; mustered in as private, Co. I, September 5, 1862; discharged, November 13, 1862.

BROOKS, JOSEPH S.— Age, 22 years. Enlisted, August 11, 1862, at Goshen, to serve three years; mustered in as private, Co. D, September 5, 1862; killed in action, May 3, 1863, at Chancellorsville Va.

BROOKS, SPENCER.— Age, 28 years. Enlisted, August 14, 1862, at Newburgh, to serve three years; mustered in as private, Co. I, September 5, 1862; promoted sergeant, November 1, 1862; discharged, August 21, 1863, from convalescent camp at Alexandria, Va., as Spencer C.

BROOKS, THOMAS M.— Age, 18 years. Enlisted, August 15, 1862, at Cornwall, to serve three years; mustered in as private, Co. C, September 5, 1862; wounded in action, November 27, 1863, at Locust Grove, Va.; died of his wounds, December 20, 1863, at McVeigh Hospital, Alexandria, Va.

BROOKS, WILLIAM S.— Age, 18 years. Enlisted, August 9, 1862, at Cornwall, to serve three years; mustered in as private, Co. C, September 5, 1862; discharged for disability, April 16, 1863, at Falmouth, Va.

BROSS, JOSEPH.— Age, 26 years. Enlisted, August 13, 1862, at Goshen, to serve three years; mustered in as private, Co. B, September 5, 1862; wounded in action, May 6, 1864, at the Wilderness, Va.; mustered out with company, June 3, 1865, near Washington, D.C.

BROWER, STEPHEN H.—Age, 24 years. Enlisted, August 4, 1862, at Goshen, to serve three years; mustered in as sergeant, Co. E, September 5, 1862; returned to ranks, prior to October 1864; transferred to Co. E, Ninety-third Infantry, June 1, 1865

BROWN, GEORGE M.—Age, 24 years. Enlisted at Goshen, to serve one year, and mustered in as private, Co. K, August 25, 1864; mustered out with company, June 3, 1865, near Washington, D.C.; also borne as George W.

BROWN, JOEL H.—Age, 25 years: Enlisted at Goshen, to serve one year, and mustered in as private, Co. D, September 3, 1864; died of chronic diarrhea, November 18, 1864, at Lincoln Hospital, Washington, D.C.

BROWN, JOHN F.—Age, 25 years. Enlisted, August 5, 1862, at Goshen, to serve three years; mustered in as private, Co. B, September 5, 1862; transferred to Co. C, Sixth Regiment, VRC, September 12, 1863; mustered out, July 10, 1865, at Cincinnati, Ohio.

BROWN, JOHN H.—Age, 32 years. Enlisted, August 16, 1862, at Newburgh, to serve three years; mustered in as private, Co. I, September 5, 1862; mustered out with company June 3, 1865, near Washington, D.C.

BROWN, JOSEPH.—Age, 21 years. Enlisted at Rochester, to serve three years, and mustered in as private, Co. D, September 24, 1864; deserted to the enemy, November 7, 1864, from Hancock Station, Va.

BROWN, MICHAEL.—Age, 39 years. Enlisted at Cambria, to serve 1 year, and mustered in as private, Co. C, September 30, 1864; mustered out June 2, 1865, at Washington, D.C.

BROWN, MILNER.—Age, 23 years. Enrolled at Albany, to serve three years, and mustered as second lieutenant, Co. I, December 30, 1862; killed in action July 2, 1863, at Gettysburg, Pa.; also borne as Milnor and J. Milner Brown. Commissioned second lieutenant, December 30, 1862, with rank from same date, vice Isaac M. Martin promoted.

BROWN STEPHEN W.—Age, 37 years. Enlisted, August 14, 1862, at Cornwall, to serve three years; mustered in as private, Co. C, September 5, 1862; died of typhoid fever, January 17, 1863, in camp, near Falmouth, Va.

BROWN, WILLIAM H.—Age, 21 years. Enlisted, August 16, 1862, at Wallkill, to serve three years; mustered in as private, Co. E, September 5, 1862; deserted, August 15, 1862, at Goshen, N.Y.

BROWN, WILLIAM H.—Age, 20 years. Enlisted, August 14, 1862, at Walden, to serve three years; mustered in as private, Co. H, September 5, 1862; wounded in action, May 3, 1863, at Chancellorsville, May 6, 1864, at the Wilderness, and May 8, 1864, at Spotsylvania Court House, Va.; promoted corporal prior to October 1864, sergeant, November 1, 1864; mustered out with detachment, May 17, 1865, at Harewood Hospital, Washington, D.C.

BROWNE, CHARLES E.—Age, 23 years. Enlisted at Goshen, to serve one year, and mustered in as private, Co. H, August 24, 1864; mustered out, June 6, 1865, at Harewood Hospital, Washington, D.C.

BROWNLY, JOSEPH—Age, 18 years. Enlisted, August 8, 1862, at Goshen, to serve three years; mustered in as private, Co. A, September 5, 1862; killed in action, May 12, 1864, at Spotsylvania, Va.

BROWNSON, WILLIAM.—Age,—years. Enrolled, August 15, 1862, at Goshen, to serve three years; mustered in as first lieutenant, Co. C, September 5, 1862, as adjutant December 31, 1862; wounded in action, May 3, 1863, at Chancellorsville; Va.; discharged for wounds, September 17, 1863.

BRUNDAGE, EZEKIEL.—Age, 45 years. Enlisted, August 23, 1862, at Goshen, to serve three years; mustered in as wagoner, Co. G, September 5, 1862; discharged, January 20, 1863, at Falmouth, Va.

BRUNSON, EDWARD.—Age, 41 years. Enlisted at New York City, to serve three years, and mustered in as private, Co. C, February 10, 1865; transferred to Co. A, Ninety-third Infantry, June 1, 1865; also borne as Brounson.

BRUSH, JAMES H.—Age, 23 years. Enlisted at Goshen, to serve one year, and mustered in as private, Co. K, August 19, 1864; died of typhoid fever, March 22, 1865, in hospital, at Point Lookout, Md.

BRUSSIE, CORNELIUS.—Age, 26 years. Enlisted at Fleming, to serve one year, and mustered in as private, Co. I, August 23, 1864; mustered out with company. June 3, 1865, near Washington, D.C.

BUCHANAN, WILLIAM.—Age, 32 years. Enlisted, August 14, 1862, at Walden, to serve three years; mustered in as private, Co. H, September 5, 1862; mustered out with company, June 3, 1865, near Washington, D.C.

BUCKLEY, JOHN G.—Age, 22 years. Enlisted, August 13, 1862, at Walden, to serve three years; mustered in as musician, Co. H, September 5, 1862; promoted second principal musician, November 7, 1863; mustered out with regiment, June 3, 1865, near Washington, D.C.

BULL, CHARLES H.—Age, 18 years. Enlisted, August 11, 1862, at Goshen, to serve three years; mustered in as private, Co. B, September 5, 1862; promoted corporal, September 1, 1864; mustered out with company, June 3, 1865, near Washington, D.C.

BULL, HARRISON.—Age, 20 years. Enlisted, August 11, 1862, at Goshen, to serve three years; mustered in as corporal, Co. B, September 5, 1862; returned to ranks prior to April 10, 1863; wounded in action, July 23, 1863, at Wapping Heights, Va.; transferred to Co. I, First Regiment, Veteran Reserve Corps, February 16, 1864; mustered out, July 6, 1865, at Albany, N.Y.

BUNCE, ALBERT J.—Age, 20 years. Enlisted. August 7, 1862, at Cornwall, to serve three years; mustered in as private, Co. C, September 5, 1862; promoted sergeant, January 1, 1865; wounded in action, April 1, 1865, before Petersburg, Va.; returned to ranks, no date; mustered out, June 2, 1863, at Douglas Hospital, Washington, D.C.

BURGESS, THOMAS.—Age, 33 years. Enlisted, July 24, 1862, at Goshen, to serve three years; mustered in as private, Co. B, September 5, 1862; deserted, October 25, 1862, at South Mountain, Md.

BURHANS, TALLMADGE.—Age, 19 years. Enlisted, August 8, 1862, at Wallkill, to serve three years; mustered in as wagoner, Co. K, September 5, 1862; grade changed to private, June 30, 1863; appointed wagoner prior to October 1864; mustered out with company, June 3, 1865, near Washington, D.C.

BURKHART, JOHN.—Age, 42 years. Enlisted at New York city, to serve one year, and mustered in as private, Co. A, February 27, 1865; transferred to Co. E, Ninety-third Infantry, June 1, 1865; also borne as John P.

BURNES, MICHAEL.—Age, 28 years. Enlisted at Rochester, to serve three years, and mustered in as private, Co. H, October 14, 1864; deserted, October 27, 1864, at Petersburg, Va.

BURNS, JOHN.—Age, 28 years. Enlisted, August 28, 1862, at Goshen, to serve three years; mustered in as private, Co. E, September 5, 1862; deserted, March 27, 1863, on expiration of furlough.

BUSH, HARVEY.—Age, 19 years. Enlisted at Goshen, to serve one year, and mustered in as private, Co. K, September 3, 1864; mustered out with company, June 3, 1865, near Washington, D.C.

BUSH, IRA S.—Age, 34 years. Enrolled, August 7, 1862, at Port Jervis, to serve three years; mustered in as captain, Co. F, September 5, 1862; wounded in action, no date; discharged for wounds, June 21, 1864.
Commissioned captain, September 10, 1862, with rank from August 20, 1862, original.

BUTTERS, GEORGE.—Age, 24 years. Enlisted, August 13, 1862, at Walden, to serve three years; mustered in as private, Co. H, September 5, 1862; promoted corporal, prior to April 10, 1863; sergeant, prior to May 1864; captured in action, May 12, 1864, at Spotsylvania Court House, Va.; no further record.

BYRNE, PETER.—Age, 19 years. Enlisted at Goshen, to serve one year, and mustered in as private, Co. D, September 19, 1864; mustered out with company, June 3, 1865, near Washington, D.C.

CABLE, CHARLES.—Age, 19 years. Enlisted at Goshen, to serve one year, and mustered in as private, Co. K, August 17, 1864; wounded in action, April 6, 1865, at Deatonsville Road, Va.; absent since at Harewood Hospital, Washington, D.C., and at muster-out of company.

CABLE, MARTIN.—Age, 25 years. Enlisted at Goshen, to serve one year, and mustered in as private, Co. K, September 3, 1864; no further record.

CABNEY, GEORGE W.—Age, 43 years. Enlisted, August 13, 1862, at Goshen, to serve three years; mustered in as private, Co. C, September 5, 1862; discharged for disability, April 16, 1863, at Falmouth, Va.

CALL, SAMUEL.—Age, 22 years. Enlisted at Goshen, to serve one year, and mustered in as private, Co. K, September 1, 1864; mustered out with detachment, June 5, 1865, at Whitehall Hospital, Philadelphia, Pa.

CALLAHAN, MICHAEL.—Age, 36 years. Enlisted at Utica, to serve three years, and mustered in as private, Co. K, September 8, 1864; transferred to Co. F, Ninety-third Infantry, June 1, 1865.

CALLISTER, WILLIAM H.—Age, 21 years. Enlisted, August 12, 1862, at Goshen, to serve three years; mustered in as private, Co. D, September 5, 1862; wounded in action, June 9, 1863, at Beverly Ford, Va.; transferred to Co. D, Ninth Regiment, Veteran Reserve Corps, September 7, 1863; mustered out with detachment, June 26, 1865, at Washington, D.C.

CALVER, JOHN M.—Age, 19 years. Enlisted, August 14, 1862, at Newburgh, to serve three years; mustered in as private, Co. G, September 5, 1862; wounded in action, May 3, 1863, at Chancellorsville, Va.; transferred to Veteran Reserve Corps, December 16, 1863.

CAMERON, JACOB.—Age, 24 years. Enlisted, August 23, 1862, at Newburgh, to serve three years; mustered in as private, Co. K, September 5, 1862; mustered out with company, June 3, 1865, near Washington, D.C.

CAMERON, JOHN.—Age, 21 years. Enlisted, August 11, 1862, at Goshen, to serve three years; mustered in as private, Co. B, September 5, 1862; deserted, October 25, 1862, at South Mountain, Md.

CAMP, JESSE F.—Age, 20 years. Enlisted, August 14, 1862, at Walden, to serve three years; mustered in as private, Co. H, September 5, 1862; wounded in action, July 2, 1863, at Gettysburg, Pa.; transferred to Veteran Reserve Corps, January 14, 1864.

CAMPBELL, MARTIN.—Age, 25 years. Enlisted at Warwick, to serve three years, and mustered in as private, Co. B, January 4, 1864; killed while on picket, September 16, 1864, at Petersburg, Va.; also borne as Martin V.

CAMPBELL, WILLIAM.—Age, 44 years. Enlisted, August 16, 1862, at Newburgh, to serve three years; mustered in as private, Co. G, September 5, 1862; killed in action, July 2, 1863, at Gettysburg, Pa.

CAMPBELL, WILLIAM H.—Age, 18 years. Enlisted, October 12, 1862, at Goshen, to serve three years; mustered in as private, Co. A, September 5, 1862; promoted corporal, December 16, 1862; first sergeant, November 15, 1864; mustered out with company, June 3, 1865, near Washington, D.C.

CANFIELD, GEORGE W.—Age, 16 years. Enlisted, August 22, 1862, at Wallkill, to serve three years; mustered in as musician, Co. K, September 5, 1862; transferred to Co. C, Ninth Regiment, Veteran Reserve Corps, September 26, 1863; mustered out with detachment, June 20, 1865, at Washington, D.C.

CANNAVAN, GEORGE.—Age, 38 years. Enlisted at Auburn, to serve one year, and mustered in as private, Co. I, August 17, 1864; mustered out with company, June 3, 1865, near Washington, D.C.

CANNON, HENRY M.—Age, 18 years. Enlisted, August 4, 1862, Goshen, to serve three years; mustered in as musician, Co. A, September 5, 1862; discharged, February 4, 1863, at St. Aloysius Hospital, Washington, D.C.

CANNON, WILLIAM E.—Age, 25 years. Enlisted, August 16, 1862, at Washingtonville, to serve three years: mustered in as private, Co. G, September 5, 1862; wounded in action, May 3, 1863, at Chancellorsville, Va.; transferred to Veteran Reserve Corps, September 30, 1868.

CAREY, JOHN.—Age, 21 years. Enlisted at Brooklyn, to serve three years, and mustered in as private, Co. I, November 12, 1864; transferred to Co. I, Ninety-third Infantry, June 1, 1865

CAREY, JOHN A.—Age, 19 years. Enlisted at New Windsor, to serve three years, and mustered in as private, Co. B, January 1864; died of chronic diarrhea, September 4, 1864, at Davids' Island, New York Harbor; borne as John N.

CARLEY, WILLIAM H.—Age, 18 years. Enlisted at Port Jervis, to serve three years, and mustered in as private, Co. F, May 5, 1864; transferred to Co. I, Ninety-third Infantry, June 1, 1865.

CARMAN, ANGUS.— Age, 23 years. Enlisted, August 14, 1862, at Walden, to serve three years; mustered in as private, Co. H, September 5, 1862; died of fever, June 30, 1862 [sic], at Walden, N.Y.

CARMAN, DANIEL N.— Age, 21 years. Enlisted, August 22, 1862, at Walden, to serve three years; mustered in as private, Co. I, September 5, 1862; wounded in action, May 6, 1868, at Chancellorsville, Va.; May 5, 1864, at the Wilderness, Va.; mustered out with company, June 8, 1865, near Washington, D.C.

CARMER, WILLIAM V.— Age, 28 years. Enlisted, August 13, 1862, at Port Jervis, to serve three years; mustered in as private, Co. F, September 5, 1862; killed in action, May 3 1863, at Chancellorsville, Va.

CARMICK, EDWARD J.— Age, 23 years. Enrolled at Brandy, Va., to serve three years, and mustered in as first lieutenant, Co. F, April 5, 1864; wounded in action, May 12, 1864, at Spotsylvania Court House, Va.; mustered in as captain, August 10, 1864; wounded in action, October 27, 1864, at Boydton Road, Va.; killed in action, April 1, 1865, near Petersburg, Va.; also borne as Cannack and Cormick; prior service as sergeant, First U.S. Sharpshooters.

CARPENTER, DANIEL.— Age, 26 years. Enlisted, August 23, 1862, at Goshen, to serve three years; mustered in as private, Co. K, September 5, 1862; promoted corporal prior to April 10, 1863; wounded in action, May 3, 1863, at Chancellorsville, Va.; transferred to Veteran Reserve Corps, April 10, 1864.

CARPENTER, DANIEL.— Age, 41 years. Enlisted at Oswego, to serve one year, and mustered in as private, Co. A, August 17, 1864; mustered out with company, June 3, 1865, near Washington, D.C.

CARPENTER, EDWARD M.— Age, 18 years. Enlisted, August 11, 1862, at Goshen, to serve three years; mustered in as private, Co. B, September 5, 1862; wounded in action, July 2, 1863, at Gettysburg, Pa.; May 19, 1864, at Spotsylvania Court House, Va.; mustered out with company, June 8, 1865, near Washington, D.C.

CARPENTER, WILLIAM.— Age, 28 years. Enlisted, July 28, 1862, at Newburgh, to serve three years, mustered in, Co. C, September 5, 1862; wounded in action, May 12, 1864, at Spotsylvania Court House, Va.; mustered out with company, June 8, 1865, near Washington, D.C.

CARPENTER, WILLIAM W.— Age, 26 years. Enlisted, August 22, 1862, at Wallkill, to serve three years, mustered in as private, Co. K. September 5, 1862: promoted corporal, October 1, 1864; sergeant, November 15, 1864; mustered out with company, June 8, 1865, near Washington, D.C.

CARR, JOHN.— Age, 21 years. Enlisted at Deer Park, to serve one year, and mustered in as private, Co. K, Sept. 13, 1864; no further record.

CARR, SOLOMON.— Age, 24 years. Enlisted, August 30, 1862, at New Windsor, to serve three years; mustered in as private, Co. E, September 5, 1862; wounded in action, May 6, 1864, at the Wilderness, Va.; transferred to Co. E, Ninety-third Infantry, June 1, 1865.

CARROLL, JOHN.— Age, 24 years. Enlisted, August 12, 1862, at Wallkill, to serve three years; mustered in as private, Co. K, September 5, 1862; killed in action, July 2, 1863, at Gettysburg, Pa.

CARSON, JAMES.— Age, place, date of enlistment and muster-in as private, Co. D, not stated; deserted to the enemy, November 9, 1864, at Hancock Station, Va.

CARTER, CHARLES.— Age, 22 years. Enlisted at Goshen, to serve one year, and mustered in as private, Co. K, August 27, 1864; no further record.

CARTY, JAMES.— Age, 30 years. Enlisted, August 15, 1862, at Port Jervis, to serve three years; mustered in as private, Co. F, September 5, 1862; mustered out with company, June 3, 1865, near Washington, D.C.

CARY, LEONARD.— Age, 28 years. Enlisted, August 7, 1862, at Cornwall, to serve three years; mustered in as private, Co. C, September 5, 1862; mustered out with company, June 3, 1865, near Washington, D.C.

CENTERBARK, CHARLES.— Age, 21 years. Enlisted at Plattsburgh, to serve one year, and mustered in as private, Co. E, September 15, 1864; mustered out with company, June 3, 1865, near Washington, D.C.

CHALMERS, SAMUEL.— Age, 24 years. Enlisted, August 22, 1862, at Newburgh, to serve three years; mustered in as private, Co. I, September 5, 1862; promoted corporal, November 1, 1862; wounded in action, July 2, 1863, at Gettysburg, Pa.; discharged, January 8, 1864.

CHAMBERS, JOHN.— Age, 35 years. Enlisted, August 13, 1862, at Washingtonville, to serve three years; mustered in as private, Co. G, September 5, 1862; died of erysipelas, April 23, 1864, at Washington, D.C.

CHANDLER, GEORGE H.— Age, 24 years. Enlisted, August 20, 1862, at Newburgh, to serve three years; mustered in as sergeant, Co. C, September 5, 1862; promoted quartermaster-sergeant, March 1, 1863; mustered out with regiment, June 3, 1865, near Washington, D.C.

CHATFIELD, CHARLES.— Age, 18 years. Enlisted, August 6, 1862, at Cornwall, to serve three years; mustered in as private, Co. C, September 5, 1862; promoted corporal, prior to April 10, 1863; killed in action, May 3, 1863, at Chancellorsville, Va.

CHATFIELD, JACOB B.— Age, 39 years. Enlisted, August 16, 1862, at Newburgh, to serve three years; mustered in as private, Co. I, September 5, 1862; returned to ranks prior to May 1864; transferred to Co. K, Sixth Regiment, Veteran Reserve Corps, May 16, 1864; promoted sergeant, no date; mustered out with detachment July 5, 1865, at Cincinnati, Ohio.

CHRISTY, WILLIAM R.— Age, 18 years. Enlisted, August 23, 1862, at Wallkill, to serve three years; mustered in as private, Co. K, September 5, 1862; transferred to Co. I, November 15, 1864; absent, sick, since April 10, 1863, and at muster-out of company; also borne as Christie.

CILES, JAMES G.— Age, 21 years. Enlisted, August 11, 1862, at Goshen, to serve three years; mustered in as private, Co. A, September 5, 1862; wounded in action, May 3, 1863, at Chancellorsville, Va., and died of his wounds, May 5, 1863, at Potomac Creek, Va., as James T. Cyles.

CLARA, JOHN.— Age, 20 years. Enlisted at Goshen, to serve one year, and mustered in as private, Co. B, September 12, 1864; mustered out with company, June 3, 1865, near Washington, D.C., as Clarny.

CLARK, CHARLES C.— Age, 24 years. Enlisted, August 7, 1862, at Newburgh, to serve three years; mustered in as private, Co. C, September 5, 1862; discharged for disability, April 16, 1863 at Falmouth, Va.

CLARK, HIRAM.— Age, 22 years. Enlisted, August 4, 1862, at Goshen, to serve three years; mustered in as private, Co. E, September 5, 1862; discharged, October 20, 1862, at Washington, D.C.

CLARK, JAMES.— Age, 22 years. Enlisted at Cambria, to serve one year, and mustered in as private, Co. I, October 4, 1864; transferred to Co. D, Ninety-third Infantry. June 1, 1865.

CLARK, JAMES H.— Age, 22 years. Enlisted August 6, 1862 at Goshen, to serve three years; mustered in as private, Co. D, Sept. 5, 1862; wounded in action May 6, 1864, at the Wilderness, Va.; promoted corporal, August 31, 1864; mustered out with company, June 3, 1865, near Washington, D.C.

CLARK, JOHN K.— Age, 23 years. Enlisted, August 12, 1862, at Goshen, to serve three years; mustered in as private, Co. D, September 5, 1862; wounded in action, May 3, 1863, at Chancellorsville, Va.; mustered out with company, June 3, 1865, near Washington, D.C.

CLARK, LEANDER.— Age, 34 years. Enrolled at Newburgh, to serve three years, and mustered in as captain, Co. I, August 20, 1862; discharged for disability, May 13, 1863.

CLARK, MOSES F.— Age, 35 years. Enlisted, August 14, 1862, at Goshen, to serve three years; mustered in as wagoner. Co. B, September 5, 1862; grade changed to private prior to April 10, 1863; transferred to Co. A, Sixth Regiment, Veteran Reserve Corps, September 26, 1863; discharged, July 6, 1863, at McLean Barracks, Cincinnati, Ohio, as Moses S.

CLARK, SAMUEL.— Age, 24 years. Enlisted, August 7, 1862, at Goshen, to serve three years; mustered in as private, Co. A, September 5, 1862; wounded in action, June 9, 1863, at Beverly Ford, Va.; died of chronic diarrhea, September 19, 1863, at Alexandria, Va.

CLARK, JR., SAMUEL.— Age, 24 years. Enlisted, August 15, 1862, at Howells, to serve three years; mustered in as private, Co. E, September 3, 1862; absent, sick at Washington, D.C., since October 20, 1862. and at muster-out of company.

CLEARWATER, NICHOLAS.— Age, 42 years. Enlisted, August 7, 1862, at Newburgh, to serve three years; mustered in as private, Co. E, September 5, 1862, absent, sick in hospital, at Washington, D.C., since October 10, 1862 and at muster-out of company.

CLEARWATER, THOMAS.— Age, 20 years. Enlisted, August 11, 1862, at Otisville, to serve three years; mustered in as private, Co. E, September 5, 1862; absent, sick in hospital, at Washington, D.C., since October 17, 1862, and at muster-out of company.

CLIFFORD, CHESTER.— Age, 19. Enlisted at Goshen, to serve one year, and mustered in as private, Co. F, September 1, 1864; transferred to Co. I, Ninety-third Infantry, June 1, 1865.

COALST, WILLIAM.— Age, 22 years. Enlisted at Warwick, to serve one year, and mustered in as private, Co. D, September 12, 1864; no further record.

CODDINGTON, ELI.— Age, 21 years. Enlisted, August 11, 1862, at Port Jervis, to serve three years; mustered in as private, Co. F. September 5, 1862; wounded in action, May 5, 1864, at the Wilderness, Va.; absent, since October 18, 1864, at Mt. Pleasant Hospital, Washington, D.C., and at muster-out of company.

CODDINGTON, JACOB M.— Age, 27 years. Enlisted, August 12, 1862, at Bloomingburg, to serve three years; mustered in as private, Co. E, September 5, 1862; mustered out with company, June 3, 1865; near Washington, D.C.

CODDINGTON, JAMES M.— Age, 23 years. Enlisted, August 12, 1862, at Bloomingburg, to serve three years; mustered in as private, Co. E, September 5, 1862; mustered out with company, June 3, 1865, near Washington, D.C.

COHEN, P.— Age, place, date of enlistment and muster-in as private, Co. I, not stated; absent, sick, since October, 1864, and at muster-out of company.

COLBY, GABRIEL.— Age, 34 years. Enlisted, August 8, 1862, at Wallkill, to serve three years; mustered in as private, Co. K, September 5, 1862; wounded in action, May 23, 1864, at North Anna, Va.; mustered out with company, June 3, 1865, near Washington, D.C.

COLE, JEREMIAH.— Age, 47 years. Enlisted, August 12, 1862, at Port Jervis, to serve three years; mustered in as private, Co. F, September 5, 1862; appointed wagoner, prior to April 10, 1863; transferred to Co. F, Ninth Regiment, Veteran Reserve Corps, February 1, 1865; mustered out as private with detachment June 26, 1865, at Washington, D.C.

COLE, JOHN N.— Age, 16 years. Enlisted, August 21, 1862, at Newburgh, to serve three years; mustered in as musician, Co. I, September 5, 1862; mustered out with company, June 3, 1865, near Washington, D.C.

COLE, JOSHUA V.— Age, 32 years. Enlisted, August 15, 1862, at Newburgh, to serve three years; mustered in as private, Co. G, September 5, 1862; promoted corporal, January 1, 1863; sergeant, September 13, 1863; first sergeant, January 1, 1864; discharged for disability, March 25, 1865; also borne as Joshua T. Commissioned, not mustered, second lieutenant, February 18, 1865, with rank from January 1, 1865, vice W. H. Benjamin promoted.

COLE, WILLIAM.— Age, 24 years. Enlisted at Schenectady, to serve one year, and mustered in as private, Co. E, August 30, 1864; mustered out with company, June 3, 1865, near Washington, D.C.

COLEMAN, GEORGE W.— Age, 43 years. Enlisted, August 22, 1862, at Goshen, to serve three years; mustered in as private, Co. G, September 5, 1862; killed in action, May 3, 1863, at Chancellorsville, Va.

COLLINS, JAMES E.— Age, 37 years. Enlisted, August 14, 1862, at Newburgh, to serve three years; mustered in as private, Co. I, September 5, 1862; died, June 30, 1863.

COMEY, JAMES.— Age, 19 years. Enlisted, August 11, 1862, at Port Jervis, to serve three years; mustered in as private, Co. F, September 5, 1862; promoted corporal, January 1, 1863; wounded in action, July 2, 1863, at Gettysburg, Pa.; mustered out with company, June 3, 1865, near Washington, D.C.

CONKLIN, HARVEY.—Age, 26 years. Enlisted at Goshen, to serve one year and mustered in as private, Co. K, September 30, 1864; see Harvey Conkling, Co. F.

CONKLIN, HENRY C.—Private, Co. K, 1st U.S. Sharpshooters; transferred to Co. H, this regiment, March 1, 1865; mustered out, May 31, 1865, from hospital, at Washington, D.C., as Henry E.

CONKLIN, ISAAC L.—Age, 25 years. Enlisted, August 8, 1862, at Chester, to serve three years; mustered in as private, Co. A, September 5, 1862; wounded in action, July 2, 1863, at Gettysburg, Pa.; absent, sick, since August 12, 1864, at De Camp Hospital, Davids' Island, New York Harbor, and at muster-out of company.

CONKLIN, JOHN H.—Age, 23 years. Enlisted, August 7, 1862, at Goshen, to serve three years; mustered in as private, Co. A, September 5, 1862; mustered out with company, June 3, 1865, near Washington, D.C.

CONKLIN, JOHN HENRY H.—Age, 21 years. Enlisted, August 18, 1862, at Goshen, to serve three years; mustered in as private, Co. A, September 5, 1862; died of typhoid fever, July 14, 1863, in hospital, at Frederick, Md.

CONKLIN, PETER.—Age, 19 years. Enlisted, August 15, 1862, at Goshen, to serve three years; mustered in as private, Co. C, September 5, 1862; wounded in action, May 3, 1863, at Chancellorsville, Va.; transferred to Veteran Reserve Corps, March 15, 1864.

CONKLIN, SAMUEL L.—Age, 25 years. Enlisted, August 1, 1862, at Goshen, to serve three years; mustered in as private, Co. A, September 5, 1862; discharged, February 2, 1864.

CONKLING, ANDREW.—Age, 22 years. Enlisted at Goshen, to serve one year, and mustered in as private, Co. K, September 2, 1864; wounded in action, April 2, 1865, before Peters. burg, Va.; absent, wounded, and in Emory Hospital, Washington, D.C., and at muster-out of company, as Conklin.

CONKLING, DANIEL.—Age, 28 years. Enlisted at Goshen, to serve three years, and mustered in as private, Co. K, September 10, 2864; mustered out with company, June 3, 1865, near Washington, D.C., as Conklin.

CONKLING, GEORGE.—Age, 19 years. Enlisted at Goshen, to serve one year, and mustered in as private, Co. K, August 24, 1864, mustered out with company, June 3, 1865, near Washington, D.C., as Conklin.

CONKLING, HARVEY.—Age, 26 years. Enlisted at Port Jervis, to serve one year, and mustered in as private, Co. F, September 3, 1864; mustered out with company, June 3, 1865, near Washington, D.C.

CONKLING, JAMES H.—Age, 26 years. Enlisted, August 21, 1862, at Goshen, to serve three years; mustered in as private, Co. K, September 5, 1862; mustered out with company, June 3, 1865, near Washington, D.C., as Conklin.

CONKLING, JOSIAH.—Age, 22 years. Enlisted at Goshen, to serve one year, and mustered in as private, Co. K, August 19, 1864; mustered out with company, June 3, 1865, near Washington, D.C., as Conklin.

CONKLING, MOSES C.—Age, 43 years. Enlisted at Goshen, to serve one year, and mustered in as private, Co. K, August 30, 1864; mustered out with company, June 3, 1865, near Washington, D.C., as Conklin.

CONKLING, NATHANIEL G.—Age, 29 years. Enlisted, August 6, 1862, at Wallkill, to serve three years; mustered in as private, Co. K, September 5, 1862; wounded in action, May 3, 1863, at Chancellorsville, Va.; deserted, July 6, 1863, at Satterlee Hospital, Philadelphia, Pa.; also borne as Nathaniel J.

CONKLING, SAMUEL.—Age, 28 years. Enlisted at Goshen, to serve one year, and mustered in as private, Co. K, September 10, 1864; no further record.

CONNELL, JOHN.—Age, 27 years. Enlisted, August 14, 1862, at Goshen, to serve three years; as private, Co. E, and deserted, August 15, 1862, at Goshen, N.Y.

CONNELLY, PATRICK.—Age, 21 years. Enlisted at Goshen, to serve one year, and mustered in as private, Co. D, September 19, 1864; mustered out with company, June 3, 1865, near Washington, D.C.

CONNELLY, JR., ROBERT.—Age, 34 years. Enlisted, August 20, 1862, at Cornwall, to serve three years; mustered in as wagoner, Co. C, September 5, 1862; promoted sergeant, Co. D, September 19, 1863; mustered out with company, June 3, 1865, near Washington, D.C.; also borne as Robert Connoly.

CONNING, JASON R.—Age, 21 years. Enlisted, August 19, 1862, at Wallkill, to serve three years; mustered in as private, Co. K, September 5, 1862; promoted corporal, January 1, 1863; sergeant, August 1, 1864; mustered out with company, June 3, 1865, near Washington, D.C.

CONOLY, WILLIAM.—Age, 22 years. Enlisted, August 21, 1862, at Wallkill, to serve three years; mustered in as private, Co. K, September 5, 1862; deserted, September 25, 1862, from camp, near Fort Bennett, Va., as Conly.

COOK, WILLIAM S.—Age, 44 years. Enlisted, August 11, 1862, at Port Jervis, to serve three years; mustered in as private, Co. F, September 5, 1862; discharged for disability, April 8, 1863, Carver Hospital, Washington, D.C.

COON, CLARK.—Age, 40 years. Enlisted, August 12, 1862, at Goshen, to serve three years; mustered in as private, Co. B, September 5, 1862; discharged, January 10, 1863.

COOPER, CHARLES G.—Age, 20 years. Enlisted, August 8, 1862, at Washingtonville, to serve three years; mustered in as corporal, Co. G, September 5, 1862; transferred to Co. B, Third Regiment, Veteran Reserve Corps, no date; mustered out, July 12, 1865, at Camp Coburn, Augusta, Maine.

COOPER, JAMES.—Age, 43 years. Enlisted, August 19, 1862, at Newburgh, to serve three years; mustered in as private, Co. I, September 5, 1862; killed in action, May 3, 1863, at Chancellorsville, Va.

CORBETT, THOMAS.—Age, 23 years. Enlisted, August 11, 1862, at Oxford, to serve three years; mustered in as private, Co. G, September 5, 1862; killed in action, July 2, 1863, at Gettysburg, Pa.; also borne as Corbitt.

COREY, HARVEY P.—Age, 18 years. Enlisted at Newburgh, to serve three years, and mustered in as private, Co. B, December 10, 1862; mustered out with detachment, May 17, 1865, at Harewood Hospital, Washington, D.C.

CORNELIUS, CHARLES T.—Age, 19 years. Enlisted, August 8, 1862, at Monroe, to serve three years; mustered in as private, Co. C, September 5, 1862; died of typhoid fever, December 23, 1862, at camp, near Falmouth, Va.

CORNELL, JAMES.—Age, 18 years. Enlisted at Rochester, to serve three years, and mustered in as private, Co. I, October 6, 1864; deserted, October 19, 1864, near Petersburg, Va.

CORTRIGHT, LEVI.— Age, 21 years. Enlisted, August 11, 1862, at Port Jervis, to serve three years; mustered in as private, Co. F, September 5, 1862; wounded in action, July 2, 1863, at Gettysburg, Pa.; mustered out with company, June 3, 1865, near Washington, D.C.

CORWIN, DAVID FL.— Age, 20 years. Enlisted, August 11, 1862, at Washingtonville, to serve three years; mustered in as private, Co. G, September 5, 1862; mustered out with company, June 3, 1865, near Washington, D.C.

CORY, JONATHAN.— Age, 26 years. Enlisted, August 9, 1862, at Wallkill, to serve three years; mustered in as private, Co. K, September 5, 1862; discharged for disability, April 1, 1863, as Corey.

COUHIG, JAMES.— Age, 18 years. Enlisted at Jamaica, to serve one year, and mustered in as private, Co. C, February 9, 1865; transferred to Co. A, Ninety-third Infantry, June 1, 1865, as Cowhig, John.

COURTER, WILLIAM H.— Age, 18 years. Enlisted, August 4, 1862, at Wallkill, to serve three years; mustered in as private, Co. K, September 5, 1862; transferred to Co. I, Third Regiment, Veteran Reserve Corps, September 1, 1863; discharged, July 27, 1865, as Corter.

COVEL, MARTIN.— Age, 25 years. Enlisted, September 2, 1864, at Port Jervis, to serve one year; mustered in as private, Co. F,. September 3, 1864; died of typhoid fever, February 13, 1865, at Division Hospital, near Petersburg, Va.

COWDREY, JR., JOHN.— Age, 21 years. Enlisted, August 16, 1862, at Goshen, to serve three years; mustered in as sergeant, Co. D, September 5, 1862; died of typhoid fever, June 9, 1863, at Falmouth, Va.

COX, GORDON B.— Age, 18 years. Enlisted, July 31, 1862, at Wallkill, to serve three years; mustered in as private, Co. K, September 5, 1862; wounded in action, May 3, 1863, and died of his wounds, May 4, 1863, at Field Hospital, Chancellorsville, Va.

COX, WILLIAM H.— Age, 26 years. Enlisted, August 15, 1862, at Walden, to serve three years; mustered in as sergeant, Co. H, September 5, 1862; wounded in action, May 3, 1863, at Chancellorsville, Va.; killed in action, July 2, 1863, at Gettysburg, Pa.

CRANS, CORNELIUS.— Age, 28 years. Enlisted, August 19, 1862, Wallkill, to serve three years; mustered in as private, Co. K, September 5, 1862; wounded in action, May 3, 1863, at Chancellorsville, Va.; wounded and captured in action, May 6, 1864, at the Wilderness, Va.; paroled prior to October, 1864; mustered out, to date June 3, 1865, at New York City.

CRANS, HERMAN.— Age, 20 years. Enlisted, August, 13, 1862, at Goshen, to serve three years; mustered in as private, Co. B, September 5, 1862; wounded in action, May 3, 1863, at Chancellorsville, Va.; transferred to Veteran Reserve Corps, September 1, 1863.

CRANSTON, JAMES.— Age, 18 years. Enlisted at Goshen, to serve one year, and mustered in as private, Co. K, August 17, 1864; no further record.

CRAWFORD, ALEXANDER.— Age, 22 years. Enlisted, August 16, 1862, at Newburgh, to serve three years; mustered in as private, Co. I, September 5, 1862; discharged, February 11, 1863.

CRAWFORD, ALEXANDER B.— Age, 23 years. Enlisted, August 13, 1862, at Newburgh, to serve three years; mustered in as private, Co. I, September 5, 1862; transferred to Veteran Reserve Corps, July 1, 1863.

CRAWFORD, GEORGE H.— Age, 27 years. Enlisted at New York City, to serve three years, and mustered in as private, Co. G, March 26, 1864; promoted sergeant, March 12, 1865; transferred to Co. D, Ninety-third Infantry, June 1, 1865; prior service in Co. I, Independent Battalion, N.Y. Vols.

CRAWFORD, JOHN J.— Age, 24 years. Enlisted, August 12, 1862 at Wallkill, to serve three years; mustered in as corporal, Co. K. September 5, 1862; promoted sergeant, May 3, 1863; returned to ranks, October 1, 1864; mustered out with company, June 3, 1865, near Washington, D.C.

CRAWFORD, JONATHAN S.— Age, 23 years. Enlisted, August 15, 1862, at Port Jervis, to serve three years; mustered in as private, Co. F, September 5, 1862; wounded in action, November 27, 1863, at Locust Grove, Va.; May 12, 1864, at Salient, Va.; again, April 6, 1865, at Deatonsville Road, Va.; mustered out, June 16, 1865, at hospital, at Annapolis, Md.

CRAWFORD, SAMUEL S.— Age, 29 years. Enlisted, August 15, 1862, at Port Jervis, to serve three years; mustered in as corporal, Co. F, September 5, 1862; returned to ranks, prior to April 10, 1863; absent, sick at Fairfax Seminary Hospital, Alexander, Va., since October 1864, and at muster-out of company.

CRAWLEY, MATHEW.— Age, 28 years. Enlisted, August 4, 1862, at Goshen, to serve three years; mustered in as private, Co. B, September 5, 1862; wounded in action, May 3, 1863, at Chancellorsville, Va.; May 6, 1864, at the Wilderness, Va.; died of chronic diarrhea, December 19, 1864, at Annapolis, Md.

CRESSY, CHARLES T.— Age, 19 years. Enrolled, August 12, 1862, at Goshen, to serve three years; mustered in as second lieutenant, Co. A, September 5, 1862; died of fever, July 14, 1864, at hospital, Davids' Island, New York.

CRIPPS, GEORGE.— Age, 18 years. Enlisted, August 15, 1862, at Salisbury Mills, to serve three years; mustered in as private, Co. G, September 5, 1862; discharged for disability, April 1, 1863, at camp, near Falmouth, Va.

CRIST, DAVID.— Age, 47 years. Enrolled at Goshen, to serve three years, and mustered in as captain, Co. H, August 23, 1862; wounded in action, May 3, 1863, at Chancellorsville, Va.; killed in action, May 30, 1864, at Totopotomy, Va.

CRIST, JAMES.— Age, 28 years. Enlisted, August 14, 1862, at Walden, to serve three years; mustered in as private, Co. H, September, 5, 1862; wounded in action, May 3, 1863, at Chancellorsville, Va.; captured, June 1, 1864, at Totopotomoy Creek, Va. died, November 11, 1864, at Andersonville, Ga.

CRIST, JEREMIAH M.— Age, 19 years. Enlisted, August 13, 1862, at Walden, to serve three years; mustered in as private, Co. H, September 5, 1862; wounded in action, May 3, 1863, at Chancellorsville, Va.; discharged for wounds, October 18, 1863.

CRIST, MILTON.—Age, 18 years. Enlisted, August 14, 1862, at Walden, to serve three years; mustered in as private, Co. H, September 5, 1862; promoted corporal, September 1, 1864; sergeant, March 20, 1865; mustered out with company, June 3, 1865, near Washington, D.C.

CRIST, MOSES.—Age, 22 years. Enlisted, August 9, 1862, at Wallkill, to serve three years; mustered in as corporal, Co. E, September 5, 1862; returned to ranks, prior to April 10, 1863; wounded in action, May 3, 1863, at Chancellorsville, Va.; promoted corporal, November 1, 1864; wounded in action, April 6, 1865, before Petersburg, Va.; mustered out, June 3, 1865, at Emory Hospital, Washington, D.C.

CRIST, VANKEUREN.—Age, 21 years, Enlisted, August 13, 1862, at Walden, to serve three years; mustered in as private, Co. H, September 5, 1862; killed in action, May 3, 1863, at Chancellorsville, Va.

CROMWELL, JAMES.—Age, 22 years. Enrolled, August 15, 1862, at Goshen, to serve three years; mustered in as captain, Co. C, August 20, 1862; as major, September 5, 1862; killed in action, July 2, 1863, at Gettysburg, Pa.; prior service in Seventh Cavalry. Commissioned captain, September 10, 1862, with rank from August 15, 1862, original; major, September 10, 1862, with rank from August 20, 1862, original.

CRONK, ABRAM J.—Age, 20 years. Enlisted at Goshen, to serve one year, and mustered in as private, Co. K, August 22, 1864; wounded in action, April 6, 1865, at Deatonsville Road, Va.; since absent at Harewood Hospital, Washington, D.C., and at muster-out of company; also, borne as Abraham.

CROTTY. NICKOLAS K.—Age, 28 years. Enlisted at Goshen, to serve one year, and mustered in as private, Co. K, September 1, 1864; promoted corporal, November 15, 1864; mustered out with company, June 3, 1865, near Washington, D.C.

CULLEN, MICHAEL.—Age, 35 years. Enlisted, August 18, 1862, at Newburgh, to serve three years; mustered in as private, Co. K, September 5, 1862; mustered out with company, June 3, 1865, near Washington, D.C.

CULLINS, THOMAS.—Age, 22 years. Enlisted at Goshen, to serve one year, and mustered in as private, Co. D, September 12, 1864; mustered out with company, June 3, 1865, near Washington, D.C.; also borne as Collins.

CULVER, GEORGE.—Age, 18 years. Enlisted, August 11, 1862, at Goshen, to serve three years; mustered in as private, Co. I, September 5, 1862; wounded in action, May 3, 1863, at Chancellorsville, Va.; transferred to Veteran Reserve Corps, April 28, 1864.

CUMMINS, FRANCIS M.—Age, 39 years. Enrolled at Goshen, to serve three years, and mustered in as lieutenant-colonel, August 16, 1862; wounded in action, July 2, 1863, at Gettysburg, Pa.; mustered in as colonel, February 11, 1864; wounded in action, May 6, 1864, at the Wilderness, Va.; discharged for wounds, September 19, 1864; prior service as captain Tenth U.S. Infantry. Commissioned lieutenant-colonel, September 10, 1862, with rank from August 16, 1862, original; colonel, October 6, 1863, with rank from July 2, 1863, vice A.V.H. Ellis, killed in action.

CUNANN, PATRICK.—Age, 30 years. Enlisted, August 18, 1862, at Newburgh, to serve three years; mustered in as private, Co. K, September 5, 1862; captured in action, June 1, 1864, at Totopotomoy Creek, Va.; paroled, no date; mustered out, July 5, 1865, at New York City, as Cunneen.

CUNNINGHAM, JAMES.—Age, 22 years. Enlisted, August 15, 1862, at Port Jervis, to serve three years; mustered in as private, Co. F, September 5, 1862; wounded in action, May 3, 1863, at Chancellorsville, Va.; absent temporarily in Veteran Reserve Corps since and at muster-out of company.

CURREN, GILES.—Age, 33 years. Enlisted, August 22, 1862, at Newburgh, to serve three years; mustered in as private, Co. I, September 5, 1862; wounded in action, July 30, 1864, at Deep Bottom, Va.; died of his wounds, August 25, 1864, in hospital, at Alexandria, Va.

CURRIE, DAVID.—Age, 41 years. Enlisted, August 26, 1862, at Goshen, to serve three years; mustered in as private, Co. D, September 5, 1862; wounded in action, July 2, 1863, at Gettysburg, Pa.; mustered out with company, June 3, 1865, near Washington, D.C.; also borne as Curry.

CURRY, JAMES.—Age, 18 years. Enlisted, August 7, 1862, at Cornwall, to serve three years; mustered in as private, Co. C, September 5, 1862; died of typhoid fever, February 17, 1863, at hospital, near Falmouth, Va.

CURRY, JOHN.—Age, 21 years. Enlisted, August 15, 1862, at Port Jervis, to serve three years; mustered in as private, Co. F, September 5, 1862; deserted, August 23, 1862, from camp, at Goshen, N.Y.

DAILY, JEREMIAH.—Age, 19 years. Enlisted at Goshen, to serve one year, and mustered in as private, Co. D, September 19, 1864; mustered out with company, June 3, 1865, near Washington, D.C.

DALEY, ISAAC W.—Age, 21 years. Enlisted, August 9, 1862, at Mount Hope, to serve three years; mustered in as private, Co. E, September 5, 1862; wounded in action, May 3, 1863, at Chancellorsville, Va.; deserted, September 1863, from Chestnut Hill Hospital, Philadelphia, Pa.

DALEY, WILLIAM J.—Age, 23 years. Enlisted, August 11, 1862, at Otisville, to serve three years; mustered in as private, Co. E, September 5, 1862; promoted corporal, prior to April 10, 1863; killed in action, May 3, 1863, at Chancellorsville, Va.

DANIELS, JAMES E.—Age, 33 years. Enlisted, August 15, 1862, at Newburgh, to serve three years; mustered in as private, Co. C, September 5, 1862; wounded in action, May 3, 1863, at Chancellorsville, Va., and August 21, 1864, in front of Petersburg, Va.; absent since and at muster-out of company.

DAVENPORT, SOLOMON.—Age, 25 years. Enlisted at Goshen, to serve one year, and mustered in as private, Co. K, October 6, 1864; killed in action, April 6, 1865, at Sailor's Creek, Va.; also borne as Devenport.

DAVENPORT, SYLVESTER.—Age, 43 years. Enlisted, August 7, 1862, at Newburgh, to serve three years; mustered in as private, Co. A, September 5, 1862; deserted, September 1862, at Goshen, N.Y.

DAVEY, JOSEPH—Age, 21 years. Enlisted, August 6, 1862, at Florida, to serve three years; mustered in as private, Co. A, September 5, 1862; promoted corporal, September 15, 1862; wounded in action, May 3, 1863, at Chancellorsville, Va.; transferred to Veteran Reserve Corps, February 2, 1865.

DAVIS, CHARLES W.—Age, 23 years. Enlisted, August 8, 1862, at Goshen, to serve three years; mustered in as private, Co. D, September 5, 1862; mustered out with company, June 3, 1865, near Washington, D.C.

DAVIS, GEORGE.—Age, 23 years. Enlisted at Warwick, to serve one year, and mustered in as private, Co. D. September 3, 1864; mustered out with company, June 3, 1865, near Washington, D.C.

DAVIS, HOWLAND W.—Age, 21 years. Enlisted, August 13, 1862, at Walden, to serve three years; mustered in as corporal, Co. H, September 5, 1862; died of typhoid fever, December 28, 1862, at Falmouth, Va.

DAVIS, JONAS G.—Age, 27 years. Enlisted, August 7, 1862, at Cornwall, to serve three years; mustered in as corporal, Co. C, September 5, 1862; discharged for disability, March 20, 1863, at Falmouth, Va.

DAVIS, WILLIAM.—Age, 21 years. Enlisted at Schenectady, to serve three years, and mustered in as private, Co. E, August 27, 1864; transferred to Co. E, Ninety-third Infantry, June 1, 1865.

DAVIS, WILLIAM.—Age, 32 years. Enlisted, March 31, 1864, at Mount Hope, to serve three years; mustered in as private, Co. I, April 1, 1864; deserted, April 30, 1864.

DAVY, SETH M—Age, 20 years. Enlisted at Minisink, to serve one year, and mustered in as private, Co. K, August 17, 1864; mustered out with company, June 3, 1865, near Washington, D.C., as Davie.

DAWKINS, WILLIAM H.—Age, 21 years. Enlisted, August 13, 1862, at Blooming Grove, to serve three years; mustered in as private, Co. G, September 5, 1862; wounded and missing in action since July 2, 1863, at Gettysburg, Pa., and at muster-out of company; supposed dead.

DAWSON, JOSIAH.—Age, 19 years. Enlisted, August 13, 1862, at Walden, to serve three years; mustered in as private, Co. H, September 5, 1862; wounded in action, May 3, 1863, at Chancellorsville, Va.; wounded and captured in action, May 8, 1864, at Spotsylvania, Va.; paroled, November 20, 1864; promoted sergeant, March 20, 1865; mustered out with company, June 3, 1865, near Washington, D.C.

DAWSON, THORNTON.—Age, 29 years. Enlisted, August 13, 1862, at Walden, to serve three years; mustered in as corporal, Co. H, September 5, 1862; returned to ranks, no date; transferred to Co. F, Eighteenth Regiment, Veteran Reserve Corps, March 1, 1864; mustered out with detachment, June 27, 1865, at Washington, D.C.

DAWSON, WILLIAM.—Age, 23 years. Enlisted, August 13, 1862, at Walden, to serve three years; mustered in as private, Co. H, September 5, 1862; transferred to Thirty-seventh Company, Second Battalion, Veteran Reserve Corps, March 15, 1865; mustered out as sergeant with detachment, June 28, 1865, at Washington, D.C.

DAWSON, WILLIAM H.—Age, 29 years. Enlisted, August 14, 1862 at Walden, to serve three years; mustered in as private, Co. H[?]. September 5, 1862; wounded in action, May 3, 1863, at Chancellorsville, Va.; discharged July 25, 1864.

DEAN, WILLIAM M.—Age, 23 years. Enlisted at Plattsburg, to serve one year and mustered in as private, Co. E, September 15, 1864; mustered out, May 26, 1865, at Albany, N.Y.

DECKER, GARRET.—Age, 18 years. Enlisted at New Windsor, to serve three years and mustered in as private, Co. D, January 15, 1864; wounded in action, May 6, 1864, at the Wilderness, Va., and June 6, 1864, at Cold Harbor, Va.; transferred to Sixteenth Company, Second Battalion, Veteran Reserve Corps, March 21, 1865; discharged for disability, June 23, 1865, at Lincoln Hospital, Washington, D.C.

DECKER, GEORGE W.—Age, 25 years. Enlisted, August 12, 1862, at Goshen, to serve three years; mustered in as private, Co. D, September 5, 1862; wounded in action, May 3, 1863, at Chancellorsville, Va., and May 12, 1864, at Spotsylvania, Va.; transferred to Co. G, Tenth Regiment, Veteran Reserve Corps, January 26, 1865; mustered out with detachment, June 28, 1865, at Washington, D.C.

DECKER, ISAAC.—Age, 24 years. Enlisted, August 31, 1862, at Goshen, to serve three years; mustered in as private, Co. K, September 5, 1862; promoted corporal, January 1, 1863; wounded in action, May 3, 1863, at Chancellorsville, Va.; killed in action, July 2, 1863, at Gettysburg, Pa.

DECKER, ISAAC.—Age, 33 years. Enlisted, August 11, 1862, at Washingtonville, to serve three years; mustered in as corporal, Co. G, September 5, 1862; promoted sergeant prior to April 10, 1863; wounded in action, July 2, 1863, at Gettysburg, Pa.; died of his wounds, August 9, 1864, at Davids' Island, New York Harbor.

DECKER, STEPHEN.—Age,23 years. Enlisted, August 11, 1862, at Warwick, to serve three years; mustered in as private, Co. G, September 5, 1862; discharged December 19, 1862, at hospital, Baltimore, Md.

DECKER, WILLIAM.—Age, 24 years. Enlisted, August 8, 1862, at Forestburgh to serve three years; mustered in as private, Co. E, September 5, 1802; discharged, April 1, 1863, near Falmouth, Va.

DECKER, WILLIAM H.—Age, 22 years. Enlisted, August 5, 1862, at Monroe, to serve three years; mustered in as private, Co. C, September 5, 1862; mustered out with company, June 3, 1865, near Washington, D.C.

DECKER, WILLIAM W.—Age, 23 years. Enlisted, August 12, 1862, at Port Jervis, to serve three years; mustered in as corporal, Co. F, September 5, 1862; died of typhoid fever, December 24, 1862, at camp, near Falmouth, Va.

DEGRAW, JOHN C.—Age, 34 years. Enlisted, August 11, 1862, at Goshen, to serve three years; mustered in as private, Co. D, September 5, 1862; wounded in action, July 2, 1863, at Gettysburg, Pa., and May 12, 1864, at Spotsylvania, Va.; mustered out May 22, 1865, at New York City.

DEGRAW, JOHN, 3d.—Age, 20 years. Enlisted, August 11, 1862, at Goshen, to serve three years; mustered in as private, Co. D, September 5, 1862; absent, sick in Second Division Hospital at Alexandria, Va., since October 1864, and at muster-out of company.

DEGRAW, SWEEZY.—Age, 21 years. Enlisted, August 15, 1862, at Goshen, to serve three years; mustered in as private, Co. C, September 5, 1862; discharged for disability, April 16, 1863, at Falmouth, Va.

DEGRAW, THOMAS J.—Age, 18 years. Enlisted, August 13, 1862, at Chester, to serve three years; mustered in as private, Co. G, September 5, 1862; deserted, September 1862, at Goshen, N.Y.

DEGROAT, HIRAM W.— Age, 23 years. Enlisted, August 21, 1862, at New Windsor, to serve three years; mustered in as private, Co. G, September 5, 1862; deserted January 1863; also borne as Degroot.

DEGROAT, NELSON.— Age, 34 years. Enlisted, August 22, 1862, at Goshen, to serve three years; mustered in as private, Co. G, September 5, 1862; died, January 4, 1864, at New Windsor, N. Y, while home on furlough; also borne as Degroott.

De HART, EDWARD.— Age, 18 years. Enlisted at Goshen, to serve one year, and mustered in as private, Co. K, August 25, 1864; mustered out with detachment, June 9, 1865, at Columbian Hospital, Washington, D.C.

DE HART, JOHN.— Age, 19 years. Enlisted at Goshen, to serve one year and mustered in as private, Co. K, August 20, 1864; mustered out with company, June 3, 1865, near Washington, D.C.

DELEMATER, JOSEPH W.— Age, 42 years. Enlisted, August 13, 1862, at Walden, to serve three years; mustered in as private, Co. H, September 5, 1862; wounded in action, May 3, 1863, at Chancellorsville, Va.; died of his wounds, May 26, 1863, in hospital.

De LONG, AMOS.— Age, 36 years. Enlisted, at Poughkeepsie, to serve one year, and mustered in as private, Co. D, September 21, 1864; wounded in action, April 6, 1865, at Sailors Creek, Va.; mustered out with company, June 3, 1865, near Washington, D.C.

DENNEY, ABRAHAM.— Age, 29 years. Enlisted, August 5, 1862, at Washingtonville, to serve three years; mustered in as private, Co. G, September 5, 1862; promoted corporal, January 1, 1863; sergeant, January 1, 1864; first sergeant, April 1, 1865; mustered out with company, June 3, 1865, near Washington, D.C.; also borne as Abram.

DENNISTON, AUGUSTUS.— Age, — years. Enrolled at Goshen, to serve three years and mustered in as first lieutenant and quartermaster, July 15, 1862; discharged for disability, January 14, 1863.

DENNISTON, JAMES OTIS.— Age, 26 years. Enrolled at Goshen, to serve three years, and mustered in as first lieutenant, Co. G, August 20, 1862; wounded in action, July 2, 1863, at Gettysburg, Pa.; mustered in as captain, July 3, 1863; discharged, October 7, 1863.

DENTON, JACOB.— Age, 27 years. Enlisted, August 15, 1862, at Wallkill, to serve three years; mustered in as first sergeant, Co. K, September 5, 1862; killed in action; May 3, 1863, at Chancellorsville, Va.

DERWIN, THOMAS.— Age, 18 years. Enlisted at Vernon, to serve one year, and mustered in as private, Co. A, September 23, 1864; mustered out with company, June 3, 1865, near Washington, D.C.

DEWITT, DAVID W.— Age, — years. Enlisted at Camp Ellis, Va., to serve three 3 years, and mustered in as private, Co. G, September 16, 1862; killed in action, July 24, 1863, at Manassas Gap, Va.; prior service in Co. I, Seventy-first Militia.

DEZENDORF, FREDERICK.— Age, 23 years. Enlisted, August 9, 1862, at Cornwall, to serve three years; mustered in as private, Co. C, September 5, 1862; wounded in action, May 3, 1863, at Chancellorsville, Va.; captured in action, June 1, 1864, at Totopotomoy Creek, Va.; released, April 28, 1865; mustered out, June 22, 1865, at New York City; also borne as Devendorf.

DICKSON, FRANCIS.— Age, 21 years. Enlisted, August 28, 1862, at New Windsor, to serve three years; mustered in as private Co. I, September 5, 1862; deserted, September 5, 1862, at Goshen, N.Y.; also borne as Dixson.

DILL, ERASTUS.— Age, 21 years. Enlisted, September 21, 1864, at Kingston, to serve one year; mustered in as private, Co. D, September 26, 1864; mustered out with detachment, June 15, 1865, at White Hall Hospital, Philadelphia, Pa.

DILL, HENRY.— Age, 31 years. Enlisted, August 9, 1862, at Blooming Grove, to serve three years; mustered in as private, Co. G, September 5, 1862; wounded and captured in action, May 6, 1864, at the Wilderness, Va.; paroled, prior to April 1865; discharged for disability, May 17, 1865, at Philadelphia, Pa.

DILL, NORMAN L.— Age, 24 years. Enlisted, August 7, 1862, at Goshen, to serve three years; mustered in as private, Co. D, September 5, 1862; wounded in action, May 3, 1863, at Chancellorsville, Va.; transferred to Co. C, Nineteenth Regiment, Veteran Reserve Corps, July 1863; mustered out with detachment, July 13, 1865, at Elmira, N.Y.

DILL, WILLIAM H.— Age, 21 years. Enlisted, August 8, 1862, at Goshen, to serve three years; mustered in as first sergeant, Co. D, September 5, 1862; returned to ranks, no date; wounded in action, May 6, 1864, at the Wilderness, Va.; discharged, August 10, 1864, for promotion to first lieutenant, One Hundred and Eighteenth U.S. Colored Troops.

DIMMICK, GEORGE W.— Age, 18 years. Enlisted, August 19, 1862. at Goshen, to serve three years; mustered in as musician, Co. D, September 5, 1862; mustered out with company, June 3, 1865, near Washington, D.C.

DINGEE, JOHN H.— Age, 18 years. Enlisted, August 11, 1862, at Goshen to serve three years; mustered in as private Co. A, September 5,

1st Sergeant William H. Dill, Company D, was wounded in action after being returned to the ranks May 6, 1864, at the Wilderness, and discharged August 10, 1864, for promotion to 1st lieutenant with the 118th U.S. Colored Troops (archive of the Historical Society of the Town of Warwick, gift of Joan and Tom Frangos).

1862; promoted corporal September 1, 1864; sergeant February 8, 1865, mustered out with company, June 3, 1865 near Washington, D.C.

DODGE, SAMUEL.— Age, 30 years. Enlisted, August 13, 1802, at Newburgh, to serve three years; mustered in as private, Co. C, September 5, 1862; killed in action, May 3, 1863, at Chancellorsville, Va.

DOLAND, WILLIAM.— Age, 25 years. Enlisted at Goshen, to serve one year, and mustered in as private, Co. K. September [?] 1864; mustered out with company, June 3, 1865, near Washington, D.C., as Dolan.

DOLD, GEORGE.— Age, 35 years. Enlisted at Wheatfield, to serve one year, and mustered in as private, Co. C, October 4, 1864; died of typhoid fever, November 25, 1864, at Corps Hospital, City Point, Va., as Dolt.

DOLSON, JESSANIAH.— Age, 20 years. Enlisted, August 9, 1862, at Goshen, to serve three years; mustered in as private, Co. D, September 5, 1862; wounded in action, May 3, 1863, at Chancellorsville, Va., and May 6, 1864, at the Wilderness, Va.; died of his wounds, May 25, 1864; also borne as Dolsen and Dolsin.

DOLSON, THEOPHILUS.— Age, 19 years. Enlisted, August 9, 1862, at Mount Hope, to serve three years; mustered in as corporal, Co. E, September 5, 1862; promoted first sergeant, prior to October 1864; mustered out with company, June 3, 1805, near Washington, D.C., as Dolsen; also borne as Dalson.

DOLSON, WILLIAM.— Age, 22 years. Enlisted, August 7, 1862, at Goshen, to serve three years; mustered in as private, Co. D, September 5, 1862; discharged, April 11, 1863; also borne as Dolsin and Dolsen.

DOOLING, ROBERT.— Private, Co. —, One hundred and Sixty-second Infantry; transferred to Co. C, this regiment, May 17, 1865; mustered out with company, June 3, 1865, near Washington, D.C.

DOTY, ORSIN E.— Private. Co. K, First U.S. Sharpshooters; transferred to Co. H, this regiment, March 1, 1865; absent missing in action, since October 27, 1864, at Boydton Road, Va., and at muster-out of company.

DOTY, REUBEN.— Age, 26 years. Enlisted, August 12, 1862, at Port Jervis, to serve three years; mustered in as private, Co. F, September 5, 1862; wounded in action, May 3, 1863, at Chancellorsville, Va.; transferred to Veteran Reserve Corps, no date; transferred to this regiment, October 1864; mustered out with company, June 3, 1865, near Washington, D.C.

DOUGHERTY, JOHN.— Age, 33 years. Enlisted at Sullivan, to serve three years; mustered in as private, Co. C, September 24, 1864; transferred to Co. A, Ninety-third Infantry, June 1, 1865.

DOUGHERTY, WILLIAM L.— Age, 26 Years. Enlisted, August 12, 1862, at Newburgh, to serve three years; mustered in as private, Co. E, September 5, 1862; wounded in action, May 3, 1863, at Chancellorsville, Va.; captured in action, October 27, 1864, at Boydton Road, Va.; no further record.

DOWNING, CHARLES.— Age, 26 years. Enlisted, September 2, 1862, at New Windsor, to serve three years; mustered in as private, Co. E, September 5, 1862; mustered out with company, June 3, 1865, near Washington, D.C.

DOYLE, JOHN.— Age, 29 years. Enlisted at Cambria, to serve one year, and mustered in as private, Co. A, October 1, 1864; absent, sick in hospital since and at muster-out of company.

DRAKE, ABRAHAM T.— Age, 26 years. Enlisted, August 12, 1862, at Port Jervis, to serve three years; mustered in as private, Co. F, September 5, 1862; transferred to Co. D, Twenty-fourth regiment Veteran Reserve Corps, March 7, 1864; mustered out with detachment, June 27, 1865, at Washington, D.C.; also borne as Abram T.

DRAKE, JOHN D.— Age, 22 years. Enlisted, August 9, 1862, at Port Jervis, to serve three years; mustered in as sergeant, Co. F, September 5, 1862; promoted first sergeant, prior to April 10, 1863; killed in action, July 2, 1863, at Gettysburg, Pa.

DRAKE, JOHN Z.— Age, 22 years. Enlisted, August 15, 1862, at Port Jervis, to serve three years; mustered in as private, Co. F, September 5, 1862; mustered out, June 7, 1863, at Satterlee Hospital West Philadelphia, Pa.; also borne as John C.

DRAKE, NICHOLAS C.— Age, 38 years. Enlisted, August 15, 1862, at Newburgh, to serve three years; mustered in as private, Co. K, September 5, 1862; discharged for disability, January 28, 1863, at Philadelphia, Pa.

DRAKE, WILLIAM W.— Age, 18 years. Enlisted, August 11, 1862, at Crawford, to serve three years; mustered in as private, Co. E, September 5,1862; discharged, November 8, 1862, at Washington, D.C.

DRILLING, HENRY.— Age, 30 years. Enlisted at Cambria, to serve one year; mustered in as private Co. C, September 27, 1864; wounded in action, October 27, 1864, at Boydton Road, Va.; died of his wounds, November 21, 1864, at Armory Square Hospital, Washington, D.C.

DUFFIE, JOHN.— Age, 21 years. Enlisted, August 13, 1862, at Walden, to serve three years; mustered in as private, Co. H, September 5, 1862; appointed wagoner prior to April 10, 1863; grade changed to private, October 1864; again appointed wagoner prior to April 1864; mustered out with company, June 3, 1865, near Washington, D.C.

DUFFIE, NATHAN H.— Age, 32 years. Enlisted, August 13, 1862, at Walden, to serve three years; mustered in as private Co. H, September 5, 1862; discharged, February 17, 1863, at Camden Street Hospital, Baltimore, Md.

DUGAN, DANIEL, P.— Age, 19 years. Enlisted, August 9, 1862, at Goshen, to serve three years; mustered in as private Co. D, September 5, 1862; wounded in action, May 3, 1861, at Chancellorsville, Va., and May 6, 1864, at the Wilderness, Va.; transferred to Co. E, Nineteenth Regiment Veteran Reserve Corps, no date; mustered out with detachment, July 13, 1865, at Elmira, N.Y.

DUNLAP, NELSON.— Age, 31 years. Enlisted, August 12, 1862, at Port Jervis, to serve three years; mustered in as private Co. F, September 5, 1862; discharged for disability, April 1, 1863, near Bellair, Va.

DUNMOODY, GEORGE.— Age, 20 years. Enlisted, August 12, 1862, at Mamakating, to serve three years; mustered in as private, Co. E, September 5, 1862; discharged, December 17, 1862, at Washington, D.C.; also borne as Dunumoody.

DUNN, EDWARD F.— Private Co. K, First United States Sharpshooters; transferred to Co. H, this regiment, March 1, 1865; mustered out with company, June 3, 1865, near Washington, D.C.

DUTCHER, BENJAMIN.— Age, 20 years. Enlisted, August 14, 1862, at Walden, to serve three years; mustered in as private, Co. H., September 5, 1862; promoted corporal prior to April 10, 1863; wounded in action, May 3, 1863, at Chancellorsville, Va.; killed in action, May 6, 1864, at the Wilderness, Va.

DUZENBERRY, ZENEPHON.— Age, 40 years. Enlisted, August 21, 1862, at New Windsor, to serve three years; mustered in as private, Co. E, September 5, 1862; promoted corporal, no date; discharged, April 1, 1863, near Falmouth, Va.

EAGER, AMOS M.— Age, 25 years. Enlisted, August 6, 1862, at Newburgh, to serve three years; mustered in as sergeant, Co. I, September 5, 1862; wounded in action, July 2, 1863, at Gettysburg, Pa.; transferred to Veteran Reserve Corps, March 16, 1864.

EAKLEY, HEZEKIAH.— Age, 21 years. Enlisted, August 8, 1862, at Chester, to serve three years; mustered in as teamster, Co. A, September 5, 1862; transferred to Thirty-sixth Infantry, December, 1862, as a deserter there from, but never joined; also borne as Ackley and Akeley.

EARL, EDWARD.— Age, 24 years. Enlisted at Warwick, to serve one year and mustered in as private, Co. G, September 5, 1864; mustered out with company, June 3, 1865, near Washington, D.C.

EASTON, EDWIN H.— Age, 18 years. Enlisted at Ward, to serve one year and mustered in as private, Co. I, October 3, 1861; transferred to Co. D, Ninety-third Infantry, June 1, 1863.

ECKER, HENRY C.— Private, Co. K, First United States Sharpshooters; transferred to Co. H, this regiment, March 1, 1865; mustered out with company, June 3, 1865, near Washington, D.C., as Henry W.

ECKERT, JOHN.— Age, 21 years. Enlisted, August 4, 1862, to serve three years; mustered in as private Co. B, September 5, 1862; promoted sergeant, no date; wounded in action, May 12, 1864, at Spotsylvania, Va., and June 18, 1864, before Petersburg, Va.; discharged, April 18, 1865, at Lovell Hospital, Portsmouth Grove, R.I.

EDGAR, WILLIAM.— Age, 26 years. Enlisted, August 18, 1862, at Newburgh, to serve three years; mustered in as private, Co. I, September 5, 1862; killed in action, May 15, 1864, at Spotsylvania, Va.

EDSALL, WILLIAM.— Age, 32 years. Enlisted at Warwick, to serve one year and mustered in as private Co. D, September 3, 1864; mustered out with company, June 3, 1865, near Washington, D.C.

EDWARDS, CHARLES.— Age, 40 years. Enlisted, August 19, 1862, at New Windsor, to serve three years; mustered in as private, Co. I, September 5, 1862; killed in action, July 2, 1863, at Gettysburg, Pa.

EDWARDS, GEORGE W.— Age, 26 years. Enlisted, August 9, 1862, at Goshen, to serve three years; mustered in as private, Co. A, September 5, 1862; promoted corporal, December 15, 1862; mustered out with company, June 3, 1865, near Washington, D.C.

EDWARDS, JOHN.— Age, 36 years. Enlisted, August 23, 1862, at Goshen, to serve three years; mustered in as private, Co. D, September 5, 1862; wounded in action, November 30, 1863, at Mine Run, Va., and May 6, 1864, at the Wilderness, Va.; died of his wounds, May 30, 1864, at Washington, D.C.

EDWARDS, NATHAN.— Age, 21 years. Enlisted, August 15, 1862, at Cornwall, to serve three years; mustered in as private, Co. C, September 5, 1862; wounded in action, July 2, 1863, at Gettysburg, Pa.; promoted corporal, December, 1864; returned to ranks, May 1, 1865; mustered out with company, June 3, 1865, near Washington, D.C.

ELLIS, A. VAN HORNE.— Age, — years. Enrolled, August 23, 1862, at Goshen, to serve three years; mustered in as colonel, September 5, 1862; killed in action, July 2, 1863, at Gettysburg, Pa.; prior service as captain, Co. I, Seventy-first Militia. Commissioned colonel, September 10, 1862, with rank from August 23, 1862, original.

ELLIS, WILLIAM L.— Age, 26 years. Enlisted, March 29, 1864, at Blooming Grove, to serve three years; mustered in as private, Co. I, March 30, 1864; deserted, April 30, 1864.

ELLISON, ISAAC.— Age, 32 years. Enlisted, August 22, 1862, at Newburgh, to serve three years; mustered in as private, Co. I, September 5, 1862; promoted corporal, no date; hospital steward, February 11, 1863; died, August 26, 1863, in camp, at Sulpher Springs, Va.

ELLISTON, GEORGE, W.— Age, 18 years. Enlisted at Goshen, to serve three years and mustered in as private, Co. K, August 25, 1864; mustered out with company, June 3, 1865, near Washington, D.C.

ELSTON, CHAUNCEY A.— Age, 19 years. Enlisted, August 15, 1862, at Port Jervis, to serve three years; mustered in as private, Co. F, September 5, 1862; discharged for disability, April 18, 1863, near Bellair, Va.

ELSTON, LEMUEL E.— Age, 33 years. Enlisted, August 13, 1862, at Port Jervis, to serve three years; mustered in as first sergeant, Co. F, September 5, 1862, discharged for disability, January 1, 1863, at College Hospital, Washington, D.C.

EMMONDS, WILLIAM.— Age, 18 years. Enlisted at Mentz, to serve one year and mustered in as private, Co. I, August 22, 1864; mustered out with company, June 3, 1865, near Washington, D.C., as Emmons.

ENSIGN, CHARLES A.— Age, 18 years. Enlisted, August 19, 1862, at Newburgh, to serve three years; mustered in as private, Co. G, September 5, 1862; promoted corporal prior to October 1864; returned to ranks, March 12, 1865; promoted sergeant, May 1, 1865; mustered out with company, June 3, 1865, near Washington, D.C.; also borne as Charles T.

ESTABROOK, HORATIO J.— Age, 26 years. Enlisted, August 14, 1862, at Newburgh, to serve three years; mustered in as sergeant, Co. G, September 5, 1862; wounded and captured in action, May 3, 1863, at Chancellorsville, Va.; paroled prior to August 1, 1863; absent at Summit House Hospital, Philadelphia. Pa., since October 1864, and at muster-out of company.

ESTABROOK, SANFORD T.— Age, 23 years. Enlisted, August 14, 1862, at Newburgh, to serve three years; mustered in as corporal, Co. G, September 5, 1862; captured in action, May 3, at Chancellorsville, Va.; paroled, May 14, 1863, at Belle Island, Va.; promoted sergeant, no date; wounded in action, 1864, at the Wilderness, Va.; died of his wounds, August 12, 1864, at Davids' Island, New York Harbor.

EVANS, CHARLES W.— Age, 26 years. Enlisted, August 13, 1862, at Walden, to serve three years; mustered in as private, Co. H, September 5, 1862; discharged, March 2, 1863, at Harewood Hospital, Washington, D.C.

EVERETT, CHARLES M .— Age, 18 years. Enlisted, August 9, 1862, at Wallkill, to serve three years; mustered in as private, Co. E, September 5, 1862; wounded in action, May 3, 1863, at Chancellorsville, Va.; transferred to Veteran Reserve Corps, May 1, 1864.

EVERETT, CHARLES M.— Age, 20 years. Enlisted, August 23, 1864, at Goshen, to serve one year; mustered in as private, Co. E, August 29, 1864; mustered out with company, June 3, 1865, near Washington, D.C.; also borne as Everitte.

EVERETT, MARTIN.— Age, 27 years. Enlisted at Monroe to serve three years and mustered in as private, Co. B, January 13, 1864; wounded in action, May 12, 1864, at Spotsylvania Court House Va.; discharged for wounds, October 1, 1864, at De Camp Hospital, Davids' Island, New York Harbor; also borne as Evert.

EWALT, LOUIS.— Age, 28 years. Enlisted at Wheatfield, to serve one year and mustered in as private, Co. C, October 5, 1864; transferred to Co. A, Ninety-third Infantry, June 1, 1865, as Ewald; also borne as Erralt.

FABOUR, PETER G.— Age, 44 years. Enlisted at Plattsburgh to serve one year, and mustered in as private, Co. E, September 13, 1864; mustered out, May 31, 1865, at Elmira, N.Y., as Faborow; also borne as Fabron.

FAIRCHILD, LYMAN.— Age, 36 years. Enlisted, August 13, 1862, at Walden, to serve three years; mustered in as private, Co. H. September 5, 1862; wounded in action, May 6, 1864, at the Wilderness, Va.; died of his wounds, May 18, 1864.

FAIRCHILD, ROBERT.— Age, 37 years. Enlisted, August 4, 1862, at Washingtonville, to serve three years; mustered in as sergeant, Co. G, September 5, 1862; discharged for fever sore, September 8, 1863, at hospital, Philadelphia, Pa.

FAIRCHILD, WILLIAM L.— Age, 21 years. Enlisted, August 3, 1862, at Walden, to serve three years; mustered in as corporal, Co. H, September 5, 1862; returned to ranks, no date; killed in action, May 3, 1863, at Chancellorsville, Va.

FARLEY, THOMAS.— Age, 18 years. Enlisted, August 14, 1862, at Newburgh, to serve three years; mustered in as private, Co. I, September 5, 1862; mustered out with detachment, June 5, 1865, at Lincoln Hospital, Washington, D.C.

FARRALL, JOHN.— Age, 22 years. Enlisted at Goshen to serve one year, and mustered in as private, Co. K, September 3, 1864; mustered out with company, June 3, 1865, near Washington, D.C., as Farrell.

FARRELL, JOHN.— Age, 19 years. Enlisted at Rochester to serve three years and mustered in as private, Co. A, September 23, 1864; transferred to Co. E, Ninety-third Infantry, June 1, 1865.

FAULKNER, WILLIAM H.— Age, 22 years. Enlisted, August 6, 1862, at Wallkill, to serve three years; mustered in as corporal, Co. K, September 5, 1862; returned to ranks, July 1, 1863; missing in action, May 12, 1864, at Spotsylvania Court House, Va.; absent since and at muster-out of company as Falkuer; reported killed.

FEHR, JOHN.— Private, Co. K, First United States Sharpshooters; transferred while prisoner of war since June 22, 1864, to Co. H, this regiment, March 1, 1865, and to Co. D, Ninety-third Infantry, June 1, 1865; also borne Fihe.

FENTON, ELIJAH.— Age, 44 years. Enlisted, August 19, 1862, at Washingtonville, to serve three years; mustered in as private, Co. G, September 5, 1862; discharged, April 20, 1863, at Falmouth, Va.; also borne as Finton.

FERGUSON, ISAAC.— Age, 41 years. Enlisted, August 4, 1862, at Goshen, to serve three years; mustered in as private, Co. E, September 5, 1862; died of consumption, December 11, 1862, in camp, near Falmouth, Va.

FINCH, JOHN H.— Age, 32 years. Enlisted, August 21, 1862, at Goshen to serve three years; mustered in as private, Co. C, September 5, 1862; appointed wagoner, prior to August, 1863; wounded in action, May 12, 1864, at Spotsylvania Court House, Va.; mustered out as private, with company, June 3, 1865, near Washington, D.C.

FINCH, JOHN H.— Age, 30 years. Enlisted at Goshen, to serve one year, and mustered in as private, Co. C, August 23, 1864; mustered out with company, June 3, 1865, near Washington, D.C.

FINLEY, JAMES.— Age, 21 years. Enlisted, August 11, 1862, at Goshen to serve three years; mustered in as private, Co. B, September 5, 1862; promoted corporal, prior to April 10, 1863; transferred to Veteran Reserve Corps, September 1, 1863.

FINNEGAN, JOHN.— Age, 20 years. Enlisted at Rochester, to serve three years, and mustered in as private Co. C, October 5, 1864; deserted, October 17, 1864.

FINNEY, HECTOR.— Age, 18 years. Enlisted, August 20, 1862, at Goshen, to serve three years; mustered in as private, Co. G, September 5, 1862; wounded and captured in action, May 3, 1863, at Chancellorsville, Va.; paroled, May 14, 1863; wounded in action, May 6, 1864, at the Wilderness, Va.; promoted corporal, March 12, 1865; mustered out with company, June 3, 1865, near Washington, D.C.

FINNIGAN, JAMES.— Age, 24 years. Enrolled, August 23, 1862, at Goshen, to serve three years; mustered in as second lieutenant, Co. K, September 5, 1862; as first lieutenant, March 7, 1863; wounded in action, July 2, 1863, at Gettysburg, Pa.; mustered in as captain, Co. C, February 18, 1864; wounded in action, October 27, 1864, at Boydton Plank Road, Va.; died of his wounds, October 28, 1864; also borne as Finnegan.

FISHER, CHARLES P. F.— Age, 28 years. Enlisted at Lovettsville, to serve three years, and mustered in as private, Co. C, October 28, 1862; wounded and captured in action, May 12, 1864, at Spotsylvania Court House, Va.; died, June 1864, at Andersonville, Ga.

FISHER, JOHN T .— Age, 21 years. Enlisted. August 13, 1862, at Port Jervis, to serve three years; mustered in as private, Co. F, September 5, 1862; wounded in action, May 3, 1863, at Chancellorsville, Va.; mustered out, May 22, 1863, at McClellan Hospital, Philadelphia, Pa.

FISHER, RINEER.— Age, 39 years. Enlisted at Goshen, to serve one year, and mustered in as private, Co. K, September 8, 1864; mustered out with company, June 3, 1865, near Washington, D.C.; also borne as Reuben Fisher.

FITZGERALD, GEORGE R.— Age, 19 years. Enlisted, August 20, 1862, at Goshen, to serve three years; mustered in as private, Co. G, September 5, 1862; promoted corporal, no date; wounded in action, June 4, 1864, at Cold Harbor, Va.; returned to ranks, July 1, 1864; mustered out with company, June 3, 1865, near Washington, D.C.

FITZGIBBONS, PATRICK.—Age, 33 years. Enlisted, August 23, 1862, at New Windsor, to serve three years; mustered in as private, Co. I, September 5, 1862; deserted, October 14, 1862, from Camp Ellis, Va.

FIXEL, JOHAN.—Age, 41 years. Enlisted, August 2, 1862, at Cornwall, to serve three years; mustered in as private, Co. C, September 5, 1862; absent, sick in hospital, since April 18, 1863, and at muster-out of company.

FLAGG, BENJAMIN P.—Age, 20 years. Enlisted, August 15, 1862, at Goshen, to serve three years; mustered in as private, Co. C, September 5, 1862; killed in action, July 2, 1863, at Gettysburg, Pa.

FLANIGAN, JAMES.—Age, 36 years. Enlisted, August 22, 1862, at Newburgh, to serve three years; mustered in as private Co. K, September 5, 1862; transferred to Co. I, September 22, 1862; wounded in action, April 6, 1865, at Deatonsville Road, Va.; absent, sick in hospital, no date, and at muster-out of company.

FLANNERY, PATRICK.—Age, 19 years. Enlisted, August 13, 1862, at Goshen, to serve three years; mustered in as private, Co. A. September 5, 1862; wounded in action, July 29, 1864, at Deep Bottom, Va.; absent at Beverly Hospital, N. J., since October 1864, and at muster-out of company.

FLINN, ANDREW.—Age, 30 years. Enlisted, August 21, 1862, at Newburgh, to serve three years; mustered in as private, Co. C, September 5, 1862; deserted, October 18, 1862, at Minors Hill, Va.

FLORENCE, GEORGE.—Age, 35 years. Enlisted, August, 14, 1862, at Cornwall, to serve three years; mustered in as private, Co. C, September 5, 1862; transferred to Veteran Reserve Corps, September 30, 1863; retransferred for punishment, February 14, 1864; mustered out, to date, May 5, 1865, at New York City, as George W.

FLYNN, JOHN.—Age, 18 years. Enlisted at Goshen, to serve one year, and mustered in as private, Co. K, September 9, 1864; mustered out with company, June 3, 1865, near Washington, D.C., as Flinn.

FOLEY, HUGH.—Age, 31 years. Enlisted, August 6, 1862, at Wallkill, to serve three years; mustered in as private, Co. K, September 5, 1862; transferred to Veteran Reserve Corps, September 30, 1863.

FOLEY, JOHN W.—Age, 21 years. Enlisted, August 8, 1862, at Newburgh, to serve three years; mustered in as sergeant, Co. C, September 5, 1862; returned to ranks, prior to April 10, 1863; wounded in action, May 3, 1863, at Chancellorsville, Va.; died of his wounds, January 12, 1864, at Newburgh, N.Y.

FOLEY, ROBERT H.—Age, 19 years. Enlisted, July 20, 1862, at Newburgh, to serve three years; mustered in as private, Co. C, September 5, 1862; killed in action, October 27, 1864, at Boydton Road, Va.

FOLEY, THOMAS.—Age, 23 years. Enlisted, July 20, 1862, at Newburgh, to serve three years; mustered in as corporal, Co. C, September 5, 1862; promoted sergeant, prior to April 10, 1863; killed in action, May 3, 1863, at Chancellorsville, Va. (as color bearer).

FOOTE, NELSON.—Age, 26 years. Enlisted, August 13, 1862, at Newburgh, to serve three years; mustered in as corporal, Co. I, September 5, 1862; transferred to Co. C, Nineteenth Regiment Veteran Reserve Corps, November 13, 1863; mustered out with detachment, July 18, 1865, at Elmira, N.Y.

FORCE, JONATHAN.—Age, 20 years. Enlisted, August 12,1862, at Otisville, to serve three years; mustered in as private, Co. E, September 5, 1862; died of fever, January 8, 1863, in hospital at Washington, D.C.

FORSHEE, ABRAM C.—Age, 19 years. Enlisted, August 8, 1862, at Goshen, to serve three years; mustered in as private, Co. D, September 5, 1862; wounded in action, May 3, 1863, at Chancellorsville, Va.; transferred to Forty-eighth Company, Second Battalion, Veteran Reserve Corps, September 11, 1863; mustered out as corporal with detachment, June 26, 1865, at Washington, D.C.

FOSBURGH, WILLIAM.—Age, 25 years. Enlisted, August 15, 1862, at Washingtonville, to serve three years; mustered in as private, Co. G, September 5, 1862; wounded in action, May 3, 1863, at Chancellorsville, Va.; deserted, August 31, 1863, at Philadelphia, Pa.; also borne as Fosbury.

FOSDICK, CHARLES L.—Age, 19 years. Enlisted, August 9, 1862, at Otisville, to serve three years; mustered in as private, Co. E, September 5, 1862; transferred to Veteran Reserve Corps, January 16, 1864.

FOSTER, CHARLES A.—Age, 24 years. Enlisted, August 13, 1862, at Walden, to serve three years; mustered in as private, Co. H, September 5, 1862; killed in action, May 3, 1863, at Chancellorsville, Va.

FOWLER, GEORGE.—Age, 21 years. Enlisted, August 11, 1862, at Newburgh, to serve three years; mustered in as private, Co. I, September 5, 1862; deserted, same date, from Goshen, N.Y.

FOWLER, JOHN S.—Age, 22 years. Enlisted, August 20, 1862, at Newburgh, to serve three years; mustered in as private, Co. I, September 5, 1862; deserted, January 22, 1863, near Falmouth, Va.

FOWLER, LEVI D.—Age, 18 years. Enlisted at Warwick, to serve three years, and mustered in as private Co. D, December 24, 1863; transferred to Co. H, Ninety-third Infantry, June 1, 1865.

FOX, EDWARD C.—Age, 27 years. Enrolled, April 7, 1865, at Burkettsville, Va., to serve three years; mustered in as assistant surgeon, April 14, 1863; mustered out with regiment, June 3, 1865, near Washington, D.C. Commissioned assistant surgeon, April 8, 1865, with rank from April 7, 1865, vice R. V. K. Montfort, promoted.

Assistant Surgeon Edward Fox joined the regiment two days before the war ended (archive of the Historical Society of the Town of Warwick, gift of Joan and Tom Frangos).

FRANCISCO, ABRAM P.— Age, 19 years. Enrolled, August 13 1862, at Port Jervis, to serve three years; mustered in as sergeant Co. F, September 5, 1862; promoted first sergeant, July 1863; mustered in as first lieutenant, January 1, 1865; mustered out with company, June 3, 1865, near Washington, D.C.

FRASHER, HENRY C.— Private, Co. K, First U.S. Sharpshooters; transferred to Co. H, this regiment, March 1, 1865; mustered out, June 6, 1865, at Washington, D.C., while in Augur Hospital, Alexandria, Va.; also borne as Henry M.

FREDERICKS, SAMUEL F.— Age, 28 years. Enlisted at Goshen, to serve one year, and mustered in as private, Co. K, September 13, 1864; mustered out with company, June 3, 1865, near Washington, D.C., as Samuel S.

FREEMAN, ARCHIBALD.— Age 18 years. Enlisted, July 4, 1862, at Newburgh, to serve three years; mustered in as private, Co. E, September 5, 1862; promoted corporal, May 1, 1864; wounded in action, May 12, 1864, at Spotsylvania Court House, Va.; promoted sergeant, March 1, 1865; mustered out with company, June 3, 1865, near Washington, D.C.; awarded medal of honor; also borne as Treman.

FROST, ALONZO S.— Age, 20 years. Enlisted, August 11, 1862, at Wallkill, to serve three years; mustered in as private Co. K, September 5, 1862; mustered out with company, June 3, 1865, near Washington, D.C.

FROST, STEPHEN W.— Age, 31 years. Enlisted, August 15, 1862, at Wallkill to serve three years; mustered in as private Co. K, September 5, 1862; discharged for disability, October 8, 1862, at Washington, D.C.

FULLER AARON W.— Private Co. K, First U.S. Sharpshooters; transferred to Co. H, this regiment, March 1, 1865; mustered out with company, June 3, 1865, near Washington, D.C.

FULLER, GEORGE O.— Age, 23 years. Enlisted, August 25, 1862, at Goshen, to serve three years; mustered in as private, Co. H, September 5, 1862; killed in action, May 3, 1863, at Chancellorsville, Va.

FURGESON, see Ferguson.

FURMANN, WILLIS.— Age, 17 years. Enlisted at Plattsburgh to serve one year, and mustered in as private, Co. E, September 13, 1864; died, February 5, 1865, in Second Corps Hospital, at City Point, Va.

GALATIAN, CLARK H.— Age, 20 years. Enlisted, August 14, 1862, at Walden, to serve three years; mustered in as private, Co. H, September 5, 1862; promoted corporal prior to April 10, 1863; sergeant, August 18, 1863; wounded in action, May 6, 1864, at the Wilderness, Va.; promoted first sergeant, September 1, 1864; wounded and captured in action, October 27, 1864, at Boydton Road, Va.; paroled, prior to April 1865; mustered out with company June 3, 1865, near Washington, D.C.; also borne as Gallation.

GALLAW, CHARLES W.— Age, 34 years. Enlisted, August 13, 1862, at Newburgh, to serve three years; mustered in as private, Co. A, September 5, 1862; wounded in action, May 12, 1864, at Spotsylvania, Va.; absent since and in McDougal Hospital, Fort Schuyler, New York Harbor, at muster-out of company; also borne as Gollaw and Gollow.

GALLAW, FRANCIS B.— Age, 30 years. Enlisted, August 13, 1862, at Newburgh, to serve three years; mustered in as private, Co. A, September 5, 1862; wounded in action, May 6, 1864, at the Wilderness, Va., and May 12, 1864, at Spotsylvania, Va.; promoted corporal, February 8, 1865; mustered out with detachment May 29, 1865, at Harewood Hospital, Washington, D.C.; also borne as Gollow.

GANNON, JOHN.— Age, 19 years. Enlisted, August 11, 1862, at Goshen, to serve three years; mustered in as private, Co. D, September 5, 1862; wounded in action, July 2, 1863, at Gettysburg. Pa.; transferred to Co. C, Twenty-fourth Regiment, Veteran Reserve Corps, March 7, 1864; mustered out with detachment June 28, 1865, at Washington, D.C.

GARDNER, DANIEL S.— Age, 20 years. Enlisted, August 11, 1862, at New Windsor, to serve three years; mustered in as private Co. C, September 5, 1862; wounded in action, May 1, 1862, at Chancellorsville, Va.; promoted corporal, no date; returned to ranks, March 31, 1865; mustered out with company, June 3, 1865, near Washington, D.C.

GARDNER, JOSEPH.— Age, 23 years. Enlisted, July 30, 1862, at Newburgh, to serve three years; mustered in as private, Co. A, September 5, 1862; wounded in action, June 9, 1863, at Beverly Ford, Va.; mustered out with company, June 3, 1865, near Washington, D.C.; also borne as Garner.

GARDNER, LEWIS.— Age, 20 years. Enlisted, August 9, 1862, at Otisville, to serve three years; mustered in as private, Co. E, September 5, 1862; mustered out with company, June 3, 1865, near Washington, D.C., as Gardiner; also borne as Garner.

GARDNER, ROBERT W.— Age, 24 years. Enlisted, August 11, 1862, at Goshen, to serve three years; mustered in as private, Co. B, September 5, 1862; promoted corporal, no date; died of chronic diarrhea, January 7, 1864, at Washington, D.C.

GARRETSON, CHARLES.— Age, 25 years. Enlisted, July 26, 1862, at Newburgh, to serve three years; mustered in as private, Co. A, September 5, 1862; deserted, October 12, 1862, at Goshen, N.Y.

GARRETT, GEORGE.— Age, 21 years. Enlisted, August 11, 1862, at Port Jervis, to serve three years; mustered in as private, Co. F, September 5, 1862; wounded in action, July 2, 1863, at Gettysburg, Pa.; mustered out with company, June 3, 1865, near Washington, D.C.

GARRISON, EDWARD H.— Age, 23 years. Enlisted, August 9, 1862, at Port Jervis, to serve three years; mustered in as private, Co. F, September 5, 1862; discharged for disability, April 18, 1863, near Bellair, Va.

GARRISON, ISAAC.— Age, 30 years. Enlisted, August 11, 1862, at Goshen, to serve three years; mustered in as private, Co. D, September 5, 1862; died of typhoid fever, December 23, 1862, at Falmouth, Va.

GARRISON, JACOB.— Age, 18 years. Enlisted, August 15, 1862, at Port Jervis, to serve three years; mustered in as private, Co. F, September 5, 1862; wounded in action, May 3, 1863, at Chancellorsville, Va.; absent since and at hospital, Philadelphia, Pa., at muster-out of company.

GARRISON, JOHN M.— Age, 23 years. Enlisted, August 22, 1862, at Goshen, to serve three years; mustered in as private, Co. D, September 5, 1862; wounded in action, May 3, 1863, at Chancellorsville, Va.; promoted corporal prior to April, 1865; mustered out with company, June 3, 1865, near Washington, D.C.

GARRISON, JOHN W.— Age, 18 years. Enlisted at Warwick to serve one year, and mustered in as private, Co. D, September 3, 1864; killed in action, April 6, 1865, at Deatonsville Road, Va.

GARRISON, JOSIAH.— Age, 37 years. Enlisted, August 15, 1862, at Port Jervis, to serve three years; mustered in as private, Co. F, September 5, 1862; discharged for disability, April 18, 1863, near Bellair, Va.

GARRISON, SAMUEL.— Age, 19 years. Enlisted, August 6, 1862, at Warwick, to serve three years; mustered in as private, Co. B, September 5, 1862; promoted corporal, January 1, 1864; sergeant, April 18, 1865; mustered out with company, June 3, 1865, near Washington, D.C.

GARRISON, SIMMERSON.— Age, 22 years. Enlisted at Warwick, to serve three years, and mustered in as private, Co. D, January 4, 1864; wounded in action, May 12, 1864, at Spotsylvania, Va.; deserted, November 20, 1864, on expiration of furlough; name transferred to Co. H, Ninety-third Infantry, June 1, 1865; also borne as Simmeons and Simmeon Garrison.

GARRISON, STEPHEN W.— Age, 22 years. Enlisted, August 11, 1862, at Goshen, to serve three years; mustered in as private, Co. D, September 5,1862; wounded in action, May 6, 1864, at the Wilderness, Va.; transferred to Co. F, Tenth Regiment, Veteran Reserve Corps, September 20, 1864; mustered out with detachment, June 26, 1865, at Washington, D.C.

GAVIN, JAMES.— Age, 24 years. Enlisted, August 11, 1862, at Newburgh, to serve three years; mustered in as private, Co. B, September 5, 1862; transferred to Co. F, Ninth Regiment, Veteran Reserve Corps, February 1, 1865, and mustered out with detachment, June 20, 1863, at Washington, D.C.; also borne as Gavan.

GIBBS, DAVID.— Age, 26 years. Enrolled, August 20, 1862, at Goshen, to serve three years; mustered in as second lieutenant, Co. G, September 5, 1862; discharged for disability, February 25, 1863.

GILES, CYRENUS.— Age, 35 years. Enlisted, August 4, 1862, at Washingtonville, to serve three years; mustered in as private, Co. G, September 5, 1862; wounded in action, May 3, 1863, at Chancellorsville, Va., and November 27, 1863, at Locust Grove, Va.; absent at Fairfax Seminary Hospital, near Alexandria, Va., since December, 1864 and at muster-out of company.

GILES, DANIEL.— Age, 44 years. Enlisted, August 4, 1862, at Washingtonville, to serve three years; mustered in as corporal, Co. G, September 5, 1862; returned to ranks, January 1, 1863; mustered out with company, June 3, 1863, near Washington, D.C.

GILLSON, ISAAC G.— Age, 28 years. Enlisted, August 15, 1862, at Port Jervis, to serve three years; mustered in as private, Co. F, September 5, 1862; wounded in action, May 3, 1863, at Chancellorsville, Va.; killed in action, July 2, 1863, at Gettysburg, Pa.

GINNER, EDWARD.— Age, 23 years. Enlisted, August 6, 1862, at Goshen, to serve three years; mustered in as private, Co. A, September 5, 1862; appointed wagoner prior to April 10, 1863; grade changed to private prior to October 1864; mustered out with company, June 3, 1865, near Washington, D.C.

GLANZ, JOHN.— Age, 27 years. Enlisted, August 8, 1862, at Goshen, to serve three years: mustered in as private Co. B, September 5, 1862; wounded in action, July 2, 1863, at Gettysburg, Pa.; absent since and at muster-out of company.

GLEN, EDWARD.— Age, 27 years. Enlisted, August 18, 1862, at New Windsor, to serve three years; mustered in as private, Co. E, September 5, 1862; wounded in action, May 3, 1863, at Chancellorsville, Va.; discharged, September 25, 1864, at Washington, D.C., as Glenn.

GOBLE, FLOYD.— Age, 20 years. Enlisted, August, 11, 1862, at Port Jervis, to serve three years; mustered in as private, Co. F, September 5, 1862; wounded in action, July 2, 1863, at Gettysburg, Pa.; mustered out with company, June 3, 1865, near Washington, D.C.; also borne as Floyd S.

GODFREY, CHARLES S.— Age, 20 years. Enlisted, August 8, 1862, at Wallkill, to serve three years; mustered in as private, Co. K, September 5, 1862; appointed wagoner, July 1, 1863; grade changed to private prior to October 1864; mustered out with company, June 3, 1865, near Washington, D.C.

GODFREY, GEORGE.— Age, 18 years. Enlisted, August 14, 1862, at Wallkill, to serve three years; mustered in as private, Co. E, September 5, 1862; promoted corporal prior to April 10, 1863; wounded in action, May 3, 1863, at Chancellorsville, Va.; captured, no date; died of fever, November 20, 1863, in prison at Richmond, Va., as George C.

GOETCHIEUS, NEWTON.— Age, 25 years. Enlisted, August 8, 1862, at Goshen, to serve three years; mustered in as private, Co. A, September 5, 1862; wounded in action, May 3, 1863, at Chancellorsville, Va.; mustered out with company, June 3, 1865, near Washington, D.C.; also borne as Goutchus.

GOLICHER, CHARLES.— Age, 18 years. Enlisted at Monroe, to serve three years, and mustered in as private, Co. B, January 4, 1864.

GOODSELL, CHARLES H.— Age, 20 years. Enlisted, August 11, 1862, at Cornwall, to serve three years; mustered in as private, Co. C, September 5, 1862; wounded in action, May 3, 1863, at Chancellorsville, Va.; died of his wounds, May 20, 1863, at Potomac Creek Hospital, Va.

GOODSELL, JOHN L.— Age, 18 years. Enlisted, August 11, 1862, at Cornwall, to serve three years; mustered in as private, Co. C, September 5, 1862; discharged for disability, March [?] 1863 at Falmouth, Va.

GOODYEAR, CHARLES O.— Age, 19 years. Enlisted at Varick, to serve one year, and mustered in as private, Co. I, August 26, 1864; promoted corporal, March 26, 1865; mustered out with company, June 3, 1865, near Washington, D.C.

GORDON, CHARLES.— Age, 22 years. Enlisted at Warwick, to serve three years, and mustered in as private, Co. D, December 30, 1863; died, February 5, 1865, at West Milford, N.J.

GORDON, IRA.—Age, 18 years. Enlisted, August 15, 1862, at Port Jervis, to serve three years; mustered in as private, Co. F, September 5, 1862; wounded in action, July 2, 1863, at Gettysburg, Pa.; discharged for disability, October 19, 1863, at hospital, Fort Schuyler, New York Harbor.

GORDON, JOHN.—Age, 21 years. Enlisted, August 14, 1862, at Newburgh, to serve three years; mustered in as private, Co. I, September 5, 1862; wounded in action, July 2, 1863, at Gettysburg, Pa.; wounded and captured in action, May 6, 1864, at the Wilderness, Va.; released, November 20, 1864 at Savannah, Ga.; mustered out, June 22, 1865, at Annapolis, Md.

GORDON, JOSEPH.—Age, 35 years. Enlisted, August 13, 1862, at Goshen, to serve three years; mustered in as private, Co. B, September 5, 1862; appointed wagoner prior to April 10, 1863; discharged as private, April 17, 1863.

GORDON, JOSEPH.—Age, 37 years. Enlisted at Monroe, to serve three years, and mustered in as private, Co. B, February 1, 1864; deserted on expiration of furlough, February 17, 1865, at Petersburg, Va.

GORDON, SANFORD L.—Age, 23 years. Enlisted, August 15, 1862, at Port Jervis, to serve three years; mustered in as private, Co. F, September 5, 1862; wounded in action, June 9, 1863, at Beverly Ford, Va.; killed in action, May 12, 1864, at Spotsylvania, Va.

GORDON, WILLIAM H.—Age, 38 years. Enlisted at Warwick, to serve three years, and mustered in as private Co. D, December 30, 1863; wounded in action, May 12, 1864, at Spotsylvania, Va.; mustered out, July 19, 1865, at Mower Hospital, Philadelphia, Pa.

GOULD, CHARLES H.—Private, Co. K. First U.S. Sharpshooters; transferred to Co. H[?] this regiment, March 1, 1865; absent, missing in action, since October 27, 1864, at Boydton Road, Va., and at muster-out of company.

GOWDY, HENRY.—Age, 25 years. Enrolled at Walden to serve three years, and mustered in as first lieutenant, Co. H, August 23, 1862; wounded in action, May 3, 1863, at Chancellorsville, Va.; died of his wounds, May 11, 1863, at Washington, D.C. Commissioned first lieutenant, September 10, 1862, with rank from August 23, 1862, original.

GRANGER, FREDERICK.—Age, 21 years. Enlisted at Royalton, to serve three years, and mustered in as private, Co. I, September 17, 1864; transferred to Co. D, Ninety-third infantry, June 1, 1865.

GRANVILLE, JOHN.—Age, 38 years. Enlisted, August 13, 1862, at Mamakating, to serve three years; mustered in as private, Co. E, September 5, 1862; discharged for disability, January 24, 1863, at Mount Pleasant hospital, Washington, D.C.

GRAY, ALFRED.—Age, 33 years. Enlisted, August 13, 1862, at Goshen, to serve three years; mustered in as wagoner, Co. D, September 5, 1862; discharged, March 5, 1863.

GRAY, BENJAMIN W.—Age, 31 years. Enlisted, August 11[?], 1862, at Goshen, to serve three years; mustered in as private, Co. D, September 5, 1862; wounded in action, May 6, 1864, at the Wilderness, Va.; mustered out with company, June 3, 1865, near Washington, D.C.

GRAY, JOHN S.—Age, 40 years. Enlisted, August 6, 1862, at Goshen, to serve three years; mustered in as private, Co. D, September 5, 1862; wounded in action, June 9, 1863, at Beverly Ford, Va.; died of typhoid fever, June —, 1864, at Washington, D.C.

GREEN, SAMUEL.—Age, 25 years. Enlisted, August 4, 1862, at Goshen, to serve three years; mustered in as private, Co. B[?], September 5, 1862; deserted, October 19, 1862, at Knoxville, Md., returned, July 25, 1863; transferred to Co. C, Ninety-third Infantry, June 1, 1865.

GRIER, JAMES A.—Age, 25 years. Enrolled, August 25, 1862, at Goshen, to serve three years; mustered in as private, Co. K, September 5, 1862; promoted sergeant-major, to date August 25, 1862; mustered in as second lieutenant, Co. C, January 15, 1863; as first lieutenant, December 11, 1863; as captain, October 28, 1864; discharged, February 26, 1865, and mustered in as second lieutenant, Co. C, same date; mustered out, June 15, 1865, at Harts Island, New York Harbor; prior service, private Co. I, Seventy-first Militia.

HAGAN, JOHN.—Age, 43 years. Enlisted, August 11, 1862, at Newburgh, to serve three years; mustered in as private, Co. C, September 5, 1862; discharged for disability, January 13, 1863, at hospital, New York Harbor.

HAGER, MICHAEL.—Age, 18 years. Enlisted, August 8, 1862, at Goshen, to serve three years; mustered in as private, Co. A, September 5, 1862; wounded in action, July 3, 1863, at Gettysburg, Pa.; transferred to First Battalion, Veteran Reserve Corps, no date; retransferred to Co. A, September 15, 1864; mustered out with company, June 3, 1865, near Washington, D.C.

HAGGERTY, JAMES C.—Age, 21 years. Enlisted, August 18, 1862, at Newburgh, to serve three years; mustered in as private, Co. I, September 5, 1862; wounded in action, May 3, 1863, at Chancellorsville, Va.; transferred to Veteran Reserve Corps, September 30, 1864, as Hagerty.

HAIGH, ARTHUR.—Age, 19 years. Enlisted, August 18, 1862, at Walden, to serve three years; mustered in as private, Co. H, September 5, 1862; appointed musician prior to April 10, 1863; mustered out with company, June 3, 1865, near Washington, D.C.

HALL, JOHN.—Age, 28 years. Enlisted, August 13, 1862, at Goshen, to serve three years; mustered in as private, Co. D, September 5, 1862; died of typhoid fever, June 11, 1863, at Fairfax Hospital, Alexandria, Va.

HALLOCK, NATHAN M.—Age, 18 years. Enlisted, August 11, 1862, at Wallkill, to serve three years; mustered in as corporal, Co. K, September 5, 1862; returned to ranks, December 31, 1862; mustered out, June 12, 1865, at Hart's Island, New York Harbor; awarded *medal of honor*.

HALLOCK, ZEBULON.—Age, 22 years. Enlisted, August 14, 1862, at Goshen, to serve three years; mustered in as private, Co. E, September 5, 1862; died of fever, January 7, 1863, in camp, near Falmouth, Va.

HALSTEAD, BENJAMIN W.—Age, 18 years. Enlisted at Goshen, to serve one year, and mustered in as private, Co. K, August 23, 1864; mustered out with company, June 3, 1865, near Washington, D.C.

HALSTEAD, DANIEL.—Age, 42 years. Enlisted, August 21, 1862, at Newburgh, to serve three years; mustered in as private, Co. B, September 5, 1862; discharged, April 16, 1863, near Falmouth, Va.

HAMILL, JOHN.—Age, 26 years. Enlisted, August 18, 1862, at Newburgh, to serve three years; mustered in as private, Co. I, September 5, 1862; wounded in action, May 3, 1863, at Chancellorsville, Va.; transferred to Veteran Reserve Corps, April 10, 1864, as Hammill.

HAMILTON, ANSON.—Age, 44 years. Enlisted, August 15, 1862, at Newburgh, to serve three years; mustered in as private, Co. I, September 5, 1862; wounded in action, May 3, 1863, at Chancellorsville, Va.; transferred to Veteran Reserve Corps, February 11, 1863.

HAMILTON, JAMES.—Age, 30 years. Enlisted, September 2, 1864, at Goshen, to serve one year; mustered in as private, Co. B, September 7, 1864; mustered out with company, June 3, 1865, near Washington, D.C.

HAMILTON, WILLIAM.—Age, 42 years. Enlisted, August 15, 1862, at Newburgh, to serve three years; mustered in as private, Co. I, September 5, 1862; wounded in action, May 3, 1863, at Chancellorsville, Va.; died of his wounds, June 30, 1863.

HAMILTON, WILLIAM.—Age, 10 years. Enlisted, August 12, 1862, at Goshen, to serve three years; mustered in as musician, Co. B, September 5, 1862; absent, sick since May 3, 1864, and at muster-out of company.

HAMMOND, HORACE.—Age, 35 years. Enlisted, August 9, 1862, at Port Jervis, to serve three years; mustered in as sergeant, Co. F, September 5, 1862; wounded in action, May 12, 1864, at Spotsylvania Court House, Va.; transferred to Third Company, Second Battalion, Veteran Reserve Corps, no date; mustered out with detachment, August 21, 1865, at Washington, D.C.

HANFORD, J. HARVEY.—Age, 24 years. Enlisted, August 11, 1862, at Goshen to serve three years; mustered in as sergeant, Co. B, September 5, 1862; mustered out, June 15, 1865, at Hart's Island, New York Harbor; also borne as Hunford.

HANFORD, NATHAN C.—Age, 25 years. Enlisted, August 15, 1862, at Goshen, to serve three years; mustered in as private, Co. B, September 5, 1862; discharged, October 4, 1862; also borne as Hunford.

HANNA, JOSEPH.—Age, 26 years. Enlisted, August 18, 1862, at Newburgh, to serve three years; mustered in as private, Co. I, September 5, 1862; wounded in action, May 3, 1863, at Chancellorsville, Va.; promoted corporal, September 1, 1863; returned to ranks, January 4, 1864; wounded in action, May 6, 1864, at the Wilderness, Va.; mustered out with company, June 3, 1865, near Washington, D.C.

HANNAKA, PETER A. F.—Age, 45 years. Enlisted, August 15, 1862, at Port Jervis, to serve three years; mustered in as private, Co. F, September 5, 1862; wounded in action, May 3, 1863, at Chancellorsville, Va.; died of his wounds, May 16, 1863, at Division Hospital.

HARMOUTH, EMILE.—Private. Co. K, First U.S. Sharpshooters; transferred to One Hundred and Seventieth Company, Second Battalion, Veteran Reserve Corps, no date, and to Company H, this regiment, March 1, 1865; absent, in general hospital, since August 15, 1864, and at muster-out of company; borne in First U.S. Sharpshooters as Harmuth.

HARRIGAN, JOHN J.—Age, 37 years. Enlisted, August 15, 1862, at Port Jervis, to serve three years; mustered in as private, Co. F, September 5, 1862; mustered out with company, June 3, 1865, near Washington, D.C.

HARRINGTON, CHARLES.—Age, 23 years. Enlisted, August 5, 1862, at Goshen, to serve three years; mustered in as private, Co. B, September 5, 1862; discharged, January 10, 1863.

HARRIS, HEZEKEL.—Age, 44 years. Enlisted, August 20, 1862, at Newburgh, to serve three years; mustered in as private, Co. E, September 5, 1862; killed in action, July 2, 1863, at Gettysburg, Pa., as Hezakiah.

HARRIS, JOSIAH.—Age, 22 years. Enlisted, August 4, 1862, at Goshen, to serve three years; mustered in as private, Co. E, September 5, 1862; killed in action, May 3, 1863, at Chancellorsville, Va.

HARRIS, JR., OSCAR.—Age, 21 years. Enlisted, August 11, 1862, at Wallkill, to serve three years; mustered in as corporal, Co. E, September 5, 1862; discharged, October 20, 1863, to enlist as hospital steward in U.S. Army, at Washington, D.C.

HART, THOMAS.—Age, 22 years. Enrolled, July 26, 1862, at Newburgh, to serve three years; mustered in as corporal, Co. A, September 5, 1862; promoted sergeant prior to October 1864: mustered in as second lieutenant, November 15, 1864; as first lieutenant, February 20, 1865; mustered out with company, June 3, 1865, near Washington, D.C.

HARTNETT, JEREMIAH.—Age, 27 years. Enlisted, August 2, 1862, at Goshen, to serve three years; mustered in as private, Co. A, September 5, 1862; deserted, July 15, 1863, at expiration of pass.

HATCH, JOHN.—Age, 18 years. Enlisted, August 14, 1862, at Walden, to serve three years; mustered in as private, Co. H, September 5, 1862; died of typhoid fever, October 15, 1862, at hospital.

HATCH, WILLIAM H.—Age, 22 years. Enlisted, August 13, 1862, at Walden, to serve three years; mustered in as private, Co. H, September 5, 1862; captured in action, July 2,1863, at Gettysburg, Pa.; died, July 8, 1864, at Andersonville, Ga.

HATFIELD, WILLIAM.—Age, 18 years. Enlisted at Sennett, to serve one year, and mustered in as private, Co. I, September 1, 1864; mustered out, June 7, 1865, at Washington, D.C.

HAWLEY, ABRAHAM.—Age, 17 years. Enlisted, August 28, 1862, at Goshen, to serve three years; mustered in as private, Co. H, September 5, 1862; wounded in action, May 3, 1863, at Chancellorsville, Va.; discharged, June 27, 1863, at Fairfax Seminary Hospital, Alexandria, Va.

HAWLEY, DAVID.—Age, 24 years. Enlisted, August 13, 1862, at Walden, to serve three years; mustered in as private, Co. H, September 5, 1862; transferred to Co. A, Twelfth Regiment, Veteran Reserve Corps, July 1, 1863; mustered out with detachment, June 27, 1865, at Washington, D.C.

HAWXHUNT, WILLIAM.—Age, 21 years. Enlisted, August 12, 1862, at Salisbury Mills, to serve three years;

mustered in as private, Co. G, September 5, 1862; killed in action, May 3, 1863, at Chancellorsville, Va.; also borne as Hawxhurst.

HAXTER, CHARLES C.—Age, 24 years. Enlisted, August 7, 1862, at Port Jervis, to serve three years; mustered in as private, Co. E, September 5, 1862; died of diarrhea, December 30, 1862, in hospital at Harpers Ferry, Va., as Haxton; also borne as Hexton.

HAYDEN, WILLIAM.—Age, 28 years. Enlisted at Deerpark, to serve one year, and mustered in as private, Co. B, September 13, 1864; no further record.

HAYES, HOMER.—Age, 19 years. Enlisted at Lagrange to serve one year, and mustered in as private, Co. I, August 31, 1864; mustered out with company, June 3, 1865, near Washington, D.C., as Hays.

HAYS, JOHN R.—Age, 22 years. Enrolled, August 14, 1862, at Walden, to serve three years; mustered in as second lieutenant, Co. H, August 23, 1862; discharged, April 8, 1864. Commissioned second lieutenant, September 10, 1862, with rank from August 23, 1862, original; first lieutenant, not mustered, December 17, 1863, with rank from May 10, 1863, vice H. Gowdy, died of wounds received in action.

HAYWARD, WILLIAM S.—Age, 21 years. Enlisted, August 14, 1862, at Goshen, to serve three years; mustered in as private, Co. A, September 5, 1862; deserted, October 25, 1862, at Berlin, Md.

HAZEN, CHARLES B.—Age, 26 years. Enlisted, August 6, 1862, at Bellvale, to serve three years; mustered in as private, Co. B, September 5, 1862; mustered out with company, June 3, 1865, near Washington, D.C.

HAZEN, JAMES N.—Age, 30 years. Enlisted, August 12, 1862, at Port Jervis, to serve three years; mustered in as private, Co. F, September 5, 1862; wounded in action, June 9, 1863, at Beverly Ford, Va.; transferred to One Hundred and Sixty-sixth Company, Second Battalion, Veteran Reserve Corps, May 31, 1864; mustered out with detachment, June 27, 1865, at Point Lookout, Md., as James R. Havagan.

HAZEN, PETER P.—Age, 22 years. Enlisted, August 9, 1862, at Cornwall, to serve three years; mustered in as corporal, Co. C, September 5, 1862; promoted sergeant, March 1, 1863; wounded in action, July 2, 1863, at Gettysburg, Pa.; returned to ranks prior to October 1864; transferred as sergeant to Fifty-first Company, Second Battalion, Veteran Reserve Corps, February 2, 1865; mustered out, September 4, 1865, at Satterlee Hospital, Philadelphia, Pa.

HAZEN, WILLIAM H.—Age, 22 years. Enlisted, August 6, 1862, at Bellvale, to serve three years; mustered in as private, Co. B, September 5, 1862; promoted corporal, prior to April 10, 1863, and sergeant, August 1863; returned to ranks, May 1, 1864; absent, sick in hospital, at Philadelphia, Pa., at muster-out of company.

HEIDT, JACOB.—Private, Co. K., First U.S. Sharpshooters; transferred to Co. H, this regiment, March 1, 1865, while absent wounded, since May 5, 1864, in hospital, at muster-out of company.

HELME, JAME S.—Age, 44 years. Enlisted at Goshen, to serve one year, and mustered in as private, Co. K, September 3, 1864; mustered out with company, June 3, 1865, near Washington, D.C.; also borne as Holme.

HELMS, JOSEPH.—Age, 21 years. Enlisted, August 11, 1862, at Monroe, to serve three years; mustered in as private, Co. C, September 5, 1862; discharged for disability, November 17, 1862, at Washington D.C.

HEPPER, DAVID.—Age, 32 years. Enlisted, August 20, 1862, at Newburgh, to serve three years; mustered in as private, Co. I, September 5, 1862; died of disease, December 16, 1863.

HERMAN, JOSEPH.—Age, 29 years. Enlisted at Warwick, to serve three years, and mustered in as private, Co. D, January 12, 1864; transferred to Co. H, Ninety-third Infantry, June 1, 1865; also borne as Herrmann.

HERMANN, PETER.—Age, 24 years. Enlisted at Lodi, to serve one year, and mustered in as private, Co. C, August 30, 1864; wounded in action, October 27, 1864, at Boydton Road, Va.; mustered out with company, June 3, 1865, near Washington, D.C.

HERRICK, HIRAM G.—Age, 20 years. Enlisted, August 6, 1862, at Goshen, to serve three years; mustered in as corporal, Co. D, September 5, 1862; wounded in action, July 2, 1863, at Gettysburg, Pa.; promoted sergeant prior to October 1864; absent, sick in Second Division Hospital at Alexandria, Va., since October 1864 and at muster-out of company.

HERRON, CORNELIUS.—Age, 19 years. Enlisted, August 29, 1862, at Goshen, to serve three years; mustered in as private, Co. K, September 5, 1862; wounded in action, May 3, 1863, at Chancellorsville. Va.; promoted corporal, October 1, 1864; mustered out with company, June 3, 1865, near Washington, D.C., as Herring.

HICKS, CHARLES E.—Private, Co. K, First U.S. Sharpshooters; transferred to Co. H, this regiment, March 1, 1865; to Co. D, Ninety-third Infantry, June 1, 1865, as Charles C.

HIGGINS, PETER.—Age, 26 years. Enlisted, August 13, 1862, at Washingtonville, to serve three years; mustered in as private, Co. G, September 5, 1862; killed in action, May 3, 1863, at Chancellorsville, Va.

HILEBRANT, MARVIN.—Corporal, Co. K, First U.S. Sharpshooters; transferred to Co. H, this regiment, March 1, 1865; mustered out with company, June 3, 1865, near Washington, D.C.

HIRST, JOHN W.—Age, 18 years. Enlisted, August 9, 1862, at Otisville, to serve three years; mustered in as private, Co. E, September 5, 1862; mustered out with company, June 3, 1865, near Washington, D.C.

HOEFLER, JOHN.—Age, 20 years. Enlisted at Schenectady, to serve one year, and mustered in as private, Co. E, September 8, 1862; deserted, November 9, 1864; arrested, December 1864; executed for desertion, February 17, 1865, near Petersburgh, Va.

HOFFMAN, CARL GUSTAVE.—Age, 32 years. Enlisted, August 9, 1862, at Goshen, to serve three years; mustered in as private, Co. D, September 3, 1862; wounded in action, May 3, 1863, at Chancellorsville, Va., and May 6, 1864, at the Wilderness, Va.; absent, since, at Columbia Hospital, Washington, D.C., and at muster out of company.

HOFFMAN, HENRY.—Age, 30 years. Enlisted, August 11, 1862 at Newburgh, to serve three years; mustered in as musician, Co. C, September 5, 1862; died of disease, September 29, 1863 at Culpepper. Va.

HOLBERT, CORNELIUS H.— Age, 25 years. Enlisted, August 7, 1862, at Goshen, to serve three years; mustered in as private, Co. D, September 5, 1862; transferred to Co. F, Ninth Regiment, Veteran Reserve Corps, January 1, 1865: mustered out with company, June 26, 1865, at Washington, D.C.

HOLBERT, EBENEZER.— Age, 20 years. Enrolled, August 8, 1862, at Goshen, to serve three years; mustered in as corporal, Co. D, September 5, 1862; promoted first sergeant, prior to August, 1863; wounded in action, May 6, 1864, at the Wilderness, Va.; mustered in as first lieutenant, July 15, 1864; again wounded in action, October 27, 1864 at Boydton Road, Va.; mustered out with company June 3, 1865, near Washington, D.C.

HOLBERT, MATHIAS T.— Age, 21 years. Enlisted, August 15, 1862, at Goshen, to serve three years; mustered in as private, Co. B, September 5, 1862; wounded in action, May 3, 1863, at Chancellorsville, Va.; discharged, October 11, 1863, at convalescent camp, Alexandria, Va.

HOLLAND, JOHN.— Age, 21 years. Enlisted, August 20, 1862, at Newburgh, to serve three years; mustered in as corporal, Co. I, September 5, 1862; deserted, September 8, 1862.

HOLLAND, JR., ROBERT.— Age, 18 years. Enlisted, August 12, 1862, at Goshen, to serve three years; mustered in as private, Co. B, September 5, 1862; wounded in action, May 3, 1863; at Chancellorsville, Va.; killed in action, July 2, 1863, at Gettysburg Pa.

HOLLODAY, PAUL.— Age, 35 years. Enlisted, August 12, 1862, at Wallkill, to serve three years; mustered in as private, Co. K, September 1, 1862; wounded in action, May 3, 1863, at Chancellorsville, Va.; mustered out with company, June 3, 1863, near Washington, D.C.; also borne as Holliday and Halladay.

HOLLY, GEORGE.— Age, 31 years. Enlisted, August 11, 1862, at Newburgh, to serve three years; mustered in as private, Co. B, September 3, 1862; mustered out with company, June 3, 1865, near Washington, D.C.

HOLLY, JOHN C.— Age, 35 years. Enlisted, August 9, 1862, at Wallkill, to serve three years; mustered in as private, Co. K, September 5, 1862; mustered out with company, June 3, 1865, near Washington, D.C.; also borne as Holley.

HOLMES, THOMAS G.— Age, 21 years. Enlisted at Brooklyn, to serve three years, and mustered in as private, Co. D, November 12, 1864; transferred to Company H, Ninety-third Infantry, June 1, 1865.

HOMAN, JAMES E.— Age, 22 years. Enlisted, August 18, 1862, at Walden, to serve three years; mustered in as private, Co. H, September 5, 1862; wounded in action, July 2, 1863, and died of his wounds, July 3, 1863, at Gettysburg, Pa.

HOMAN, WILLIAM A.— Age, 22 years. Enlisted, August 13, 1862, at Newburgh, to serve three years; mustered in as private, Co. C, September 5, 1862; mustered out with company, June 3, 1865, near Washington, D.C.

HOTCHKISS, SAMUEL W.— Age, 35 years. Enrolled, August 9, 1862, at Port Jervis, to serve three years; mustered in as second lieutenant, Co. F, August 20, 1862; discharged, April 2, 1864. Commissioned second lieutenant, September 10, 1862, with rank from August 20, 1862, original.

HOUGH, ALVA.— Age, 44 years. Enlisted at Port Jervis, to serve one year, and mustered in as private, Co. F, August 20, 1864; mustered out, June 10, 1865, at New York City; also borne as Alba.

HOUSTON, JOHN W.— Age, 20 years. Enrolled at Goshen, to serve three years, and mustered in as second lieutenant, Co. D, August 16, 1862; wounded in action, June 9, 1863, at Beverly Ford, Va.; mustered in as first lieutenant, December 12, 1863; wounded in action, May 12, 1864, at Spotsylvania Court House, Va.; Discharged for disability, August 10, 1864.

HOWARD, AUGUSTUS.— Age, 26 years. Enlisted at Deer Park, to serve one year, and mustered in as private, Co. B, September 13, 1864; no further record.

HOWARD, GEORGE L.— Age, 23 years. Enlisted at Goshen, to serve one year, and mustered in as private, Co. K, August 31 1864; wounded in action, April 6, 1865, at Sailors Creek, Va.; mustered out with detachment, June 15, 1865, at White Hall[?] Hospital, Philadelphia, Pa.

HOWARD, GILBERT S.— Age, 21 years. Enlisted, August 14, 1862, at Goshen, to serve three years; mustered in as private, Co. D, September 5, 1862; discharged, March 5, 1863, at Carve Hospital, Washington, D.C.

HOWELL, HENRY M.— Age, 20 years. Enlisted, August 9, 1862, at Otisville, to serve three years; mustered in as private, Co. E, September 5, 1862; wounded in action, May 12, 1864, at Spotsylvania Court House, Va.; mustered out, June 8, 1865, at Lincoln Hospital, Washington, D.C.

HOWELL, PETER D.— Age, 20 years. Enlisted at Warwick, to serve three years, and mustered in as private, Co. D, January 2, 1864; transferred to Co. H, Ninety-third Infantry, June 1, 1865.

HOWELL, WILLIAM H.— Age, 21 years. Enlisted, August 7, 1862, at Goshen, to serve three years; mustered in as corporal, Co. E, September 5, 1862; killed in action, May 12, 1864, at Spotsylvania, Va.

HOYT, RUFUS S.— Age, 21 years. Enlisted at Goshen to serve one year, and mustered in as private, Co. K, September 10, 1864; mustered out with company, June 3, 1865, near Washington, D.C.

HUGHES, CORNELIUS.— Age, 18 years. Enlisted, August 11, 1862, at

2nd Lieutenant Samuel Hotchkiss, Company F. He was discharged April 2, 1864, before the start of Grant's Overland Campaign (archive of the Historical Society of the Town of Warwick, gift of Joan and Tom Frangos).

Craigsville, to serve three years; mustered in as private, Co. G, September 5, 1862; wounded in action, July 2, 1863, at Gettysburg, Pa.; July 30, 1864, in front of Petersburgh, Pa.; promoted corporal, March 12, 1865; mustered out with company, June 3, 1865, near Washington, D.C.

HUGHES, ELI.— Age, 19 years. Enlisted, August 11, 1862, at Craigsville, to serve three years; mustered in as private, Co. G, September 5, 1862; wounded in action, May 3, 1863, at Chancellorsville, Va., and died of his wounds, in hospital, May 25, 1863.

HULBERT, AMBROSE S.— Age, 18 years. Enlisted, July 31, 1862, at Wallkill, to serve three years; mustered in as corporal, Co. K, September 5, 1862; returned to ranks, June 1, 1863; killed in action, July 2, 1863, at Gettysburg, Pa.; also borne as Holbert.

HULL, BENJAMIN.— Age, 21 years. Enlisted, August 9, 1862, at Wallkill, to serve three years; mustered in as corporal, Co. E, September 5, 1862; promoted sergeant prior to October 1864; mustered out with company, June 3, 1865, near Washington, D.C.; also borne as Hall.

HULL, CHARLES H.— Age, 32 years. Enlisted, August 11, 1862, at Port Jervis, to serve three years; mustered in as corporal, Co. F, September 5,1862; promoted sergeant prior to April 10, 1863; transferred to Co. E, Tenth Regiment, Veteran Reserve Corps, June 29, 1865; mustered out with detachment, February 1, 1865, at Washington, D.C.

HUMPHREY, ORLANDO.— Age, 21 years. Enlisted, August 11, 1862, at Goshen, to serve three years; mustered in as private, Co. D, September 5, 1862; wounded in action, May 3, 1863, at Chancellorsville, Va.; transferred to Veteran Reserve Corps, September 30, 1864, as Orlando A.

HUNT, JOSEPH.— Age, 21 years. Enlisted at Goshen, to serve one year, and mustered in as private, Co. K, October 8, 1864; transferred to Co. F, Ninety-third Infantry, June 1, 1865.

HUNT, NATHAN.— Age, 38 years. Enlisted, August 9, 1862, at Goshen, to serve three years; mustered in as private, Co. D, September 5, 1862; transferred to Co. C, Twelfth Regiment, Veteran Reserve Corps August 19, 1863; mustered out with detachment, June 28, 1865, at Washington, D.C.

HUNT, ROBERT C.— Age, 26 years. Enlisted, August 7, 1862, at Goshen, to serve three years; mustered in as private, Co. A, September 5, 1862; promoted corporal, November 1, 1862; wounded in action, May 12, 1864, at Spotsylvania Court House. Va.; mustered out, May 16, 1865, at Patterson Park Hospital, Baltimore, Md.

HUNT, WILLIAM H. H.— Age, 22 years. Enlisted, August 12, 1862, at Port Jervis, to serve three years; mustered in as private, Co. F, September 5, 1862; died of typhoid fever, April 12, 1863, at camp, near Falmouth, Va.

HUNTER, EDWARD.— Age, 18 years. Enlisted, August 18, 1862, at Walden, to serve three years; mustered in as private, Co. H, September 5, 1862; wounded in action, June 16, 1864, before Petersburg, Va., and died of his wounds, June 30, 1862

HUNTER, JESSE.— Age, 22 years. Enlisted, August 6, 1862, at Bellvale, to serve three years; mustered in as private, Co. B, September 5, 1862; wounded in action, May 6, 1864, at the Wilderness, Va.; mustered out with company, June 3, 1865, near Washington, D.C.

HURDER, JOHN C.— Private, Co. H, Second U.S. Sharpshooters; transferred to Co. H, this regiment, March 1, 1865; mustered out with company, June 3, 1865, near Washington, D.C.

HURSHLER, NATHAN.— Age, 19 years. Enlisted, August 22, 1862, at Port Jervis, to serve three years; mustered in as private, Co. F, September 5, 1862; promoted corporal, December 1, 1862, and first sergeant, March 1, 1865; mustered out with company, June 3, 1865, near Washington, D.C., as Hershler.

HYATT, ABRAM.— Age, 44 years. Enlisted, August 2, 1862, at Goshen, to serve three years; mustered in as private, Co. A, September 5, 1862; discharged, February 2, 1864, at Brandy Station, Va.

HYATT, EZRA.— Age, 22 years. Enlisted, August 10, 1862, at Goshen, to serve three years; mustered in as private, Co. D, September 5, 1862; promoted corporal, prior to April 10, 1863; wounded in action, July 2, 1863, at Gettysburg, Pa.; transferred to Veteran Reserve Corps, no date.

HYATT, HENRY H.— Age, 25 years. Enlisted, August 12, 1862, at Goshen, to serve three years; mustered in as corporal, Co. D, September 5, 1862; wounded in action, June 9, 1863, at Brandy Station, Va.; returned to ranks, September 1, 1864; mustered out as corporal May 23, 1865, at hospital, Frederick, Md., as Henry C.

HYATT, JAMES W.— Age, 33 years. Enlisted, August 7, 1862, at Warwick, to serve three years; mustered in as private, Co. D, August 11, 1862; discharged for disability, October 15, 1862, at Morris Hill, Va.

HYATT, THOMAS M.— Age, 21 years. Enlisted, August 11, 1862, at Goshen, to serve three years; mustered in as corporal, Co. D, September 5, 1862; returned to ranks prior to April 10, 1863; wounded in action, July 2, 1863, at Gettysburg, Pa.; promoted corporal, March 1, 1865; mustered out with company, June 3, 1865, near Washington, D.C.

HYATT, WILLIAM E.— Age, 22 years. Enlisted, August, 12, 1862, at Goshen, to serve three years; mustered in as private, Co. D, September 5, 1862; promoted corporal, August 18, 1863, and sergeant, no date; killed in action, May 12, 1864, at Spotsylvania Court House, Va.

IRWIN, JAMES G.— Age, 22 years. Enlisted, August 11, 1862, at Goshen, to serve three years; mustered in as sergeant, Co. D, September 5, 1862; promoted first sergeant, August 31, 1864; mustered out with company, June 3, 1865, near Washington, D.C.

ISBELL, ANDREW J.— Age, 24 years. Enlisted, July 31, 1862, at Goshen, to serve three years; mustered in as private, Co. B, September 5, 1862; deserted, same date, at Goshen, N.Y.; also borne as Isbeel.

JACKSON, JOSEPH D.— Age, 30 years. Enlisted at Goshen, to serve one year, and mustered in as private, Co. K, September 8, 1864; promoted corporal, October 31, 1864; mustered out with company, June 3, 1865, near Washington, D.C.

JACKSON, LEONARD L.— Age, 39 years. Enlisted, August 11, 1862, at Newburgh, to serve three years; mustered in as private, Co. A, September 5, 1862; wounded in action, May 5, 1864, at the Wilderness, Va.; mustered out, June 16, 1865, at Mount Pleasant Hospital, Washington, D.C.

JACKSON, NATHANIEL. — Age, 19 years. Enlisted, August 14, 1862, at Newburgh, to serve three years; mustered in as private, Co. I, August 15, 1862; wounded in action, July 2, 1863, at Gettysburg Pa.; absent since and at muster-out of company.

JACKSON, WILLIAM . — Age, 18 years. Enlisted, August 20, 1862, at Hamptonburg, to serve three years; mustered in as private, Co. G, September 5, 1862; wounded in action, July 30, 1864, before Petersburg, Va.; mustered out with company, June 3, 1865, near Washington, D.C.

JACKSON, WILLIAM A. — Age, 23 years. Enrolled, August 23, 1862, at Goshen, to serve three years; mustered in as captain, Co. K, September 5, 1862; killed in action, June 18, 1864, at Petersburg, Va. Commissioned captain, September 10, 1862, with rank from August 23, 1862, original.

JAMES, STEPHEN C. — Corporal, Co. D, First U.S. Sharpshooters; transferred to Co. H, this regiment, March 1, 1865; discharged, June 5, 1865, at general hospital, Albany, N.Y., as of Co. D, First N.Y. Sharpshooters.

JAYCOX, ISAIAH. — Age, 31 years. Enlisted at Goshen, to serve one year, and mustered in as private, Co. K, August 18, 1864; mustered out with company, June 3, 1865, near Washington, D.C.

JEFFRY, THOMAS H. — Age, 18 years. Enlisted, August 15, 1862, at Port Jervis, to serve three years; mustered in as private, Co. F, August 20, 1862; killed in action, May 3, 1863, at Chancellorsville, Va.

JENKINS, ENOS. — Age, 19 years. Enlisted, August 9, 1862, at Goshen, to serve three years; mustered in as private, Co. A, September 5, 1862; captured by guerrillas, December 12, 1864, during the Weldon raid; paroled, prior to April 1865, and mustered out with company, June 3, 1865, near Washington, D.C.

JENNINGS, DANIEL C. — Age, 18 years. Enlisted, August 11, 1862, at Newburgh, to serve three years; mustered in as private, Co. C, September 3, 1862; discharged for disability, February 12, 1863, at convalescent camp, Alexandria Va.

JOHNSON, CHARLES. — Age, 24 years. Enlisted at Goshen, to serve one year, and mustered in as private, Co. K, August 23, 1864; mustered out with company, June 3, 1865, near Washington, D.C.

JOHNSON, JAMES L. — Age, 18 years. Enlisted at Ithaca, to serve one year, and mustered in as private, Co. A, September 1, 1864; killed in action, March 31, 1865, at Boydton Plank Road, Va.

JOHNSON, JOHN. — Age, 18 years. Enlisted at Porter, to serve three years, and mustered in as private, Co. D, September 19, 1864; mustered out with company, June 3, 1865, near Washington, D.C.

JOHNSON, JOHN H. — Age, 27 years. Enlisted at Wayland, to serve one year, and mustered in as private, Co. A, September 21, 1864; mustered out with company, June 3, 1865, near Washington, D.C.

JOHNSON, JOSEPH. — Age, 22 years. Enlisted, August 13, 1862, at Chester, to serve three years; mustered in as private, Co. A, August 7, 1862; mustered out with company, June 3, 1865, near Washington, D.C., as Joseph L.

JOHNSON, ROBERT. — Age, 23 years. Enlisted at Sullivan, to serve three years, and mustered in as private, Co. A, August 20, 1864; transferred to Co. E, Ninety-third Infantry, June 1, 1865.

JOHNSTON, JOSEPH H. — Age, 18 years. Enlisted, August 13, 1862, at Newburgh, to serve three years; mustered in as private, Co. E, September 5, 1862; wounded in action, May 5, 1864, at the Wilderness, Va., absent since and in hospital at Washington, D.C., at muster-out of company; also borne as Johnson.

JOHNSTON, WAKEMAN. — Age, 45 years. Enlisted, August 8, 1862, at Goshen, to serve three years; mustered in as musician, Co. B, September 5, 1862; discharged, March 16, 1863, at hospital, Philadelphia, Pa.; also borne as Johnson.

JOHNSTON, WILLIAM. — Age, 21 years. Enlisted, August 19, 1862, at Goshen, to serve three years; mustered in as private, Co. E, September 5, 1862; deserted, September 8, 1862, at Baltimore, Md., as Johnson.

JONES, ALEXANDER. — Age, 45 years. Enlisted, August 6, 1862, at Goshen, to serve three years; mustered in as private, Co. G, September 5, 1862; promoted corporal, January 1, 1863; captured in action, May 3, 1863, at Chancellorsville, Va.; paroled, May 14, 1863, at Belle Island, Va.; wounded in action, June 16, 1864, before Petersburg, Va.; mustered out with company, June 3, 1865, near Washington, D.C.

JONES, CHAUNCEY B. — Age, 24 years. Enlisted, July 28, 1862, at Goshen, to serve three years; mustered in as corporal, Co. A, September 5, 1862; returned to ranks, September 12, 1862; discharged, October 4, 1862, at Miner's Hill, Va.

JONES, JAMES. — Age, 43 years. Enlisted, July 28, 1862, at Goshen, to serve three years; mustered in as private, Co. A, September 5, 1862; wounded in action, June 9, 1863, at Beverly Ford, Va.; discharged, September 17, 1863.

JONES, JOSEPH. — Age, 18 years. Enlisted, August 14, 1862, at Newburgh, to serve three years; mustered in as private, Co. G, September 5, 1862; promoted corporal, March 12, 1865; mustered out with company, June 3, 1865, near Washington, D.C.

JORDAN, JACOB F. — Age, 18 years. Enlisted, August 13, 1862, at Walden, to serve three years; mustered in as private, Co. H, August 20, 1862; wounded in action, November 30, 1863, at Mine Run, Va.; absent since and at Fairfax Seminary Hospital, Va., at muster-out of company.

JOUBIN, HENRY — Private, Co. K, First U.S. Sharpshooters; transferred to Co. H, this regiment, March 1, 1865; mustered out with company, June 3, 1865, near Washington, D.C., as Jonbin; also borne as Jubin.

JOYCE, JOHN. — Age, 44 years. Enlisted, August 18, 1862, at Newburgh, to serve three years; mustered in as private, Co. I, September 5, 1862; transferred to One Hundred and Forty-fifth Company, Second Battalion, Veteran Reserve Corps, June 15, 1864; mustered out with detachment, August 9, 1865, at Davids' Island, New York Harbor.

JUDSON, CHESTER.— Age, 18 years. Enlisted, August 14, 1862, at Walden, to serve three years; mustered in as private, Co. H, August 20, 1862; promoted corporal, no date; killed while on picket, September 14, 1864, at Petersburg, Va.

JUDSON, GRANDASON.— Age, 30 years. Enlisted, August 14, 1862, at Walden, to serve three years; mustered in as private, Co. H, September 5, 1862; wounded in action, May 3, 1863, at Chancellorsville, Va.; transferred to Co. F, Ninth Regiment, Veteran Reserve Corps, February 1, 1865; mustered out with detachment, June 26, 1863, at Washington, D.C.

JUDSON, JOHN H.— Age, 18 years. Enlisted, August 11, 1862, at Goshen, to serve three years; mustered in as private, Co. A, September 5, 1862; killed in action, May 3, 1863, at Chancellorsville, Va.

KALBFUS, JOHN L.— Age, 32 years. Enlisted, August 9, 1862, at Port Jervis, to serve three years; mustered in as corporal, Co. F, September 5, 1862; promoted second lieutenant, Sixteenth West Virginia Infantry, September 26, 1862.

KANOFF, ISAAC.— Age, 26 years. Enlisted, August 9, 1862, at Wallkill, to serve three years; mustered in as private, Co. K, September 5, 1862; wounded and captured in action, May 3, 1863, at Chancellorsville, Va.; paroled, May 13, 1863; wounded in action, May 14, 1864, at Spotsylvania, Va.; discharged for wounds, May 29, 1865, at Columbian Hospital, Washington, D.C.

KEAN, BERNARD F.— Age, 18 years. Enlisted, August 15, 1862, at Port Jervis, to serve three years; mustered in as private, Co. F, September 5, 1862; wounded in action, May 3, 1863, at Chancellorsville, Va.; died of his wounds, June 2, 1863, at Harewood Hospital, Washington, D.C.

KEANE, PATRICK.— Age, 39 years. Enlisted, August 12, 1862, at Newburgh, to serve three years; mustered in as private, Co. I, September 5, 1862; wounded in action, June 15, 1864, at Petersburg, Va.; discharged, August 31, 1864, at hospital; also borne as Kane.

KEARNS, WILLIAM.— Age, place and date of enlistment and muster-in as private, Co. K, not stated; discharged, October 1863; subsequent service in Thirteenth Artillery.

KEITH, ISAAC.— Age, 19 years. Enlisted at Schenectady, to serve one year, and mustered in as private, Co. E, August 30, 1864; promoted corporal, March 1, 1863; mustered out with company, June 3, 1865, near Washington, D.C.

KELLEY, JUDSON.— Age, 19 years. Enlisted, August 12, 1862, at Mount Hope, to serve three years; mustered in as private, Co. E, September 5, 1862; wounded in action, May 3, 1863, at Chancellorsville, Va.; discharged for disability, September 4, 1863, at hospital, Philadelphia, Pa., as Kelly.

KELLY, EDWARD.— Age, 27 years. Enlisted at Schenectady, to serve one year, and mustered in as private, Co. E, September 2, 1864; mustered out with company, June 3, 1865, near Washington, D.C.

KELLY, THOMAS.— Age, 29 years. Enlisted, August 4, 1862, at Goshen, to serve three years; mustered in as prvate, Co. A, September 5, 1862; company muster-roll of April 10, 1863, remarks; died, no date, at Philadelphia, Pa.

KERR, STEPHEN B.— Age, 21 years. Enlisted, August 5, 1862, at Wallkill, to serve three years; mustered in as private, Co. K, September 5, 1862; wounded in action, May 3, 1863, at Chancellorsville, Va.; transferred to Co. D, November 15, 1864; to Co. F, Eighteenth Regiment, Veteran Reserve Corps, no date; mustered out as corporal with detachment, June 27, 1865, at Washington, D.C.

KETCHAM, HIRAM.— Age, 19 years. Enlisted, August 9, 1862, at Mount Hope, to serve three years; mustered in as private, Co. E, September 5, 1862; promoted corporal, prior to April 10, 1863; wounded in action, May 3, 1863, at Chancellorsville, Va.; discharged for disability, February 8, 1864, at hospital, Davids' Island, New York Harbor; also borne as Ketchum.

KETCHAM, IRA S.— Age, 18 years. Enlisted, August 20, 1862, at Wallkill, to serve three years; mustered in as private, Co. K, August 22, 1862; wounded, no date; transferred to Co. D, Seventh Regiment, Veteran Reserve Corps, November 15, 1863; mustered out as corporal with detachment, June 30, 1865, at Washington, D.C.

KETCHAM, JAMES M.— Age, 20 years. Enlisted, August 14, 1862, at Newburgh, to serve three years; mustered in as private, Co. G, September 5, 1862; mustered out with company, June 3, 1865, near Washington, D.C.; also borne as Ketchum.

KIDD, DAVID L.— Age, 21 years. Enlisted, August 5, 1862, at Newburgh, to serve three years; mustered in as corporal, Co. I, September 5, 1862; returned to ranks, November 1, 1862; transferred to Co. A, Tenth Regiment, Veteran Reserve Corps, September, 1863; mustered out with detachment as corporal, June 28, 1865, at Washington, D.C.

KIDD, JR., HENRY.— Age, 44 years. Enlisted, August 13,1862, at Walden, to serve three years; mustered in as private, Co. H, September 3, 1862; discharged, January 17, 1863.

KIDD, JOHN E.— Age, 24 years. Enlisted, August 15, 1862, at Walden, to serve three years; mustered in as corporal, Co. H, September 5, 1862; returned to ranks, no date; wounded in action, July 2, 1863, at Gettysburg, Pa.; mustered out with company, June 3,1865, near Washington, D.C.

KIMBALL, HERVEY.— Age, 24 years. Enlisted August 8, 1862, at Goshen, to serve three years; mustered in as private, Co. A, September 5, 1862; discharged, August 28, 1863.

KIMBARK, NOAH B.— Age, 31 years. Enlisted, August 13, 1862, at Walden, to serve three years; mustered in as private, Co. H, September 5, 1862; promoted corporal, prior to April 10, 1863; wounded in actions, May 3, 1863, at Chancellorsville, Va., and July 2, 1863, at Gettysburg, Pa.; transferred to Co. H, Eleventh Regiment, Veteran Reserve Corps, January 21, 1865; discharged, June 29, 1865, at Albany, N.Y.

KINCAID, THOMAS.— Age, 35 years. Enlisted, August 20, 1862, at Wallkill, to serve three years; mustered in as private, Co. K, September 5, 1862; wounded in action, July 30, 1864, before Petersburg, Va.; promoted corporal, October 1, 1864; mustered out, June 8, 1865, at Washington, D.C., while in Slough Hospital, Alexandria, Va.

KING, GEORGE G.—Age, 32 years. Enlisted, August 13, 1862, at Newburgh, to serve three years; mustered in as private, Co. C, September 5, 1862; killed in action, September 10, 1864, before Petersburg, Va.

KING, JOHN S.—Age, 23 years. Enrolled, September 15, 1864, at Albany, to serve three years; mustered in as first lieutenant, Co. K, October 22, 1864; wounded in action, March 31,1865, near Hatcher's Run, Va.; discharged for disability to date, October 28, 1865; prior service as first lieutenant, Co. D, Eighteenth Infantry. Commissioned first lieutenant, December 17, 1864, with rank from September 15, 1864, vice Thomas W. Bradley, promoted.

KING, WILLIAM.—Age, 13[?] years. Enlisted, August 13, 1862, at Newburgh, to serve three years; mustered in as private, Co. C, September 5, 1862; discharged for disability, April 16, 1863, at Falmouth, Va.

KINNEY, GEORGE B.—Age, 22 years. Enlisted, August 8, 1862, at Goshen, to serve three years; mustered in as private, Co. D, September 5, 1862; wounded in action, July 2, 1863, at Gettysburg, Pa.; mustered out with company, June 3, 1865, near Washington, D.C.

KIPP, PETER H.—Private, Co. K, First U.S. Sharpshooters; transferred to Co. H, this regiment, March 1, 1865; to Co. D, Ninety-Third Infantry, June 1, 1865; veteran.

KIRK, CHARLES P.—Age, 21 years. Enlisted, August 15, 1862, at Port Jervis, to serve three years; mustered in as private, Co. F, September 5, 1862; wounded in action, May 3, 1863, at Chancellorsville, Va.; transferred to Co. H, Tenth Regiment, Veteran Reserve Corps, January 10, 1865; mustered out with detachment, June 27, 1865, at Washington, D.C.

Corporal Thomas Kincaid was wounded July 30, 1864, at Petersburg (Michael J. McAfee collection).

KLINE, CHARLES S.—Age, 21 years. Enlisted, August 12, 1862, at Newburgh, to serve three years; mustered in as private, Co. A, September 5, 1862; deserted, April 15, 1863, at expiration of furlough.

KNAPP, CHARLES.—Age, 22 years. Enlisted, August 15, 1862, at Goshen, to serve three years; mustered in as private, Co. C, September 5, 1862; promoted corporal, March 1, 1863; wounded in action, May 3, 1863, at Chancellorsville, Va.; returned to ranks, prior to October 1864; discharged for wounds, December 9, 1864, at DeCamp Hospital, Davids' Island, New York Harbor; also borne as Charles C.

KNAPP, JOHN N.—Age, 23 years. Enlisted, August 20, 1862, at Newburgh, to serve three years; mustered in as private, Co. I, September 5, 1862; promoted corporal, January 1, 1865; returned to ranks, March 15, 1865; mustered out with company, June 3, 1865, near Washington, D.C.

KNAPP, ORLANDO U.—Age, 27 years. Enlisted, August 11, 1862, at Port Jervis, to serve three years; mustered in as corporal, Co. F, August 20, 1862; killed in action, July 2, 1863, at Gettysburg, Pa.

KNIFFEN, SAMUEL.—Age, 22 years. Enlisted, August 25, 1862, at Goshen, to serve three years; mustered in as private, Co. D, September 5, 1862; discharged, February 28, 1863, at Providence, R.I.

KNOX, CHARLES.—Private, Co. K, First U.S. Sharpshooters; transferred to Co. H, this regiment, March 1, 1865; to Co. D, Ninety-third Infantry, June 1, 1865; veteran.

LADUE, HENRY.—Age, 43 years. Enlisted, September 5, 1864, at Baxter, to serve one year; mustered in as private, Co. A, September 29, 1864; mustered out with company, June 3, 1865, near Washington, D.C.

LAFOUNTAIN, ANDRE W.—Age, 23 years. Enlisted at Plattsburg, to serve one year, and mustered in as private, Co. E, September 15, 1864; mustered out with company, June 3, 1865, near Washington, D.C.

LAIN, EDWARD N.—Age, 19 years. Enlisted, August 7, 1862, at Goshen, to serve three years; mustered in as private, Co. B, September 5, 1862; killed in action, May 3, 1863, at Chancellorsville, Va.; also borne as Lane.

LAMOREAUX, AUSTIN W.—Age, 18 years. Enlisted, August 9, 1862, at Mt. Hope, to serve three years; mustered in as private, Co. E, September 5, 1862; promoted corporal, prior to October, 1864; wounded in action, June 16, 1864, in front of Petersburg, Va., and April 6, 1865, at Sailor's Creek, Va.; died of his wounds, April 15, 1865, at Douglas Hospital, Washington, D.C.; also borne as Lamaraux.

LAMOREUX, FREDERICK R.—Age, 18 years. Enlisted, August 12, 1862, at Monroe, to serve three years; mustered in as private, Co. C, September 5, 1862; wounded in action, July 2, 1863, at Gettysburg, Pa.; died of disease, October 4, 1864, at hospital, Washington, D.C.

LAMOREUX, RANSLER S.—Age, 23 years. Enlisted, August 9, 1862, at Goshen, to serve three years; mustered in as private, Co. D, September 5, 1862; promoted sergeant, August 31, 1864; mustered out with company, June 3, 1865, near Washington, D.C.; also borne as Rensselaer S. Lamereux.

LAMOREUX, WILLIAM.—Age, 43 years. Enlisted, August 9, 1862, at Goshen, to serve three years; mustered in as private, Co. B, September 5, 1862; killed in action, July 2, 1863, at Gettysburg, Pa.

LANCASTER, BENJAMIN.—Age, 26 years. Enlisted, August 6, 1862, at Goshen, to serve three years; mustered in as private, Co. A, September 5, 1862; deserted, April 15, 1863, on expiration furlough.

LANG, SYLVANUS.—Age, 24 years. Enlisted at Avon, to serve three years, and mustered in as private, Co. H, August 31, 1864; transferred to Co. D, Ninety-third Infantry, June 1, 1865.

LANGTON, GEORGE H.— Age, 26 years. Enlisted, August 15, 1862, at Port Jervis, to serve three years; mustered in as private, Co. F, September 5, 1862; wounded in action, July 2, 1863, at Gettysburg, Pa.; transferred to One Hundred and Sixty-second Company, Second Battalion, Veteran Reserve Corps, May 1, 1864; mustered out with detachment, July 7, 1865, at Philadelphia, Pa.

LANNING, STEPHEN.— Age, 18 years. Enlisted, August 23, 1862, at Wallkill, to serve three years; mustered in as private, Co. K, September 5, 1862; discharged, September 6, 1862, as a minor; also borne as Laning.

LARISIE, JAMES.— Age, 35 years. Enlisted at Lodi, to serve one year; mustered in as private, Battery M, Third Artillery, September 3, 1864; transferred to Co. I, this regiment, May 10, 1865; mustered out with company, June 3, 1865, near Washington, D.C.; also borne as Larressey.

LAROE, JOHN T.— Age, 19 years. Enlisted, August 19, 1862, at Newburgh, to serve three years; mustered in as private, Co. I, September 5, 1862; wounded in action, July 2, 1863, at Gettysburg, Pa.; mustered out, June 29, 1865, at hospital, Annapolis, Md., as John S.; also borne as Larone and Laroc.

LATHAM, SAMUEL D.— Age, 33 years. Enlisted, August 12, 1862, at Blooming Grove, to serve three years; mustered in as private, Co. G, September 5, 1862; discharged for disability, May 20, 1863, at Lincoln Hospital, Washington, D.C.

LAWSON, SYLVESTER.— Private, Co. C, Second U.S. Sharpshooters; transferred to Co. H, this regiment, February 18, 1865; mustered in as second lieutenant, March 19, 1865; mustered out with company, June 3, 1865, near Washington, D.C.; prior service as private, Co. I, Seventy-first Militia. Commissioned second lieutenant, March 14, 1865, with rank from March 3, 1865, vice W. T. Ogden, promoted.

LEE, BOWDEWINE C.— Age, 33 years. Enlisted, August 14, 1862, at Goshen, to serve three years; mustered in as sergeant, Co. B, September 5, 1862; discharged, as private, March 18, 1863, at Camden Hospital, Baltimore, Md.; also borne as Bodervine C.

LEE, FRANCIS.— Age, 19 years. Enlisted, August 12, 1862, at Newburgh, to serve three years; mustered in as private, Co. B, September 5, 1862; promoted corporal, prior to April 10, 1863; captured in action, May 3, 1863, at Chancellorsville, Va.; paroled, May 14, 1863, at Belle Island, Va.; promoted sergeant, September 17, 1863; returned to ranks, May 1, 1864; discharged to date, May 3, 1864.

LEECH, PATRICK.— Age, 23 years. Enlisted, August 9, 1862, at Goshen, to serve three years; mustered in as private, Co. B, September 5, 1862; wounded in action, May 10, 1864, at Spotsylvania Court House, Va.; mustered out with company, June 3, 1865, near Washington, D.C., as Leach.

LEEPER, JOHN W.— Age, 24 years. Enlisted, August 8, 1862, at Goshen, to serve three years; mustered in as private, Co. D, September 5, 1862; wounded and captured in action, July 2, 1863, at Gettysburg, Pa.; paroled and died, no date, at Annapolis, Md.

LEEPER, ROBERT C.— Age, 22 years. Enlisted, August 9, 1862, at Goshen, to serve three years; mustered in as private, Co. D, September 5, 1862; discharged, March 25, 1863, at camp hospital.

LEGG, GOUVERNEUR M.— Age, 31 years. Enlisted, August 22, 1862, at Goshen, to serve three years; mustered in as private, Co. H, September 3, 1862; wounded in action, May 6, 1864, at the Wilderness, Va.; mustered out, June 6, 1865, at Harewood Hospital, Washington, D.C., as Governeur M.

LEHNING, PHILIP.— Age, 18 years. Enlisted at Goshen, to serve one year, and mustered in as private, Co. K, August 17, 1864; mustered out with company, June 3, 1865, near Washington, D.C.

LENT, JACOB.— Age, 18 years. Enlisted, August 11, 1863, at Goshen, to serve three years; mustered in as private, Co. A. September 5, 1862; promoted corporal, no date; killed in action, July 2, 1863, at Gettysburg, Pa.

LEWIS, AMSY.— Age, 21 years. Enlisted, August 2, 1862, at Goshen, to serve three years; mustered in as private, Co. A, September 5, 1862; deserted, October 25, 1862, at Berlin, Md., as Amzy.

LEWIS, JAMES.— Age, 21 years. Enlisted, August 12, 1862, at Goshen, to serve three years; mustered in as private, Co. B, September 5, 1862; deserted, October 25, 1862, at Berlin, Md.

LEWIS, JAMES.— Age, 18 years. Enlisted at Warwick, to serve three years, and mustered in as private, Co. B, January 15, 1864; wounded in action, May 6, 1864, at the Wilderness, Va.; transferred to Co. G, Sixth Regiment, Veteran Reserve Corps, September 20, 1864; mustered out with detachment, August 5, 1865, at Johnson's Island.

LEWIS, JOHN.— Age, 23 years. Enlisted, August 12, 1862, at Goshen, to serve three years; mustered in as private, Co. A, September 5, 1862; captured in action, May 3, 1863, at Chancellorsville, Va.; paroled, May 14, 1863; mustered out with company, June 3, 1865, near Washington, D.C.

LEWIS, SAMUEL.— Age, 28 years. Enlisted, August 13, 1862, at Monroe, to serve three years; mustered in as private, Co. C, September 5, 1862; deserted, June 25, 1863, while en route to Gettysburg, Pa.

LEWIS, SAMUEL.— Age, 28 years. Enlisted at Bethel, to serve one year, and mustered in as private, Co. K, September 19, 1864; wounded in action, April 6, 1865, at Sailor's Creek, Va.; died of his wounds, May 3, 1865, at Jarvis Hospital, Baltimore, Md.

LEWIS, THOMAS.— Age, 25 years. Enlisted, August 6, 1862, at Goshen, to serve three years; mustered in as private, Co. A, September 5, 1862; transferred to Forty-ninth Company, Second Battalion, Veteran Reserve Corps, December 27, 1864; mustered out with detachment, June 26, 1865, at Washington, D.C.

LEWIS, WILLIAM H.— Age, 19 years. Enlisted at Bethel, to serve one year, and mustered in as private, Co. K, September 19, 1864; mustered out with company, June 3, 1863, near Washington, D.C.

LITTLE, BENJAMIN M.— Age, 40 years. Enlisted, August 8, 1862, at Goshen, to serve three years; mustered in as private, Co. B, September 5, 1862; wounded in action, October 19, 1864, in front of Petersburg, Va.; mustered out with company, June 3, 1865, near Washington, D.C.; also borne as Benjamin H.

LITTLE, JOHN H.— Age, 44 years. Enlisted, August 15, 1862, at Wallkill, to serve three years; mustered in as corporal, Co. E, September 5, 1862; returned to ranks, prior to April 10, 1863; transferred to Veteran Reserve Corps, April 25, 1864.

LOCKE, GEORGE.—Age, 18 years. Enlisted at New York City, to serve one year; mustered in as private, Co. G, March 8, 1865; transferred to Co. D, Ninety-third Infantry, June 1, 1865.

LOGAN, ISAAC.—Age, 28 years. Enlisted at Goshen, to serve one year, and mustered in as private, Co. K, August 19, 1864; mustered out with company, June 3, 1865, near Washington, D.C.

LOOMIS, PHILITUS.—Age, 26 years. Enlisted at Plattsburgh, to serve one year, and mustered in as private, Co. E, September 5, 1864; missing in action, April 1, 1865, at Boydton, Va., and at muster-out of company.

LORD, WILLIAM.—Age, 26 years. Enlisted, August 21, 1862, at Goshen, to serve three years; mustered in as private, Co. H, September 5, 1862; deserted, November 26, 1862, from hospital, at Berlin, Md.

LOSEY, HENRY.—Age, 21 years. Enlisted, August 18[?], 1862, at Newburgh, to serve three years; mustered in as private, Co. I, September 5, 1862; captured, June 30, 1863, at Emmitsburg, Pa.; died, January 27, 1865, at Richmond, Va.

LOSEY, JAMES T.—Age, date, place of enlistment, term, and muster-in as private, Co. K, not stated; joined company, October 20, 1864; died, March —, 1865, at Armory Square Hospital, Washington, D.C.

LOUGHRIGE, DANIEL.—Age, 18 years. Enlisted, August 18, 1862, at Newburgh, to serve three years; mustered in as private, Co. I, September 5, 1862; wounded in action, May 3, 1863, at Chancellorsville, Va.; promoted corporal, April 80, 1864; sergeant, December 1, 1864; mustered out with company, June 3, 1865, near Washington, D.C., as Loughridge.

LOVETT, GEORGE.—Age, — years. Enlisted at Montgomery, to serve three years; mustered in as private, Co. K, August —, 1862. (From personal record not on rolls.) Discharged for disability, no date.

LOWERS, DAVID.—Age, 28 years. Enlisted, August 12, 1862, at Blooming Grove, to serve three years; mustered in as private, Co. G, September 5, 1862; wounded in action, June 9, 1863, at Beverly Ford, Va.; discharged, October 16, 1863.

LOZIER, CHARLES.—Age, 19 years. Enlisted, August 13, 1862, at Newburgh, to serve three years; mustered in as private, Co. I, September 5, 1862; mustered out with company, June 3, 1865, near Washington, D.C.; also borne as Losier.

LUCKEY, WILLIAM H.—Age, 29 years. Enlisted, August 13, 1862, at Warwick, to serve three years; mustered in as private, Co. B, September 5, 1862; discharged, September 7, 1863, at convalescent camp, Alexandria, Va.

LUPTOK, JUDSON B.—Age, 21 years. Enlisted, August 13, 1862, at Walden, to serve three years; mustered in as private, Co. H, September 5, 1862; wounded in action, June 17, 1864, at Petersburg, Va.; mustered out with company, June 3, 1865, near Washington, D.C.

LUTES, CALVIN CHARLES.—Age, 21 years. Enlisted, August 9, 1862, at Goshen, to serve three years; mustered in as private, Co. A, September 5, 1862; mustered out with company, June 3, 1865, near Washington, D.C.

LYNN, JAMES.—Age, 26 years. Enlisted at Goshen, to serve one year, and mustered in as private, Co. K, August 23, 1864; promoted corporal, October 31, 1864; mustered out with company, June 3, 1865, near Washington, D.C.; also borne as Linn.

MABEE, THOMAS G.—Age, 21 years. Enrolled, August 7, 1862, at Goshen, to serve three years; mustered in as sergeant, Co. D, September 5, 1862; promoted sergeant-major, September 1, 1863; mustered in as second lieutenant, Co. B, September 27, 1864; mustered out with company, June 3, 1865, near Washington, D.C. Commissioned second lieutenant, November 15, 1864, with rank from July 21, 1864, vice E. Holbert, not mustered.

MACKAY, WILLIAM.—Age, 38 years. Enlisted, August 6, 1862, at Wallkill, to serve three years; mustered in as private, Co. E, August 16, 1862; missing in action, October 13, 1863, near Auburn, Va.; no further record.

MACKENY, ROBERT.—Age, 17 years. Enlisted, August 18, 1862, at Wallkill, to serve three years; mustered in as private, Co. H, September 5, 1862; missing in action, October 14, 1863, at Auburn, Va.; no further record; also borne as Mackiney.

MACKEY, JAMES B.—Age, 44 years. Enlisted, August 6, 1862, at Wallkill, to serve three years; mustered in as private, Co. E, September 5, 1862; no further record.

MADDEN, JOHN.—Age, 21 years. Enlisted at Goshen, to serve one year, and mustered in as private, Co. E, September 29, 1864; mustered out to date, June 3, 1865, at New York City.

MAGIE, JOHN C.—Age, 25 years. Enlisted, August 15,

2nd Lieutenant Thomas G. Mabee. He was mustered as sergeant of Company D, promoted to sergeant major, promoted again to 2nd lieutenant of Company B, and mustered out with the regiment June 3, 1865 (archive of the Historical Society of the Town of Warwick, gift of Joan and Tom Frangos).

1862, at Port Jervis, to serve three years; mustered in as private, Co. F, September 5, 1862; promoted corporal, September 23, 1863; returned to ranks, November 1, 1863; mustered out with company, June 3, 1865, near Washington, D.C.; also borne as Magee.

MAJOR, HUGH.—Age, 34 years. Enlisted, August 18, 1862, at Newburgh, to serve three years; mustered in as private, Co. K, September 5, 1862; deserted, September 25, 1862, from camp, near Fort Bennett, Va.

MALCOLM, SAMUEL.—Age, 25 years. Enlisted, August 18, 1862, at Newburgh, to serve three years; mustered in as private, Co. K, September 5, 1862; wounded in action, May 3, 1863, at Chancellorsville, Va.; transferred to Co. D, November 15, 1864; absent since in general hospital and at muster-out of company; also borne as Malcom and Macolm.

MALONE, ROBERT A.—Age, 26 years. Enrolled at Albany, to serve three years, and mustered in as second lieutenant, Co. K, August 18, 1864, as captain, September 15, 1864; mustered out with company, June 3, 1865, near Washington, D.C.; prior service as captain, Co. D, Eighteenth Infantry.

MALONEY, MICHAEL.—Age, 22 years. Enlisted, September 26, 1864, at Royalton, to serve three years; mustered in as private, Co. D, September 26, 1864; deserted to the enemy, November 11, 1864, at Hancock Station, Va.

MANN, WILLIAM M.—Age, 23 years. Enlisted, August 11, 1862, at Goshen, to serve three years; mustered in as private, Co. D, September 5, 1862; mustered out with company, June 3, 1865, near Washington, D.C.

MANNY, MATHEW.—Age, 28 years. Enlisted, August 13, 1862, at Newburgh, to serve three years; mustered in as private, Co. I, September 5, 1862; wounded and captured in action, May 6, 1864, at the Wilderness, Va.; paroled, no date; wounded in action, April 6, 1865, at Sailor's Creek, Va.; mustered out with company, June 3, 1865, near Washington, D.C.

MANY, WILLIAM H.—Age, 18 years. Enlisted, August 11, 1862, at Cornwall, to serve three years; mustered in as first sergeant, Co. C, September 5, 1862; transferred to Co. D, Twenty-fourth Regiment, Veteran Reserve Corps, March 15, 1864.

MAPES, EDWARD T.—Age, 21 years. Enlisted, August 11, 1862, at Goshen, to serve three years; mustered in as private, Co. B, September 5, 1862; promoted corporal, no date; transferred to Co. B, Eighteenth Regiment, Veteran Reserve Corps, April 22, 1864; mustered out with detachment, June 17, 1865.

MAPES, WILLIAM E.—Age, 21 years. Enrolled at Goshen, to serve three rears, and mustered in as second lieutenant, Co. B, August 14, 1862; as first lieutenant, February 9, 1863; wounded in action, May 12, 1864, at Spotsylvania Courthouse, Va.; mustered in as captain, Co. H, May 31, 1864; wounded in action, 14, 1864, at Strawberry Plains, Va.; discharged for wounds, December 15, 1864. Commissioned second lieutenant, September 10, 1862, with rank from August 14, 1862, original; first lieutenant, February 27, 1863, with rank from February 8, 1863, vice W.E. Wygant, resigned; captain, December 17, 1863, with rank from July 2, 1863, vice H.S. Murray, promoted.

MARSHALL, EDWARD G.—Age, — years. Enrolled, August 28, 1862, at Goshen, to serve three years; mustered in assistant surgeon, September 5, 1862; dismissed, August 7, 1863. Commissioned assistant surgeon, September 10, 1862, with rank from September 5, 1862, original.

MARTIN, ISAAC M.—Age, — years. Enrolled, August 20, 1862, at Newburgh, to serve three years; mustered in as second lieutenant, Co. I, September 5, 1862; promoted first lieutenant, December 30, 1862; dismissed May 15, 1863.

MARVIN, HENRY.—Age, 28 years. Enlisted, August 8, 1862, at Goshen, to serve three years; mustered in as private, Co. A, September 5, 1862; deserted, September —, 1862, at Goshen, N.Y.

MASON, GEORGE.—Age, 18 years. Enlisted, August 7, 1864, at Aurelius, to serve one year; mustered in as private, Co. A, August 30, 1864; died of typhoid fever, March 14, 1865, at division hospital.

MATHEWS, PETER.—Age, 29 years. Enlisted, August 7, 1862, at Goshen, to serve three years; mustered in as private, Co. A, September 5, 1862; deserted, September, 1862, at Goshen N.Y.; also borne as Matthews.

MATTHEWS, GEORGE F.—Age, 19 years. Enlisted, August 25, 1864, at Goshen, to serve one year; mustered in as private, Co. K, August 25, 1864; mustered out with company, June 3, 1865, near Washington, D.C.

MATTHEWS, HENRY.—Age, 20 years. Enlisted, August 13, 1862, at Walden, to serve three years; mustered in as private, Co. H, September 5, 1862; wounded in action, May 3, 1863, at Chancellorsville, Va.; deserted July 12, 1863, from camp distribution, at Alexandria, Va.

MAYETTE, HENRY H.—Age, 19 years. Enlisted, August 5, 1862, at Wallkill, to serve three years; mustered in as private, Co. K, September 5, 1862; promoted corporal, March 5, 1864; wounded in action, May 23, 1864, at North Anna, Va.; promoted sergeant, November 15, 1864; mustered out with company, June 8[?], 1865, near Washington, D.C.

McBRIDE, THOMAS.—Age, 27 years. Enlisted, August 20, 1862, at Newburgh, to serve three years; mustered in as private, Co. I, September 5, 1862; mustered out with company, June 3, 1865, near Washington, D.C.

McBURNEY, WILLIAM A.—Age, 23 years. Enrolled, August 19, 1862, at Goshen, to serve three years; mustered in as captain, Co. E, September 5, 1862; discharged, March 9, 1863. Commissioned captain, September 10, 1862, with rank from August 19, 1862, original.

McCALLISTER, JOHN H.—Age, 18 years. Enlisted, August 22, 1862, at Newburgh, to serve three years; mustered in as private, Co. I, September 5, 1862; wounded in action, May 3, 1863, at Chancellorsville, Va.; transferred to Seventh Company, Second Battalion, Veteran Reserve Corps, November 16, 1864; mustered out, June 29, 1865, with detachment, at Washington, D.C., as McAllister.

McCANN, JOEL.—Age, 21 years. Enlisted, August 14, 1862, at Goshen, to serve three years; mustered in as private, Co. D, September 5, 1862; wounded in action, May 3, 1863, at Chancellorsville, Va.; mustered out with company, June 3, 1865, near Washington, D.C.

McCANN, JOHN.—Age, 32 years. Enlisted, August 13, 1862, at Walden, to serve three years; mustered in as private, Co. H, September 5, 1862; wounded in action, May 3, 1863, at Chancellorsville, Va.; discharged for disability caused from wounds, October 17, 1863.

McCARTNEY, ROBERT.—Age, 42 years. Enlisted, August 14, 1862, at Newburgh, to serve three years; mustered in as private, Co. K, September 5, 1862; wounded in action, May 3, 1863, at Chancellorsville, Va.; transferred to Co. D, Third Regiment, Veteran Reserve Corps, June 15, 1864; mustered out for disability, July 6, 1865.

McCARTY, ANDREW J.—Age, 25 years. Enlisted, August 25, 1862, at Port Jervis, to serve three years; mustered in as private, Co. F, September 5, 1862; wounded in action, May 3, 1863, at Chancellorsville, Va., and May 5, 1864, at the Wilderness, Va.; absent, in general hospital, at Philadelphia, Pa., at muster-out of company.

McCLELLAN, KENNETH.—Age, 44 years. Enlisted, December 25, 1863, at Newburgh, to serve three years; mustered in as private, Co. D, December 25, 1863; transferred to Co. I, no date; to Co. D, Ninety-third Infantry, June 1, 1865.

McCOLLUM, JAMES.—Age, 45 years. Enlisted, August 6, 1862, at Goshen, to serve three years; mustered in as sergeant, Co. A, September 3, 1862; discharged, February 16, 1863, in camp near Falmouth, Va.

McCORMICK, DENNIS.—Age, 28 years. Enlisted, August 6, 1862, at Goshen, to serve three years; mustered in as private, Co. B, September 5, 1862; wounded in action, May 3, 1863, at Chancellorsville, Va.; transferred to Co. I, Sixth Regiment, Veteran Reserve Corps, April 10, 1864; discharged, July 3, 1865, at Lytle Barracks, Cincinnati, Ohio.

McCOY, JAMES.—Age, 22 years. Enlisted, August 16, 1862, at Newburgh, to serve three years; mustered in as private, Co. K, September 5, 1862; promoted corporal, prior to March 1863; furloughed from Falmouth, Va., and deserted on its expiration while home, April 2, 1863.

McCULLOUGH, JOSEPH.—Age, 44 years. Enlisted, September 15, 1864, at Plattsburgh, to serve one year; mustered in as private, Co. E, September 15, 1864; mustered out with detachment, May 29, 1865, at Harewood Hospital, Washington, D.C., as McCullock.

McDERMOTT, JOHN.—Age, 26 years. Enlisted, August 26, at Goshen, to serve three years; mustered in as private, Co. K, September 3, 1862; mustered out with company, June 3, 1865, near Washington, D.C.

McDOUGAL, ANDREW D.—Age, 23 years. Enlisted, August 13, 1862, at Walden, to serve three years; mustered in as first sergeant, Co. H, September 5, 1862; discharged, February 10, 1863, as sergeant; prior service in Co. I, Seventy-first Regiment Militia.

McELROY, JAMES H.—Age, 18 years. Enlisted, August 7, 1862, at Goshen, to serve three years; mustered in as private, Co. D, September 5, 1862; appointed musician, no date; discharged, October 10, 1863.

McGARRAH, WILLIAM.—Age, 24 years. Enlisted, August 11, 1862, at Goshen, to serve three years; mustered in as private, Co. D, September 5, 1862; wounded in action, May 3, 1863, at Chancellorsville, Va.; discharged for disability, August 1863, from Augur general hospital, Washington, D.C.

McGAW, JOHN.—Age, 31 years. Enlisted, August 22, 1862, at Newburgh, to serve three years; mustered in as private, Co. I, September 5, 1862, mustered out with company, June 3, 1865, near Washington, D.C.

McGRAGOR, CHARLES A.—Age, 20 years. Enlisted, August 19, 1862, at Walden, to serve three years; mustered in as private, Co. H, September 5, 1862; wounded in action, May 3, 1863, at Chancellorsville, Va.; again, November 30, 1863, and died of his wounds, December 1, 1863, at Mine Run, Va.; also borne as McGregor.

McGRATH, JAMES.—Age, 18 years. Enlisted, August 11, 1862, at Goshen, to serve three years; mustered in as private, Co. A, September 5, 1862; wounded in action, May 6, 1864, at the Wilderness, Va.; mustered out with company, June 3, 1865, near Washington, D, C.

McGRATH, JOHN.—Age, 19 years. Enlisted, February 24, 1864, at Goshen, to serve three years; mustered in as private, Co. A, February 24, 1864; wounded in action, May 6, 1864, at the Wilderness, Va.; transferred to Co. E, Ninety-third Infantry, June 1, 1865.

McGRIGOR, JAMES.—Age, 21 years. Enlisted, August 11, 1862, at Newburgh, to serve three years; mustered in as private, Co. I, September 5, 1862; discharged, August 14, 1863; also borne as McGregor.

McGULPIN, WILLIAM H.—Age, 19 years. Enlisted, August 1, 1864, at Conquest, to serve one year; mustered in as private, Co. I, August 1, 1864; mustered out with company, June 5[?], 1865, near Washington, D.C.; also borne as Magulpin.

McLALLEN, STEPHEN.—Private, Co. H, First U.S. Sharpshooters; transferred to Co. H, this regiment, March 1, 1865; on detached duty at New York City since July 28, 1863, and at muster-out of company.

McMAHON, FRANCIS.—Age, 21 years. Enlisted, September 3, 1862, at Goshen, to serve three years; mustered in as private, Co. G., September 5, 1862; wounded in action, November 30, 1863, at Mine Run, Va., and May 12, 1864, at Spotsylvania, Va.; mustered out with company, June 3, 1865, near Washington, D.C.; also borne as McMahan.

McMORRIS, MICHAEL.—Age, 18 years. Enlisted, January 4, 1864, at Warwick, to serve three years; mustered in as private, Co. D, January 4, 1864; wounded in action, May 5, 1864, at the Wilderness, Va.; died of his wounds, May 30, 1864, at Washington, D.C.

McNEIL, SIDNEY.—Private, Co. K, First U.S. Sharpshooters; transferred to Co. H, this regiment.—March 1, 1865; absent, in general hospital, wounded, since November 30, 1863, and at muster-out of company.

McNITT, WILLIAM L.—Age, 18 years. Enlisted, August 5, 1864, at Castile, to serve one year; mustered in as private, Co. A, August 5, 1864; mustered out with company, June 3, 1865, near Washington, D.C.

McQUAID, SAMUEL.—Age, 27 years. Enlisted, August 15, 1862, at Newburgh to serve three years; mustered in as private, Co. I, September 5, 1862; promoted corporal, November 1, 1862; wounded in action, May 3, 1863, at Chancellorsville, Va.; July 3, 1863, at Gettysburg, Pa.; transferred to One Hundred and Thirty-first Company,

Second Battalion, Veteran Reserve Corps, September 30, 1864; discharged for disability, as sergeant, April 12, 1865, at Summit House Hospital, Philadelphia, Pa.

McQUOID, JR., WILLIAM.—Age, 18 years. Enlisted, August 5, 1862, at Chester, to serve three years; mustered in as private, Co. A, September 5, 1862; promoted corporal, September 15, 1862; discharged February 8, 1864, at Washington, D.C.

McSHANE, HUGH.—Age, 35 years. Enlisted, August 12, 1862, at Goshen, to serve three years; mustered in as private, Co. B, September May 5, 1862; wounded in action, May 3, 1863, at Chancellorsville, Va., and May 6, 1864, at the Wilderness. Va.; discharged, March 27, 1865, at general hospital, Alexandria, Va.

McVAY, WILLIAM.—Age, 36 years. Enlisted, August 14, 1862, at Walden, to serve three years; mustered in as private, Co. I, September 5, 1862; promoted corporal, prior to October 1864; mustered out with company, June 3, 1865, near Washington D.C.

McVEIGH, CHARLES.—Age, 19 years. Enlisted, August 11, 1862, at Newburgh, to serve three years; mustered in as private, Co. A, September 5, 1862; died of typhoid fever, December 27, 1862, in camp, near Falmouth, Va.

MEAD, CHARLES.—Age, 19 years. Enlisted, October 1, 1864, at Rochester, to serve three years; mustered in as private, Co. I, October 1, 1864; transferred to Co. D, Ninety-third Infantry, June 1, 1865.

MEAD, FRANCIS.—Age, 24 years. Enlisted, August 15, 1862, at Walden, to serve three years; mustered in as sergeant, Co. H, September 5, 1862; discharged, March 18, 1863, from general hospital, West Building, Baltimore, Md.

MEAD, WILLIAM.—Age, 30 years. Enlisted, August 6, 1862, at Cornwall, to serve three years; mustered in as private, Co. C, September 5, 1862; promoted corporal, March 1, 1863; returned to ranks, no date; promoted corporal, January 1, 1865; mustered out with company, June 3, 1865, near Washington, D.C.

MEEHAN, JOHN B.—Age, 41 years. Enlisted, August 20, 1862, at Newburgh, to serve three years; mustered in as private, Co. K, September 5, 1862; discharged for disability, April 17, 1863, at Falmouth, Va., as John R. Mehan.

MERMAN, JOSEPH.—Age, 21 years. Enlisted, August 6, 1862, at Goshen, to serve three years; mustered in as private, Co. A. September 5, 1862; deserted, October 25, 1862, at Berlin, Md.

MERRIAN, JAMES.—Age, 22 years. Enlisted at Goshen, to serve one year, and mustered in as private, Co. K, August 22, 1864; mustered out with company, June 3, 1865, near Washington, D.C.; also borne as Merriam.

MERRITT, ABRAM.—Age, 25 years. Enlisted, August 5, 1862, at Monroe, to serve three years; mustered in as private, Co. C, September 5, 1862; discharged for disability, March 20, 1863, at Falmouth, Va.

MERRITT, ANDREW H.—Age, 26 years. Enlisted, August 22, 1862, at Blooming Grove, to serve three years; mustered in as private, Co. G, September 5, 1862; mustered out with company, June 3, 1865, near Washington, D.C.; also borne as Merret.

MERRITT, CHAUNCEY W.—Age, 28 years. Enlisted, August 22, 1862, at Washingtonville, to serve three years; mustered in as corporal, Co. G, September 5, 1862; returned to ranks, no date; discharged for disability, March 3, 1863, at Continental Hotel Hospital, Baltimore, Md.

MERRITT, FRANCIS E.—Age, 32 years. Enlisted, August 22, 1862, at Washingtonville, to serve three years; mustered in as private, Co. G, September 5, 1862; discharged for disability, December 19, 1862, from hospital at Baltimore, Md.

MERRITT, JAMES M.—Age, 27 years. Enlisted, August 11, 1862, at Goshen, to serve three years; mustered in as private, Co. B, September 5, 1862; wounded in action, June 16 to 22, 1864, in front of Petersburg, Va.; promoted corporal, September 1, 1864.

MERRITT, JOHN M.—Age, 38 years. Enlisted, August 22, 1862, at Washingtonville, to serve three years; mustered in as musician, Co. G, September 5, 1862; discharged, January 31, 1863, at hospital, Philadelphia, Pa.

MERRITT, WILLIAM E.—Age, 18 years. Enlisted, December 30, 1863, at Warwick, to serve three years; mustered in as private, Co. D, December 30, 1863; transferred to Co. H, Ninety-third Infantry, June 1, 1865.

MERRITT, WILLIAM H.—Age, 22 years. Enlisted, August 20, 1862, at Goshen, to serve three years; mustered in as private, Co. B, September 5, 1862; promoted first sergeant, September 1, 1864; mustered out with company, June 3, 1865, near Washington, D.C.

MESLER, ANDREW J.—Age, 33 years. Enlisted, August 20 1862, at Port Jervis to serve three years; mustered in as private, Co. F, September 5, 1862; transferred to Co. G, Third Regiment, Veteran Reserve Corps, October 20, 1863; mustered out, July 10, 1865, at U.S. Barracks, Burlington, Vt., as Messler.

MESSENGER, ANDREW J.—Age, 25 years. Enlisted, August 7, 1862, at Florida, to serve three years; mustered in as private, Co. B, September 5, 1862; wounded in action, May 3, 1863, at Chancellorsville, Va., May 12, 1864, at Spotsylvania, Va.; deserted September 4, 1864, from Haddington Hospital, Philadelphia, Pa.

MESSENGER, JOHN J.—Age, 18 years. Enlisted, July 31, 1862, at Goshen, to serve three years; mustered in as private, Co. I, September 5, 1862; wounded in action, May 3, 1863, at Chancellorsville, Va., April 2, 1865, near Boydton Road, Va.; mustered out with company, June 3, 1865, near Washington, D.C.

MEYER, JOHN A.—Age, 19 years. Enlisted, August 18, 1862, at Newburgh, to serve three years; mustered in as private, Co. I, September 5, 1862; mustered out with company, June 3, 1865, near Washington, D.C., as Meyers; also borne as John Myer.

MEYERS, JOHN F.—Age, 25 years. Enlisted, March 26, 1864, at New York City, to serve three years; mustered in as private, Co. G, March 26, 1864; wounded in action, December 7, 1864, during Weldon raid; deserted, March 17, 1865, on expiration of furlough; also borne as Myers; veteran.

MEYERS, WILLIAM.—Age, 25 years. Enlisted, August 12, 1862, at Newburgh, to serve three years; mustered in as private, Co. A, September 5, 1862; discharged, February 15, 1864, at Washington, D.C.

MILES, WILLIAM J.—Age, 22 years. Enlisted, August 14, 1862, at Goshen, to serve three years; mustered in as private, Co. D, September 5, 1862; wounded in action, June 4, 1864, at Cold Harbor, Va.; mustered out, June 5, 1865, from Lincoln Hospital at Washington, D.C.

MILLER, ADAM W.— Age, 25 years. Enlisted, August 15, 1862, at Howells, to serve three years; mustered in as private, Co. E, September 5, 1862; wounded in action, May 2, 1863, at Chancellorsville, Va.; promoted corporal, no date; killed in action, May 12, 1864, at Spotsylvania, Va.

MILLER, ALANSON W.— Age, 19 years. Enlisted, August 12, 1862, at Wallkill, to serve three years; mustered in as private, Co. K, September 5, 1862; killed in action, May 3, 1863, at Chancellorsville, Va.

MILLER, HENRY S.— Age, 18 years. Enlisted, September 8, 1864, at Utica, to serve three years; mustered in as private, Co. K, September 8, 1864; transferred to Co. F, Ninety-third Infantry, June 1, 1865, as Henry L.; also borne as Henry Miller.

MILLER, JAMES M.— Age, 25 years. Enlisted, August 4, 1862, at Washingtonville, to serve three years; mustered in as corporal, Co. G, September 5, 1862; discharged as private, January 6, 1864, at Alexandria, Va., as Millier.

MILLER, JOHN F.— Age, 19 years. Enlisted, August 14, 1862, at Otisville, to serve three years; mustered in as private, Co. E, September 5, 1862; transferred to Veteran Reserve Corps, November 15, 1863, as John H.

MILLER, JOSEPH.— Age, 33 years. Enlisted, August 5, 1862, at Washingtonville, to serve three years; mustered in as private, Co. G, September 5, 1862; wounded in action, May 3, 1863, at Chancellorsville, Va.; discharged, March 20, 1864, at New York city.

MILLER, LEWIS P.— Age, 27 years. Enlisted, August 14, 1862, at Newburgh, to serve three years; mustered in as private, Co. G, September 5, 1862; promoted corporal, prior to April 10, 1863; wounded in action, May 3, 1863, at Chancellorsville, Va.; transferred to One Hundred and Forty-fifth Company, Second Battalion, Veteran Reserve Corps, April 6, 1864; mustered out, August 13, 1865, at DeCamp Hospital, Davids' Island, New York Harbor.

MILLER, OLIVER.— Age, 34 years. Enlisted, August 4, 1862, at Washingtonville, to serve three years; mustered in as private, Co. G. September 5, 1862; captured in action, November 27, 1863, at Locust Grove, Va., and reported dead.

MILLER, REUBEN C.— Age, 22 years. Enlisted, August 13, 1862, at Wallkill, to serve three years; mustered in as private, Co. K, September 5, 1862; discharged for disability, February 11, 1863, at Falmouth, Va.

MILLER, WILLIAM L.— Age, 44 years. Enlisted, August 28, 1862, at Goshen, to serve three years; mustered in as private, Co. G, September 5, 1862; discharged, August 30, 1863, at Alexandria, Va.

MILLIGAN, WILLIAM.— Age, 31 years. Enlisted, August 22, 1862, at Newburgh, to serve three years; mustered in as private, Co. I, September 5, 1862; wounded in action, May 3, 1863, at Chancellorsville, Va.; May 5, 1864, at the Wilderness, Va.; captured in action, October 27, 1864, near Petersburg, Va.; paroled, no date; mustered out with company, June 3, 1865, near Washington, D.C.

MILLIKEN, JOHN A.— Age, 20 years. Enlisted, August 13, 1862, at Walden, to serve three years; mustered in as private, Co. H, September 5, 1862; discharged for disability, November 17, 1862.

MILLIKEN, WILLIAM H.— Age, 18 years. Enlisted, August 13, 1862, at Newburgh, to serve three years; mustered in as private, Co. I, September 5, 1862; transferred to Forty-ninth Company, Second Battalion, Veteran Reserve Corps, September 16, 1863; mustered out with detachment, June 29, 1865, at Washington, D.C.

MILLSPAUGH, ANDREAS P.— Age, 23 years. Enlisted, August 11, 1862, at Newburgh, to serve three years; mustered in as corporal, Co. I, September 5, 1862; wounded in action, May 3, 1863, at Chancellorsville, Va.; promoted sergeant, September 1, 1863; wounded in action, May 10, 1864, at Spotsylvania, Va.; mustered out with company, June 3, 1865, near Washington, D.C., as Andreas S.

MILLSPAUGH, ANDREW A.— Age, 18 years. Enlisted, August 18, 1862, at Wallkill, to serve three years; mustered in as musician, Co. K, September 5, 1862; mustered out with company, June 3, 1865, near Washington, D.C.

MILLSPAUGH, ARCHIBALD.— Age, 19 years. Enlisted, January 1, 1864, at Goshen, to serve three years; mustered in as private, Co. G, January 1, 1864; transferred to Co. D, Ninety-third Infantry, June 1, 1865; veteran.

MILLSPAUGH, W. DEWITT.— Age, 20 years. Enlisted, August 13, 1862, at Warwick, to serve three years; mustered in as corporal, Co. B, September 5, 1862; discharged, February 4, 1863, as William D.

MILLSPAUGH, JEDUTHAN.— Age, 33 years. Enlisted, August 11, 1862, at Newburgh, to serve three years; mustered in as wagoner, Co. I, September 5, 1862; grade changed to private, no date; wounded and captured in action, May 3, 1863, at Chancellorsville, Va.; paroled, May 1863; wounded in action, May 12, 1864, at Spotsylvania, Va.; captured in action, October 27, 1864, near Petersburg, Va.; mustered out with company, June 3, 1865, near Washington, D.C.; also borne as Jedutha.

MILLSPAUGH, PETER.— Age, 21 years. Enlisted, August 14, 1862, at Walden, to serve three years; mustered in as private, Co. H, September 5, 1862; deserted, November 15, 1862, at Waterloo, Va.

MILLSPAUGH, STEPHEN.— Age, 28 years. Enlisted, August 12, 1862, at Goshen, to serve three years; mustered in as private, Co. B, September 5, 1862; discharged, February 13, 1863, at convalescent camp, Alexandria, Va.

MILSON, THOMAS.— Age, 38 years. Enlisted, August 12, 1862, at Newburgh, to serve three years; mustered in as corporal, Co. C, September 5, 1862; mustered out with company, June 3, 1865, near Washington, D.C.

MONELL, WILLIAM H.— Age, 18 years. Enlisted, August 25, 1864, at Goshen, to serve one year; mustered in as private, Co. K, August 25, 1864; mustered out with company, June 3, 1865, near Washington, D.C.

MONTFORT, ROBERT V. K.— Age, 27 years. Enrolled, August 23, 1862, at Goshen, to serve three years; mustered in as assistant surgeon, September 5, 1862; as surgeon, March 27, 1865; mustered out with regiment, June 3, 1865, near Washington, D.C. Commissioned assistant surgeon, September 10, 1862, with rank from September 4, 1862, original; surgeon, March 22, 1865, with rank from March 14, 1865, vice J. H. Thompson, failed to muster.

MONTGOMERY, JAMES.— Age, 21 years. Enlisted, August 14, 1862, at Newburgh, to serve three years; mustered in as private, Co. C, September 5, 1862; discharged for disability, January 12, 1864, at convalescent camp, Alexandria, Va.

MONTROSS, HEZEKIAH.— Age, 18 years. Enlisted at Warwick, to serve three years, and mustered in as private, Co. B, January 12, 1864; wounded in action, June 16, 1864, before Petersburg, Va.; promoted corporal, September 1, 1864; transferred to Co. C, Ninety-third Infantry, June 2, 1865; also borne as Hezekiah H.

MOONEY, MICHAEL.— Age, 18 years. Enlisted, August 11, 1862, at Goshen, to serve three years; mustered in as private, Co. B, September 5, 1862; transferred to Thirty-third Company, Second Battalion, Veteran Reserve Corps, February 2, 1865; mustered out with detachment, June 25, 1865, as of Co. G, Ninth Regiment, Veteran Reserve Corps, at Washington, D.C.

MOORE, JOHN.— Age, 20 years. Enlisted, September 2, 1864, at Goshen, to serve one year; mustered in as private, Co. E, September 2, 1864; mustered out with detachment, May 10, 1864, at Hart's Island, New York Harbor.

MOORE, THOMAS H.— Age, 41 years. Enlisted, August 20, 1864, at Goshen, to serve one year; mustered in as private, Co. K, August 20, 1864; mustered out with company, June 3, 1865, near Washington, D.C.

MOORE, WILLIAM.— Age, 38 years. Enlisted, August 20, 1862, at Newburgh, to serve three years; mustered in as private, Co. I, September 5, 1862; killed in action, July 3, 1863, at Gettysburg, Pa.

MOORES, JAMES B.— Age, 30 years. Enlisted, August 7, 1862, at Newburgh, to serve three years; mustered in as private, Co. E, September 5, 1862; wounded in action, July 2, 1863, at Gettysburg, Pa.; died of his wounds, July 8, 1863; also borne as Moore.

MORGAN, CHARLES.— Age, 22 years. Enlisted, September 9, 1864, at Williamston, to serve one year; mustered in as private, Co. D, September 9, 1864; mustered out with company, June 3, 1865, near Washington, D.C.

MORGAN, DANIEL.— Age, 19 years. Enlisted, August 6, 1862, at Goshen, to serve three years; mustered in as private, Co. A, September 5, 1862; wounded in action, April 6, 1865, at Sailors' Creek, Va.; mustered out with detachment, May 17, 1865, from Harewood Hospital, Washington, D.C.

MORGAN, DANIEL.— Age, 26 years. Enlisted, August 12, 1862, at Goshen, to serve three years; mustered in as private, Co. B, September 5, 1862; deserted, October 19, 1862, at Knoxville, Md.

MORGAN, GEORGE.— Age, 22 years. Enlisted, August 30, 1862, at New Windsor, to serve three years; mustered in as private, Co. E, September 5, 1862; mustered out with company, June 3, 1865, near Washington, D.C.

MORGAN, JOHN.— Age, 19 years. Enlisted, January 12, 1864, at Warwick, to serve three years; mustered in as private, Co. B, January 12, 1864; wounded in action, May 6, 1864, at the Wilderness, Va.; transferred to Co. C, Ninety-third Infantry, June 2, 1865.

MORGAN, THOMAS.— Age, 18 years. Enlisted, February 10, 1864, at Warwick, to serve three years; mustered in as private, Co. B, February 10, 1864; wounded in action, May 6, 1864, at the Wilderness, Va.; transferred to Co. C, Ninety-third Infantry, June 2, 1865.

MORGAN, WESTLEY.— Age, 26 years. Enlisted, August 12, 1862, at Goshen, to serve three years; mustered in as private, Co. A, September 5, 1862; wounded in action, July 3, 1863, at Gettysburg, Pa.; absent, sick at Fairfax Seminary Hospital, Va., since August 25, 1864, and at muster-out of company; also borne as Wesley.

MORGAN, WILLIAM H.— Age, 21 years. Enlisted, December 21, 1863, at Warwick, to serve three years; mustered in as private, Co. D, December 21, 1863; wounded in action, May 8, 1864, at Spotsylvania, Va.; transferred to Co. H, Ninety-third Infantry, June 1, 1865.

MORRIS, COLEMAN.— Age, 21 years. Enlisted, August 25, 1862, at Goshen, to serve three years; mustered in as private, Co. D, September 3, 1862; wounded in action, May 3, 1863, at Chancellorsville Va.; promoted corporal, August 31, 1864; mustered out with company, June 3, 1865, near Washington, D.C.

MOULD, DAVID.— Age, 21 years. Enlisted, August 22, 1862, at Montgomery, to serve three years; mustered in as private, Co. H, September 5, 1862; promoted corporal prior to April 10, 1863; killed in action, May 3, 1863, at Chancellorsville, Va.

MOULD, MARTIN.— Age, 21 years. Enlisted, August 14, 1862, at Newburgh, to serve three years; mustered in as corporal, Co. I, September 5, 1862; discharged, February 5, 1863.

MOULTON, JAMES P.— Age, 31 years. Enlisted, August 13, 1862, at Monroe, to serve three years; mustered in as private, Co. C, September 5, 1862; promoted corporal, March 1, 1863; wounded in action, May 5, 1864, at the Wilderness, Va.; mustered out with company, June 3, 1865, near Washington, D.C.; also borne as Molton.

MULLEN, NATHAN B.— Age, 19 years. Enlisted, August 5, 1862, at Wallkill, to serve three years; mustered in as private, Co. K, September 5, 1862; wounded in action, May 3, 1863, at Chancellorsville, Va.; died of his wounds, July 22, 1863, in Armory Square Hospital, at Washington, D.C.

MULVEHILL, MARTIN.— Age, 21 years. Enlisted, August 22, 1862, at Goshen, to serve three years; mustered in as private, Co. D, September 5, 1862; captured in action, November 6, 1862, at Front Royal, Va.; paroled, November 22, 1862, at City Point, Va.; reported at Parole Camp, Md., November 24, 1862; no further record.

MUNHALL, JOHN.— Age, 26 years. Enlisted, August 11, 1862, at Washingtonville, to serve three years; mustered in as private, Co. G, September 5, 1862; deserted, August 30, 1863, at Washington, D.C., as Monhall.

MUNROE, JONATHAN.— Age, 23 years. Enlisted, September 26, 1864, at Royalton, to serve three years; mustered in as private, Co. D, September 26, 1864; absent, sick in general hospital since April 30, 1865, and at muster out of company.

MUNROE, WILLIAM.— Age, 22 years. Enlisted at Royalton, to serve one year, and mustered in as private, Co. D, September 26, 1864; mustered out with company, June 8[?], 1865, near Washington, D.C.

MURPHY, JOHN.— Age, 33 years. Enlisted at Royalton, to serve one year, and mustered in as private, Co. D,

September 20, 1864; wounded in action, April 6, 1865, at Sailor's Creek, Va.; mustered out with company, June 3, 1865, near Washington, D.C.

MURRAY, HENRY S.— Age, 22 years. Enrolled, August 14, 1862, at Goshen, to serve three years; mustered in as captain, Co. B, September 5, 1862; wounded, captured in action, and paroled, May 3, 1863, at Chancellorsville, Va.; mustered in as major, September 20, 1861; wounded and captured in action, October 27, 1864, at Boydton Road, Va.; paroled, February 1865; discharged, March 30, 1865. Commissioned captain, September 10, 1862, with rank from August 14, 1862, original; major, October 6, 1863, with rank from July 2, 1863, vice C. H. Weygant, promoted; lieutenant-colonel, not mustered, January 11, 1865, with rank from September 19, 1864, vice C. H. Weygant, promoted.

MURRAY, ROBERT R.— Age, 20 years. Enlisted, August 11, 1862, at Goshen, to serve three years; mustered in as corporal, Co. B, September 5, 1862; promoted sergeant, prior to April 10, 1863; wounded in action, May 3, 1863, at Chancellorsville, Va.; transferred to Twenty-seventh Company, Second Battalion, Veteran Reserve Corps, September 1, 1863; mustered out with detachment, June 29, 1865, at Washington, D.C.

MYER, EDWARD.— Age, 24 years. Enlisted at Goshen, to serve one year, and mustered in as private, Co. K, August 18, 1864; wounded, December 9, 1864; mustered out with company, June 3, 1865, near Washington, D.C.; also borne as Meyer and Mayer.

NEWELL, CHARLES.— Age, 21 years. Enlisted, August 14, 1862, at Wallkill, to serve three years; mustered in as private, Co. E, September 5, 1862; killed in action, May 3, 1863, at Chancellorsville, Va.

NEWKIRK, JOHN.— Age, 18 years. Enlisted, July 29, 1862, at Warwick, to serve three years; mustered in as private, Co. G, September 5, 1862; mustered out with company, June 3, 1865, near Washington, D.C.

NEWTON, JOHN.— Age, 23 years. Enlisted, August 11, 1862, at Goshen, to serve three years; mustered in as corporal, Co. A, September 5, 1862; returned to ranks, no date; deserted, October 25, 1862, at Berlin, Md.

NICHOL, GEORGE.— Age, 26 years. Enlisted, August 15, 1862, at Wallkill, to serve three years; mustered in as private, Co. E, September 5, 1862; mustered out with company, June 3, 1865, near Washington, D.C.; also borne as Nichols.

NICHOLS, JACOB.— Age, 18 years. Enlisted at Goshen, to serve one year, and mustered in as private, Co. K, September 7, 1864; mustered out with detachment, May 17, 1865, at Satterlee Hospital, West Philadelphia, Pa., as Jacob J.

NICHOLS, MARTIN T.— Corporal, Co. K, First United States Sharpshooters; transferred as private to Co. H, this regiment, March 1, 1865; absent, missing in action, since May 6, 1864, at the Wilderness, Va., and at muster-out of company.

NICOLL, ISAAC.— Age, 22 years. Enrolled, August 20, 1862, at Goshen, to serve three years; mustered in as captain, Co. G, September 5, 1862; killed in action, July 2, 1863, at Gettysburg, Pa. Commissioned captain, September 10, 1862, with rank from August 20, 1862, original.

NICOLL, JAMES.— Age, 22 years. Enlisted, August 15, 1862, at Newburgh, to serve three years; not mustered in as private, Co. K; claimed and taken as a deserter by the Thirty-sixth Infantry prior to muster-in of company; also borne as James C.

NIXON, JAMES.— Age, 19 years. Enlisted, August 6,1862, at Goshen, to serve three years; mustered in as private, Co. A, September 5, 1862; deserted, September 19, 1862, at Camp Ellis, Va.

NIXON, JOHN.— Age, 18 years. Enlisted, August 4, 1862, at Goshen, to serve three years; mustered in as private, Co. A, September 5, 1862; deserted, September 19, 1862, at Camp Ellis, Va.

NOLL, PETER.— Age, 43 years. Enlisted, August 7, 1862, at Wallkill, to serve three years; mustered in as private, Co. K, September 5, 1862; discharged for disability, April 16, 1863, at Falmouth, Va.; also borne as Nall.

NORTON, FREDERICK E.— Age, 18 years. Enlisted at Plattsburgh, to serve one year, and mustered in as private, Co. E, September 17, 1864; mustered out with company, June 3, 1865, near Washington, D.C.

O'BRIEN, JOHN.— Age, 19 years. Enlisted, August 16, 1862, at Wallkill, to serve three years; mustered in as private, Co. K, September 5, 1862; wounded and captured in action, May 3, 1863, at Chancellorsville, Va.; paroled, May 18, 1863; discharged for wounds, April 1, 1864, at Washington, D.C.; also borne as O'Brian.

O'CONNELL, THOMAS.— Age, 23 years. Enlisted, August 13, 1862, at Walden, to serve three years; mustered in as private, Co. H, September 5, 1862; wounded in action, July 2, 1863, at Gettysburg, Pa.; absent since, and in hospital at Philadelphia, Pa., at muster-out of company.

ODELL, DAVID.— Age, 33 years. Enlisted, August 13, 1862, at Cornwall, to serve three years; mustered in as private, Co. C, September 5, 1862; accidentally wounded, no date; discharged for wounds, December 12, 1862, at Washington, D.C.

ODELL, GEORGE W.— Age, 22 years. Enlisted, August 6, 1862, at Chester, to serve three years; mustered in as private, Co. D, September 5, 1862; promoted corporal, prior to April 10, 1863; wounded in action, May 3, 1863, at Chancellorsville, Va.; transferred to Forty-eighth Company, Second Battalion, Veteran Reserve Corps, December 14, 1863, and mustered out as sergeant with detachment, June 20, 1865, at Washington, D.C.

ODELL, ISAAC.— Age, 35 years. Enlisted, August 13, 1862, at Cornwall, to serve three years; mustered in as private, Co. C. September 5, 1862; accidentally wounded, no date; transferred to Co. D, Third Regiment, Veteran Reserve Corps, March 15, 1864, and discharged, July 6, 1865.

ODELL, JABES.— Age, 18 years. Enlisted, August 25, 1862, at Goshen, to serve three years; mustered in as private, Co. A, September 5, 1862; wounded in action, May 12, 1864, at Spotsylvania Court House, Va.; mustered out with company, June 3, 1865, near Washington, D.C.; also borne as Jabez Alwood Odell.

ODELL, JAMES.— Age, 23 years. Enlisted, August 5, 1862, at Goshen, to serve three years; mustered in as private, Co. B, September 5, 1862; mustered out with company, June 3, 1865, near Washington, D.C.

ODELL, MOWALDEN.—Age, 36 years. Enlisted, August 20, 1862, at Newburgh, to serve three years; mustered in as private, Co. C, September 5, 1862; promoted corporal, May 1, 1865; mustered out with company, June 3, 1865, near Washington, D.C.

ODELL, NAPOLEON B.—Age, 18 years. Enlisted, August 23, 1862, at Goshen, to serve three years; mustered in as private, Co. G[?], September 5, 1862; discharged, January 31, 1863, at camp near Falmouth, Va.

ODELL, WILLIAM.—Age, 19 years. Enlisted, August 8, 1862, at Goshen, to serve three years; mustered in as private, Co. A, September 5, 1862; killed in action, May 3, 1863, at Chancellorsville, Va.

OGDEN, WOODWARD T.—Age, 20 years. Enrolled, August 5, 1862, at Wallkill, to serve three years; mustered in as corporal, Co. K, September 5, 1862; promoted sergeant, January 1, 1863; wounded in action, May 3, 1863, at Chancellorsville, Va.; July 2, 1863, at Gettysburg, Pa.; and May 12, 1864, at Spotsylvania Court House, Va.: promoted first sergeant, July 4, 1864; mustered in as second lieutenant, November 15, 1864; mustered out with company, June 3, 1865, near Washington, D.C. Commissioned second lieutenant, November 15, 1864, with rank from July 21, 1864, vice T. M. Roberson, promoted; first lieutenant, not mustered, February 18, 1865, with rank from January 1, 1865, vice T. M. Roberson, promoted.

OGG, JOHN G.—Age, 23 years. Enlisted, August 12, 1862, at Port Jervis, to serve three years; mustered in as private, Co. F, September 5, 1862; wounded in action, May 2, 1863, at Chancellorsville, Va.; died of his wounds, June 20, 1863, at Alexandria. Va.

OGG, PHILIP M.—Age, 20 years. Enlisted, August 9, 1862, at Port Jervis, to serve three years; mustered in as private, Co. F, September 5, 1862; transferred to Co. D, Ninth Regiment, Veteran Reserve Corps, September 7, 1863; mustered out with detachment, June 20, 1865, at Washington, D.C.

O'HARA, DANIEL.—Age, 22 years. Enlisted, August 15, 1862, at New Windsor, to serve three years; mustered in as private, Co. C, September 5, 1862; promoted corporal, prior to April 10, 1863; wounded in action, May 3, 1863, at Chancellorsville, Va.; transferred to Veteran Reserve Corps, October 28, 1863.

OLDS, ALEXANDER R.—Age, 35 years. Enlisted at Goshen, to serve one year, and mustered in as private, Co. K, August 22, 1865; mustered out with company, June 3, 1865, near Washington, D.C.

O'NEAL, PATRICK.—Age, 39 years. Enlisted, August 14, 1862, at Newburgh, to serve three years; mustered in as private, Co. I, September 5, 1862; discharged, February 7, 1863.

ONEY, EDWARD.—Age, 40 years. Enlisted, August 18, 1862, at New Windsor, to serve three years; mustered in as private, Co. I, September 5, 1862; discharged, October 7, 1863.

O'REILLY, GEORGE J.—Age, 19 years. Enlisted at Goshen, to serve one year, and mustered in as private, Co. K, August 20, 1864; mustered out with company, June 3, 1865, near Washington, D.C.

OSBORN, EDWARD P.—Age, 35 years. Enlisted at Lyons, to serve three years, and mustered in as private, Co. A, August 10, 1864; transferred to Co. E, Ninety-third Infantry, June 1, 1865.

OSTRAM, STEPHEN E.—Age, 45 years. Enlisted, August 19, 1862, at Goshen, to serve three years; mustered in as private, Co. E, September 5, 1862; discharged, February 21, 1863, near Falmouth, Va., as Ostrom; also borne as Ostrum.

OSTRANDER, JOHN.—Age, 30 years. Enlisted, August 14, 1862, at Newburgh, to serve three years; mustered in as private, Co. G[?], September 5, 1862; discharged, January 11, 1864, at Alexandria, Va.

OWEN, ALLEN.—Age, 24 years. Enlisted, August 11, 1862, at Goshen, to serve three years; mustered in as private, Co. A, September 5, 1862; wounded in action, August 14, 1864, at Deep Bottom, Va.; transferred to Twelfth Company, Second Battalion, Veteran Reserve Corps, December 19, 1864; mustered out with detachment, June 26, 1865, at Washington, D.C.

OWEN, CHARLES E.—Age, 18 years. Enlisted at Hamptonburg, to serve three years, and mustered in as private, Co. G, January 1, 1864; transferred to Co. D, Ninety-third Infantry, June 1, 1865; also borne as Owens.

OWENS, WILLIAM R.—Age, 32 years. Enlisted, August 11, 1862, at Newburgh, to serve three years; mustered in as private, Co. C, September 5, 1862; promoted corporal, no date; killed in action, May 14, 1864, at Spotsylvania, Va.

PARET, HORACE D.—Age, 37 years. Enlisted, August 5, 1862, at Wallkill, to serve three years; mustered in as private, Co. K, September 3, 1862; mustered out with company, June 3, 1865, near Washington, D.C., as Parrot; also borne as Parrett.

PARKER, ALBERT W.—Age, 22 years. Enlisted, August 11, 1862, at Washingtonville, to serve three years; mustered in as private, Co. G, September 5, 1862; mustered out with company, June 3, 1863, near Washington, D.C.

PARKER, ISAAC W.—Age, 19 years. Enlisted, August 11, 1862, at Washingtonville, to serve three years; mustered in as private, Co. G, September 5, 1862; captured, October 1863; died, July 3, 1864, at Andersonville, Ga. [The Andersonville records give the cause of his death as diarrhea and say that he is in grave #2819.]

PARKER, JOHN.—Age, 23 years. Enlisted at Goshen, to serve one year, and mustered in as private, Co. B, September 12, 1864; mustered out with company, June 3, 1865, near Washington, D.C.

PARKER, NATHAN W.—Age, 19 years. Enlisted at Montgomery, to serve three years, and mustered in as private, Co. G, February 5, 1864; wounded in action, May 12, 1864, at Spotsylvania, Va.; died of his wounds, May 17, 1864.

PARKS, JOHN W.—Age, 32 years. Enlisted, August 8, 1862, at Wallkill, to serve three years; mustered in as private, Co. K, September 5, 1862; promoted corporal, October 1, 1864; mustered out with company, June 3, 1865, near Washington, D.C.

PARLIMENT, NATHANIEL.—Age, 23 years. Enlisted, August 15, 1862, at Goshen, to serve three years; mustered in as private, Co. C, September 3, 1862; deserted, September 6, 1862, at Jersey City, N.J.; apprehended, November 18, 1863, and sent to Fort Columbus, New York Harbor; absent since and at muster-out of company, also borne as Parlemnent.

PARSONS, JAMES N.—Age, 20 years. Enlisted, August 9, 1862, at Otisville, to serve three years; mustered in as private, Co. E, September 5, 1862; died of typhoid fever, July 1, 1863, at Chestnut Hill Hospital, Philadelphia, Pa.; also borne as Parson.

PARSONS, WINFIELD W.—Age, 18 years. Enlisted, August 12, 1862, at Wallkill, to serve three years; mustered in as sergeant, Co. K, September 5, 1862; promoted first sergeant, no date; wounded in action, May 5, 1864, at the Wilderness, Va.; died of his wounds, July 3, 1864, at Armory Square Hospital, Washington, D.C.

PARTINGTON, JAMES.—Age, 22 years. Enlisted, August 15, 1862, at Newburgh, to serve three years; mustered in as private, Co. I, September 5, 1862; wounded in action, July 2, 1863, at Gettysburg, Pa.; died of his wounds, July 8, 1863.

PATTERSON, WILLIAM H.—Age, 40 years. Enlisted, August 11, 1862, at Port Jervis, to serve three years; mustered in as corporal, Co. F, September 5, 1862; returned to ranks, no date; transferred to Veteran Reserve Corps, January 15, 1864.

PAYNE, DANIEL P.—Age, place, date of enlistment and muster-in as private, Co. D, not stated; wounded in action, May 6, 1864, at the Wilderness, Va.; no further record.

PAYNE, HENRY C.—Age, 24 years. Enlisted, August 11, 1862, at Goshen, to serve three years; mustered in as musician, Co. B, September 5, 1862; grade changed to private, prior to April 10, 1863; mustered out as musician, with company, June 3, 1865, near Washington, D.C.; also borne as Paine.

PAYNE, JOHN K.—Age, 24 years. Enlisted at Goshen, to serve three years, and mustered in as private, Co. B, December 18, 1863; wounded and captured in action, May 3, 1864, at the Wilderness, Va.; paroled, no date; discharged, May 7, 1865; also borne as John Paine.

PECK, ERASTUS M. B.—Age, 25 years. Enlisted, August 11, 1862, at Port Jervis, to serve three years; mustered in as sergeant, Co. F, September 5, 1862; wounded in action, May 10, 1864, at Spotsylvania, Va.; mustered out with company, June 3, 1865, near Washington, D.C.

PECK, THOMAS B.—Age, 35 years. Enlisted, August 15, 1862, at Port Jervis, to serve three years; mustered in as private, Co. F, September 5, 1862; discharged for disability, February 9, 1863, at Harewood Hospital, Washington, D.C.

PEET, GILBERT.—Age, 45 years. Enlisted, August 12, 1862, Washingtonville, to serve three years; mustered in as private, Co. G, September 5, 1862; wounded in action, July 2, 1863, Gettysburg, Pa.; transferred to Veteran Reserve Corps, August 20, 1864; also borne as Peit.

PELTON, GIDEON H.—Age, 21 years. Enlisted, August 2, 1862, at Goshen, to serve three years; mustered in as corporal, Co. D, September 5, 1862; wounded in action, July 2, 1863, at Gettysburg, Pa.; transferred to One Hundred and Second Company, Second Battalion, Veteran Reserve Corps, January, 1865, and mustered out with detachment, June 30, 1865, at Washington, D.C., while in Augur Hospital, near Alexandria, Va.

PEMBLETON, JAMES.—Age, 28 years. Enlisted, August 11, 1862, at Goshen, to serve three years; mustered in as private, Co. D, September 5, 1862; killed in action, July 2, 1863, at Gettysburg, Pa., as Pemberton.

PERRY, ROBERT.—Age, 19 years. Enlisted at Porter, to serve one year, and mustered in as private, Co. A, September 15, 1864; mustered out with company, June 3, 1865, near Washington, D.C.

PETERS, CHARLES.—Age, 35 years. Enlisted, August 12, 1862, at Port Jervis, to serve three years; mustered in as corporal, Co. F, September 5, 1862; wounded in action, May 3, 1863, at Chancellorsville Va.; promoted sergeant, July 3, 1863; mustered out with company, June 3, 1865, near Washington, D.C.

PETIT, LUKE.—Age, 20 years. Enlisted at Royalton, to serve three years, and mustered in as private, Co. C, September 26, 1864; wounded in action, April 1, 1865, near Boydton Road, Va.; mustered out, June 7, 1865, at Elmira, N.Y.

PETREY, JOHN.—Age, 21 years. Enlisted at Morristown, N.J., to serve one year, and mustered in as private, Co. K, October 3, 1864; transferred to Co. F, Ninety-third Infantry, June 1, 1865; also born as Petry.

PIERSON, NEWTON B.—Age, 23 years. Enlisted, August 6, 1862, at Goshen, to serve three years; mustered in as private, Co. A, September 5, 1862; transferred to Co. I, September 6, 1862; absent, sick at Taneytown, Md., since August, 1863, and at muster-out of company.

PINE, DANIEL.—Age, 31 years. Enlisted, August 13, 1862, at Newburgh, to serve three years; mustered in as private, Co. C, September 5, 1862; mustered out with company, June 3, 1865, near Washington, D.C.

PITTS, ELI W.—Age, 17 years. Enlisted, August 13, 1862, at Crawford, to serve three years; mustered in as private, Co. E, September 5, 1862; deserted, October 25, 1862, on the march to Berlin, Md.

PITTS, JOHN W.—Age, 18 years. Enlisted, August 8, 1862, at Wallkill, to serve three years; mustered in as private, Co. K, September 5, 1862; wounded in action, May 3, 1863, at Chancellorsville, Va.; promoted corporal, July 1, 1863; sergeant, October 1, 1864; mustered out with company, June 3, 1865, near Washington, D.C.

POINT, JOSEPH.—Age, 21 years. Enlisted, August 22, 1862, at Newburgh, to serve three years; mustered in as private, Co. K, September 5, 1862; wounded in action, May 24, 1864, at North Anna, Va.; mustered out, May 23, 1865, at Ladies Home Hospital, New York City.

POLHAMUS, JOHN.—Age, 36 years. Enlisted, July 26, 1862, at Newburgh, to serve three years; mustered in as private, Co. A, September 5, 1862; wounded in action, June 9, 1863, at Beverly Ford, Va., and April 6, 1865, at Sailor's Creek, Va.; died of his wounds, April 17, 1865.

PORTER, NATHAN W.—Age, 23 years. Enlisted at Goshen, to serve three years, and mustered in as private, Co. F, August 22, 1864; deserted, no date; returned, under President's Proclamation, May 10, 1865; transferred to Co. I, Ninety-third Infantry, June 1, 1865.

POST, DAVID D.—Age, 24 years. Enlisted, August 15, 1862, at Walden, to serve three years; mustered in as private, Co. H, September 5, 1862; wounded in action, May 3, 1863, at Chancellorsville, Va.; mustered out with company, June 3, 1865, near Washington, D.C.

POST, ELLIS.—Age, 21 years. Enrolled, August 8, 1862, at Goshen, to serve three years; mustered in as private, Co. A, September 5, 1862; promoted commissary sergeant to date, September 4, 1862; mustered in as first lieutenant and quartermaster, September 9, 1863; mustered out with regiment, June 3, 1865, near Washington, D.C. Commissioned first lieutenant quartermaster, August 21, 1863, with rank from April 21, 1863, vice H. T. Travis, promoted.

POST, JOHN R.—Age, 20 years. Enlisted, August 13, 1862, at Walden, to serve three years; mustered in as corporal, Co. H, September 5, 1862; wounded in action, May 3, 1863, at Chancellorsville, Va.; returned to ranks, no date; mustered out with company, June 3, 1865, near Washington, D.C.

POTTER, ROBERT.—Age, 24 years. Enlisted, August 2, 1862, at Goshen, to serve three years; mustered in as private, Co. A, September 5, 1862; wounded in action, May 3, 1863, at Chancellorsville, Va.; transferred to Veteran Reserve Corps, November 1, 1863.

POTTER, SAMUEL.—Age, 18 years. Enlisted, August 8, 1862, at Goshen, to serve three years; mustered in as private, Co. A, September 5, 1862; killed in action, May 23, 1864, at North Anna, Va.

POTTS, NATHAN B.—Age, 37 years. Enlisted, August 9, 1862, at Monroe, to serve three years; mustered in as corporal, Co. C, September 5, 1862; transferred to First U.S. Engineers, April 16, 1863.

POWELL, HENRY J.—Age, 29 years. Enlisted, August 7, 1862, at Goshen, to serve three years; mustered in as private, Co. B, September 5, 1862; discharged, November 17, 1862, at St. Aloysius Hospital, Washington, D.C.

POWELL, THOMAS P.—Age, 26 years. Enlisted, August 6, 1862, at Goshen, to serve three years; mustered in as private, Co. D, September 5, 1862; wounded in action, June 16, 1864, in front of Petersburg, Va.; died of smallpox, November 30, 1864, at Fifth Corps Hospital, City Point, Va.

PRATT, JOSEPH.—Age, 23 years. Enlisted, August 14, 1862, at Goshen, to serve three years; mustered in as private, Co. A, and transferred to Co. B[?], September 5, 1862; wounded in action, September 18, 1864, in front of Petersburg, Va.; mustered out with company, June 3, 1865, near Washington, D.C.

PRICE, ALONZO.—Age, 28 years. Enlisted, August 31, 1862, at Goshen, to serve three years; mustered in as private, Co. K, September 5, 1862; wounded in action, May 3, 1863, at Chancellorsville, Va.; mustered out with company, June 3, 1865, near Washington, D.C.

PRICE, ANTHONY.—Age, 48 years. Enlisted at Goshen, to serve three years, and mustered in as private, Co. K, January 13, 1864; died of chronic diarrhea, July 28, 1864, at De Camp Hospital, Davids' Island, New York Harbor.

PRICE, JEHIEL.—Age, 18 years. Enlisted, August 13, 1862, at Port Jervis, to serve three years; mustered in as musician, Co. F, September 5, 1862; transferred to Third Regiment, Veteran Reserve Corps, no date, and discharged for disability, May 5, 1865.

PRICE, WILLIAM.—Age, 29 years. Enlisted, August 9, 1862, at Otisville, to serve three years; mustered in as sergeant, Co. E, September 5, 1862; wounded in action, May 3, 1863, at Chancellorsville, Va.; transferred to Twelfth Company, Second Battalion, Veteran Reserve Corps, May 1, 1864, and mustered out with detachment, June 30, 1865, at Washington, D.C.

PUFF, EGBERT S.—Age, 20 years. Enlisted, August 5, 1862, at Wallkill, to serve three years; mustered in as private, Co. K, September 5, 1862; wounded in action, May 3, 1863, at Chancellorsville, Va.; discharged for wounds, September 18, 1863, at Philadelphia, Pa.

PULLMAN, BYRAN J.—Private, Co. K, First U.S. Sharpshooters; transferred to Co. H, this regiment, March 1, 1865; mustered out with company, June 3, 1865, near Washington, D.C.

PULLMAN, CORNELIUS.—Private, Co. K, First U.S. Sharpshooters; transferred to Co. H, this regiment, March 1, 1865; wounded in action, April 1, 1865, near Boydton Road, Va.; mustered out, June 3, 1865, at Harewood Hospital, Washington, D.C.

PULLMAN, DOUGLAS.—Private, Co. K, First U.S. Sharpshooters; transferred to Co. H, this regiment, March 1, 1865; mustered out with company, June 3, 1865, near Washington, D.C.

PURDY, DAVID S.—Age, 23 years. Enlisted, August 15, 1862, at Newburgh, to serve three years; mustered in as private, Co. K, September 5, 1862; deserted on expiration of furlough, given December 18, 1863.

QUACKENBUSH, HENRY S.—Age. 22 years. Enlisted, August 11, 1862, at Goshen, to serve three years; mustered in as private, Co. D, September 5, 1862; mustered out with company, June 3, 1865, near Washington, D.C.

QUACKENBUSH, JONAS F.—Age, 20 years. Enlisted, August 11, 1862, at Goshen, to serve three years; mustered in as private, Co. D, September 5, 1862; wounded in action, May 3, 1863, at Chancellorsville, Va.; discharged for disability, October 2, 1863; also borne as Jonah F.

QUACKENBUSH, JOSEPH.—Age, 18 years. Enlisted at Warwick, to serve three years, and mustered in as private, Co. D, December 23, 1863; wounded in action, May 12, 1864, at Spotsylvania Court House, Va.; transferred to Co. H, Ninety-third Infantry, June 1, 1865.

QUACKENBUSH, RICHARD.—Age, 22 years. Enlisted, August 7, 1862, at Goshen, to serve three years; mustered in as private, Co. D, September 5, 1862; discharged, August 2, 1863.

QUACKENBUSH, SYLVESTER.—Age, 18 years. Enlisted at Warwick, to serve three years, and mustered in as private, Co. D, December 24, 1863; transferred to Co. H, Ninety-third Infantry, June 1, 1865.

QUACKENBUSH, WILLIAM F.—Age, 22 years. Enlisted, August 11, 1862, at Goshen, to serve three years: mustered in as private, Co. D, September 5, 1862; promoted corporal, prior to October, 1864; sergeant, March 1, 1865; mustered out with company, June 3, 1865, near Washington, D.C.

Sergeant William Quackenbush, Company D. He mustered out with the company June 3, 1865, near Washington, D.C. (archive of the Historical Society of the Town of Warwick, gift of Joan and Tom Frangos).

QUICK, AMSEY W.— Age, 24 years. Enlisted, August 24, 1862, at Port Jervis, to serve three years; mustered in as private, Co. F, September 5, 1862; killed in action, July 2, 1863, at Gettysburg, Pa.

QUICK, DAVID U.— Age, 21 years. Enrolled, August 14, 1862, at Wallkill, to serve three years; mustered in as private, Co. K, September 5, 1862; wounded in action, May 3, 1863, at Chancellorsville, Va.; promoted corporal, March 5, 1864; wounded in action, August 14, 1864, at Deep Bottom, Va.; promoted sergeant, October 1, 1864; wounded in action, October 27, 1864, at Boydton Road, Va.; mustered in as second lieutenant, Co. B, November 15, 1864; as first lieutenant, January 1, 1865; mustered out with company, June 3, 1865, near Washington, D.C. Commissioned second lieutenant, November 15, 1864, with rank from July 21, 1864, vice S. W. Hotchkiss, resigned; first lieutenant, February 18, 1865, with rank from January 1, 1865, vice Thomas Taft, promoted.

QUICK, GEORGE T.— Age, 29 years. Enrolled at New York City, to serve three years, and mustered in as second lieutenant, March 18, 1864 (conditionally); no further record; prior service as first lieutenant, Co. A, Enfants Perdus.

QUICK, MARTIN V.— Age, 21 years. Enlisted, August 15, 1862, at Port Jervis, to serve three years; mustered in as private, Co. F, September 5, 1862; discharged for disability, January 9, 1864, at convalescent camp, Alexandria, Va.

QUICK, THOMAS J.— Age, 23 years. Enrolled, August 13, 1862, at Port Jervis, to serve three years; mustered in as first lieutenant, Co. F, August 20, 1862; wounded in action, May 3, 1863, at Chancellorsville, Va.; mustered in as Captain, Co. G, January 1, 1864; mustered out with company, June 3, 1865, near Washington, D.C. Commissioned first lieutenant, September 10, 1862, with rank from August 20, 1862, original; captain, December 17, 1863, with rank from December 10, 1863, vice H. P. Ramsdell, honorably discharged.

QUINN, FRANCIS.— Age, 25 years. Enlisted, September 12, 1864, at Lodi, to serve three years; mustered in as private, Co. H, September 17, 1864; wounded and captured in action, October 27, 1864, at Boydton Plank Road; paroled, December 1864; discharged for disability, February 27, 1865, at Mount Pleasant Hospital, Washington, D.C.

RAKE, WILLIAM.— Age, 21 years. Enlisted August 6, 1862, at Chester, to serve three years; mustered in as private, Co. G, September 5, 1862; killed in action, May 3, 1863, at Chancellorsville, Va.

RAMSDELL, HENRY P.— Age, 18 years. Enrolled at Goshen, to serve three years, and mustered in as second lieutenant, Co. C, August 15, 1862; promoted first lieutenant, December 31, 1862; mustered in as such, April 1, 1863; discharged for disability, December 13, 1862.

RANDALL, ALFRED G.— Age, 24 years. Enlisted, August 12, 1862, at Wallkill, to serve three years; mustered in as private, Co. K, September 5, 1862; deserted, December 15, 1862, in front of the enemy, at Fredericksburg, Va.

RANDALL, GEORGE.— Age, 19 years. Enlisted, August 21, 1862, at Wallkill, to serve three years; mustered in as private, Co. K, September 5, 1862; died of typhoid fever, December 28, 1862, at camp, near Falmouth, Va.

RAPALJE, ABRAHAM B.— Age, 25 years. Enlisted, August 14, 1862, at Walden, to serve three years; mustered in as corporal, Co. H, September 5, 1862; returned to ranks, no date; promoted corporal, November 1, 1864; mustered out with company, June 3, 1865, near Washington, D.C.

RAPELYE, ABRAHAM.— Age, 27 years. Enlisted, August 5, 1862, at Blooming Grove, to serve three years; mustered in as private, Co. G, September 5, 1862; discharged, April 16, 1864, at Culpeper Va., as Rapelyea; also borne as Rapalye.

RAYMOND, DAVID F.— Age, 21 years. Enlisted, August 11, 1862, at Goshen, to serve three years; mustered in as private, Co. D, September 5, 1862; wounded in action, Mar 3, 1863, at Chancellorsville, Va., and May 19, 1864, at Spotsylvania, Va.; mustered out with detachment, June 9, 1865, at Columbian Hospital, Washington, D.C.

RAYMOND, JOHN.— Age, 19 years. Enlisted, August 9, 1862, at Goshen, to serve three years; mustered in as private, Co. H, September 5, 1862; wounded in action, June 9, 1863, at Beverly Ford, Va., and May 6, 1864, at the Wilderness, Va.; mustered out with company, June 3, 1865, near Washington, D.C.

REDEKER, JOHN.— Age, 22 years. Enlisted, August 14, 1862, at Walden, to serve three years; mustered in as private, Co. H, September 5, 1862; mustered out with company, June 3, 1865, near Washington, D.C.

REED, JOHN.— Age, 18 years. Enlisted at Goshen, to serve three years, and mustered in as private, Co. K, September 10, 1864; mustered out with company, June 3, 1865, near Washington, D.C.; also borne as Reid.

REED, WILLIAM.— Age, 35 years. Enlisted at Goshen, to serve one year, and mustered in as private, Co. K, August 20, 1864; mustered out with company, June 3, 1865, near Washington, D.C.; also borne as Reid.

REEVS, COE L.— Age, 18 years. Enlisted, August 11, 1862, at Goshen, to serve three years; mustered in as corporal, Co. B, September 5, 1862; promoted sergeant, prior to April 10, 1863; wounded in action, May 3, 1863, at Chancellorsville, Va.; promoted hospital steward, July 1, 1864; mustered out with regiment, June 3, 1865, near Washington, D.C.; also borne as Reeves.

RENSLER, MICHAEL.— Age, 21 years. Enlisted, August 15, 1862, at Port Jervis, to serve three years; mustered in as corporal, Co. F, August 20, 1862; discharged for disability, September 15, 1863, at convalescent camp, Alexandria, Va.; also borne as Rensselaer.

RETALICK, WILLIAM H.—Age, 36 years. Enlisted at Lockport, to serve one year, and mustered in as private, Co. A, September 23, 1864; wounded in action, April 1, 1865, before Petersburg, Va.; mustered out, July 11, 1865, at Armory Square Hospital, Washington, D.C.

RHINDFIELD, FRANCIS.—Age, 19 years. Enlisted, August 8, 1862, at Goshen, to serve three years; mustered in as private, Co. A, September 5, 1862; killed in action, June 9, 1863, at Beverly Ford, Va.

RHINEHEART, ALDER R.—Age, 26 years. Enlisted, August 9, 1862, at Walden, to serve three years; mustered in as corporal, Co. H, September 5, 1862; promoted sergeant, prior to April 10, 1863; wounded in action, May 3, 1863, at Chancellorsville, Va.; died of his wounds, May 20, 1863.

RHODES, CORNELIUS L.—Age, 44 years. Enlisted, August 9, 1862, at Canterbury, to serve three years; mustered in as private, Co. C, September 5, 1862; discharged for disability, April 16, 1863, at Falmouth, Va.

RHODES, WILLIAM H.—Age, 22 years. Enlisted, August 13, 1862, at Canterbury, to serve three years; mustered in as private, Co. C, September 5, 1862; wounded in action, May 12, 1864, at Spotsylvania Court House, Va.; mustered out with company, June 3, 1865, near Washington, D.C.

RICE, EDWARD.—Age, 43 years. Enlisted at Newburgh, to serve three years, and mustered in as private, Co. A, August 1, 1862; wounded in action, June 9, 1863, at Beverly Ford, Va.; transferred to Veteran Reserve Corps, September 30, 1864.

RIDER, DANIEL.—Age, 25 years. Enlisted, August 6, 1862, at Washingtonville, to serve three years; mustered in as private, Co. G, September 5, 1862; wounded in action, November 27, 1863, at Locust Grove, Va.; transferred to One Hundred and Sixteenth Company, Second Battalion, Veteran Reserve Corps, March 13, 1865; mustered out with detachment, July 17, 1865, at Augur Hospital, Washington, D.C.

RIDER, DANIEL C.—Age, 23 years. Enlisted, August 7, 1862, at Cornwall, to serve three years; mustered in as private, Co. C, September 5, 1862; discharged for disability, December 7, 1863, at hospital, Philadelphia, Pa.; also borne as Ryder.

RIGGENBAUGH, DANIEL.—Age, 38 years. Enlisted, August 18, 1862, at Blooming Grove, to serve three years; mustered in as private, Co. G, September 5, 1862; mustered out with company, June 3, 1863, near Washington, D.C.

RIKER, RALPH R.—Age, 44 years. Enlisted, July 31, 1862, at Chester, to serve three years; mustered in as private, Co. G, September 3, 1862; absent in hospital since November 16, 1862, and at muster-out of company.

RILEY, FRANKLIN.—Age, 18 years. Enlisted at Big Flats, to serve one year, and mustered in as private, Co. I, August 23, 1864; mustered out with company, June 3, 1865, near Washington, D.C.

RILEY, THOMAS.—Age, 21 years. Enlisted, September 3, 1864, at Cornwall, to serve one year; mustered in as private, Co. I, September 16, 1864; mustered out with company, June 3, 1865, near Washington, D.C.

RITCH, WATSON W.—Age, 21 years. Enlisted, August 6, 1862, at Wallkill, to serve three years; mustered in as corporal, Co. K, September 5, 1862; promoted sergeant, January 1, 1863; wounded in action, June 18, 1864, at Petersburg, Va.; died of his wounds, July 20, 1864, at Alexandria, Va.

ROAK, JAMES.—Age, 32 years. Enlisted, August 13, 1862, at Blooming Grove, to serve three years; mustered in as private, Co. B[?], September 5, 1862; killed in action, July 2, 1863, at Gettysburg, Pa., as Roke.

ROAT, GILBERT D. W.—Age, 29 years. Enlisted, August 12, 1862, at Newburgh, to serve three years; mustered in as private, Co. A, September 5, 1862; mustered out with company, June 3, 1865, near Washington, D.C.

ROBBINS, GILBERT E.—Age, 22 years. Enlisted at Goshen, to serve one year, and mustered in as private, Co. K, August 23, 1864; mustered out with company, June 3, 1865, near Washington, D.C., as Robbens; also borne as Robins.

ROBERSON, GEORGE H.—Age, 21 years. Enlisted at Goshen, to serve one year, and mustered in as private, Co. K, September 2, 1864; mustered out with detachment, May 12, 1865, at Jervis Hospital, Baltimore, Md.

ROBERSON, THEODORE M.—Age, 22 years. Enrolled, August 19, 1862, at Goshen, to serve three years; mustered in as first sergeant, Co. E, September 5, 1862; as second lieutenant, March 7, 1863; wounded in action, May 3, 1863, at Chancellorsville, Va.; mustered in as first lieutenant, September 26, 1863; as captain, Co. H, January 1, 1865; mustered out with company, June 3, 1865, near Washington, D.C.; also borne as Robertson and Robinson. Commissioned second lieutenant, May 26, 1863, with rank from March 6, 1863, vice A. Wittenbeecher, dismissed; first lieutenant, December 17, 1863, with rank from September 25, 1863, vice W. A. Verplank, resigned; captain, February 18, 1865, with rank from January 1, 1865, vice D. Crish, killed in action.

Captain Theodore Roberson, Company E. He was wounded in action May 3, 1863 at Chancellorsville, and promoted to captain of Company H. He mustered out with the regiment June 3, 1865. Col. Weygant referred to him as "a model soldier" (archive of the Historical Society of the Town of Warwick, gift of Joan and Tom Frangos).

ROBERTSON, JOHN.—Age, 29 years. Enlisted at Wheatfield, and mustered in as private, Co. A, August 4, 1864; transferred to Co. E, Ninety-third Infantry, June 1, 1865.

ROBERTSON, SAMUEL R.—Age, 40 years. Enlisted at Groton, to serve one year, and mustered in as private, Co. A, September 2, 1864; mustered out with company, June 3, 1865, near Washington, D.C.

ROBERTY, CHARLES.—Age, 39 years. Enlisted August 12, 1862, at Port Jervis, to serve three years; mustered in as private, Co. F, September 5, 1862; absent, detached as guard at Corps Headquarters at City Point, Va.; since April, 1865, and at muster-out of company.

ROBINSON, JOHN.—Age, 29 years. Enlisted at Goshen, to serve three years, and mustered in as private, Co. A, September 5, 1862; died of typhoid fever, January 18, 1863, in camp, near Falmouth, Va.

RODMAN, THOMAS.—Age, 18 years. Enlisted, August 11, 1862, at Newburgh, to serve three years; mustered in as private, Co. C, September 5, 1862; wounded in action, May 3, 1863, at Chancellorsville, Va.; promoted sergeant prior to October 1864; mustered out with company, June 3, 1865, near Washington, D.C.

ROGERS, ABRAM.—Age, 29 years. Enlisted, August 13, 1862, at Crawford, to serve three years; mustered in as private, Co. E, September 5, 1862; wounded in action, May 3, 1863, at Chancellorsville, Va.; promoted corporal, March 1, 1865; mustered out with company, June 3, 1865, near Washington, D.C.; also borne as Abraham Rodgers.

ROLLINGS, RICHARD.—Age, 27 years. Enlisted, August 12, 1862, at Goshen, to serve three years; mustered in as private, Co. A, August 14, 1862; wounded in action, May 3, 1863, at Chancellorsville, Va., and May 12, 1864, at Spotsylvania, Va.; mustered out with company, June 3, 1865, near Washington, D.C.

ROLLINGS, SAMUEL.—Age, 23 years. Enlisted, August 11, 1862, at Goshen, to serve three years; mustered in as sergeant, Co. A, September 5, 1862; wounded, in action, May 3, 1863, at Chancellorsville, Va.; May 12, 1864, at Spotsylvania Court House, Va., and August 14, 1864, at Deep Bottom, Va.; mustered out with company, June 3, 1865, near Washington, D.C., as Samuel T.

ROMER, BENJAMIN P.—Age, 28 years. Enlisted at Cornwall, to serve one year, and mustered in as private, Co. K, September 29, 1864; mustered out with company, June 3, 1865, near Washington, D.C., as Roomer.

ROMER, JOSEPH P.—Age, 32 years. Enlisted at Cornwall, to serve one year, and mustered in as private, Co. K, September 29, 1864; mustered out with company, June 3, 1865, near Washington, D.C., as Roomer; also borne as Roome.

ROMINE, RICHARD.—Age, 24 years. Enlisted, August 12, 1862, at Goshen, to serve three years; mustered in as private, Co. D, September 5, 1862; discharged, February 28, 1863.

ROOSA, JAMES H.—Age, 21 years. Enrolled at Goshen, to serve three years, and mustered in as first lieutenant, Co. K, August 23, 1862; discharged, March 7, 1863, as James F. Commissioned first lieutenant, September 10, 1862, with rank from August 23, 1862, original.

ROSE, JOHN N.—Age, 44 years. Enlisted, August 11, 1862, at Goshen, to serve three years; mustered in as private, Co. D, September 5, 1862; discharged, April 11, 1863.

ROSE, JOSEPH.—Age, 17 years. Enlisted at Warwick, to serve one year, and mustered in as private, Co. I, August 31, 1864; mustered out with company, June 3, 1865, near Washington, D.C.

ROSE, PETER.—Age, 20 years. Enlisted, July 29, 1862, at Goshen, to serve three years; mustered in as sergeant, Co. A, September 5, 1862; wounded in action, May 3, 1863, at Chancellorsville, Va., and June 17, 1864, before Petersburg, Va.; transferred to Veteran Reserve Corps, February 8, 1865; also borne as Peter H.

ROSE, ROBERT.—Age, 21 years. Enlisted, August 20, 1862, at Newburgh, to serve three years; mustered in as private, Co. I, September 5, 1862; captured in action, December 11, 1862, at Fredericksburg, Va.; paroled, no date; mustered out with company, June 3, 1865, near Washington, D.C.

ROSS, MOSES P.—Age, 23 years. Enlisted, August 4, 1862, at Chester, to serve three years; mustered in as private, Co. A, September 5, 1862; appointed musician, no date; promoted principal musician, October 31, 1863; mustered out with regiment, June 3, 1865, near Washington, D.C.

ROSSMAN, FREEMAN H.—Age, 20 years. Enlisted, August 12, 1862, at Port Jervis, to serve three years; mustered in as private, Co. F, September 5, 1862; absent, sick at Fairfax Seminary Hospital, Alexandria, Va., since August, 1864, and at muster-out of company.

ROWLAND, JOHN.—Age, 25 years. Enlisted, August 13, 1862, at Walden, to serve three years; mustered in as sergeant, Co. H, September 5, 1862; promoted first sergeant prior to April 10, 1863; wounded in action, May 3, 1863, at Chancellorsville, Va.; died of his wounds, June 22, 1863, at Washington, D.C., as sergeant.

ROY, JOSEPH B.—Age, 23 years. Enlisted, August 8, 1862, at Goshen, to serve three years; mustered in as private, Co. D, September 5, 1862; transferred to Veteran reserve Corps, February 1864.

ROYCE, EDWARD.—Age, 43 years. Enlisted, August 14, 1862, at Goshen, to serve three years; mustered in as private, Co. D, September 5, 1862; mustered out with company, June 3, 1865, near Washington, D.C.

ROYKE, WILLIAM.—Age, 19 years. Enlisted at Goshen, to serve one year, and mustered in as private, Co. D, September 19, 1864; discharged for disability, January 1865, at Augur Hospital, Washington, D.C., as Rouke; also borne as Rorke.

RUBY, JOHN.—Age, 22 years. Enlisted at Rochester, to serve three years, and mustered in as private, Co. C, September 26, 1864; transferred to Co. A, Ninety-third Infantry, June 1, 1865.

RUFFIN, JOHN.—Age, 27 years. Enlisted at Deer Park, to serve one year, and mustered in as private, Co. B, September 12, 1864; mustered out, June 14, 1865, at Washington, D.C., while in Slough Hospital, Alexandria, Va.; also borne as Raffin.

RUMSEY, ISAIAH.—Age, 18 years. Enlisted, August 15,1862, at Newburgh, to serve three years; mustered in as private, Co. C, September 5, 1862; died of typhoid fever, February 22, 1863, at Falmouth, Va.

RUMSEY, MOSES.— Age, 22 years. Enlisted at Newburgh, to serve three years, and mustered in as private, Co. B, December 24, 1863; transferred to Co. C, Ninety-third Infantry, June 2, 1865.

RUNDLE, FREDERICK.— Age, 32 years. Enlisted, August 12, 1862, at Port Jervis, to serve three years; mustered in as private, Co. F, August 20, 1862; wounded in action, July 2, 1863, at Gettysburg, Pa.; mustered out with company, June 3, 1865, near Washington, D.C.

RUSH, ROBERT.— Age, 42 years. Enlisted, August 15, 1862, at Cornwall, to serve three years; mustered in as private, Co. C, September 5, 1862; killed in action, May 3, 1863, at Chancellorsville, Va.

RUSSELL, WILLIAM.— Age, 18 years. Enlisted, August 16, 1862, at Mount Hope, to serve three years; mustered in as private, Co. E, September 5, 1862; deserted, September 6, 1862, at Goshen, N.Y.

RYAN, JAMES.— Age, 17 years. Enlisted, August 15, 1862, at New Windsor, to serve three years; mustered in as private, Co. C, September 5, 1862; wounded in action and deserted, July 2, 1863, at Gettysburg, Pa.

RYAN, JAMES.— Age, 22 years. Enlisted at Rochester, to serve one year, and mustered in as private, Co. I, September 30, 1864; mustered out with company, June 3, 1865, near Washington, D.C.

RYAN, PATRICK.— Age, 21 years. Enlisted, August 6, 1862, at Newburgh, to serve three years; mustered in as private, Co. I, September 5, 1862; wounded in action, May 3, 1863, at Chancellorsville, Va.; mustered out with company, June 3, 1865, near Washington, D.C.

RYERSON, JAMES.— Age, 28 years. Enlisted at Warwick, to serve three years, and mustered in as private, Co. D, December 14, 1863; died of heart disease, October 31, 1864, at Third Division Hospital.

RYERSON, JOHN.— Age, 18 years. Enlisted, August 11, 1862, at Goshen, to serve three years; mustered in as private, Co. B, September 5, 1862; discharged, January 10, 1863.

RYNDER, REUBEN.— Age, 21 years. Enlisted, August 7, 1862, at Goshen, to serve three years; mustered in as private, Co. B, September 5, 1862; promoted sergeant, September 1, 1864; mustered out with company, June 3, 1865, near Washington, D.C.

SAGER, MATTHIAS.— Age, 33 years. Enlisted, August 18, 1862, at Newburgh, to serve three years; mustered in as private, Co. G, September 5, 1862; mustered out with company, June 3, 1865, near Washington, D.C.; also borne as Sayer and Sagar.

SALLSBURY, JAMES.— Age, 21 years. Enlisted at Schenectady, to serve three years, and mustered in as private, Co. E, August 30, 1864; mustered out with company, June 3, 1865, near Washington, D.C.; also borne as Salisbury.

SANDERS, JOHN S.— Age, 22 years. Enlisted at Goshen, to serve one year, and mustered in as private, Co. K, August 30, 1864; mustered out with company, June 3, 1865, near Washington, D.C.

SANDERS, WILLIAM.— Age, 19 years. Enlisted, August 7, 1862, at Goshen, to serve three years; mustered in as private, Co. A, September 5, 1862; wounded in action, May 12, 1864, at Spotsylvania, Va.; wounded and at Mansion Hospital, Baltimore, Md., at muster-out of company.

SARVIS, JOHN H.— Age, 25 years. Enlisted, August 12, 1862, at Newburgh, to serve three years; mustered in as private, Co. E, September 5, 1862; absent, sick in hospital, Washington, D.C., since February 5, 1864, and at muster-out of company.

SAYER, DANIEL.— Age, 43 years. Enrolled, August 16, 1862, at Goshen, to serve three years; mustered in as first lieutenant, Co. D, September 5, 1862; wounded in action, May 3, 1863, at Chancellorsville, Va.; mustered in as captain, Co. E, January 1, 1864; mustered out with company, June 3, 1865, near Washington, D.C. Commissioned first lieutenant, September 10, 1962, with rank from August 16, 1862, original; captain, December 17, 1863, with rank from March 6, 1863, vice W. A. McBurney resigned.

SAYER, DAVID D.— Age, 19 years. Enlisted at Warwick, to serve three years, and mustered in as private, Co. D, January 1, 1864; transferred to Co. H, Ninety-third Infantry, June 1, 1865, as David S.

SCERING, GEORGE.— Age, 39 years. Enlisted, August 6, 1862, at Goshen, to serve three years; mustered in as private, Co. A, September 5, 1862; mustered out, May 11, 1865, at Albany, N.Y.

SCHOFIELD, MOSES.— Age, 21 years. Enlisted at Goshen, to serve one year, and mustered in as private, Co. K, August 17, 1864; absent, sick in hospital, Division No. 1, Annapolis, Md., since January 26, 1865, and at muster-out of company, as Scofield.

SCHULTZ, SAMUEL.— Age, 33 years. Enlisted, August 9, 1862, at Goshen, to serve three years; mustered in as private, Co. B, September 5, 1862; deserted, October 26, 1862, at Berlin, Md., as Shultz; reported as having died of disease prior to May 3, 1863.

SCOFIELD, JOHN.— Age, 27 years. Enlisted at Warwick, to serve three years, and mustered in as private, Co. D, December 29, 1863; transferred to Co. H., Ninety-third Infantry, June 1, 1865.

SCOFIELD, WILLIAM H.— Age, 18 years. Enlisted, August 15, 1862, at Port Jervis, to serve three years; mustered in as private, Co. F, September 5, 1862; discharged for disability, October 27, 1863; also borne as Schofield.

SCOTT, GEORGE D.— Age, 19 years. Enlisted, August 9, 1862, at Newburgh, to serve three years; mustered in as corporal, Co. I, September 5, 1862; promoted sergeant, November 1, 1862; returned to ranks, December 17, 1862; wounded in action, May 3, 1863, at Chancellorsville, Va.; transferred to Veteran Reserve Corps, January 10, 1865.

SCOTT, JAMES.— Age, 29 years. Enlisted, August 4, 1862, at Goshen, to serve three years; mustered in as private, Co. B, September 5, 1862; promoted corporal prior to July 1863; wounded in action, July 2, 1863, at Gettysburg, Pa.; discharged, July 29, 1863, at Patterson Park Hospital, Baltimore, Md.

SCOTT, JOHN.— Age, 21 years. Enlisted, August 4, 1862, at Goshen, to serve three years; mustered in as private, Co. E, September 5, 1862; promoted corporal, prior to April 10, 1863; killed in action, July 2, 1863, at Gettysburg, Pa.

SCOTT, JOHN J.— Age, 23 years. Enlisted, August 8, 1862, at Wallkill, to serve three years; mustered in as sergeant, Co. E, September 5, 1862; returned to ranks, August 1, 1863; killed in action, May 12, 1864, at Spotsylvania, Va.

SEAMEN, HENRY.— Age, 45 years. Enlisted, August 14, 1862, at Walden, to serve three years; mustered in as wagoner, Co. H, September 5, 1862; discharged, April 2, 1863, at Camp Stoneman, Va.

SEEMAN, CHARLES.— Age, 26 years. Enlisted, August 14, 1862, at Walden, to serve three years; mustered in as private, Co. H, September 5, 1862; killed in action, May 3, 1863, at Chancellorsville, Va.; also borne as Seaman.

SERVIS, PHILLIP.— private, Co. K. First U.S. Sharpshooters; transferred to Co. S[?], this regiment, March 1, 1865; mustered out with company, June 3, 1865, near Washington, D.C.

SEYMOUR, JOHN.— Age, place, date of enlistment, term and mustered in as private, Co. C, not stated; joined company, October 7, 1864; transferred to Co. A, Ninety-third Infantry, June 1, 1865.

SHARP, EDWARD.— Age, 21 years. Enlisted, August 9, 1862, at Port Jervis, to serve three years; mustered in as private, Co. F, September 5, 1862; wounded in action, June 9, 1863, at Beverly Ford, Va.; absent, sick in hospital, Alexandria, Va., at muster-out of company.

SHAW, JOHN S.— Age, 32 years. Enlisted at Goshen, to serve one year, and mustered in as private, Co. K, September 2, 1864; promoted corporal, November 15, 1865; mustered out with company, June 3, 1865, near Washington, D.C.; also borne as Shore.

SHAW, JOSEPH H.— Age, 15[?] years. Enlisted at New York City, to serve three years, and mustered in as private, Co. G, February 23, 1865; transferred to Co. D, Ninety-third Infantry, June 1, 1865.

SHAW, THEODORE A.— Age, 15 years. Enlisted, August 20, 1862, at Goshen, to serve three years; mustered in as musician, Co. C, September 5, 1862; deserted, same date.

SHAW, WILLIAM H.— Age, 21 years. Enlisted, August 14, 1862, at Greenville, to serve three years; mustered in as private, Co. E, September 5, 1862; mustered out with company, June 3, 1865, near Washington, D.C.

SHAWCROSS, GEORGE.— Age, 31 years. Enlisted. August 6, 1862, at Bellvale, to serve three years; mustered in as private, Co. B, September 5, 1862; promoted corporal, prior to April 10, 1863; killed in action, May 3, 1863, at Chancellorsville, Va.

SHELP, WILLIAM.— Age, 20 years. Enlisted, August 13, 1862, at Walden, to serve three years; mustered in as private, Co. H, September 5, 1862; died of typhoid fever, January 30, 1863, at Falmouth, Va.

SHEPERD, JOHN.— Age, 19 years. Enlisted, August 9, 1862, at Chester, to serve three years; mustered in as private, Co. A, September 5, 1862; deserted. September 6, 1862, at New York City, as Shepard.

SHERMAN, ALMOND P.— Age, 31 years. Enlisted at Culpeper Va., to serve three years, and mustered in as private, Co. D, September 21, 1863; promoted hospital steward, September 1863; discharged for disability, no date.

SHERMAN, SAMUEL L.— Age, 23 years. Enlisted, July 22, 1862, at Newburgh, to serve three years; mustered in as private, Co. B, September 5, 1862; wounded in action, May 12, 1864, at Spotsylvania, Va.; died of his wounds, May 19, 1864, at Washington, D.C.

SHERMAN, SAMUEL L.— Age, 23 years. Enlisted July 26, 1862, at Goshen, to serve three years. Mustered in as private, Co. A, July 28, 1862; no further record.

SHERMAN, WILLIAM B.— Age, 33 years. Enlisted, August 15, 1862, at Walden, to serve three years; mustered in as private, Co. H, September 3, 1862; discharged for disability, December 31, 1862, while in insane asylum, Washington, D.C.

SHIELDS, FRANCIS.— Age, 24 years. Enlisted, August 15, 1862, at Newburgh, to serve three years; mustered in as private, Co. K, September 5, 1862; deserted, September —, 1862, at New York City.

SHULTZ, LOUIS T.— Age, 31 years. Enrolled, August 4, 1862, at Washingtonville, to serve three years; mustered in as sergeant, Co. G, September 5, 1862; returned to ranks, January 1, 1863; wounded in action, May 12, 1864, at Spotsylvania, Va.; promoted corporal, July 20, 1864; sergeant, August 1, 1864; wounded in action, August 14, 1864, at Deep Bottom, Va.; mustered in as second lieutenant, March 1, 1865; mustered out with company, June 3, 1865, near Washington, D.C.; also borne as Lewis T.

SILLIMAN, WILLIAM.— Age, 25 years. Enrolled at Goshen, to serve three years, and mustered in as first lieutenant and adjutant, July 16, 1862; as captain, Co. C, August 15, 1862; mustered out, February 1, 1864, for promotion to colonel, Twenty-sixth U.S. Colored troops; prior service as first lieutenant, Co. D, Seventh Cavalry.

SIMPSON, JOSEPH L.— Age, 18 years. Enlisted, August 6, 1862, at Goshen, to serve three years; mustered in as private, Co. A, September 5, 1862; wounded in action, May 6, 1864, at the Wilderness, Va.; mustered out with company, June 3, 1865, near Washington, D.C.

SISCO, JEREMIAH.— Age, 25 years. Enlisted, August 15, 1862, at Port Jervis, to serve three years; mustered in as private, Co. F, September 5, 1862; captured in action, June 19, 1863, at Beverly Ford, Va.; paroled, same day; wounded in action, June 1, 1864, at Totopotomoy Creek, Va.; mustered out with company, June 3, 1865, near Washington, D.C.; also borne as Cisco.

SKELTON, JOHN.— Age, 21 years. Enlisted, August 12, 1862, at Wallkill, to serve three years; mustered in as private, Co. K, September 5, 1862; mustered out with company, June 3, 1865, near Washington, D.C.

SLAWSON, JOHN.— Age, 18 years. Enlisted, February 6, 1864, at New York City, to serve three years; mustered in as private, Co. B, February 16, 1864; transferred to Co. C, Ninety-third Infantry, June 2, 1865; also borne as Slauson.

SLAWSON, WILLIAM.— Age, 38 years. Enlisted, August 13, 1862, at Goshen, to serve three years; mustered in as private, Co. B, September 5, 1862; died of chronic diarrhea, October 17, 1864, at Washington, D.C.; also borne as Slauson.

SLOAT, JAMES.—Age, 19 years. Enlisted, August 13, 1862, at Crawford, to serve three years; mustered in as private, Co. E, September 5, 1862; promoted sergeant, September 1, 1864; mustered out with company, June 3, 1865, near Washington, D.C.

SLY, NORMAN A.—Age, 21 years. Enlisted, August 9, 1862, at Goshen, to serve three years; mustered in as private, Co. D, September 5, 1862; wounded in action, May 5, 1864, at the Wilderness, and May 13, 1864, at Spotsylvania Court House, Va.; transferred to One hundred and Fifty-second Infantry, February 1865, for promotion to second lieutenant.

SMITH, CLARK.—Age, 45 years. Enlisted, August 9, 1862, at Cornwall, to serve three years; mustered in as private, Co. C, September 5, 1862; captured in action, May 3, 1863, at Chancellorsville, Va.; paroled, May 14, 1863; transferred to Co. F, Eighteenth Regiment, Veteran Reserve Corps, no date; mustered out with detachment, June 27, 1865, at Washington, D C.; also borne as Clark Smith, Jr.

SMITH, DANIEL.—Age, 27 years. Enlisted, August 12, 1862, at Blooming Grove, to serve three years; mustered in as private, Co. G, September 5, 1862; wounded in action, May 23, 1864, at North Anna, Va.; transferred to Co. H, Sixteenth Regiment, Veteran Reserve Corps, January 25, 1865; mustered out, July 5, 1865, at Harrisburg. Pa.

SMITH, HENRY O.—Age, 35 years. Enlisted, August 4, 1862, at Goshen, to serve three years; mustered in as private, Co. B, September 5, 1862; promoted corporal, prior to April 10, 1863; killed in action, May 3, 1863, at Chancellorsville, Va.

SMITH, HENRY W.—Age, 19 years. Enlisted, August 13, 1862, at Wallkill, to serve three years; mustered in as private, Co. K, September 5, 1862; wounded in action, July 2, 1863, at Gettysburg, Pa.; mustered out, July 27, 1865, at Hospital Division No. 2, Annapolis, Md.

SMITH, HORACE A.—Age, 23 years. Enlisted at Ontario, to serve one year, and mustered in as private, Co. I, September 3, 1864; mustered out with company, June 3, 1865, near Washington, D.C.

SMITH, ISAAC.—corporal, Co. K, First U.S. Sharpshooters; transferred to Co. H, this regiment, March 1, 1865; to Co. D, Ninety-third Infantry, June 1, 1865; veteran.

SMITH, JACOB F.—Age, 35 years. Enlisted, August 11, 1862, at Wallkill, to serve three years; mustered in as private, Co. K, September 1862; wounded in action, May 3, 1863, at Chancellorsville, Va.; discharged for wounds, August 17, 1863, at Washington, D.C.

SMITH, JAMES.—Age, 20 years. Enlisted, December 4, 1863, at Goshen, to serve three years; mustered in as private, Co. B, January 4, 1864; wounded and captured in action, October 27, 1864, at Boydton Road, Va.; paroled, no date; transferred to Co. C, Ninety-third infantry July 2, 1865

SMITH, JAMES A.—Age, 19 years. Enlisted August 22, 1862, at Newburgh, to serve three years; mustered in as private, Co. I, September 5, 1862; promoted corporal, February 1, 1863; sergeant, May 1, 1864; wounded in action, May 24, 1864, at North Anna, Va.; mustered out with company, June 3, 1865, near Washington, D.C.

SMITH, JOHN.—Age, 30 years. Enlisted, at Goshen, to serve one year, and mustered in as private, Co. K, September 10, 1864; mustered out with company, June 3, 1865, near Washington, D.C.

SMITH, JOHN W.—Age, 18 years. Enlisted, August 7, 1862, at Goshen, to serve three years; mustered in as private, Co. D, September 5, 1862; discharged for disability, August 21,1863; subsequent service in Co. L, Fifteenth Cavalry

SMITH, JOSEPH T.—Age, 39 years. Enlisted at Oswego, to serve one year, and mustered in as private, Co. H, September 1, 1864; mustered out with company, June 3, 1865, near Washington, D.C.

SMITH, JOSIAH.—Age, 45 years. Enlisted at Warwick, to serve three years, and mustered in as private, Co. B, December 30, 1863; transferred to Co. C, Ninety-third Infantry, June 2, 1865.

SMITH, NIAL.—Age, 18 years. Enlisted at Goshen, to serve one year, and mustered in as private, Co. G, February 13, 1865; transferred to Co. D, Ninety-third Infantry, June 1, 1865; also borne as Niel Smith.

SMITH, SOLOMON W.—Age, 18 years. Enlisted, August 22, 1862, at Wallkill, to serve three years; mustered in as private, Co. K, September 5, 1862; promoted corporal, January 1, 1863; wounded in action, May 3, 1863, at Chancellorsville, Va.; promoted sergeant, March 5, 1864; first sergeant, November 15, 1864; mustered out with company, June 3, 1865, near Washington, D.C.

SMITH, STEPHEN B[?].—Age, 25 years. Enlisted, August 6, 1862, at Goshen, to serve three years; mustered in as private, Co. B, September 5, 1862; died of apoplexy, November 28, 1862, at Bellair, Va.

SMITH, THEODORE.—Age, 30 years. Enlisted, August 11, 1862, at Goshen, to serve three years; mustered in as private, Co. A, September 5, 1862; promoted corporal, September 1, 1864; wounded in action, October 15, 1864, in front of Petersburg, Va.; absent at McDougal Hospital, Fort Schuyler, New York Harbor, since and at muster-out of company; also borne as Theodore S.

SMITH, THOMAS.—Age, 23 years. Enlisted at Rochester, to serve three years, and mustered in as private, Co. A, September 26, 1864; transferred to Co. E, Ninety-third Infantry. June 1, 1865.

SMITH, WILLIAM S.—Age, 35 years. Enlisted at Deer Park, to serve one year, and mustered in as private, Co. G, August 31, 1864: mustered out with company, June 8, 1865, near Washington, D.C.

SMITH, WILLIAM W.—Age, 19 years. Enrolled, August 4, 1862, at Newburgh, to serve three years; mustered in as first sergeant, Co. I, August 20 1862; wounded in action, May 4, 1864, at the Wilderness, Va.; returned to ranks, December 4, 1864; discharged, May 4, 1865, at Filbert Street Hospital, Philadelphia, Pa. Commissioned not mustered second lieutenant, April 13, 1864, with rank from September 7, 1863, vice C. Stewart, promoted.

SNELL, JOB M.—Age, 18 years. Enlisted, August 12, 1862, at Port Jervis, to serve three years; mustered in as private, Co. F, September 5, 1862; wounded in action, May 3, 1863, at Chancellorsville Va.; transferred to Twelfth

Company Second Battalion, Veteran Reserve Corps, October 1, 1863; mustered out with detachment, June 30, 1865, at Washington, D.C.

SNIDER, HARVEY H.—Age, 18 years. Enlisted, August 13, 1862, at Newburgh, to serve three years; mustered in as private, Co. I, September 5, 1862; deserted at Camp Parole, Annapolis, Md., about August 1863; also borne as Snyder.

SNIDER, WILLIAM.—Age, 18 years. Enlisted, August 14, 1862, at Goshen, to serve three years; mustered in as private, Co. B, September 5, 1862; killed in action, May 3, 1863, at Chancellorsville, Va., as Snyder.

SNYDER, ALFRED.—Age, 29 years. Enlisted, August 19, 1862, at Newburgh, to serve three years; not mustered in as private, Co. K; deserted, August 30, 1862, at Goshen, N.Y., as Alfred G.

SOULE, LEWIS H.—Private, Co. K, First U.S. Sharpshooters; transferred to Co. H, this regiment, March 1, 1865; mustered out, May 25, 1865, at New York City, as of Co. K, First U.S. Sharpshooters.

SPACE, JOHN A.—Age, 21 years. Enlisted, August 11, 1862, at Goshen, to serve three years; mustered in as private, Co. B, September 5, 1862; deserted, April 1, 1863, at Alexandria, Va.

SPEIR, NELSON.—Age, 30 years. Enlisted, August 13, 1862, at Goshen, to serve three years; mustered in as private, Co. D, September 5, 1862; discharged for disability, February 23, 1863, at Haddington Hospital, Philadelphia, Pa., as Speer.

STACK, JAMES.—Age, 31 years. Enlisted at Wheatfield, to serve one year, and mustered in as private, Co. F, September 24, 1864; transferred to Co. I, Ninety-third Infantry, June 1, 1865.

STACY, JOEL H.—Age, 26 years. Enlisted at Plattsburg, to serve one year, and mustered in as private, Co. E, September 16, 1864; mustered out with detachment, June 29, 1865, at White Hall Hospital, Philadelphia, Pa.

STAFFORD, EDWARD.—Age, 18 years. Enlisted at Goshen, to serve one year, and mustered in as private, Co. K, August 22, 1864; mustered out with company, June 3, 1865, near Washington, D.C.

STAFFORD, JOHN J.—Age, 21 years. Enlisted, August 21, 1862, at New Windsor, to serve three years; mustered in as private, Co. E, September 5, 1862; discharged for disability, March 28, 1863, at hospital, Philadelphia, Pa.

Private Job Snell, Company F, was wounded at the Battle of Chancellorsville and transferred to the Veteran Reserve Corps (Michael J. McAfee collection).

STALBIRD, JOHN M.—Age, 19 years. Enlisted, August 5, 1862, at Wallkill, to serve three years; mustered in as private, Co. K, September 5, 1862; died of consumption, February 7, 1863, in Division Hospital, near Falmouth. Va.

STALTER, ABRAM.—Age, 44 years. Enlisted, August 14, 1862, at Washingtonville, to serve three years; mustered in as private, Co. G, September 5, 1862; wounded in action, May 3, 1863, at Chancellorsville, Va.; transferred to Veteran Reserve Corps, July 30, 1863; also borne as Abraham Stalters.

STALTER, PETER T.—Age, 45 years. Enlisted, August 27, 1862, at New Windsor, to serve three years; mustered in as private, Co. E, September 5, 1862; discharged, November 3, 1862, at Washington, D.C.

STANBROUGH, JOHN B.—Age, 32 years. Enrolled, August 20, 1862, at Newburgh, to serve three years; mustered in as first lieutenant, Co. I, September 5, 1862; discharged, November 12, 1862.

STANTON, JOHN.—Age, 18 years. Enlisted at Blooming Grove, to serve three years, and mustered in as private, Co. B, January 12, 1864; transferred to Fifty-second Company, Second Battalion, Veteran Reserve Corps, August 13, 1864; mustered out with detachment, September 11, 1865, at Mower Hospital, Philadelphia, Pa.

STANTON, JOHN H.—Age, 25 years. Enlisted, August 15, 1862, at Newburgh, to serve three years; mustered in as corporal, Co. I, September 5, 1862; discharged, November 24, 1863.

STANTON, PETER.—Age, 21 years. Enlisted, August 22, 1862, at Goshen, to serve three years; mustered in as private, Co. K, and deserted, September 5, 1862, at Goshen, N.Y.

STANTON, WILSON R.—Age, 22 years. Enlisted, August 22, 1862, at Goshen, to serve three years; not mustered in as private, Co. K; deserted, August 29, 1862, at Goshen, N.Y.

STAPLES, JOHN C.—Age, 19 years. Enlisted, August 12, 1862, at Otisville, to serve three years; mustered in as private, Co. E, September 5, 1862; killed in action, May 3, 1863, at Chancellorsville, Va.

STEPHENS, EPHRAIM.—Age, 22 years. Enlisted, August 6, 1862, at Chester, to serve three years; mustered in as private, Co. A, September 3, 1862; mustered out with company, June 3, 1865, near Washington, D.C.

STEPHENS, GEORGE H.—Age, 19 years. Enlisted, August 20, 1862, at Newburgh, to serve three years; mustered in as private, Co. K, September 5, 1862; killed in action, July 2, 1863, at Gettysburg, Pa.

STEPHENS, ROBERT L.—Age, 16 years. Enlisted, August 15, 1862, at Goshen, to serve three years; mustered in as musician, Co. B, September 5, 1862; mustered out with company, June 3, 1865, near Washington, D.C.

STEVENS, CHARLES H.—Age, 25 years. Enlisted, August 13, 1862, at Walden, to serve three years; mustered in as private, Co. H, September 5, 1862; discharged April 18, 1863.

STEVENS, DANIEL.—Age, 35 years. Enlisted, August 29, 1862, at Goshen, to serve three years; mustered in as private, Co. D, September 5, 1862; transferred to Co. G, Ninth Regiment, Veteran Reserve Corps, February 1, 1865; mustered out with detachment, June 26, 1865, at Washington, D.C.

STEWART, CHARLES.—Age, 33 years. Enrolled, August 15, 1862, at New burgh, to serve three years; mustered in as sergeant, Co. I, September 5, 1862; wounded in action, May 3, 1863, at Chancellorsville, Va.; promoted second lieutenant, July 2, 1863; mustered in as first lieutenant, October 18, 1863; captured in action June 1, 1864, at Totopotomoy, Va.; paroled, March 1865; discharged, May 15, 1865.

STICKNEY, GEORGE.—Age, 19 years. Enlisted at Lodi, to serve three years, and mustered in as private, Co. C, September 26, 1864; captured in action, October 27, 1864, at Boydton Road, Va.; released, May 1865; transferred to Co. A, Ninety-third Infantry, June 1, 1865.

STOCKWELL, SAMUEL S.—Age, 20 years. Enlisted at Plattsburgh, to serve one year, and mustered in as private, Co. B, September 12, 1864; mustered out with company, June 3, 1865, near Washington, D.C.

STORMS, DAVID.—Age, 19 years. Enlisted, August 19, 1862, at Goshen, to serve three years; mustered in as private, Co. I, September 5, 1862; wounded in action, May 3, 1863, at Chancellorsville, Va.; mustered out, June 9, 1863, at Finley Hospital, Washington, D.C.

STORMS, DAVID.—Age, 26 years. Enlisted at Goshen, to serve one year, and mustered in as private, Co. K, September 9, 1864; mustered out with company, June 3, 1865, near Washington, D.C.

STORMS, GEORGE N.—Age, 22 years. Enlisted at Warwick, to serve three years, and mustered in as private, Co. D, December 14, 1863; transferred to Co. H, Ninety-third Infantry, June 1, 1865.

STORMS, HARRISON H.—Age, 28 years. Enlisted, August 21, 1862, at Goshen, to serve three years; mustered in as private, Co. B, September 5, 1862; killed in action, July 2, 1863, at Gettysburg, Pa.

STORMS, JOHN C.—Age, 26 years. Enlisted, August 1, 1862, at Goshen, to serve three years; mustered in as private, Co. B, September 5, 1862; promoted corporal, prior to April 10, 1863; discharged for disability, July 15, 1863, at convalescent camp, Fairfax Seminary, Va.

STORMS, THOMAS S.—Age, 25 years. Enlisted, August 11, 1862, at Goshen, to serve three years; mustered in as private, Co. D, September 5, 1862; wounded in action, July 2, 1863, at Gettysburg Pa.; discharged for disability, December 28, 1863.

STORMS, WESLEY.—Age, 18 years. Enlisted, August 20, 1862, at Florida, to serve three years; mustered in as private, Co. B, September 5, 1862; wounded in action, July 2, 1863, at Gettysburg, Pa.; transferred to Co. H, Fourteenth Regiment, Veteran Reserve Corps, January 10, 1865; mustered out with detachment, June 29, 1865, at Washington, D.C.

STUDER, JOHN.—Age, 31 years. Enlisted, August 11, 1862, at Wallkill, to serve three years; mustered in as private, Co. K, September 5, 1862; wounded in action, May 16, 1864, at Spotsylvania, Va.; discharged for wounds, September 22, 1864, at Washington, D.C., as Studor; also borne as Studar.

SULLIVAN, JAMES.—Age, 18 years. Enlisted, August 4, 1862, at Blooming Grove, to serve three years; mustered in as private, Co. G, September 5, 1862; deserted, October 26, 1862, at Berlin, Md.; joined regulars.

SULLIVAN, JESSE.—Age, 21 years. Enlisted, August 4, 1862, at Goshen, to serve three years; mustered in as private, Co. B, September 5, 1862; deserted, October 25, 1862, at South Mountain, Md.

SULLIVAN, JOHN.—Age, 45 years. Enlisted, August 14, 1862, at Newburgh, to serve three years; mustered in as private, Co. C, September 5, 1862; discharged for disability, April 16, 1863, at Falmouth, Va.

SUTHERLAND, WILLIAM.—Age, 34 years. Enlisted, August 14, 1862, at Newburgh, to serve three years; mustered in as private, Co. I, September 5, 1862; promoted corporal, November 7, 1864; wounded in action, April 6, 1865, at Sailor's Creek, Va.; mustered out with company, June 3, 1865, near Washington, D.C.; also borne as Southerland.

SWIMM, JOHN W.—Age, 23 years. Enlisted, August 6, 1862, at Goshen, to serve three years; mustered in as private, Co. A, September 5, 1862; wounded in action, June 9, 1863, at Beverly's Ford, Va.; mustered out with company, June 3, 1865, near Washington, D.C.

SWIMM, WILLIAM.—Age, 20 years. Enlisted at Rochester, to serve three years, and mustered in as private, Co. A, October 3, 1864; transferred to Co. E, Ninety-third Infantry, June 1, 1865.

SYERS, ROSWELL.—Age, 18 years. Enlisted at Newburgh, to serve one year, and mustered in as private, Co. B, February 8, 1865; mustered out with detachment, May 10, 1865, at Hart's Island, New York Harbor.

TAFT, THOMAS.—Age, 21 years. Enrolled, August 7, 1862, at Cornwall, to serve three years; mustered in as sergeant, Co. C, September 5, 1862; wounded in action, July 2, 1863, at Gettysburg. Pa.; mustered in as first lieutenant, Co. H, July 20, 1864; as captain, Co. C, September 22, 1864; mustered out with company, June 8, 1865, near Washington, D.C. Commissioned first lieutenant, August 2, 1864, with rank from July 20, 1864, vice C. T. Cressy, deceased; captain, November 15, 1864, with rank from September 21, 1864, vice C. B. Wood, honorably discharged.

TAMELSON, CHARLES.—Age, 18 years. Enlisted, August 24, 1864, at Victory, to serve one year; mustered in as private, Co. H, August 24, 1864; wounded in action, October 27, 1864, at Boydton Plank Road, Va.; died of typhoid fever, January 4, 1865, at Armory Square Hospital, Washington, D.C., as Timerson.

TAYLOR, GEORGE G.—Age, 29 years. Enlisted, August 6, 1862, at Cornwall, to serve three years; mustered in as sergeant, Co. C, September 5, 1862; discharged for disability, January 23, 1864, at Hammond Hospital, Point Lookout, Md.

TAYLOR, JAMES H.—Age, 22 years. Enlisted, August 11, 1862, at Port Jervis, to serve three years; mustered in as private, Co. F, September 5, 1862; promoted corporal, September 15, 1862; wounded in action, July 2, 1863, at Gettysburg, Pa., and August 1, 1864, near Petersburg, Va.; promoted sergeant, March 1, 1865; mustered out with company, June 3, 1865, near Washington, D.C.

TAYLOR, JOHN J.—Age, 37 years. Enlisted, August 4, 1862, at Washingtonville, to serve three years; mustered in as corporal, Co. O, September 5, 1862; returned to ranks, February 1, 1863; captured in action, November 27, 1863, at Locust Grove, Va.; paroled, no date; wounded in action, May 7, 1864, at the Wilderness, Va.; absent, in Armory Square Hospital, Washington, D.C., since October 30, 1864, and at muster-out of company.

TAYLOR, JOHN W.—Age, 21 years. Enlisted, August 12, 1862, at Newburgh, to serve three years; mustered in as private, Co. E, September 5, 1862; died of typhoid fever, July 25, 1863, at hospital, Alexandria.

TAYLOR, JOHN W.—Age, 26 years. Enlisted, August 11, 1862, at Chester, to serve three years; mustered in as private, Co. A, September 5, 1862: promoted corporal, September 15, 1862; wounded in action, May 8, 1863, at Chancellorsville, Va.; mustered out with company, June 3, 1865, near Washington, D.C.

TEARS, DANIEL T.—Age, 22 years. Enlisted, August 13, 1862, at Walden, to serve three years; mustered in as private, Co. H, September 5, 1862; discharged, January 10, 1863.

TERRY, DAVID.—Age, 44 years. Enlisted, August 16, 1862, at Newburgh, to serve three years; mustered in as private, Co. I, September 5, 1862; discharged, January 28, 1863.

TERWILLEGER, CHARLES L.—Age, 25 years. Enlisted, August 13, 1862 at Walden, to serve three years; mustered in as private, Co. H, September 5, 1862; deserted, November 26, 1862, from temporary hospital at Berlin, Md., as Charles T.

TERWILLIGAR, WHITMORE.—Age, 18 years. Enlisted, August 15, 1862, at Newburgh, to serve three years; mustered in as private, Co. I, September 5, 1862; wounded in action, May 6, 1864, at the Wilderness, Va.; promoted corporal, August 1, 1864, and sergeant, November 7, 1864; wounded in action, April 6, 1865, at Deatonsville Road, Va.; mustered out with company, June 3, 1865, near Washington, D.C.

TERWILLIGER, JESSE.—Age, 26 years. Enlisted, August 11, 1862, at Port Jervis, to serve three years; mustered in as private, Co. F, September 5, 1862; died of typhoid fever, January 1, 1863, at camp near Falmouth, Va.

TERWILLIGER, JOHN I.—Age, 19 years. Enlisted, September 2, 1864, at Goshen, to serve three years; mustered in as private, Co. K, September 2, 1864; mustered out with company, June 3, 1865, near Washington, D.C.

TERWILLIGER, OSCAR.—Age, 21 years. Enlisted, August 15, 1862, at Goshen, to serve three years; mustered in as corporal, Co. C, September 5, 1862; wounded while on picket, April 2, 1863, near Falmouth, Va.; accidentally wounded, no date; transferred to One Hundred and Twenty-ninth Company Second Battalion, Veteran Reserve Corps, March 15, 1864; mustered out, July 14, 1865, at Washington, D.C.; prior service in Co. D, Seventh Cavalry.

THITCHNER, JAMES T.—Age, 25 years. Enlisted, August 16, 1862, at Newburgh, to serve three years; mustered in as private, Co. I, September 5, 1862; discharged, August 29, 1863; also borne as Thitchener.

THOMPKINS, BENJAMIN L.—Age, 23 years. Enlisted, August 11, 1862, at Port Jervis, to serve three years; mustered in as private, Co. F, September 5, 1862; mustered out with detachment, June 2, 1865, at Washington, D.C.; also borne as Tompkins.

THOMPKINS, GEORGE W.—Age, 20 years. Enlisted, August 11, 1862, at Port Jervis, to serve three years; mustered in as private, Co. F, September 5, 1862; promoted corporal, March 1, 1865; mustered out with company, June 3, 1865, near Washington, D.C.; also borne as Tompkins; awarded *medal of honor*.

THOMPKINS, JOHN.—Age, 35 years. Enlisted, August 15, 1862, at Cornwall, to serve three years; mustered in as private, Co. C, September 5, 1862; captured while on picket, June 23, 1864, near Petersburg Va.; released, May 1865, and at Annapolis, Md., at muster-out of company.

THOMPSON, Alexander.—Age, 25 years. Enlisted, August 14, 1862, at Newburgh, to serve three years; mustered in as private, Co. I, September 5, 1862; discharged, December 27, 1863.

THOMPSON, CHARLES T.—Corporal, Co. K, First U.S. Sharpshooters; transferred to Co. H, this regiment, March 1, 1865; mustered out with company, June 8, 1865, near Washington, D.C.

THOMPSON, JOHN.—Age, 22 years. Enlisted, August 13, 1862, at Newburgh, to serve three years; mustered in as private, Co. C, September 5, 1862; wounded, May 3, 1863, at Chancellorsville, Va.; captured in action, June 22, 1864, in front of Petersburg, Va.; released, April 29, 1865; mustered out, June 24, 1865, at New York City.

THOMPSON, JOHN H.—Age, — years. Enrolled, July 26, 1862, at Goshen, to serve three years; mustered in as surgeon, September 5, 1862; dismissed November 25, 1864, for disability; removed January 26, 1865. Commissioned surgeon, September 10, 1862, with rank from July 26, 1862, original; recommissioned, not mustered, surgeon, February 15, 1865, with rank from same date, vice himself, dismissed.

THOMPSON, ROBERT.—Age, 23 years. Enlisted, September 27, 1864, at Avon, to serve three years; mustered in as private, Co. D, September 27, 1864; deserted to the enemy, November 7, 1864, at Hancock's Station, Va.

THORNE, GEORGE J.—Age, 29 years. Enlisted, August 11, 1862, at Cornwall, to serve three years; mustered in as private, Co. C, September 5, 1862; transferred by enlistment to First U.S. Engineers, April 16, 1863.

THORP, CORNELIUS.—Age, 27 years. Enlisted, August 2, 1862, at Goshen, to serve three years; mustered in as private, Co. B, September 5, 1862; deserted, October 24, 1862, at South Mountain, Md.

THORP, WILLIAM H.—Age, 30 years. Enlisted, August 12, 1862, at Goshen, to serve three years; mustered in as private, Co. B, September 5, 1862; deserted, September 4, 1862, at Goshen; returned to duty, April 21, 1863; transferred to Co. C, Ninety-third infantry, June 2, 1865.

THORPE, WILLIAM H. G.—Age, 39 years. Enlisted, August 15, 1862, at Cornwall, to serve three years; mustered in as private, Co. C, September 5, 1862; discharged for disability, March 29, 1863, at Baltimore, Md.

TIDD, SAMUEL V.—Age, 20 years. Enlisted, August 12, 1862, at Wallkill, to serve three years; mustered in as private, Co. K, September 5, 1862; captured in action, June 1, 1864, at Totopotomoy Creek, Va.; released, April 28 1865; mustered out, June 29, 1865, at New York City.

TILTON, JAMES D.—Age, 34 years. Enlisted, August 11, 1862, at Newburgh, to serve three years; mustered in as private, Co. C, September 5, 1862; killed in action, May 3, 1863, at Chancellorsville, Va.

TINDALL, CHARLES W.—Age, 25 years. Enlisted, August 14, 1862, at Walden, to serve, three years; mustered in as private, Co. H, September 5, 1862; wounded in action, July 2, 1863, at Gettysburg, Pa.; promoted sergeant, August 1863; captured in action, May 12, 1864, at Spotsylvania Va.; paroled, April 1865; mustered out with company, June 3, 1865, near Washington, D.C.

TITSWORTH, DAVID.—Age, 4 [?] years. Enlisted, August 11, 1862, at Port Jervis, to serve three years; mustered in as private, Co. F, September 5, 1862; died of typhoid fever, December 28, 1862, at camp, near Falmouth, Va.

TITUS, WILLIAM E.—Age, 18 years. Enlisted, August 11, 1862, at Goshen, to serve three years; mustered in as private, Co. B, September 5, 1862; transferred to Veteran Reserve Corps, April 20, 1864.

TOMER, WILLIAM H.—Age, 21 years. Enlisted, August 9, 1862, at Goshen, to serve three years; mustered in as private, Co. D, September 5, 1862; wounded in action, May 3, 1863, at Chancellorsville, Va.; transferred to Co. I, Twenty-first Regiment, Reserve Corps, April 6, 1864; discharged, July 14, 1865, at Trenton, N.J.

TOMPKINS, EPHRAIM.—Age, 28 years. Enlisted, August 8, 1862, at Cornwall, to serve three years; mustered in as private, Co. C, September 3, 1862; wounded in action, May 3, 1863, at Chancellorsville Va.; transferred to Fourteenth Company, Second Battalion, Veteran Reserve Corps, March 15, 1864: mustered out with detachment, June 30, 1865, at Stone Hospital, Washington, D.C.; also borne as Tompkins.

TOMPKINS, WILLIAM.—Age, 19 years. Enlisted, August 11, 1862, at Goshen, to serve three years; mustered in as private, Co. A, September 5, 1862; deserted, October 24, 1862, at Berlin, Md.

TOPPING, HUGH.—Age, 30 years. Enlisted, August 11, 1862, at Newburgh, to serve three years; mustered in as private, Co. A, September 5, 1862; discharged, June 18, 1863, at Stoneman's Switch, Va.

TOULON, LEWIS M.—Age, 18 years. Enlisted, August 14, 1862, at Wallkill, to serve three years; mustered in as private, Co. E, September 5, 1862; deserted, September 1, 1863, from Chestnut Hill Hospital, Philadelphia, Pa.; arrested, January 24, 1864; returned to duty, awaiting trial; wounded in action, April 6, 1865, at Sailor's Creek, Va.: transferred to Co. B, Ninety-third Infantry, June 1, 1865.

TRAINER, ALEXANDER.—Age, 21 years. Enlisted, August 9, 1862, at Blooming Grove, to serve three years; mustered in as private, Co. 0[?], September 5, 1862; wounded in action, May 3, 1863, at Chancellorsville, Va.; transferred to Co. G, Twelfth Regiment, Veteran Reserve Corps, December 31, 1864; mustered out with detachment, June 29, 1863, at Washington, D.C.

TRAINER, JOHN.—Age, 24 years. Enlisted, August 12, 1862, at Blooming Grove, to serve three years; mustered in as private, Co. G, September 5, 1862; wounded in action, May 6, 1864, at the Wilderness, Va.; mustered out with company, June 3, 1865, near Washington, D.C.

TRAINER, WILLIAM A.—Age, 23 years. Enlisted at Royalton, to serve three years, and mustered in as private, Co. D, September 23, 1864; absent, sick in hospital, since April 1865, and at muster-out of company.

TRAINER, WILLIAM H.—Age, 28 years. Enlisted, August 11, 1862, at Blooming Grove, to serve three years; mustered in as private, Co. G, September 5, 1862; wounded in action, May 12, 1864, at the Wilderness, Va.; promoted corporal, October 25, 1864; mustered out with company June 3, 1865, near Washington, D.C.

TRANT, JOHN B.—Age, 19 years. Enlisted at Victory, to serve one year, and mustered in as private, Co. H, August 24, 1864; mustered out with company, June 3, 1865, near Washington, D.C.; also borne as John P.

TRAPHAGEN, DANIEL.—Age, 18 years. Enlisted, August 15, 1862, at Walden, to serve three years; mustered in as private, Co. H, September 5, 1862; transferred to Co. I, Sixth Regiment, Veteran Reserve Corps, April 16, 1864; mustered out with detachment, July 3, 1865, at Cincinnati; also borne as David.

TRAVER, RICHARD.—Age, 21 years. Enlisted, August 13, 1862, at Newburgh, to serve three years; mustered in as private, Co. E, September 3, 1862; discharged, December 19, 1862, at Washington, D.C., as Travor; also borne as Travers.

TRAVIS, HENRY F.—Age, 21 years. Enrolled, August 22, 1862, at Newburgh, to serve three years; mustered in as private, Co. I, September 5, 1862; promoted quartermaster sergeant, September 21, 1862; mustered in as first lieutenant and quartermaster, January 15, 1863; as captain, Co. I, September 3, 1863; mustered out with company, June 3, 1865, near Washington, D.C.; prior service as corporal, Co. I, Seventy-first Militia. Commissioned first lieutenant and quartermaster, February 27, 1863, with rank from January 14, 1863, vice A. Denniston, resigned; captain, August 21, 1863, with rank from April 21, 1863, vice L. Clark, discharged.

TRAVIS, JOHN.—Age, 24 years. Enlisted at Goshen, to serve one year, and mustered in as private, Co. D, September 12, 1864; died of chronic diarrhea, November 18, 1864, at hospital, Washington, D.C.; also borne as John A.

TRAVIS, ROBERT.—Age, 17 years. Enlisted, August 11, 1862, at Port Jervis, to serve three years; mustered in as musician, Co. F, September 5, 1862; mustered out with company, June 3, 1865, near Washington, D.C.; also borne as Robert L.

TRISLER, LEWIS.—Age, 35 years. Enlisted, August 6, 1862, at Deer Park, to serve three years; mustered in as private, Co. E, September 5, 1862; discharged, April 16, 1863, near Falmouth, Va.

TUCKER, ALBERT W.—Age, 18 years. Enlisted, August 11, 1862, at Goshen, to serve three years; mustered in as private, Co. B, September 5, 1862; promoted corporal, March 7, 1865; mustered out with company, June 3, 1865, near Washington, D.C.

TUCKER, GEORGE N.—Age, 19 years. Enlisted, August 15, 1862, at Newburgh, to serve three years; mustered in as private, Co. I, September 5, 1862; mustered out with company, June 3, 1865, near Washington, D.C.

TUCKER, WILLIAM E.—Age, 33 years. Enlisted, to serve one year; mustered in as private, Co. K, September 3, 1864; mustered out with company, June 3, 1865, near Washington, D.C.

TUOHEY, PATRICK.—Age, 19 years. Enlisted, August 11, 1862, at Blooming Grove, to serve three years; mustered in as Co. G, September 5, 1862; wounded in action, May 3, 1863, at Chancellorsville, Va.; discharged for disability, December 26, 1863, at Philadelphia, Pa.; also borne as Twohey and Touhey.

TURNER, HENRY R.—Age, 18 years. Enlisted, August 18, 1862, at Newburgh, to serve three years; mustered in as private, Co. I, September 5, 1862; promoted corporal, April 20, 1865; mustered out with company, June 3, 1865, near Washington, D.C.

TURNER, JR., JAMES.—Age, 28 years. Enlisted, August 20, 1862, at Newburgh, to serve three years, and mustered in as private, Co. I, September 5, 1862; deserted, October 18, 1862, at Miners Hill, Va.

TURNER, REUBEN.—Age, 45 years. Enlisted, August 20, 1862, at Goshen, to serve three years; mustered in as private, Co. G, September 5, 1862; discharged, April 20, 1863, at Falmouth, Va.

TURNER, JR., REUBEN.—Age, 24 years. Enlisted, August 15, 1862, at Newburgh, to serve three years; mustered in as private, Co. G, September 5, 1862; discharged, February 11, 1863, at Columbia College Hospital, Washington, D.C.

TUTHILL, EZRA F.—Age, 24 years. Enlisted, August 11, 1862, at Goshen, to serve three years; mustered in as private, Co. B, September 5, 1862; wounded in action, May 3, 1863, at Chancellorsville, Va.; discharged for disability, June 29, 1863, at Fairfax Seminary, Alexandria, Va.

TUTHILL, GABRIEL.—Age, 24 years. Enrolled, August 13, 1862, at Goshen, to serve three years; mustered in as first sergeant, Co. B, September 5, 1862, as second lieutenant, February 9, 1863; discharged to date, February 23, 1864, having accepted an appointment as second lieutenant, One Hundred and Ninth Co., Second Battalion Veteran Reserve Corps. Commissioned second lieutenant, February 27, 1863, with rank from February 8, 1863, vice W. E. Mapes, promoted.

TWIGGS, WILLIAM.—Age, 19 years. Enlisted, August 20, 1862, at Goshen, to serve three years; mustered in as private, Co. C, September 5, 1862; transferred to First U.S. Engineers, April 16, 1863.

TYSOE, WILLIAM.—Age, 20 years. Enlisted, August 27, 1862, at Newburgh, to serve three years; mustered in as private, Co. G, September 5, 1862; promoted corporal, December 1, 1863, sergeant, October 1, 1864; mustered out with company, June 3, 1865, near Washington, D.C.

UPTEGROVE, WILLIAM P.—Age, 19 years. Enlisted, August 9, 1862, at Otisville, to serve three years; mustered in as private, Co. E, September 5, 1862; appointed wagoner prior to April 10, 1863; promoted sergeant, August 1, 1863; commissary sergeant, September 3, 1863; mustered out with regiment, June 3, 1865, near Washington, D.C.; also borne as Uptergrove.

UTTER, HENRY S.—Age, 33 years. Enlisted at Goshen, to serve one year, and mustered in as private, Co. D, September 3, 1864; mustered out with company, June 3, 1865, near Washington, D.C.

VALENTINE, CHARLES H.—Age, 18 years. Enlisted, August 8, 1862, at Chester, to serve three years; mustered in as private, Co. A, September 5, 1862; wounded in action, July 3, 1863, at Gettysburg, Pa.; transferred to Co. H, Twenty-second Regiment, Veteran Reserve Corps, April 10, 1864; mustered out with detachment, July 1, 1865, at Tod Barracks, Columbus, Ohio.

VALENTINE, WILLIAM.—Age, 32 years. Enlisted, August 4, 1862, at Goshen, to serve three years; mustered in as corporal, Co. B, September 5, 1862; promoted sergeant, prior to April 10, 1863; wounded in action, May 3, 1863, at Chancellorsville, Va., and died of his wounds, May 29, 1863, at Bellair, Va.

VALET, ALEXANDER M.—Age, 23 years. Enlisted, August 11, 1862, at Newburgh, to serve three years; mustered in as private, Co. I, September 5, 1862; promoted corporal, November 1, 1862; returned to ranks, August 1, 1864; mustered out, June 2, 1865, at Washington, D.C., while in Augur Hospital, Alexandria, Va.

VANCE, ELI.—Age, 44 years. Enlisted, August 18, 1862, at Newburgh, to serve three years; mustered in as private, Co. I, September 5, 1862; discharged, March 28, 1863.

VANCE, MILES.—Age, 18 years. Enlisted, August 12, 1862, at Otisville, to serve three years; mustered in as private, Co. E, September 5, 1862; killed in action. June 9, 1863, at Beverly Ford, Va.

VANDERLYN, ABRAHAM T.—Age, 21 years. Enlisted, August 14, 1862, at Newburgh, to serve three years; mustered in as sergeant, Co. I, September 5, 1862; wounded in action, July 2, 1863, at Gettysburg Pa., and May 6, 1864, at the Wilderness, Va.; died, November 7, 1864, at Fairfax Seminary Hospital, Alexandria, Va.

VAN GORDON, CHARLES H.—Age, 18 years. Enlisted, August 16, at Washingtonville, to serve three years; mustered in as musician, Co. G, September 5, 1862; mustered out with company, June 3, 1865, near Washington, D.C.

VAN GORDON, DAVID R. P.—Age, 21 years. Enlisted, August 2, 1862, at Goshen, to serve two years; mustered in as private, Co. B, September 5, 1862; transferred to Co. D, Ninth Regiment, Veteran Reserve Corps, September 7, 1863; mustered out, July 17, 1865, at Washington, D.C.

VAN HORN, JOHN.—Age, 18 years. Enlisted, August 11, 1862, at Wallkill, to serve three years; mustered in as private, Co. K, September 5, 1862; promoted hospital steward, to date, August 11, 1862; discharged for disability, February 11, 1863.

VAN HOUGHTEN, JOHN.—Age, 36 years. Enlisted, August 9, 1862, at Port Jervis, to serve three years; mustered in as private, Co. F, September 5, 1862; discharged for disability, July 1863, from hospital, at Washington, D.C., as Van Houten.

VAN HOUTEN, JOHN.—Age, 36 years. Enlisted, August 9, 1862, at Goshen, to serve three years; mustered in as private, Co. A, September 5, 1862; deserted. September, 1862, at Goshen, N.Y.

VAN HOUTEN, WILLIAM B.— Age, 28 years. Enrolled, August 13, 1862, at Goshen, to serve three years; mustered in as sergeant, Co. D, September 5, 1862; promoted sergeant-major, May 1, 1863; mustered in as first lieutenant, Co. I, July 1,1863; appointed adjutant, same date; discharged, January 23, 1865, as Van Horten.

VAN KEUREN, ELISHA I.— Age, 29 years. Enlisted, August 18, 1862, at Walden, to serve three years; mustered in as private, Co. H, September 5, 1862; discharged, July 1, 1865, at Fort Delaware, Del.

VAN SCIVER, GEORGE.— Age, 23 years. Enlisted, July 31, 1862, at Wallkill, to serve three years; mustered in as corporal, Co. K, September 5, 1862; wounded in action, May 3, 1863, at Chancellorsville, Va.; transferred to Veteran Reserve Corps, April 10, 1864: also borne as Van Seiver.

VAN SICKLE, WILLIAM C.— Age, 43 years. Enlisted, August 15, 1862, at Port Jervis, to serve three years; mustered in as private, Co. F, September 5, 1862; wounded in action, July 2, 1863, at Gettysburg, Pa.; discharged for disability, January 7, 1864, from hospital at Philadelphia, Pa.

VANSTRANDER, THOMAS.— Age, 34 years. Enlisted, August 13, 1862, at Walden, to serve three years; mustered in as private, Co. H, September 15[?], 1862; discharged for disability, January 16, 1863.

VAN TASSEL, THEODORE R.— Age, 31 years. Enlisted, August 16, 1862, at Newburgh, to serve three years; mustered in as private, Co. I, September 5, 1862; discharged, March 24, 1863.

VAN ZILE, ANDREW I[?].— Age, 24 years. Enlisted, August 11, 1862, at Washingtonville, to serve three years; mustered in as private, Co. B[?], September 5, 1862; mustered out with company, June 3, 1865, near Washington, D.C.

VAN ZILE, JOHN C.— Age, 28 years. Enlisted, August 14, 1862, at Newburgh, to serve three years; mustered in as private, Co. I, September 5, 1862; promoted corporal, July 26, 1863; mustered out, June 15, 1865, at Harts Island, New York Harbor.

VEDDENBURG, JOSEPH.— Age, 33 years. Enlisted at Goshen, to serve three years, and mustered in as private, Co. G, January 2, 1864; wounded in action, May 18, 1864, at Spotsylvania Court House, Va.; transferred to Co. D, Ninety-third Infantry, June 1, 1865, as Vreddenburg.

VERMILYA, JOHN C.— Age, 22 years. Enlisted, August 7, 1862, at Wallkill, to serve three years; mustered in as private, Co. K, September 5, 1862; promoted corporal, July 1, 1863; wounded in action, May 12, 1864, at Spotsylvania Court House, Va.; died of his wounds, May 28, 1864, at Washington, D.C.

VERDENBURGH, SAMUEL.— Age, 26 years. Enlisted, August 13, 1862, at Newburgh, to serve three years; mustered in as private, Co. C, August 15, 1862; no further record.

VERPLANK, WILLIAM A.— Age, 29 years. Enrolled, August 19, 1862, at Goshen, to serve three years; mustered in as first lieutenant, Co. L, September 5, 1862; discharged for disability, September 28, 1863. Commissioned first lieutenant, September 10, 1862, with rank from August 19, 1862, original.

VOLENTINE, STEPHEN E.— Age, 18 years. Enlisted at Warwick, to serve three years, and mustered in as private, Co. D, December 24, 1863; transferred to Co. H, Ninety-third Infantry, June 1, 1865, as Valentine.

VOOHERS, ALONZO.— Private, Co. K., First United States Sharpshooters; transferred to Co. H, this regiment, March 1, 1865; mustered out with company, June 3, 1865, near Washington, D.C.

VREELAND, HENRY J.— Age, 45 years. Enlisted, August 18, 1862, at Goshen, to serve three years; mustered in as private, Co. G, September 5, 1862; rejected same date.

WADE, SILAS.— Age, 28 years. Enlisted at Plattsburg, to serve one year, and mustered in as private, Co. E, September 5, 1864; mustered out with company, June 3, 1865, near Washington, D.C.

WALKER, GEORGE.— Age, 26 years. Enlisted at Sullivan, to serve one year, and mustered in as private, Co. A, October 1, 1864; absent, sick in hospital, at muster-out of company.

WALKER, JOHN.— Age, 22 years. Enlisted at Goshen, to serve three years, and mustered in as private, Co. E, May 7, 1864; transferred to Co. E, Ninety-third Infantry, June 1, 1865.

WALLACE, JOHN.— Age, 43 years. Enlisted at Goshen, to serve one year, and mustered in as private, Co. K, September 1, 1864; died of typhoid fever, February 16, 1865, at Baltimore, Md.

WALLACE, WILLIAM.— Age, 24 years. Enlisted, August 18, 1862, at Newburgh, to serve three years; mustered in as private, Co. I, September 5, 1862; promoted corporal, November 1, 1862; killed in action, May 3, 1863, at Chancellorsville, Va.

WARD, JAMES A.— Age, 18 years. Enlisted, August 13, 1862, at Unionville, to serve three years; mustered in as private, Co. C, September 5, 1862; killed in action, May 3, 1863, at Chancellorsville, VA.

WARFORD, JOHN H.— Age, 21 years. Enlisted, August 12, 1862, at Newburgh to serve three years; mustered in as private, Co. A, August 15, 1862; wounded in action, May 3, 1863, at Chancellorsville, Va., and May 12, 1864, at Spotsylvania Court House, Va.; promoted corporal, September 1, 1864; sergeant, November 15, 1864; wounded in action, April 6, 1865, at Deatonsville Road, Va.; absent since and in Jarvis Hospital, Baltimore, Md., at muster-out of company.

WARNERMAKER, CHARLES.— Age, 23 years. Enlisted at Wallkill, to serve one year, and mustered in as private, Co. B, August 17, 1864; deserted, March 28, 1865, at Dinwiddie, Va., as Wannemaker.

WARREN, WILLIAM G.— Age, 23 years. Enlisted, August 15, 1862, at Newburgh, to serve three years; mustered in as private, Co. I, September 5, 1862; died of typhoid fever, February 8, 1863, at Stoneman's Station, Va.

WEBB, DANIEL E.— Age, 21 years. Enlisted, August 12, 1862, at Wallkill, to serve three years; mustered in as sergeant, Co. K, August 14, 1862; returned to ranks, January 1, 1863; wounded and captured in action, May 3, 1863, at Chancellorsville, Va.; paroled, May 14, 1863; died of his wounds, August 24, 1863, at Methodist Church Hospital, Alexandria, Va.

WEBSTER, CHARLES.— Private, Co. K, First United States Sharpshooters; transferred to Co. H, this regiment, March 1, 1863; mustered out with company, June 3, 1865, near Washington, D.C.

WEEDEN, SAMUEL M.— Age, 26 years. Enlisted, August 12, 1862, at Goshen, to serve three years; mustered in as private, Co. D, September 5, 1862; appointed musician, no date; mustered out with company, June 3, 1863, near Washington, D.C.

WEEKS, ANDREW J.— Age, 31 years. Enlisted, August 11, 1862, at Blooming Grove, to serve three years; mustered in as private, Co. G, September 5, 1862, and deserted, same date, at Goshen, N.Y.

WELCH, MICHAEL.— Age, 21 years. Enlisted at Rochester, to serve three years, and mustered in as private, Co. D, September 27, 1864; mustered out with company, June 3, 1865, near Washington, D.C.

WELLER, CHARLES M.— Age, 19 years. Enlisted at Wallkill, to serve three years; mustered in as private, Co. K, September 5, 1862; discharged for disability, February 5, 1863, at Philadelphia, Pa.

WELLS, JOSEPH.— Age, 44 years. Enlisted at Plattsburg to serve one year, and mustered in as private, Co. E, September 14, 1864; mustered out with company, June 3, 1865, near Washington, D.C.

WELLS, SAMUEL S.— Age, 25 years. Enlisted, August 7, 1862, at Goshen, to serve three years; mustered in as private, Co. A, September 5, 1862; deserted, September 1862, at Goshen, N.Y.

WELSH, JOHN.— Age, 27 years. Enlisted, August 12, 1862, at Monroe, to serve three years; mustered in as private, Co. A, August 14, 1862; no further record.

WERNER, FRANCIS M.— Age, 18 years. Enlisted, August 8, 1862, at Goshen, to serve three years; mustered in as private, Co. D, September 5, 1862; discharged for hernia, January 12, 1863.

WESCOTT, DAVID L.— Age, 41 years. Enlisted, August 11, 1862, at Cornwall, to serve three years; mustered in as private, Co. C, September 5, 1862; wounded in action, May 3, 1863, at Chancellorsville, Va.; died of his wounds, May 24, 1863, at Potomac Creek Hospital.

WESTERVELT, ANDREW.— Private, Co. K, First United States Sharpshooters; transferred to Co. H, this regiment, March 1, 1865, to Co. D. Ninety-third Infantry, June 1, 1865; veteran.

WEYGANT, CHARLES H.— Age, 23 years. Enrolled, August 12, 1862, at Goshen, to serve three years; mustered in as captain, Co. A, September 5, 1862; wounded in action, May 3, 1863, at Chancellorsville, Va.; mustered in as major, September 16, 1863; as lieutenant-colonel, February 11, 1864; wounded in action, May 12, 1864, at Spotsylvania Court House, Va., and October 27, 1864, at Boydton Road, Va.; mustered out with regiment, June 3, 1865, near Washington, D.C. Commissioned captain, September 10, 1862, with rank from August 12, 1862, original; major, September 14, 1863, with rank from July 2, 1863, vice James Cromwell, killed in action; lieutenant-colonel, October 6, 1863, with rank from July 2, 1863, vice F. M. Cummins, promoted; colonel, not mustered, January 11, 1865, with rank from September 19, 1864, vice F. M. Cummins, honorably discharged.

WEYGANT, WINES E.— Age, 22 years. Enrolled, August 14, 1862, at Goshen, to serve three years; mustered in as first lieutenant, Co. B, September 5, 1862; discharged, February 9, 1863. Commissioned first lieutenant, September 10, 1862, with rank from August 14, 1862, original; adjutant, not mustered, January 31, 1865, with rank from same date, vice W. B. Van Houten, resigned.

WEYMER, JOHN B.— Age, 40 years. Enlisted, August 11, 1862, at Goshen, to serve three years; mustered in as private, Co. D, September 5, 1862; captured in action, November 27, 1863, at Mine Run, Va.; exchanged, prior to December 1864; mustered out with company, June 3, 1865, near Washington, D.C.

WEYMER, OSCAR S.— Age, 18 years. Enlisted at Warwick, to serve three years, and mustered in as private, Co. D, December 30, 1863; wounded in action, May 12, 1864, at Spotsylvania, Va.; discharged for disability, May 27, at hospital, Washington, D.C.

WHALEN, WILLIAM.— Age, 18 years. Enlisted at Goshen, to serve one year, and mustered in as private, Co. K, August 17, 1864; mustered out, May 16, 1865, at hospital, York, Pa., as Whalon.

WHAN, WILLIAM.— Age, 30 years. Enlisted, August 11, 1862, at Newburgh, to serve three years; mustered in as private, Co. I, September 5, 1862; killed in action, July 2, 1863, at Gettysburg, Pa.

WHEAT, DANIEL B.— Age, 32 years. Enlisted, August 20, 1862, at Wallkill, to serve three years; mustered in as private, Co. E, September 5, 1862; discharged, January 11, 1863, near Falmouth, Va., as David B.

WHEAT, SIMEON.— Age, 28 years. Enlisted, August 9, 1862, at Mount Hope, to serve three years; mustered in as private, Co. E, September 15, 1862; wounded in action, May 12, 1864, at Spotsylvania, Va.; transferred to Veteran Reserve Corps, January 9, 1865.

WHEELER, CHARLES A.— Age, 35 years. Enlisted at Rochester, to serve three years, and mustered in as private, Co. A, September 7, 1864; mustered out with detachment, May 17, 1865, at Setterle Hospital, W. Philadelphia, Pa.

WHEELER, HORACE.— Age, 21 years. Enlisted, August 15, 1862, at Bethel, to serve three years; mustered in as private, Co. E, September 5, 1862; wounded in action, May 1864, at Spotsylvania, Va.; died of fever, November 10, 1864, in hospital, near Petersburg, Va.

WHITE, DANIEL S.— Age, 18 years. Enlisted, August 14, 1862, at Newburgh, to serve three years; mustered in as private, Co. G, September 5, 1862; promoted corporal, prior to April 10, 1863; wounded in action, May 3, 1863, at Chancellorsville, Va.; returned to ranks, December 1, 1864; transferred to Veterans Reserve Corps, January 1, 1865.

WHITE, JOHN.— Age, 22 years. Enlisted at Goshen, to serve three years, and mustered in as private, Co. B, December 23, 1863; transferred to Co. C, Ninety-third Infantry, June 2, 1865.

WHITE, JOHN H.— Age, 24 years. Enlisted, August 14, 1862, at Newburgh, to serve three years; mustered in as private, Co. G, September 5, 1862; died of typhoid fever, December 10, 1862, at camp near Falmouth, Va.

WHITE, RICHARD L.— Age, 22 years. Enlisted, August 14, 1862, at Port Jervis, to serve three years; mustered in as private, Co. F, September 5, 1862; discharged for disability, December 24, 1863, at convalescent camp, Alexandria, Va.

WHITE, SAMUEL A.—Age, 43 years. Enlisted, August 14, 1862, at Newburgh, to serve three years; mustered in as private, Co. I, September 5, 1862; discharged, April 4, 1864.

WHITE, WILLIAM.—Age, 28 years. Enlisted, August 7, 1862, at Cornwall, to serve three years; mustered in as private, Co. C, September 5, 1862; promoted corporal, prior to February 1863; deserted, on expiration of furlough, February 21, 1863.

WHITE, WILLIAM G.—Age, 21 years. Enlisted, August 7, 1862, at Goshen, to serve three years; mustered in as corporal, Co. B, September 5, 1862; discharged, January 12, 1863.

WHITEHEAD, CHARLES.—Age, 20 years. Enlisted, August 18, 1862, at Walden, to serve three years; mustered in as musician, Co. H, September 5, 1862; mustered out with company, June 3, 1865, near Washington, D.C.

WHITESIDE, WILLIAM H.—Age, 19 years. Enlisted, August 19, 1862, at Walden, to serve three years; mustered in as private, Co. H, September 5, 1862; mustered out with company, June 3, 1865, near Washington, D.C.

WHITNEY, OSBORNE H.—Age, 20 years. Enlisted, July 31, 1862, at Goshen, to serve three years; mustered in as corporal, Co. A, September 5, 1862; promoted sergeant, December 15, 1862; mustered out with company, June 3, 1865, near Washington, D.C., as Osborne A.

WICKHAM, ISRAEL H.—Age, 24 years. Enlisted at Poughkeepsie, to serve three years, and mustered in as private, Co. K, July 20, 1864; transferred to Co. F, Ninety-third Infantry, June 1, 1865.

WIGHTMAN, JOSEPH P.—Age, 31 years. Enlisted, August 18, 1862, at Newburgh, to serve three years; mustered in as private, Co. I, September 5, 1862; wounded in action, May 3, 1863, at Chancellorsville, Va.; died of his wounds, May 25, 1863.

WILKESON, HENRY.—Age, 18 years. Enlisted at Goshen, to serve one year, and mustered in as private, Co. K, August 27, 1864; mustered out with company, June 3, 1865, near Washington, D.C., as Wilkinson.

WILKINS, DAVID.—Age, 36 years. Enlisted. August 15[?], 1862, at Newburgh, to serve three years; mustered in as private, Co. K, September 5, 1862; discharged for disability, December 13, 1862, at Washington, D.C., as David M.

WILLCOX, IRA.—Age, 21 years. Enlisted, August 15, 1862, at Port Jervis, to serve three years; mustered in as private, Co. F, September 5, 1862; wounded in action, May 3, 1863, and died of his wounds, May 3, 1863, at Chancellorsville, Va.

WILLCOX, RANSOM.—Age, 24 years. Enlisted, August 12, 1862, at Port Jervis, to serve three years; mustered in as private, Co. F, September 5, 1862; discharged for disability, January 13, 1865, at hospital, Davids' Island, New York Harbor.

WILLIAMS, EZRA.—Age, 40 years. Enlisted at Goshen, to serve three years, and mustered in as private, Co. I, April 6, 1864; transferred to Co. D, Ninety-third Infantry, June 1, 1865.

WILLIAMS, JOHN.—Age, 34 years. Enlisted, August 13, 1862, at Goshen, to serve three years; mustered in as corporal, Co. B, September 5, 1862; transferred to Co. H, Twenty-fourth Regiment, Veteran Reserve Corps, March 16, 1864; mustered out, July 3, 1865, at Washington, D.C.

WILLIAMS, LEWIS.—Age, 26 years. Enlisted, August 15, 1862, at Port Jervis, to serve three years; mustered in as private, Co. F, September 5, 1862; discharged for disability, April 1, 1863, near Bellair, Va.

WILSON, JACOB.—Age, 44 years. Enlisted, August 11, 1862, at Goshen, to serve three years; mustered in as private, Co. A, September 5, 1862; wounded in action, May 6, 1864; died of his wounds, May 12, 1864, at the Wilderness, Va.

WILSON, ROBERT.—Age, 29 years. Enlisted, August 14, 1862, at Newburgh, to serve three years; mustered in as private, Co. I, September 5, 1862; captured in action, May 3, 1863, at Chancellorsville, Va.; paroled, no date; deserted, June, 1863, from Camp Parole, Annapolis, Md.

WILSON, ZOPHER.—Age, 21 years. Enlisted, August 12, 1862, at Goshen, to serve three years; mustered in as private, Co. D, September 5, 1862; killed in action, May 3, 1863, at Chancellorsville, Va.

WINTERS, AMOS.—Age, 18 years. Enlisted at Plattsburgh, to serve one year, and mustered in as private, Co. E, September 13, 1864; mustered out, June 7, 1865, from hospital, at Washington, D.C.

WINTERS, JAMES E.—Age, 36 years. Enlisted at Plattsburgh, to serve one year, and mustered in as private, Co. E, September 5, 1864; mustered out with company, June 3, 1865, near Washington, D.C.

WINTERS, PETER.—Age, 18 years. Enlisted at Goshen, to serve three years, and mustered in as private, Co. K, October 10, 1864; transferred to Co. F, Ninety-third Infantry, June 1, 1865.

WISE, ALBERT.—Age, 38 years. Enlisted, August 15, 1862, at New Windsor, to serve three years; mustered in as private, Co. C, September 5, 1862; wounded in action, May 3, 1863, at Chancellorsville, Va.; mustered out with company, June 3, 1865, near Washington, D.C.

WISNER, LEWIS S.—Age, 21 years. Enrolled, August 12, 1862, at Wallkill, to serve three years; mustered in as sergeant, Co. K, September 5, 1862; as second lieutenant, May 3, 1863, and wounded in action, same date, at Chancellorsville, Va.; mustered in as first lieutenant, February 2, 1864; as captain, July 14, 1864; discharged, August 6, 1864; awarded *medal of honor*; also borne as Lewis G. and Lewis M. Commissioned second lieutenant, August 21, 1863, with rank from May 3, 1863, vice Jacob Denton, killed in action; first lieutenant, February 23, 1864, with rank from February 1, 1864, vice J. Finnegan, promoted; captain, July 15, 1864, with rank from July 14, 1861, vice W. A. Jackson, killed in action.

WITTENBEECHER, ADOLPHUS.—Age, 30 years. Enrolled, August 19, 1862, at Goshen to serve three years, mustered in as second lieutenant, Co. E. September 5, 1862; dismissed, March 6, 1863; also borne as Wettenbeecher; prior service as private, Co. I, Seventy-first Militia.

WOOD, ABNER A.—Age, 21 years. Enlisted, August 13, 1862, at Goshen, to serve three years; not mustered in as private, Co. B; deserted, August 24, 1862, at Goshen, N.Y.

WOOD, CHARLES B.—Age, 24 years. Enrolled at Goshen, to serve three years, and mustered in as first lieutenant, Co. A, August 12, 1862; as captain, July 3, 1863; wounded in action, May 12, 1864, at Spotsylvania Court House, Va.; discharged for wounds, September 21, 1864 ; also borne as Charles E.; prior service as private, Co. I, Seventy-first Militia. Commissioned first lieutenant, September 10, 1862, with rank from August 12, 1862, original; captain, October 6, 1863, with rank from July 2, 1863, vice C. H. Weygant, promoted.

WOOD, FREDERICK F.—Age, 20 years. Enlisted, August 14, 1862, at Washingtonville, to serve three years; mustered in as sergeant, Co. G, September 5, 1862; wounded in action, May 3, 1863, at Chancellorsville, Va.; died of his wounds, June 3, 1863, at Falmouth, Va.

WOOD, JAMES H.—Age, 25 years. Enlisted, August 14, 1862, at Goshen, to serve one year; mustered in as private, Co. K, August 24, 1864; mustered out with company, June 3, 1865, near Washington, D.C.

WOOD, JOHN C.—Age, 25 years. Enrolled, July 26, 1862, at Newburgh, to serve three years; mustered in as first sergeant, Co. A, September 5, 1862; as first lieutenant, August 1, 1864; as captain, January 1, 1865; mustered out with company, June 8, 1865, near Washington, D.C. Commissioned first lieutenant, November 15, 1864, with rank from August 1, 1864, vice L. S. Wisner, promoted; captain, February 18, 1865, with rank from January 1, 1865, vice J.W. Benedict, promoted.

WOOD, JOSEPH.—Age, 26 years. Enlisted, August 11, 1862, at Goshen, to serve three years: mustered in as private, Co. D, September 5, 1862; promoted corporal, prior to April 1863; mustered out with company, June 3, 1865, near Washington, D.C.

WOOD, MATHEW W.—Age, 24 years. Enlisted, August 9, 1862, at Otisville, to serve three years; mustered in as private, Co. E, September 5, 1862; wounded and captured in action, July 2, 1863, at Gettysburg, Pa.; paroled, prior to August 1863; deserted, September 1863, at home on expiration of parole furlough.

WOOD, PETER L.—Age, 21 years. Enlisted, August 6, 1862, at Chester, to serve three years; mustered in as sergeant, Co. A, September 5, 1862; died of typhoid fever, March 18, 1863, in camp, near Falmouth, Va.

WOOD, WILLIAM B.—Age, 22 years. Enlisted, August 13, 1862, at Goshen, to serve three years; mustered in as private, Co. A, September 5, 1862; mustered out, September 29, 1865, at Richmond, Va.

WOOD, WILLIAM H. H.—Age, 22 years. Enlisted, August 6, 1862, at Wallkill, to serve three years; mustered in as private, Co. K, September 5, 1862; wounded in action, May 3, 1863, at Chancellorsville, Va.; discharged for wounds, March 30, 1864, at Washington, D.C.

WRIGHT, CHARLES H.—Age, 33 years. Enlisted, August 5, 1862, at Washingtonville, to serve three years; mustered in as corporal, Co. G, September 5, 1862; returned to ranks, prior to April 10, 1863; transferred to Co. C., Sixteenth Regiment, Veterans Reserve Corps, November 2, 1863; mustered out, July 6, 1865, at Harrisburg, Pa.

WRIGHT, DAVID.—Age, 36 years. Enlisted, August 11, 1862, at Cornwall, to serve three years; mustered in as private, Co. C, September 5, 1862; transferred to Veteran Reserve Corps, October 26, 1863.

WRIGHT, HENRY J.—Age, 34 years. Enlisted, August 12, 1862, at Wallkill, to serve three years; mustered in as corporal, Co. K, September 5, 1862; deserted to the enemy, December 15, 1862, at Fredericksburg, Va.

WRIGHT, WILLIAM.—Age, 21 years. Enlisted, September 4, 1862, at Goshen, to serve three years; mustered in as private, Co. D, September 5, 1862; promoted corporal, prior to April 10, 1863; deserted, August 1863, from hospital at Philadelphia, Pa.

WRIGHT, WILLIAM W.—Age, 22 years. Enlisted at Plattsburg, to serve three years, and mustered in as private, Co. E, September 12, 1864; mustered out with company, June 3, 1865, near Washington, D.C.

WYGANT, GEORGE.—Age, 20 years. Enlisted, August 12, 1862, at Newburgh, to serve three years; mustered in as private, Co. I, September 5, 1862; killed in action, May 3, 1863, at Chancellorsville, Va.; also borne as Weygant.

WYGANT, WILSON.—Age, 22 years. Enlisted, August 12, 1862, at Newburgh, to serve three years; mustered in as sergeant, Co. I, September 5, 1862; died of disease, October 18, 1862.

WYLES, KINGSLEY.—Age, 30 years. Enlisted, July 30, 1862, at Goshen, to serve three years; mustered in as corporal, Co. B, September 5, 1862; deserted, October 19, 1862, at Georgetown, D.C.

YOUMANS, ALFRED.—Age, 27 years. Enlisted, August 12, 1862, at Goshen, to serve three years; mustered in as private, Co. B, September 5, 1862; died of typhoid fever, June 22, 1863, at hospital, Fairfax Seminary, Va.

YOUMANS, JOSEPH J.—Age, 30 years. Enlisted at Monroe, to serve three years, and mustered in as private, Co. D, December 18, 1863; transferred to Co. H, Ninety-third Infantry, June 1, 1865; also borne as Joseph I.

YOUNG, JOHN M.—Age, 21 years. Enlisted, August 11, 1862, at Port Jervis, to serve three years; mustered in as private, Co. F, September 5, 1862; promoted corporal, September 23, 1863; mustered out with company, June 3, 1865, near Washington, D.C.

YOUNGBLOOD, GEORGE B.—Age, 32 years. Enlisted, August 13, 1862, at Walden, to serve three years; mustered in as sergeant, Co. H, September 5, 1862; transferred to Sixty-fifth Company, Second Battalion, Veteran Reserve Corps, September 30, 1863; mustered out with detachment as first sergeant, June 29, 1865, at Washington, D.C.

YOUNGBLOOD, SAMUEL S.—Age, 18 years. Enlisted, August 13, 1862, at Walden, to serve three years; mustered in as private, Co. H, September 5, 1862; wounded in action, May 3, 1863, at Chancellorsville, Va.; transferred to Co. F, Twentieth Regiment, Veteran Reserve Corps, February 15, 1864; mustered out, July 4, 1865, at Camp Cadwallader, Philadelphia, Pa.

YOUNGS, ALBERT.—Age, 18 years. Enlisted, August 5, 1862, at Goshen, to serve three years; mustered in as private, Co. B, September 5, 1862; discharged, September 8, 1863, at convalescent camp, Alexandria, Va.

Chapter Notes

Abbreviations Used in the Notes

ABC	Alfred Booth Collection.
AC	Author's Collection.
CCC	Cheri Cardone Collection.
COL	Colonel Charles and Tavy Umhey Collection.
CUL	Courtesy of the Division of Rare and Manuscript Collections, Cornell University Libraries.
DBC	Dennis Buttacavoli Collection.
DHC	David Handzel Collection/Civil War Between the States Collectibles.
SM	Family Collection of Shirley A. Mearns.
GPLHSC	Goshen Public Library and Historical Society Collection. Courtesy of Pauline Kehoe, Director.
HHS	Historic Huguenot Street Archives, New Paltz, New York.
HSMWP	Historical Society of Middletown and the Wallkill Precinct. Marvin H. Cohen, President.
JTFC	Courtesy of the Benedict Family Collection, Archive of the Histori- cal Society of the Town of War- wick, Gift of Joan and Tom Frangos.
LCC	The Clance 124th Regiment N.Y.S.V. Civil War Collection.
LWC	Lynne Whealton Collection.
MHHSC	Mount Hope Historical Society Col- lection.
NYHS	Courtesy of the New-York Historical Society Collection.
OR	*The War of the Rebellion; A Compila- tion of the Official Records of the Union and Confederate Armies.* 130 vols. Washington, D.C.: Govern- ment Printing Office, 1880–1901.
PLRC	Paul and Lynne Ruback Collection.
RC	Ruttenbur Collection.
RCC	Robert Cammaroto Collection.
RSRC	Robert W. and Sandra J. Rodman Collection.
SKC	Stuart Kessler Collection.
USAMHI	U.S. Army Military History Institute, Carlisle Barracks, Pennsylvania.

Preface

1. Don Graham, *No Name on the Bullet: A Biography of Audie Murphy* (New York: Penguin Books, 1989).

Chapter 1

1. James McPherson, *Battle Cry of Free- dom* (New York: Oxford University Press, 1988), pp. 436–7.

2. Frederick Phisterer, *New York in the War of the Rebellion* (Albany, NY: J.B. Lyon, 1912), pp. 32–33.

3. Phisterer, p. 33.

4. Phisterer, pp. 33–34.

5. *Newburgh Telegraph,* July 31, 1862.

6. *Newburgh Telegraph,* July 31, 1862.

7. *Goshen Democrat,* July 17, 1862.

8. Charles H. Weygant, *History of the One Hundred and Twenty-Fourth Regiment New York State Volunteers* (Newburgh, NY: Journal Printing House, 1877), 12–13.

9. *Goshen Democrat,* July 17, 1862.

10. National Archives, Washington D.C.

11. *Newburgh Telegraph,* July 14, 1862.

12. *Newburgh Telegraph,* July 12, 1862.

13. *Goshen Democrat,* July 17, 1862.

14. *Newburgh Telegraph,* July 14, 1862.

15. *Newburgh Telegraph* July 24th 1862.

16. Colonel A. Van Horne Ellis to Col- onel Thomas B. Arden, July 20, 1862. RC.

17. Colonel A. Van Horne Ellis to Col- onel Thomas B. Arden, July 14, 1862. RC.

18. Colonel A. Van Horne Ellis to Col- onel Thomas B. Arden, August 4, 1862. RC.

19. *Newburgh Telegraph,* August 7, 1862.

20. *Goshen Democrat,* August 18, 1862.

21. *Newburgh Telegraph,* August 8, 1862.

22. Diary of William Howell, AC.

23. Diary of William Howell, AC.

24. *Goshen Democrat,* August 7, 1862.

25. John Fisk and William Blake, *A Con- densed History of the 56th Regiment New York Veteran Volunteer Infantry* (New- burgh, NY: Journal Printing House and Bindery, 1906), pp. 24–37; Amanda Mc- Ginnis and Cynthia Rapp, "Our Name Is Legion!" *America's Civil War* (Septem- ber 1990), pp. 10, 62–66.

26. *Goshen Democrat,* August 14, 1862.

27. Franklin B. Williams, *Middletown A Biography* (Middletown, NY: Lawrence A. Toepp, 1928), p. 63.

28. *Goshen Democrat,* August 7, 1862.

29. Colonel Ellis to Colonel Arden, July 14, 1862. RC.

30. *Goshen Democrat,* August 14, 1862.

31. *Newburgh Telegraph,* August 8, 1862.

32. It was a military tradition that in- fantry regiments had no company J. There are differing opinions on the reason, but the one that makes the most sense is that in cursive writing, the letters I and J look too much alike, which could lead to con- fusion in written documents. As very few officers of the 124th had any military ex- perience whatsoever, and because all the company officers were mustered within a few days of each other, the seniority issue was really one of form rather than sub- stance.

33. Phisterer, p. 694.

34. *Newburgh Telegraph,* July 31, 1862.

35. Weygant, p. 31.

36. Descriptive Muster Book of the One Hundred and Twenty Fourth Regiment N.Y. Vols., National Archives.

37. Captain John Wood Houston, "Short Sketch of the 124th New York Vols.," 1893, COL.

38. *Newburgh Daily Telegraph,* August 14, 1862.

39. *Goshen Democrat* August 14, 1862.

40. Houston.

41. *Goshen Democrat,* August 21, 1862.

42. *Goshen Democrat,* Sept 11, 1862.

43. *Goshen Democrat,* August 21, 1862.

44. Sergeant William W. Bailey, September 25, 1862, HSMWP. Sergeant Bailey's letters home were transcribed by his brother Edwin into a notebook donated to the society by Mr. and Mrs. Richard O. Hall of Ridgebury, N.Y.

45. Bailey, Sunday July 21, 1862.

46. Henry Dill, November 30, 1862, CCC.

47. Houston.

48. Houston.

49. Private John Z. Drake, August 27, 1862, in Robert and Megan Simpson, *The Civil War Letters of John Zephaniah Drake* (Goshen, New York: 1996).

50. Colonel A. Van Horne Ellis to Colonel Thomas B. Arden, August 4, 1862, RC.

51. Weygant, pp. 17–29.

52. Special Orders No. 488, Adjutant General Thomas Hillhouse, and Special Orders, Headquarters; "American Guard," Goshen, August 12, 1862; *Newburgh Telegraph,* August 21, 1862. These orders were published in all the local newspapers in Orange and Sullivan counties.

53. Hannah Johnston, August 19, 1862, HHS.

54. *Goshen Democrat,* September 11, 1862.

55. *Goshen Democrat,* September 11, 1862.

56. *Goshen Democrat,* August 28, 1862.

57. *Newburgh Telegraph,* September 4, 1862.

58. *Newburgh Telegraph,* August 28, 1862.

59. *Newburgh Telegraph,* August 28, 1862.

60. *Whig Press,* September 3, 1862.

61. *Goshen Democrat,* August 1862.

62. *Whig Press,* September 3, 1862.

63. *Goshen Democrat,* August 1862.

64. *Whig Press,* September 3, 1862.

65. *Goshen Democrat,* August 28, 1862.

66. *Whig Press,* September 3, 1862.

67. *Newburgh Telegraph,* September 4, 1862.

68. Rodman, Sept 2, 1862, RSRC.

69. Phisterer, p. 3470.

70. Phisterer, p. 3475. Both Cromwell and Silliman enrolled in Company D, 7th New York Cavalry, October 12, 1861. Cromwell served as the captain of D and Silliman as first lieutenant. Both were mustered out with the company March 31, 1862, "when, not having been mounted, it was honorably discharged and mustered out."

71. Rodman, Goshen, Sept. 2, 1862; RSRC.

72. Weygant, pp. 31–32.

Chapter 2

1. *Goshen Democrat,* September 11, 1862.

2. Houston, COL.

3. Bailey, "Park Barracks Sunday, Sept. 7, 1862, HSMWP.

4. Bailey, "October 5, 1862," HSMWP.

5. Irwin, "Camp Ellis Sept 15th 1862," RCC and Sergeant John D. Drake, *Whig Press,* September 17, 1862.

6. *Goshen Democrat,* September 18, 1862, "Army Correspondence from the 124th Regiment. Baltimore, Sept 8th, 1862," T.S. Bradner, chaplain.

7. Bailey, "Park Barracks Sunday, Sept. 7, 1862," HSMWP and Sergeant John D. Drake, *Whig Press,* Sept 17, 1862.

8. *Annual Report of the Adjutant-General for the State of New York for the Year 1903. No. 36* (Albany, NY: Oliver Quayle, 1904).

9. Corporal William W. Decker, "Washington, September, 9th 1862," *Whig Press* and Weygant, p. 92. Three months later, on Christmas Eve, the twenty-three-year-old William Decker died of typhoid fever in camp at Falmouth, Virginia, one of thirty men to succumb to the dreaded disease that winter.

10. *Annual Report of the Commissary General of Ordinance, S.N.Y. #66 1863* (for 1862) (Albany, NY: January 27, 1863), provided by Robert Braun and Roger Strucke.

11. Irwin, "Camp Ellis Sept 15th 1862," RCC.

12. Simpson, p. 6.

13. Bradner, *Goshen Democrat,* September 18, 1862 and James Moore, M.D., *History of the Cooper Shop Volunteer Refreshment Saloon* (Philadelphia: Jas. Rodgers, 1866), p. 158.

14. Sergeant John D. Drake, September 17, 1862, *Whig Press* and Corporal William Decker, September 9, 1862, *Whig Press.*

15. *Watchman & Democrat,* October 1, 1862.

16. Captain James Benedict, September 11, 1862, JTFC.

17. *Watchman & Democrat.*

18. Corporal William Decker, September 9, 1862.

19. Corporal William Howell September 10, 1862, AC.

20. Weygant, p. 34.

21. Simpson, p. 6.

22. Rodman, September 11, 1862, RSRC.

23. Diary of Henry Howell, AC.

24. *Watchman & Democrat,* Oct. 1, 1862.

25. *Goshen Democrat,* September 18, 1862.

26. Corporal William Howell, "Camp Chase, Va., Sept 10th 1862," AC.

27. *Watchman & Democrat.*

28. Thomas Rodman, September 11, 1862, RSRC.

29. Simpson, p. 6.

30. Bailey, Camp Chase, September 10, 1862, HSMWP.

31. Houston, COL.

32. Captain William Jackson, September 14, 1862, CUL.

33. Benedict, October 9, 1862, JTFC.

34. Weygant, pp. 34–35.

35. William Howell, "Sep 19th 62 Arlington Heights, Va.," AC.

36. Private Joseph H. Johnston, September 18, 1862, HHS.

37. Weygant, p. 36 and Phisterer, p. 2955.

38. Jackson, Camp Ellis, Sept 14, 1862, CUL.

39. Ezra J. Warner, *Generals in Blue* (Baton Rouge: Louisiana State University Press, 1964), p. 554.

40. Weygant, p. 36.

41. Warner, pp. 227–8.

42. Diary of Henry Howell, AC.

43. Brig. Gen. Silas Casey, *Infantry Tactics for the Instruction, Exercise, and Maneuvres of the Soldier, A Company, Line of Skirmishers, Battalion, Brigade, or Corps D'Armee* (New York: D. Van Nostrand, 1862).

44. Diary of Henry Howell, AC.

45. Private Joseph Brooks, October 9, 1862, GPLHS.

46. Bailey, "Camp Dekalb, September 22, 1862," HSMWP.

47. Bailey, October 8, 1862, HSMWP.

48. Simpson, p. 8.

49. Jackson, September 14, 1862, CUL.

50. Corp. William Howell, Arlington Heights, Va., September 19, 1862 and Private Henry Howell, Georgetown Heights, Va., September 23, 1862, AC.

51. Bailey, "Camp Dekalb, Sunday 21st. Va.," HSMWP.

52. Diary of William Howell, AC.

53. Jackson, September 20, 1862, CUL.

54. Jackson, September 20, 1862, CUL.

55. Rodman, October 3, 1862, RSRC.

56. Rodman, October 3, 1862, RSRC.

57. Weygant, p. 35–36.

58. Bailey, September 22, 1862. HSMWP.

59. *Revised United States Army Regulations of 1861,* p. 37–38.

60. Article of agreement between the firm of C.W. Reevs & Son and Nathaniel J. Kelsey. GPLHS.

61. Henry Howell, September 23, 1862, AC.

62. Bailey, September 26, 1862. HSMWP.

63. Bailey, October 5, 1862. HSMWP.

64. Bailey, September 21, 1862. HSMWP.

65. "Consolidated Return of Clothing, Camp and Garrison Equipage," AC.

66. Bailey, September 12, 1862, HSMWP.

67. Bailey, September 21, 1862, HSMWP.

68. Rodman, September 26, 1862, RSRC.

69. Rodman, October 10, 1862, RSRC.

70. Simpson, p. 7.

71. Bailey, September 24, 1862, HSMWP.

72. Henry Howell, September 23, 1862, AC.

73. Bailey, September 17, 1862, HSMWP.

74. Bailey, September 22, 1862, HSMWP.

75. Simpson, p. 8.

76. Rodman, October 3, 1862, RSRC.

77. Jackson, October 7, 1862, CUL.

78. Diary of Henry Howell, AC.

79. Lieutenant William E. Mapes, Sept. 26, 1862, Lynne Whealton Collection.

80. Mapes, September 28, 1862, LWC.

81. Mapes, September 26, 1862, LWC.

82. Jackson, October 7, 1862, CUL.

83. Mapes, October 15, 1862, LWC.

84. Descriptive Book of the 124th NYSV, National Archives, Washington, D.C.

85. Weygant, p. 43.

86. Bailey, October 3, 1862, HSMWP.

87. Benedict, Minor's Hill, Sept 30, 1862, JTFC.

88. Joseph Brooks, October 9, 1862, GPLHS. Private Clark was not put before a firing squad, was wounded in battle the following May at Chancellorsville, and

survived the war to be mustered out with the regiment.

89. Bailey September 21, 1862, HSMWP.
90. Bailey, October 5, 1862, HSMWP.
91. Bailey, Camp De Kalb, September 21, 1862, HSMWP.
92. Bailey, September 26, 1862, HSMWP.
93. Bailey, October 5, 1862, HSMWP.
94. *Newburgh Daily Telegraph,* October 14, 1862.
95. Bailey, October 3, 1862, HSMWP.
96. Bailey, October 3, 1862, HSMWP.
97. Private Nathan Hallock, October 12, 1862, HSMWP.
98. Rodman, September 26, 1862, RSRC.
99. Bailey, October 15, 1862, HSMWP.
100. Lieutenant James Roosa, October 14, 1862, HSMWP.
101. Jackson, October 7, 1862, CUL.
102. Bailey, Minor's Hill, October 8, 1862, HSMWP.
103. Diary of Henry Howell, AC.
104. Bradner, *Goshen Democrat,* October 23, 1862.
105. Bradner, *Goshen Democrat,* October 23, 1862.
106. Henry Howell, October 11, 1862, AC.
107. William Howell, October 15, 1862, AC.
108. Henry Howell, Knoxville, Md., October 18, 1862, AC.
109. Dan Webb, October 16, 1862.
110. Simpson, p. 8.
111. Bailey, October 8, 1862, HSMWP.
112. Rodman, October 3, 1862, RSRC.

Chapter 3

1. Weygant, p. 45.
2. Henry Howell, "Dear Mother," October 18, 1862. AC.
3. Henry Howell.
4. Sergeant William Van Houten, "Nov. 20, 62," *Goshen Democrat,* November, 27, 1862.
5. Benedict, October 20, 1862, JTFC.
6. Irwin, October 29, 1862, RCC.
7. Rodman, October 25, 1862, RSRC.
8. Van Houten, *Goshen Democrat,* November 27, 1862.
9. Journal of Isaac Decker, RC.
10. Weygant, p. 47.
11. Irwin, October 29, 1862, RCC.
12. Van Houten, *Goshen Democrat,* November 20, 1862.
13. Captain Henry Murray, November 3, 1862, LCC.
14. Journal of Isaac Decker, November 7, 1862, RC.
15. Murray, November 5, 1862, LCC.
16. Van Houten and Weygant, p. 52, and Henry Howell's diary, AC.
17. Henry Howell, November 9, 1862, AC.
18. Van Houten, *Goshen Democrat,* November 20, 1862.
19. Piatt, OR, Vol. 19, Part 2, p. 138.
20. Journal of Isaac Decker.
21. Van Houten, *Goshen Democrat,* November 20, 1862.
22. Captain Henry Murray, November 3, 1862, LCC.
23. Report of Brigadier General A. Sanders Piatt, U.S. Army, of reconnais-

sance to Manassas Gap, and skirmish, OR, Series I, Vol. 19, Part 2, pages 138–39.
24. Simpson, p. 9.
25. Rodman, November 9, 1862, RSRC.
26. Van Houten and Weygant, p. 55.
27. Henry Howell, November 9, 1862, AC.
28. Simpson.
29. *Goshen Democrat,* November 20, 1862.
30. Irwin, December 10, 1862, RCC.
31. Mapes, October 15, 1862, LWC.
32. Henry Howell November 9, 1862, AC.
33. Henry Howell, November 15, 1862, AC.
34. Henry Howell, November 15, 1862, AC.
35. Benedict, November 16, 1862, JTFC.
36. Weygant, p. 57.
37. Weygant, p. 58.
38. Simpson, p. 10.
39. Benedict, November 27, 1862, JTFC.
40. Henry Dill, November 30, 1862, CCC.
41. Irwin, November 25, 1862, RCC.
42. Sergeant John D. Drake, *Port Jervis Union,* November 25, 1862.
43. *Descriptive Muster Book of the One Hundred and Twenty Fourth Regiment N.Y. Vols.* Microfilm, National Archives, Washington, D.C.
44. Memorandum of Captain Leander Clark, RC.
45. Benedict, December 6, 1862, JTF.
46. Clark, RC.
47. Clark, RC, and Irwin, December 10, 1862.
48. Clark, RC.
49. Simpson, p. 11.
50. Irwin, December 10, 1862, RCC. According to knife expert Richard Langston, the knife Irwin requested was a folding combination knife, fork, and spoon manufactured not in Walden, N.Y., but in Kingston, just up the Hudson River from Newburgh.
51. Clark, RC.
52. Captain Murray, *Goshen Democrat,* December 25, 1862.
53. Brigadier General A.W. Whipple, OR, Vol. 21, Part 1, pp. 392–394.
54. Weygant, p. 62.
55. Weygant, p. 63.
56. Weygant, p. 64.
57. Captain Murray, *Goshen Democrat,* December 25, 1862.
58. Jackson, December 17, 1862, CUL.
59. Murray.
60. Jackson, Dec. 17, 1862, CUL.
61. Benedict, December 17, 1862, JTFC.
62. Jackson.
63. Benedict.
64. Journal of Isaac Decker, RC.
65. Rodman, December 18, 1862, RSRC.
66. Murray, *Goshen Democrat,* December 25, 1862
67. Whipple, OR, and Weygant, p. 71.
68. Weygant, p. 71.
69. Murray.
70. Weygant, p. 67.
71. Murray.
72. Weygant, p. 67.
73. Jackson, December 17, 1862, CUL.
74. Simpson, p. 12.

75. Diary of Pvt. James Haggerty, Family Collection of Shirley A. Mearns, FCSM.
76. Private Daniel Dugan, December 17, 1862, GPLHS.
77. Rodman, December 18, 1862, RSRC.
78. "The 124th at Fredericksburg," December 27, 1862; *Whig Press,* January 7, 1863.
79. Haggerty, and Rodman, December 18, 1862.
80. Weygant, p. 72.
81. Murray.
82. Mapes, Fredericksburg, Va., December 15, 1862. LWC.
83. Jackson, December 17, 1862. CUL.
84. Jackson, and *Annual Report of the Adjutant-General for the State of New York for the Year 1903. No. 36* (Albany, NY: Oliver Quayle, 1904), pages 500–666.
85. Haggerty.
86. Murray.
87. Weygant, p. 68.
88. Murray.
89. Haggerty, December 16, 1862, FCSM.
90. Jackson, CUL.
91. Weygant, pp. 73–74.
92. Weygant.
93. *Daily Telegraph,* January 9, 1863.
94. "The 124th at Fredericksburg," *Whig Press,* January 7, 1863.
95. Jackson, CUL.
96. Whipple, OR.
97. Rodman, RSRC.

Chapter 4

1. Rodman, Christmas Morning, 1862. RSRC.
2. Rodman, January 8, 1863. RSRC.
3. Private Joseph Brooks, January 4, 1863, GPLHS.
4. Simpson, p. 12.
5. Private G. Legg, Sunday, January 4, 1863, AC.
6. *Descriptive Muster Book of the One Hundred and Twenty Fourth Regiment N.Y. Vols.* Microfilm, National Archives, Washington, D.C.
7. Private Andrew Bowman, December 9, 1862, GPLHS.
8. *Daily Telegraph,* January 8, 1863.
9. *Daily Telegraph,* January 15, 1863.
10. Sergeant Charles Stewart, *Newburgh Daily Telegraph,* January 28, 1863.
11. John Cowdrey, "A Visit to the 124th Regiment," *Goshen Independent Republican,* January 15, 1863.
12. Rodman, January 8, 1863, RSRC.
13. Brooks, January 14, 1863, GPLHS.
14. "A Soldier Boy's Letters: Extracts from the home letters of a member of the Orange Blossoms," *Warwick Advertiser,* December 18, 1890. One of a series of letters published in the local newspaper located by Sue Gardner, local history librarian, Albert Wisner Public Library, Warwick, New York.
15. Weygant, pp. 79–80.
16. Captain Henry Murray, January 12, 1863, NYHS.
17. Brooks, January 14, 1863, GPLHS.
18. During the Civil War all weapons used the same propellant — black powder — and therein lay one drawback of the

Enfield. After any Civil War–era muzzle-loader fired a number of rounds, the inside of the barrel became fouled with powder residue. As that fouling built up, it was progressively harder to ram the next round home. This was true for old weapons and for American-made arms as well. If the barrel were not cleaned, at some point the ball would become lodged part way down, rendering the weapon unusable. Because the diameter of the Enfield's bore was ever so slightly smaller (.577 caliber, or 577/1000th inch) than that of the American-made Springfield (.58 caliber), that critical point would be arrived at sooner with the Enfield. Civil War soldiers were wont to complain that the Enfield "clogged" more easily than the Springfield, a fact that had more to do with the ammunition than with the quality of the weapon.

19. Weygant, p. 80.
20. Rodman, January 8, 1863, RSRC.
21. Weygant, p. 83.
22. Andrew Bowman, January 31, 1863, GPLHS.
23. Weygant, pp. 80–81.
24. Weygant, p. 81.
25. Bowman, January 31, 1863, GPLHS.
26. William H. Shaw, January 25, 1863, DBC.
27. Rodman Saturday, January 24, 1863, RSRC.
28. Bowman, January 31, 1863, GPLHS.
29. James Irwin, January 25, 1863, RCC.
30. Weygant, pp. 83–84.
31. Bowman, January 31, 1863, GPLHS.
32. Irwin, January 25, 1863, RCC.
33. "A Soldier Boy's Letters: Extracts from the home letters of a member of the Orange Blossoms," *Warwick Advertiser,* December 18, 1890, Albert Wisner Public Library, Warwick, New York.
34. Rodman, Saturday January 24, 1863.
35. Bowman, January 31, 1863.
36. Murray, January 27, 1863, NYHS.
37. Nathan Hallock, April 6, 1863, HSMWP. Private McCoy was listed as a deserter on April 2, 1863.
38. "Head Quarters 124th NYV Camp Belleair Jan'y 25th-/63." National Archives, Washington, D.C. Located by Howard Bertholf.
39. George C. Shiver, HSMWP.
40. "From the 124th Regiment. Camp of 124th Regiment Near Falmouth, Va., Feb. 18, 1863," *Independent Republican,* March 5, 1863. Butter Hill is a locale in Cornwall, Corporal Davis's hometown, which apparently was not a very good place to grow potatoes. Thanks to Cornwall town historian Janet Dempsey and Cornwall library director Karen Fels.
41. Daniel Dugan, March 9, 1863, GPLHS.
42. *Newburgh Daily Telegraph,* April 23, 1863.
43. Lieutenant William E. Mapes, February 23, 1863, LWC.
44. *Montgomery Standard,* February 14, 1863.
45. Edward Carpenter, March 3, 1863, Lorraine Booth collection.
46. Report of Brigadier General Fitzhugh Lee, C.S. Army Headquarters, Lee's

Cavalry Brigade, Culpeper Court-House, Virginia, February 27, 1863.
47. Weygant, p. 85.
48. Henry Howell, March 9, 1863. AC.
49. Carpenter.
50. Report of Colonel Benajah P. Bailey, Eight-sixth New York Infantry, commanding First Brigade, Third Division, OR.
51. Weygant, p. 85.
52. Report of Brigadier General Fitzhugh Lee, C.S. Army, Lee's Cavalry Brigade, Culpeper Court-House, Virginia, February 27, 1863, OR.
53. Sickles, OR.
54. Henry Howell, Feb. 14 and 21, 1863, AC.
55. Henry Howell, March 8, 1863, AC.
56. Henry Howell.
57. Sergeant Stewart, *Newburgh Daily Telegraph,* April 16, 1863.
58. Dugan, March 9, 1863, GPLHS.
59. Bailey, March 19, 1863, HSMWP.
60. Bailey, March 27, 1863, HSMWP.
61. Weygant, p. 86.
62. John Z. Drake, Company F, "Camp Near Stonmons Switch," April 7, 1863.
63. Henry Howell and William Howell, "Camp Near Falmouth Va. March 21, 1863," AC.
64. William Howell, "Camp of the 124th, Stonemans Switch, March 31, 1863," AC.
65. William Howell.
66. Thomas Rodman, "In Camp Near Falmouth, Va.," March 21, 1863, RSRC.
67. William Howell, "Camp of the 124th, Stonemans Switch," March 31, 1863, AC.
68. John Z. Drake, "Camp Near Stonmons Switch," April 19, 1863.
69. Diary of Henry Howell, AC.
70. Diary of Henry Howell, AC.
71. Weygant, p. 86.
72. Weygant, p. 87.
73. Diary of Henry Howell, AC.
74. Rodman, "In Camp Near Falmouth, Va.," April 9, 1863, RSRC.
75. Weygant pp. 87–88.
76. Diary of Henry Howell, AC.
77. Weygant, p. 88.
78. Diary of Henry Howell, AC.
79. Nathan Hallock, April 18, 1863, HSMWP.
80. Rodman, "In Camp Near Falmouth April 16th 1863," RSRC.
81. Hallock, April 18, 1863, HSMWP.
82. Diary of Henry Howell, April 17, 1863, AC.
83. *Newburgh Daily Telegraph,* April 23, 1863.
84. Jackson, Camp of the 124th, April 25, 1863, CUL.
85. "Camp Correspondence, Camp Near Falmouth April 27, 1863," *Newburgh Daily Telegraph,* May 2, 1863.

Chapter 5

1. *Whig Press,* May 6, 1863.
2. General E. Porter Alexander, *Fighting for the Confederacy, The Personal Recollections of General Edward Porter Alexander,* edited by Garry W. Gallagher (Chapel Hill: University of North Carolina Press, 1989), p. 195.

3. Weygant, p. 90.
4. Diary of Henry Howell, April 28, 1863. AC.
5. *Newburgh Telegraph,* May 14, 1863.
6. "Middletown Volunteers in Battle" *Whig Press,* May 27, 1863.
7. Corporal William Howell, "Sickles Corps on Battlefield, May 4, 1863," AC.
8. "Felix," *Newburgh Telegraph,* May 14, 1863.
9. Weygant, p. 90.
10. *Whig Press,* May 27, 1863.
11. Sergeant Peter P. Hazen, "Out in a Thick Woods, Virginia, May 2, 1863," *Newburgh Journal,* NYSMHM.
12. Lewis S. Wisner, "An Open Letter to Comrade John T. Ogden and Others," Scrapbook #2, GPLHS.
13. Leander Clark, "The Orange Ribbon," *Middletown Daily Press,* August 22, 1877, HSMWP.
14. Stephen W. Sears, *Chancellorsville* (New York: Houghton Mifflin, 1996), p. 116.
15. *Whig Press,* May 8, 1863.
16. *Goshen Democrat,* May 21, 1863.
17. *Whig Press,* May 8, 1863.
18. *Whig Press,* May 8, 1863.
19. Hazen.
20. *Goshen Democrat,* May 21, 1863.
21. Hazen.
22. Hazen.
23. Weygant, p. 95; *Annual Report of the Adjutant-General for the State of New York for the Year 1903 No. 36* (Albany, NY: Oliver Quayle, 1904), pp. 500–666.
24. Weygant, pp. 26 and 99; *Annual Report of the Adjutant-General for the State of New York for the Year 1903.*
25. Colonel Ellis's report May 7, 1863, handwritten document, AC.
26. Sears, *Chancellorsville,* p. 212.
27. Ibid.
28. John Bigelow, *The Campaign of Chancellorsville: A Strategic and Tactical Study* (New Haven, CT: Yale University Press, 1910), p. 261.
29. Hazen.
30. Diary of Henry Howell, May 2, 1863, AC.
31. Corporal A.M. Valet, "Camp of the 124th Regiment, N.Y.S.V. Near Falmouth Va. May 7th, 1863," *Montgomery Standard,* May 23, 1863.
32. Hazen.
33. Corporal A.M. Valet, loc. cit.
34. Weygant, p. 104.
35. Hazen.
36. Weygant, pp. 106–107.
37. Ellis report, AC.
38. Valet.
39. Captain William Jackson, "In Our Old Camp, May 8, 1863," *Whig Press,* May 27, 1863.
40. William Howell, "Sickles Corps on the battlefield," May 4, 1863, AC.
41. William Howell.
42. Report of Captain Henry R. Dalton, assistant adjutant-general, Third Division, "Hdqrs. Third Div., Third Army Corps," May 10, 1863, No. 159, OR Vol. 25, Part 1, p. 490.
43. Ellis.

44. Colonel Emlen Franklin, OR Vol. 25, Part 1, pp. 494–495.

45. Lieutenant Colonel Edward McGovern, OR Vol. 25, Part 1, pp. 498–499.

46. Sgt. George F. Sprenger, *A Concise History of the Camp and Field Life of the 122nd Regiment, Penn'a Volunteers* (Lancaster, PA: The New Era Steam Book Print, 1885), p. 287.

47. William Howell, May 4, 1863, AC.

48. Sergeant Coe Reevs, "Division Hospital Near Potomac Creek, May 16th, 1863," *Goshen Democrat*, May 21, 1863.

49. Henry Howell, "Camp Stoneman" May 29, 1863, AC.

50. Ellis.

51. Valet.

52. Sears, 272.

53. Ellis.

54. Esculapius, "Headquarters, 124th Reg't N.Y.S.V.," *Goshen Independent Republican*, May 12, 1863.

55. Esculapius.

56. General Daniel Sickles, OR Vol. 25, Part 1, pp. 384–395.

57. Henry Howell, "In Camp, May 7, 1863," AC.

58. McGovern, OR.

59. Ben Dutcher, "Mt. Pleasant Hospital Wash. D.C. May 7, 1863," National Archives, Washington, D.C.

60. Dalton.

61. Henry Howell, May 7, 1863, AC.

62. Diary of Henry Howell, May 3, 1863, AC.

63. Howell, May 7, 1863, AC.

64. William Howell, May 4, 1863, AC.

65. William Howell, May 4, 1863, AC.

66. Valet.

67. Weygant, p. 110.

68. Weygant, p. 111.

69. Weygant, p. 113.

70. "Stonewall Jackson — A New York Man's Claim," *National Tribune*, August 30, 1888.

71. John Bigelow, *The Campaign of Chancellorsville: A Strategic and Tactical Study* (New Haven, CT: Yale University Press, 1910), p. 346.

72. Weygant, p. 114.

73. Weygant, p. 115.

74. Valet, May 7, 1863.

75. Henry Howell, "In Camp, May 8, 1863."

76. *Whig Press*, May 27, 1863.

77. *Montgomery Standard*, May 16, 1863, Marcus Millspaugh collection.

78. Ernest Furguson, *Chancellorsville 1863: The Souls of the Brave* (New York: Alfred A. Knopf, 1992), p. 230.

79. Bigelow, p. 347, note.

80. Bigelow, 352.

81. *Whig Press*, May 27, 1863.

82. Weygant, p. 116.

83. Weygant.

84. William Howell, May 4, 1863.

85. *Montgomery Standard*, May 16, 1863, Marcus Millspaugh collection.

86. *Whig Press*, May 27, 1863.

87. Valet, May 7, 1863.

88. Ellis.

89. "Felix," *Newburgh Telegraph*, May 14, 1863.

90. "How Our Orange Boys Fought" *Whig Press*, June 3, 1863.

91. William Howell, "Sickles Corps on Battlefield, May 4, 1863," AC.

92. William Howell, May 4, 1863, AC.

93. William Howell, May 4, 1863, AC.

94. *Goshen Democrat*, May 21, 1863.

95. *Goshen Democrat*, May 21, 1863.

96. *Montgomery Standard*, May 23, 1863.

97. Bigelow, pp. 356–7.

98. Bigelow, p. 358.

99. *Montgomery Standard*, May 23, 1863.

100. Ellis.

101. *Whig Press*, May 27, 1863.

102. Valet, May 7, 1863.

103. William Howell, May 4, 1863.

104. *Montgomery Standard*, May 23, 1863.

105. *Montgomery Standard*, May 30, 1863, Marcus Millspaugh collection.

106. William Howell, May 4, 1863; *Montgomery Standard*, May 23, 1863.

107. Weygant, p. 120.

108. Captain Jacob Lansing, 86th NY, OR. The after-action report of the 86th New York was written by a company commander, Captain Jacob Lansing, because Lieutenant Colonel Barna Chapin, who led the 86th into battle, was killed in the charge. The second in command, Major Higgins, was wounded in the same charge and presumably had not recovered sufficiently to write it.

109. Dalton.

110. Bigelow, pp. 364–365.

111. Weygant, p. 120.

112. William Howell, May 4, 1863.

113. Valet, May 7, 1863.

114. Frank Lee, "Camp Stoneman, Falmouth, Va.," June 4, 1863.

115. Ellis.

116. Jackson, *Whig Press*, May 27, 1863.

117. Jackson.

118. "A Hero with His Face to the Foe," *Antiques Digest*, 1902.

119. Lieutenant Hart, cited in "A Hero with His Face to the Foe."

120. "A Hero."

121. "A Hero."

122. *Montgomery Standard*, May 23, 1863.

123. William Howell, "Sickles Corps on Battlefield, May 4, 1863," AC.

124. Diary of William Howell, AC.

125. Diary of Henry Howell, AC.

126. Weygant, p. 121; Ellis.

127. Diary of Henry Howell, AC.

128. Weygant, pp. 121–22.

129. *Whig Press*, May 27, 1863.

130. William Howell, "Sickles Corps on Battlefield, May 4, 1863," AC.

131. William Howell, "Sickles Corps on Battlefield, May 4, 1863," AC.

132. Diary of William Howell, AC.

133. Diary of Henry Howell, AC.

134. *Montgomery Standard*, May 30, 1863.

135. Henry Howell, "In Camp, May 7th, 1863," AC.

136. *Whig Press*, May 27, 1863

137. "Middletown Volunteers in Battle," *Middletown Whig Press*, May 27, 1863.

138. "Felix," *Newburgh Telegraph*, May 14, 1863.

139. "How Our Orange Boys Fought," *Middletown Whig Press*, June 3, 1863.

140. "In Our Old Camp May 8, 1863," *Middletown Whig Press*, May 27, 1863.

Chapter 6

1. "Camp Near Falmouth, May 14, 1863," *Whig Press*, May 27, 1863.

2. Rodman, "In Camp Near Falmouth, Va. May 13, 1863," RC.

3. "Potomac Creek, May 9, 1863," *Whig Press*, May 25, 1863.

4. "How Our Orange Boys Fought," *Whig Press*, June 3, 1863.

5. Jackson, "In Our Old Camp," *Whig Press*, May 27, 1863.

6. Jackson.

7. Jackson.

8. *Newburgh Daily Telegraph*, May 8, 1863.

9. *Montgomery Standard*, May 16, 1863, Marcus Millspaugh collection.

10. *Montgomery Standard*, May 16, 1863, Marcus Millspaugh collection.

11. Gouvernor Legg, May 16, 1863, AC.

12. Weygant, p. 134.

13. Weygant.

14. Weygant, p. 135.

15. "Letter from the 124th Regiment," *Newburgh Telegraph*, May 21, 1863.

16. *Newburgh Telegraph*, June 4, 1863.

17. *Middletown Whig Press*, June 17, 1863.

18. *Newburgh Telegraph*, June 4, 1863.

19. *Annual Report of the Adjutant-General for the State of New York for the Year 1903.*

20. Frank Lee, "Camp Stoneman, Near Falmouth, Va. June 4th, 1863."

21. Richmond *Examiner*, May 11, 1863, LCC.

22. Frank Lee.

23. Bailey, Division Hospital, May 17, 1863, HSMWP.

24. Henry Howell, "Camp Stoneman, May 29 1863," AC.

25. Henry Howell.

26. Henry Howell.

27. Henry Howell.

28. Weygant, p. 136.

29. Weygant, p. 137.

30. OR Vol. 35, Pt. 2, p. 528.

31. Weygant, p. 156.

32. Diary of William Howell, AC.

33. Weygant, p. 138.

34. Diary of Henry Howell, SKC.

35. Diary of William Howell, AC.

36. Weygant, p. 138.

37. Diary of Henry Howell, SKC.

38. Diary of William Howell, AC.

39. Weygant, p. 138.

40. Mapes, "Saturday June 6th 1863," LWC. Mapes was obviously mocking "Mitt." Daniel Webster was famous for his eloquence but Gov. Seymour, a Democrat, was reviled by Mapes as no better than a Copperhead. Clement Vallandigham was a Copperhead congressmen jailed for his opposition to the war and sent across the lines to the Confederacy for his actions. Mapes is also quite laudatory in his opinion of black troops.

41. Diary of Henry Howell, SKC.

42. Diary of William Howell, AC.

43. Weygant, pp. 140–41; Esculapius, "Letter from the 124th Regiment Camp Near Bealeton Station, on Orange & Alexandria R.R., June 10, 1863," Goshen *Independent Republican*, June 18, 1863.

44. Weygant, p. 143.
45. Diary of Henry Howell, SKC.
46. Diary of William Howell, AC.
47. Diary of Henry Howell, SKC.
48. Major General Joseph Hooker, OR Vol. 27, Pt. 3, pp. 27–28.
49. Stephen Z. Starr, *The Union Cavalry in the Civil War* (Baton Rouge: Louisiana State University Press, 1979), p. 373.
50. Hooker, OR.
51. *New York Times,* June 11, 1863.
52. Esculapius, June 10, 1863.
53. "Bealeton Station, Va. June 11 1863." This letter is missing the last page or pages so the author is not known. The owner of the letter, Larry Clance, and I have discussed who it might be. The letter may have been written by an officer, perhaps Captain Jackson of Company K, but there is no way to tell for sure. The letter gives a detailed account of the action of the 124th New York at Brandy Station, LCC.
54. Weygant, pp. 144–5.
55. "Bealton Station," LCC.
56. Esculapius.
57. Journal of Isaac Decker, "Bealton, on the O. & A. R.R. June 10, '63," RC.
58. Henry Dill, "Gum Springs Virginy, June the 20, 1863," CCC.
59. Diary of William Howell, AC.
60. Starr, p. 378.
61. Diary of Henry Howell, SKC.
62. "Bealton Station," LCC.
63. Weygant, p. 145.
64. Weygant, p. 146.
65. Weygant, 146–7.
66. Weygant, p. 146.
67. Weygant, p. 150.
68. Weygant.
69. Weygant.
70. Journal of Isaac Decker, RC.
71. "Bealton Station," LCC.
72. Diary of Henry Howell, SKC.
73. Journal of Isaac Decker, RC.
74. "Bealton Station," LCC.
75. Weygant, p. 151.
76. Dan Beattie, *Brandy Station 1863: First Step Towards Gettysburg* (Oxford: Osprey Publishing, 2008), pp. 143–146.
77. "Bealton Station," LCC.
78. "Bealton Station," Decker.
79. Decker.
80. "Bealton Station," LCC. According to Mike Block of the Brandy Station Foundation, this was the house of Cunningham's overseer. "The Cunningham house was on a hill (not Buford's Knoll), closer to the confluence of the Hazel and Rappahannock. It was burned in August 1862 by Federals retreating after being chased out of Culpeper County at the start of the Second Manassas Campaign. But the author [of the anonymous letter] would not have known this."
81. Journal of Isaac Decker.
82. Diary of Henry Howell, SKC.
83. Weygant, pp. 151–2.
84. Diary of William Howell.
85. Report of Brigadier General Adelbert Ames, U.S. Army Headquarters Infantry, Bealton Station, June 10, 1863, OR.
86. Weygant, p. 158.
87. Weygant, p. 159.
88. "Seminary Hospital, Georgetown D.C. June 10th 1863," collection of Colonel Charles and Tavey Umhey.
89. Goshen *Independent Republican,* June 18, 1863.
90. Weygant, pp. 151–152.
91. Diary of Henry Howell, SKC.
92. Captain William Jackson, "Bealeton Station, June 10th 1863," CUL.
93. Diary of Henry Howell, SKC.
94. Journal of Isaac Decker, RC.

Chapter 7

1. Henry Howell, "Bull Run Creek, June 16th," DBC.
2. Diary of Henry Howell, SKC.
3. Diary of Henry Howell, SKC; Henry Howell, DBC.
4. Warner, *Generals in Blue*, pp. 537–8.
5. Warner, p. 34.
6. Weygant, p. 161.
7. Diary of William Howell, AC; Diary of Henry Howell, SKC.
8. Henry Howell, "Bull Run Creek June 16th," DBC.
9. Henry Howell, "Bull Run Creek June 16th," DBC.
10. Diary of Henry Howell, SKC; Henry Howell, "Bull Run Creek June 16th," DBC.
11. Weygant, p. 162.
12. Henry Howell, "Bull Run Creek June 16th," DBC.
13. Henry Howell, "Bull Run Creek June 16th," DBC.
14. Diary of William Howell.
15. Weygant, p. 162–3.
16. Howell, "Bull Run Creek, June 14th," DBC.
17. Howell, "Bull Run Creek, June 14th," DBC.
18. Diary of Henry Howell, SKC.
19. Diary of William Howell, AC.
20. Diary of Henry Howell, SKC.
21. Weygant, p. 164.
22. Diary of Henry Howell, SKC.
23. Weygant, p. 164.
24. Weygant, p. 165.
25. Diary of William Howell, AC.
26. Diary of Henry Howell, SKC.
27. Private Henry Dill, "Gum Springs Virginy June the 20 1863," CCC.
28. Diary of Henry Howell, SKC.
29. Captain William Jackson, "Gum Springs, June 21st Sunday 1863," CUL.
30. Diary of Henry Howell, SKC.
31. Weygant, pp. 165–66; Diary of Henry Howell, SKC.
32. Diary of Henry Howell, SKC.
33. Diary of William Howell, AC.
34. Diary of Henry Howell, SKC.
35. Weygant, p. 167.
36. Diary of Henry Howell, SKC.
37. Civilwararchive.com.
38. Lieutenant Brown carried orders addressed to Colonel Ellis dated March 28, 1863. What post he had held between that date and the previous December 30 has yet to be determined. In his regimental history, Colonel Weygant referred to Brown as a "civilian" which, considering his service in the 7th NY Militia, was incorrect. PLRC.
39. Weygant, p. 167.
40. Diary of Henry Howell, SKC.
41. Diary of William Howell.
42. Diary of Henry Howell, SKC.
43. Weygant, p. 168.
44. Color Sergeant D.G. Crotty, *Four Years Campaigning in the Army of the Potomac, Third Michigan Volunteer Infantry* (Grand Rapids, MI: Dygert Bros. & Co., 1874), pp. 87–88.
45. Diary of William Howell, AC.
46. Henry Howell, June 28, 1863, HSMWP.
47. Diary of Henry Howell, SKC.
48. Weygant, p. 168.
49. Diary of William Howell, AC.
50. Diary of Henry Howell, SKC.
51. Weygant, p. 169.
52. R.G. 156 *Summary of Quarterly Returns of Ordnance 124th N.Y.V.I.*, National Archives, Washington, D.C., p. 3.
53. Weygant, p. 171.
54. Meade to Sickles, OR Series 1, Vol. 27, Pt. 3, p. 420.
55. Weygant, p. 169.
56. Meade to Sickles, OR Series 1, Vol. 27, Pt. 3, p. 422.
57. Richard Sauers, *A Caspian Sea of Ink: The Meade-Sickles Controversy* (Baltimore: Butternut and Blue, 1989), p. 19.
58. Major General John Reynolds to Sickles, OR Series 1, Vol. 27, Pt. 3, p. 424.
59. Sickles to Reynolds, OR Series 1, Vol. 27, Pt. 3, p. 425.
60. "Battlefield, July 5, 1863," *Whig Press,* July 22, 1863; Diary of William Howell, AC.
61. Diary of Henry Howell, SKC.
62. Weygant, p. 169.
63. "Battlefield, July 5, 1863," *Whig Press,* July 22, 1863.
64. Ward, OR. V01.27, Part 1, [S# 43]—Gettysburg Campaign.
65. Peter B. Ayars, "The 99th Pennsylvania," *National Tribune,* February 4, 1886.
66. Sauers, p. 20.
67. Sauers.
68. Weygant, p. 171.
69. Weygant.
70. Diary of Henry Howell, SKC.
71. Weygant, p. 172.
72. Weygant.
73. Brigadier General Hobart Ward, OR, Vol. 27, Part 1, #43.
74. Ayars.
75. Diary of Henry Howell, SKC.
76. Braun, p. 5; Maj. John Moore, OR No. 148, Vol. 27, Pt. 1, p. 513.
77. Sergeant Harvey Hanford, "Gettysburg," *National Tribune,* Sept 24, 1885.
78. Henry Howell, "Battlefield, July 5, 1863," *Whig Press.*
79. Hanford.
80. Sickles, OR, Vol. 27 Pt. 3, p. 466.

Chapter 8

1. Craft, 118.
2. Diary of Henry Howell, July 5, 1863, SKC.
3. Hanford.
4. A.W. Tucker, "Orange Blossoms," *National Tribune,* January 21, 1886.
5. Tucker.

6. Birney, OR, Series 1, Vol. 27, #43.

7. Sauers; David Downs, "His Left Was Worth a Glance," *Gettysburg Magazine* 7.

8. Vermilyea, p. 41. General Buford reported for July 2, "The division became engaged with the enemy's sharpshooters on our left, and held its own until relieved by General Sickles' corps, after which it moved to Taneytown, and bivouacked for the night." Report of Brig. Gen. John Buford, U.S. Army, commanding First Division. Battle of Gettysburg.

9. Daniel M. Laney, "Wasted Gallantry: Hood's Texas Brigade at Gettysburg," *Gettysburg Magazine* 16, p. 33.

10. Troy Harman, *Lee's Real Plan at Gettysburg* (Mechanicsburg, PA: Stackpole Books, 2003).

11. Sauers, pp. 27–28.

12. Harry Pfanz, *Gettysburg The Second Day* (Chapel Hill: University of North Carolina Press, 1987), pp. 94–97.

13. Pfanz, pp. 96–97; Edward Coddington, *The Gettysburg Campaign: A Study in Command* (New York: Scribner's, 1968), p. 344.

14. Brevet Major-General Henry J. Hunt, "The Second Day at Gettysburg," *Battles and Leaders of the Civil War* Vol. 3, p. 303.

15. Birney, OR.

16. Birney, OR.

17. Weygant, p. 172.

18. Tucker.

19. Hanford.

20. Kathleen Georg Harrison, "Our Principal Loss Was in This Place," *Gettysburg Magazine*, July 1, 1989, p. 45.

21. John W. Busey and David G. Martin, *Regimental Strengths and Losses at Gettysburg* (Hightstown, NJ: Longstreet House, 1986), p. 207.

22. Birney, OR.

23. Captain George Randolph, OR Vol. 27, Pt. 1, pp. 581–585, report number 181. Randolph, chief of artillery for the 3rd Corps, wrote that Smith's position was "very rough and rocky" and that Smith's men "continued their fire till their supports were compelled to retire" at which point Smith's men were forced to leave three guns in place. "Captain Smith says he supposed the hill would be immediately retaken by our troops, and that, as it was a place most difficult of access, it was wiser to leave them where they could be used against the enemy immediately we regained the hill. I regret the loss, but from my knowledge of the position and of the gallantry displayed by Captain Smith, I am convinced that it was one of those very unpleasant, but yet unavoidable, results that sometimes attend the efforts of the most meritorious officers."

24. Captain James E. Smith, *A Famous Battery and Its Campaigns, 1861–'64* (Washington, DC: W.H. Lowdermilk & Co., 1892), p. 102.

25. Major Thomas W. Bradley, "At Gettysburg," *National Tribune,* February 4, 1886.

26. Brigadier General Hobart Ward, OR, Series 1, Vol. 27, Pt. 1, p. 493.

27. Harrison, p. 45.

28. Smith, p. 102.

29. Weygant, p. 173.

30. *Maine at Gettysburg* (Portland: Lakeside Press, 1898), p. 181.

31. Weygant, p. 173.

32. Weygant.

33. Edward Coddington, *The Gettysburg Campaign: A Study in Command* (New York: Scribner's, 1968), p. 346.

34. Hanford.

35. Captain William Jackson, "Near Gettysburg July 5th 1863," CUL.

36. "Old Orange Musters Few for Reunion," unknown local newspaper, month unknown, date 28th, 1929, AC.

37. Hunt, OR.

38. Ward, OR Vol. 27 Pt. 1, pp. 493–495.

39. Smith.

40. Tucker. It should be noted that Private Tucker put the left of the regiment behind the guns. Other witnesses, including Captain Weygant, put the regiment in front of the guns. The placement of the regiment at an angle running northwest to southeast explains the discrepancy. From the right flank of the regiment, where Weygant was, the guns did appear to be behind the regiment while from the left flank, where Tucker and Hanford were posted, they were to the front.

41. Tucker.

42. Tucker.

43. Tucker.

44. Bradley, *National Tribune,* February 4, 1886.

45. Hanford.

46. J.B. Polley, *Hood's Texas Brigade* (Dayton, OH: Morningside Bookshop, 1988), p. 180.

47. Daniel Laney, "Wasted Gallantry: Hood's Texas Brigade at Gettysburg," *Gettysburg Magazine* 16, p. 40.

48. General J.B. Robertson in Polley, p. 163.

49. Major John P. Bane's report in Polley, p. 184.

50. Polley, p. 167.

51. "Battle of Gittesburgh — Statement of Thomas M. Ries," RC.

52. Pfanz, p. 173.

53. Smith, p. 103.

54. Jackson.

55. Polley, pp. 179–181.

56. Busey and Martin.

57. Polley, p. 180.

58. Polley, p. 169.

59. Polley, p. 181.

60. Ward, OR.

61. Ward, OR.

62. Pfanz, pp. 183–184.

63. Garry E. Adelman and Timothy H. Smith, *Devil's Den: A History and Guide* (Gettysburg, PA: Thomas Publications, 1997), p. 31. The account written by Col. Work of the 1st Texas mentions but one charge and does not mention the initial charge made by the 124th New York which drove the Texans back to the bottom of the Weikert Field. This being the case, events of the two charges may have been blended together into one. However, Adelman and Smith place these events in the first advance of Work's regiment.

64. "Veteran H.M. Howell on Gettysburg," *Daily Argus,* July 12, 1913.

65. Tucker.

66. Tucker.

67. Tucker.

68. Ward, OR.

69. Silliman's account.

70. Silliman's account.

71. Weygant, p. 175.

72. Silliman's account.

73. *Newburgh Daily Telegraph,* July 24, 1863.

74. Weygant, p. 176.

75. Silliman's account.

76. Weygant, p. 176.

77. Hanford.

78. Ward, OR.

79. Tucker. The command "charge bayonet" is not an order to charge at all but to simply throw the rifle forward, bayonet at eye level in a threatening manner. It is usually accompanied by a loud "Hurrah!" the "charging shout of the Union men," as Weygant likes to describe it. The purpose is to frighten the enemy and nerve the men prior to or while advancing to a charge.

80. Weygant, p. 176.

81. Henry Howell, "Battlefield, July 5, 1863."

82. Polley, p. 171. Private Bradfield mixed the two advances of the 1st Texas against Smith's Battery and also intermingled the story with that of the fight later in the day between the Texans and the 40th New York along Plum Run on the east side of Houck's Ridge. But Daniel Laney, who wrote the article on the 1st Texas in *Gettysburg Magazine,* is of the opinion that "the passage quoted here clearly refers to Cromwell." This author agrees.

83. Silliman's account.

84. Silliman's account.

85. "Hon. Elihu Root, Sec'ty. of War…," Middletown, N.Y., October 2nd, 1899, application for Medals of Honor. There are two of these applications, one in support of the other. The author has not been able to determine why the applications did not go forward, especially since Thomas Bradley, a 124th New York comrade of the men mentioned who himself was wounded at Gettysburg had political connections with fellow Republican (and Civil War veteran) William McKinley, who was president at the time. The documents are in the collection of Larry Clance, who made them, as well as many others, available to me for this book.

86. Adelman and Smith, p. 36.

87. Tucker.

88. Jackson.

89. Weygant, p. 177.

90. Letter from Richard Cyrus Yarbrough to Henry Howell, June 15, 1913, AC.

91. Adelman and Smith, p. 38.

92. Ward, OR.

93. Adelman and Smith, pp. 39–40.

94. Adelman and Smith, pp. 40–43.

95. Major John W. Moore, 99th Pennsylvania Infantry, OR, Series 1, Vol. 27, Pt. 1, p. 513.

96. Tucker.

97. Polley, 177.

98. Henry Howell, Battlefield, July 5,

1863, *Middletown Whig Press*, July 22, 1863.

99. Tucker.
100. Hanford.
101. Hanford; Weygant, p. 178.
102. Weygant, p. 178.
103. William C. Hart, *In a Beautiful Country: Historic Wallkill and Hudson River Valleys*. Walden, New York: Wallkill Valley Publishing Association, 1906, p. 77.
104. "Old Regiment Musters Few for Reunion."
105. Weygant, p. 179.
106. Weygant, p. 179.
107. Weygant, p. 180.
108. Corporal William Howell, "On the Battlefield, July 5, 1863," in Ethel B. Gage, "Orange County in the Civil War," *Views* (a publication of the Orange County Community of Museums and Galleries) 2:2, April 1963.
109. Henry Howell, *Whig Press*, July 22, 1863.
110. Weygant, p. 181.
111. Lieutenant William Mapes, "Battle field Gettysburg Pa Monday July 6th, 1863," Lynne Whealton collection.
112. The Kearny Cross was a medal awarded by General Birney to enlisted members of the First Division, 3rd Corps, who had displayed unusual bravery on the field. Named for General Phil Kearny who once commanded the division, the cross was an unofficial military honor and the medals were paid for by General Birney himself. Like the Kearny Cross, the red diamond badge of the same division and corps was a well-known symbol of courage. Captain Jackson wrote on July 5, "Gen. Ward who commanded our brigade said we earned the red patch and Kearney cross," CUL. From these comments and others, it is obvious that both symbols of bravery were coveted by the soldiers.
113. Weygant, p. 181.
114. Sergeant Harvey Hanford, "Gettysburg," *National Tribune*, September 24, 1885.
115. Private Jeremiah Hartnett, *Goshen Democrat*, July 16, 1863.
116. Diary of Henry Howell, SKC.
117. Diary of Henry Howell, SKC.
118. Diary of William Howell, July 3, 1863.
119. William Howell, July 5, 1863, LCC.
120. Weygant, p. 184.
121. William Howell, July 5, 1863.
122. Henry Howell, Battlefield, July 5, 1863, *Middletown Whig Press*, July 22, 1863.
123. Diary of Henry Howell, SKC.
124. Corporal William Howell, in Ethel B. Gage, "Orange County in the Civil War," *Views* (a publication of the Orange County Community of Museums and Galleries) 2:2, April 1963.
125. Diary of Henry Howell SKC.
126. Captain James Benedict, *Whig Press*.
127. Jackson, "Near Gettysburg July 5th 1863," CUL.
128. *Whig Press*, July 29, 1863.
129. Weygant, p. 181.
130. Major Thomas W. Bradley, "At Gettysburg," *National Tribune*, February 4, 1886.
131. Thomas Rodman, RSRC.
132. Richard Cyrus Yarbrough, AC.
133. Memoir of Stephen D. Chase.

Chapter 9

1. Mapes, "Battle Field Gettysburg Pa Monday July 6th, 1863," LWC.
2. Mapes.
3. Corporal William Howell, "On the Battlefield, July 5, 1863, in Ethel B. Gage, "Orange County in the Civil War," *Views* (a publication of the Orange County Community of Museums and Galleries) 2:2, April 1963.
4. Diary of William Howell, AC.
5. Weygant, p. 185.
6. Weygant, p. 185.
7. Henry Howell, "Battlefield, July 5, 1863," *Middletown Whig Press*, July 22, 1863.
8. Diary of Henry Howell, SKC.
9. *Newburgh Journal*, July 1893.
10. *Newburgh Daily Telegraph*, Oct. 23, 1863.
11. Weygant, p. 195.
12. Diary of Henry Howell, SKC.
13. Weygant, p. 196.
14. Diary of William Howell, AC.
15. Rodman, July 17, 1863, RSRC.
16. Rodman, July 27, 1863, RSRC.
17. Rodman, July 29, 1863, RSRC.
18. Diary of William Howell, AC.
19. Weygant, p. 197.
20. Weygant, p. 197.
21. Diary of William Howell, AC.
22. Warner, pp. 161–2; Report of Major General William H. French, OR Vol. 27, Pt. 1, pp. 488–491.
23. Diary of William Howell, AC.
24. Weygant, p. 198.
25. Weygant, p. 201.
26. Stephen Sears, *Gettysburg* (New York: Houghton Mifflin, 2004), pp. 490–491.
27. Weygant.
28. Weygant, pp. 202–3.
29. Weygant.
30. Sears, *Gettysburg*, p. 493.
31. Sears.
32. Weygant, p. 205.
33. Henry Howell, July 17, 1863, MHHSC.
34. Jackson, "Near Hillsboro Va. July 18th 1863," CUL. Wood & Company is a reference to Mayor Fernando Wood who, at the start of the war, suggested that New York should declare itself a "free city" and secede so that it might keep up a lucrative cotton trade with the South.
35. Henry Howell, July 18, 1863, MHHSC.
36. Weygant, p. 206.
37. French, OR.
38. Brigadier General Hobart Ward, OR Vol. 27, Pt. 1, pp. 495–496.
39. Weygant, pp. 206–7.
40. Weygant.
41. Weygant.
42. Weygant.
43. French, OR.
44. Weygant, p. 207.
45. French, OR.
46. Weygant, p. 209.
47. Weygant.
48. Henry Dill, August 14, 1863, CCC.
49. Weygant, p. 209.
50. Weygant, p. 210.
51. Ward, OR.
52. Weygant, p. 211.
53. National Park Service Web site, Civil War Sites Advisory Commission Battle Summaries.
54. John W. Pitts, "White Sulphur Springs Va Sept. 8 1863," *Middletown Whig Press*, September 16, 1863.
55. Sears, *Gettysburg*, pp. 496–7.
56. Col. Vincent Esposito, chief editor, *The West Point Atlas of the Civil War* (New York: Frederick A. Praeger, 1962), p. 117.
57. Weygant, p. 216.
58. William Howell, August 5, 1863, MHHSC.
59. Weygant, p. 216.
60. Jackson, August 9, 1863, CUL.
61. Mapes, "Camp Near Sulphur Springs Va, August 10th, 1863," LWC.
62. Mapes, "Camp Near Sulphur Springs Va, August 13th 1863," LWC.
63. Henry Dill, August 14, 1863, CCC.
64. Henry Howell, August 23, 1863, MHHSC.
65. William Howell, September 5, 1863, MHHSC.
66. William Howell, September 28, 1863, MHHSC.
67. Corporal William Howell, "Sulphur Springs Sept 11th 63," DBC.
68. Benedict, "Sulphur Springs, Va, Sep 13, 1863," JTFC.
69. Benedict, "Sulphur Springs, Sept 14, 1863," JTFC.
70. Weygant, p. 217.
71. Captain William Jackson, "Camp Near Culpepper C. H. Sept 20, 1863," CUL.
72. Henry Dill, "September 18, 1863 Culpeper Virginy," CCC.
73. G.C. Godfrey, "Culpepper Sept 23rd. 1863," CCC. Godfrey, who had been wounded at Chancellorsville and present at Gettysburg, was captured about a month later. He was sent as a prisoner of war to Richmond, where he contracted a fever and died November 20, 1863.
74. Henry Howell, Sept 26, 1863, MHHSC.
75. *New York Tribune*, July 15, 1863.
76. Mapes, September 27, 1863, Culpeper, Va., LWC. *The Daily News* was owned by Benjamin Wood, brother of Mayor Fernando Wood of New York City. Mapes considered both to be traitors.
77. Weygant, p. 218.
78. Jackson, Camp Near Culpeper, October 2, 1863, CUL.
79. Jackson, Camp Near Culpeper, October 2, 1863, CUL.
80. Weygant, p. 223.
81. Mapes, "Cullpicker Va, Oct. 8th 1863," LWC.
82. Weygant, p. 224.

Chapter 10

1. Esposito, 118.
2. Captain Ira Bush to C. Thomas, Esq., "Camp Near Brandy Station Va. Nov 11th./63," USAMHI.
3. Bush.

4. Report of Major General David B. Birney, U.S. Army, commanding First Division, Third Army Corps. OR Vol. 41, p. 311.

5. T. Scott Bradner, *Goshen Democrat*, Oct. 29, 1863. Mike Block of the Brandy Station Foundation found Bradner's description a little confusing. "You must cross Welford's Ford on the Hazel, before Freeman's. It appears the 124th crossed Welford's on a pontoon bridge, camped for the night near Presque Ile, then continued on toward Freeman's Ford on the Rappahannock."

6. Birney, OR.

7. Bush, USMHI.

8. Bradner. Mike Block says that Bradner has the correct sequence here. "They watched the fight from Fleetwood Hill [about a mile from the fighting], continued toward and past Farley [Welford House], crossed the Hazel, past Presque Ile on the Freeman Ford Road, and crossed at Freeman's the next morning."

9. Bradner.

10. Bush, USMHI. According to Mike Block, Bush is referring to Freeman's Ford.

11. Bradner.

12. Birney, OR.

13. Bradner.

14. Lieutenant William Mapes, Oct. 14, 1863, LWC.

15. Bradner.

16. Bush.

17. Bradner.

18. Esposito, 118. The firing heard that morning was General Stuart's cavalry trying to escape the trap. According to Mike Block, "He was caught in a ravine just south of Auburn, between the 3rd Corps and the cavalry. He escaped in the foggy dawn when Confederate infantry arrived to extricate him. This action was known as the Battle of Coffee Hill."

19. Mapes, October 14, 1862, LWC.

20. Bush.

21. Bradner.

22. Esposito, 118.

23. William Howell, Oct. 26, 1863, MHHSC.

24. Henry Howell, October 22, 1863, MHHSC.

25. Weygant, p. 227.

26. Henry Howell, October 22, 1863, MHHSC.

27. Rodman, Fairfax Station, Va., October 17, 1863, RSRC.

28. Rodman, Fairfax Station, Va., October 17, 1863, RSRC.

29. Esposito, 118.

30. Martin Graham and George Skoch, *Mine Run: A Campaign of Lost Opportunities October 21, 1863–May 1, 1864* (Lynchburg, VA: H.E. Howard, 1987), pp. 3–4.

31. Weygant, p. 227.

32. Weygant, pp. 227–8.

33. Henry Howell, October 22, 1863.

34. William Howell, October 26, 1863, MHHSC.

35. Rodman, "Camp Near Brandy Station, Va Thursday Nov 12th 1863," RSRC

36. Weygant, p. 228.

37. Weygant, p. 229.

38. Weygant, pp. 229–30.

39. Graham and Skoch, p. 8.

40. Graham and Skoch, p. 9.

41. Weygant, p. 232.

42. Bush. Mike Block places this move at November 7.

43. Bush.

44. Weygant, p. 234.

45. Weygant, pp. 234–5.

46. Bush.

47. Graham and Skoch, pp. 38–39.

48. Weygant, p. 235.

49. Jackson, Nov. 14, 1863, CUL.

50. William Howell, Nov. 23, 1863, MHHSC.

51. Weyant, p. 236.

52. Mapes, Nov. 20, 1863, LWC.

53. William Howell, Nov. 23, 1863, MHHSC.

54. Graham and Skoch, pp. 40–41.

55. Weygant, p. 236.

56. Weygant, pp. 236–7.

57. Graham and Skoch, pp. 44–45.

58. Weygant, p. 237.

59. Anonymous, "Camp Near Brandy Station, Va. December 3d, 1863," *Goshen Democrat*, December 17, 1863.

60. William B. Jordan, *Red Diamond Regiment: The 17th Maine Infantry, 1862–1865* (Shippensburg, PA: White Mane Publishing, 1996), p. 101.

61. Birney, OR.

62. Weygant, p. 237.

63. Weygant.

64. Weygant, p. 238.

65. Weygant.

66. Weygant, p. 239.

67. Anonymous, "Camp Near Brandy Station, Va. December 3d, 1863," *Goshen Democrat*, December 17, 1863.

68. Birney, OR.

69. Weygant, p. 241.

70. Anonymous, "Camp Near Brandy Station, Va. December 3d, 1863," *Goshen Democrat*, December 17, 1863.

71. Weygant, p. 242.

72. Weygant.

73. Weygant, p. 243.

74. William Howell, December 3, 1863, MHHSC.

75. Birney, OR.

76. William Howell, December 3, 1863, MHHSC.

77. Weygant, p. 243.

78. Birney, OR.

79. Weygant, p. 244.

80. William Howell, December 3, 1863, MHHSC.

81. Weygant, p. 247.

82. Anonymous, "Camp Near Brandy Station, Va. December 3d, 1863," *Goshen Democrat*, December 17, 1863.

83. Anonymous.

84. William Howell, December 3, 1863, MHHSC.

85. Weygant, p. 247.

Chapter 11

1. Weygant, p. 247.

2. Weygant.

3. Jackson, December 5, 1863, CUL; William Reeder, *From a True Soldier and Son: The Civil War Letters of William Reeder*, commentary by Carolyn Reeder, edited by Jack Reeder (Brandy Station, VA: Brandy Station Foundation, 2008), p. 174; Weygant, pp. 247–248. Private Birdsall was sent to Fort Jefferson, Dry Tortugas, Florida, to serve his sentence. He returned to the company January 11, 1865 and mustered out with company June 3, 1865, near Washington, D.C.

4. Weygant, p. 248.

5. Mapes, December 8, 1863, LWC.

6. Rodman, "In Camp Near Brandy Station Va Dec 8th 1863," RSRC.

7. Weygant, p. 248.

8. Rodman, "In Camp Near Brandy Sta Va December 16, 1863," RSRC.

9. Weygant, p. 249.

10. Weygant.

11. Weygant, p. 249.

12. Henry Howell, January 6, 1864, MHHSC.

13. Weygant, p. 251.

14. Weygant.

15. Jackson, January 10, 1864, CUL.

16. "R.G. 156 Summary of Quarterly Returns of Ordnance," December 1863–Early 1864, National Archives, Washington, D.C.

17. Weygant, p. 252.

18. Private Horace D. Paret, "Letter from the 124th Regiment, Camp Near Brandy Station, Va.," *Middletown Whig Press*, January 17, 1864.

19. William Howell, "Camp of the 124th, January 17th 64," AC.

20. William Howell.

21. William Edgar, "Camp of the 124th Regiment N.Y.S.V. Near Brandy Station, Va. Feb 18, 1864," *Newburgh Journal*, February 29, 1864.

22. William Jackson, January 19, 1864. CUL.

23. Weygant, p. 252.

24. Chaplain Bradner, "Near Culpepper Va Wednesday, September 30th 1863," GPLHS.

25. "The 124th Regiment, One of the Daughters of Orange," *Goshen Democrat*, January 6, 1864, NYSMHM.

26. Weygant, pp. 252–3.

27. "F.M. Cummins, Colonel 124th Regt. N.Y. Vols., Camp 124th Regt N.Y. Vol., Culpeper, Va., April 20th 1864," GPLHS.

28. "Camp Near Culpeper Jan. 28, 1864," transcribed by Steve Haas, National Archives, Washington, D.C.

29. Weygant, p. 253.

30. Rodman, Camp near Brandy Station, Virginia. RSRC.

31. Private Horace D. Paret, "Letter from the 124th Regiment, Camp Near Brandy Station, Va.," *Middletown Whig Press*, February 3, 1864.

32. Weygant, pp. 253–4.

33. William Edgar, "Camp of the 124th Regiment N.Y.S.V. Near Brandy Station, Va. Feb 18, 1864," *Newburgh Journal*, February 29, 1864.

34. William Howell, "On Picket, Feb 9th 1864," AC.

35. William Edgar.

36. Weygant, pp. 253–4.

37. William Howell.

38. William Edgar.

39. William Howell.

40. "On Picket Feb 9th 1864," AC.

41. Weygant, p. 255.
42. Rodman, "In Camp Near Brandy Station Va.," February 16, 1864, RSRC.
43. Rodman, February 22, 1864, RSRC.
44. Henry Howell, "Headquarters Feb 15th (1864)," AC.
45. Henry Howell.
46. Henry Howell.
47. William Howell, "Camp 124th N.Y. Vols. March 3d, 1864," *Middletown Whig Press*.
48. William Howell.
49. Rodman, "In Camp Near Culpeper Va., March 5th 1864," RSRC.
50. Sidney David Brummer, *Political History of New York State During the Period of the Civil War*, doctoral dissertation, Columbia University, 1911, pp. 351–352.
51. *The Daily Journal*, March 3, 1864.
52. William Howell, "In Camp, March 5th 1864," AC
53. Henry Howell, "Camp of the 124th N.Y. Vols," March 11, 1864.
54. Private William Luckey, "A Letter from a Soldier Camp of the 124th NY Vols., March 13th, 1864," *Middletown Whig Press*, April 23, 1864.
55. E.B. Long, *The Civil War Day by Day: An Almanac 1861–1865* (Garden City, NY: Doubleday, 1971), p. 473.
56. Weygant, p. 261.
57. Henry Howell, "In Camp March 25th 1864," AC.
58. Rodman, "Camp Near Culpeper Va., March 29th 1864," RSRC.
59. Weygant, p. 261.
60. Weygant, p. 262
61. Weygant, pp. 262–3.
62. Weygant, p. 264.
63. Weygant.
64. Horace D. Paret, "Camp Near Culpeper, Va., April 4, 1864," *Middletown Whig Press*.
65. Rodman, "In Camp Near Culpeper Va, April 5th 1864," RSRC.
66. Rodman, "Camp Near Culpepper April 13, 1864," RSRC.
67. David W. Lowe, editor, *Meade's Army: The Private Notebooks of Lt. Col. Theodore Lyman* (Kent, OH: Kent State University Press, 2007), p. 119.
68. Weygant, pp. 266–69.
69. Documents pertaining to the question of Colonel Cummins's sobriety are from the National Archives, Washington, D.C., provided by Howard Berthoff.
70. Ben Dutcher, "Camp Near Brandy Station," April 14, 1864.
71. William Howell, "On Picket, Apr 17th 1864," AC.
72. Henry Howell, "Camp of American Guard April 23d 1864," AC.
73. Henry Howell, "Camp of American Guard April 23d 1864," AC.
74. Rodman, "In Camp Near Brandy Station Va, April 25th 1864," RSRC.

Chapter 12

1. Lyman, p. 124.
2. Lyman, 126.
3. Warner, pp. 202–4.
4. Weygant, pp. 284–5.
5. Warner, pp. 541–2.

6. Warner, 430–1.
7. Weygant, p. 270.
8. Weygant, p. 284; Norman Augustus Sly, *"Rambling Thoughts on the 1864 Campaign: Father's speech at the Warwick Historical Society — of which he was a member,"* Part 1: The Wilderness, HSMWP. Norman Sly is an ancestor of former Orange County Historian Ted Sly, who, together with Marvin Cohen of the Middletown Historical Society, brought this handwritten document to my attention.
9. David Craft, *History of the One Hundred Forty-First Regiment Pennsylvania Volunteers 1862–1865* (Towanda, PA: Reporter-Journal Printing Company, 1885), p. 175.
10. Lincoln to Halleck, September 19, 1863, OR Vol. 29, Pt. 2, pp. 207–208.
11. Craft, p. 176.
12. Gordon Rhea, *The Battle of the Wilderness: May 5–6, 1864* (Baton Rouge: Louisiana State University Press, 1994), p. 52.
13. Andrew A. Humphreys, *The Virginia Campaign '64–'65* (New York: Charles Scribner's Sons, 1883), pp. 10–13.
14. Mark Grimsley, *And Keep Moving On: The Virginia Campaign, May–June 1864* (Lincoln: University of Nebraska Press, 2002), pp. 9–10; Rhea, pp. 53–56.
15. Rhea, pp. 55–56.
16. Esposito, p. 121.
17. Sly, *Rambling Thoughts*, HSMWP, p. 2.
18. Sly.
19. Weygant, p. 271.
20. Sly, p. 3.
21. Craft, p. 176.
22. Weygant, p. 271.
23. Sly, p. 4.
24. Weygant, pp. 271–2.
25. Craft, p. 176.
26. Charles LaRocca, editor, *The Red Badge of Courage: An Historically Annotated Edition* (New York: Purple Mountain Press, 1995), p. 131.
27. Weygant, p. 272.
28. Sly, p. 6.
29. Weygant, pp. 278–80.
30. Rhea, p. 94.
31. Weygant, p. 285.
32. OR Vol. 36, Pt. 2, p. 403 as quoted in Rhea, p. 102.
33. Weygant, p. 285.
34. Rhea, p. 161.
35. Rhea, p. 188.
36. Esposito, p. 122.
37. Sly, p. 6.
38. Craft, p. 177.
39. Weygant, p. 286.
40. Sly, p. 7.
41. Order cited in Rhea, p. 189.
42. Hancock's Report in OR Vol. 36, Pt. 1, p. 318.
43. Weygant, p. 286; Hancock, OR.
44. Weygant, p. 286.
45. Hancock, OR.
46. Earl J. Hess, *Trench Warfare Under Grant & Lee, Field Fortifications in the Overland Campaign* (Chapel Hill: University of North Carolina Press, 2007), p. 19.
47. Hess, pp. xiii–xviii.

48. Craft, p. 178.
49. Edward Steere, *The Wilderness Campaign* (Harrisburg, PA: Stackpole, 1987), p. 203.
50. Steere.
51. Hancock, OR.
52. Steere, p. 207.
53. Sly, p. 8.
54. Sly.
55. Steere, pp. 206–7.
56. Steere, pp. 207–208.
57. Craft, p. 178.
58. Steere, pp. 212–214.
59. Brigadier General Silas Casey, *Infantry Tactics for the Instruction, Exercise, and Maneuvres of the Soldier, a Company, Line of Skirmishers, Battalion, Brigade, or Corps D'Armee* Vol. 2 (New York: D. Van Nostrand, 1862), p. 36.
60. Steere, p. 214.
61. Chaplain Cudworth, quoted in Steere, p. 214.
62. Colonel McAlister, quoted in Steere, p. 215.
63. Weygant, p. 287.
64. The Web site dcnyhistory.org lists the 144th New York as camped at Jacksonville, Florida, on May 5, 1864; the regimental history of the 144th also places the regiment on duty in Florida in May 1864. James H. McKee, *"Back in War Times." History of the 144th Regiment, New York Volunteer Infantry* (Unadilla, NY: Robert Rutter & Son's Bindery, 1903).
65. Steere, p. 215.
66. Weygant, p. 287.
67. Lyman, p. 135.
68. Steere, p. 224.
69. Weygant, p. 287.
70. Weygant, pp. 287–288.
71. Sly, p. 10.
72. Sly.
73. Weygant, p. 288.
74. Sly, p. 10.
75. Weygant, p. 288.
76. Sly, p. 14.
77. Sly, p. 15.
78. Sly, p. 16.
79. Sly, p. 17.
80. Rhea, pp. 263–4.
81. Hancock, OR Vol. 48, p. 320.
82. Weygant, p. 290.
83. Sly, p. 18.
84. Steere, pp. 328–330; Rhea, pp. 283–290.
85. Weygant, p. 291.
86. Sly, p. 17.
87. Sly, p. 19.
88. Sly, p. 20.
89. Sly, pp. 20–21.
90. Weygant, p. 291.
91. Francis A. Walker, *History of the Second Army Corps of the Army of the Potomac* (New York: Scribner's, 1991), p. 422.
92. Weygant, p. 291.
93. Sly, p. 21.
94. Weygant, p. 293.
95. Sly, pp. 21–22.
96. Sly, pp. 23–24.
97. Weygant, p. 293.
98. Sly, pp. 24–25
99. Weygant, p. 294.
100. Sly, p. 25.
101. Weygant, p. 294.

102. Rhea, pp. 370–72.
103. Rhea.
104. Weygant, pp. 294.
105. Weygant, pp. 295–6.
106. Sly, pp. 25–26.
107. Weygant, p. 296.
108. Weygant.
109. Weygant, p. 297.
110. Weygant p. 298.
111. Weygant.
112. Sly, p. 27.
113. Walker, p. 432.
114. Walker.
115. Walker, p. 432–33.
116. Warren Wilkinson and Steven E. Woodworth, *A Scythe of Fire, A Civil War Story of the Eighth Georgia Infantry Regiment* (New York: William Morrow, 2002), p. 287.
117. Hess, p. 42.
118. Weygant, pp. 299–300.
119. Captain Henry Travis, "Near Todds Tavern Va May 8th 1864," Larry Clance collection. Among the wounded were 1st Sergeant W.W. Smith, Sergeant A.T. Vanderlyn, Corporal Joseph Hanna, Corporal Whitmore Terwilliger, Private Rensellaer D. Beard, Private John Gordon, and Private William Milligan. The eighth man must have been Private Mathew Manney, who was listed in Weygant's history of the regiment. Of those, Beard (listed as Baird in the muster rolls) was captured and paroled, Gordon was captured on May 6, and Vanderlyn, who had been wounded, would linger until November, when he died of his wound.
120. Henry Howell, "On the battlefield, May 8th, 1864," AC.
121. Lyman, 139.
122. Lyman, p. 141.
123. Horace Porter, *Campaigning with Grant* (Lincoln: University of Nebraska Press, 2000), p. 98.
124. Ida M. Tarbell, *A Reporter for Lincoln The Story of Henry E. Wing* (New York: Macmillan, 1927), p. 13.

Chapter 13

1. Sly, *Rambling Thoughts, from the Wilderness to the Po River*, HSMWP, p. 1.
2. Lyman, p. 142.
3. Lyman, 143.
4. Lyman, 145.
5. General Sir James Marshall-Cornwall, *Grant as Military Commander* (New York: Van Nostrand Reinhold, 1970), pp. 153–4.
6. Ulysses S. Grant, *Memoirs and Selected Letters* (Camp Hill, PA: The Library of America), p. 540.
7. Walker, p. 442.
8. Weygant, p. 303.
9. Gordon Rhea, *The Battles for Spotsylvania Court House and the Road to Yellow Tavern; May 7–12, 1864* (Baton Rouge: Louisiana State University Press, 1997), p. 43.
10. William D. Matter, *If It Takes All Summer: The Battle of Spotsylvania* (Chapel Hill: University of North Carolina Press, 1988), p. 28.
11. Weygant, p. 300.

12. Weygant, 301.
13. Sly, p. 2.
14. Sly.
15. Weygant, pp. 303–4.
16. Esposito, p. 125.
17. Sly, p. 3.
18. Rhea, 86–7.
19. Brigadier General P. Regis de Trobriand, OR Vol. 36, Pt. 1, p. 469.
20. Weygant, 305.
21. Weygant, p. 306.
22. Rhea, 109–110.
23. Weygant, p. 306.
24. Weygant. In his regimental history, Weygant quoted from an "official report" of the action, presumably General de Trobriand's account of the move. De Trobriand was not in command for this action but would later take command of Ward's Brigade after Ward was dismissed. He would be the one writing the after-action reports for the battles, not Ward.
25. Hancock, OR Vol. 36, Pt. 1, p. 330.
26. Matter, p. 124.
27. Weygant, pp. 306–7.
28. Hancock, OR.
29. Sly, p. 5.
30. Roger D. Hunter and Jack R. Brown, *Brevet Brigadier Generals in Blue* (Gaithersburg, MD: Olde Soldier Books, 1990), p. 77.
31. Sly, p. 6.
32. Sly, p. 7.
33. Alexander, p. 370.
34. Rhea, p. 127; Grant, p. 546.
35. Alexander, p. 371.
36. Hancock, OR Vol. 36, Pt. 1, pp. 331–332.
37. *Memoirs of Stephen D. Chase 86th New York*, U.S. Army Military History Institute, Carlisle Barracks, PA, USMHI.
38. Weygant, p. 308.
39. Hancock, OR.
40. De Trobriand, OR Vol. 36, Pt. 1, p. 470.
41. Sly, p. 8.
42. Hancock, OR.
43. Sly, p. 9.
44. Weygant, p. 309.
45. Sly, p. 11.
46. Sly, p. 12.
47. Grant, p. 546; Humphreys, pp. 80–82.
48. Rhea, p. 143.
49. Noah A. Trudeau, *Bloody Roads South: The Wilderness to Cold Harbor, May–June 1864* (Boston: Little, Brown, 1989), p. 153.
50. Angelina V. Winkler, *The Confederate Capital and Hood's Texas Brigade* (Austin, TX: E. Von Boeckmann, 1879), p. 171.
51. Hancock, OR Vol. 36, Pt. 1, p. 334.
52. Grant, p. 549; Hess, p. 56.
53. Trudeau, pp. 156–158.
54. Trudeau, pp. 158–162.
55. Rhea, p. 177.
56. Rhea, pp. 149–150.
57. Weygant, p. 310.
58. *Memoir of Stephen D. Chase*, page 101.
59. Rhea, p. 177.
60. Weygant, p. 310.
61. Polley, J.B. *Hood's Texas Brigade*

(Dayton, OH: Morningside Bookshop, 1988), p. 237.
62. Rhea, p. 179.
63. Rhea.
64. Weygant, p. 310.
65. Weygant.
66. Weygant, pp. 310–11.
67. Polley, pp. 237–8.
68. Winkler, p. 171.
69. Chase, p. 102.
70. Rhea, p. 180.
71. Weygant, p. 311.
72. Weygant.
73. Polley, p. 238.
74. Weygant, p. 311.
75. De Trobriand, OR.
76. Winkler, p. 171.
77. Polley, pp. 237–8.
78. Polley, pp. 237–9.
79. Hancock, OR Vol. 36, Pt. 1, p. 344.
80. Hess, p. 54.
81. Rhea, pp. 180–181.
82. Walker, pp. 460–61.
83. Weygant, p. 311.
84. Sly, p. 13.
85. Sly, pp. 13–14.
86. Walker, p. 465.
87. Grant, p. 552.
88. William Howell, undated but most likely written May 11, 1864, the day before he was killed in action. LCC.
89. Rifle or artillery fire on one side of the salient cannot be brought to bear on an enemy attacking the other side. Another problem lies in the fact that it is hard to bring guns beyond the salient to bear on an enemy attacking the tip. A salient is also vulnerable to being overrun should the enemy attack the base from either or both sides and successfully cut off the troops inside the bulge.
90. Craft, p. 193.
91. Craft, p. 192.
92. Weygant, pp. 312–313.
93. Craft, p. 192.
94. Weygant, p. 313.
95. Weygant, pp. 313–4.
96. Sly, pp. 14–15.
97. Weygant, pp. 319–21.
98. Weygant, p. 320.
99. Hancock, OR Vol. 36, Pt. 1, p. 355; Grant, p. 553.
100. Weygant, p. 319; Hancock, OR.
101. Weygant, p. 283.
102. Rhea, p. 226.
103. Weygant, p. 320.
104. Sly, p. 15.
105. Weygant, p. 322.
106. Sly, p. 15.
107. Jordan, p. 148.
108. Weygant, pp. 321–3.
109. Rhea, p. 235.
110. Craft, p. 193.
111. Weygant, p. 322.
112. Henry Howell, Fredericksburg, May 14, 1864, AC.
113. Hancock, OR Vol. 36, Pt. 1, p. 336.
114. Matter, p. 197.
115. Weygant, p. 323.
116. Hancock, OR Vol. 36, Pt. 1, pp. 335–336.
117. Sly, p. 16.
118. Lyman, pp. 153–4.
119. Weygant, p. 333.

120. Weygant, pp. 332–3.
121. Henry Howell, May 14, 1864.
122. Matter, p. 198.
123. Weygant, p. 323.
124. Weygant, p. 324.
125. Sly, p. 16.
126. Sly, p. 17.
127. Weygant, p. 325.
128. Rhea, pp. 250–252.
129. Rhea, pp. 243–244.
130. Sly, p. 18.
131. Sly.
132. Walter Frederick Beyer and Oscar Frederick Keydel, editors, *Deeds of Valor* (Detroit, MI: Perrien-Keydel, 1906).
133. Lyman, p. 155.
134. Sly, p. 19.
135. Lyman, pp. 155–56.
136. Jackson, May 17, 1864, CUL.
137. Henry Howell, May 14, 1864, AC.
138. Henry Howell, May 17, 1864, AC.

Chapter 14

1. Lyman, p. 157.
2. Sly, p. 20.
3. Sly, pp. 21–22.
4. Sly, p. 23.
5. Grant, pp. 556–561; Rhea, *Spotsylvania*, p. 310.
6. Gordon Rhea, *To the North Anna River; Grant and Lee, May 13–25, 1864* (Baton Rouge: Louisiana State University Press, 2000), pp. 72–75; Walker, pp. 480–482; Humphreys, pp. 106–109.
7. Sly, pp. 24–25.
8. Sly, pp. 26–27.
9. Diary of James G. Irwin, RCC.
10. Weygant, pp. 337–8.
11. Walker, p. 482; Weygant, pp. 338–339.
12. Weygant, p. 343.
13. Sly, p. 27.
14. Sly, pp. 28–29.
15. Matter, pp. 306–312.
16. Weygant, p. 340.
17. Diary of James G. Irwin, RCC.
18. De Trobriand, OR Vol. 36, Pt. 1, p. 475.
19. Weygant, pp. 340–1.
20. Lyman, p. 164; Warner, pp. 515–6.
21. Walker, p. 488.
22. Weygant, 341.
23. Weygant.
24. Rodman, "May 20th 1864," RSRC.
25. DeTrobriand, OR Vol. 36, Pt. 1, pp. 471–472.
26. Captain Madison M. Cannon, OR Vol. 47, p. 475.
27. Diary of James G. Irwin, RCC.
28. Mark Grimsley, *And Keep Moving On: The Virginia Campaign, May–June 1864* (Lincoln: University of Nebraska Press, 2002), p. 135.
29. Rhea, pp. 219–222; Grant, pp. 562–564.
30. Rhea, pp. 288–89.
31. Walker, p. 493.
32. Diary of James G. Irwin, May 23, 1864, RCC.
33. General Andrew A. Humphreys, *The Virginia Campaign '64–'65* (New York: Charles Scribner's Sons, 1883), p. 128.

34. Grimsley, pp. 139–40.
35. Grimsley.
36. Hancock, OR Vol. 36, Pt. 3, p. 115.
37. J. Michael Miller, *The North Anna Campaign: "Even to Hell Itself" May 21–26, 1864* (Lynchburg, VA: H.E. Howard, 1989), pp. 57–60.
38. Hancock, OR, p. 119.
39. Hess, 124.
40. Hess.
41. William Swinton, *Campaigns of the Army of the Potomac* (New York: C.B. Richardson, 1866), pp. 475–76.
42. Walker.
43. Hess, p. 125.
44. Travis quoted in Weygant, p. 343.
45. Memoir of Stephen D. Chase.
46. Chase.
47. Travis quoted in Weygant, pp. 343–4.
48. Chase.
49. Travis letter quoted in Weygant, pp. 343–4.
50. Walker, pp. 493–494.
51. Chase.
52. Weygant; *Annual Report of the Adjutant-General for the State of New York for the Year 1903*, No. 36 (Albany, NY: Oliver Quayle, 1904), pp. 500–666.
53. Grimsley, p. 140; de Trobriand, OR Vol. 36, Pt. 1, pp. 471–472.
54. Walker, p. 494.
55. Captain Madison M. Cannon, OR Vol. 47, p. 475.
56. Diary of James G. Irwin, May 24, 1864, RCC.
57. Hess, p. 131.
58. Walker, p. 496.
59. Diary of James G. Irwin, May 25, 1864, RCC.
60. Walker, p. 497.
61. Weygant, p. 345.
62. Craft, p. 206.
63. Gordon Rhea, *Cold Harbor: Grant and Lee May 26–June 3, 1864* (Baton Rouge: Louisiana State University Press, 2002), p. 36.
64. Diary of James G. Irwin, May 26, 1864, RCC.
65. Captain Madison M. Cannon, OR Vol. 47, p. 475.
66. Craft, p. 207.
67. Rhea, pp. 43–45.
68. "J.H.T., South Side Pamunky River Twelve Miles from Richmond, Va. May 30th 1864," *Independent Republican*.
69. J.H.T.
70. Diary of James G. Irwin, May 28, 1864, RCC.
71. Hess, p. 140.
72. Walker, p. 499.
73. Grant, p. 575.
74. Hancock, OR Vol. 36, Pt. 1, No. 67; Walker, p. 500.
75. Hancock, OR.
76. Lyman, p. 181.
77. Craft, p. 207.
78. Diary of James G. Irwin, May 29, 1864, RCC.
79. Chase.
80. De Trobriand, OR Vol. 36, Pt. 1, p. 472; Craft, p. 208; Hancock, OR.
81. Weygant, p. 345; Chase.
82. Craft, p. 208.

83. Weygant, pp. 345–6.
84. Lyman, p. 182.
85. Hancock, OR Vol. 36, Part 1, No. 67.
86. Grant, p. 575.
87. Rhea, p. 150; Hancock, OR.
88. Craft, p. 208.
89. Diary of James G. Irwin, May 30, 1864, RCC.
90. Weygant, p. 346.
91. Weygant.
92. Weygant.
93. Captain Henry Travis, "124th New York Vols., June 4th 1864," LCC. Captain Travis cited the date of Captain Crist's death as June 1, but he was dead and buried by then.
94. "J.H.T., South Side Pamunky River Twelve Miles from Richmond, Va. May 30th 1864," Goshen *Independent Republican.*
95. Captain William Jackson, "South of the Pamunkey River P. M. May 30th 1864," CUL.
96. Weygant, p. 347.
97. Rhea, 151.
98. Diary of James G. Irwin, May 31, 1864, RCC.
99. Craft, p. 208.
100. De Trobriand, OR, p. 472.
101. Hancock, OR Vol. 36, Part 1, No. 67.
102. Hancock, OR Vol. 36, Part 1, No. 67.
103. Craft, p. 208.
104. Hancock, OR Vol. 36, Part 1, No. 67.
105. Diary of James G. Irwin, June 1, 1864, RCC.
106. Weygant, p. 347.
107. Craft, p. 209.
108. Walker, p. 506.
109. Diary of James G. Irwin, June 2, 1864, RCC.
110. Hancock, OR Vol. 36, Part 1, No. 67.
111. Diary of James G. Irwin, June 2, 1864, RCC.
112. Walker, p. 510.
113. Walker, p. 516.
114. Diary of James G. Irwin, June 3, 1864, RCC.
115. Hancock, OR Vol. 36, Part 1, No. 67.
116. Hancock, OR Vol. 36, Part 1, No. 67.
117. Walker, p. 521.
118. Rhea, *Cold Harbor*, p. 362.
119. Grant, p. 588.
120. Grant, p. 584.
121. Diary of James G. Irwin.
122. Craft, p. 209.
123. Chase memoir.
124. Rodman, "In the Trenches About 4 miles from Coal Harbor Va, June 6th/64," RSRC.
125. Diary of James G. Irwin, June 7, 1864, RCC.
126. Sergeant George Brewster, June 22, 1864, *Middletown Whig Press.*
127. Captain William Jackson, "June 8th 1864 Place where I don't know but In Rifle Pits north of the Chickahominy with the rebs Between it and us." CUL. The refer-

ence to taking the shine off the 56th New York implies that its soldiers had not seen the same sort of action or suffered the battle casualties of the 124th New York. While it was true that the 56th did not have the combat experience that the 124th New York had, the unit lost more men during the war to disease than did the Orange Blossoms to enemy fire. The 56th spent the last years of the war on the coast of South Carolina, but did see action in a number of battles there.

128. Diary of James G. Irwin, June 8–10, 1864, RCC.
129. Simpson, p. 38.
130. Diary of James G. Irwin, June 12, 1864, RCC.
131. Esposito, p. 137.
132. Esposito.
133. Esposito. Robert E.L. Krick of the Richmond National Battlefield Park wrote, "Lee suspected the truth, but could not prove it and did not dare guess, as a wrong guess would have exposed Richmond."
134. Diary of James G. Irwin, June 14, 1864, RCC.
135. Weygant, p. 349
136. Diary of James G. Irwin, June 14, 1864, RCC.
137. Walker, p. 522.
138. Walker, p. 523.

Chapter 15

1. Trudeau, p. 36.
2. Craft, pp. 212–13.
3. Beauregard, General Pierre T.G., "Four Days of Battle at Petersburg," in *Battles and Leaders of the Civil War* Vol. 4, p. 540.
4. Trudeau, p. 38; Earl J. Hess, *In the Trenches at Petersburg, Field Fortifications & Confederate Defeat* (Chapel Hill: University of North Carolina Press, 2009), pp. 18–19.
5. Noah Trudeau, *The Last Citadel: Petersburg, Virginia June 1864–April 1865* (Boston: Little, Brown, 1991), p. 36.
6. Diary of James G. Irwin, June 15, 1864, RCC.
7. John, Howe, *The Petersburg Campaign: Wasted Valor June 15–18, 1864* (Lynchburg, VA: H. E. Howard, 1988), p. 30; Weygant, p. 349; Humphreys, pp. 208–09.
8. Humphreys, pp. 207–10.
9. Chase.
10. Trudeau, p. 42.
11. Howe, p. 37.
12. Howe, p. 43.
13. Chase.
14. Howe, 44 and note 15.
15. Ruth, L. Silliker, editor, *The Rebel Yell and Yankee Hurrah, The Civil War Journal of a Maine Volunteer* (Camden, ME: Down East Books, 1885), p. 171.
16. Diary of James G. Irwin, RCC.
17. De Trobriand, OR Vol. 40, p. 391.
18. De Trobriand.
19. Howe, p. 44; Silliker, p. 141.
20. Silliker, p. 172.
21. Weygant, pp. 349–350.
22. Howe, p. 48.
23. Howe, pp. 49–51. Historian Jimmy Blankenship of the Petersburg National

Battlefield notes, "The Hare Plantation House was west of the Prince George Court House Road but some of the land was south of the road. The road goes east to west from Confederate Battery 9 and then makes a 90-degree turn to the north just east of the house."

24. Howe, pp. 52–54.
25. Meade, OR 40, Pt. 2, p. 117.
26. Howe, p. 59.
27. Craft, p. 215.
28. Diary of James G. Irwin, June 17, 1864, RCC.
29. Edwin C. Bearss, *Meade's June 18 Assault Fails and the Investment Begins* (National Park Service, 1964), pp. 1–2.
30. Bearss, p. 4.
31. Meade, OR Series 1, Vol. 40, Pt. 2, p. 120.
32. Lyman.
33. Howe, pp. 110–11.
34. Meade, OR Vol. 40, Pt. 2, p. 164.
35. Weygant, p. 350.
36. Meade to Birney, OR Vol. 40, Pt. 2, p. 165.
37. Bearss, pp. 11–12.
38. Hess, p. 130.
39. Birney, OR Vol. 40, Pt. 2, p. 168.
40. Craft, p. 216.
41. Howe, pp. 130–132; Bearss, pp. 18–31.
42. Howe; Bearss.
43. Craft, p. 216.
44. Bearss.
45. Chase.
46. William F. Fox, *Regimental Losses in the American Civil War 1861–1865* (Dayton, OH: Morningside Books, 1985), p. 125.
47. Bearss, p. 21.
48. Chase, p. 127.
49. OR Vol. 40, Pt. 2, p. 168.
50. Sergeant Ben Hull, "Camp of the 124th NY Vols July 17/64," HSMWP.
51. *Goshen Democrat*, June 23, 1864.
52. *Whig Press*, July 6, 1864.
53. Sergeant Ben Hull, "Camp of the 124th NY Vols July 17/64." Jackson was buried at the Hamptonburg Cemetery, a short distance from his boyhood home at "Hill Hold" in Orange County. HSMWP.
54. Frank Wilkeson, *Recollections of a Private Soldier in the Army of the Potomac* (New York: G.P. Putnam's Sons the Knickerbocker Press, 1887), pp. 180–1.
55. Thomas Rodman, "In the Breastworks Near Petersburg Va, June 19th 1864," RSRC.
56. Weygant, p. 351.
57. Weygant.
58. D.P.Q., "On Picket Near Petersburg, Va., June 26th, 1864," *Whig Press*.
59. Weygant, p. 357.
60. Weygant, pp. 356–57.
61. Weygant, p. 358.
62. Thomas Rodman, "In Camp Near Petersburg Va., July 2 1864," RSRC.
63. Thomas Rodman, "In Camp Near Petersburgh Va., July 6 1864," RSRC.
64. Ben Hull July 18, 1864, HSMWP.
65. William Mapes, "Camp of 124th NY Vols. Near Petersburg Va. Sunday, July 17, 1864," LWC.
66. Weygant, p. 359.

67. Captain Henry Travis, July 25, 1864, LCC.
68. Hess, pp. 82–83.
69. Weygant, p. 360.
70. Grant, p. 613.
71. Captain Henry Travis, July 30, 1864, LCC.
72. Hess, *In the Trenches at Petersburg*, pp. 90–106.
73. Travis. Chaos reigned inside the crater as hundreds of Union troops were pushed forward in a desperate attempt to break through the enemy line. Determined counterattacks by the Confederate defenders stopped any attempt to exploit the situation. It is small wonder that in viewing the total confusion from a quarter mile away, Captain Travis got the sequence of events wrong.
74. Weygant, p. 362.
75. P., "Camp Before Petersburgh, Va., Sunday, Aug. 7th, 1864," *Whig Press*.
76. "From the One Hundred and Twenty-Fourth Regiment," August 8, 1864, *Newburgh Daily Journal*, August 16, 1864, NYSMHM.
77. Hess, p. 124.
78. Weygant, p. 362.
79. Hess, 124–5; Weygant pp. 363–4.
80. Weygant, p. 364.
81. Weygant, p. 365.
82. Historian Jimmy Blankenship noted that Confederate spies at City Point knew that the steamers had turned about and were headed upriver. "Lee sent troops from the Petersburg front to counter this move and that's why Grant faced more CSA troops than he thought were there originally."
83. Weygant, pp. 365–6.
84. Weygant, pp. 368–9.
85. Weygant, p. 371.
86. Weygant, pp. 372–3.
87. Thomas Rodman, "In Bomb Proofs Near Petersburg Va., Sept 7th/64," RSRC.
88. Weygant, p. 374.
89. Weygant, p. 375.
90. William E. Mapes, "Hospital, Ward 7, Fort Monroe, Sept 8th 1864," LWC.
91. William E. Mapes, "U.S. Genl Hospital, Ward 7, Fort Monroe, Va., Sunday (Sept) 18th 1864," LWC.
92. Thomas Rodman, "In Front of Petersburgh Va., Sept 20th/64," RSRC.
93. Weygant, p. 378.
94. J.H.W., "The Feeling of the Army, Camp Near Reams' Station, Va., October 3d, 1864," *Middletown Whig Press*, October 19, 1864.
95. Thomas Rodman, "In Camp Near Petersburg Va., Oct 20th/64," RSRC
96. Weygant, p. 382.
97. Weygant.
98. Weygant, p. 383.
99. Thomas Rodman, "In Camp Near Petersburgh Va., Nov 9th 1864," RSRC.
100. Weygant, pp. 390–91.
101. Alan Damon, "Surgeon Thompson's Separate Peace," *American Heritage* Vol. 26, No. 1 (December, 1974), pp. 70–71.
102. Damon, p. 71.
103. Damon, p. 72.
104. Damon, p. 73.
105. Weygant, pp. 392–3.

106. Weygant, p. 394.
107. Warner, p. 204.
108. Thomas Rodman, "In Camp Near Petersburg Va., November 18 & 19, 1864," RSRC.
109. Private Charles O. Goodyear, "Letter from a Soldier, Camp of the 124th N.Y.V., Near Petersburgh, Nov. 21, 1864," RC.
110. Weygant, p. 403.
111. Weygant.
112. Weygant, p. 405.
113. Weygant, p. 407.
114. Weygant, p. 407.
115. Weygant, p. 412.
116. Weygant, p. 413.
117. Sam Duvall, "Incident at Hatcher's Run," *Alabama Heritage* 63 (Winter 2002), pp. 18–19.
118. Weygant, pp. 415–16; Duvall, p. 20.
119. Duvall, pp. 20–22.
120. Duvall, p. 24.
121. Duvall, pp. 24–25. Colonel Troy survived his wound and was paroled June 16, 1865, after signing a loyalty oath and swearing that he would not take up arms against the United States again. He was so well treated at Lincoln Hospital in Washington, D.C., by the Sisters of Charity that he converted to Catholicism. He returned to his law practice in Montgomery, Alabama, where he died in 1895. The flag of the 59th Alabama became a war trophy and was stored in Washington until being returned in 1905 to the state of Alabama.

122. Weygant, p. 415; Captain Thomas Taft as quoted in Weygant, p. 416.
123. Weygant, p. 417.
124. Weygant, 418–9.
125. Weygant, p. 421.
126. Weygant, pp. 422–424.
127. Weygant, p. 425.
128. Weygant, p. 426.
129. Weygant, pp. 435–6.
130. Weygant, p. 437.
131. Weygant, p. 438.
132. Weygant, p. 442.

Epilogue

1. Weygant, pp. 444–445.
2. Henry Howell, April 15, 1865, Washington, D.C., AC.
3. Henry Howell, May 2, 1865, AC; Weygant, p. 466.
4. *Newburgh Daily Journal*, June 13, 1865.
5. Weygant, p. 447.
6. *Newburgh Daily Journal*, June 14, 1865.
7. Weygant, p. 448.
8. *Newburgh Daily Journal*, June 14, 1865.
9. *Newburgh Daily Journal*, June 14, 1865.
10. Weygant, p. 452.
11. Weygant, p. 451.
12. *Newburgh Daily Journal*, June 15, 1865.
13. *Newburgh Daily Journal*, June 16, 1865.

Bibliography

Letters and Diaries

Bailey, Sergeant William Wirt. Letters, edited by Edna Raymond. Historical Society of Middletown and the Wallkill Precinct. (HSMWP)

Benedict, Captain James. Courtesy of the Benedict Family Collection, Archive of the Historical Society of the Town of Warwick, gift of Joan & Tom Frangos. (JTFC)

Bowman, Private Andrew. Letter. Historical Society of Walden and Wallkill Valley.

———. Letters. Goshen Public Library and Historical Society Collection. (GPLHSC)

Brooks, Private Joseph. Letters. Goshen Public Library and Historical Society Collection. (GPLHSC)

Bush, Captain Ira. Letter. U.S. Army Military History Institute, Carlisle Barracks, Pennsylvania. (USMHI)

Carpenter, Private Edward M. Letter. Alfred Booth Collection. (ABC)

Chase, Stephen D. *Memoir of Stephen D. Chase.* U.S. Army Military History Institute, Carlisle Barracks, Pennsylvania. (USMHI)

Clark, Captain Leander. "Extracts from the Journal of Capt. Leander Clark, Co. I...." *Fifth Annual Report of the Chief of the Bureau of Military Statistics.* C. Van Benthuysen & Sons, 1868.

Decker, Isaac. Journal. Ruttenbur Collection. (RC)

Dill, Private Henry. Letters. Cheri Cardone Collection. (CCC)

Drake, Private John Z. *The Civil War Letters of John Zephaniah Drake, August 1862–April 1865,* edited by Robert Drew Simpson and Megan Demarest Simpson. Privately printed, 1996.

Godfrey, Private G.C. Letters. Cheri Cardone Collection. (CCC)

Haggerty, Private James. Diary. Family Collection of Shirley A. Mearns. (FCSM)

Hallock, Private Nathan. Letters. Francis Wooster Collection, Historical Society of Middletown and the Wallkill Precinct. (HSMWP)

Houston, Lieutenant John. Letters. Col. Charles and Tavy Umhey Collection. (COL)

———. "Short Sketch of the 124th New York Vols." Col. Charles and Tavy Umhey Collection. (COL)

Howell, Private Henry. Diary, September 1862–1863. Author's Collection. (AC)

———. Diary, June 1863–August 1864. Stuart Kessler Collection. (SKC)

———. Letters, Author's Collection. (AC)

———. Letters. The Clance 124th Regiment N.Y.S.V. Civil War Collection. (LCC)

———. Letters. David Handzel Civil War Between the States Collectibles. (DHC)

———. Letters. Dennis Buttacavoli Collection. (DBC)

———. Letters. Mount Hope Historical Society Collection. (MHHSC)

Howell, Corporal William. Letters. Author's Collection. (AC)

———. Diary. Author's Collection. (AC)

———. Letters. The Clance 124th N.Y.S.V. Civil War Collection. (LCC)

———. Letters. Dennis Buttacavoli Collection. (DBC)

———. Letters. Mount Hope Historical Society Collection. (MHHSC)

Irwin, Private James. Letters and diary. Robert Cammaroto Collection. (RCC)

Jackson, Captain William. William Augustus Jackson's Letters 1862–1864. Courtesy of the Division of Rare and Manuscript Collections, Cornell University Libraries. Archives 4200. (CUL)

Johnson, Private Joseph. Historic Huguenot Street Archives, New Paltz, New York. (HHS)

Mapes, Lieutenant William. Lynne Whealton Collection. (LWC)

Murray, Captain Henry S. Letters. Larry Clance Collection. (LCC)

———. American Historical Manuscript Collection — Murray, Henry S. Courtesy of the New York Historical Society. (NYHS)

Parsons, Winfield W. Letters. Frances Wooster Collection, Historical Society of Middletown and the Wallkill Precinct. (HSMWP)

Ramsdell, Lieutenant Henry. Letters. Paul and Lynne Ruback Collection. (PLRC)

Rich, Watson. Letters. Frances Wooster Collection, Historical Society of Middletown and the Wallkill Precinct. Marvin H. Cohen, president. (HSMWP)

Ries, Thomas M. "Battle of Gittesburgh — Statement of Thomas M. Ries." Ruttenburr Collection. (RC)

Rodman, Sergeant Thomas. Letters. Robert W. and Sandra J. Rodman Collection. (RSRC)

Roosa, Lieutenant James. Letters. Historical Society of Middletown and the Wallkill Precinct. (HSMWP)

Shaw, Private William H. Letters. Dennis Buttacavoli Collection. (DBC)

Silliman, William. "Silliman's Account of the 124th at Gettysburg." Author's Collection. (AC)

Sly, Norman Augustus. "Rambling Thoughts on the 1864 Campaign: Father's speech at the Warwick Historical Society — of which he was a member." Part I: The Wilderness; Part II: From the Wilderness to the Po River. Ruth Masten Collection. Historical Society of Middletown and the Wallkill Precinct. Marvin H. Cohen, president, and Office of the Orange County Historian. (HSMWP)

Travis, Captain Henry. Letters. Larry Clance Collection. (LCC)

Van Sciver, George. Letters. Historical Society of Middletown and the Wallkill Precinct. (HSMWP)

Yarbrough, Private Richard Cyrus. Letter. Author's Collection. (AC)

Manuscripts and Records

Annual Report of the Adjutant-General for the State of New York for the Year 1903. No. 36. Albany, NY: Oliver Quayle, 1904.

Annual Report of the Commissary General of Ordinance, S.N.Y. #66 1863 (for 1862) January 27, 1863, Albany, N.Y. Provided by Robert Braun and Roger Strucke.

Berthoff, Howard. Documents pertaining to charges of drunkenness against F.M. Cummins. National Archives, Washington, D.C.

Descriptive Muster Book of the One Hundred and Twenty Fourth Regiment N.Y. Vols. Microfilm, National Archives, Washington, D.C.

Newspapers

Goshen Democrat. Microfilm copies, Goshen Public Library and Historical Society, Goshen, New York. Courtesy of Pauline Kehoe, director.

Independent Republican. Microfilm copies, Goshen Public Library and Historical Society, Goshen, New York. Courtesy of Pauline Kehoe, director.

Middletown Daily Press. Historical Society of Middletown and Wallkill Precinct, Middletown, New York.

Middletown Whig Press. Microfilm copies, author's collection.

Montgomery Standard. Microfilm copies, New York State Library, Albany, NY; and original copies, Marcus Millspaugh Collection.

National Tribune. Microfilm copies, author's collection.

New York Times.

Newburgh Daily Telegraph. Microfilm copies, author's collection.

Newburgh Journal. Reprints in various newspapers and scrapbook collections. Sometimes seen as *Newburgh Daily Journal* or *Daily Journal.*

Newburgh Telegraph. Microfilm copies, author's collection.

"Old Orange Musters Few for Reunion." Unknown local newspaper, month unknown, date 28th, 1929, author's collection.

Scrapbook collection of various Orange County Civil War–era newspapers. New York State Military History Museum and Veterans Research Center, Saratoga, New York. Courtesy of Tom DuClose and Michael Aikey. (NYSMHM)

Warwick Advertiser. "A Soldier Boy's Letters: Extracts from the home letters of a member of the Orange Blossoms." A series of letters published in the 1890s located by Sue Gardner, local history librarian, Albert Wisner Public Library, Warwick New York.

Watchman & Democrat. Sullivan County, NY.

Official Compilations

Maine at Gettysburg, Report of Maine Commissioners Prepared by the Executive Committee. Portland, ME: Lakeside Press, 1898.

New York Monument Commission. *New York at Gettysburg: final Reports on the Battlefield of Gettysburg.* 3 vols. Albany, NY: J.B. Lyon Co., 1900.

Phisterer, Frederick. *New York in the Rebellion 1861–1865.* Albany, NY: J.B. Lyon Co. State Printer, 1912.

Revised United States Army Regulations of 1861. Washington, DC: Government Printing Office, 1863.

The War of the Rebellion; A Compilation of the Official Records of the Union and Confederate Armies. 130 vols. Washington, DC: Government Printing Office, 1880–1901. (OR)

Books and Articles

Adelman, Garry E., and Timothy H. Smith. *Devil's Den: A History and Guide.* Gettysburg, PA: Thomas Publications, 1997.

Alexander, Gen. E. Porter. *Fighting for the Confederacy, the Personal Recollections of General Edward Porter Alexander.* Edited by Garry W. Gallagher. Chapel Hill: University of North Carolina Press, 1989.

Bearss, Edwin C. *Meade's June 18 Assault Fails and the Investment Begins.* National Park Service, 1964. Made available by Jimmy Blankenship, Petersburg National Military Park.

Beattie, Daniel J., and Adam Hook. *Brandy Station 1863: First Step Towards Gettysburg.* Oxford: Osprey Publishing, 2008.

Beauregard, General Pierre T.G. "Four Days of Battle at Petersburg." In *Battles and Leaders of the Civil War,* Vol. 4, edited by Robert Underwood Johnson and Clarence Clough Buel of the editorial staff of *The Century* magazine, compiled from reproductions of articles. Whitefish, MT: Kessinger Publishing, 2010.

Beyer, W.F., and O.F. Keydel, editors. *Deeds of Valor.* Detroit, MI.: Perrien-Keydel, 1906.

Bigelow, John. *The Campaign of Chancellorsville: A Strategic and Tactical Study.* New Haven, CT: Yale University Press, 1910.

Bradley, Major Thomas W. "At Gettysburg." *National Tribune,* February 4, 1886.

Brummer, Sidney David. "Political History of New York State During the Period of the Civil War." Doctoral dissertation, Columbia University, 1911.

Busey, John W., and David G. Martin. *Regimental Strengths and Losses at Gettysburg.* Hightstown, NJ: Longstreet House, 1986.

Casey, Brigadier General Silas. *Infantry Tactics for the Instruction, Exercise, and Maneuvres of the Soldier, a Company, Line of Skirmishers, Battalion, Brigade, or Corps D'Armee.* New York: D. Van Nostrand, 1862.

Coddington, Edward. *The Gettysburg Campaign: A Study in Command.* New York: Scribner's, 1968.

Craft, David. *History of the One Hundred Forty-First*

Regiment Pennsylvania Volunteers 1862–1865. Towanda, PA: Reporter-Journal Printing Company, 1885.

Crotty, D.G. Four Years Campaigning in the Army of the Potomac, Third Michigan Volunteer Infantry. Grand Rapids, MI: Dygert, 1874.

Damon, Alan. "Surgeon Thompson's Separate Peace." American Heritage XXVI, December 1974.

Downs, David. "His Left Was Worth a Glance." Gettysburg Magazine 7, July 1993.

Duvall, Sam. "Incident at Hatcher's Run." Alabama Heritage 63, Winter 2002.

Esposito, Col. Vincent, chief editor. The West Point Atlas of the Civil War. New York: Frederick A. Praeger, 1962.

Furgurson, Ernest. Chancellorsville 1863: The Souls of the Brave. New York: Alfred A. Knopf, 1992.

Gage, Ethel B. "Orange County in the Civil War." Views (the official publication of the Orange County Community of Museums and Galleries) 2:2, April 1963.

Graham, Don. No Name on the Bullet: A Biography of Audie Murphy. New York: Penguin Books, 1989.

Graham, Martin F., and George F. Skoch. Mine Run: A Campaign of Lost Opportunities, October 21, 1863– May 1, 1864. Lynchburg, VA: H.E. Howard, 1987.

Grant, Ulysses S. Memoirs and Selected Letters. New York: Literary Classics of the United States, 1990.

Grimsley, Mark. And Keep Moving On: The Virginia Campaign, May–June 1864. Lincoln: University of Nebraska Press, 2002.

Hanford, Sergeant Harvey. "Gettysburg." National Tribune, September 24, 1885.

Harman, Troy. Lee's Real Plan at Gettysburg. Mechanicsburg, PA: Stackpole Books, 2003.

Harrison, Kathleen Georg. "Our Principal Loss Was in This Place." Gettysburg Magazine 1, July 1, 1989.

Hart, Thomas. "A Hero with His Face to the Foe." Antiques Digest, 1902.

Hart, William C. In a Beautiful Country: Historic Wallkill and Hudson River Valleys. Walden, NY: Wallkill Valley Publishing Association, 1906.

Hess, Earl J. In the Trenches at Petersburg: Field Fortifications and Confederate Defeat. Chapel Hill: The University of North Carolina Press, 2009.

_____. Trench Warfare Under Grant and Lee: Field Fortifications in the Overland Campaign. Chapel Hill: The University of North Carolina Press, 2007.

Hessler, James A. Sickles at Gettysburg. New York: Savas Beatie, 2009.

Howe, John. The Petersburg Campaign: Wasted Valor, June 15–18, 1864. Lynchburg, VA: H.E. Howard, 1988.

Humphreys, Andrew A. The Virginia Campaign of '64–'65, the Army of the Potomac and the Army of the James. New York: Charles Scribner's, 1883.

Hunt, Brevet Major-General Henry J. "The Second Day at Gettysburg," In Battles and Leaders of the Civil War, Vol. 3. New York: Castle, 1985.

Hunter, Roger D., and Jack R. Brown. Brevet Brigadier Generals in Blue. Gaithersburg, MD: Olde Soldier Books, 1990.

Jordan, William B. Red Diamond Regiment: The 17th Maine Infantry, 1862–1865. Shippensburg, PA: White Mane, 1996.

Laney, Daniel. "Wasted Gallantry: Hood's Texas Brigade at Gettysburg." Gettysburg Magazine 16, January 1997.

LaRocca, Charles. This Regiment of Heroes. Montgomery, NY: C.J. LaRocca, 1991.

_____, ed. The Red Badge of Courage: An Historically Annotated Edition. Fleischmanns, NY: Purple Mountain Press, 1995.

Long, E.B. The Civil War Day by Day: An Almanac, 1861–1865. Garden City, NY: Doubleday, 1971.

Lowe, David W., ed. Meade's Army: The Private Notebooks of Lt. Col. Theodore Lyman. Kent, OH: Kent State University Press, 2007.

Matter, William D. If It Takes All Summer: The Battle of Spotsylvania. Chapel Hill: University of North Carolina Press, 1988.

Marahall-Cornwall, General Sir James. Grant as Military Commander. New York: Van Nostrand Reinhold, 1970.

McGinnis, Amanda, and Cynthia Rapp. "Our Name Is Legion!" America's Civil War, September 1990.

McPherson, James M. Battle Cry of Freedom: The Civil War Era. New York: Oxford University Press, 1988.

Miller, J. Michael. The North Anna Campaign: "Even to Hell Itself," May 21–26, 1864. Lynchburg, VA: H.E. Howard, 1989.

Pfanz, Harry. Gettysburg: The Second Day. Chapel Hill: University of North Carolina Press, 1987.

Polley, J.B. Hood's Texas Brigade. Dayton, OH: Morningside Bookshop, 1988.

Porter, Horace. Campaigning with Grant. Lincoln: University of Nebraska Press, 2000.

Reeder, William. From a True Soldier and Son: The Civil War Letters of William Reeder. Commentary by Carolyn Reeder, edited by Jack Reeder. Brandy Station, VA: Brandy Station Foundation, 2008

Rhea, Gordon C. The Battle of the Wilderness: May 5– 6, 1864. Baton Rouge: Louisiana State University Press, 1994.

_____. The Battles for Spotsylvania Court House and the Road to Yellow Tavern: May 7–12, 1864. Baton Rouge: Louisiana State University Press, 1997.

_____. Cold Harbor Grant and Lee: May 26–June 3, 1864. Baton Rouge: Louisiana State University Press, 2002.

_____. To the North Anna River; Grant and Lee: May 13–25, 1864. Baton Rouge: Louisiana State University Press, 2000.

Rogers, James Moore, M.D. History of the Cooper Shop Volunteer Refreshment Saloon. Philadelphia: Jas. Rodgers, 1866.

Sauers, Richard. A Caspian Sea of Ink: The Meade-Sickles Controversy. Baltimore: Butternut and Blue, 1989.

Sears, Stephen W. Chancellorsville. New York: Houghton Mifflin, 1996.

_____. Gettysburg. New York: Houghton Mifflin, 2004.

Silliker, Ruth L., ed. The Rebel Yell and Yankee Hurrah, the Civil War Journal of a Maine Volunteer. Camden, ME: Down East Books, 1885.

Smith, Captain James E. A Famous Battery and Its Campaigns, 1861–'64. Washington, DC: W.H. Lowdermilk, 1892.

Sprenger, Sgt. George F. A Concise History of the Camp and Field Life of the 122nd Regiment, Penn'a Volunteers. Lancaster, PA: New Era Steam Book Print, 1885.

Starr, Stephen Z. The Union Cavalry in the Civil War.

Baton Rouge: Louisiana State University Press, 1979.

Steere, Edward. *The Wilderness Campaign.* Harrisburg, PA: Stackpole, 1987.

Styple, William B., ed. *Our Noble Blood: The Civil War Letters of Major-General Regis de Trobriand.* Kearny, NJ: Belle Grove, 1997.

Swinton, William. *Campaigns of the Army of the Potomac.* New York: C.B. Richardson, 1866.

Tarbell, Ida M. *A Reporter for Lincoln: The Story of Henry E. Wing.* New York: McMillan, 1927.

Trudeau, Noah A. *Bloody Roads South: The Wilderness to Cold Harbor, May–June 1864.* Boston: Little, Brown, 1989.

_____. *The Last Citadel: Petersburg, Virginia, June 1864–April 1865.* Boston: Little, Brown, 1991.

Tucker, A.W. "Orange Blossoms," *National Tribune,* January 21, 1886.

Vermilyea, Peter C. "The Pipe Creek Effect: How Meade's Pipe Creek Circular Affected the Battle of Gettysburg." *Gettysburg Magazine* 42, January 2010.

Walker, Francis A. *History of the Second Army Corps of the Army of the Potomac.* New York: Scribner's, 1991.

Warner, Ezra J. *Generals in Blue.* Baton Rouge: Louisiana State University Press, 1964.

_____. *Generals in Gray.* Baton Rouge: Louisiana State University Press, 1959.

Weygant, Charles. *History of the One Hundred and Twenty-fourth Regiment New York State Volunteers.* Newburgh, NY: Journal Printing House, 1877.

Wilkeson, Frank. *Recollections of a Private Soldier in the Army of the Potomac.* New York: G.P. Putnam's Sons (Knickerbocker Press), 1887.

Wilkinson, Warren, and Steven E. Woodworth. *A Scythe of Fire, a Civil War Story of the Eighth Georgia Infantry Regiment.* New York: William Morrow, 2002.

Williams, Franklin B. *Middletown: A Biography.* Middletown, NY: Lawrence A. Toepp, 1928.

Winkler, Angelina V. *The Confederate Capital and Hood's Texas Brigade.* Austin, TX: E. Von Boeckmann, 1879.

Index

Numbers in *bold italics* indicate pages with photographs.